Management for Professionals

The Springer series *Management for Professionals* comprises high-level business and management books for executives, MBA students, and practice-oriented business researchers. The topics span all themes of relevance for businesses and the business ecosystem. The authors are experienced business professionals and renowned professors who combine scientific backgrounds, best practices, and entrepreneurial vision to provide powerful insights into how to achieve business excellence.

Uwe Hannig • Uwe Seebacher
Editors

Marketing and Sales Automation

Basics, Implementation, and Applications

Springer

Editors
Uwe Hannig
Institute for Sales and Marketing
Automation (IFSMA)
Viernheim, Germany

Uwe Seebacher
FYNEST International
Frankfurt, Germany

ISSN 2192-8096 ISSN 2192-810X (electronic)
Management for Professionals
ISBN 978-3-031-20039-7 ISBN 978-3-031-20040-3 (eBook)
https://doi.org/10.1007/978-3-031-20040-3

This Springer imprint is published by the registered company Springer Nature Switzerland AG
The registered company address is: Gewerbestrasse 11, 6330 Cham, Switzerland

Preface

Although the first edition of the German version of this book, published in mid-2017, was still by far the most successful German-language book on the subject, with around half a million chapter downloads by now, it was time for a revised second edition of the German version due to developments in the market as well as the general conditions, such as the introduction of the General Data Protection Regulation already mentioned above. Against this background and in the absence of an international, comparable book on this so important topic, it was obvious to make this unique collection and scientifically based expertise available to the entire international community through an English edition.

How to Read This Book?

The book is intended to be a companion on the journey in terms of a change management process towards digitized marketing, sales, but also the entire corporate interaction. With this in mind, this book contains carefully selected contributions with direct practical relevance to ensure easy and simple application and implementation. As publishers, we have placed particular emphasis on ensuring the evidence and validity of the content as well as the profound, proven expertise of the authors and contributors.

This book therefore does not necessarily have to be read from beginning to end, but is intended—depending on the situation of the reader in his or her own organization—to be an ongoing guide and signpost in the various activities surrounding the all-important digitization. The sequence in the book with regard to the complexity of the topics is designed in such a way that simpler content and concepts can be found at the beginning of each of the various sections of the publication.

How Can This Book Support?

This book supports with many new approaches and concepts based on concrete examples from practice and shows what can be achieved with marketing, sales but also communication automation. The focus is on concrete, measurable results, in order to make it clear that digitization is not a cost factor, but a decisive turnover and profit factor when approached correctly and in synergy with concept and competence.

However, this book goes one step further and for the first time also offers a comprehensive insight and overview of everything that is still to come and will have to come in the context of the digitization of marketing, sales, and communication. This means that, for the first time, this publication also illuminates all practice-relevant content against the backdrop of a visionary, predictive big picture. This is essential in order to be able to assess and understand today's measures and projects in relation to next developments already today. Digitization is not a goal, but a task, because the actual goal is to optimize processes in order to sustainably increase the efficiency and effectiveness of distribution functions with the aim of maximizing return on sales (RoS).

From ABM to CRO to Predictive Intelligence

On the road to digitization, Körner's comments on his "Marketing Automation Roadmap" and those of Burkholz and Heinzelbecker on customer expectations provide decisive impetus. Especially for the business-to-business (B2B) sector, the contributions by Braun, Herrmann, and Heinzelbecker in the context of account-based marketing (ABM) should be valuable reading. Whether talking about social selling, digital selling, or conversion rate optimization (CRO), lead management along the customer and then the buyer journey is crucial. In this context, the article by Trummer impressively shows the results of a laboratory test project for conversation-rate-optimized (CRO) marketing and sales automation for which a new company with off-the-shelf products was launched and grown within few weeks from 0 to almost 100,000 euros in sales. The case demonstrates marketing and sales automation at next level.

In this regard, the contributions by Hannig, Huttelmaier, and Heigl, but also Kacar, who critically discusses Customer Experience Management in relation to the use of artificial intelligence (AI), provide aspects and information on the latest state of knowledge. Looking into the future, Geiger, Rach, and Seebacher introduce "Machine Augmented Marketing" or "Predictive Intelligence" into the discourse in order to be able to precisely predict and assess future developments through the application and use of AI technologies.

With this book, we hope to make a valuable contribution to the all-important daily work of the entire community, because the efficiency and effectiveness of digitization in the entire area of the distribution function according to Meffert will make a lasting difference between the success and failure of companies. What has been happening for years in the areas of the production functions must ultimately also find its way into marketing, sales, and communication on a broad basis. If we can contribute to this development with this publication and thereby help and support you, dear reader, then our efforts have been worthwhile, and we have been able to achieve our goal for this book. In this spirit, we wish you an interesting and informative read.

Viernheim, Germany
Frankfurt, Germany
July 2022

Uwe Hannig
Uwe Seebacher

Acknowledgement

We would like to thank all the authors for their contributions and their willingness to share their knowledge with others—despite full order books and the turmoil of the Corona period during which this book was written. In doing so, they are making a significant contribution to further increasing transparency and competence in the market for marketing and sales automation.

We would also like to thank Springer Verlag, and in particular Prashanth Mahagaonkar and Rolf-Günther Hobbeling, for their valuable thoughts and inputs, which contributed significantly to the selection and structuring of the contributions to this publication. It is so helpful and value-creating for us as editors and authors alike to always have someone at one's side when it comes to publishing aspects and topics to enable a conspiratorial exchange. Thank you Prashanth and Rolf-Günther!

Contents

Introduction

Uwe Seebacher and Uwe Hannig

If automation succeeds, humans can save themselves "monkey work" and invest the time they gain in tasks with greater benefits. The latest developments in the context of ChatGPT and consorts can be seen by the launch of the first artificial intelligence (AI) combining and integrating MarCom-on-Demand (MoD) respectively MarCom-as-a-Services (MaaS) platforms such as www.fynest.agency. Automation therefore always makes sense when repetitive tasks can be performed more cost-effectively by a machine or system even more so when now latest AI technology is used not in a "gagdetary" but a real adding-value manner. This is not a new insight, but its acceptance and implementation is still surprisingly difficult, especially in marketing and sales. What is the reason for this? Is it the lack of imagination that processes in marketing and sales can be automated? Or is it the lack of imagination as to what the new tasks with greater benefits could be, in which the freed-up time could be invested? Is it due to the multitude of sometimes loud messages from an almost unmanageable number of solution providers, which are constantly growing at breakneck speed, and which confuse more than they clarify? It is due to all of the above and, of course, other reasons (data protection, management of change projects, reliable best practice examples, etc.) that are addressed in this first international English-language edition of this book.

U. Seebacher (✉)
University of Applied Sciences Munich, Munich, Germany
e-mail: uwe.seebacher@hm.edu

U. Hannig
Institute for Sales and Marketing Automation (IFSMA), Viernheim, Germany
e-mail: hannig@ifsma.de

U. Hannig, U. Seebacher (eds.), *Marketing and Sales Automation*, Management for Professionals, https://doi.org/10.1007/978-3-031-20040-3_1

1 The Definitional Starting Position

The Institute for Sales and Marketing Automation defines marketing and sales automation as the IT-supported execution of recurring marketing and sales tasks with the aim of increasing the efficiency of processes and the effectiveness of decisions in these areas. When looking for processes to automate, the focus must always be on the company as a whole. After all, even a process that only runs once a year in one branch office lends itself to automation if it is used in many locations worldwide.

Despite the demonstrable benefits of marketing and sales automation, companies have been slow to embrace the digitization of marketing and sales. A major reason for this was the fear of data protection problems when using cloud-based IT solutions. Since the introduction of the General Data Protection Regulation, however, a reliable set of rules for the use of such systems is now available.

The necessity of digital transformation in marketing and sales became clear even to the biggest skeptics due to the global Corona-related shutdowns in 2020. Visiting customers was no longer possible overnight. The promotion of one's own offer took place almost exclusively online, even in the B2B sector. And selling and support at a distance worked because new technologies were finally being used. Along the way, environmentally damaging car journeys could be avoided and parents in particular learned to appreciate the advantages of working in a home office. But the pandemic is only a catalyst for the digitization of sales and marketing. The decisive reason for its success is that it pays off.

2 Marketing and Sales Automation Is Not an IT Issue

The fact that the automation of marketing and sales goes far beyond the introduction of an IT tool runs like a thread through all the contributions with practical examples. The critical success factor is to manage a change process that is ideally driven equally by marketing, communication, sales, service, and management. Anyone who chooses this path will register as a major success the improvement of cooperation between the departments, including IT, but especially between marketing and sales. However, this requires that all departments involved do their own homework so that a solid basis for cross-departmental collaboration in the context of digitization or automation becomes possible in the first place. We refer here to the instrument of the marketing or communication process library, which maps and presents all relevant activities in the form of processes and interfaces as the basis for IT-supported automation. On this basis, roles and responsibilities are precisely defined and transparent. Based on this any kind of automation or digitization activity can then happen efficiently and effectively.

3 About the Structure of the Book

To optimize the reader experience in line with the user or customer experience (UX or CX), we have decided to divide the final contributions to this book into four sections that build on each other. In the sense of a top-down approach, we approach the topic from the big picture via a journey thought from the customer's point of view, in order to build on this and look toward the future and trends.

The first section, "Digital Transformation in Marketing and Sales," provides current insights of a general nature and concludes with a current case study in the area of the new hot topic of conversion-rate-optimization (CRO). The first section deals with organizational issues in the context of change management aspects of digital transformation.

Building on this, the second section "The Customer Side of Marketing and Sales Automation" is dedicated to the customer perspective. What expectations do B2C and B2B customers have and how can we deal with them in the context of automation and what needs to be considered. Automation does not equal standardization, because that would neglect the customer experience and put it at risk. On the contrary, marketing, sales, and communication automation should improve CX. This topic is also referred to in the second section.

The section on the customer side also addresses the topic of data as the new gold and the important customer group of key customers. How can data be used and processed in order to successfully set up and implement omni-channel marketing in the context of the rapid transformation from 1-2-1 to All-2-All (A2A) interaction? Data also plays an essential role in the context of account-based marketing (ABM). Therefore, the ABM concept in the interaction of CRM and marketing automation is also critically discussed in the second section.

The third section of the book on "Customer Journey Management" provides the latest insights from research on customer touchpoints, strategies for increasing and optimizing the quality of leads, through to innovative approaches from the field of artificial intelligence (AI) for optimizing the customer experience (CX). Most examples come from lead management and focus on shaping the customer journey with the goal of creating a consistently positive customer experience across all channels. In the future, however, tool providers will offer solutions and apps for all areas of marketing and sales. These will then generally be made available in sales or marketing clouds.

"Beyond Sales and Marketing Automation" rounds off the book with visionary, innovative approaches, and concepts. Topics such as Automated and Social Selling show how a completely automated buyer journey can be realized from marketing and sales automation to optimize the return on sales (RoS). In the future, AI will have an even greater impact on the field of marketing and sales automation, but the greatest challenge in this context will not be AI, but HI—human intelligence. Because only in symbiosis of concept and competence can AI as an enabler in the sense of an instrument—and that's all AI is—enable the realization of Predictive Intelligence (PI) as the all-important tool for sustainable economic, precisely predictable success. Things get exciting at the end of the fourth section, when the topic of marketing and sales automation is enriched by a facet, namely communication automation. This is because current research results show that many findings from the field of marketing and sales automation can be adopted directly in the context of a seemingly more than overdue reengineering of corporate communication (RCC). This article manages to close the circle to Meffert's distribution function and shows how companies must proceed in order not to be fit for the future in terms of marketing and sales through marketing and sales automation, but to drown in the shitstorm tsunami of 24/7 interaction arenas in the absence of an adequate A2A corporate interaction.

In addition to approaches, concepts, and further literature references, all sections contain many practical examples, templates, process models, and pointed lessons learned, but also recommendations for action.

Uwe Seebacher is a methods and structural scientist. He holds a doctorate in economics and business administration and is Professor for Predictive Intelligence at the University of Applied Sciences Munich, Professor for Marketing and Communications at the University of Applied Sciences for Marketing and Communication at Vienna and Professor for Data Science, Predictive Intelligence, Sales and Distribution Management at the Institute of Management Technology Ghaziabad and Dubai. He has more than 30 years of experience as a business angel and investor, consultant, leader but also entrepreneur in the media, manufacturing, and service industries. He is a popular keynote speaker and panelist.

He has authored more than 50 books in many leading publishing houses, such as "Reengineering Corporate Communications" (Springer Cham), "Assets-as-Service" (Springer Gabler 2021), "Data-driven Management" (Springer Gabler 2021), "Predictive Intelligence for Managers" (Springer 2021), "B2B Marketing Guidebook" (Springer 2021), "Marketing Resource Management" (AQPS 2021), "Leadership Development" (Linde 2006) or "Template-based Management (Springer 2020) or "European Human Resource Management" (HBM 2009).

For his innovative concepts and initiatives, e.g., with Allianz, the European Union, the Austrian Federal Economic Chamber, Bayer Leverkusen, and BASF, he received various awards, such as the Diskobolos Innovation Award of the European Chamber of Commerce and the 2016 Export Award of the Austrian Federal Economic Chamber. For more information, visit www.uweseebacher.org.

Uwe Hannig is scientific director of the Institute for Sales and Marketing Automation (IFSMA) in Ludwigshafen. The professor for Information and Performance Management has many years of experience in marketing and sales in theory and practice.

The Institute for Marketing and Sales Automation has set itself the goal of paving the way for sales and marketing automation in the DACH region. It monitors the market, promotes the exchange of experience and knowledge transfer at specialist events, and takes care of the training of urgently needed specialists. The common focus of the institute's activities is to improve efficiency and effectiveness in marketing and sales with the help of scientific and practice-relevant methods, instruments, and systems.

Part I

Digital Transformation in Marketing and Sales

Automation of Repetitive Processes in Marketing and Sales

Uwe Hannig

1 From Automating to Automation

In contrast to the Anglo-American countries, Central Europe for a long time only reluctantly engaged in marketing and sales automation. Business was excellent and sales went from success to success. Thus, there was little need and, especially in medium-sized B2B companies, no inclination to change the status quo.

However, the shutdown caused by Corona abruptly changed business life, especially in the SME sector. Customer visits were suddenly no longer possible and thus lost their significance for winning orders. Since then, communication with customers and, in particular, the promotion of the company's own products and services have taken place almost exclusively online. And to the surprise of sales staff in particular, selling at a distance using new technologies works and even makes their lives easier, for example by avoiding hours of travel to customers.

Even after the pandemic has been overcome, neither customers nor suppliers will return to pre-Corona business practices as a result of the positive experience. The entire sales process, from contact acquisition to customer care, will be automated wherever possible. Personal contact on site will permanently lose importance in the B2B sector as well. This is due not least to the fact that digital natives do not like to negotiate anyway. Instead, they prefer to use portal forms, regardless of whether they are buying a new car or selling their old smartphone.

In general, automation is the state achieved through automating parts of or total processes transferring recurring activities from humans to machines or IT systems, or at least the intervention of humans has been minimized. Marketing and sales consist of a sequence of interlocking processes for the profitable satisfaction of demand requirements.

U. Hannig (✉)
Institute for Sales and Marketing Automation (IFSMA), Viernheim, Germany
e-mail: hannig@ifsma.de

U. Hannig, U. Seebacher (eds.), *Marketing and Sales Automation*, Management for Professionals, https://doi.org/10.1007/978-3-031-20040-3_2

Against this background, the Institute for Sales and Marketing Automation (IFSMA) defines (Hannig, 2016, p. 27):

▶ Marketing automation is the IT-supported execution of recurring marketing tasks with the aim of increasing the efficiency of marketing processes and the effectiveness of marketing decisions.

For the distribution sector, the definition by IFSMA is analogous:

▶ Sales automation is the IT-supported execution of recurring sales tasks with the aim of increasing the efficiency of sales processes and the effectiveness of sales decisions.

The goal of automation is thus not only to improve the input/output ratio, but also to increase the effectiveness of the measures implemented, e.g., through personalized communication geared to individual needs. Automation is always useful when repetitive tasks are carried out more cost-effectively by a machine, freeing up time for more value-adding activities for the employees previously tasked with performing them.

When looking for processes to automate, it is important to keep the entire company in mind. Even a process that is triggered only once a year in a subsidiary company or is required in a branch office may well lend itself to automation if it is used at hundreds of locations worldwide. A campaign developed for one product can be used for several other products. Advertising can be created in one language and placed in several in different countries. Thus, the reusability of processes or process components represents a significant savings potential.

It is advisable to create a list of all recurring activities in marketing and sales sorted by their frequency, e.g. weekly, monthly, quarterly, or annually. The next step is to determine which processes or process steps can be automated. For these, the savings effects and the effort of automation must then be estimated. The corresponding comparison shows where automation is most worthwhile and thus with which processes to start.

2 Investments in MarTech and Sales IT Are Imperative

The prerequisite for a concerted approach to digital transformation in marketing and sales is the existence of a digitization strategy. While more than half of the companies participating in the above-mentioned study already have one (Hannig et al., 2021), more than a third are planning to introduce a strategy. This means that most companies will soon be systematically tackling digitization on the sales side. The ground is thus prepared for the automation of marketing and sales.

The strategic approach already pays off. More than two-thirds of the outperformers have a digitization strategy, while this is not even the case for one in five of the underperformers. For more than a third of the outperformers,

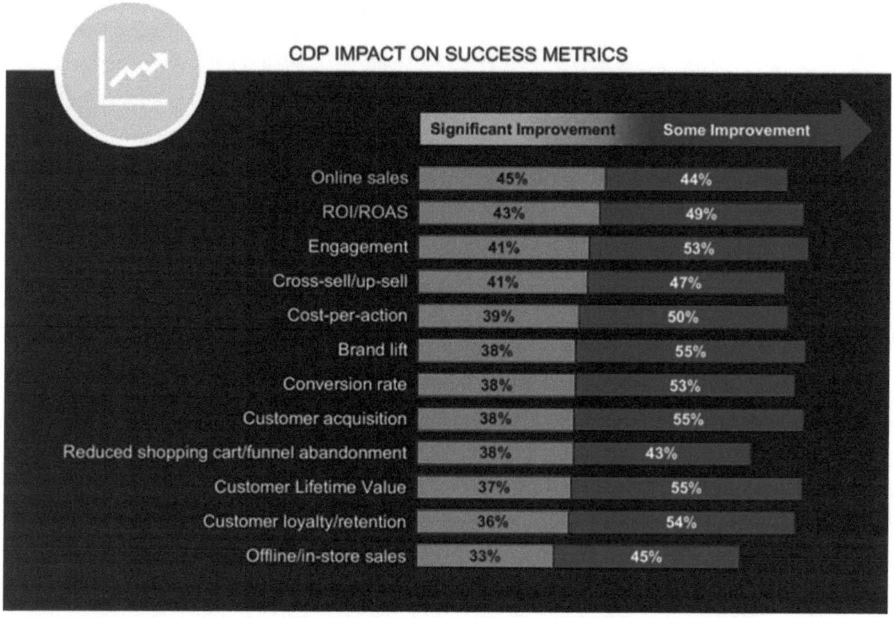

Fig. 1 CDP impact on success metrics (Source: Treasure Data, 2020)

digitization is already the key driver of their market success. The digital transformation of marketing and sales is therefore not only worthwhile, but is often a key factor for success.

Competitive advantages can only be achieved by investing in the necessary technology. However, the assessment of the status quo in this respect is sobering in many companies. More than half of the companies are convinced that they still have major gaps in their IT infrastructure for marketing and sales. Only around one in eight companies considers itself to be well-positioned today.

The IT basis for targeted market development is a Customer Data Platform (CDP). This is database software that allows customer data to be stored and used across all tools, giving marketing and sales a coherent view of the customer. This development began with the introduction of customer relationship management (CRM) systems in the mid-1980s. Then in 2013, the term CDP appeared for the first time. The need to create a consistent customer database is illustrated by the statement of the founder of the CDP Institute, David Raab; "A company can easily have over 100 systems in place, pulling in customer data. And they don't necessarily talk to each other." (CDP Institute).

The CDP Institute expects the global market for CDPs to grow to $20.5 billion by 2027. This growth is due to the benefits of CDP deployment (see Fig. 1). In more than 80% of the cases, all performance measures showed a positive development.

The range of highly developed technologies, tools, and applications for marketing and sales, which are summarized under the terms MarTech or SalesTech, has

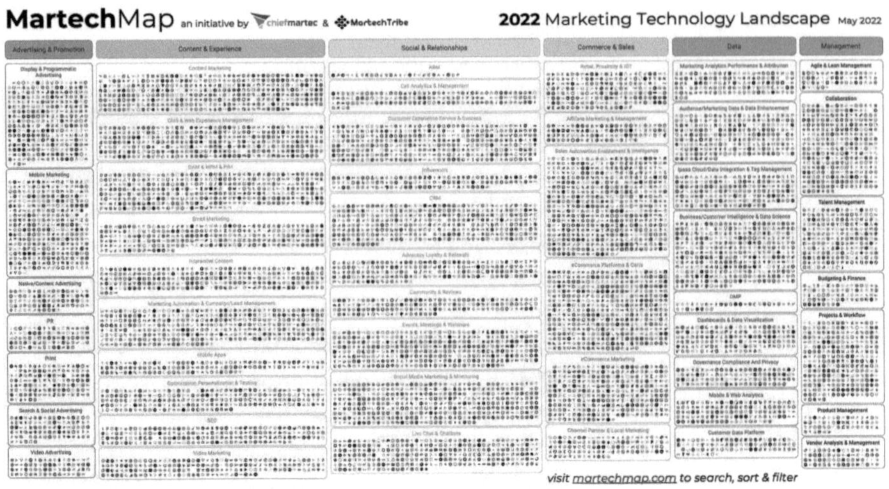

Fig. 2 Marketing technology landscape 2022 (Source: chiefmartech)

virtually exploded in the last 10 years. For example, the number of IT solutions for marketing has risen from around 150 in 2011 to 9932 in 2022 (Brinker, 2022). The offerings are so numerous and varied that they have become virtually impossible to represent in a chart (cf. Fig. 2). The situation is no different for sales solutions.

In view of the huge range on offer, it is not surprising that many companies are uncertain about the right marketing or sales technology stack for them. A technology stack is a set of hardware and software building blocks, such as servers, programming language, and frameworks, for developing an IT solution to a specific problem. In larger companies, the marketing technology stack consists of dozens of solutions and apps. Usually, the Marketing Automation System forms the core of the Marketing Technology Stack.

Before investing in MarTech and sales IT, it is necessary to take stock of the marketing and sales solutions already in place. In most companies, no corresponding overviews are available at the highest corporate level. As a result, gaps in the IT portfolio are identified too late and redundant investments are made.

In the Hannig et al. study, the greatest short-term need for investment was in lead management (see Fig. 3). More than half of the companies need to invest in appropriate IT solutions as quickly as possible. Likewise, more than two-fifths of the companies have an acute need for action in the areas of social media engagement, customer journey mapping, and content management.

The quickest way to address these shortcomings is to implement cloud-based systems.

The study by Hannig et al. proves that it pays to invest in MarTech and sales IT. While almost all underperformers have large gaps in their IT portfolio for marketing and sales, this applies to just one in four outperformers.

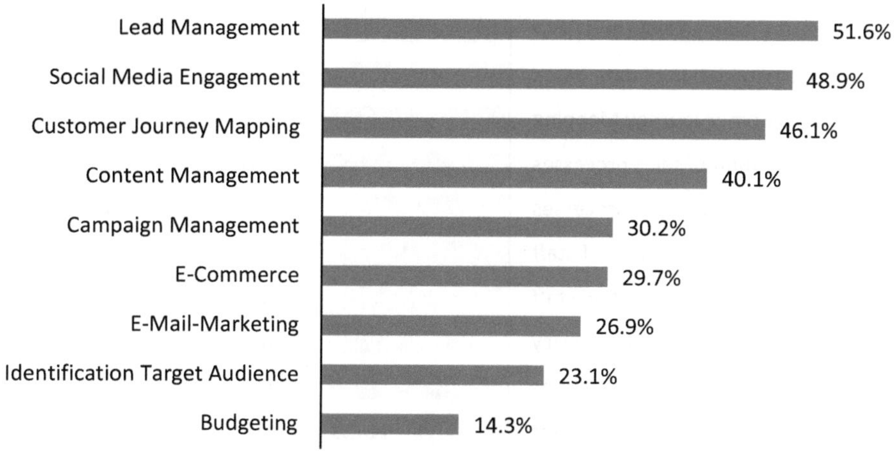

Fig. 3 Areas with short-term investment needs (Hannig et al., 2021, p. 16)

3 The Road to Automation

Despite the advantages of digitizing marketing and sales, implementation is not imminent in many companies. The reasons cited for this reluctance are cost, lack of support from management, and lack of sufficient in-house expertise.

However, even companies that are planning to use an MAS and are intensively searching for information often encounter problems. There is a lack of transparency with regard to costs, benefits, and offerings. Accordingly, more than one third of businesses surveyed complain about problems in estimating costs/benefits and determining the realizable benefits (Hannig et al., 2021, p. 33).

Even greater challenges arise when planning the introduction of a marketing automation system. Most frequently, the linking of the MAS with the CRM system is considered critical to success (Hannig et al., 2021). This is followed by the adaptation of processes in marketing and sales and the merging of different data sets.

When implementing MAS, many companies rely on their own employees. Most of them carry out the implementation predominantly with internal resources. In around two-thirds of the cases studied, project management lies with marketing (Hannig et al., 2021, p. 35).

The challenges to be overcome during implementation largely coincide with those previously expected in terms of their order of importance. The linking of the MAS with the CRM system is also named most frequently by the MAS user companies (see Fig. 4). Before the adaptation of processes in sales and marketing, the merging of different data sets in second place. On the positive side, the willingness to change processes as part of the MAS implementation has increased in recent years.

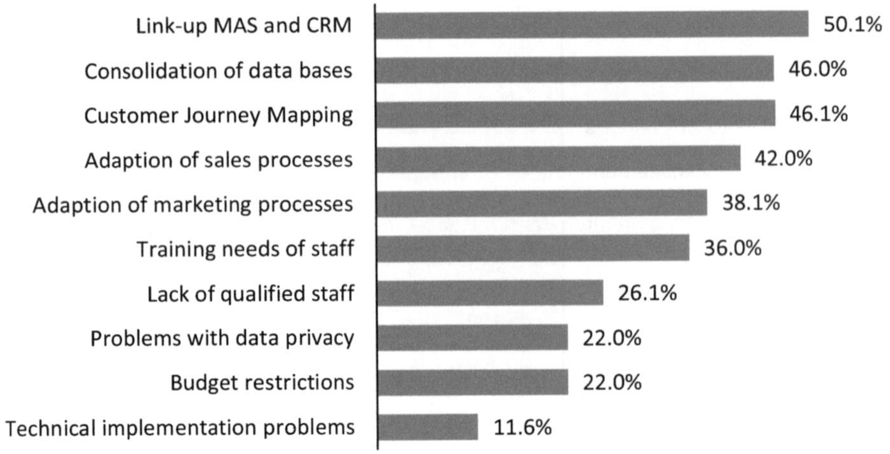

Fig. 4 Obstacles at implementing a marketing automation system (Hannig et al., 2021, p. 36)

4 Automation Pays Off

The central goal of process automation is generally to save time and money by optimizing the use of human resources. After all, employees in marketing and sales are the most expensive resource, whose productive daily use is limited, while hardware and software run around the clock with consistent quality. The time saved through marketing and sales automation also opens up the possibility of creating improved processes and thus improving the impact of the use of resources in marketing and sales.

The Institute for Sales and Marketing Automation (IFSMA) studied the impact of marketing and sales automation on corporate success in 2021 (Hannig et al., 2021). It was proven that systematic, IT-supported market preparation improves performance. For one third of the companies with above-average success, digitization is already the central driver of market success.

Outperformers have implemented a marketing automation system (MAS) more than twice as often as underperformers. In the first place in the decision for a MAS is the automation of marketing processes (see Fig. 5). Improving lead management follows in the second place ahead of creating personalized campaigns.

Most user companies are obviously getting what they expected. Accordingly, almost 73% of them are very satisfied or satisfied with the level of target achievement. Here, too, it is interesting to compare satisfaction with target achievement with the development of the company. All outperformers are satisfied with the achievement of the goals they set themselves, i.e., they have successfully implemented the MAS and are now reaping the rewards of their efforts. The situation is quite different for the underperformers. Of these, not a single one is satisfied with target achievement.

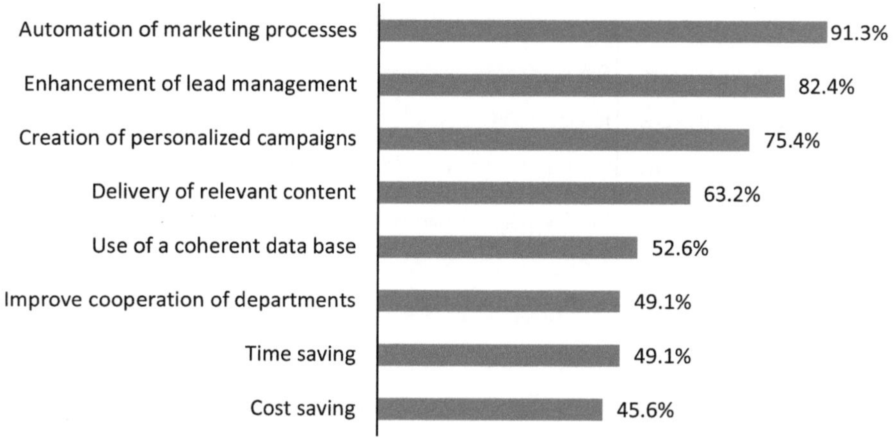

Fig. 5 Objectives of using a marketing information system (Hannig et al., 2021, p. 37)

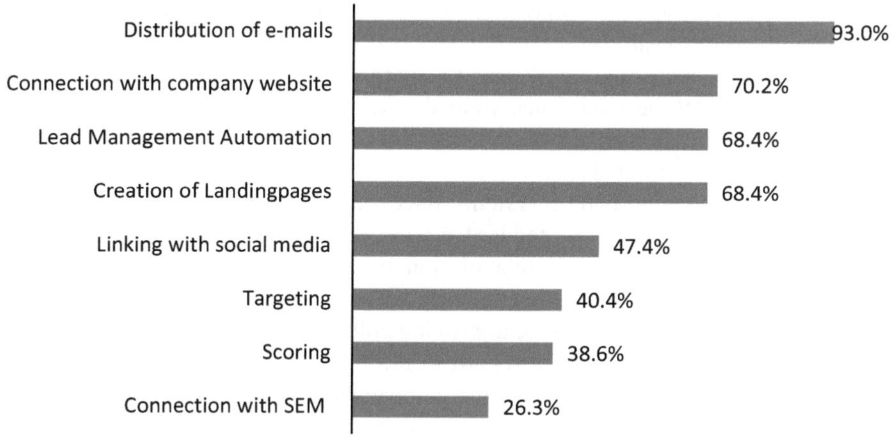

Fig. 6 Frequently used MAS functions (Hannig et al., 2021, p. 37)

Overall, satisfaction with the MAS tool used is even better than with regard to target achievement. More than 85% of all companies are at least satisfied with the system used. Here, too, the outperformers are at least satisfied, while a third of the underperformers are less satisfied with the tool used and the rest are even dissatisfied. This result suggests that in the underperforming companies, even a good tool does not produce satisfactory results because of a lack of the necessary human resources and sensible implementation.

As in previous years, the most frequently used MAS function by far is automated e-mailing (see Fig. 6). The connection to the company's own website is increasing significantly and relegates the automation of the lead management process to the third place. In general, the longer the MAS is used, the more complex functions are

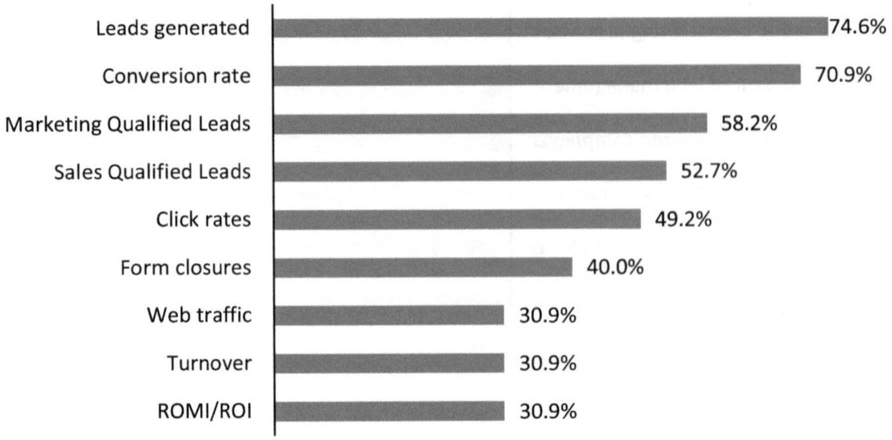

Fig. 7 Measures of MAS success (Hannig et al., 2021, p. 39)

used more frequently. The connection to social media in particular has increased sharply in the last 2 years.

More qualified metrics are now used to determine the success of the use of MAS than in the past. While click rates were the measure of all things for years, the generated leads and the conversion rate now dominate (see Fig. 7). The focus is still on easy-to-measure variables.

Most marketing automation systems have integrated reporting. Analyses are carried out automatically and standard reports sent to the decision-makers. This does not allow the quality of collaboration between marketing and sales to be determined. This is why the study explicitly addressed this issue.

For about half of the companies, improving collaboration between marketing and sales was an important goal with regard to the introduction of MAS. This is also achieved in a good three quarters of the companies with MAS deployment. While none of the underperformers could determine a real effect regarding the MAS employment on the co-operation of marketing and selling, approximately 90% of the above-average successful enterprises registered a more effective co-operation of the two departments. This result alone justifies the use of marketing and sales automation systems.

5 Automation Will Come from the Cloud in the Future

The terms Marketing Cloud and Sales Cloud are not primarily derived from the fact that the tools are cloud-based. That applies to every IT tool sooner or later. Rather, it is a company's cloud-based portfolio of offerings from which users select exactly the tools, functionalities, and solutions they need at any given time.

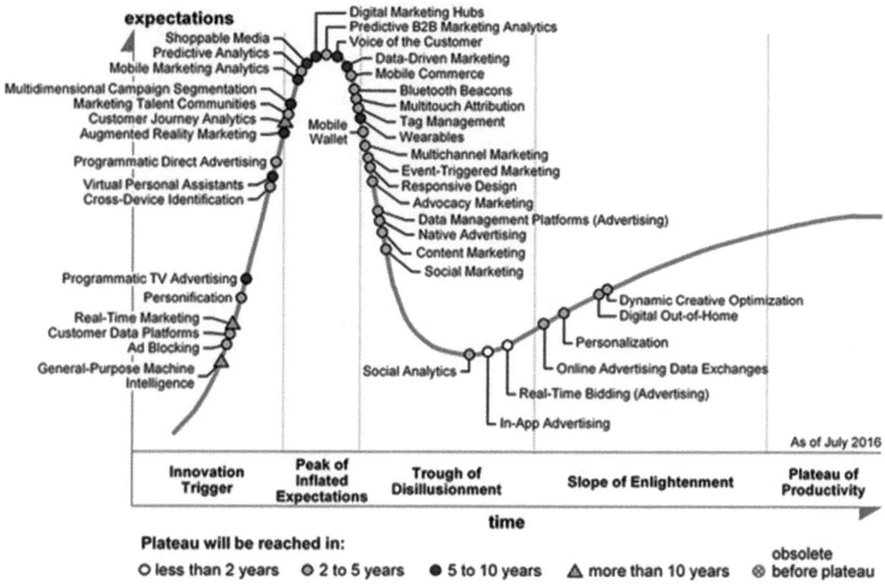

Fig. 8 Gartner's (2016) hype cycle for digital marketing and advertising (Source: Gartner, 2016)

Definition of Marketing Cloud: A Marketing Cloud is a platform for digital marketing. The terms "marketing hub," "digital marketing platform," and "marketing portal" are also used synonymously.

According to Gartner, the topic of marketing clouds and digital marketing hubs was already at the peak of the hype cycle in the USA in 2016 (see Fig. 8).

In Europe, and especially in Germany, there was still a great deal of mistrust of cloud-based solutions at that time for data protection reasons. Accordingly, the spread of marketing and sales automation tools still lags behind other industrialized nations. This must change. After all, the share of cloud-based systems is around three times higher among outperformers than among underperformers (Hannig et al., 2021, p. 16).

The major marketing automation vendors Adobe, Salesforce, and Oracle are ranked by Gartner as leaders in the Magic Quadrant for Marketing Hubs (see Fig. 9). These enterprise-grade platforms for marketing tools and solutions are driving concentration in this market. They represent the evolution of the suite idea. Customers should be able to find everything they need for marketing on the marketing hubs. These can be tools as well as solutions developed by partners with them, e.g. for a specific industry. The range of solutions for marketing increases over time without any major intervention by the platform operator, making the platform more and more interesting. As a result, concentration in the market increases at the expense of smaller companies.

Adobe describes its own Marketing Cloud as a central, unified platform for anyone who is tired of working with individual puzzle pieces in marketing and

Fig. 9 Magic quadrant for multichannel marketing hubs (Source: Gartner, 2021)

promises: digital marketing from a single source. The offering includes tools for organizing and personalizing the marketing of medium and large B2B and B2C companies. The original Adobe Marketing Cloud has since been merged into Adobe Experience Cloud. The key offerings for marketers are (Adobe, 2022):

- Experience Manager: This is about delivering and managing personalized content to create consistent customer experiences, such as on customized landing pages. Experience Manager Sites aims to ensure that content is consistent and personalized for each customer. Experience Manager Forms links form and communication processes, and Experience Manager Assets provides target group and channel-oriented content.
- Campaign: This allows campaigns to be planned, designed, and managed across all channels. Data on target groups, customers, customer journey, transactions,

etc. converge here (order data, order values, etc.) and improve interaction with customers. Emails, ads, and campaigns are centrally managed and automated. With AI support, open rates and optimal dispatch times are predicted.
- Target: Helps users optimize individual customer experience through A/B testing and multivariate testing. The goal is to provide a consistent and personalized experience throughout the customer journey across channels by using a single customer profile.
- Marketo Engage: Following the acquisition of Marketo, the company integrated its Engagement Platform for planning, execution, and engagement with customers and prospects for lead management and account-based marketing. Complementary offerings include Adobe Advertising Cloud for media optimization and Adobe Analytics Cloud for audience targeting and predictive analytics.

The second major fixed star in the marketing cloud sky is Salesforce.com. The Salesforce Marketing Cloud is a digital platform for personalized marketing for B2C and B2B companies of all sizes (Salesforce.com, 2022). It helps target the right audience at the right time with the right message at every stage of the interaction. The essential tools are:

- Journey Builder: Design of personalized customer journeys across all touchpoints and channels. Supports the networking of marketing, sales, and customer service.
- Email Studio: Allows you to run personalized email campaigns using data from any source, such as the CRM system.
- Marketing Cloud Customer Data Platform: Platform for merging, segmenting, and analyzing customer data. Facilitates lead management as a common database for marketing and sales.
- Marketing Cloud Advertising: Provides support for planning and implementing advertising campaigns. The Salesforce Marketing Cloud also includes tools for interacting with prospects on social networks, Google Analytics 360, and access to external marketing data.

Oracle, the third heavyweight in the major marketing cloud league, says CX Marketing offers an integrated portfolio of digital marketing solutions that enable B2B and B2C marketers to leverage real-time information and customer signals to deliver personalized experiences (Oracle, 2022). The CX Marketing Suite has the key components:

- Eloqua Marketing Automation: Widely used marketing automation tool for B2B companies to create and execute campaigns that promote customer experience.
- Responsys Campaign Management: Supports the management of B2C campaigns to create cross-channel customer experiences.
- Maxymiser Testing and Optimization: tool for optimizing campaigns through real-time personalization and A/B as well as multivariate testing and generates heatmaps.

- Audience Segmentation: Tool for segmentation, data management, and analysis of large audiences to improve performance.
- Content Management: Helps create personalized content and consistent experiences with AI support. There are also solutions for accessing external data sources and Big Data analytics.

The other vendors listed by Gartner in the Leaders quadrant are not in the same marketing cloud league as Adobe, Salesforce, and Oracle, particularly with regard to marketing automation. As a result, the three full-service marketing cloud providers are currently under little threat from other software companies. They should be able to expand their market position in digital marketing accordingly.

References

Adobe. (2022). *Adobe experience cloud for marketers.* https://business.adobe.com/de/solutions/role/marketer.html

Brinker, S. (2022). *Marketing technology landscape 2022. Search 9,932 solutions on martechmap.com.* https://chiefmartec.com/2022/05/marketing-technology-landscape-2022-search-9932-solutions-on-martechmap-com/

CDP Institute. *The history of the CDP & CRM.* https://cdp.com/articles/basics/the-history-of-the-cdp/

Gartner. (2016, November 3). *Gartner's 2016 hype cycle for digital marketing and advertising identifies four forces driving a data-centric future for marketers.* https://www.gartner.com/en/newsroom/press-releases/2016-11-03-gartners-2016-hype-cycle-for-digital-marketing-and-advertising-identifies-four-forces-driving-a-data-centric-future-for-marketers

Gartner. (2021, May 10). *2021 Magic quadrant for mulitichannel marketing h*ubs. https://www.pega.com/de/gartner-mmh-2021

Hannig, U. (2016). More than basic mental attitude. *Acquisa, 11–12*, 26–27.

Hannig, U., Heinzelbecker, K., & Foell, T. (2021). *Mission digital transformation. Automation in Marketing and Sales 2021.* White Paper, Institute for Sales and Marketing Automation, Viernheim.

Oracle. (2022). *Oracle marketing.* https://www.oracle.com/de/cx/marketing/.

Salesforce.com. (2022). *Marketing cloud. Digital Marketing Platform.* https://www.salesforce.com/de/products/marketing-cloud/products/.

Treasure Data. (2020). *State of Customer Data Platforms 2020.* https://cdp.com/articles/basics/cdp-industry-statistics/

Uwe Hannig is scientific director of the Institute for Sales and Marketing Automation (IFSMA) in Ludwigshafen. The professor for Information and Performance Management has many years of experience in marketing and sales in theory and practice.

The Institute for Marketing and Sales Automation has set itself the goal of paving the way for sales and marketing automation in the DACH region. It monitors the market, promotes the exchange of experience and knowledge transfer at specialist events, and takes care of the training of urgently needed specialists. The common focus of the institute's activities is to improve efficiency and effectiveness in marketing and sales with the help of scientific and practice-relevant methods, instruments, and systems.

Roadmap to Marketing Automation

Alexander Körner

1 Setup, Scoping, and Readyness

Marketing automation is a technically supported marketing process that is often regarded as the technical backbone of disciplines such as inbound marketing, lead management, or content marketing. Marketing automation is oriented to the customer or buyer journey. It encompasses and links all market-oriented business units that operate along this path within the company (Fig. 1).

Setup

As a rule, successful implementation requires that the silo mentality of the business units, which can be found in many places, be broken down and that all affected functions be involved. This must be considered when setting up the project team. At the very least, marketing and sales should be represented in the project team right from the start.

The first task of this team is to develop a common understanding of the challenges, goals, and possible solutions. This is particularly essential for the interaction between marketing, sales. It is often the case that the initial situation is perceived very differently.

It is in the nature of a rather young discipline that breaks with many previous rules that central terms, contents, mechanisms of action, and possibilities are still interpreted very differently. Therefore, clarity or a common sense must be created from the beginning. This avoids later irritations and costly readjustments in the advanced project status.

A. Körner (✉)
b.relevant – Agile Digital Marketing Agency GmbH, Mainz, Germany
e-mail: a.koerner@b-relevant.agency

U. Hannig, U. Seebacher (eds.), *Marketing and Sales Automation*, Management for Professionals, https://doi.org/10.1007/978-3-031-20040-3_3

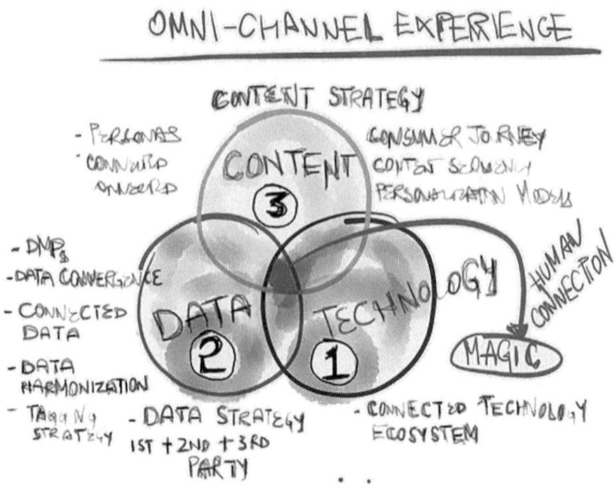

Fig. 1 Content, data, technology as the foundations of marketing automation. (Source: Gupta, 2015)

Scoping

If the setup is successful, the goals to be pursued must be defined together. Furthermore the team has to have a common idea of the impact of Marketing Automation. The range of applications for marketing and sales is very broad (see Fig. 2). For this reason, the team should select three of the possible goals, prioritize them, and align them with each other. Only then can a consistent set of goals be determined which increases effectiveness and avoids efficiency-robbing conflicts of objectives.

Beyond the explicit goals, it is important to find out what expectations the players from marketing, sales, and other involved areas associate with the project and what restrictions they see. It is also very important to identify any existing "red lines" that must not be crossed, otherwise this will result in showstoppers for the entire project.

Readyness

Before starting with the implementation, it is important to take a self-critical look at where the company stands with regard to the following success criteria:

- Mindset
  Marketing Automation is a data-driven, iterative process. Constant trial and error, measurement, and learning are the DNA of this approach. Classic, campaign-oriented long-term planning is not compatible with this. Marketing Automation maps a data-driven and insight-driven understanding of marketing. The philosophy and working method of "Agile Marketing," on the other hand, corresponds exactly to the requirements. In order to be successful with marketing automation, it is necessary to think consistently from the perspective of the target customer. Only in this way can the purchase decision process be optimally supported with relevant content.

Fig. 2 Marketing and sales goals that can be supported with marketing automation (Source: Own presentation)

- Knowledge
  Beyond attitudes and beliefs, it's about tangible knowledge in areas that are critical to the success of the marketing automation program. Content marketing know-how can be considered a key factor. Relevant content is the fuel for the marketing machine. The marketing team still needs experience with process automation. Without experience in analyzing and interpreting data, it is difficult to extract the insights from the marketing automation system data that are permanently needed in the context of program management.

- Culture
  Marketing automation means constant trial and error and learning. A corporate culture that is fault-tolerant and positively embraces goal-oriented experimentation is a good match for this. Marketing automation stands for an integrated, cross-divisional process. The culture therefore also includes horizontal permeability, i.e., openness to and interaction with the neighboring areas of sales, support, and IT.
- Top management buy-in
  As always with strategic initiatives, the support of top management is enormously important, e.g., to overcome cultural hurdles and achieve the necessary opening. The more top management views marketing automation as a strategic initiative rather than a tool decision, the more likely it is that the conditions critical to success will be created and the necessary changes initiated.
- Marketing Authority
  Marketing must have a high priority in the company to successfully introduce marketing automation. In medium-sized companies, however, marketing today often still plays the role of sales support. There, the marketing department is often still seen as a "coloring-in department" that is responsible for awareness and image at best. In order to initiate a strategic process, however, it must be assigned relevance and responsibility for customer acquisition. It is essential to turn marketing from a cost-into a sales engine.
- Marketing and Sales Alignment
  Marketing automation is based on the customer journey, which begins in marketing and ends in sales with successful customer acquisition. This requires close cooperation and constant coordination between marketing and sales. So that marketing can make a measurable contribution to success, e.g., in the form of qualified leads for the sales department. Common goals, processes, and key performance indicators (KPIs) are required for this.
- Knowledge of and access to target customers
  Successful marketing automation establishes a direct line to the end customer without jeopardizing established sales structures. Thus, sales partners are the recipients of the leads generated by business-to-business (B2B). Knowing the preferences of their customers is crucial for developing relevant content. The Internet affinity of the target customers is decisive for reaching them in the first place and for obtaining the data required to control the marketing automation program.
- Buyer Persona and Customer Journey
  In order to produce relevant content and offer it in the right context, the application of the buyer persona model and mapping to the customer journey is crucial. While the buyer persona model corresponds to the further development of the target group model, the customer journey is about the information and purchase decision process of the target customers or buyer personas. In combination, this results in model maps for marketing automation and content marketing activities.

- Complexity of the purchase decision
  The more complex and in need of explanation a product or service is, the more intensively a decision-maker must familiarize himself with the decision-making process and with relevant decision parameters. And the more he has to learn what a solution to his problem looks like, the higher the added value that marketing automation achieves. This is because with marketing automation, the decision-supporting content can be offered to the respective buyer persona at the right time in the appropriate context.
- Marketing and sales targets
  Marketing automation is not the right approach for every target picture. The higher the congruence with the goals listed above, the more can be expected from marketing automation.
- Marketing Communications
  If a company is already active beyond promotional communication, it will be easy to enter a buyer persona oriented communication characterized by relevance and utility, as the necessary change of perspective is easier to achieve.
- Technical ecosystem (Martech and Salestech)
  If a company already has a CRM or ERP system, then it can dovetail customer and transaction data with the marketing automation system. This opens the opportunity to track the customer's entire customer journey from orientation to purchase and setting up a closed loop. In this way, every activity of the marketing automation program, every touch point can be evaluated and predicted for its contribution to results and budget resources can be allocated where it will generate the highest return on marketing investment (ROMI). However, you only have a valid basis for the use of business intelligence systems if you have accurate data. The better the systems are networked, exchange data and interact with each other, and the more cloud solutions are used, the easier it is to integrate cloud-based marketing automation systems and achieve a new control center for your marketing.
- Marketing budget
  Marketing automation systems are inexpensive. A license is available for as little as a few hundred euros per month. However, the setup and operation of a marketing automation solution requires considerable resources and budget. The setup will not be accomplished for less than 20,000 euros, and it will be difficult to get anything going with less than 5000 euros per month for the ongoing operation, including content marketing and lead management.
- Team/Headcounts
  Experienced specialists are needed to implement marketing automation. The involvement of external service providers or a full-service provider is always the more promising solution when required employees cannot be procured at short notice to complete the team.
- Digital Maturity
  Fully integrated marketing automation is the high-end solution for marketing. Companies from the USA are writing one success story after another with it. However, they also have very different prerequisites than German companies.

Many of them lag considerably behind the required digital status quo. It is difficult to achieve great success with marketing automation if the fax machine is still in use for customer traffic at the same time.

- Industry and market environment
  Internationality, many market participants, providers, solution variants, and substitutes, coupled with perceived lack of transparency for solution seekers, indicate a strong need for information and orientation on the part of customers. In this context, marketing automation can play to its strengths.

2 Buyer Persona and Customer Journey

If one, like most companies, wants to use marketing automation in the context of inbound marketing and lead management to gain visibility and qualified leads, defining buyer personas and determining their customer journey are key tasks. While the buyer persona determines what, i.e., what content, needs to be communicated, the customer journey represents the step-by-step accompaniment of the leads through their purchase decision process.

Buyer Persona

The buyer persona concept is a further development of classic target group models. In contrast to these, the focus is not on socio-demographic characteristics of the target person, but on motives or needs as triggers for the purchase decision process. The core of the buyer persona approach is to determine the motives of the function holder, which could lead to the procurement consideration for a product.

Today, more than 80% of all purchasing decisions begin with an Internet search. The starting point for these searches is increasingly less brands and products than problem or need situations, which are reflected in corresponding search phrases. The challenge is to create context to appear in the search result set of Google & Co. and thus on the radar of the target customers. The starting point in the development of buyer personas are the most valuable customers, from whom one would like to acquire more. Step by step, the essential questions are answered for the following headings:

- Profile
  To whom does this buyer persona report? What is she measured by? Which are trustworthy sources?
- Trigger
  What business situation or change triggers the information and decision-making process that could provide the solution for the prospect?
- Success factors
  What added value does the buyer persona expect from the product? What would inspire them, what would disappoint them? What would be a disaster for them?

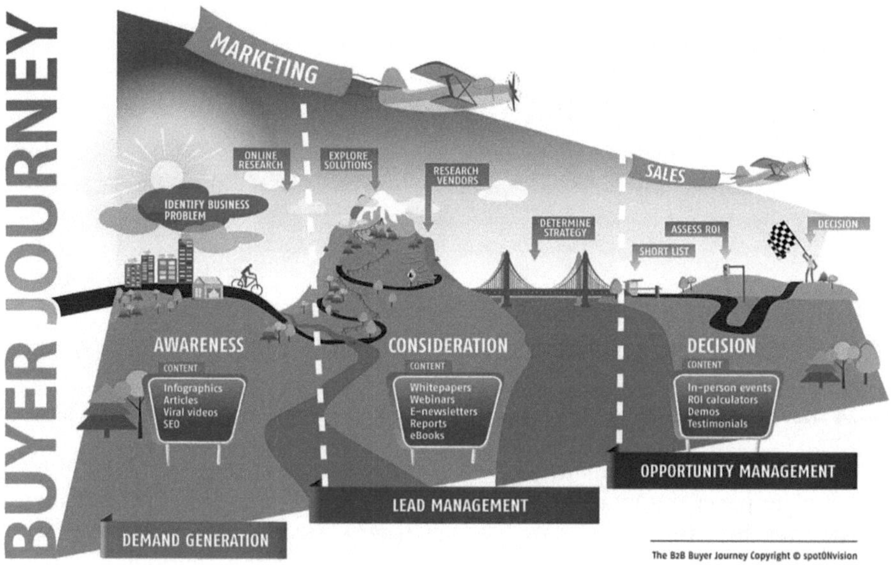

Fig. 3 Buyer journey. (Source: SpotOnVision)

- Barriers
  What attitudes or concerns might prevent the Buyer Persona from buying the specific solution? Why might she not buy it from this company?
- Decision criteria
  Which features and criteria of the solution does the buyer persona evaluate when comparing with procurement alternatives?
- Customer Journey
  What role does the buyer persona play in the decision-making process? Who else influences this?

The result is a clear profile of requirements in terms of content, orientation, and tonality of the content required for the respective buyer persona.

Customer Journey

The customer or buyer journey describes the journey of a buyer persona through the purchase decision process (see Fig. 3). It is the blueprint for the content (content) and process (channel, touch points) orientation of marketing and sales activities.

At the content level, the buyer journey enables conclusions to be drawn about when the buyer persona deals with which questions and which content can be used in this context to capture their attention and provide them with added value. At the process level, it outlines at which touch points you can pick up the buyer persona and on which channels (e-mail, social media, etc.) you should act with which media for

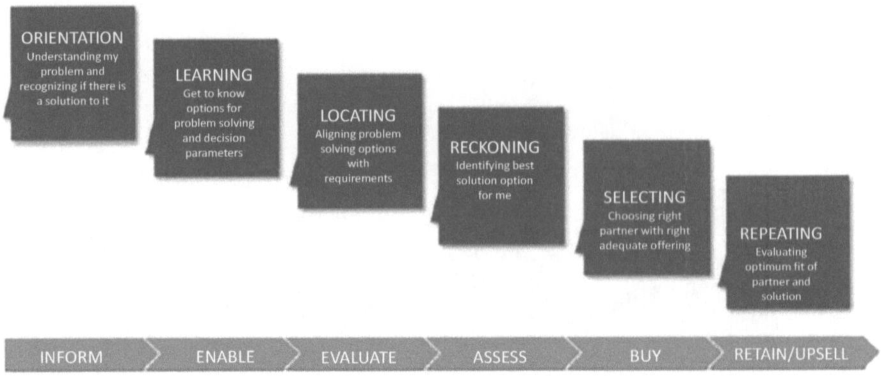

Fig. 4 Key needs and questions in the course of the customer journey (Source: Own presentation)

mats (white paper, infographic, app, etc.) in the respective phase of the customer journey (see Fig. 4).

If possible, all departments of an organization that have direct customer contact or customer knowledge should be involved in the development of the buyer persona and customer journey. In addition to marketing and sales, this also includes customer service and market research. Parallel customer interviews are a good way to validate the results of their work and gain additional insights.

3 Inbound Search Engine Optimization

Purchase decisions by target customers today begin self-determinedly on the Internet in places that the provider does not control and at times that he does not know. The potential customer thus flies under the radar and eludes systematic processing. This is why it is crucial for success to be findable when the target person is looking for content that is relevant to them in the context of their mostly motive-driven search. An inbound SEO analysis provides the answers to the questions of what the buyer persona is looking for, what relevant offers would be for them, and what chance the provider has of being found in this context. In the first step, the subject of this analysis is the analysis of the:

- User perspective
  What is important for the buyer persona? Which phrases or keywords does she use to search for it (relevance)?
- Brand Perspective
  In which context is your own company and its service portfolio currently located by search engines (authority)?

The second step is to identify the intersection of the two perspectives, the so-called content sweet spot (see Fig. 5).

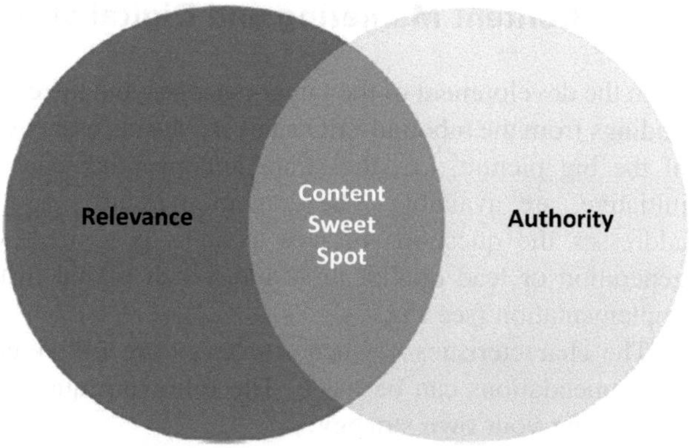

Fig. 5 Content sweet spot as a result of the inbound SEO analysis (Source: Own presentation)

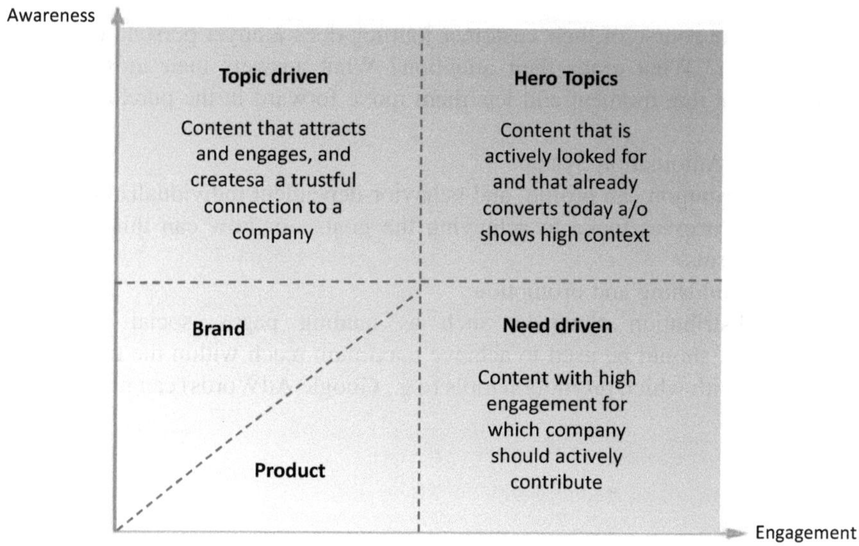

Fig. 6 The topic matrix (Source: Own presentation)

Content that addresses this area is equally relevant for the buyer persona and beneficial for the company's own visibility in the search result ranking. The inclusion of social media in the analysis provides additional insight into which content, topics, and content formats are shared and to what extent.

The result of this phase is the topic matrix. This provides a comprehensive overview of the topics in which the buyer persona is interested, the topics with which they are intensively concerned against the background of their needs, and where the existing content of their own company is to be classified according to this consideration of relevance. The topic matrix thus represents the basis and the guiding principle for the content strategy (see Fig. 6).

4 Content Marketing and Digital Strategy

With the development of the buyer personas and the customer journey as well as the findings from the inbound SEO analysis, the necessary elements for the development of the big picture, i.e., the strategic-conceptual core of a marketing automation initiative, are available. The content marketing and digital strategy essentially addresses the questions of how content is to be used for awareness and lead generation or lead qualification and which digital instruments are to be used for implementation (see Fig. 7).

The characteristics of such a strategy are individual. Accordingly, no general recommendations can be made. The following questions must be answered when developing your own strategy:

- Content
  When in the course of their customer journey does a buyer persona need which information? What grabs their attention? What answers their most important questions at that moment and lets them move forward in the purchase decision process?
- Marketing Automation System
  What contribution can profile- and behavior-dependent individualization of content and processes make to achieving the goals—or how can this be done in concrete terms?
- Content publishing and promotion
  Which distribution channels, such as landing pages, social media, and influencers, should be used to achieve maximum reach within the target group? How and with which promotion tools (e.g., Google AdWords) can momentum be

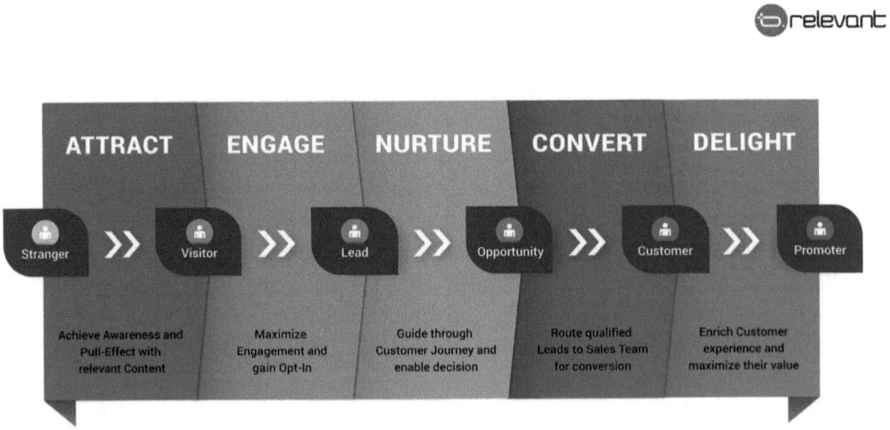

Fig. 7 The content marketing and digital strategy. (Source: Own presentation based on Hubspot, 2015)

quickly built up in the awareness building for the content and retargeting be carried out in the course of lead qualification?

- Digital platforms and tools
  What role should digital platforms (e.g., website), presences (e.g., own social media accounts), and instruments (e.g., newsletter) play? What contribution can they make in the course of the customer journey? How can they interact with existing marketing and sales activities (e.g., trade fair participation)?

Despite all the complexity and the tendency to counter it with a comprehensive strategic approach, it must always be remembered that marketing automation is an iterative process. It thrives on secured, continuous learning. The strategy should therefore focus on guiding ideas that can be validated and further developed during application.

5 Lead Management Concept

Lead management is essentially about the question of what makes a contact a qualified lead for sales. In detail, this involves three areas: the profile of a lead (lead profile), the insights that both the lead and the sales department should gain per customer journey phase (educational critical path), and the underlying lead management processes (see Fig. 8).

The next tasks are the step-by-step enrichment of the lead profile (progressive profiling), the evaluation of the lead profile to determine the lead quality (lead scoring), and for the specific use of content and the tools for knowledge-based qualification of the lead (nurturing). The lead profile determines what information the sales department needs to process a lead successfully and at what point in time. To start working on the profile together with colleagues from sales, it is a good idea to answer the following questions:

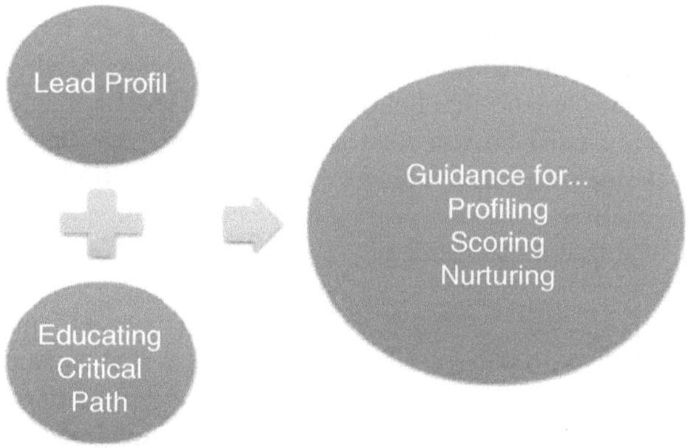

Fig. 8 Basics of lead management (Source: Own presentation)

- What is the minimum set of information about the lead (e.g., person, company, project/product use)?
- What is the optimal set of information about the lead?
- Which parameters with which characteristics determine the value of a lead?
- Which signals or indicators turn a lead into a hot lead that needs to be prioritized?
- Where should the sales-ready lead be routed?

The Educational Critical Path, the success-critical insight process along the customer journey, is also best determined in the interaction between marketing and sales. The following questions help to gain the necessary insights:

- What, i.e., which topics, does the lead deal within which phase?
- From his point of view, what is interesting, what is important, and what is indispensable in the respective phase?
- Which aspects should the lead have necessarily dealt with in each case from the point of view of his own company?
- What specific questions should he have asked himself and answered with the help of relevant content?
- What information should he receive and process from our company and when?

If the results of the previous phase are available, one has the prerequisites to derive the following three levels of the lead management process:

- Progressive profiling
  As a rule, valuable content should be the so-called gated content, i.e., its download should require registration by the prospective customer. The customer journey consists of many questions that the lead is given the opportunity to answer with appropriate content offers. Each of these touch points opens the opportunity to further complete the lead's profile by asking customized questions as part of the next registration process. Knowing when the lead needs what information and what insights sales wants to gain in the same breath provides the blueprint for Progressive Profiling.
- Lead scoring
  Answering the question of when a lead is ready for sales is the task of lead scoring based on lead profile and educational critical path. In lead scoring, each profile characteristic (explicit characteristics such as name, e-mail, decision authority, etc.) must be weighted according to its relevance and assigned a quantitative value. The same applies to the lead's interactions (implicit characteristics such as opening an e-mail, visiting a website, downloading a content module), which map the lead's engagement.

If the sum of the ratings reaches a defined threshold, the lead becomes a marketing qualified lead and can be transferred to Sales for further processing (see Fig. 9). Experience shows that the final result cannot yet be achieved in the first impact. This can be understood as a qualified working hypothesis that is

Fig. 9 Lead scoring matrix (Source: Own presentation)

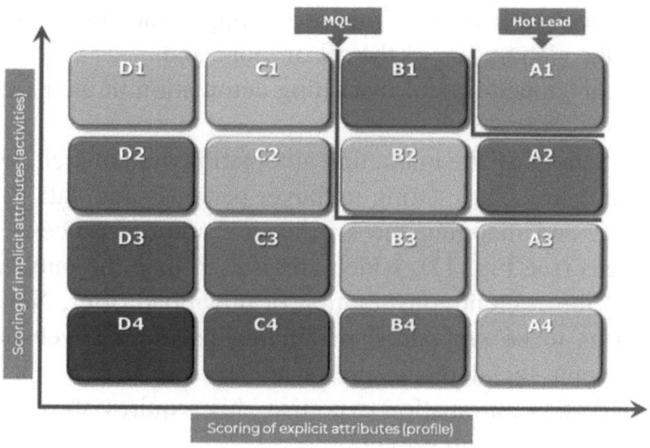

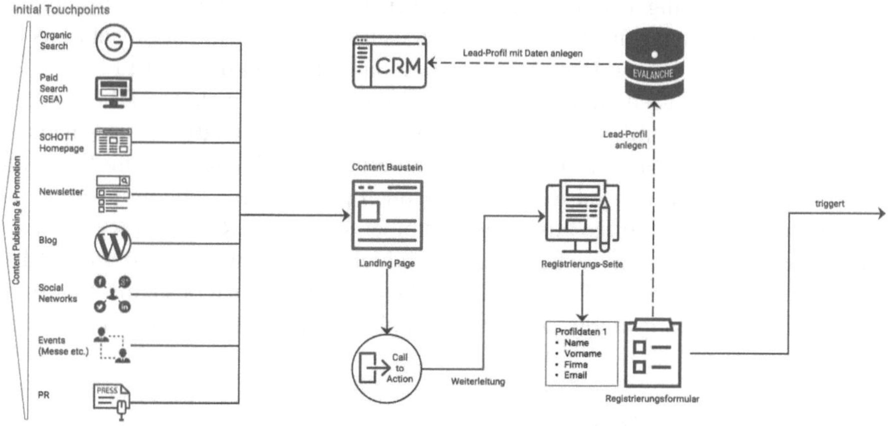

Fig. 10 Sample lead nurturing process (Source: Own presentation)

continuously optimized together with Sales. The joint learning process will lead to an increasingly accurate evaluation model that can be used to reliably determine the qualification status and the optimum handover time to sales.

If profiling and scoring are combined against the background of the selected strategy, the result is the lead nurturing process. This detailed process model of lead management must then be mapped in the marketing automation system (see Fig. 10).

6 Marketing Automation Setup

Tangible results are achieved from the start of the marketing automation setup phase. The setup can be divided into three action circles:

- the establishment of the marketing automation system,
- the elaboration of the set of tools, and
- the embedding of marketing automation in their technical ecosystem.

Setting up the marketing automation system includes, for example, creating users and their rights, setting up buyer personas and data fields, importing any inventory data, and mapping the scoring and nurture processes. The tools include landing pages (see Fig. 11), which are used to map the publication of content, registration, and the content consumption or download offer. Newsletter and e-mail templates, forms to be embedded in landing pages and websites, and the establishment of relevant social media presences are also part of the basic toolkit. In addition to marketing automation expertise, this requires above all experience in the development of web and e-mail objects.

The more the marketing automation system is integrated into the existing systems as the control center of marketing, the greater the achievable utility value. In the course of creating landing pages and web forms, it is obligatory to interlock with the content management system, which usually provides the technical basis for the website. In the second step, the marketing automation system must be linked to all systems that are used along the customer journey. These include CRM and ERP systems, but also business intelligence systems and social media and ad management. The goal should be to be able to continuously track and measure the entire customer journey of the lead from the first touch point (e.g., a landing page) to the successful conversion to the customer (customer status in CRM and ERP). Then it can be determined exactly which measure, which content, which process, etc. has achieved which value contribution. This makes it possible to allocate the marketing budget where it demonstrably achieves the highest return on marketing investment.

7 Agile Realization

Now that the strategic-conceptual foundation is in place and the lead generation and qualification machine has been built with the marketing automation setup, the task is to achieve the optimal output. Instead of developing a comprehensive concept and waiting for the output of the campaign after pushing the start button (linear process), marketing automation with agile realization enables and conditions a more promising approach (see Fig. 12).

In traditional marketing, the findings on the success of a campaign are only available at the end of the campaign or after a further analysis period with the help of market research. With marketing automation, the results are available in real time. This makes it possible to intervene in the ongoing process to optimize it. It also has an effect on planning and conception. Instead of a big bang, you start with small steps. Long planning periods thus become a series of short cycles that enable faster learning from the test results.

Marketing automation thus breaks with many traditional and familiar characteristics of marketing. New impact mechanics, a changed interaction with

Fig. 11 Landing page mockup (Source: Own presentation)

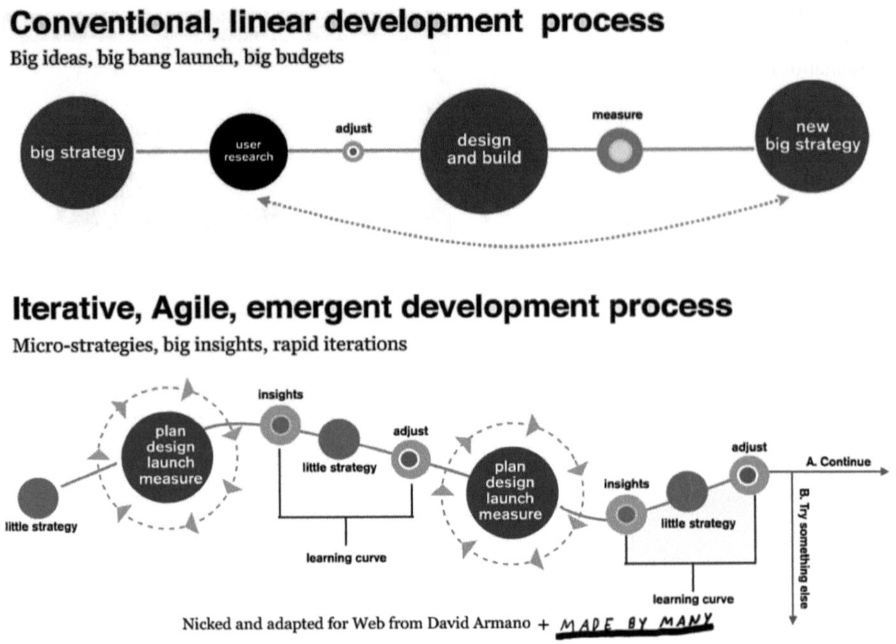

Fig. 12 Linear vs. agile project management processes (Source: Armano, 2015)

other corporate divisions, and new expertise pose not inconsiderable challenges when embarking on this path. The roadmap presented here cannot exhaustively answer all the questions that arise on the path to greater marketing and sales success with marketing automation. However, it should make it possible to target the milestones that lead to success and draw attention to the biggest pitfalls along the way.

References

Armano, D. (2015). *Agile methodologies*. Accessed April 04, 2017, from http://agilemarketingmanifesto.org/values/adaptive-and-iterative-campaigns-over-big-bang-campaigns

Gupta, M. (2015). *Marketing technology*. Accessed May 18, 2015, http://www.martechadvisor.com/interviews/marketing-technology/founding-principles-of-enabling-an-omni-channel-strategy/

Hubspot. (2015). *Inbound methodology*. White paper. Hubspot. Accessed April 04, 2017, from http://www.hubspot.de/inbound-marketing

Alexander Körner is the founder and managing director of b. relevant – Agile Digital Marketing Agency GmbH and a member of the board of the Institute for Marketing and Sales Automation. He has been working for years on the customer journey, which has been changed by the Internet, and its impact on marketing and sales.

Dovetailing of Marketing and Sales Automation

Manfred Aull

1 Digitalization Is Changing Procurement Behavior Permanently

Every day we experience how digitalization influences our lives. More tasks can be completed faster and with less effort. This is also particularly true for procurement processes. Anyone who needs a printer today, for example, enters the term "color laser" into an Internet search engine, checks the functionalities, sets a price range, looks at the customer reviews for the two or three favorites that have been filtered out in the meantime, and possibly completes the purchase directly online without having sought personal contact with a sales consultant.

The vast majority of future private, but also business customers use the possibilities of the Internet to obtain information in the early phase of the emergence of a need, in order to get a first idea, a first approach to his requirement within seconds. Thanks to the Internet with its powerful search engines and databases, basic access to information is easier than ever. The Allensbach Institute for Public Opinion Research writes in a recent study that over 90% of purchasing decisions are influenced by the Internet (Köcher & Bruttel, 2011). The behavior described here has thus found its way into our procurement routines in the long term.

The period in which interested parties anonymously obtain information on the Internet can be used excellently to understand their search behavior and, building on this, to deliver situationally adequate information morsels in a digestible form. In this way, a provider establishes itself as a competent and active, but at the same time unobtrusive, solution partner long before a contact is made. This results in valuable clues for the purchase-critical decision parameters, the form of the information desired or still required by the interested party, as well as the stage reached by the

M. Aull (✉)
Manfred Aull Sales Success, Düsseldorf, Germany
e-mail: manfred@aulls2.de

U. Hannig, U. Seebacher (eds.), *Marketing and Sales Automation*, Management for Professionals, https://doi.org/10.1007/978-3-031-20040-3_4

latter in the purchase cycle. In the course of the interactions, a profile of the prospective customer is automatically created on the basis of prefabricated documents and queries. This prepares the personal contact of the sales staff in the best possible way. The optimal accompaniment and retention of the prospect in the period just described is an essential goal of Marketing Automation (MA), which marks the waypoints for this "customer journey," as exemplified in Fig. 1.

2 The Marketing Automation Opportunity

Due to the increasing relevance of the aforementioned customer behavior before a first contact with potential suppliers, companies should deal with marketing automation and especially with the opportunities it offers for early prospect retention and needs-based support.

The Institute for Sales and Marketing Automation defines the term "marketing automation" as follows:

- "Marketing automation is the IT-supported execution of recurring marketing tasks with the goal of increasing the efficiency of marketing processes and the effectiveness of marketing decisions" (Hannig, 2016).

In concrete terms, marketing automation supports the creation of attention, the need-based information, and the binding of target customers already in the very early information phases in the purchase cycle. The prospective customer can be confronted with attractive messages and performance promises after the provider has become visible in the search processes of the consumer.

According to an unpublished study by the Chair of Marketing at the University of Erlangen-Nuremberg, Marketing Automation is about automating processes in decentralized marketing. Examples of this can be automated execution of personal one-to-one campaigns or interest-based promotional content. Marketing automation maintains integrated communication across different channels with mailings, banner placements, the generation of landing pages, emails, etc. (Walla, 2016).

A customer who is tackling the solution of a requirement enters his first vague idea for a solution into an Internet search engine. He browses the first, sometimes the second, and only in very rare cases more than the third page of results. Interesting sounding offers are clicked on by him. If he finds what he is looking for there and if approaches that fit his solution are described clearly, then he is prepared to have further useful information, such as a white paper, sent to him in a first contact step and to disclose initial data about himself, at least his e-mail address. And if this proves helpful, then his interest is aroused to embark on the customer journey with further helpful content, such as e-books or videos, and to contribute to the refinement of his profile information. On this journey, the customer wants to be able to call up the information that suits him best and to have his individual situation acknowledged by an adapted offer. Once he has gained enough trust in his solution partner, he finally places his order.

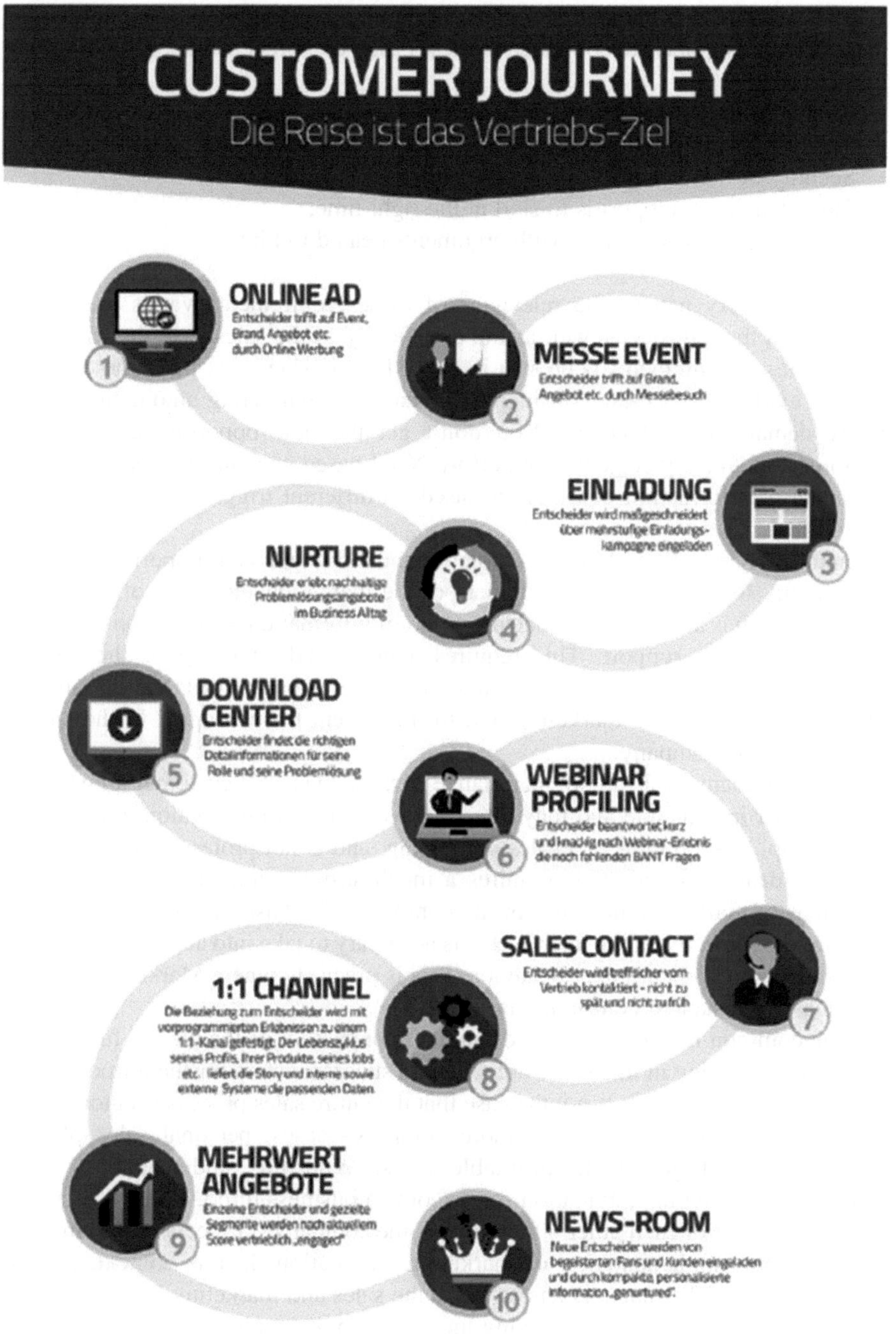

Fig. 1 The customer journey (Source: SC-Networks o.J.)

The essential requirements for good marketing automation and any subsequent personal sales support are contained in these easily comprehensible personal wishes:

- Timing of the information is selectable by the customer;
- The type of information and contact can be controlled by the customer;
- Security of the data provided by the customer is guaranteed;
- Individual sales support is to start at the right time;
- The customer is convinced with arguments geared to him.

By their very nature, the relevance of these requirements varies greatly and depends on the industry as well as the complexity of the sales case. In principle, a mix of these requirements is present in every B2B business. At the same time, it is already evident from these considerations that good marketing automation is definitely demanding and costly. You don't get the new opportunities to engage customers at an early stage without effort. Need-based content must be created and a system of information distribution based on different trigger situations must be established.

In the early retention of interested parties and individualized support lies the great opportunity for the further development of the market development of companies. Specifically, it is about the automated support of information-seeking consumers and their active sales support. This requires a good understanding of the changed customer behavior and the openness to consider new possibilities that digitalization also offers in sales and marketing and to implement them adapted to the specific situation of the company.

After all, many deals do not materialize because the target customer knows about the provider in principle and may already have gathered information, but he is not "picked up," i.e. brought to a sales processing, and is not professionally supported until the deal is closed. This requires a much stronger integration of the classic functions of marketing and sales in the company. The basic focus of the functions remains the same, but at the interfaces it is necessary to take into account the changed information and procurement behavior. This is precisely where Marketing Automation makes substantial contributions.

The common understanding and mutual appreciation of the classic functions of sales and marketing in this sense are essential success factors for the introduction of marketing automation. It is not the case that the entire sales process is automated by marketing. In many—especially more complex—cases, personal sales play the decisive role in generating profitable sales. With this understanding of the disciplines, marketing automation can become a business turbo. Mutual respect for the performance of each other's functions in the company is especially important for the profitable implementation of marketing automation. In this context, it is the responsibility of the management to value the sales and marketing functions and to get them on board with the following messages, for example.

- Message for Marketing:
  "Marketing can make a better contribution to the positioning of our company with marketing automation, especially with new customers who are not yet known to us today and who have not yet personally outed themselves as prospects. This is achieved in particular by providing these prospects with needs-based information at the right time. At the same time, valuable profile information, including the status of the purchase process, can be collected. As a result, the acquisition process can be supported much better."
- Message for Sales:
  "It's about our firm taking advantage of the evolving changes in how we gather information from target customers and adapting in the best way possible to position ourselves with them early and generate better leads, both quantitatively and qualitatively. Sales continues to be the critical entity for personalized trust and business generation."

3 Getting Started with Sales Automation in B2B Sales Organizations

In B2B practice, one often experiences that the sales department, as an extended workbench, is somehow supposed to sell what is developed and produced. A good product will sell itself. Systematic control of sales or even dovetailing with marketing are often treated stepmotherly because there are supposedly no good procedures and techniques for this.

First and foremost, customers want their requirements to be fulfilled by an efficient and trustworthy supplier that they can rely on even in the event of difficulties. This trust cannot be fully created by an automated process, especially in the case of complex requirements, even if it is personalized through marketing automation.

In a demand situation, the target customer wants to be looked after personally and in this way led to good decisions. He is happy to have someone who takes care of this individual need and its background, proposes convincing solutions, and conveys security.

It would therefore be a fatal mistake to believe that sales could be abolished through marketing automation. The opposite is the case. Many sales cases still require a personal relationship of trust and the competence of the sales manager. The more complex the relationships are, the earlier and more intensively individual sales support should be involved. Automation cannot do this. But automation can "take care" of the needy in the "anonymous" phase of the buying cycle far better than it can without it. The sales employee can work more effectively because he receives significantly more qualified contacts—in addition to his other possibilities for identifying business opportunities from his personal network of decision-makers, trade fair contacts or as a result of other market activities.

In order to be able to profitably use the advantages achieved through marketing automation, the sales manager needs a positive attitude based on inner drive, discipline, and sales systematics. He must focus his attention on the right topics

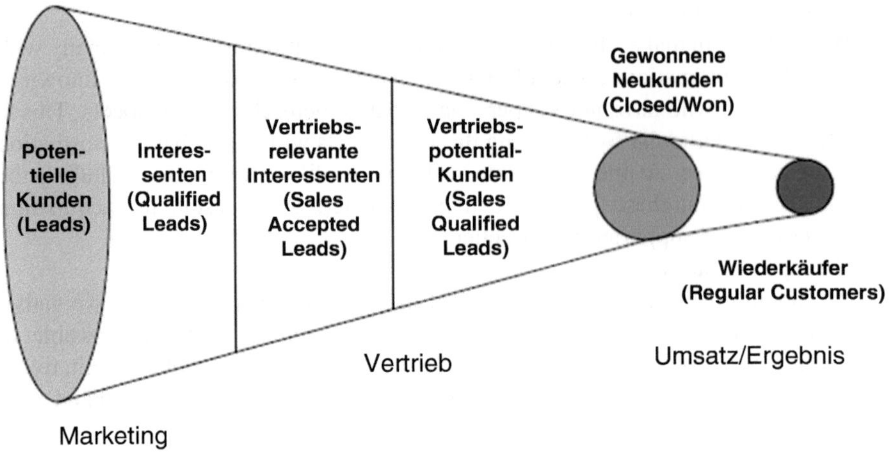

Fig. 2 The sales funnel

with the right people at the right time. To be helpful and successful for the target customer, the sales person needs contact skills, conversational skills, negotiation skills, and closing skills as tools of the trade. The right combination of attitude, good behavior, and sales systematics is important.

In any case, it is important to create transparency with the sales management; not only for reporting purposes, but also for the planning of market development. It is important to avoid wasting sales energy on supposed business opportunities that never become orders or that cannot be won. The filling of the sales funnel (see Fig. 2) and the movement of potential business through to closing can be mapped and tracked by sales automation systems.

- "Sales automation (SA) is the IT-supported execution of recurring sales tasks with the goal of increasing the efficiency of sales processes and the effectiveness of sales decisions" (IFSMA, 2016).

In practice, self-developed solutions still today, as the study of the Institute for Sales and Marketing Automation proves. It is to be expected that their functionalities will be technically covered by CRM and MA systems in the future. Therefore, essential application mechanisms of SA solutions in sales practice are described below, independent of a specific software solution.

Goal of a sales organization should be become familiar with the fundamental mechanisms of action that ultimately underlie all SA solutions. In this way, initial experience is gained in day-to-day management, the first feelings of success are achieved and the motivation for a more efficient solution is created. And the company learns much better what to look for in an SA solution and what it must offer.

Decisive for the success of such systems are the inherent mechanisms of action in sales, namely the focus of attention of the sales team on the right topics with the right people at the right time, and the management discipline of follow-up, constructive questioning, and thus improvement of the sales work. These core aspects are already addressed in intermediate step described below. In particular, it affects attitude as well as systematic behavior and thus prepares a more efficient system in the best possible way.

Due to the intermediate step of introducing sales automation with a negligible technical system effort—only tools that have already been introduced, are used—the focus is placed from the very beginning on the central mechanisms of sales automation and not on its technical implementation. The focus is on the development of the sales behavior and the communication between the operationally responsible sales department and its management. The discipline, the focus of the sales managers on the essential sales topics, and the systematic sales approach are thus promoted. Same applies to the discipline of follow-up with targeted exchange between sales staff and their sales management. Furthermore, the low implementation effort and the work with familiar tools significantly increase the acceptance of the systematic sales approach. As a result, it is often much easier to get people enthusiastic about it in practice.

For the company, it is important that sales work is systematic and consistently successful and transparent. The tools used to achieve this are of secondary importance. The main goal of sales automation is ultimately to generate more profitable business. For sales practice, this can be broken down into the three sub-goals of sales automation:

1. Clarification of the question: "Who should be our customer?" And this in the aspects "Who do you approach sales-wise?" and "In which business opportunities do you not put any further sales energy?";
2. Focusing the attention of sales managers on the most important sales aspects that are critical to winning orders;
3. Transparency of market development and expected business.

With a target customer radar of any kind (see Fig. 3), the concrete target customer landscape can be mapped, i.e. the companies with which one would like to do business in the future. The existing customers plus the target customer radar including the leads from the marketing automation result in the target market. It is excellent for planning market cultivation as well as making it transparent and is also mapped in different ways in more complex SA solutions. It makes sense to assign priorities for the processing of the target customers and to underlay the sales measures with deadlines.

The following data, which also form the data basis of an SA solution, must at least be included in the mapping of the target customers:

Column 1: Sales manager VB

The sales manager is responsible for market cultivation and the action defined in column 4. His task is to go "with his search beam" over the defined target market and discover business potentials.

Zielkundenradar Datum 20xx/yy/zz					
VB	Prio	Zielkunde	Maßnahme: Wann? Was? Bei wem?	Aktueller Status - Ergebnis	Potenzial p.a.
VB1	1	Unternehmen 1	20xx/10/14 Telefontermin mit Leiter Technik Herr Bauer zur Bedarfsklärung	Telefontermin mit Herrn Bauer via Assistenz	500,000 €
VB1	1	Unternehmen 2	20xx/10/15 Besuchstermin zur geschäftlichen Qualifizierung bei CFO Herrn Epple	Interesse geweckt im Ersttelefonat	300,000 €
VB1	1	Unternehmen 3	20xx/10/10 Akquisebrief Geschäftsführerin Frau Lowinger	Brief bei Assistenz angekündigt	200,000 €
VB1	1	Unternehmen 4	20xx/10/22 Ansprache Geschäftsführer Herr Brunswick auf Branchenkonferenz	Erscheint auf Teilnehmerliste der Konferenz	200,000 €
VB1	1	Unternehmen 5	20xx/10/22 Ansprache technische Leitung Frau Bäumer auf Branchenkonferenz	Erscheint auf Teilnehmerliste der Konferenz	200,000 €
VB1	2	Unternehmen 6	20xx/10/22 Ansprache Abteilungsleiter Hellmann auf Branchenkonferenz	Erscheint auf Teilnehmerliste der Konferenz	80,000 €
VB1	2	Unternehmen 7	20xx/12/13 Erstbesuch CTO Herr Lampe		70,000 €
VB1	2	Unternehmen 9	20xx/11/18 Telefontermin Qualifikation Geschäftsmöglichkeiten		70,000 €
VB1	3	Unternehmen 10	20xx/11 Telemarketing – Firma beauftragt und gebrieft		50,000 €
VB1	3	Unternehmen 11	20xx/11 Telemarketing – Firma beauftragt und gebrieft		50,000 €
VB1	3	Unternehmen 12	20xx/11 Telemarketing – Firma beauftragt und gebrieft		50,000 €
VB1	3	Unternehmen 13	20xx/11 Telemarketing – Firma beauftragt und gebrieft		
VB1	3	Unternehmen 14	20xx/11 Telemarketing – Firma beauftragt und gebrieft		
VB1	2	Unternehmen 15	20xx/11/11 Akquisebrief Leiter Werke Ausland Herr Paul	Bestehendes Geschäft mit Werken Inland	100,000 €

Farblegende
Potenzielle Geschäftsmöglichkeit, muss weiter qualifiziert werden
Kaufender Kunde, Cross- und Upselling
Kein Zielkunde, kein Geschäft möglich

Fig. 3 The target customer radar (Source: Aull, 2016)

Column 2: Priority

The Priority column describes the order in which market cultivation should take place. The priority results, on the one hand, from the importance and size of the customer, on the other hand, from the existing accesses of the sales manager.

Column 3: Target customer

This column is about facts about the target customer company. There are two versions of the target customer radar, depending on whether an existing address directory is established in the CRM system or whether the addresses are managed in the target customer radar.

Column 4: Scheduled action

It has proven useful to start entries in this column with the specified date format "year/month/day." After that, the target result of the action is described as concisely as possible. Here are some wording suggestions for the entry in the action column of the target customer radar:

- Telephone call with the aim of making an appointment for an introduction and business qualification;
- Visit;
- Acquisition letter individual or campaign;
- Acquisition email individual or campaign;
- Fair invitation;
- Presentation;
- Addressing industry conference;
- Fair date;
- Telemarketing with the goal of initial qualification.

Projekt / Segment	Volumen in €	Wettbewerber & deren Strategie	Verkaufsziel	Vertriebsstrategie
•	•	•	•	•

Zwingendes Kaufmotiv, Geschäftsziel des Kunden
•

Unser Mehrwert
•

Entscheider beim Kunden & Entscheidungstiming
•

Entscheidungsmächtige Unterstützung
•

Wichtigste Entscheidungskriterien des Kunden
•

Kritische Erfolgsfaktoren für Projektgewinn
•

Fig. 4 The most important sales aspects (Source: Aull, 2016)

Column 5: Current status—result

The result of the most recently performed measures is recorded here, e.g.:

- Interest aroused;
- Follow-up appointment arranged;
- does not fit, because: ....

Column 6: Potential

Here is an indicator of the possible size of sales with the customer. This will initially be a rough estimate, because far too little is known about the target customer. The most concrete in this column is certainly the estimation of a euro value.

If business opportunities are identified during this market cultivation with the support of the target customer radar, then these must be systematically processed: In sales practice, focusing on the key aspects of a business opportunity has proven to be effective in order to position oneself, assess the probability of closing and, above all, increase it. These key points are shown in the fields of the following diagram (see Fig. 4).

First field: Compelling motive to buy

This is a description of the motivation to act, ideally derived from the customer's business objectives. The pressure to act on the part of the customer should be expressed briefly and succinctly here. It is often particularly informative to consider what happens if no purchase decision is made. If there are no noticeable consequences, the buying motive is too weak. Mentioning relevant project examples of successful companies can help to motivate action. It is important that only what is expressed by the customer is recorded and not the customer's own wishful thinking.

Field 2: Decision-making process

In this field it is entered by whom the decision is made at the partner and when this happens. For this, exact research, great attention, and the best possible precision are decisive. The way in which the decision is actually taken should be recorded in bullet points.

Field 3: Decision criteria
Here are the effectively effective and indispensable decision criteria of the customer. These are not necessarily congruent with the published criteria. The focus is on the "must-haves", not on the "nice-to-haves". Very often, buyers or other representatives of the operational level present extensive catalogs of requirements in order to make the incoming offers comparable on the basis of as many criteria as possible. In the decision-making circles, however, often only a handful of criteria are effectively discussed and evaluated. In the course of the informational interviews, focus on prioritizing the criteria.

Field 4: Business added value
It is precisely these actual decision criteria in the third field that must now be used to build the business added value and formulate it as far as possible "in the language of the customer." The customer should be able to see a clear connection between the solution offered, his strategic priorities, and his pressing problems. The basis for the formulation is the services and special features of the customer's company and of the company's own offering, which are precisely tailored to the project requirements and genuine decision-making criteria. This added value must then be formulated in the customer's conceptual world.

Field 5: Decision-making support
This maps who among the key decision-makers recognizes the value and wants to see the vendor as a partner. If an executive of the customer says that he sees the provider as a partner, he should ideally describe his preference on the basis of the business added value that has been developed.

Field 6: Critical success factors
Here it is necessary to describe what has to be done concretely in order to get the order. This also includes the courage to ask for a commitment.

Closer to the order placement, this section of the sales plan becomes more important. Even with positive signals about the company and its performance, it is worth paying close attention and asking questions such as: "Thank you for your assessment. What specifically needs to be done now to turn this into an order?". This is ultimately an invitation to the interlocutor to help. This demands something from him, but is justified by a committed and professionally managed sales campaign and the courage to ask for a commitment. Asking questions and asking for support will guide you through the process. This is an intense exchange—ideally a win-win situation that benefits both partners. And sometimes it's a matter of helping the customer to his happiness and the liberating conclusion and removing the obstacles on the way to the order together with him.

Forecast Datum 20xx/05/29									
VB	Kunde	Business-Status	Geschäfts-möglichkeit	Potenzial	Auftrags-eingang	Wahrschein-lichkeit	Auftragseingang gewichtet	Auftrags-monat	Nächste Aktion
Schmitz	Unternehmen A	neu	CPE	400,000 €	70,000 €	50%	35,000 €	20xx/06	20xx/06/11 Präsentation bei GF E. Löw, Ziel Überzeugung auf Top-Ebene
Schmitz	Unternehmen B	bestehend	CPE	350,000 €	120,000 €	70%	84,000 €	20xx/07	20xx/07/08 Nachweis Managebarkeit CPE im Kundenlabor
Schmitz	Unternehmen C	neu	CPE	200,000 €	80,000 €	40%	32,000 €	20xx/08	20xx/07/06 Kennenlernen CEO Frau Bäumer auf Konferenz, Kontaktaufbau
Schmitz	Unternehmen D	neu	Umrüstung HE	250,000 €	25,000 €	30%	7,500 €	20xx/12	20xx/08/03 Gespräch AL Heil zur Bestätigung Entscheidungskriterien
Schmitz	Unternehmen E	neu	POPs Region 1	200,000 €	150,000 €	40%	60,000 €	20xx/09	20xx/07/05 Schlussverhandlung mit Einkaufsleiter Herr Panzel
Schmitz	Unternehmen F	bestehend	EDFA	80,000 €	10,000 €	70%	7,000 €	20xx/11	20xx/07/20 Gespräch Prod-mgmt, Ziel Überzeugung von Design & Funktion
Schmitz	Unternehmen G	bestehend	Netz Werk 3	100,000 €	31,000 €	60%	18,600 €	20xx/11	20xx/07/08 Besuch Leiter Werk 3 bei unserer Referenzinstallation Werk1
Schmitz	Unternehmen H	neu	CPE	100,000 €	48,000 €	35%	16,800 €	20xx/12	20xx/08/27 Präsentation 3D-Print CPE Innovation für CTO und Mitarbeiter
Schmitz	Unternehmen I	bestehend	Modem	100,000 €	15,000 €	50%	7,500 €	20xx/09	20xx/09/05 Teststellung Nachweis 1Gbps Durchsatz und Stabilität bei Last
Schmitz	Unternehmen J	neu	CPE	70,000 €	10,000 €	50%	5,000 €	20xx/10	20xx/06/23 Besuch Zentrallabor mit dem Technischen GF Rutz: CPE Demo
Summe				1,850,000 €	559,000 €	49%	273,400 €		

Fig. 5 The forecast form (Source: Aull, 2016)

The business opportunities processed with this system as a constant mental companion of the sales work are summarized in the instrument "Forecast." The sales process supported by Sales Automation has the core functions "filling the sales funnel" (target customer radar) and "successful movement of sales opportunities through the sales funnel to closing" (forecasting). In this respect, the forecast is at the heart of the sales process. It is not just a reporting tool, but rather a guidepost in sales. The sales manager is accountable to himself and to his sales management for his future business and is at the same time reminded of the important focus topics for the business profit. An empty field in the forecast form (see Fig. 5) is to be understood as a hint and should be filled in as soon as possible. Only through regular follow-up does the format develop its effect. Because then the sales manager knows what to expect in these monthly, bi-weekly, or even weekly sales meetings. And therefore he questions his own knowledge about the positioning in the business opportunity and will already strive in advance to determine the essential information, to implement the measures of the last meeting and overall to increase the order probability. The same questions over and over again imprint themselves and result in actions. On the one hand, a forecast that is taken seriously and handled professionally can help in estimating future business. On the other hand, it also initiates measures to improve the order probability or the release of resources through the qualification of business opportunities that are not or not positively developing.

Customer Name

Business status New business or a new business opportunity with an existing customer

Business opportunity A name that is as self-explanatory as possible should be chosen for the business opportunity.

Potential An estimated cumulative sales potential of the customer in a period of time customary in the industry is to be entered here as an indicator of the possible size and relevance of the customer.

Incoming orders Incoming orders refer to the value of the specific business processed, for which a decision is made and an order is placed.

Order probability Probability that the order under consideration will be won.

Weighted incoming orders This is the probability-weighted incoming orders in euros. The sum of the weighted incoming orders is particularly meaningful.

Because the better the forecast quality and the more business opportunities are in the forecast, the better the informative value of this column due to the law of large numbers.

Month of order entry Only those who know the decision-making and commissioning process well are in a position to forecast the time of commissioning. Caution is advised with projects that are repeatedly delayed. Either the project is not that important or the sales manager does not really have a good understanding of the processes and responsible persons at the customer.

Next action The operational and action-oriented character of the forecast format becomes visible here. Ideally provided with a defined date format (year/month/day), the next sales action is recorded in bullet point form. This makes the forecast even more action-oriented.

Regardless of whether one decides directly for an SA solution or takes the intermediate step with on-board resources, the focus must be on the right topics with the right people at the right time. Especially when companies have little experience with sales systematics, the intermediate step helps to focus on the essential content and not on system properties or requirements, to deepen the understanding as well as the mechanisms of action of SA and thus to prepare the introduction of a software solution.

References

Aull, M. (2016). *B2B - Or not to be? The path to sales success and profitable growth.* Springer Gabler.

Hannig, U. (2016, September 02). *What is Marketing Automation? - Marketing Automation concerns all recurring processes.* acquisa. https://www.haufe.de/marketing-vertrieb/online-marketing/was-ist-eigentlich-marketing-automation/marketing-automation-betrifft-alle-wiederkehrenden-prozesse_132_374262.html

IFSMA. (2016). *The customer value funnel.* http://imis.de/portal/ifsma/de/dt.jsp?seite=institut_fuer_sales_und_marketing_automation

Köcher, R., & Bruttel, O. (2011). *Social media IT & society 2011.* 1st Infosys study, Institut für Demoskopie, Allensbach.

Walla, K. (2016). *Marketing Automation – Identification of positive and negative effects on consumer behavior.* Unpublished study by the Chair of Marketing at the University of Erlangen-Nuremberg, Nuremberg.

Manfred Aull is a graduate physicist (TU Munich), Executive MBA (Duke University), and Systemic Organizational Consultant (Prof. Dr. Fritz B. Simon). He is the owner of the Aull Sales Success Institute, which has focused on sales concepts and sales training in the B2B environment for more than ten years.

CRM, CXM, and Marketing Automation

Klaus Heinzelbecker

The use of CRM systems is now a standard application in Germany and Switzerland. This is shown by studies conducted by the Institute for Sales and Marketing (IFSMA). In the 2016 survey, 76 percent of responding companies said they already had a CRM system in place and a further 17 percent were planning to introduce one. The latest study from 2021 shows that around 80% in Germany now have a CRM system in place and a further 13% are planning to introduce one in the next 24 months (Hannig et al., 2021).

In contrast, the IFSMA study from the year 2021 shows that marketing automation systems (MAS) are still relatively uncommon in Germany. Only 35% of the companies already use a MAS, but another 30% said they are planning to implement it in the next 1–2 years (Hannig et al., 2021).

Some users are likely to assume that the requirements of marketing are already sufficiently covered by the CRM system. This conclusion can be drawn from the IFSMA study of 2021. It shows, that in 75% of cases, marketing is user of the CRM system.

However, whether all of the CRM systems currently used in practice are also useful for marketing can be doubted on the basis of the development status of many systems. Almost half of the companies surveyed in the IFSMA study by 2019 stated that they had been working with their CRM system for more than 5 years. Accordingly, it is not surprising that around 23% of the companies already using a CRM system today are planning to replace it in the next 2 years. This concerns above all also the self-developed systems which have at present still a portion of 9% (Hannig et al., 2019). The benchmarks are the goals mentioned in the IFSMA study of 2016: Increasing efficiency (cited by 73%) and increasing effectiveness (cited by 57%).

K. Heinzelbecker (✉)
Institute for Sales and Marketing Automation (IFSMA), Ludwigshafen, Germany
e-mail: heinzelbecker@ifsma.de

U. Hannig, U. Seebacher (eds.), *Marketing and Sales Automation*, Management for Professionals, https://doi.org/10.1007/978-3-031-20040-3_5

How these goals are achieved depends on whether the CRM implemented is already at the development stage of CRM 4.0 or is still more or less far away from it.

1 From CRM 0.0 to CRM 4.0

Current CRM development is moving in the direction of comprehensive customer experience management that covers all points of contact with customers and prospects. The aim is to turn satisfied customers into loyal customers and to turn them into referrers. However, the road to such a concept is still long in most companies, and in many cases the established CRM system is still rather at the level of the first or second system generation.

The forerunners of today's CRM systems were still called sales force reporting and sales force management systems in the 1980s (see Fig. 1). The objective was to ensure market-oriented sales force management which is not only based on sales, contribution margins, etc., but above all on market potential and the competitive situation (Heinzelbecker, 1985). In most cases, these systems failed because the sales force did not want to be abused as market researchers, nor did they want to reveal too much information about their activities. The enthusiasm of the sales staff toward such a "control instrument" was accordingly very limited. Excessively time-consuming data entry and bureaucratic forms were readily cited as reasons for the lack of use.

CRM systems of the first generation (CRM 1.0) emphasized the principle of customer retention. The effort and cost of retaining customers was set against the higher cost of repeatedly acquiring new customers. In addition to classic instruments, such as bonus and discount programs, the key role was assigned to sales, especially in the industrial goods sector. The core idea was to retain profitable customers over the long term.

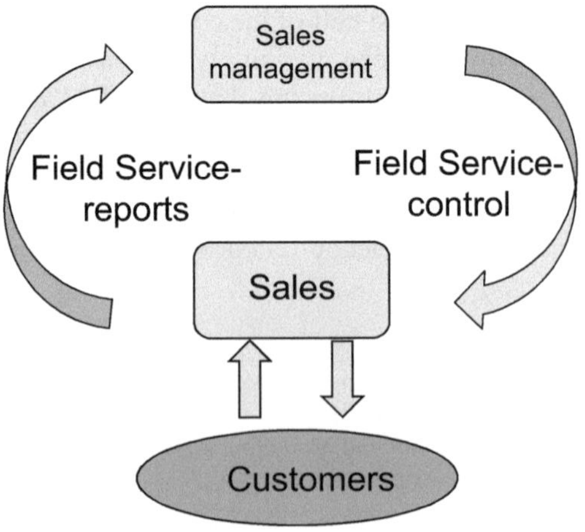

Fig. 1 Field service reporting and control systems (CRM 0.0) (Source: Own representation)

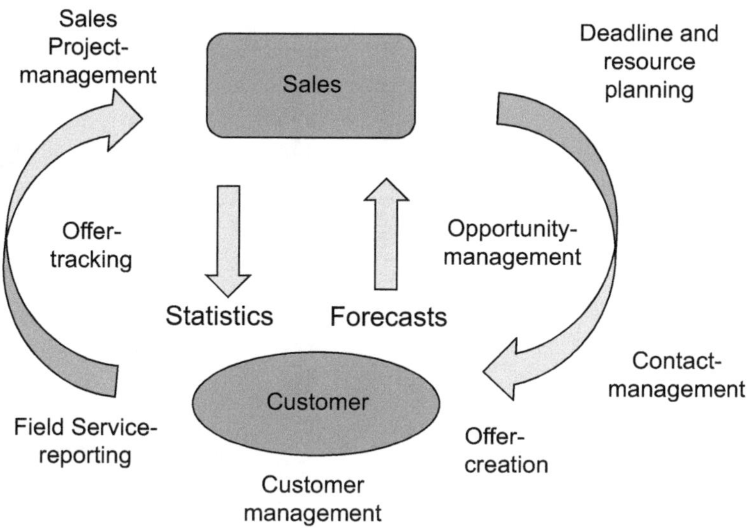

Fig. 2 Sales automation systems (CRM 1.0) (Source: Own representation)

The motivation of sales to use the CRM system has been attempted more or less successfully with the argument of relieving them of routine tasks, e.g., by creating standard quotations, automating approvals, or automatically carrying out sales forecasts (see Fig. 2). The term Sales Automation or Sales Force Automation (SFA) or the term CAS for Computer Aided Selling has become established in some cases.

First-generation CRM systems frequently helped to increase the efficiency of customer care. However, a positive correlation between CRM use and market success could not be demonstrated in most cases (Müller, 2004, p. 250ff.).

Second-generation CRM systems (CRM 2.0) already live up to the name Customer Relationship Management (see Fig. 3). The potential for improving customer care and loyalty was recognized with the help of targeted support for sales staff in customer care. In some cases, this support was also extended to the area of customer service and to call centers, resulting in a more or less integrated customer support center (Customer Service Center).

From an IT perspective, linking the CRM system to the company's basic systems for order processing and sales logistics (ERP system, SCM system) is a key prerequisite for successful use. Above all, the connection of the basic systems supports the sales department in essential aspects of customer management:

- faster access to customer information;
- better overview of customer transactions;
- Data exchange between field service and back office.

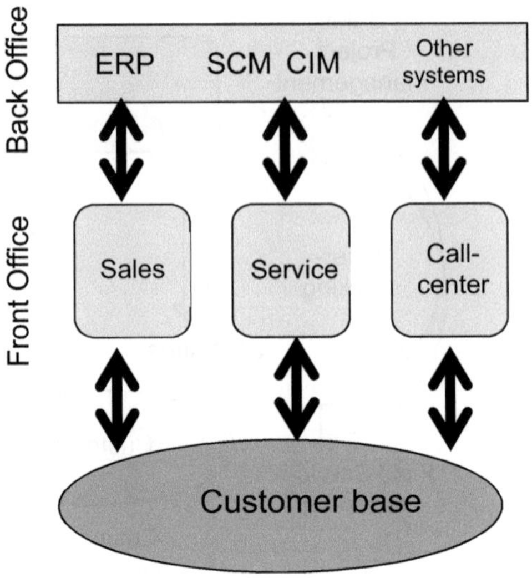

Fig. 3 Traditional CRM systems (CRM 2.0) (Source: Own representation)

With the increasing importance of electronic sales channels and social media (especially Facebook, WhatsApp, YouTube, Instagram, and Xing), complexity has been increased in many companies and the challenges of multi-channel management have had to be mastered with more advanced CRM systems. In addition to the online sales channel and dialog with customers via e-mails, etc. customer contact is increasingly taking place via the webpage and social media.

Prospects increasingly start buying processes on the homepage, go to social networks in the next step to obtain reviews and experiences, then possibly participate in an active expert chat, and perhaps only after that are ready for a personal appointment with a sales representative. Accordingly, it is necessary for all those responsible in marketing, sales, and service to have the information exchanged with the prospect or customer available across all channels and for all phases of communication.

The focus of third-generation CRM systems (CRM 3.0) is on online sales and online marketing (see Fig. 4). Third-generation CRM systems, such as Microsoft Dynamics CRM, Oracle Siebel CRM, Pegasystems CRM, Salesforce, SAP CRM, or Sugar CRM, go beyond pure support of sales and services but also support marketing in its routine tasks.

The aim of online marketing support is primarily to improve efficiency in the area of e-mail marketing and campaign management. Advanced systems take all communication channels into account (multi-channel campaign management). This is where traditional CRM system providers meet marketing software providers, e.g. Adobe, and providers from the field of business analytics, e.g. SAS. This is where the limitations of traditional CRM systems become clear. In many companies, therefore, the realization is gaining ground that it is time to say goodbye to the paradigm of customer loyalty. The following questions are being asked more and more frequently:

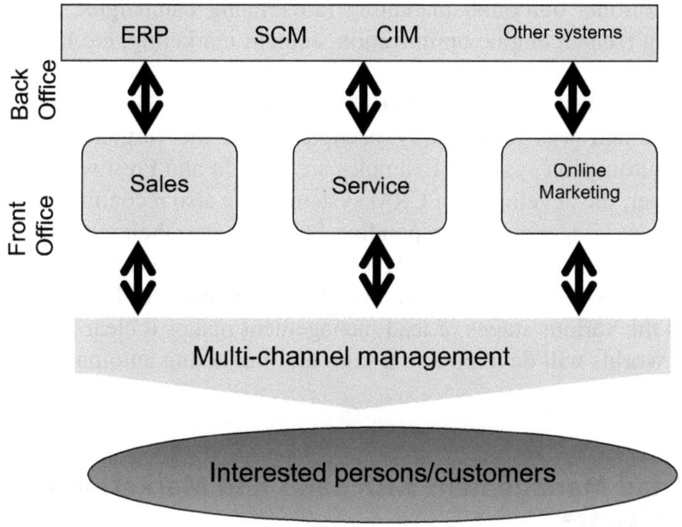

Fig. 4 Multi-channel CRM systems (CRM 3.0) (Source: Own representation)

- How many of our customers really stay loyal?
- How will the share of our regular customers develop in the future?
- Is sales our most important tool for acquiring new customers?
- Is our marketing prepared for the digital opportunities and risks?

A major concern of German business leaders at present is declining customer loyalty. This is the finding of KPMG's CEO Outlook (KPMG, 2015). 88% of CEOs assume that customers are more or less willing to switch. Only 12% are not worried about this at all.

In the B2B sector, the so-called millennials or digital natives now form the majority of buyers (Snyder, 2015):

- Before making a purchasing decision, they obtain intensive information on the Internet (Demand Gen, 2014), increasingly even via mobile access (Huff, 2014).
- It is only after more than 50% of the time in the overall purchasing decision process that contact is made with sales (CEB, 2012).
- Buyers are looking not only for information on products, prices, and technical details, but first for case studies, white papers, and articles (Huff, 2014).
- In some cases, up to eight elements are retrieved (Demand Gen, 2014).

As the need to win back customers and acquire new ones increases, the balance shifts:

- from sales with a focus on customer retention to marketing with a focus on customer acquisition;

- from traditional outbound marketing (advertising campaigns, etc.) to inbound marketing (search engine optimization, content marketing, etc.).

This development was recognized early on by the providers of software for lead management and was consistently occupied with the further development into marketing automation systems. Examples are Act-On and Freshworks. In the meantime, however, the developers of CRM systems have also recognized the importance of this topic and integrated corresponding functions into their systems, so that these systems could be referred to as CRM 4.0. Typical examples are Creatio, CRMNext, HubSpot, Pegasystems, SugarCRM, and Zoho (Gartner, 2021). A look at the sales funnel and the various stages of lead management makes it clear how the sales and marketing worlds will develop into a sales and marketing automation system in the future.

2 Lead Management with Sales and Marketing Automation Software

Lead management software is the term used to describe IT systems that enable sales and marketing teams to evaluate, filter, and selectively route any contacts from a variety of sources to direct, indirect, or e-commerce sales channels for sales initiation. Marketing Automation software supports automatic email generation in this process and, in more sophisticated systems, information and buying behavior analysis, Search Engine Optimization (SEO), and content management. Ideally, marketing automation and the CRM system are linked and directly integrated in the lead management process (see Fig. 5).

This can overcome the thinking still found in many companies in silos for marketing, sales, service and IT that are sealed off from one another. It is no coincidence that there is the saying: "Marketing is responsible for spending money. Sales then has to recoup the money."

In any case, the view of digital transformation in marketing and sales varies widely across silos:

- Marketers think first of web pages, email marketing, campaign management, etc.—and, of course, especially of the challenges created by social media and networks.
- Salespeople think first of online sales and e-commerce and the use of mobile devices.
- IT specialists think of CRM systems and their linkage with ERP systems and, of course, cloud computing.

All these aspects are correct and important. But they only ever describe one perspective of the digital marketing and sales world. But what often comes up short is the holistic view of marketing and sales.

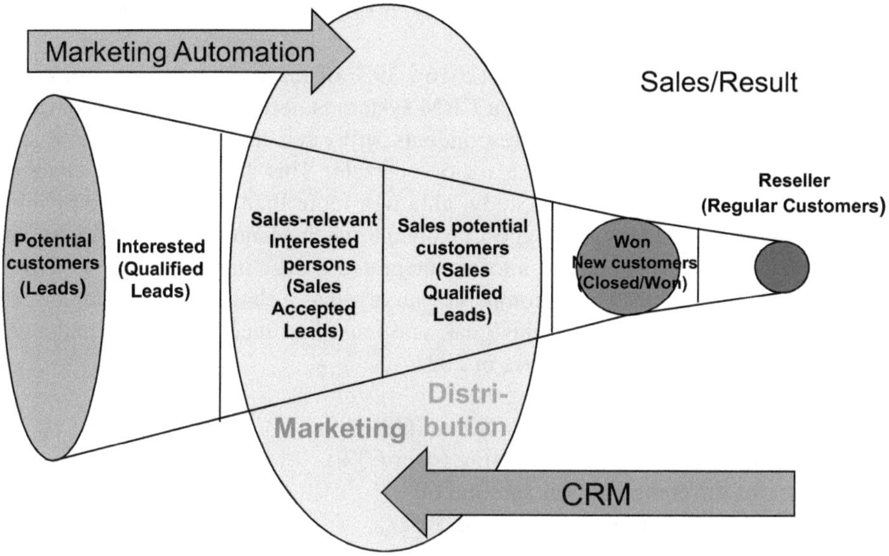

Fig. 5 Integrated sales and marketing automation system (Source: Own representation)

With integrated systems, the traditional divide between marketing and sales can be overcome. Therein lies the real opportunity of digital transformation in marketing and sales. An end-to-end customer value chain creates a common mindset despite different roles. According to this, marketing has product responsibility and sales has customer responsibility in the customer value chain. The joint responsibility for success prevents conflicting goals with a uniform performance measurement system and a joint incentive system. This philosophy is at the core of account-based marketing for B2B companies, in which the CRM system plays a central role and MAS can also be used effectively (see Chap. 28).

Integrated marketing and sales planning coordinates goals, strategy, and measures that joint project teams implement for product launches and market initiatives. The integrated marketing and sales view thus does not consider individual tasks and areas of responsibility, but focuses on the overall process. The goals are to improve:

- Effectiveness: Optimization of all customer-related decisions by focusing on the right target persons and their purchasing behavior;
- Efficiency: Utilization of all rationalization potentials in the customer value chain by minimizing time and costs while ensuring quality.

The minimum requirement in this area is the central storage of all customer and prospect information across all communication and sales channels with access for all employees in marketing, sales, and service. As BARC's, 2015 CRM Survey shows, this requirement is currently met by only 60% of the customers surveyed in Germany.

In the IFSMA study in Germany (2016), 39% of respondents from companies with productive MAS stated that their CRM system is networked with the MAS. In the 2017 IFSMA study, 47% of respondents still cited the linking of CRM and marketing automation system as a major obstacle. This figure has not changed significantly in the 2021 IFSMA study, although more than half of the companies surveyed identified this as the biggest challenge when planning their MAS implementation. Further development into an integrated marketing and sales system is only cited by around 40% of the companies surveyed as a challenge in implementing MAS, since in order to achieve this goal, one must first meet the other challenges cited with the following frequencies in 2021:

- Adaptation of processes in sales (around 60%)
- Adaptation of processes in marketing (over 60%)
- Merging of different data sets (around 60%)
- Training needs of employees (around 30%)

In the USA, the integration of CRM and marketing automation is already more advanced. In a survey of 500 U.S. companies by Capterra, 44% of CRM users said they had integrated marketing automation solutions (Hollar, 2015). But even there, in the B2B sector, access to a uniform customer database is still considered the greatest challenge by 95% of MAS users (ACT-ON & Gleanster Research, 2015).

3 Future Developments and Challenges

If you follow the current trends in CRM and marketing automation, you will see that system providers are increasingly focusing on combining these two areas. While CRM providers are supplementing their marketing portfolios primarily through acquisitions, marketing automation providers are ensuring that interfaces to as many CRM systems as possible are available. In addition, they are adapting to the same trends in both fields:

- on the legal side: the specific challenges in data protection in Germany and the EU;
- on the social side: the continuing growth in the importance of social media;
- on the technical side: the increasing importance of mobile applications and cloud computing;
- on the analytical side: the increasing requirements for meaningful key figures and future-oriented methods and models (predictive intelligence);
- on the communication side: taking into account communication between employees, sales partners, cooperation partners, end customers, suppliers, etc. across all stages of the market value chain (collaborative CRM, collaborative marketing).

The greatest momentum is currently taking place on the systems provider side of marketing. Since Gartner analyst Laura McLellan predicted at the 2014 Martech conference that in 2017 chief marketing officers (CMOs) will spend more money on IT than chief information officers (CIOs), the marketing sector has been in particular focus. The new buzzword for this is the marketing cloud, which makes it easier for marketing to procure its own software. Marketing Cloud vendors include Adobe, IBM, Mapp, Marketo, Oracle, and Salesforce, SAP Hybris, SAS, and many others (Forrester, 2016; Gartner, 2017).

But there are also interesting new approaches in the further development of IT support for sales. Of particular interest here is the range of sales engagement software or sales engagement platforms (SEP). These complement traditional CRM systems and offer support in the following areas:

- Individualization of emails and email tracking
- Push notifications
- Provision of presentation aids
- Telephone management support
- Create content for personalized customer engagement
- Sales empowerment tools (training, coaching, internal communication)
- Analyses, e.g., A/B content tests
- Machine learning based on customer responses
- Interfaces to CRM and Marketing Automation

Well-known providers of SEPs are Outreach, Groove, ClearSide, and Showpad. But the providers of marketing and sales clouds have also already discovered this topic. Corresponding offerings are available, for example, from Sales Force (High Velocity Sales), HubSpot (Sales Hub), and SAP CEC (Heinzelbecker, 2020).

If you look at the further development of CRM systems and the still hesitant use of software for the area of marketing and sales in practice, you will notice again and again a clear contradiction between the claim as signaled in the terms and the reality as it shows up in the systems offered and the implementation in the companies. With the terms "Sales Automation" and "Marketing Automation" one is reminded of old buzzwords, such as marketing information and marketing decision system and of the early dreams of method and model supported decisions in marketing and sales (Montgomery & Urban, 1969). But even today we are still far away from this vision. But due to advances in artificial intelligence, predictive intelligence (Seebacher, 2021), Big Data, etc., don't the technical possibilities for realizing this vision already exist? Is it not rather the inhibition thresholds in management and the deficits in human resources that prevent us from realizing this vision?

The systems currently available for sales and marketing automation serve to relieve sales and marketing managers of routine tasks and standardized processes. In the best case, they also support well-structured decisions with relevant information. But what about the automation of more sophisticated marketing decisions, where well-founded assumptions about future market shares, sales development, and profit forecasts are required?

The key question of reliably quantifying the marketing ROI (return on investment) usually remains unanswered. The sales and marketing automation systems currently available only provide highly simplified methods for estimating ROI based on key figures from lead management. However, a link to incoming orders, sales, and earnings figures is usually not made. For more reliable concepts based on market modeling, some vendors, e.g. Marketo and SAS, do provide the necessary analytical tools. However, there are only few publications about the successful application so far.

It is therefore not surprising that in the IFSMA survey 2021 only around 12% of respondents said they had all the IT systems they needed for marketing, and 5% said they had large gaps, 5% stated that there were large gaps.

It can be stated that CRM systems are already widespread in German corporate practice. In most cases, people are also largely satisfied with the available solutions. However, the development level of the systems in use covers a broad spectrum. From first-generation systems designed to relieve sales staff of routine tasks, to second-generation systems with links to basic IT systems, to third-generation systems with more comprehensive support for sales, service and marketing, everything can be found in practice. However, fourth generation CRM systems in the sense of integrated marketing and sales systems are still the exception.

The challenge of the digital age, with declining customer loyalty and the need to constantly acquire new customers or win back old ones, calls into question the traditional division of roles between sales and marketing. Above all, the silo mentality still frequently present in corporate practice, with more or less compartmentalized departmental boundaries, is proving to be a critical bottleneck for a successful digitization strategy.

With the increasing importance of the Internet for purchasing and for the entire procurement process, also and especially in the B2B sector, the emphasis is shifting toward online sales and online marketing. In this context, the central importance of IT support for lead management becomes particularly clear.

In addition, since marketing is becoming less and less dependent on central IT departments due to the penetration of cloud solutions, the use of systems for marketing automation is becoming more and more prevalent. With the dovetailing of MAS with CRM systems, the traditional separation between marketing and sales can be overcome. Ideally, an integrated sales and marketing automation system is created. But, this requires not only technical integration, but also the end-to-end design of the customer acquisition and retention process. However, this needs a common understanding and shared responsibility in marketing, sales, and service. This addresses the central challenge of a digitization strategy for marketing, sales, and ultimately for the entire company: digital customer focus!

The new buzzword in this context is customer experience management (CEM or CXM). If we consider not only the strategic side of this holistic customer orientation, but also the associated digital challenges, we speak of Digital Customer Experience Management (DXM). DXM refers to the integration of all digital instruments with which a customer comes into contact over the entire course of his direct and indirect contacts with the company (customer journey). This refers not only to marketing and

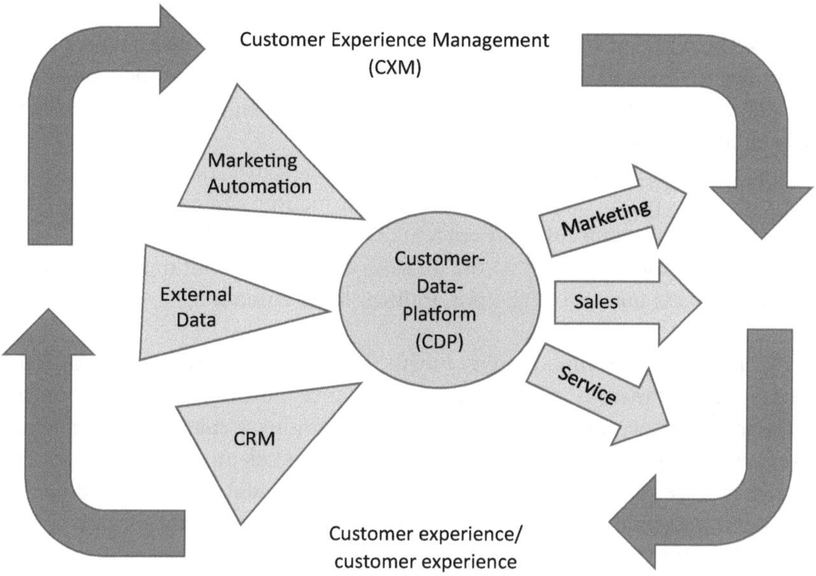

Fig. 6 CDP and customer experience management (Source: Own representation)

sales functions, but also to logistics and service. Accordingly, the goal is to make all accruing external and internal customer data from all marketing and sales systems (CRM, marketing automation, etc.), as well as from the ERP system, available in an integrated customer database for all employees with customer contact. Customer Data Platforms (CDP) are offered as a solution to this problem. These platforms are intended to provide marketing, sales, and service with a common view of the customer and, with a 360-degree perspective, to include data from external sources in addition to the company's internal data (see Fig. 6). Crucial here are the available tools for data reconciliation and consistency checking (Casey et al., 2021).

This not only overcomes traditional data silos, but also overcomes classic departmental barriers. The reality in corporate practice is still far from this as various studies (IDG, 2017; CX Network, 2018; DMV, 2018) make clear. However, the growing offer of digital experience platforms (DXPs) shows the interest in comprehensive digitization solutions that include marketing and sales and service as well as other business areas (Cicman, 2021; Guseva & MacComascaigh, 2021).

The main reason for the still relatively low penetration rate of customer experience management is not so much on the technical side, but rather on the strategic side and the challenge of establishing a holistic customer-centric mindset in the company. Although this has actually been demanded in modern marketing for a long time, today, with the new technologies mentioned, a variety of instruments are available to facilitate the implementation of this demand:

- Comprehensive storage of all relevant customer information across all touch points in the course of the information and procurement process (customer

journey). For example, from the first contact of a prospective customer on the web page, to the retrieval of a white paper, to a trade fair contact and a contact with the field sales force, to the order via a call center and ultimately payment and delivery, and perhaps afterward a service request. Privacy and sales opportunities need not be mutually exclusive (Litz, 2020).
- Personalized addressing of the customer on the basis of a personality profile (persona concept) or on the basis of the information gained in the course of the customer journey with relevant content (Heinzelbecker, 2021).
- Uniform customer approach across all sales channels and all marketing, sales and service contacts and use of the possibilities for automation.

While automation in marketing is mostly viewed positively in terms of relieving the burden of routine tasks, reluctance and resistance are still frequently noticeable in sales (Heinzelbecker, 2019). Aligning the company to a customer-centric mindset requires rethinking in all areas and at all levels. It forces an adjustment of business processes, requires a changed team-oriented organizational structure, and needs new management principles based on a comprehensive measurement of customer satisfaction and customer lifetime value (Kuen & Philipp, 2020).

References

ACT-ON, & Gleanster Research. (Eds.). (2015). *Rethinking the role of marketing*. https://www.act-on.com/whitepaper/gleanster-report-rethinking-the-role-of-marketing/

BARC. (Ed.). (2015). *CRM Survey 2015*. http://barc.de/docs/barc-crm-survey-20152015

Casey, S., et al. (2021). *The Forrester new wave: B2B CDP*. Forrester Reprint.

CEB. (Ed.). (2012). *Customer purchase research survey*. https://www.cebglobal.com/content/dam/cebglobal/us/EN/best-practices-decision support/marketing-communications/pdfs/CEB-Mktg-ThinkB2B-Presentation.pdf

Cicman, J. (2021). *The Forrester wave: Digital experience platforms*. Forrester Reprints.

CX Network. (Ed.). (2018). *The global state of customer experience 2018*. WWW.kontakta.se/upl/files/154366

Demand Gen. (Ed.). (2014). *The 2014 b2b buyer behavior survey report*. http://www.demandgenreport.com/industry-resources/research/2508-the-2014-b2b-buyer-behavior-survey2014

DMV. (Ed.). (2018). *Marketing Survey Report Dec. 2018*. https://www.marketingverband.de/marketingkompetenz/studien/customer-experience-studie/

Forrester. (Ed.). (2016). *The Forrester wave: Enterprise marketing software suites 2016*. https://www.forrester.com/report/The+Forrester+Wave+Enterprise+Marketing+Software+Suites+Q2+2016/-/E-RES122622

Gartner. (Ed.). (2017). *Magic quadrant for digital marketing hubs 2017*. https://www.gartner.com/doc/reprints?id=1-3T5J67Y&ct=170209&st=sb

Gartner. (Ed.). (2021). *Magic quadrant for B2B marketing automation platforms*. Gartner Reprint. https://www.gartner.com/doc/reprints?id=1-27ILIPXH&ct=210923&st=sb

Guseva, I., & MacComascaigh, M. (2021). *Magic quadrant for digital experience platforms*. Gartner Reprint.

Hannig, U., Heinzelbecker, K., & Foell, T. (2019). *Digital safety first – marketing automation in DACH*. White Paper, Institute for Sales and Marketing Automation, Ludwigshafen.

Hannig, U., Heinzelbecker, K., & Foell, T. (2021). *Mission digital transformation*. IFSMA Whitepaper, Ludwigshafen

Heinzelbecker, K. (1985). *Marketing information systems*. .

Heinzelbecker, K. (2019). *How much automation can sales tolerate?* https://www.ifsma.de/2019/12/31/914/

Heinzelbecker, K. (2020). *Sales engagement, the bridge between marketing automation and CRM*. https://www.ifsma.de/2020/08/02/

Heinzelbecker, K. (2021). Digital personalization in the B2C and B2B sectors. In S. Lacher, P. Tachkov, & R. Völker (Eds.), *Digitalization in marketing*.

Holler, K. (2015, July). *CRM industry user research report*. http://www.capterra.com/customer-relationship-management-software/user-research

Huff, D., & KoMarketing Associates. (Eds.). (2014). *B2B web usability report*. www.komarketingassociates.com/B2B-Web-Usability-Report

IDG. (Ed.). (2017). *Digital customer experience study*. https://www.cobra.de/fileadmin/downloads/Whitepaper_pdf-Downloads/Studie_IDG_DCX_2017.pdf

KPMG. (Ed.). (2015). *CEO outlook*. https://www.kpmg.com//global-ceo-outlook-2015

Kuen, T., & Philipp, N. (2020). *Customer experience management*.

Litz, J. (2020). *Next. CRM goes CXM* (2nd ed.).

Montgomery, D. B., & Urban, G. L. (1969). *Management science in marketing*. .

Müller, H. (2004). *Deployment of customer relationship management systems*. .

Seebacher, U. (2021). *Predictive intelligence for data-driven managers: Process model, assessment-tool, IT-blueprint, competence model and case studies*. Springer.

Snyder, K. (2015). *The changing face of B2B marketing*. https://www.thinkwithgoogle.com/consumer-insights/the-changing-face-b2b-marketing/

Klaus Heinzelbecker Co-Founder and Member of the Board of the Institute for Sales and Marketing Automation (IFSMA).

With his book “Marketing Information Systems,” published in 1985, he is considered to be a pioneer in the area of IT support in sales and marketing in Germany.

After studying business administration at the University of Mannheim, he received a PhD at the technical university of Aachen (RWTH).

During the course of his management career, he worked as marketing consultant in the electrical industry (ABB), as manager of marketing research, and as director of strategic planning in the chemical industry (BASF). He has many years of experience in international consulting in Europe, Asia, and the Americas and he has dealt with the challenges of many different industries, particularly in automotive, construction, packaging, nutrition, and healthcare.

After retirement, he worked as strategy consultant and in the area of futuring for the German think-tank Z-Punkt. His current focus is on new markets, new business models, online marketing, and digital transformation.

He is chairman of the Supervisory Board of the Future Management Group.

As lecturer at the University of Business and Society Ludwigshafen, he teaches Strategic Management and HR Management.

Marketing Automation Changes Sales

Norbert Schuster

1 Man Versus Machine

The word "automation" in "marketing automation" suggests that marketing automation platforms (MAP) are only intended to automate existing processes and thus make marketing and sales staff redundant and rationalize them away. But that was not the intention when these platforms were developed, nor is that the purpose of their use. They have come into being because digitization has drastically changed the buying process of potential customers and thus brought about a new method of marketing.

Jobs in marketing will change and some will go away. However, this is not due to the marketing automation platforms, but to the changed buying processes. At this point, one must not confuse cause and effect. Prospects search, decide, and buy differently today than in the past. Particularly in the B2B sector, potential customers want to obtain undisturbed information before making a purchase. They look for relevant and helpful content in "self-service mode" to get an overview of solution variants and providers.

The Internet and social media platforms have made the pure "brochure-deliverer" obsolete. Customers want to get information at their leisure and not be constantly harassed by sales staff when they don't even need them yet. In my view, sales will never lose its justification, but its field of activity has already changed and will continue to change.

The sales department has a particular justification for activities that a machine cannot perform optimally and where the human factor can play to its strengths. After all, there are tasks that a human being can perform much better than a machine:

N. Schuster (✉)
strike2 GmbH, Kleinostheim, Germany
e-mail: n.schuster@strike2.de

U. Hannig, U. Seebacher (eds.), *Marketing and Sales Automation*, Management for Professionals, https://doi.org/10.1007/978-3-031-20040-3_6

- Verification of the needs analysis
  Has the prospect been interested in the "right" information and solutions? The salesperson must "match" the real need with his company's offer in the early phase of the sales process.
- Individual advice
  What challenges and requirements does the potential customer have and which solution fits best?
- Identification of the members of the buying center
  In B2B, it is often not an individual who buys, but a purchasing panel. The B2B sales representative identifies the members of the panel and manages them according to their individual issues and perspectives.
- Quotation creation
  In the B2B area, the supplier often needs detailed information in order to create a suitable quotation. These offers are usually complex, individual and cannot be created automatically.
- Price negotiation
  Humans are also better suited than machines for negotiating conditions and prices.
- Representation of the company
  Ultimately, the sales representative is also the face of the company and influences whether the "chemistry" between supplier and customer is right.

2 Marketing Automation Platforms/PreSales Automation Platforms

Marketing automation tools provide the technical platform for a new way of marketing. On this, the focus is really on the customer and the content relevant to him. Marketing automation (Seebacher, 2021a) helps generate prospects, qualify them, and develop them until they are ready to buy (e.g., web store in B2C or B2B aftersales) or sell in an automated but individualized way. In this scenario, the marketing automation platform acts as "PreSales Automation." For sales, this means that they receive highly developed and well-qualified leads from marketing. They can base their sales strategy and benefit arguments on the detailed lead profiles and thus close more deals faster.

Marketing and sales automation platforms act as an incubator for sales. After the transfer of prospects from marketing to sales, processes accompanying sales (sales automation/funnel automation) can also run in the marketing automation platform. One example is the phase in which the sales employee has to wait for a specification from a potential customer. Classically, the sales employee has only two options here. He waits for the customer's response and requirements specification, or he calls the customer permanently to get the requirements specification. The latter approach is usually not very pleasant for the customer and the sales representative. With the support of an automation platform, the sales representative now has the option of

Fig. 1 The classic marketing model (Source: strike2.de)

offering the customer a process with suitable content that helps him to go through the requirements specification phase faster and more efficiently.

In the classic marketing model, marketing did not bother with leads at all or generated the prospects with outbound marketing (Seebacher, 2021b, p. 47) measures and then handed them over directly to sales without prospect development and qualification (see Fig. 1). An approach that today usually causes dissatisfaction in three areas:

- The sales rep is frustrated because the prospect is usually not ready to buy at this stage of their buying process.
- The customer is annoyed because he only wants to get information first and does not want to be addressed (yet).
- Marketing is frustrated because they are getting poor feedback on the quality of leads from sales.

In addition to the dissatisfaction with the quality of the prospects, many companies also have to deal with the insufficient quantity of leads generated. With outbound marketing measures alone, such as advertisements or cold calling, very few companies today still achieve the number of leads they want. It doesn't help to do more of the same and simply increase the pressure on the players. If prospects were then generated and not "chased away" despite the aforementioned challenges, the prospect has by no means bought. The development to the point of purchase or sales maturity is usually a long-term process in the B2B sector.

3 Challenges in Sales

In addition to the challenges that digitization has brought to sales, there are also general hurdles to overcome:

- Who among the prospects is far enough along in their buying process that they want to talk to sales? After all, sales should only deal with prospects who are ready to sell.

- The sales department must quickly identify the pain points and requirements of the prospect and how he is "wired." They must base their sales strategy and argumentation on this.
- Who among the contacts from the Buying Center is responsible for which topics? To whom do they have to answer which questions, which information do they have to provide?
- A good sales representative is busy with current projects/offers. How is he supposed to generate new leads or look after B and C customers during this time?
- What does the sales department do with prospects it has qualified, but who are not yet ready for sales or have even been lost?

These classic and the new challenges in sales require a mindshift, a new method for marketing, lead generation, and prospect development. In the modern marketing model (Seebacher, 2021c, p. 53), responsibilities are shifting. Marketing is challenged to stop focusing only on "decorative marketing." That is, not just producing "pretty" results, such as a "pretty" website or "pretty" ads. Marketing is challenged to provide sales with qualified leads and to support the achievement of business goals in a measurable and scalable way. This requires close collaboration (marketing/sales alignment) with sales.

In the new marketing model, marketing and sales must define an end-to-end, coordinated lead process. Successful implementation of marketing automation is only possible if marketing and sales work together.

The sales department has two main tasks. On the one hand, it is the "supplier of knowledge and experience." It must support marketing with its knowledge and experience in order to create realistic customer profiles and relevant content, as well as to set up suitable prospect development processes. Content creation, addressing potential prospects and pure implementation are of course marketing jobs. But without the customer and market knowledge of sales, marketing can't do it.

In my workshops, I often hear statements like this from sales: "What are we supposed to do here? Are we supposed to be doing marketing tasks now?" The more realistic perspective is: sales helps marketing help sales so that marketing can deliver better leads to sales, which sales can use to realize more revenue, faster, and achieve their goals. The better Marketing can implement Marketing Automation with the help of Sales, the more successful Sales will be and achieve their bonuses/ commissions faster and easier.

The second block of tasks facing sales is adjusting to the change in lead quality. Leads developed using marketing automation processes are much more mature and a lot of information is already available that sales used to have to painstakingly find out. No matter what sales method you are working with, such as Solution Selling (Sulliva, 2022), Challenge Sales (Dixon & Adamson, 2011), SPIN Selling (Rackham, Neil, 1998), or simply the BANT questions:

- B = Budget: Is budget available
- A = Authority: Am I talking to the right person?

- N = Need: How well does my offer fit the prospect's need?
- T = Time: When does the prospect want to buy/book?

Each model is based on sales gathering information from the potential customer in order to optimize the acquisition process. This task is usually time-consuming and reduces sales efficiency. A large part of this task can be automated, but done individually, with the help of marketing automation.
As part of prospect development processes (lead nurturing, Wenger, 2021) running in the Marketing Automation platform, information is captured from the potential customer. This profile building is one of the main features of Marketing Automation (Klaus, 2021). In each step of the nurturing processes, the prospect voluntarily reveals information. He does this through his behavior, information in forms, and answering questions:

- Click in an email or on a landing page,
- Enter, e.g., his position or industry in a form field,
- Deciding on content building blocks,
- Click on a selection of options: "Which of the following topics are you most interested in?".

This is not about "stalking" or spying on the prospect. It is about getting to know the prospect better in order to provide them with better content offers or to assign them to the appropriate sales representative.

In the first stages of the process, you should request as little information as possible so as not to negatively influence the conversion rate. In each subsequent stage, you can ask for more information (progressive profiling). The prospect himself controls how much he reveals or even whether he opts out of the process. From my experience, the prospect's trust increases with each stage of the process if you offer relevant content. You'll be surprised how much information a prospect is willing to provide at the end of the process if you've provided them with helpful content. In Fig. 2, you can see the entire lead process, the handoff point from marketing to sales, and the responsibilities for each:

- Lead
  Lead refers to a new prospect or an existing customer who may be interested in further offers. Marketing generates these leads with inbound and outbound marketing measures.
- Marketing Qualified Lead (Seebacher, 2021c, p. 45)
  Marketing develops the generated prospect to the status "MQL—Marketing qualified Lead." When this status is reached, the prospect is transferred to Sales.
- Sales Accepted Lead
  If the sales department accepts this lead, the status changes to "SAL—Sales accepted Lead." If the sales department knows the company and knows, for example, that it has no budget or that it has only requested comparative offers

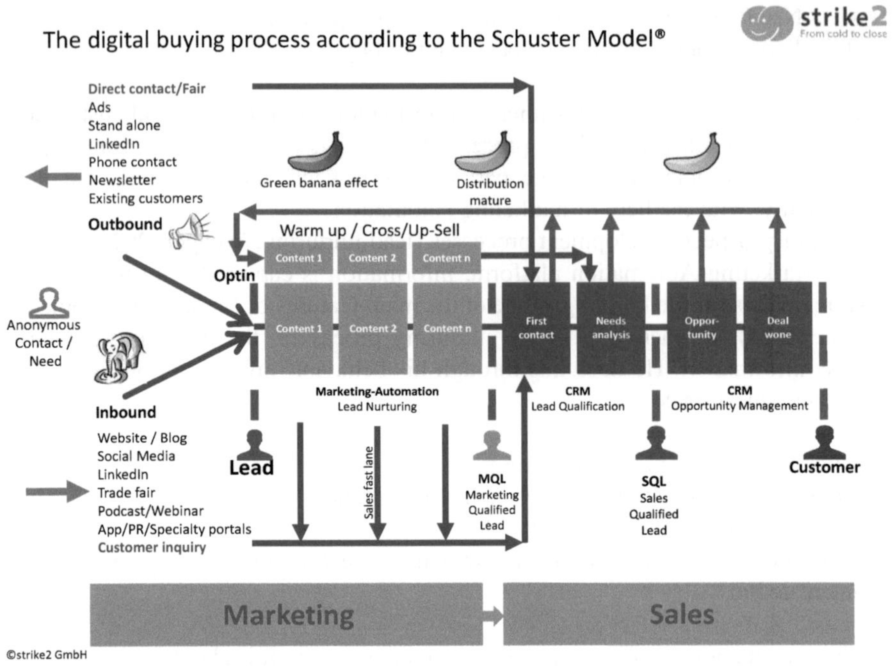

Fig. 2 The entire buying process in the B2B sector (Source: "Digitalisierung in Marketing und Vertrieb," Norbert Schuster, Haufe Verlag, 2020)

in order to reduce the price of the regular supplier, it can also reject a lead. In this case, it must be clarified how to proceed with these leads.

- Sales Qualified Lead (Seebacher, 2021c, p. 49f)
  When Sales takes responsibility for the lead, they begin to qualify it. The status then changes to SQL (Sales Qualified Lead).
- Closing/sale
  If the sale was successful, the prospect reaches the status "Closing/Sale" and becomes a customer.

Once the customer stage has been reached, the process should not end but move on to further stages, which can be supported by prospect development processes (nurturing):

- After-sales: Depending on the solution area and portfolio of offerings, services such as education, training, maintenance, and consumables can be offered to the customer in this phase.
- Repurchase: If your customer uses your solution, is satisfied with it, and in principle he can use more of it, you can offer him more of the original purchased.
- Up/cross-selling (Njenga, 2020): If it fits your portfolio of offerings and your customer's needs, offer them "higher value" or "additional" solutions.

- Recommendation generation: If your customer is satisfied with your solution or offer, don't miss out on asking him for a recommendation. He can recommend you and possibly even become a brand ambassador for you.
- Customer recovery: If you have lost a customer, this does not have to be the end of your customer relationship. If you take care of these customers and prepare the appropriate content and approach, you may also win these customers back.

On the far left is the unknown prospect or existing customer with an "anonymous" need that has not yet been expressed or does not yet exist. The basis for all activities in digital marketing and sales are desired customer profiles (buyer personas). However, it is important to create a detailed Buyer Persona profile, i.e. a "Deep Buyer Persona" profile with the relevant parameters (e.g., pain points, target states, decision criteria, behavioral preferences) that support to design the approach, content, and processes for the marketing automation processes. Based on these Buyer Persona (Revella, 2015) profiles, you create the appropriate content building blocks—i.e., a document or video that matches the Buyer Persona's "pain points" and/or target states and the respective sales goals. Then define the inbound (Watering Hole Strategy) and outbound marketing efforts that will drive leads or existing customers to this content building block. The goal of this content building block is not to sell yet, but first to move leads or existing customers into the digital process.

Definition: Waterhole Strategy (Source: "Digitalisierung in Marketing und Vertrieb," Wasserloch-Strategie®, Norbert Schuster, Haufe Verlag, 2020)

What does the Waterhole Strategy describe? Imagine you are a photographer, and you have the assignment to photograph elephants in the wild. What could you do to fulfill this assignment? You could walk through the jungle, the bush, or the savannah to find and photograph elephants. This is the picture of outbound efforts such as telephone canvassing. Ideally, you have shots of elephants in the camera after what is usually a long search. Figuratively speaking you have generated a new prospect.

Even if you have been able to photograph elephants or attract prospects, the process starts all over again with new "picture assignments" and you don't know if you will be lucky enough to find elephants each time with an acceptable amount of time and resources. How would you feel about building a "prospect watering hole," "magically" attracting elephants (clients) to take pictures of elephants at any time? Then build a "watering hole" for prospects and make sure the scent of the water spreads to the "elephants." Put up signs that say, "Here's delicious water for elephants. Take a look!".

Behind the image of the water hole is, on the one hand, the difference in approach, i.e. the method used to generate leads or existing customer sales. In

(continued)

one case you go hunting for prospects, in the other case you create a state that ensures that leads find their way to you. That's a different mindset.

In the picture, the water hole stands for your "presences" (website, blog, webshop, microsites, professional articles, etc.), which ideally have a magnetic effect on your leads or existing customers. The water in the waterhole is your content and added values that you offer. Each of these content like ...

- Text on your web pages
- Articles in your blog
- Guest articles on other people's blogs
- Professional articles on portals
- Mention in foreign media
- YouTube videos
- Podcasts in the popular portals

properly applied, increases your water hole and the corresponding effect.
The Waterhole Strategy not only works for new prospects. It can also be used to be (re)found by existing customers with an anonymous need, for example if up- and cross-selling or account-based marketing (Bacon, 2021) is your goal. You can use it to be found by existing customers on your own (website, newsletter, blog, etc.) and "foreign" (Linkedin, professional portals, etc.) media when they are looking for a solution or just moving around there.

If the content module is effective and a lead enters the process, the corresponding sales representative can make direct contact. Depending on the customer's situation and offer, however, the customer is probably not even ready for a conversation or closing. If the content module has generated initial interest, but there is not yet a need for sales support, the "Green Banana Effect®" will strike.

Definition: Green Banana Effect (Source: "Digitalisierung in Marketing und Vertrieb", Grüne Bananen Effekt®, Norbert Schuster, Haufe Verlag, 2020)
What happens when you peel a green banana and bite into it? You will probably not like the banana. Is the banana bad or broken? No, it was just opened too early and is not ripe yet.

This is often the case with leads that you pass on to sales. If they are not yet mature, they "clog" your funnel and impair your efficiency and sales success. The maturation of the need and the readiness of leads to close are promoted with nurturing processes (automated customer development processes) in a marketing automation platform.

If the "green banana effect occurs, the content modules of the automated nurturing process come into play and develop the lead to sales maturity. The content modules must be designed according to the customer journey of the buyer persona. Once the lead has reached the MQL (marketing qualified lead) stage, the sales department comes back into play to analyze the need and develop the customer to the point of closure.

At each stage of this process, the customer can use the shortcut to sales ("Sales fast lane"), for example, to request a consultation, price indication, or online demo. In the diagram, the "Sales fast lane" is shown with the red arrows.

Definition: Sales fast lane

With the "sales fast lane," the customer can signal at any stage in the digital development process that they want to contact sales. To support this process, you include offers in the content modules, emails, and landing pages that indicate sales-readiness.

Examples:

- Consultation
- Price indication
- Online demo
- Implementation Note
- Checklist for the selection of a solution

If the customer chooses one of the offers, the options for direct contact are provided.

If it becomes apparent in personal contact that a lead handed over to sales is not yet ready to take the next steps in the personal sales process, the blue arrows come into play. They stand for nurturing processes in marketing automation that further inform the lead with relevant content and keep the contact up to the point of concrete buying interest. A special blue arrow is the last one on the right above the Order process step. It stands for the start of a new automated development process for after-sales, repurchase or cross- and up-selling.

The exemplary process steps using the example: Sales of a machine/plant

- Using the appropriate performance measures, a lead is generated and passed to the marketing automation platform for development.
- *Automated*: A prospect for a machine, for example, was developed to sales maturity using an automated lead-nurturing process.
- *Personal*: The sales department has accompanied the prospective customer until the purchase of the machine and thus to the status of customer.
- *Automated:* After a reasonable waiting period, the automated process started to prepare for the repurchase of the same machine.

- *Personal*: After the needs analysis for the use of the machine in another production area, the sales department accompanies the customer until the purchase of the second machine.
- *Automated:* After an appropriate waiting period, an automated process started again to address and generate interest in the feeding of components to the machine and the packaging of the manufactured parts.
- *Personal*: After the customer has gone through the process to MQN (Marketing qualified Need) status, Sales takes over again to close the deal.
- *Automated:* Other automated processes can follow to provide additional offerings such as implementation support, consumables, maintenance, training, etc.

4 The Strategy Process

The Marketing Automation Strategy lays the foundation for successful implementation and operation. This model has evolved from many years of consulting practice and guides through the most important elements of successful strategy development (Fig. 3).

Kick-Off

The first step is to take stock of the situation in a kick-off meeting so that everyone involved is brought up to speed and understands:

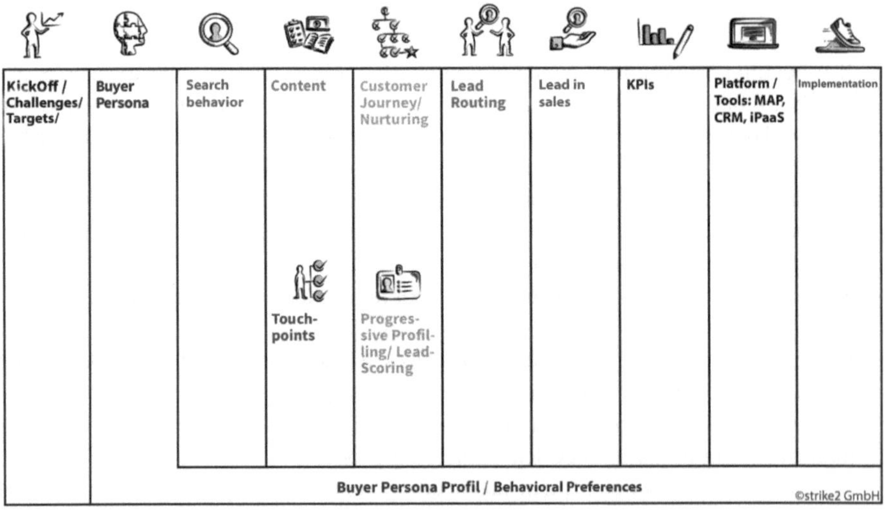

Fig. 3 From cold to close®—strategy canvas according to the Schuster model (Source: "Digitalisierung in Marketing und Vertrieb", Schuster-Modell®, Norbert Schuster, Haufe Verlag, 2020)

- what marketing or PreSales Automation is.
- what automation platforms can do and where the leverage for marketing lies.
- where the limits of automation are.
- who will take on which part in the new marketing process.
- what implementation means for everyone.

Furthermore, it is important in this phase to define the goals and challenges in an understandable way. These can be, for example:

- "We need to become more visible in our market segment and increase our reach."
- "We need more leads."
- "We have enough leads. But we don't know which ones are sales-ready and how to develop you to sales-readiness."
- "We need to better leverage our inventory addresses to generate more sales."
- "We want to become more successful in AfterSales and sell more training, service and spare parts."
- "We need to do a better job of serving our B and C customers."

Representatives from sales should be involved in strategy development to contribute their view of the situation, customers, and the market.

Buyer Persona

In the second stage of the strategy process, you define who you actually want to reach. In other words, who your ideal customers are in detail. With the help of "deep buyer persona" profiles based on the Schuster Model, these ideal customers are described in detail (see Fig. 4).

Demographic data, such as industry, company size or position, the persona's knitting pattern (performer, innovator, supporter, preserver) and detailed behavioral data are incorporated into these profiles. An important element of the buyer persona profiles is also the buying process of the buyer persona. What are the stages of your persona's buying process and what information is important to them? The lead process should not be based on internal departmental responsibilities or desires, but on the buying process of the buyer persona. In the B2B area, a buying process can be structured as shown in Fig. 5.

The phases of a B2B buying process are:

- Inform: The prospect has a pain point or challenge and seeks information about possible solutions.
- Empower: If the interested party encounters terms or methods that he does not know or cannot adequately assess for his own implementation, he must empower himself in order to make a decision.

(continued)

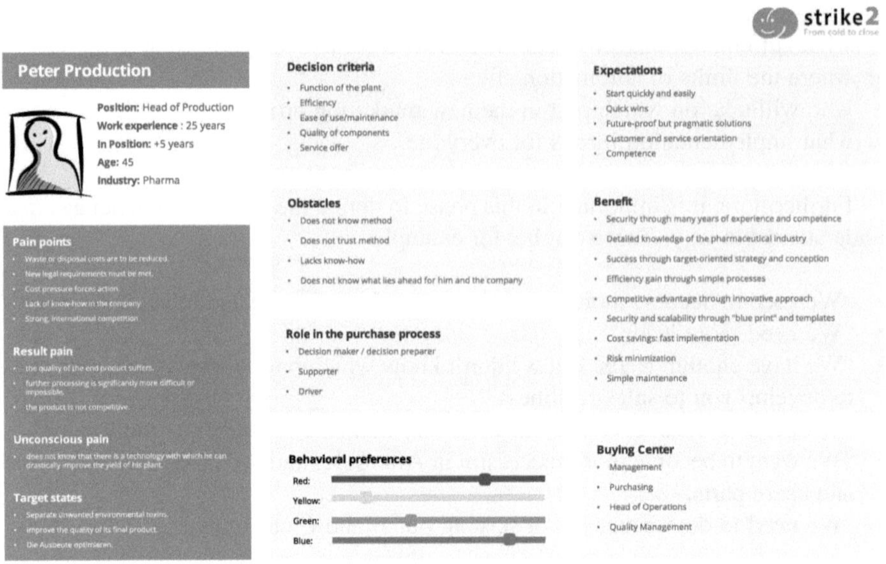

Fig. 4 First page of a buyer-persona profile (Source: "Digitalisierung in Marketing und Vertrieb", Norbert Schuster, Haufe Verlag, 2020)

Fig. 5 strike2 Customer Journey flywheel (Source: "Digitalisierung in Marketing und Vertrieb, Norbert Schuster, Haufe Verlag, 2020)

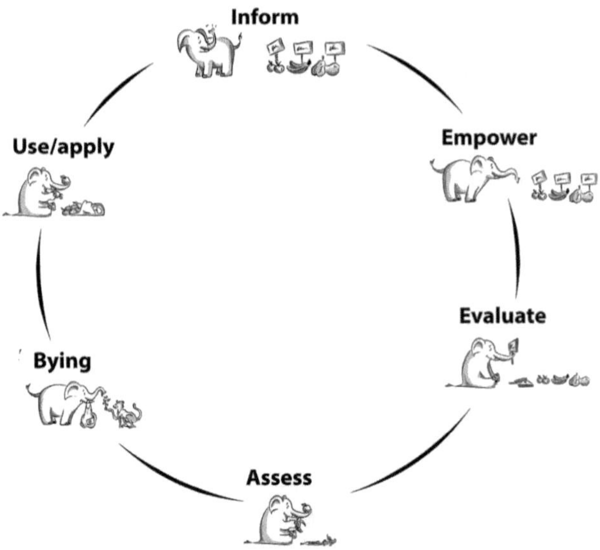

- Evaluate: Once he has found the right solution option, he evaluates corresponding solution variants, offers, and providers.
- Assess: Once he has decided on a selection of offers, he begins to assess it according to his criteria (quality, competence, ability to deliver, scope of services, price, etc.).
- Buying: In this phase, he begins to enter the buying process and negotiate with one or a few vendors.
- Use/apply: Once the prospective customer has decided on and purchased a solution, he uses the offer or the solution. After a short time, he begins to evaluate his purchase decision and makes a decision whether he is satisfied and open to a recommendation or further purchases/bookings.

Marketing uses this information to create appropriate content modules, define the process, and use suitable performance measures with the right approach.

Please note: Superficial buyer persona profiles do not help you derive suitable content building blocks and lead-nurturing processes. A good buyer persona profile has a length of 6–10 pages. After profiling, you should verify your profiles in interviews with representatives of the buyer persona type and expand them if necessary. These detailed ideal customer profiles will also help you to do this:

- Optimize general communication with your prospects and customers.
- To improve your products or your offer.
- Make websites, landing pages, and blogs more customer centric.
- Optimize your advertising campaigns (AdWords, Ads, Facebook Ads, etc.).

Based on the profiles, marketing can research the search behavior (keywords and search volume) of the desired customer types, create relevant content, and offer it at the appropriate customer touchpoints.

Search behavior

Your SEO managers will be happy about buyer-persona profiles because they can use them to optimize their keyword strategy. In this phase, sales play a rather subordinate role. However, in conversations with prospects or existing customers, they can find out which keywords they originally used to search for a solution (Enge et al., 2015).

Content

Buyer-persona relevant content is the fuel for successful marketing automation. The word "relevant" is crucial. Potential prospects won't respond to your outreach, request content, and opt-in (permission to send emails) if your content isn't relevant, helpful, or entertaining (Polizzi, 2013).

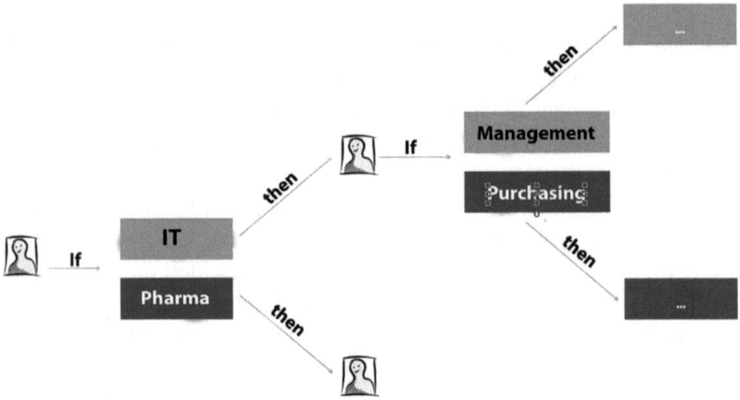

Fig. 6 If/then principle in the lead-nurturing process (Source: "Marketing Automation," Norbert Schuster, Haufe Verlag, 2022)

In the marketing automation process, each content component has a task and a goal (Barrett & Herten, 2021). Think about the content first, and then the delivery method (video, whitepaper, etc.) and channels (website, Facebook, etc.). Create content building blocks that map the buying process and the information needs of your prospects at each stage. The first building block is especially important, as it determines whether a prospect will opt-in and enter your "system." You have a second chance in all further stages, but not in the first stage.

Sales can support marketing in this phase with feedback on the content modules created. If a customer is interested in your first content module and gives you permission to send him information, he enters a lead-nurturing process. In this process, they are offered additional content modules that match their buyer persona profile based on their behavior. These lead-nurturing processes work according to the if/then principle (see Fig. 6).

Nurturing

If switches have been built into the nurturing processes (example: management, purchasing, etc.), the interested party controls which further content modules are offered to him based on his "click decision." Of course, the prospect can also withdraw the opt-in at any time and log out of the processes.

With every click and every entry made by the prospect, a profile is built up and expanded in the background. This profile is the basis for further nurture processes and provides sales with detailed information about the prospect after the transfer. However, it is not advisable to harass prospects at will with content offers. This is spam and the prospect will quickly opt out of the process.

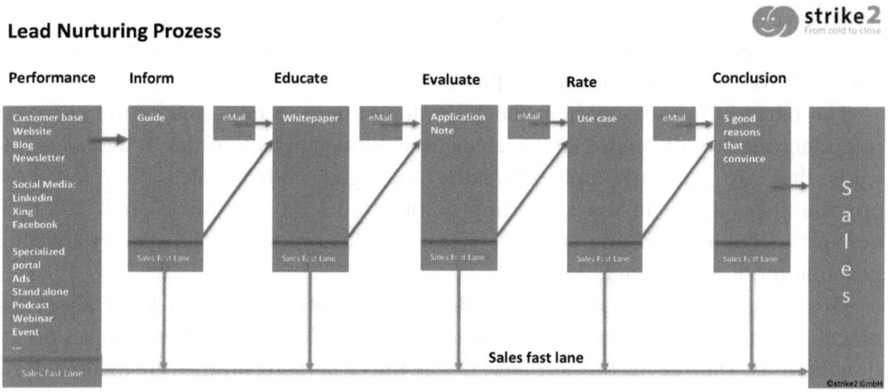

Fig. 7 Exemplary lead-nurturing process (Source: strike2.de)

The lead-nurturing processes only achieve their effect of developing the prospect to sales maturity if they map the buying process (customer journey) of the potential customer (customer journey mapping) and offer him relevant content. It is therefore essential to work with marketing and sales to create a target-oriented strategy for the use of marketing and sales automation platforms. Sales plays a crucial role in this process, as it is usually the only one with the knowledge to incorporate customers and the market into the strategy to be developed. It is the guarantor for the customer and reality proximity of the marketing and sales automation activities. Figure 7 shows an example of a lead-nurturing process.

In general, there are several scenarios in which sales can use marketing or sales automation platforms:

- Welcome-Nurture: New prospects are generated with content offers and developed to sales maturity until they are handed over to sales.
- Warm-up Nurture: Interested parties or existing customers who are not currently interested in a purchase usually end up in a salesperson's resubmission. However, due to ongoing projects, further support often fails to materialize, and the potential is not exploited. With this process, the prospect continues to be provided with relevant content and is developed until renewed interest and a renewed handover to the sales department.
- B/C customer nurture: Sales usually only manages to actively manage A customers. B and C customers are rarely sufficiently appreciated. Nurturing can be done through an appropriate nurturing process. Customers are automated but individually developed to renewed sales maturity.
- Trade show follow-up: In the context of optimal trade show execution and follow-up, leads do not end up in the sales staff's jacket pockets ("jacket leads"), but in a marketing automation process. In this process, leads are motivated to visit the trade show booth before the trade show, receive initial information during the trade show visit, and receive further information at appropriate intervals with relevant content after the trade show.

To give sales the assurance that prospects who are ready to buy do not have to go through the entire nurture process, a "sales fast lane" identifies these prospects and passes them directly to sales for further support.

The nurturing processes help the sales department to take care of the currently important leads with high closing chances without neglecting the potential of the leads that are currently not personally managed. When sales discover these opportunities, they can use marketing automation as a "nurturing pool" for their new prospects and existing addresses (existing customers and prospects) and thus generate more deals faster.

Of course, the question remains: How do potential prospects learn about the processes and content components? Where are the relevant customer contact points (touchpoints, Halb & Seebacher, 2021)? The buyer persona profiles are again helpful here. There, it was determined where the respective desired customers move, where they can be reached or addressed. The most important touchpoint in the B2B sector is the company website. It should be found by the desired customers and encourage them to contact the company with relevant content modules. Other relevant touchpoints are:

- Being found with the waterhole strategy
  - Blogs,
  - Social media,
  - Specialized portals,
  - Press,
  - Email Signature,
  - Podcasts.
- Active Address:
  - LinkedIn,
  - Company Newsletter,
  - Stand-alone newsletter
  - Ads, AdWords, SEA,
  - Telephone Acquisition,
  - Fair and events,
  - Field Service.

Sales can also become active here on several levels. It can:

- Share the content that Marketing has created and placed on its channels, such as LinkedIn.
- Optimize its profiles in LinkedIn to address the desired customers.
- Share the content on the company's social media channels.
- Point out the content building blocks in conversations, phone calls, and emails.

Sales leads

With the help of marketing automation, sales does not necessarily get more leads. Since the prospects are developed in marketing automation, the leads that are not ready for sales and are not transferred to sales naturally crystallize there. So, sales will probably get fewer leads at first. Only with the ongoing optimization of lead generation will the number of leads increase again.

The decisive factor, however, is that sales receives higher-quality leads. With the information from the buyer persona profiles and the lead-nurturing process, sales can optimally prepare its strategy and benefit arguments for contact with the potential customer. It would be fatal if the sales department ignored this information and did not contact the prospect according to his lead history. It is their task to optimally adapt their approach and communication to the prospect's history and built-up profile and to guide the prospect through the appropriate phases of their buying process.

System integration

An important lever for the effect of marketing automation is the integration of MAP with other systems and platforms. Performance platforms such as Linkedin, Google, or Facebook must be connected before the lead-nurturing process. After the nurturing process, the leads are transferred to the CRM system (lead routing) for optimal and rapid further support. Other possible subsequent systems are ERP, PIM, or store systems.

Even more exciting is the integration of systems for existing customer business. The movements of existing customers as part of their customer journey are usually easier to measure than those of prospects. Once the systems and platforms are integrated, leads and customers leave behind a large amount of data that companies can use to their advantage:

- The data becomes and remains consistent.
- Processes can be controlled and automated across all systems.
- Signals from customers are captured, leading to insights and triggering activities.
- Sales obtains an overall picture of customers, their activities, and sales opportunities in "R/U/C" (Repeat-/ Up-/ Cross-Selling) selling.

Another important aspect is the opportunities that consistent and enriched data open up for management (Seebacher, 2021a). They provide insights into the behavior of leads and customers that help management:

- evaluate success.
- Obtain a basis for decision-making and planning certainty.
- Be able to make action deductions.

Supplemented with AI/machine learning components, management receives an early warning system in the context of Predictive Intelligence (Seebacher, 2021d) to, for example:

- detect customer churn tendencies at an early stage
- identify clusters in customer data
- better estimate the probability of a deal being closed

and to initiate appropriate actions and activities.

To integrate the systems easily and quickly, it is advisable to use an iPaaS integration platform (Integration Platform as a Service, API Middleware, exemplary Marini Systems No-Coding Integration platform), which has existing adapters for the common systems in marketing and sales. This allows changes to be made flexibly and new systems to be integrated without programming knowledge (no-code approach).

In order to optimally map and evaluate the data from all systems and platforms, it makes sense to use a CDP (Customer Data Platform). A CDP is a platform that brings together data from prospects and customers from all systems along the customer journey with the help of an iPaaS integration platform. It supports marketing and sales in keeping the customer in focus across all systems. In this context a comprehensive, valid, operational but also strategic discussion on the required Marketing Technology Stack (MarTechStack) can be found at Seebacher (2021e) exploring also a growth path on how to best draft and deploy a such MarTechStack minimizing costs and risks and optimizing the Return-on-Marketing-Investment (RoMI, Güpner & Seebacher, 2021).

Conclusion

The bottom line is that marketing and sales automation platforms do not make sales superfluous. On the contrary, with their help you can offer your desired customers relevant content at the appropriate touchpoints and support sales with more qualified prospects and reactivated existing customers. With lead-nurturing processes in the automation platforms, you develop these prospects individually and automatically until they are ready to be sold or closed. In this way, automation helps sales to shorten acquisition times and significantly increase sales success.

References

Bacon, A. (2021). Strategic account-based marketing: How to tame this beast. In U. G. Seebacher (Ed.), *B2B marketing. Management for professionals*. Springer. https://doi.org/10.1007/978-3-030-54292-4_17

Barrett, J., & Herten, M. (2021). From keywords to contextual frameworks: New take on B2B SEO enabling next level content. In U. G. Seebacher (Ed.), *B2B marketing. Management for professionals*. Springer. https://doi.org/10.1007/978-3-030-54292-4_16

Dixon, M., & Adamson, B. (2011). *The challenger sale: Taking control of the customer conversation* (1st ed.). Portfolio.

Enge, E., Spencer, S., & Stricciola, J. (2015). *The art of SEO: Mastering search engine optimization*. O'Reilly Media.

Güpner, A., & Seebacher, U. (2021). *Marketing resource management: Guidebook for organizational development with many examples, explanations and instructions for action*. AQPS.

Halb, F., & Seebacher, U. G. (2021). User experience and touchpoint management: A touchpoint performance management toolkit for the buyer journey. In U. G. Seebacher (Ed.), *B2B marketing. Management for professionals*. Springer. https://doi.org/10.1007/978-3-030-54292-4_12

Klaus, L. (2021). Marketing automation: Exploring the process model for implementation. In U. G. Seebacher (Ed.), *B2B marketing. Management for professionals*. Springer. https://doi.org/10.1007/978-3-030-54292-4_9

Njenga, G. (2020). *THE ART OF THE CROSS-SALE: Learn how to grow your Insurance Agency through cross-selling and up-selling*. Independently published.

Pulizzi, J. (2013). *Epic content marketing: How to tell a different story, break through the clutter, and win more customers by marketing less*. McGraw Hill.

Rackham, N. (1998). *SPIN selling* (1st ed.). McGraw Hill.

Revella, A. (2015). *Buyer Personas: How to gain insight into your customer's expectations, align your marketing strategies, and win more business* (1st ed.). Wiley.

Schüller, A. M., & Schuster, N. (2017). *Marketing automation for existing customers. More sales with the waterhole strategy®*.

Schuster, N. (2020). *Digitalization in marketing and sales*. Haufe-Verlag.

Seebacher, U. (2021a). *Data-driven Management: A primer for modern corporate decision making*. AQPS.

Seebacher, U. (2021b). *Praxishandbuch B2B-Marketing: Neueste Konzepte, Strategien und Technologien sowie praxiserprobte Vorgehensmodelle –mit 11 Fallstudien*. Springer Gabler.

Seebacher, U. G. (2021c). The B2B marketing ecosystem: Finding your way through the world of colorful B2B terms! In U. G. Seebacher (Ed.), *B2B marketing. Management for professionals*. Springer. https://doi.org/10.1007/978-3-030-54292-4_2

Seebacher, U. (2021d). *Predictive intelligence for data-driven managers: Process model, assessment-tool, IT-blueprint, competence model and case studies*. Springer.

Seebacher, U. G. (2021e). MarTech 8000: How to survive in Jurassic Park of dazzling marketing solutions. In U. G. Seebacher (Ed.), *B2B marketing. Management for professionals*. Springer. https://doi.org/10.1007/978-3-030-54292-4_4

Sullivan, T. (2022). *Solution selling transformed: The revolutionary sales process that is changing the way people sell* (3rd ed.). McGraw Hill.

Wenger, S. (2021). Successful lead management: Nothing's gonna stop us now. In U. G. Seebacher (Ed.), *B2B marketing. Management for professionals*. Springer. https://doi.org/10.1007/978-3-030-54292-4_10

Norbert Schuster (www.strike2.de) was a sales manager and sales director in the B2B sector for 25 years. Since 2011, he has been intensively involved with marketing automation and modern lead management. In his seminars and consulting projects, he has trained, advised, and supported the implementation of several thousand marketing and sales managers.

Norbert Schuster is a strategy consultant for digitalization in marketing and sales, helping companies to leverage the potential of digitalization for their marketing. He advises and supports companies in the strategy/concept development and implementation of lead management, marketing automation, the Waterhole Strategy, SalesTech, Customer Data Platform (CDP), and Enterprise Data Integration.

He is a speaker, lecturer, and author of the books "Digitalization in Marketing and Sales," "Marketing Automation for Existing Customers," "Lead Management," and The Inbound Marketing Method."

Automation and Social Selling, Can It Work?

Philipp Schmid

1 The Specific Features of Sales and Marketing in a B2B Environment

It is essential to clarify and distinguish B2B and B2C sales and marketing and what social selling is before diving into the topic of marketing automation. Until these two terms are clear, marketing automation, its importance, and its uses will be lost on the reader.

Sales and marketing are generally classified into B2B (business to business) and B2C (business to consumers) marketing and sales. While one might employ similar digital vehicles in both cases, the strategy, processes, and techniques differ based on their specific features.

1.1 Business to Consumer (B2C) Businesses

B2C companies sell their goods or services to end-users or consumers. The goods are typically finished products which the customers use. They involve relatively small sums of money and goods that people use daily. Many purchasing decisions can be made consciously or subconsciously on an average day, the buyer often making the decisions alone.

In many cases, B2C customers do not need to invest much thought into the buying process or decision except when making high-value purchases, such as a car or house.

P. Schmid (✉)
Kempten University of Applied Sciences, Kempten, Germany
e-mail: philipp@drphilippschmid.com

U. Hannig, U. Seebacher (eds.), *Marketing and Sales Automation*, Management for Professionals, https://doi.org/10.1007/978-3-031-20040-3_7

1.2 Business to Business (B2B) Businesses

Firms that operate B2B marketing typically sell to other businesses. According to Seebacher, B2B marketing occurs between market participants who, due to their original business function in a defined market, are suppliers or subcontractors and buyers of raw materials and semi-finished products, and therefore, not end customers or end consumers (Seebacher, 2021).

In more practical terms, B2B sales mainly cover goods needed to produce and resell other goods and services instead of finished goods required for consumption.

These differences are crucial as they affect the social selling (and other marketing) strategies employed. For example, when selling to business customers, the salesperson deals with a buying centre, which includes all the relevant people involved in a purchasing decision, as opposed to one person, which is typical in a B2C transaction.

It is the norm that, in business, several people make the purchase decision (or, at least, influence it). For a classic example, when buying a machine used to manufacture goods, the designated buyer, a developer, a production manager and management may be involved. In addition, users of the machine, for example, workers at the factory, may also be asked about their opinions and wishes. Normally we are talking about 5–7 people.

These people often have different desires and goals. For example, a buyer's goal may be to get the lowest possible purchase price. The production manager will be more interested in availability and high output The machine operator may want it to be simple to handle. These goals are often in conflict with each other. In the end, management has to decide on a product or service taking all requirements into consideration.

In these situations, the first step in the procurement process is to summarise the technical requirements on a specification sheet, obtain offers from potential suppliers based on the specification sheet, and then evaluate whether they meet the technical specifications. Only then are the commercial requirements checked. These can be the price, delivery times or warranties for example. Further discussions are held with the suppliers to achieve price reductions or other commercial goals based on a shortlist. Only then is the official order triggered with an official purchase order. As a result, purchasing decisions often take a long time and are delayed by internal voting rounds.

As for the technical requirements, one can see that the products and purchasing processes are often complex and make high demands on the seller. The seller has to be able to answer technical questions. For this reason, engineers very often sell technical goods and programmers sell software. The customer is accustomed to speaking with a technically experienced contact person and exchanging possible problems and solutions.

Another crucial reason (or difference) is that B2B sales often involve more significant investment sums. Machines and fixed assets cost from several thousand Euros to several million Euros. Accordingly, the purchase decisions are made carefully and influenced by a committee, the already mentioned Buying Centre.

2 How Social Selling Works

Having highlighted the environment in which B2B sales and marketing work and the B2B social seller must operate, let us now talk about social selling itself.

Social selling is about deepening relationships as well as finding and acquiring new contacts for your business and engaging with them through social media (and other digital platforms). It allows salespersons and firms to find their target audience, network and build a relationship with them, nurture them and then move over to the "regular" sales process of a company.

The term social selling describes the establishment and expansion of a customer relationship as part of the sales process. The goal is to strengthen the customer relationship with other members through active social media behaviour (posting pictures, articles, social listening, and more) and thereby generating leads (Ancillai et al., 2019). However, at a certain point, the lead needs to be transferred into the "regular" sales process. This is a critical step.

With these definitions, it becomes clear that social selling is not a stand-alone sales process but one integrated into the company's sales process. This is especially the case in B2B businesses. As already mentioned, a salesperson has to deal with different people in the buying centre of the customer. These people all have varying interests and contribute differently to the decision-making process and ultimately to the purchase of the product or service.

With this in mind, a crucial starting point in social selling is to create Buyer Personas. These are semi-fictional representations of a company's ideal customers based on data and research (Hubspot, 2022).

The better a salesperson understands the personas' needs, goals, and aspirations, the better they can identify and address those people. Also, a clear understanding of the personas' job titles will help identify them and know what role they play in making the buying decision.

The goal for a salesperson (and social selling) in B2B is to build a relationship with all relevant people in the buying centre. This way, a salesperson can manage to influence the internal decision-making processes in their favour. For example, the technical requirements that a development manager includes in the specifications are already aligned with the company's solutions. If a salesperson is connected with many people, they can be available early in the decision-making process to answer questions from stakeholders and respond to their different interests.

The advent of professional social networks, such as LinkedIn, has resulted in an unprecedented opportunity to identify and build relationships with decision-makers in the sales process.

I should mention here that this relationship building is a long-term process and should be done strategically. For those in the buying centre to perceive the salesperson as a competent contact partner, it is recommended to proceed in the following steps when establishing the budding customer relationship (Fig. 1):

Adopting social selling and sales and marketing automation is often made very complex by different people. But it should not be. It can be as simple as assigning a

Fig. 1 The five Cs of social selling by Professor Philipp Schmid

few salespeople to the task, creating a social selling department, and helping them develop and execute a winning social selling strategy.

For the social seller to develop a winning social selling strategy (as an individual or social selling department), they must have a clear concept. This concept must include precise answers to the following questions:

- Who is your target group?
- Who are the stakeholders you have to reach to influence the sale or purchase decisions?

One must develop a clear roadmap of how to use the answers to these questions to create a strategy that will enable one to succeed in the social selling endeavour.

The marketing and sales process is an information-gathering process. The more information one has regarding the customer, the better one can tailor the offer to match the company's needs and goals.

Some other parts of one's final concept will emerge as one engages in social selling. These include gathering answers to questions such as:

- What are the current trends in the market?
- What are your customer's competitors doing?
- What other solutions have your customer tried?
- Why did they terminate their use of that solution?
- What are their goals, needs, and challenges?
- And more

Companies and individuals publish plenty of helpful information on social media. Reading such posts helps to prepare for customer conversations. This is part of Social Listening.

With the answer to the questions above, one might find that the best offer for the customer might be to build a custom-made machine (if offered by the company) instead of selling one with general specifications.

The strategy one employs should also include gathering information on the different officials and personnel involved at the buying centre.

Once the salesperson has the basic concept in place, it is time to begin demonstrating competence on the social media platform of choice, in this case, LinkedIn. To do this, he has to upload a profile and a background (or cover) photo which are attractive, professional, and current. The background picture must be related to the industry in which he operates in. With both images in place, he writes a headline summarising the value he delivers to the customer. The headline should be meaningful, i.e. more than just a job title. Then comes the summary. A summary told as a story helps the profile visitors to learn more about him. It is also essential to emphasise the relevant skills and industry knowledge on his profile (Dehan, 2022).

Ultimately, a seller's LinkedIn profile is his digital business card. It should be professionally complete and personable so that the customer's contacts will want to interact with him. A poor profile drives away connections and makes it difficult for them to initiate interaction with or reach out to the social seller.

Demonstrating competence also includes bringing solutions to some of the problems that prospects and connections might have. This might be through the posts or the comments one leaves in groups or on other people's posts.

Once a salesperson has done his homework, and the LinkedIn profile is professional, the next step is to build up contacts (or connections, as they are called on LinkedIn). This should be done strategically, i.e., in line with his concept. A possible goal could be that a salesperson is in contact with as many people as possible at the customer's company and thus achieves high customer penetration.

In addition, he should identify the relevant contacts who are involved in a decision. He can achieve this by using the search function and filters for the company name and job titles. If he is already talking to some of the people involved, he can find out who else has an interest in his product or is involved in the decision-making process.

Building connections and making contacts is beneficial. Yet, because of how the LinkedIn algorithm and platform work, it is advisable not to send a contact request directly. A recommendation from a third party is the surest way. The social seller can also try to initially meet them in person in a face-to-face meeting at a trade fair, seminar, professional associations, or at the customer's office.

Note: This is not to say that sending requests directly never works or that it is forbidden to send a contact request; however, a recommendation is the best way as the party one seeks to connect with has a mutual connection to the person doing the recommending. Recommendations and prior meetings reduce the possibility of having your requests turned down. When someone has several requests ignored, left pending, or marked as spam, LinkedIn penalises the person, hence the earlier advice. Still, if a person has no mutual connection to recommend him, sending a connection request directly is one of his few options.

That said, instead of sending a connection request out of the blue, you should have a strategy to get the contact's attention and get the prospect to "pre-know" or like you before the request. And when you do send a request, it must never be without an accompanying message.

A good network with the customer is always the perfect basis for making connections and to send them messages. But to generate new contacts (contacts with whom you have no previous affiliations), it is recommended to publish content on LinkedIn consistently. This content should establish the salesperson as an expert. It should, therefore, fit the target group's needs and be relevant and valuable to them. This is what is meant by consistency.

The fifth piece of a winning social selling strategy is constancy. The social seller needs to stay on topic, publish valuable content related to the customer's industry, needs, and goals, and build a relationship over several months as he attempts to make contacts. If he does this well, it will help him get links to several people at the customers' buying centres and influence their buying decisions in his favour. Hence the salesperson has to get a publishing strategy that helps him achieve the primary objectives.

Lastly, the salesperson will be able to influence these decisions over time as focusing on quick decisions is typically not feasible with B2B customers. This is because no singular person has power over the budget and all the other components needed to decide in a business setting. At least a second person has to look it over (the four-eyed principle).

3 Basic Functions of LinkedIn and Its Regulation

A salesperson's success on LinkedIn has much to do with understanding the platform, its features, and regulations. Even regarding marketing and sales automation, without understanding what is allowed or disallowed, one's social selling campaign will be filled with many perils and headaches.

First, it is essential to note that LinkedIn's features and functions are constantly changing due to its improvements to the platform. Its regulations are also continually evolving, so wisdom entails that the salesperson familiarises himself with them periodically.

LinkedIn is the world's largest professional network, with 810 million members worldwide in more than 200 countries and territories (LinkedIn, 2022). Therefore it is the most relevant platform for B2B business.

Below, I will discuss some of the most basic but critical functions for social selling. I have already mentioned some of them, including creating a professional yet personable profile, so I will not touch on these again.

One of the essential features of the platform for a social seller is the search function. It gives him the ability to search for contacts specifically, using different filters. A salesperson can use the search function and enter the contact's name. He can also enter other search terms related to the role or position of the prospect at the customer's company. After that, it is possible to visit the profile with one click and get all the information one needs about the contact's occupational history and more; as long as the prospect has made them publicly available.

This search function is not only limited to individuals. A salesperson can also search for companies. For example, a search for BMW on LinkedIn shows you all the official information the company has made available on its page (or account). This includes their official website, those who have indicated BMW as their employer, and more.

From this simple search, if BMW happens to be his customer, he can get an overview of the people he needs to connect with and tries to influence. He can use the search function to gather further information regarding roles and responsibilities within BMW and their different locations relevant to him.

For the best results, the social seller should follow the official LinkedIn page of the customer (or company) that he targets. This way, publications, events, and other relevant information regarding things going on at the customer's will show up in his feed. These can be used as conversation starters when he decides to reach out to contacts at the customer's company.

Once a salesperson has identified a contact, he can send them a networking request. It is advisable (as earlier stated) to include a short text in that request. Of course, a contact who already knows the salesperson personally is more likely to answer this networking request than an unknown person. Therefore, the first step is to add all relevant contacts one already knows as "connections." Should the contact search the salesperson's profile and notice that they have several mutual connections, it increases the likelihood that he will accept the request.

Another important feature of LinkedIn, which is essential to establish authority and influence connections, is the ability to publish posts. LinkedIn allows one to share information in different formats, including videos, text, pdfs, polls, graphics, and more.

When a post is shared on the platform, it is first shown to a small percentage of contacts. When many people from this first group view, like, or comment on it, LinkedIn's algorithm classifies the content as relevant and shows it to other participants in their feed. Thus, the content is also shown to the sharer's second and third-degree contacts. However, this content has to be considered relevant by the members.

LinkedIn offers numerous other features that the social seller can take advantage of, including groups, InMail, Sales Navigator, and more. Some of these are available in their basic (free) plan. Others are available only within their premium (paid) plans.

3.1 LinkedIn Regulations Regarding the Use of Bots or Third-Party Software

As we have learned above, there are various ways to interact with customers and potential customers on LinkedIn. The reader should note that this interaction is individual and time-consuming. The question here is whether and how to automate these functions. One thing to note upfront: LinkedIn is very restrictive, and its guidelines prohibit the use of software to automate interactions (LinkedIn, 2018).

As a result, it is crucial to clarify LinkedIn's guidelines and rules on using bots and third-party software. LinkedIn prohibits bots or other automated methods to access its services, add or download contacts, and send or redirect messages.

This poses some problems since all the tasks associated with social selling can be very repetitive and time-consuming. The question then becomes, "Is there no way out?"

While LinkedIn prohibits using bots and several third-party software in contacting people on the platform, it also allows integration with several other third-party software that makes one's work easy. The software these partners offer is deemed safe to use. LinkedIn's restrictions are aimed at protecting its users and platform. This is the environment in which we discuss automation in the next section.

4 Solutions and Software Where Automation Makes Sense

To answer the question posed in this chapter's title, "Automation and Social Selling, can it work?" the answer is yes, it can. Social selling needs automation to deliver outstanding results in record time.

Sales and marketing automation is a way to save time and perform repetitive tasks on autopilot (or, at least, something close to that). Building relationships, nurturing those relationships, and moving a prospect through the customer journey can be scaled when you automate using customer relationship management software (CRM).

Suppose one is still sceptical or unsure why they should use automation for their business, marketing, and sales endeavour. In that case, the simple answer lies in the fact that they are currently doing business in a fast-paced, ever-changing, digitalised world. However, it is important to mention that before automating any process it is vital to make sure that the process works. This means before automating check wisely and use tests to improve the process.

If one is to meet the demands of digitalisation, they must learn to adopt automation. Marketing Automation should not be seen as a new software alone. Instead, it is a fundamental approach to meeting the changing requirements of digitalisation and protecting the core business (Klaus, 2021).

According to Klaus, some other things that marketing automation can help you achieve include:

- Increase sales and generate a measurable contribution from marketing through more leads
- Optimisation of the customer experience through personalisation
- Increased productivity through automation of formerly manual tasks
- Creation of a modern working atmosphere to increase the attractiveness from the employee's point of view
- Implementation of Data-Driven Marketing as a preliminary stage of a Data-Driven Business (Klaus, 2021)

For social selling on LinkedIn, the list of things one can achieve using marketing automation is endless and includes scaling and automating content creation and publishing, funnelling prospects through a pre-designed series of content aimed at nurturing and building a thriving relationship, while simultaneously influencing prospects to favour one when they decide which product or brand to choose.

As noted earlier, LinkedIn allows the use of some third-party software. For example, one can connect CRM to the LinkedIn Sales Navigator. This will automate the process of updating customer and prospect information. It will not have to be done manually. So, whenever a contact updates their information or changes company, without the salesperson doing anything, the company can use LinkedIn for data validation, as long as the prospect or customer makes that change in their LinkedIn profile. That means he can send personalised messages to that contact and even get a new company to do business with, because he now has a contact with the new customer.

Since we have listed some of the reasons you should be using marketing automation and specified that LinkedIn does restrict some applications while allowing others, it is only fitting that we state what the platform allows. The reader can find a list of software the social network allows for each region by following this link https://business.linkedin.co/marketing-solutions/marketing-partners/find-a-partner#specialty/service-type/region-support.

I have included the link in case LinkedIn has updated the list by the time the reader sees this.

The list includes software that performs various business and marketing related tasks, including

- Customer Relationship Management
- Content creation
- Business and marketing analytics
- Data-driven analytics
- Campaign creation and optimisation
- Advertising ROI measurement
- Advertising management
- Branding and standardising your message throughout all communication channels
- And more

A few of these solutions work on the platform itself. Others work as background processes but use the data they collate from LinkedIn.

While automation is essential for marketing and business in our digital age, it does not replace human communication. One still has to comment on a post, reply to messages in person, and more. Contacts can easily detect when all the messages one sends are sent using software, even when it is personalised with their names, company names and addresses. Sometimes, when people feel that they are communicating with bots, they stop responding.

To say this differently, the best way to use marketing automation is to enhance and scale one's social selling activities. Marketing automation should not replace the social seller on LinkedIn. It will only have the opposite effect of what one is trying to achieve.

LinkedIn is currently the most important platform for B2B connections globally. However, this can change. New platforms maybe with different focuses may arise in future.

Conclusion

B2B marketing and sales are about the individual identification and addressing of different people in the customer's buying centre. Deciding on these purchases is often lengthy and involves many people with different goals and objectives and high transaction volumes or prices. As a result, to get these types of sales, one needs to connect with several contacts at the customer's company, build relationships with them, and influence their decision-making while also creating content and messaging for different roles. This process is frequently time-consuming and repetitive. This is where marketing automation comes in. Marketing automation helps to scale and optimise one's business, sales and marketing activities and results, while also meeting the demands of doing business in a fast-paced, digitalised world.

Personal notes:

I want to thank Timo Buck, Lutz Klaus for their feedback and Okesiri Oveh for his input and editing of this article.

References

Ancillai, C., HarriTerho, S. C., & Pascucci, F. (2019). Advancing social media-driven sales research: Establishing conceptual foundations for B-to-B social selling. *Industrial Marketing Management, 82*, 293–308. ISSN 0019-8501. https://doi.org/https://doi.org/10.1016/j.indmarman.2019.01.002

Deehan, J. (2022). *20 steps to a better LinkedIn profile in 2022, 01/01/2022*. Retrieved March 08, 2022, from https://www.linkedin.com/business/sales/blog/profile-best-practices/17-steps-to-a-better-linkedin-profile-in-2017

Hubspot. (2022). *How to create detailed buyer personas for your business*. Retrieved April 2022, from https://blog.hubspot.com/marketing/buyer-persona-research

Klaus, L. (2021). Marketing automation: Exploring the process model for implementation. In U. G. Seebacher (Ed.), *B2B marketing. Management for professionals*. Springer. https://doi-org.hske.idm.oclc.org/10.1007/978-3-030-54292-4_9

LinkedIn. (2018). *Prohibited software and extensions*. Retrieved March 08, 2022, from https://www.linkedin.com/help/linkedin/answer/56347/prohibited-software-and-extensions?lang=en

LinkedIn. (2022). *About LinkedIn*. Retrieved March 08, 2022, from https://about.linkedin.com/de-de?lr=1

Seebacher, U. G. (2021). The B2B marketing ecosystem: Finding your way through the world of colorful B2B terms! In U. G. Seebacher (Ed.), *B2B marketing. Management for professionals*. Springer. https://doi-org.hske.idm.oclc.org/10.1007/978-3-030-54292-4_2

Philipp Schmid is a Professor of Business Development and Sales at the Faculty of Mechanical Engineering at Kempten University of Applied Sciences. He has served as the Marketing Manager for an international group in the engineering sector. While there, he built up a large network on LinkedIn, which he leveraged to generate many leads for the group.

Professor Philipp Schmid is also a social selling expert. He has trained more than one hundred sales engineers on how to use social selling to generate leads and meet their goals.

From 0 to 5-Digit-Profit in 10 Weeks with Conversion-Rate-Optimized Marketing and Sales Automation

Bernd Trummer

1 From SEO to RoS with CRO

The COVID pandemic has given the entire digital business an enormous boost. In the period from 2020 to 2023, the volume of total global online trade will more than double, from USD4200 billion to USD6500 billion (Fig. 1). This corresponds to growth of more than 55% or an average annual growth rate (CAGR) of around 15.67%. Even the global B2B e-commerce market, which is more conservative, is recording a growth rate of 18.7%, as marketing and sales automation can significantly optimize return on sale (RoS). The advantage in B2B marketing (Seebacher, 2022) lies in the generally better and more easily defined target group, whereas the end customer segment, i.e., the Business-2-Consumer (B2C) segment, is defined by less easily defined and thus more difficult to reach target groups and buyer groups.

Thus, the attractive growth of online retailing is both a blessing and a curse, as it is becoming increasingly difficult for companies in the sense of suppliers to reach customers in the ever-denser jungle. The rapidly increasing number of providers is making it more and more expensive to reach relevant customers at the right time via the right channels through paid advertisements and campaigns, and to persuade them to make a purchase.

In many places, the term *Search Engine Optimization* (SEO) (Barrett & Herten, 2021) is used in this context. But the SEO concept is no longer sufficient to generate sales in eCommerce in the context of Marketing and Sales Automation (MSA) and this especially with an attractive high Return-on-Sales (RoS).

SEO helps to be found by search engines. In contrast, conversion-rate-optimization (CRO) as a concept helps to take the decisive step further in the buyer journey

B. Trummer (✉)
Fynest International, Graz, Austria

Frankfurt, Germany
e-mail: bernd@fynest.at

U. Hannig, U. Seebacher (eds.), *Marketing and Sales Automation*, Management for Professionals, https://doi.org/10.1007/978-3-031-20040-3_8

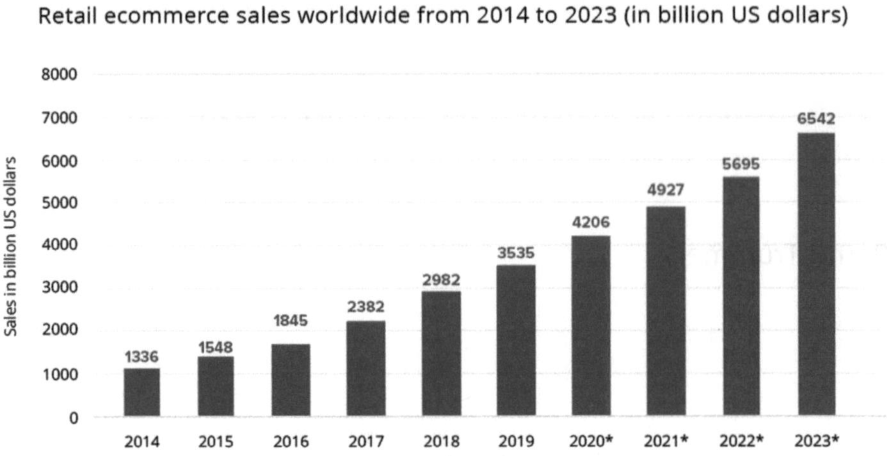

Fig. 1 Retail eCommerce sales worldwide (Source: Statista)

(Halb & Seebacher, 2021) in the direction of revenue generation. After all, what is it all about in the end—cash through sales and profit maximization? Being found by search engines is undoubtedly important for visibility in terms of brand development and branding, but the goal of every company and every marketer must be to transform marketing from a cost factor into a revenue generator through the application and proper use of CRO as Seebacher puts and describes it in his book "How to turn your marketing from a cost into a Sales Engine" (2020).

What is conversion rate optimization? Seebacher in the B2B marketing guidebook (2021a) in this context states:

> For conversion rate optimization, measuring customers in relation to conversions is one of the most important key figures. The CRO is usually part of the search engine optimization. It can improve lead generation, turnover and sales figures. Marketing experts generally assume an average CR of 1% in e-commerce, including B2C and B2B (Ryte, 2020). Thus, on average, every 100th visitor to an e-commerce shop becomes a customer. The level of the conversion rate depends on many different factors and especially for B2B these values are often significantly below those of B2C.

Another source[1] uses following definition for CRO:

> Conversion rate optimization (CRO) is the practice of increasing the percentage of users who perform a desired action on a website. Desired actions can include purchasing a product, clicking "add to cart", signing up for a service, filling out a form, or clicking on a link.
>
> Standard definitions of CRO, like the one we just wrote above, place their focus on conversion percentages, averages, and benchmarks. This emphasis on a numerical approach comes with a downside—the more you look at spreadsheets full of conversion data points and actions, the less you think of the individuals behind them.

[1] https://www.hotjar.com/conversion-rate-optimization/. Retrieved: Aug. 11th, 2022.

$$\text{Conversation rate} = \frac{\text{Number of sales}}{\text{Total number of visitors}} \times 100$$

Fig. 2 Conversion rate (CR) formula (Source: Own illustration)

$$\text{Conversation rate Optimization} = \frac{\text{Conversation rate period 2}}{\text{Conversation rate period 1}} \times 100$$

Fig. 3 Conversion rate optimization (CRO) formula (Source: Own illustration)

$$\text{Cash conversation rate (CCR)} = \frac{\text{Online sales}}{\text{CRO costs}} \times 100$$

Fig. 4 Cash Conversion rate optimization (CCR) formula (Source: Own illustration)

$$\text{Dynamic CCR optimization} = \frac{\text{CCR period n}}{\text{CCR period 1}} \times 100$$

Fig. 5 Dynamic CCR optimization formula (Source: Own illustration)

> Here is an alternative, more holistic and user-centric way of defining CRO: think of it as the process of focusing on understanding what drives, stops, and persuades your users, so you can give them the best user experience possible—and that, in turn, is what makes them convert and ultimately improves your website conversion rate.

These formulas determine the percentage values for CR and CRO. In the context of data-driven management (Seebacher, 2021b) and the development of predictive intelligence as part of central business intelligence (Strohmeier, 2021), these values can also be calculated and evaluated in absolute monetary amounts for CR and CRO. This absolute view allows the impact of the application of CRO to be presented even more clearly and transparently in terms of the economic effects. This is not possible with SEO as a concept, since the degree of visibility or its rate of increase or decrease can be measured, but not a direct financial benefit in terms of revenue generated from it.

If this last definition in the context of marketing and sales is interpreted purely in terms of revenue, the formulas in Figs. 2 and 3 result for CRO.

Based on these index formulas, however, absolute values for CRO can also be determined, namely performance indicators for Cash Conversation Rate (CCR) (Fig. 4) and the Dynamic CCR Optimization (Fig. 5).

With these indicators, the efficiency and effectiveness of all CRO activities can easily and transparently be measured and documented.

2 CRO at a Glance

In the following section, the complex topic of CRO is briefly and succinctly summarized so that you, the reader, can quickly understand what CRO all is about and what is important. This concise theoretical basis will then help you to better understand and comprehend the CRO case study presented below.

In general, a distinction is made between three levels regarding CRO. CRO in the *narrowest sense* refers to specific touchpoints, such as websites or landing pages. CRO in the *broader sense* focuses on the entire buyer journey and thus considers the optimization of conversion along the entire buyer journey, but also subsequently along the customer journey. This includes terms and topics such as up-selling and cross-selling for existing customers. CRO in the *broadest sense* focuses on optimizing the entire return on sales (RoS) or the marketing and sales resources used. Seebacher and Güpner (2021) have defined the methodological foundation for this with their Marketing Resource Management approach (Fig. 6).

CRO in the narrowest sense uses measures such as the following:

- Shopping cart or checkout process
  - Optimization of the ordering process
  - Optimization of checkout process
  - Measures result from a
    Hypothetical measure and also the
    Previous analysis through appropriate programs
- Customer registrations
  - Landing page registrations,
  - Registrations for SaaS solutions
  - Improvement of the newsletter registration
  - Heatmap tools are used

The operational objectives of CRO in the narrowest sense are:

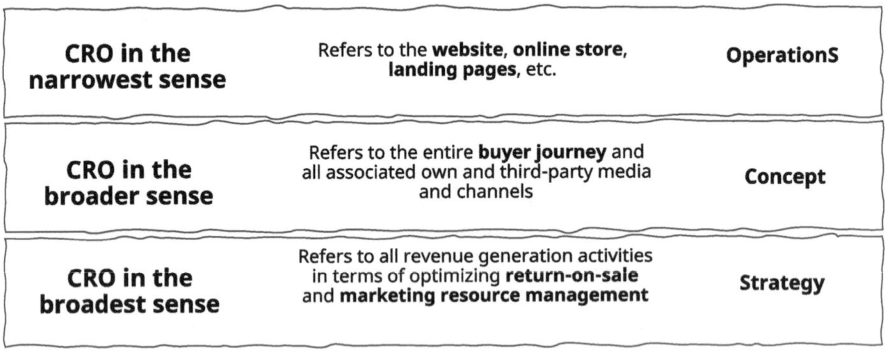

Fig. 6 Different dimensions of CRO (Source: Own illustration)

- Conversion of search results in search engines into page views of a website
- Conversion of the user of a search engine into a visitor of a website
- Conversion of a visitor to a website into a prospective customer for a download offer
- Conversion of website visitors into contact requests
- Registration for a newsletter on a website
- Filling out a quote request in an online store

but also...

- Converting a prospect into a Marketing Qualified Lead (MQL)
- Conversion of a Marketing Qualified Lead (MQL) into a Sales Qualified Lead (SQL)
- Conversion of a SQL into a buyer
- The request for information by means of a coupon of an advertisement
- The response to a contest (addresses are generated)
- Ordering a catalog after a mailing

When asking why CRO is needed in addition to all other and so many concepts and tools in the context of marketing and sales automation then again, the reference to the utmost goal, realizing and optimizing sales and profit, must be made. After the click is before the purchase. This means that a good click rate does not necessarily mean a good sale. Increasing competition leads to continuously rising customer acquisition costs in online marketing which is why CRO must be used to stringently reduce costs and keep these costs at the minimum level. Online marketing is (only) efficient when the entire process is optimally structured and continuously optimized.

3 What Do Consider for CRO Strategies and Tactics

In regard to strategy, CRO must consider two core aspects, content management and IT management. Both can and will only perform jointly as good content will not be found by the target groups if not played out adequately in regard to channel, time, and manner. Also, an ideal Interaction Technology Stack (InTechStack) as introduced into the discourse by Seebacher (2022) as part of his Reengineering Corporate Communication (RCC) approach will and cannot perform and convert with poor content.

In regard to best practice content management the following articles can be of help to design and deploy a performing content management:

- *Buyer-centric content approach*: Design thinking for more empathetic marketing in the B2B world (Ender, 2021)
- *Contingency-Centric Content Management* (CCCM): Smart Content Marketing against Content Overload (Mörk, 2021)

Fig. 7 QRC for accessing the mentioned articles (Source: Own illustration)

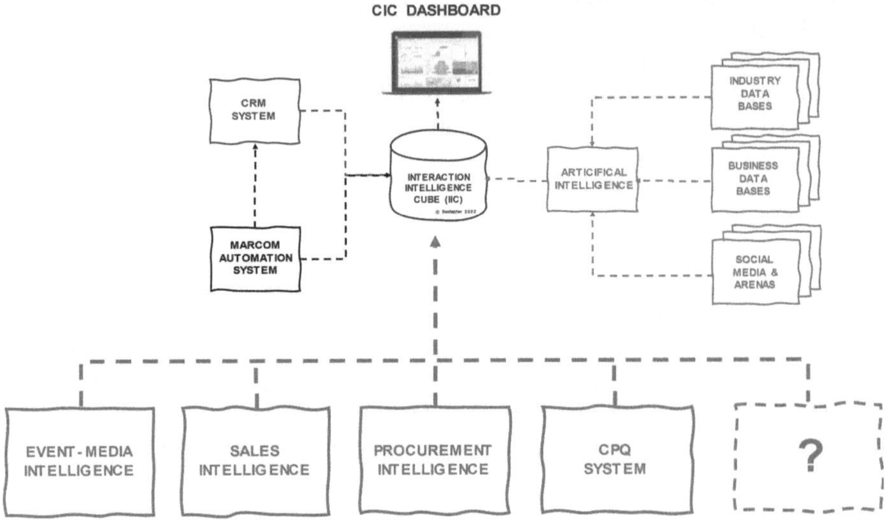

Fig. 8 Blueprint for ideal integrated InTechStack (Source: Own illustration)

- *Content Marketing Process Optimization*: How to Master the Symbiosis of Art and Science (Kosuniak, 2021)
- *Social Selling in B2B*: How Sales Benefits and the Sales Process Flourishes via Social Media (Ermer & Kleine, 2021)

Using the QR-Code in Fig. 7 directly leads you to the guidebook containing all four publications.

For ensuring a performing content playout a modern stable integrated InTechStack must be developed step by step. A blueprint is provided by Seebacher (2022, p. 196) as shown in Fig. 8. The core element is the Interaction Intelligence Cube (IIC) as the central part consolidating all data. These data must also contain all performance and conversion data as only then the key performance indicators (KPI) can be ongoingly monitored and predictively optimized. All CRO-relevant tools at the different touchpoints must be tracked and stored in the IIC as only then the evaluation can show which combination content, channel, design, and playout-time perform and convert best. This data stack is also the basis for A/B testing in order to ongoingly skip less performing combinations and continue with always the better converting options. The complexity behind is the fact that we must deal with multi-dimensional data models containing information on content, channel, design, and play-out time as well as region.

4 How to Develop CRO Texts!

The most important aspects in this context can be summarized as shown in the following list. All aspects will be explained and shown practically in the later section when the entire project of the Minimal Fashion[2] showcase company is illustrated and described:

- Communicate your value proposition.
- Put the needs of your target group and potential clients in the foreground and be empathetic about what their problem is and how you or your product can solve their problem. In most of the cases there are three things which are at the core:
  - Increase sales
  - Reduce costs
  - Save time
- Integrate trustificational elements in order to create trust by using references, testimonials, etc.
- Critically analyze what the core objective of the respective touchpoint is in the sense of the intended behavior for optimizing your conversation. Once you have identified and defined it then stringently lead your prospect to this objective.

Stringently implement above-the-fold optimization which means that the most important content must be placed on top as shown in Fig. 9. Users spend 80% of their time in the upper directly displayed area of the touchpoint. This means that “above-the-fold” the most important content must be placed as this ensures the user not having to scroll down for finding the core information.

> Note: In this context, you must also consider that depending on the browser or displaying tool the screen size and screen resolution differ which means that also the aspect of tool optimization must be playing a decisive role in your activities when it comes to successful CRO. CRO-checks and free-to-use web evaluation tools such as Google Optimize, Optimizely, or Eyequant are easy-to-use tools in the context of CRO.

[2] https://en.minimal-fashion.eu/. Retrieved: Aug. 11th, 2022.

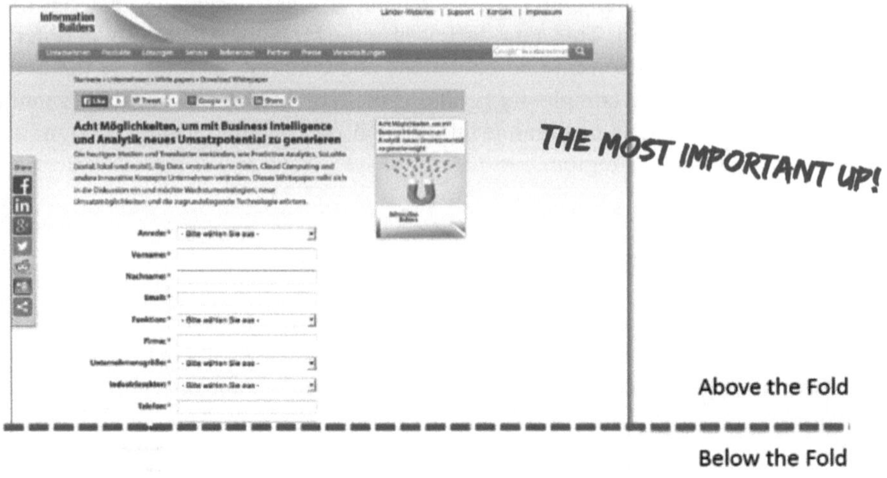

Fig. 9 Above-the-fold illustration (Source: Own illustration)

Position your value-add communication (VAC) together with the response element or the call-to-action (C2A) directly at the upper section of the screen. Also, the template or form for realizing the conversation in the sense of the intended behavior should also be placed above-the-fold. If you face space issues, then better go for a two-column form design in which you place the VAC on the left side and the form for completion on the left side. Do not hesitate to position a button twice on your touchpoint if the respective page is longer due to more required and additional information.

When putting together the content for your touchpoint you should use the below checklist for strong converting sales texts:

- Use a direct approach, active wordings, and specific formulations such as:
  - "With this software you reduce your retour costs by 20 percent" instead of
  - "This software helps to reduce return costs!"
- On all digital touchpoints text is being "scanned" and not "read"
  - Users search for headlines, highlights, and links
  - On average only 20 (!) % of all words are being read
  - Avoid nested sentences
- Speak the language of your target group
  - What are the needs for your prospects ("What is in for me?")
  - Use the terms your prospects are searching for and identify those terms through web analyzes and internal evaluations
  - Test different terms and formulations with Google AdWords

- Define and position clear and precise call-to-actions (C2A) such as
  "Request now without obligation!"
  "Download now for free!"
- Be short and to the point and avoid superfluous texts

5 How to Identify CRO Images!

Also, pictures and illustrations can impact the conversion in both ways, negatively as well as positively. Nothing worse could happen then to scrutinize a great and converting content by the wrong graphics. Therefore, it is essential to also focus on the selection and identification of strong selling images. The following checklist raises the most essential aspects:

- Does the motive communicate your unique selling proposition (USP)?
- Is the model authentic?
  - Is this what your typical customer looks like?
  - Use pictures from real clients and employees rather than stock images
- Is the motive supporting the call-to-action (C2A)?
  - Take into account the course of the gaze of the person(s) depicted
- Or does the image distract from the conversion goals?

Figure 10 shows the result of an eye-tracking evaluation of a picture from an Australian advertisement. The red spots show the areas, where the visitors spend time looking or reading. Green shadings show areas where the prospect rather scans only the content which means that essential value-adding information will not be percepted. A positive aspect of this example is that the baby's gaze is directed at the essential information, which is highly likely to have a positive effect on conversion. However, this is under the assumption that the important added-value communication or information is positioned at the top right next to the baby and that this information in turn corresponds to the criteria of strongly converting texts, as shown above.

6 What You Need to Know About CRO Landing Pages!

Basically, you need to distinguish in the context of marketing and sales automation between three types of landing pages:

- *Main website:* The main website is part of the corporate website and uses the same navigation as the corporate website. A main website in most of the cases is an integral part of the corporate website structure.

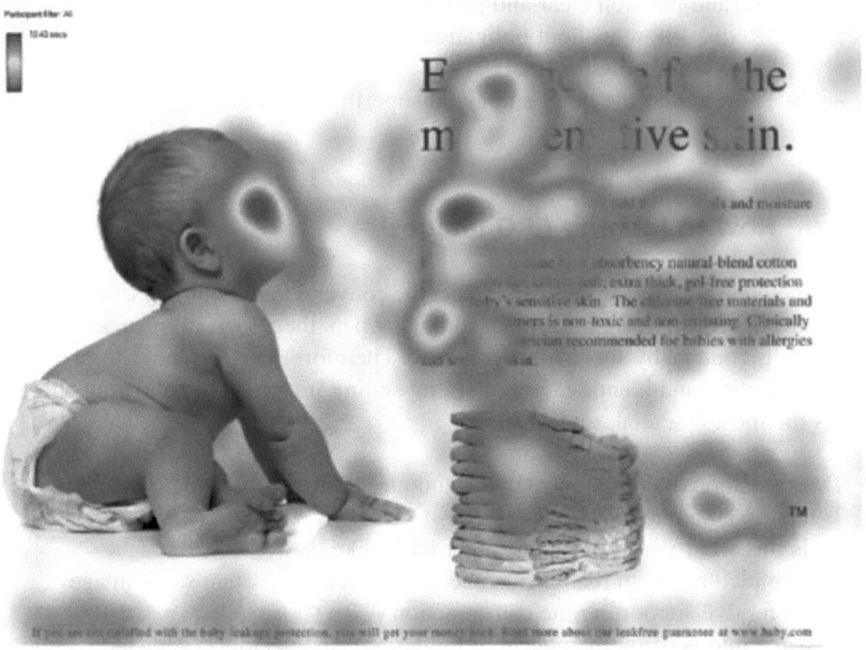

Fig. 10 Eye-tracking evaluation from Australian advertisement (Source: Own illustration)

- *Microsite:* The microsite is not part of the corporate website and in most cases uses its own navigation.
- *Standalone page:* Such pages are technically as well as optically fully independent. Mostly no navigation is used and no direct relation to the main or corporate website is existing.

Following five core functions can be defined for landing pages:

1. Registration
2. Purchase
3. Download
4. Knowledge Transfer
5. Call

The following variations of landing pages are the most used in the context of CRO:

1. Preview of new products
2. WLAN landing page
3. Event landing page
4. "Book Demo" landing page for software

5. Landing page for special promotions
6. Webinar landing page
7. Ebook/Whitepaper Landing Page
8. Product launch landing page

Based on different studies and papers the following checklist on how to conceptualize and design perfectly converting landing pages has been evolved:

1. A meaningful headline is half the battle
2. Less is more
3. Content must inspire the reader
4. Observe short loading times
5. Explain videos—inspire images
6. Pay attention to correct spelling
7. The call-to-action needs to be eye-catching and build in a value proposition right away!
8. All elements must be visible when the page is opened

Figure 11 shows a simple LinkedIn post that resulted in over six-digit impressions only applying a few but essential criteria of both texting and illustrating the value-add information. Less is more but authentic in an attractive narrative and the right framing.

Also useful in the context of CRO is the below checklist for Google Ads optimized landing pages. This is what you must consider for developing converting landing pages:

1. Adopt keywords from the Google Ads ad
2. Text optimization of the landing page (choose meaningful subheadings, include bulleted lists, one statement per paragraph, start with the most important statements)
3. Skimming (look, know what it is about!)
4. Scanning (skimming text and picking out data)
5. Reading (read carefully)
6. Keep promises
7. Formulate clear offer
8. The call-to-action function
9. Sort listing correctly (name advantages before product features!)
10. Transparency and seriousness
11. Uniform corporate identity
12. Standstill is regression: test your landing page

Finally, as already indicated above, also the landing page optimization for different touchpoints is an important element of conversion rate optimization. Especially mobile devices do play an ever more important role. Due to this, we provide you the below checklist on crucial elements to consider for ensuring conversion rate optimized mobile device landing pages:

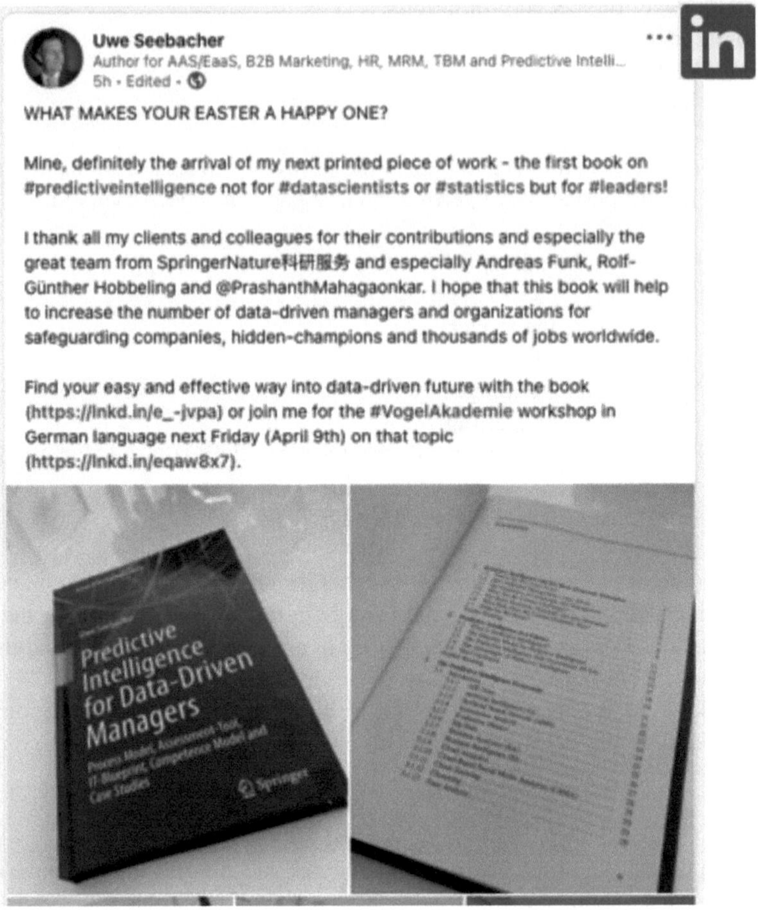

Fig. 11 Sample LinkedIn post as micro landing page (Source: Own illustration)

1. Pay attention to readability
2. Pay attention to different screen sizes
3. As little as possible, as much as necessary
4. Be reachable
5. Finger-friendly buttons: Images should be between 38×38 pixels and 44×44 pixels—depending on the device—to be clickable without problems
6. Use responsive design: It is best to design your mobile landing page in only one column—i.e., fullwidth.
7. Think regional
8. Simple forms
9. Pay attention to the loading speed
10. Go for web standards
11. Point to your app

12. Test!
13. Do not lock out search engines

7 How to Gain More Leads with Optimized Forms!

Forms in the sense of templates are at the core for optimizing your landing pages' conversion. The decisive groundbreaking work on templates for CRO has been brought into the discourse by Seebacher (2021c) with the Template-based Management (TBM) concept, which was first published in 2003 and since then has been the underlying reference framework for leading-edge concepts and tools such as Agile, Blueprints, Canvas, Design Thinking, or even Kanban.

Seebacher defines five essential aspects for good templates which are also at the core for conversion rate optimizing forms. These key success factors are (Fig. 12):

- User friendliness
- Precise in expression
- Self-explanatory
- Comprehensiveness
- Consistency

User friendliness focuses the customer experience (CX) for easy understanding and easy usage of provided forms. Less is more! Precision in expression refers to the already provided hints in regard to converting texts. A high user friendliness goes hand in hand with self-explanatory forms and used fields in the sense of terminology. Ensure also that CRO forms are comprehensive containing all details on usage, used terms and information on what will happen after completion of the respective form. This is important as nobody wants to be left standing in the dark unknowing what comes next.

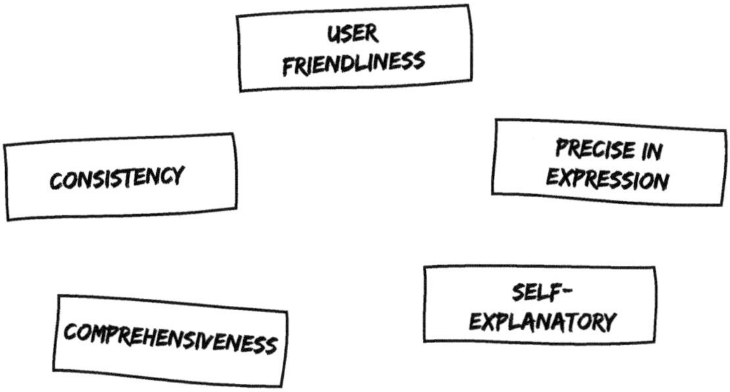

Fig. 12 Key factors for good forms (Source: Seebacher, 2021a, p. 113)

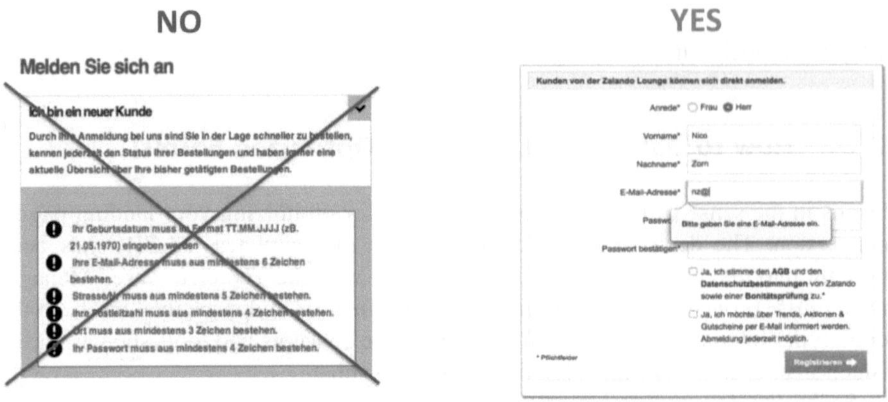

Fig. 13 Correct positioning of error messages (Source: Own illustration)

TIP: In the context of the above-mentioned success factors for good templates we recommend setting error messages above or even use inline validation (Fig. 13). In addition, consider the following tips for efficient and performing templates:

- Expectation-compliant arrangement and grouping such as
  - First name, family name
  - Street and number
  - ZIP code, city
- Clearly mark mandatory fields ideally with the label “mandatory field” above or directly next to the field instead of using a superscript asterisk (*)
- Avoid “conversion killer” such as “reset”-button and Captchas
- Use trust symbols directly next to the templates referring to data protection, trusted shops, SSL, TÜV, etc.
- Position cursor automatically at the beginning of the first field of the template
- Avoid fancy design elements in templates distracting and maybe irritating the user
- Position the C2A stringently above-the-fold and also at the end of the touchpoint page. Do not hesitate to use the C2A more often on the page to easen the conversion
- Be clear and precise in telling the user what to do!
- Proactively anticipate conversion objection with micro copy elements (Fig. 14)
  - Referring to low time expenditure
  - Renewed reference to free offer
  - Guarantees (data protection, satisfaction guarantees, etc.)
- Use value-added statements as they create instant conversion rate optimization (Fig. 15)

Fig. 14 Sample for micro copy elements (Source: Own illustration)

Fig. 15 Sample for value-add statement conversion rate optimization (Source: Own illustration)

Figure 16 shows the result of an A/B testing with an impressive outcome. By only eliminating the "controlling" three items at the top of the form, the provider could optimize the conversion rate by 11 times.

The conscious and rational customer is a myth as current studies show that 95% of buying behavior is controlled unconsciously! This means that using *Social Proof* (Blokdyk, 2021) is also essential in the context of CRO. The social proof concept is about how the actions of other people influence the decision-making of the visitors on the landing pages. Social proof in marketing is not new because it has always been around. New York Times Best Selling lists, sporting brand Nike gear, or anything Oprah touched in the early 2000s must be already considered in the context of the social proof concept. Nowadays almost all brands are taking advantage of social proof learnings (Fig. 17).

But now it is no longer only famous people and influencers telling customers what to buy or nurturing interested people and target groups with their personal recommendations. Social proof is any- and everywhere, may it be on Instagram, TikTok, or Facebook. Social proof also takes place through Google Reviews giving first-hand accounts from previous customers. Recently also YouTubers are playing a

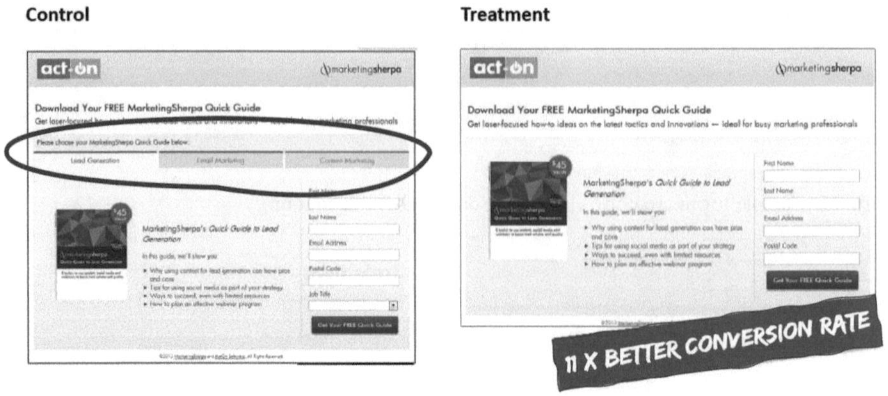

Fig. 16 Control versus treatment CRO example (Source: Own illustration)

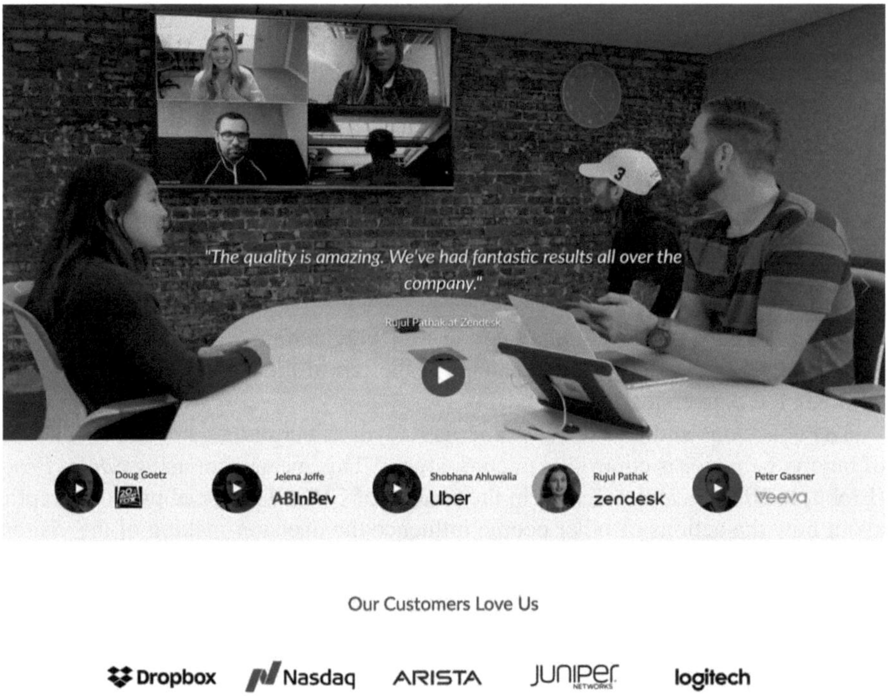

Fig. 17 Social proof example from Zoom (Source: https://www.mailerlite.com)

vital role when it comes to social proofing by telling their followers which products are their favorites.

In the context of CRO seven forms of social proof are relevant and must be considered when it comes to conversion rate optimizing measures:

1. Customer testimonial
2. Customer reviews
3. Expert, influencer, and celebrity endorsements
4. Media mentions
5. Brand stats
6. Customer favorites
7. User-generated content

In regard to best practice in marketing automation, microsite optimization and conversion rate optimizing persona utilization following articles might be of interest:

- *From Zero to Hero: B2C Practices as Revenue Drivers in B2B (Kleinemass,* 2021*)*
- *365 Days Turnaround in B2B Marketing: A Fact-Based Guide to Success (Negovan & Seebacher,* 2021*)*
- *Sales Channel Excellence: An SME Marketing Success Story from Mechanical Engineering (Gölles & Seebacher,* 2021*)*
- *From Key Words to Contextual Models: How to Successfully Implement Next Level Content Optimization (Barrett & Herten,* 2021*).*

8 Testing Is Everything!

Even the most experienced CRO-managers use testing for ongoingly increasing the conversion. In the Minimal Fashion case study, testing was at the core of an initially non-definable target group. Without testing thousands of marketing dollars can easily be wasted. The recipe for success is "test and scale"! Testing everything and step-by-step scaling the marketing money spent for campaigns. How powerful this golden rule of CRO is can easily be seen by the later presented results of the Minimal Fashion endeavor.

In order to generate added value from testing the guiding principle must be to always run tests in parallel and never sequentially. This is essential as external factors such as traffic sources, offers and pricing, competitive environment and others are ongoingly influencing the test results. By parallel testing, the likelihood of different contingency situations and thus false results can be minimized, and test results can be compared with a high degree of validity (Fig. 18).

The following checklist was put together based on many different projects and thus provides a framework for conversion rate optimizing testing. These are the elements that should be tested in the context of CRO:

- Call-to-action (C2A) and order buttons
- Headlines (content, size, color, direct vs. indirect approach, questions vs. no questions, emotional vs. rational approach, sub-header vs. no sub-header)
- Text (running text vs. bullet points, length of text)

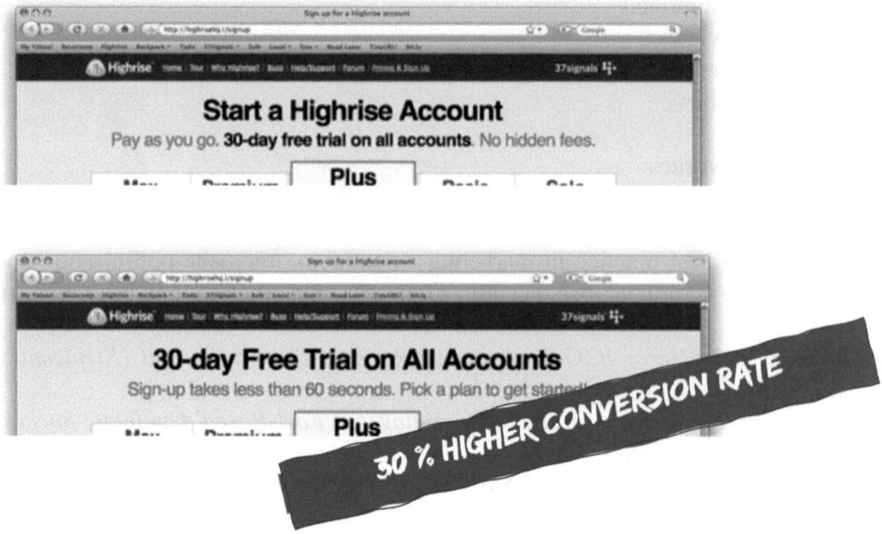

Fig. 18 Value-add communication as conversion rate optimizer (Source: Own illustration)

- Pictures, graphics, illustrations (and captions) (age, gender, "mood picture" vs. added-value communication)
- Trust elements (usage, positioning)
- Templates (number of fields, mandatory fields, template labeling, one-step vs. multiple step process, positioning above- vs. below-the-fold)
- Pricing and discounts
- Added-value communication (product advantage A, B, *or* C vs. A, B, *and* C)
- Lead process (product order vs. non-binding information request, webinar vs. video)
- Social proof elements
- References and testimonials
- Response amplifier (early bird, artificial shortage, raffle)

9 The Minimal Fashion Project

In order to explore the limits of programmatic CRO in the context of marketing and sales automation in April 2022 a joint project with Prof. Dr. Uwe Seebacher[3] from the University of Applied Science in Munich and the FYNEST Agency based in Frankfurt was started. The project aim was to show what programmatic CRO can achieve when stringently and correctly used and applied right from the beginning in the context of a B2C eCommerce online shop. For this project, the label Minimal

[3] https://uweseebacher.org/. Retrieved: Aug. 12th, 2022.

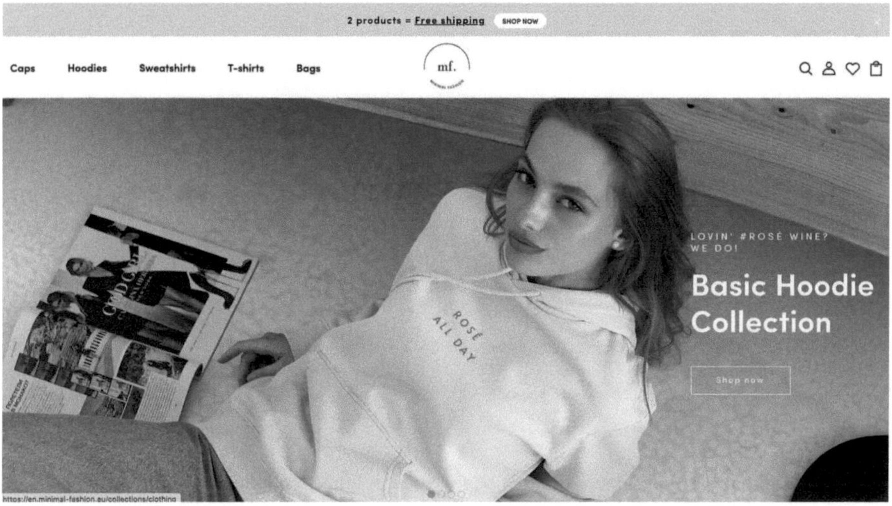

Fig. 19 Start screen Minimal Fashion company (Source: https://en.minimal-fashion.eu/)

Fashion (Fig. 19) was established without any prior products, processes, or client data. This was part of the laboratory test.

10 The Products

To as best as possible create product-independent test results, commodity me-too products were used such as caps, hoodies, or bags (Figs. 20 and 21). These products were chosen from a third-party print-on-demand online store providing a direct interface to the Minimal Fashion online shop with integrated production initiation and delivery to the end client.

These off-the-shelf products were only supplemented with upbeat slogans. These slogans were rendered into the product picture by a graphic designer. The slogans were created on the fly with no big effort and were then part of A/B testing in regard to their performance in regional but also age groups.

11 The Case Study TechStack

The test store was set up within four workdays by one IT specialist using Shopify.[4] This product was equipped with the Elementor[5] plug-in for better and conversion rate optimizing designs (Fig. 22). The texts were generated and developed by a

[4] https://www.shopify.com/. Retrieved: Aug. 12th, 2022.

[5] https://elementor.com/. Retrieved: Aug. 12th, 2022.

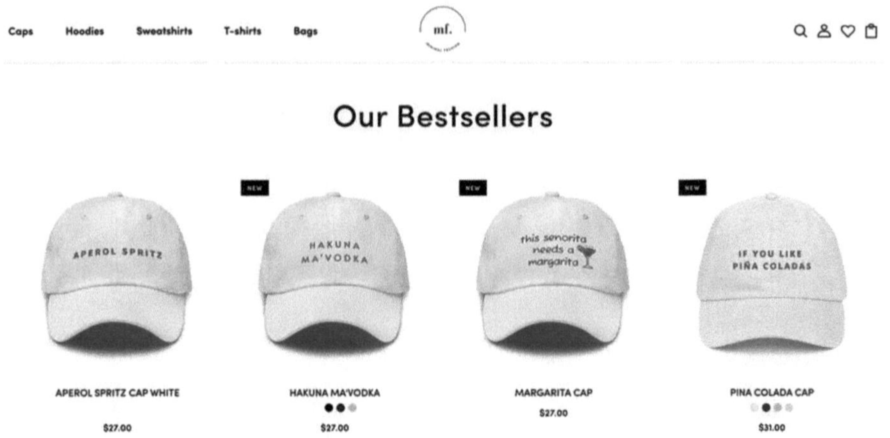

Fig. 20 Minimal Fashion sample product page (Source: https://en.minimal-fashion.eu/)

Fig. 21 Minimal Fashion sample collection page (Source: https://en.minimal-fashion.eu/)

CRO-experienced Content Manager who also then was provided with all product images by the graphic designer.

The entire system was set up as lean and cost-effective as possible for ensuring a maximum return-on-sale (RoS) and also a short break-even-period (BEP) which was in the end realized with a BEP of 2.3 weeks (!) for the Minimal Fashion project.

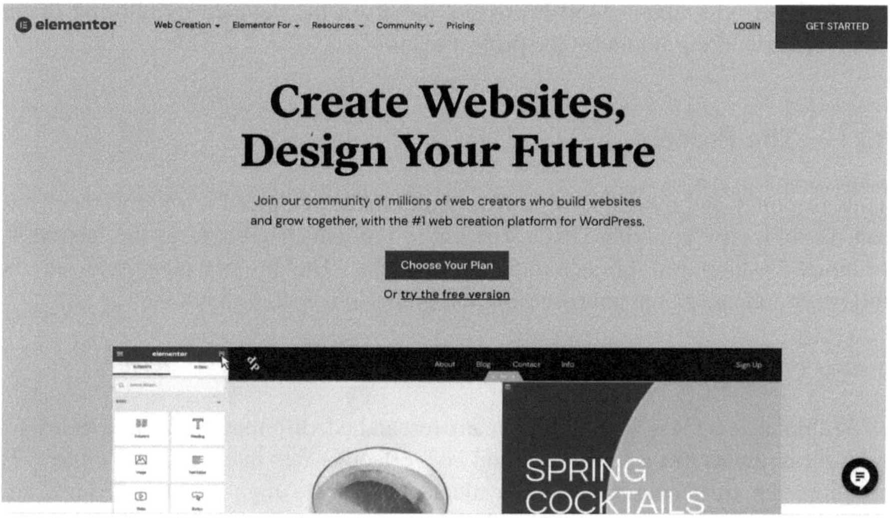

Fig. 22 Elementor landing page (Source: https://elementor.com/)

12 The Challenge

For a bulletproof reality check, all contingency factors were defined as challenging as possible. The following list provides an overview of the complex and challenging start of the laboratory Minimal Fashion project:

- *Target group:* The target group was almost non-definable as the products were not dedicated to certain buyer groups.
- *Case study products:* In order to really test the limits for CRO commodity and easy-to-copy standard products off the shelf were used. This product strategy allowed for the elimination of any competitive advantages through unique products in the sense of a result distortion through unique selling propositions (USP).
- *Competitive situation:* In the fashion segment, the project can be expected to be characterized by a high level of competition, which will have a massive negative impact on achieving and increasing sales.
- *Branding:* To also eliminate any kind of competitive advantages through using an already existing brand or an already existing online shop a completely new artificial brand was established and with this a completely new eCommerce online shop.
- *Client base:* The showcase label had to start with no existing client base or any kind of buying community.
- *Investment and budget:* The label was equipped with a funding of 1500 Euros marketing budget. The initial setup for the online store, the texts and designs were

calculated with about 3450 Euros net based on the detailed monitoring of the invested working hours by the project team.

13 The Process

Time is money and money is what we want to make and profit is what we need and can maximize by applying CRO. The entire pre-launch process of the laboratory Minimal Fashion test project took us 2 weeks. The project team realized the following nine steps for jump-starting the going-live of this showcase:

Step 1: Print-on-demand (PoD) provider selection and products selection

Within a few days, the design team researched different PoD companies for relevant products but also reliable and cost-effective fast international delivery. In addition, the trust elements were evaluated to ensure high-quality products and delivery not to cause any issues with a bad customer experience. No direct talks and negotiations were held with the finally selected PoD supplier for arranging better purchasing conditions or any kind of preferred agreements. Standard official purchasing prices are used!

As part of the PoD supplier selection also the PoD-specific available Automated Programming Interfaces (API) were checked as the entire workflow from purchase to pay, production and delivery had to be fully integrated and automated. This fully automated marketing and sales process was part of the defined pre-conditions for this marketing and sales automation (MSA) laboratory test project. This complete marketing and sales automation ensures that no human activity is required for the entire customer journey which must be considered as the highest development stage of state-of-the-art marketing and sales automation.

Step 2: Topic research with Google Trends

At the same time the team realized market research using Google Trends to find out the currently most popular topics. The findings were used to cross-check available products of the short-listed PoD supplier. Also, the findings were used to derive catchy slogans and claims that were then used to refine and finish the otherwise standard off-the-shelf products.

Step 3: Competitor research

Together with the above-described two steps, the team investigated competitors regarding their products but also their landing pages and e-shops. For this, a specific CRO testing was used, which enabled the project team to precisely analyze and evaluate the customer experience, the buying process, and the weak spots of the competitors. The findings were used to proactively optimize the customer journey and their customer experience.

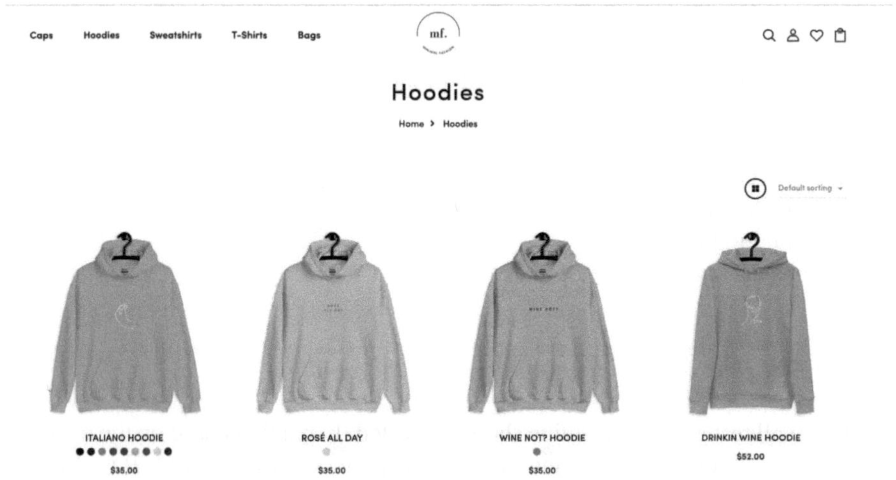

Fig. 23 Hoodies product page (Source: https://en.minimal-fashion.eu/collections/clothing/)

Step 4: Target group research

The next step focused on a first definition of possible target groups. One strategic aspect ad been defined for this test project, that the focus could only lie on so-called *impulse buys*. This is because the brand was new and the price of the products was in the range of between 20 and 40 euros, which fully falls into the segment of fast and intuitive buying decision. This circumstance also had to be considered for the efficient and effective advertising scale-up strategy to target the potential buyers at the right time through the right channel.

Step 5: Price clarification with competitors

Regarding the pricing strategy, the findings from the prior steps were consolidated and aggregated. The price corridor was defined and cross-checked with the provided PoD prices also adding the shipment fees and the defined profit margin of 30% before tax. The final price range was 25 euros for caps, bags, and t-shirts up to 35 euros for all hoodies (Fig. 23).

Step 6: Create store

Step 6 was the setup of the operational online store using the Shopify solution with the already mentioned Elementor plug-in. The shop was created and fully set up within 4 days from a technical point. All content management elements were added and proofread by the content management. Also, the touchpoint-specific optimization was realized as part of this step, in accordance with the before described different aspects. The activities covered CRO-based image selection, CRO-based mobile optimization and CRO-best contexting of marketing texts as well as product descriptions. The payment process and interfaces were set up and tested.

Step 7: Create products

The next field of activities covered product creation. Operationally this step consisted of:

- Slogan creation
- Adding slogans to PoD product screenshots
- Finishing and rendering
- CRO-based landing page optimization

Step 8: Test store and run user survey about the handling

With a small test group, the online shop was tested. In parallel based on the testing, a user survey about touchpoint and customer experience was realized. Based on the feedback the workflows, designs, and texts were optimized to increase the performability and conversion of the shop. This test stage was realized over a weekend as this was the best time frame for targeting and reaching the potential test buyer group.

Step 9: Install tracking and start advertising campaign

The following 15 steps were then realized for developing and growing the store. These steps are the result of many different smaller test projects and can be considered as best practice in CRO-based eCommerce. The method can easily be applied to any kind of online shop regardless of products, regions, or target groups:

1. The most popular theme (cap design): Create five adsujets
2. Play out these ads to an open target group
   (budget: €5–10 per day)
   (a) No age
   (b) No gender
   (c) No place
   (d) No interests
   (e) Only citeria setting was "Language German"
3. Duplicate best performing subject 5× and create 5 target groups each with 1 user area, e.g.:
   User area: Interest
   (a) Cocktails
   (b) Drinks
   (c) Beach
   (d) Vacation
   (e) Online Shopping
4. Play out subject on these properties
   (budget: €5–10 per day per user area)
   The period until clear data can be read is about 3–4 days

5. Repeat task 4 for all user areas mentioned in task 2
   (budget: €5–10 a day per user area on 3–4 days), e.g.:
   Property: Age
   (a) 18–25
   (b) 25–30
   (c) 30–35
   (d) 35–40
   (e) 40–45
6. After all user areas have been tested, take the best from each user area and form two target groups, e.g.:
   (a) Target group A
       Age: 18–25
       Gender: Female
       Location: Germany
       Interest: Cocktails
       Language: German
   (b) Target group B
       Age: 18–25
       Gender: Female
       Location: Germany
       Interest: Online shopping
       Language: German
7. Duplicate the best adsujet on five other products (same design)
8. Play out these five new subjects including the previously used subject on the two new target groups
   (budget: €5–10 per day per target group on 3–4 days)
9. Verify results. Here the first interactions should take place and a user group should be built up that is interested in the brand. If this is not the case, then we had to go back to the start and look for a new product or create new subjects. In Minimal Fashion project, we could continue due to the establishment of the required user group.
10. Duplicate each of the two target groups and test the display options *(budget: €5–10 per day per target group)*, e.g.:
    (a) Target group A
        Instagram feed
        Facebook Feed
        No instant experience
    (b) Target group B
        Instagram feed
        Facebook Feed
        With instant experience
11. Keep the best display option and increase budget weekly by a maximum of 20% until the market will not allow for more.

12. Simultaneously monitor store tracking and find out where users are lost. Optimize these steps in the customer journey, gladly also play off different designs on product pages against each other, e.g.:
    (a) Product page A
        Product image above
        Short product description
        Popup opens when you click "Add to cart"
    (b) Product page B
        Product image above
        Long product description
        By clicking on "Add to cart" the user is directly forwarded to the checkout
13. Simultaneously correct CRO mistakes, e.g.:
    (a) When you lose many people at the shopping cart then resize checkout button and make it larger.
    (b) When you lose many people on the product page then check if the page performance is fast enough. Do users find their important information? Is the price adequate?
    (c) When you lose many people at the checkout then check the trust elements on the page. Is the checkout trustworthy? Are the shipping costs too high?
    (d) If you are losing people at the store page, then check if your customers can find their products? Is the store clearly arranged? Is the core information above-the-fold? Are the trust elements adequately positioned and converting?
    (e) Etc.
14. Generate and ongoingly maximize profit through stringently extending the daily budget until you realize a stagnant sales increase. Then it is time to keep daily budget stable and have the shop running with a continuous monitoring.
15. Grow the shop by adding new designs a/o products and maybe categories. The essential element is the stringent and slow scaling of spent daily advertising budget to ensure correct training and learning of engaged algorithms.

14 The Results

Since its launch the laboratory test project "Minimal Fashion" brand realized over 90,000 Euros in sales (Fig. 24). More than 100,000 sessions were tracked, and 2.36% over time are returning customers. The conversion rate is 1.72% which is slightly below the B2C eCommerce average of 2.5–3%.[6] But these benchmark values are covering eCommerce shops being online for many years. For the showcase company, this means that such a high conversion rate after only such a short

[6]https://www.ruleranalytics.com/blog/insight/conversion-rate-by-industry/. Retrieved: Aug. 17th, 2022.

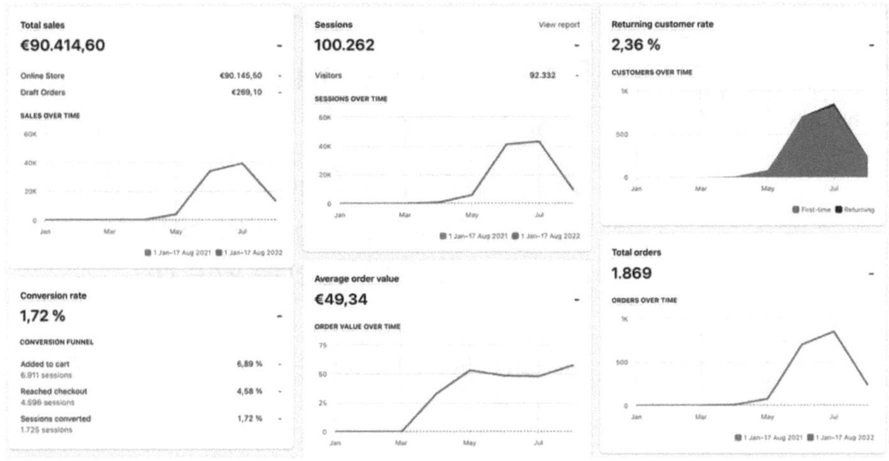

Fig. 24 Performance dashboards (Source: https://minimalfashion-eu.myshopify.com/admin/dashboards)

Fig. 25 Conversion rate increase (Source: https://minimalfashion-eu.myshopify.com/admin/dashboards)

period of time can be considered best-in-class. By now the conversion rate reached 6.15% (Fig. 25) which outperforms the B2C eCommerce industry benchmark by approximately 100% after only 3 months of operations.

This also is confirmed by the fact that the Minimal Fashion shop is ranked by Shopify itself as among the top 1% of all parallel launched Shopify online stores (Fig. 26). As Shopify releases such evaluations as updates and the Minimal Fashion project was realized in German language this screenshot is unfortunately only available in German language stating that the shop performs under the Top 1% of all shops that have been launched the same week as the Minimal Fashion project.

A significant value is also the average order size. With CRO the aim is and must be to quickly grow the average order value (AOV) as this positively impacts the return-on-sales (RoS). Special package deals and offers must be defined and distributed to proactively grow the AOV. During the project, three such packages and special deals were used to achieve this high AOV growth.

The "sales attributed to marketing" (SAM) value shows sales that can be attributed to traffic driven to the storefront(s) by marketing efforts. With a value of 5425.20 Euros, the SAM performs at 6% which is double digit lower than the B2C eCommerce industry average. This again is an indicator of the strong target group community that the test project team could establish with the project setting. This is

Fig. 26 Top 1% ranking for Minimal Fashion (Source: https://minimalfashion-eu.myshopify.com/admin/dashboards)

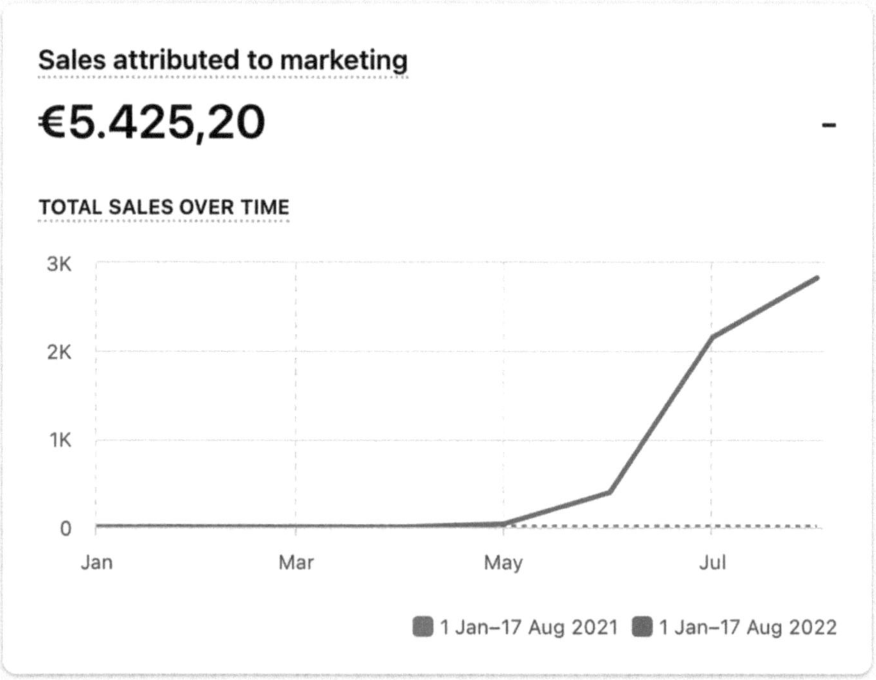

Fig. 27 Performance dashboards (Source: https://minimalfashion-eu.myshopify.com/admin/dashboards)

only possible with the consistent application of the 15-step scaling method described before. If the marketing budget is scaled-up too fast the SAM increases which means that the RoS decreases, and the community must be considered to be "artificial" and less "organic." This also negatively impacts the returning customer rate (RCR) (Fig. 27).

Device type	Visitors	↑ Sessions
	92.353	100.283
Mobile	74.484	95.963
Desktop	3.136	3.771
Other	299	368
Tablet	154	181

ult(s).

Fig. 28 Performance dashboards (Source: https://minimalfashion-eu.myshopify.com/admin/dashboards)

Sales by social source		
Instagram	€25.590,00	-
Facebook	€2.863,96	-
Snapchat	€29,82	-

Sessions by social source	View report	
Instagram	12.983	-
Facebook	9.249	-
Youtube	10	-
LinkedIn	6	-
Snapchat	5	-

Fig. 29 Comparison of sessions and sales by social sources (Source: https://minimalfashion-eu.myshopify.com/admin/dashboards)

How important the in-depth touchpoint optimization especially to different devices and linked contingency factors is shows the report "session by device" as 95.5% of all sessions came from mobile devices (Fig. 28). When designing and defining an eCommerce business in the context of CRO-based marketing and sales automation then the connex between products, kind of intended buying behavior (impulse vs. planned and rational buying) and adequate channel as well as device must be anticipated. In this Minimal Fashion showcase, the ex-ante defined combination of product, the resulting impulse buying, and thus most likely mobile devices as major interaction source was stringently deployed by the mobile device optimization of the online shop.

An interesting detail is also the comparison between "sessions by social source" and "sales by social source" as this clearly shows that one can easily burn marketing advertising money when betting on the wrong horse. The stats show that Facebook does not convert since there were many sessions (9.249 or 9.2%), but they generated insufficient and disproportionate small revenue of only 2863.96 Euros equaling only 3.2%. This means a channel underperformance of Facebook of approximately 6 percentage points. On the contrary, Instagram outperformed Facebook significantly with 12,983 sessions (12.9%) but generating 25,590.00 Euros (28.3%) of entire sales (Fig. 29).

The sales conversion of social source nevertheless in the context of CRO-based MSA only plays a minor role as—when all CRO principles are stringently applied

Sessions by traffic source	View report	
Direct	70.501	-
Social	22.261	-
Search	7.353	-
Unknown	163	-
Email	15	-

Fig. 30 Sessions by traffic source ranking (Source: https://minimalfashion-eu.myshopify.com/admin/dashboards)

and deployed—most generated sales must be coming directly. But this requires a consistent buyer journey, conversion rate optimized touchpoints, and perfect targeting and advertising. For the Minimal Fashion project, the direct sales ratio (DSR) is 70.3% which is a proof of the good job the entire project team delivered in this context. This impressive DSR shows that the buyers were directly engaged following the defined buyer journey (Fig. 30).

15 What the Minimal Fashion Has Shown!

Nothing is impossible. With a start budget of not even 5000 Euros, a sales volume of almost 100,000 Euros and a net profit of 27,953.21 Euros within 12 weeks were realized. Where and how else can you get such a yield of almost 30% within 3 months.

Minimal Fashion has shown that if one has done the homework, stringently applies the CRO principles and works smart and not hard, even with little money one can easily start to scale online sales in any kind of industry, segment, target group or region. The Minimal Fashion case study was realized in the very complex B2C environment and nevertheless within only a few weeks and off-the-shelf products a five-digit order intake growth was realized.

What does this mean for B2B marketers and sellers? The answer is rather clear and promising. In B2B segment target groups are defined and sharp. This means that in comparison to the Minimal Fashion project companies know their clients, their needs, and their pain points. Thus, the targeting of their potential buyers is much easier than in the B2C showcase. In addition, in 90% of the cases, the relevant products are no off-the-shelf me-too products, which means that certain unique selling propositions and arguments ease the marketing and selling process substantially—but only if these aspects are being considered during the

CRO-oriented texting and designing stage. Still in the context of CRO content remains king.

What does the Minimal Fashion showcase reveal for B2C online marketers and sellers? The answer is quite easy and maybe not the one that one wants to hear. Because the learning is that marketing and sales automation still do need the *human intelligence*, as also being considered as the biggest challenge in the context of artificial intelligence (AI) by Seebacher (2022). The reason for this is simple as big budgets do not help to scale online sales because to approach, reach and sharpen a target group for product(s) requires time as the algorithms of search engines as well as of social media channels must be trained slowly.

Many online marketers and online sellers burn their money by too fast jump-starting their campaigns. The result is that the algorithms of Google et al. are trained badly and wrongly what then causes the targeting of wrong target groups not buying the products. In the end, the advertising budget is burned with no sales. Overall, Minimal Fashion has shown that CRO has almost no limits as scaling can be done almost endlessly. The only limiting factor is the lack of concept and competence—but this is no gain in knowledge as this is the case in almost all areas of life in our automated and digitalized world.

The project team is already on its way to launch the next eCommerce online stores. If you feel like having an idea for a such initiative, do not hesitate to contact us as we are more than happy to assist, support, and be at your hand with our expertise.

References

Barrett, J., & Herten, M. (2021). From keywords to contextual frameworks: New take on B2B SEO enabling next level content. In U. G. Seebacher (Ed.), *B2B marketing. Management for professionals*. Springer. https://doi.org/10.1007/978-3-030-54292-4_16

Blokdyk, G. (2021). *Social proof. A complete guide*. 5StarCooks.

Ender, A. (2021). Buyer-centric content approach: Design thinking to market to humans in the B2B world. In U. G. Seebacher (Ed.), *B2B marketing. Management for professionals*. Springer. https://doi.org/10.1007/978-3-030-54292-4_15

Ermer, B., & Kleine, J. (2021). Social selling in B2B: How to get jump started. In U. G. Seebacher (Ed.), *B2B marketing. Management for professionals*. Springer. https://doi.org/10.1007/978-3-030-54292-4_19

Gölles, K., & Seebacher, U. G. (2021). Sales channel management: A low-cost quick win showcase for external salesforce excellence. In U. G. Seebacher (Ed.), *B2B marketing. Management for professionals*. Springer. https://doi.org/10.1007/978-3-030-54292-4_29

Halb, F., & Seebacher, U. G. (2021). User experience and touchpoint management: A touchpoint performance management toolkit for the buyer journey. In U. G. Seebacher (Ed.), *B2B marketing. Management for professionals*. Springer. https://doi.org/10.1007/978-3-030-54292-4_12

Kleinemaß, M. (2021). From zero to hero: B2C practice as revenue generator in B2B. In U. G. Seebacher (Ed.), *B2B marketing. Management for professionals*. Springer. https://doi.org/10.1007/978-3-030-54292-4_31

Kosuniak, Ł. (2021). Content marketing process: Embrace art and science. In U. G. Seebacher (Ed.), *B2B marketing. Management for professionals*. Springer. https://doi.org/10.1007/978-3-030-54292-4_13

Mörk, O. (2021). Contingency-centric content management: Mastering content overload with smart content marketing. In U. G. Seebacher (Ed.), *B2B marketing. Management for professionals*. Springer. https://doi.org/10.1007/978-3-030-54292-4_14

Negovan, M., & Seebacher, U. G. (2021). 365 Days B2B marketing turnaround: A fact-driven, bullet-proof showcase guide. In U. G. Seebacher (Ed.), *B2B marketing. Management for professionals*. Springer. https://doi.org/10.1007/978-3-030-54292-4_32

Ryte Wiki. (2020). *Conversion rate*. Retrieved July 22, 2022, from https://de.ryte.com/wiki/Conversion_Rate

Seebacher, U. (2020). *B2B marketing essential: How to turn your marketing from a cost into a sales engine*. AQPS.

Seebacher, U. (2021a). *B2B marketing guidebook*. Springer.

Seebacher, U. (2021b). *Data-driven management: A primer for modern corporate decision making*. AQPS.

Seebacher, U. (2021c). *Template-based management: A guide for an efficient and impactful professional practice*. Springer.

Seebacher, U., & Güpner, A. (2021). *Marketing resource management: Guidebook for organizational development with many examples, explanations and instructions for action*. AQPS.

Seebacher, U. (2022). *Reengineering corporate communication: A marketer's perspective offering new concepts, processes, tools, and templates*. Springer.

Strohmeier, L. (2021). Central business intelligence: A lean development process for SMEs. In U. G. Seebacher (Ed.), *B2B marketing. Management for professionals*. Springer. https://doi.org/10.1007/978-3-030-54292-4_30

Bernd Trummer, CEO and co-founder of the leading agency in conversation-rate-optimization (CRO) FYNEST International and one of the master minds of the first multiple AI combining and integrating MarCom-on-Demand (MoD) and MarCom-as-a-Service (MaaS) platform, is a passionate and experienced digital native with many years of successful projects in all kinds of digital business models and start-ups. With different successful exits, Bernd knows what it takes to effectively scale business with the minimum amount of money and limited budgets. He is an internationally booked speaker, trainer, and companion for Performance Marketing and Conversion-rate-optimization.

Part II

The Customer Side of Marketing and Sales Automation

On Buyers' Expectations, Buyers' Goals, and the Improvement of the Customer Experience

Roland Burkholz

1 The Apple I, the Apple II ...

Innovative products (or services) can give companies a huge growth boost. Apple is a prime example of a company that owes its enormous success largely to outstanding products. Think of the Apple II personal computer (introduced in 1977), the aesthetically very felicitous cube-like Macintosh with a mouse and an operating system with a graphical user interface (introduced in 1984),[1] the iPod (introduced in 2001) or the iPhone (introduced in 2007). By the end of 2002, for example, Apple had sold 600,000 iPods. Later generations of the iPod had more storage capacity and more features. Apple sold a total of 350 million units of this product.[2] The iPhone, which had a touch screen and apps instead of a space-hogging physical keyboard that allowed only a small screen, was also a huge success for the Cupertino-based company. At the presentation of the iPhone, Steve Jobs said:

[1]The Macintosh was not the first Apple computer with a graphical user interface and mouse. The 1983 Apple Lisa already had a mouse, but it was very expensive and sold only moderately. The Apple Lisa cost $9995 in 1983, the Apple Macintosh $2495 in 1984, but even the Lisa was not the first personal computer with a graphical user interface. An icon-based graphical user interface and mouse had previously been introduced by Xerox. The Xerox Star 8010, launched in 1981, was the first commercial computer with this type of user interface. (Cf. Xerox Star 8010 Information System - The Interface Experience: Bard Graduate Center (interface-experience.org); https://interface-experience.org/objects/xerox-star-8010-information-system/.) The Xerox Star was yet again significantly more expensive than the Lisa. It cost $16,595. The mouse, by the way, was invented back in the early 1960s by Doug Engelbart in his research lab at Stanford Research Institute. The first prototype was developed in 1964. (Cf. Firsts: The Mouse - Doug Engelbart Institute; https://dougengelbart.org/content/view/162).

[2]Cf. Larry Downes, Paul Nunes, "Big Bang Disruption. Business Survival in the Age of Constant Innovation", Portfolio Penguin, 2014, p. 125.

R. Burkholz (✉)
University of Media, Communication and Business, Frankfurt, Germany

U. Hannig, U. Seebacher (eds.), *Marketing and Sales Automation*, Management for Professionals, https://doi.org/10.1007/978-3-031-20040-3_9

> Every once in a while a revolutionary product comes along and changes everything. [...] Apple has been very fortunate. It has been able to introduce a few of these into the world. 1984 we introduced the Macintosh. It didn't just change Apple. It changed the whole computer industry. In 2001 we introduced the first iPod ... [...] Today, today, Apple is going to reinvent the phone.[3]

Outstanding end-user experience was the primary driver of growth for these products. But a product's outstanding performance profile is not a purely engineering achievement. The user experience will only be positive if the product's functionality fits the expectations and goals of the target segment. And, of course, the product surround also plays an important role—for example, buying advice and customer service. The fact that knowledge of customer expectations and good customer support can play an important role in product success can be demonstrated by the early Apple computers.

The personal computer market virtually emerged with the Altair 8800 by Micro Instrumentation and Telemetry Systems (MITS), based in Albuquerque, New Mexico.[4] The Altair was introduced in January 1975 by "Popular Electronics" magazine and was offered via advertisements as an inexpensive kit. Just 1 year later, Steve Wozniak and Steve Jobs presented the Apple I at a meeting of the Homebrew Computer Club. However, only about 200 units of the Apple I were sold. The home computer was a new product category and no one knew what the buyers—hobbyists with electronics expertise—intended to do with it, what they would use such a microcomputer for. Market research was not possible, because the potential users themselves did not yet know what exactly they would do with such a thing. They were technology enthusiasts and simply fascinated that they could now buy their own computer for home. Even if the Apple I was not a sales success, it was still important for the just-founded Apple company, because Jobs and Wozniak learned a lot from this project. Joseph Bower and Clayton Christensen make this point. In their essay "Disruptive Technologies: Catching the Wave" (1995), they write:

> The company's original product, the Apple I, was a flop when it launched in 1977 [1976, R.B.]. But Apple had not placed a huge bet on the product and had gotten at least *something* into the hands of early users quickly. The company learned a lot from the Apple I about the new technology and about what customers wanted and did not want. Just as important, a

[3]Steve Jobs introduces iPhone in 2007 – YouTube; https://www.youtube.com/watch?v=MnJzXM7a6o. The iPhone is not Apple's first mobile phone. In 2005, Apple had already launched the ROKR E1 in cooperation with Motorola—the first mobile phone to integrate iTunes. Apple discontinued support after just 1 year. (Cf. Learn How Apple's First Smartphone Came to Be (thoughtco.com); https://www.thoughtco.com/who-invented-the-iphone-1992004 and "Project Purple": How the Motorola ROKR E1 became the first iPhone - ComputerBase; https://www.computerbase.de/2021-10/apple-iphone-project-purple-motorola-rokr-e1/).

[4]For the following information on early personal computers, cf. Paul Freiberger, Michael Swaine, "Fire in the Valley. The Making of the Personal Computer", Osborne/McGraw-Hill, 1984.

> group of *customers* learned about what they did and did not want from personal computers. Armed with this information, Apple launched the Apple II quite successfully.[5]

So the Apple II does not owe its success to a pure engineering achievement. A fair amount of customer knowledge had already gone into this second Apple product—knowledge about users' expectations, wants, and goals.

Established computer manufacturers, such as IBM, entered the nascent personal computer market late. But that does not mean that in the early years only MITS, Apple, and Commodore developed, produced, and sold personal computers. There were numerous companies competing with each other in this just emerging market. Here is a selection: Apple Computer, Atari, Commodore, Digital Microsystems, Cromemco, IMSAI, MITS, Ohio Scientific, NorthStar (formerly Kentucky Fried Computers[6]), Sinclair, Tandy/RadioShack.

Why did Apple prevail? Not only because of the products. There were two other important reasons. Presumably, the second is a consequence of the first. Reason number 1: Apple had experienced management compared to the other young personal computer companies. For Jobs and Wozniak were able to win over the experienced Mike Markkula early on. Freiberger and Swaine write in "Fire in the Valley":

> Within months, Markkula decided to join the corporation [...] Thereafter, Markkula set the tone for the company. He helped Jobs with the business plan. He obtained a line of credit for Apple at the Bank of America. He told Woz and Jobs that neither of them had the experience to run a company and hired Mike Scott as its president.[7]

Reason number 2: Unlike its direct competitors, the young Apple company was not purely product-centric. Apple focused on customer support from the very beginning. Adam Osborne, a contemporary witness and founder of the Osborne Computer Corporation, writes in "Hypergrowth" (1984):

> Technology had nothing to do with Apple Computer Corporation's success; nor was the company an aggressive price leader. Rather, this company was the first to offer real customer support and to behave like a genuine business back in 1976 when other manufacturers were amateur shoe-string operations.[8]

Toward the end of the book it says:

---

[5] Joseph L. Bower, Clayton M. Christensen, "Disruptive Technologies: Catching the Wave" (1995), in: "Seeing Differently. Insights on Innovation", edited by John Seely Brown, Harvard Business Review Book, 1997, p. 136.

[6] Fast-food poultry chain Kentucky Fried Chicken did not find the company name funny and sent a letter demanding the company to stop using it. Cf. Paul Freiberger, Michael Swaine, "Fire in the Valley", op. cit., p. 117.

[7] Ibid., p. 215.

[8] Adam Osborne, John Dvorak, "Hypergrowth. The Rise and Fall of Osborne Computer Corporation", Idthekkethan Publishing Corporation 1984, p. 11.

> Under the expert guidance of Mike Markkula, Apple quickly became the company that sinned the least. They had customer service representatives who could give meaningful answers when competitors had no customer service department at all. They acknowledged defective product and made good on it when such obvious policies were unknown elsewhere.[9]

2 The iPhone 1 and the Japanese Market

But Apple did not always have buyers' expectations in mind. The iPhone 1[10] was a huge sales success in the USA and Europe—but not in Japan. Adele Revella writes in her book "Buyer Personas" (2015) that the iPhone's introduction to tech-obsessed Japan was a classic lesson in the importance of understanding buyers' expectations.[11] The iPhone first hit the market in the U.S. in 2007 and was then launched in Europe. By summer 2008, it was available in 22 countries. When the iPhone was introduced in Japan in 2008, its success seemed preordained because 50 million mobile phones had been sold in Japan the year before. But in fact, only 200,000 units of the iPhone were sold in 2008—mainly to users of Apple computers. Why only 200,000 units? Because the first iPhone failed to meet the expectations of Japanese mobile phone users. Revella writes:

> With a minimum of research, Apple could have discovered that by 2008 the Japanese were accustomed to using their personal phones to shoot videos and to watch digital TV programs.[12]

But the iPhone 1 did not have a video camera. In addition, Revella writes, Apple could have anticipated the difficulties of competing in a market where many phones routinely included chips for debit card transactions and train tickets.[13]

Four years later—in 2012—Forbes magazine reported that the iPhone 5s had captured 34% of the Japanese smartphone market:

> The dramatic difference this time: Apple was keenly aware of what its Japanese buyers were expecting.[14]

---

[9] Ibid., p. 167 f.

[10] Other names for the first iPhone are: first generation iPhone, iPhone (original), iPhone 2 G and iPhone EDGE.

[11] Cf. Adele Revella, "Buyer Personas. How to Gain Insight into Your Customer's Expectations, Align Your Marketing Strategies, and Win More Business", Wiley 2015, p. 3. The following information on the iPhone 2 G (which Revella erroneously calls iPhone 3 G) is taken from Revella's book.

[12] Ibid., p. 4.

[13] Ibid.

[14] Ibid.

3 Customer Type Research

Great product performance, reliability, ease of use, and strong customer service are undoubtedly important for a company's success. However, in order to market products (or services) as successfully as possible, it is also important to build up knowledge about the typical expectations and goals of buyers. To do this, you have to ask people from the target customer segment in some detail. Unscripted in-depth interviews are a very suitable instrument for this purpose.[15]

What name is chosen for this knowledge about these target customers is not important. Whether companies talk about market research, buyer behavior research, buyer persona development, customer type research, segmentation studies, jobs-to-be-done investigations, buyer insights research, buying center analyses, or experiential research—it basically does not matter. What matters is that the relevant expectations, desires, attitudes, approaches, and goals of the people who make up the target segment is represented in these studies. Revella chooses the term buyer persona to describe this knowledge about buyers.[16] And she captures those expectations with her interview-based approach. She generates, as she says, buying insights.[17]

---

[15] Qualitative interviews need to be interpreted. I have this interpretation, you have another. Who is right? Everyone thinks they are right, right? Are not these interpretations hopelessly subjective? Where is the scientific objectivity? Answer: Interpretations are carried out by subjective minds, but they are not arbitrary. Utterances have meaning. Linguistic Meaning is not the same as the communicative intention of the speaker (which is locked in his mind). One can only speculate about communicative intention. It is different with linguistic meaning. Linguistic Meaning is rule-governed. If I say (under ordinary conditions) that I have 20 bucks in my wallet, then in English it means that I have 20 bucks in my wallet (even if I have memorized the sentence and do not understand what I am uttering). But of course, I will usually want to communicate that I have 20 bucks in my wallet when I perform the utterance "I have 20 bucks in my wallet." If uttered meaningfully these words have conventional linguistic meaning ("objective meaning") and intended speaker meaning ("subjective meaning") as well. A native speaker interpreting a qualitative interview knows the linguistic rules and can therefore grasp the linguistic meaning of the interviewee's utterances. And these inferred meanings can then be used to draw further conclusions. Drawing conclusions from data and developing convincing chains of arguments is what scientists try to do when they do research. (Cf. Michael Dummett, "Origins of Analytical Philosophy", Bloomsburg Academic 2014, chapter 13, p. 121 ff, John R. Searle, "Mind, Language and Society. Philosophy in the Real World", Basic Books 1998, p. 141 and Roland Burkholz, "Problemlösende Argumentketten. Ein Modell der Forschung", Velbrück Wissenschaft 2008).

[16] The term buyer persona is systematically ambiguous. It is used for the description of a homogeneous group of buyers (customer knowledge) as well as for the group of buyers the description is about. Thus, the term can refer both to the designation (the linguistic representation) and to what is designated. Customer knowledge is of course also systematically ambiguous. It can refer to knowledge about customers (genetivus objectivus) or knowledge of the customer (genetivus subjectivus)—knowledge that customers possess. Here, customer knowledge always refers to knowledge about customers (genetivus objectivus).

[17] Tony Zambito, who claims to be the founder of the interview-based buyer persona concept, speaks of *buyer* insights instead of *buying* insights. (Cf. Tony Zambito, "Buyer Insights Research And Market Research that Create Opportunities"; https://tonyzambito.com/engage/buyer-research-

But many buyer personas, which are created by companies—Revella also points out—do not include these buying insights. Revella refers to them as buyer profiles. There are numerous blog posts with titles like "Get to a Buyer Persona in 5 Minutes" that make developing a buyer persona seem like child's play. Just download the buyer persona template, fill it out, and you are done. But of course, it is not that simple. Without good empirical research, you do not capture these expectations, desires, attitudes, goals, and ways of acting. Like Revella, Tony Zambito makes a clear distinction between buyer profiling and buyer persona development. In a podcast, he says:

> A rookie mistake is to take that kind of a profiling, slap a picture on it and then call it a buyer persona. That's a bad rookie mistake.[18]

In the blog post "What is a Buyer Persona?" he says about buyer persona development:

> ... this has nothing to do with profiling. And it has everything to do with buying behavior.[19]

Neither having marketing staff fill out a template nor conducting an internal company workshop with a facilitating buyer persona expert and marketing, sales, and customer service staff will result in this needed customer knowledge. Organizations must not map the internal perspective onto the external customers, but rather capture the perspective of the customers themselves—the external experiential reality—and bring that knowledge into the organization and entrench it there. In other words, it is not about how employees think the company's customers are structured, it is about how customers really think and act—about how they actually interact with the company and how they interpret those interactions ("touchpoints"), how they evaluate them.

This customer knowledge must answer the following questions: How do the target customers want to be supported in the purchase decision process (and afterward), what questions do they have, what do they expect, what do they consider desirable, what do they consider helpful and what not, what bothers them, what

---

and-buyer-insights-that-create-opportunities/). The buyer persona concept grew out of the user persona concept of Alan Cooper, who is also known as an "UX guru." Cooper has been one of the important players in the user-centered design movement that emerged in the 1980s.

UX—User Experience—design is a precursor and special case of Customer Experience Management (CXM). On user personas cf. Alan Cooper, "The Inmates are Running the Asylum. Why High-Tech Products Drive Us Crazy and How to Restore Sanity", Pearson Education US, 2004.

[18] Tony Zambito, "Improving Sales Effectiveness With Buyer Personas. #SalesChats Episode 10"; https://salespop.net/sales-professionals/buyer-personas-for-effective-sales/ [#SalesChats: Buyer Personas, with Tony Zambito by Tony Zambito - SalesPOP!].

[19] Tony Zambito, "What is a Buyer Persona? Why the Original Definition Still Matters to B2B, May 27, 2013; https://tonyzambito.com//buyer-persona-original-definition-matters/; [What is a Buyer Persona? Why the Original Definition Still Matters to B2B - Tony Zambito].

problems do they want to solve, respectively what goals do they want to achieve with the help of the product or service?

Template personas and workshop personas do not contain this knowledge. They primarily contain demographic data, because these are readily available within the company. Templates ask about gender, age, marital status, income, and profession. Sometimes there is also a section called challenges or goals. But when you look at what is filled in there, it is disappointing. For a B2B persona, for example: *Skills shortage; sets personal goals; scarce resources in an increasingly complex set of measures*. These are generic statements that are virtually information-less. They apply to virtually every industry. Is there any manager who does not set personal goals? What good is the information to a software company that the IT director sets goals?

Or take the demographic data: The fact that Japanese consumers did not buy the iPhone in 2008 was not due to their age, income, gender, or profession. Nor was it due to their hobbies, educational status, or geographic region as such. It was primarily because Japanese folks expected a smartphone to have a video function, and the first iPhone did not have one. It would not have been difficult to acquire that knowledge. A few qualitative interviews with Japanese mobile phone users would have sufficed. But from demographic (and similar) data, this knowledge cannot be inferred. In short, you have to go outside the company and talk to (actual or potential) customers to build up this important customer knowledge.

4 Purchase Expertise and Goals

What does this knowledge look like in concrete terms? How should we imagine buyer personas that contain buying insights? I would like to present two studies on this. One is by Adele Revella—a study that her Buyer Persona Institute did for the Caterpillar company. The second study I want to outline here is by Malcolm McDonald, who conducted a segmentation study for a fertilizer manufacturer. McDonald does not use the term buyer persona. He talks about "segmentation," about "purchase combinations," and about "types of farmers." But as I said, which expressions are chosen to denote this knowledge does not matter. It is not the label that counts, but the content. And both studies describe customer types—different customer groups that are homogeneous in relevant respects. These studies thus contain the kind of customer knowledge we are talking about here. In a next step, I will then derive a customer-type "matrix" from these two studies.

Adele Revella reports on this buyer persona study for Caterpillar in the webinar "Personas: Everything You've Heard Is Wrong" (2018).[20] Caterpillar makes snow removal vehicles, agricultural vehicles, and construction vehicles. Caterpillar tells Revella that it needs a buyer persona for each of these three product categories: the

[20] Adele Revella, "Personas: Everything You've Heard Is Wrong" (2018); https://vimeo.com/270746719 [Personas: Everything You've Heard Is Wrong on Vimeo].

snow removal persona, the agriculture persona, and the construction persona. What does Revella say? She says, "Maybe, maybe. Let's go find out."

These three product categories can easily be reinterpreted as customer segments/ target audiences: The customer segment of agricultural vehicle buyers/farmers, etc. And there are numerous buyer persona blog posts with titles like "Put a face to your target audience." The logic behind this: target segments do not buy products or services, people do. So it was natural for Caterpillar to assume that a Caterpillar buyer persona study would result in exactly three different buyer personas.

What are the findings of Revella's institute? Here is the answer: There are exactly two buyer personas in this case. And they have nothing to do with these three product categories. Two buyer personas here means: two different types of customers who need different support, different assistance from the supplier in the purchase decision process in order to reach (probably) correct purchase decisions. The way of optimal support, in the case of Caterpillar, is related to the level of purchase experience that buyers have.

There are two types among Caterpillar buyers, which I would like to call the novice and the veteran. The novice is the buyer who is buying an excavator or a tractor for the first time, and the veteran is the type of buyer who has made such purchase decisions more often. The person who is buying this type of vehicle for the first time does not really know what he needs, what his exact requirements are, and what functionalities can be used to optimally meet these requirements. Accordingly, he wants to be informed and advised in detail by the dealer. This type, as Revella's institute has found out, wants to be connected immediately on the phone, for example, with an employee who knows his stuff and takes a lot of time for him. "Needs a lot of handholding," Revella says. First buyer persona. Experienced buyers, on the other hand, want clear comparisons of the available equipment and want to reach their goals quickly. They know what is important, which technical parameters must be met and which performance profile they need. "Side by side comparisons," says Revella. Second buyer persona. That is it. Both groups need different kinds of information from the vendor, different types of input, in order to arrive at the right purchase decision. The supplier who has this knowledge and provides optimal support for group A and provides different but also optimal support for group B has a clear advantage here. The customer experience will be much better than with a company that does not have this customer knowledge or that has not drawn any practical conclusions from it. Revella points out that neither Caterpillar nor its direct competitors did a good job of supporting these two customer groups in the decision-making process. She says in this webinar: "Neither Caterpillar nor their competitors were serving these buyers well. The buyer experience for both of these buyers were terrible."[21]

The level of purchasing experience and product (or service) knowledge will naturally only play a role in customer type formation if the product or service category is reasonably complex. If I am buying a bottle opener, a key case, or printer

[21] Ibid.

paper, then as a socialized individual I will have sufficient knowledge to make a purchase decision that is right for me. Whether I buy a screwdriver for the first time or for the tenth time makes practically no difference. But even with complex products, with major purchases, it is not a priori certain that a high and a low level of purchasing knowledge will necessarily lead to two types of customers. When it comes to buying ERP software, for example, the lead decision-makers are usually IT managers.[22] The fact that some IT managers are selecting an ERP system for a company for the second or third time and others for the first time does not mean that these IT managers need different support in the purchasing decision process. Because they have already purchased other business software systems, the IT managers selecting an ERP system for the first time will usually have sufficient experience to be able to identify the requirements and the matching functionality profile about as well as the "ERP veterans."

Now let us look at the segmentation study Malcom McDonald did for a fertilizer manufacturer. Here, all farmers—the potential customers—will have enough knowledge about the product category that a high or low level of buying experience will not play a role in the type formation. Thus, other characteristics must be present here to justify different types. McDonald identified more than two types of farmers, but I pick out only two of those customer types here: the price-sensitive farmer and the scientific farmer. The fertilizer manufacturer had assumed that the farmer market was homogeneous—one big target group: farmers—and that low price was *the* purchasing decision criterion. McDonald found that this market was actually heterogeneous. He discovered that not all farmers thought and acted alike, but that the market could be segmented according to different needs. One group of farmers, a segment, had need A, another group need B, and so on. McDonald chooses to use the term need here. But one can just as well speak instead of different problems or of different goals. Segment 1 wants to solve a different problem than segment 2, or, again, in other words, segment 1 has a different goal than segment 2. The fertilizer manufacturer had assumed that all farmers had the same goal: to fertilize their soil as

[22]The key users, external ERP consultants, and purchasing can also exert an influence—possibly a great one—on the purchasing decision-making process. If this is the case, then the buying center consists of the IT manager, the key users, the ERP consultant and the purchaser. In a buyer persona study, one interviews the lead decision maker, usually a senior executive, who has a high level of expertise in the product (or service) to be purchased. In the case of business software, this is the IT director. If you interview the IT director, then you naturally also ask about co-decision-makers and thus gain insights into the composition of the buying center. The role-based buying center model was developed by Frederick E. Webster, Jr. and Yoram Wind in "Organizational Buying Behavior," Prentice Hall, 1972. This model does not state that all B2B buying decisions are true group decisions, that there is always a formal equal decision-making body with regular meetings. This is—as Webster and Wind explicitly state—a buying center special case. The occasional argument that the buyer persona concept is obsolete because in B2B companies today it is no longer a single person who buys, but a buying center, is consequently a poor argument. Even 50 years ago, companies had buying centers. And, as we have just seen, the buying center model is well compatible with the buyer persona approach.

cheaply as possible. Of course, there were farmers who were extremely price sensitive. McDonald christened this group Arthur. He writes about Arthur:

> [Arthur] ... bought on price alone but represented only 10 per cent of the market, not the 100 per cent put about by everyone in the industry, especially the sales force.[23]

Another type ("Oliver") is the scientific farmer who drives around his fields in a tractor with an on-board computer and satellite-based controls. A fertilizer rep has the best chance of success with this type, McDonald says, if he chooses a technical sales pitch.

Oliver, by the way, was considered particularly price-sensitive by the fertilizer industry because he bought the fertilizer's phosphorus (P), nitrogen (N), and potassium (K) components individually, which was particularly cheap. In fact, however, he did this only to get the maximum yield from his soils, the nature of which he had previously analyzed. Some of his soils needed more P than K, for others it was the other way around, and so on. But the fertilizer manufacturers only offered the ready-mix:

> ...Oliver was a scientific farmer, but the supply industry believed he was buying on price because he bought his own ingredients as cheaply as possible. He did this, however, because none of the suppliers bothered to understand his needs.[24]

What is the difference between "Oliver," the scientific farmer John Doe, and the group of scientific farmers? First, about the difference between "Oliver" and Joe Doe. "Oliver" is the type—an abstract. He is not flesh and blood, John Doe is. The type "Oliver" is a concept—like 4-leaf shamrock or 17-leaf shamrock. The concept does not live, the clover (if it has not been pulled out) does. The type singles out a property or bundle of properties: the property of being a farmer and the property of being scientific (or the property of being a shamrock and of being four-leafed). John Doe is a guy who fits this bundle of properties that make up the type: John Doe is a farmer and John Doe runs his farm in a scientific way. The group is the population that consists of people like John Doe. All guys in this population have the two characteristics mentioned above. The group is also not flesh and blood, but its members are. The group can consist of 0, 1, 2 ... people, for example, John Doe, Jane Doe, Joe Public, Joe Average, and Joe Sixpack.[25]

---

[23] Malcom McDonald, "On Marketing Planning", 2nd edition, KoganPage 2017, p. 80.

[24] Ibid.

[25] Because there are abstract properties or concepts—for example, that of the unicorn—that we can conceive, some philosophers (e.g., Gottlob Frege, in the twentieth century Roderick Chisholm) have assumed that a realm of abstract objects exists. An abstract property that exists in this realm may or may not be instantiated in the material or psycho-social world. For example, the property of being a unicorn—the concept of unicorn—is not instantiated, that is, there are no flesh and blood unicorns. However, the concept is in the world, it is an abstract object that we can grasp with our minds. But the assumption of such an objective realm of abstract entities (properties, numbers and the like) is unnecessary and can therefore fall to Occam's razor. The non-instantiated property of

In McDonald's segmentation study, the criterion used to create types is the goal of the particular farmer, not the level of product knowledge and buying experience. The more clearly distinguishable goals there are in the large group of farmers, the more farmer types (homogeneous subgroups) there are. In the Caterpillar case, the two types of customers expected buying advice tailored to their different buying-related knowledge. For example, with the novice, the salesperson must first ensure purchase enablement. These two buyer personas will certainly not provide Caterpillar with input for product development. It may be different for customer types linked to goals. For example, if Apple had known the expectations of Japanese mobile phone users before the launch of the iPhone 1, this would have had an impact on the functionality of the product. The functionality profile of the first iPhone would have been changed before launch. It would have been adapted to the expectations of Japanese buyers. And these expectations here related to what the Japanese wanted to do with a smartphone. In the fertilizer case, customer type knowledge provides input to R & D as well. The ready-mix fits the goal of the price-sensitive farmer but not that of the scientific farmer. The job that the scientific farmer wants to get done with fertilizer requires variable mixtures of the ingredients P, N, and K. If knowledge is acquired about the specific goals that a customer type wants to achieve with a product (or service), then this goal knowledge can be used for goal-oriented product innovation. This is a very interesting point, which I will come back to.

So the types of farmers differ according to the goals they want to achieve with the purchase and use of the fertilizer. What if Revella's institute had found out that there are, for example, two groups of construction companies. One group wants to buy excavators to move soil from A to B, and the other group wants to buy excavators to impress potential customers and investors? The buyers of the excavators (and other Caterpillar vehicles) would then have different jobs to do. Group A—the "diggers"—would buy excavators to dig holes, Group B—the "impressors"—to attract important people. In this case, four types of customers would result (assuming B novices, need different advice than B routiniers):

being a unicorn and the instantiated property of being a clover are abstract entities generated in a process of mental abstraction, which are represented in biological (or artificial) brains (and can be externalized linguistically). If a child sees several objects—for example, balls, cones, and blocks—that all have a red color, then the child can abstract the concept redness from them. From the fact that the child can do this, it does not follow that redness is an eternal object. Only the red balls, cones and blocks do exist in the external world.

On this "Platonist" ontology of eternal abstract objects cf. Gottlob Frege, "Der Gedanke," in Gottlob Frege, "Logische Untersuchungen," ed. by Günther Patzig, 3rd edition, Vandenhoeck u. Ruprecht 1986; Gottlob Frege, "Funktion und Begriff", in Gottlob Frege, "Funktion, Begriff und Bedeutung," ed. by Günther Patzig, 6th edition, Vandenhoeck u. Ruprecht 1986, pp. 19 f; Roderick Chisholm, "First Person, Essay on Reference and Intentionality (Studies in Philosophy)", Branch Line, 1981, chapter 2.

		Purchase expertise	
		Low	High
Goals	A	Customer type 1[a]	Customer type 2
	B	Customer type 3	Customer type 4

[a]Here this "matrix" is related to the Caterpillar case. In a generalized form, the type 1 and type 2 fields must read: *potential* customer type 1 and *potential* customer type 2, because, as already mentioned, it does not follow from the fact that there are buyer novices and buyer routiniers that these two type fields are actually both occupied. Whether this is the case or not is an empirical question. If, despite differences in purchase experience, no different purchase decision support is required, then exactly one customer type ("type1/2") results per goal.

5 Jobs to Be Done

I made the point that knowledge about the goals customers want to achieve can provide ideas for innovation. In doing so, I made use of the phrase "job to be done," alluding to a theory of the highly influential innovation researcher Clayton Christensen. This "goal-innovation link," which I inferred from the farmer-type "Oliver" forms the core of Christensen's Jobs to Be Done theory ("JTBD").[26] Christensen and Raynor write in "The Innovator's Solution":

> ... customers—people and companies—have "jobs" that arise regularly and need to get done. When customers become aware of a job that they need to get done in their lives, they look around for a product or service that they can "hire" to get the job done. This is how customers experience life. Their thought processes originate with an awareness of needing to get something done, and then they set out to hire something or someone to do the job as effectively, conveniently, and inexpensively as possible.[27]

"Oliver" wants to get a different job done with the fertilizer than "Arthur" does. And knowledge about "Oliver's" job provides information on how to change the product to do this job better for "Oliver" than the current ready-mix does.

The Jobs to Be Done theory is—and Christensen concedes this—quite old in its essence. It goes back to Theodore Levitt. Levitt uses the expression "problem" instead of the expression "job to be done." But these are—and Christensen is also aware of this—merely two different expressions to designate the same thing. A problem/job to be done is nothing more than a discrepancy between the current reality and desired results. If the gap between the actual state and the target state is

[26]I return to the connection between job to be done and innovation in Chap. 7. For JTBD, see: Clayton M. Christensen, Michael E. Raynor, "The Innovator's Solution. Creating And Sustaining Successful Growth", Harvard Business Review Press, 2003, p. 75 ff. and Clayton M. Christensen, Teddy Hall, Karen Dillon, David S. Duncan, "Competing Against Luck. The Story of Innovation and Customer Choice", Harper Business, 2016.

[27]Clayton M. Christensen, Michael E. Raynor, "The Innovator's Solution", op. cit., p. 75.

closed, the problem is solved/the goal is achieved/the job is done.[28] Professional dart players, for example, who have won their game, like to say "I got the job done" in the subsequent interview. The job to be done here is to beat the opponent. In other words, the problem is to win more legs and sets in this match than the other player. In other words, the goal is to walk off the stage a winner.

Christensen attributes the following statement to Theodore Levitt, which reflects Levitt's views very pointedly: *People don't want to buy a quarter-inch drill. They want a quarter inch hole!*[29]

Customers are not interested in the product as such, but buy it as a tool to solve a problem they have. Or, as Christensen puts it, they hire it to get a job done. Of course, drill buyers do not just want to drill a few holes. The holes are also a means to an end. What they ultimately want is, for example, to mount a mirror or shelf on the wall of their home. To do this, they need a drill, drill bits, dowels, and screws. They want to solve a problem, i.e., they want to do a job, i.e., they want to achieve a goal. When the mirror is on the wall, the problem is solved, the job is done, the goal is achieved. Levitt (and McDonald) use the expressions problem (or need) to denote this. The customer has a problem that he needs to solve. And the company that wants to retain that customer also has a problem that it needs to solve. The company's problem is to understand the customer's problem (the job to be done). In the famous essay "Marketing Myopia" (1960), in which Levitt criticizes the product-centric (he says product-oriented) attitude of companies, he writes:

> The reason that the customer (and the satisfaction of his deepest needs) is not considered as being "the problem" is not because there is any certain belief that no such problem exists, but because an organizational lifetime had conditioned management to look in the opposite direction. [...] Management must think of itself not as producing products but as providing customer-creating value satisfactions.[30]

6 Customer Value

At the end of the quote, Levitt uses the term "value satisfactions" to refer to what customers get (in the best case) in exchange for the dough they have to shell out for the products or services they want to use. Customers basically do not pay for the products themselves (they do not really care about those, as I said), but for the values

---

[28] In practice, of course, the term problem often comes to mean only an unexpected obstacle that must be overcome on the way to achieving the goal. "Houston, we have a problem!"

[29] Levitt himself, in "The Marketing Mode: Pathways To Corporate Growth" (1969), attributes this statement to Leo McGivena (1947). But as early as 1942, an advertisement in a Somerset, Pennsylvania newspaper stated:

Hardware stores report that over one million men bought one-quarter inch drills in one year. Not one of those million men wanted the drills. They wanted quarter inch holes in metal or wood. Cf. No One Wants a Drill. What They Want Is the Hole, https://quoteinvestigator.com/2019/03/23/drill/#note-22083-9. [No One Wants a Drill. What They Want Is the Hole – Quote Investigator].

[30] Theodore Levitt, "Marketing Myopia", Harvard Business Review, July–August 1960, p. 55 f.

they have for them and the satisfactions they provide them as a result of those values. Levitt thus refers to value from the customer's perspective—to customer value.

From the customer's perspective, a product or service has a non-price value and a price value.[31] If the price of a product falls, then the price value increases, and vice versa. When the two brothers Richard ("Dick") and Maurice ("Mac") McDonald opened a walk-up hamburger stand in 1948, a hamburger cost 15 cents and a cheeseburger 19 cents—about half as much as in a sit-down restaurant.[32] So the price value for a McDonald's hamburger was much higher than the price value for a hamburger at a Mom & Pop diner. If a Budweiser tastes better to me than a Heineken and the only thing that counts for me besides the price is the taste of the beer, then the Budweiser has a higher non-price value for me than the Heineken. If a Heineken tastes better to me, then it is the other way around. Customer value is thus equal to price value plus non-price value.

The user-friendly Apple Lisa (1983) and the Apple Macintosh (1984) both had a mouse and a graphical user interface. What was the difference? The Apple Macintosh had a lower non-price value than the Apple Lisa. It was effectively an "undersized" version of the Lisa. For example, it had significantly less memory, lower graphical resolution, and a smaller monitor. But the Macintosh had two important advantages over the Lisa. Advantage 1: The Macintosh was relatively small. It fits into a bag and could be carried from A to B in a bicycle basket, for example. Advantage 2: It had a much higher price value than the Lisa. The Macintosh changed the computer world, the Lisa did not. So price value matters even for a non-price value brand like Apple, which can charge high prices for its products. Even for Apple, a very low price value of a device has the consequence that it is gathering dust on store shelves. Stephen Hackett in the blog post "The Lisa" (2017):

> The Mac sold 50,000 units in its first 100 days; the Lisa sold only a few thousand in its first year. No doubt the Mac's $2,495 price tag was a major factor.[33]

Let us substitute price and non-price value with numbers (higher number = higher value) to quantify the customer value. The Lisa has a slightly higher non-price value than the Mac, but a much lower price value. Let us set the non-price value of the Lisa arbitrarily equal to 20, that of the Mac equal to 15—it must be somewhat lower than 20. And let us set the price value of the Lisa arbitrarily equal to 5 and that of the Mac equal to 20—it must be significantly higher than 5. The Lisa then has a customer value of: 20 + 5 = 25 and the Mac of 15 + 20 = 35. 35 is greater than 25, so the overall customer value of the Mac is higher than that of

---

[31] Cf. Michael E. Raynor, Mumtaz Ahmed, "The Three Rules. How Exceptional Companies Think", Portfolio/Penguin 2013, p. 60 f.

[32] Cf. Lauren Cahn, "Here's What the McDonald's Menu Looked Like the Year You Were Born", updated: Jul. 30, 2021; https://www.rd.com/list/mcdonalds-menu-year-born/ [A Look Back at the McDonald's Menu Through the Years | Reader's Digest (rd.com)].

[33] Stephen Hackett, "The Lisa", DEC 14, 2017; https://www.macstories.net/mac/the-lisa/ [The Lisa – MacStories.

the Lisa. There is another "customer value formula." It goes like this: *customer value = benefits minus costs.*[34] Let us ignore transaction costs such as information costs, initiation costs, etc. and equate costs with price. We can then perform the Lisa-Mac calculation with this formula as well: If we set the benefits of the Lisa equal to 45, the price equal to 20 and the benefits of the Mac equal to 40 (slightly lower) and the price equal to 5 (significantly lower), then we get 45 – 20 = 25 for the Lisa and 40 – 5 = 35 for the Mac. How are benefit and price value related? A low price (high price value) is also beneficial to me, because I have more bucks in my wallet. I like having more bucks, because then I can buy a better charging station and a protective case in addition to my desired smartphone (a Google Pixel), and also go to my favorite Italian restaurant and eat a delicious plate of spaghetti diavolo and sip a glass of Barolo with it.

The word benefit is another expression that is closely related to the problem to be solved or the job to be done. For example, the bottle opener has a benefit for me because it helps me remove the crown cork from the beer bottle. It does a job for me—with my help—and it does it better than a disposable lighter, a table knife or a fork. So the bottle opener has value for me because it is useful when I want to drink a bottle of beer. I was, therefore, willing to spend money on it. But if my bottle opener broke and suddenly every bottle opener became as expensive as an iPhone, I would not buy a new bottle opener but a cheap disposable lighter: Value = benefits *minus costs*. So I can reduce the customer value for a product or service by increasing the price and I can increase the value by reducing the price. Alternatively, I can reduce or increase the benefits and thus reduce or increase the customer value. Why do I have to subtract the price I pay from the benefit? Answer: If the price of the Google Pixel was zero, then I would have even more bucks in my wallet and then I could, for example, also buy a (used) Omega watch (and feel like James Bond)—more value.

The Nomad Jukebox digital music player (2001) weighed twice as much as a portable CD player, had a slow, hard-to-use interface for transferring music files, and poor battery life.[35] And then came the iPod ... Apple's iPod did the job it was supposed to do for virtually all of its target customers significantly better than the Nomad Jukebox. The iPod had a higher non-price value. Non-price value is therefore closely related to the job to be done, i.e., the problem to be solved, i.e., the goal to be achieved. The better the job is done from a customer's point of view, the higher the non-price value.

Is the non-price value of a high-priced Porsche 911 higher than the non-price value of a low-priced Renault Grand Scénic? That depends. On what? On the job the car is supposed to do. If I have a large family and often want to transport a lot of

[34] Cf. Neil Rackham, John De Vincentis, "Rethinking the Sales Force. Redesigning Selling to Create and Capture Customer Value", McGraw-Hill Education, 1999, p. 12; Tom Snyder, Kevin Kearns, "Escaping the Price-Driven Sale. How World Class Sellers Create Extraordinary Profit", McGraw-Hill Education, 2007, p. 28.

[35] Cf. Larry Downes, Paul Nunes, "Big Bang Disruption", op. cit., p. 124.

people, then a Renault Grand Scénic will do the job, because it has (a maximum of) seven seats, but a fancy Porsche 911 will not.

Companies can position themselves accordingly in the price value space—being "aggressive price leaders" (Adam Osborne)—, like Dick and Mac McDonald or they can position themselves in the non-price space—like Apple.

Non-price value is not only created by the well-known features and benefits (functionality) of the product. Ease of use, aesthetic form ("good design"), materials used/processing and the product surround also play an important role.[36] When I—Roland Burkholz—buy a new TV set, for example, I do not just want a first-class picture, good workmanship, a beautiful device, an intuitive handling and a convenient purchase process, but I also want the new set to be brought to my apartment on the fourth floor (no elevator), the broken old TV to be taken away and disposed of professionally, my old Bose music system to be connected to the new smart TV right away and I to be given a brief introduction to how to operate the new set because I hate reading instruction manuals.

If an electronics retailer offers me these additional services, then his offer has a higher non-price value for me than an electronics retailer who offers me the same smart TV but not these additional services. The informativeness of a vendor's website, the competence and availability of the salespeople (at a bricks-and-mortar retailer) ...—in short, the quality of support in the purchase decision process—can possibly increase the non-price value considerably. And for major sales in the B2B sector, the implementation phase (including training of key users) by the vendor is also an important factor. Differences in performance here can have a big impact for the customer company. If a company gets the most out of a mediocre product as a result of a very good implementation phase, then the non-price value for the company is higher than for a first-class product whose potential users can only exploit by 10%. User support, maintenance and repair should also be mentioned here. There can be significant differences between providers here.

So: The better a provider helps me to do the job I want to get done well and in a pleasant way, the higher the non-price value I get as a customer. But of course, the product (or service) itself is an essential factor in this calculation, because it is the product (or service), with the participation of the customer, that has to do the job.

Customer value is value from the customer's perspective. Customer value is therefore not equal to the labor hours used to produce the good, nor is it equal to the market value the good has. Something can have a high market value (e.g., a superb sounding audiophile tube amplifier) but be of little value to me (e.g., if I am almost deaf or hardly ever listen to music). Is customer value therefore a subjective concept? Is this kind of value exclusively in the eye of the beholder? Nope! Customer *experience* is an intrinsically subjective concept—customer *value* is not. When FC Bayern Munich scores a goal against Manchester City in a Champions

[36]Materials used and aesthetic design are of course not independent of each other. A notebook made of aluminum looks nicer (and it feels better) than a notebook made of silver-colored plastic simply because of the material.

League match, I experience it positively as a Bayern Munich supporter and negatively as a Man City supporter. One state of affairs (a goal scored by Bayern Munich)—two different ways of experiencing it. If a customer service employee is incompetent and makes an incompetent impression on me, then as a customer I have a negative "incompetence experience." If the customer service employee is competent but makes an incompetent impression on me (for whatever reason), then I have an equivalent "incompetence experience." Two distinct objective realities—one consistent customer experience. Value is different because of its relation to the job I want to do. Suppose I now use product (or service) A and attribute value x to it because it does the job I want to get done. Further, suppose there is a product (or service) A' that does the job better, but I do not know that. In this case, I will assign a value of less than/equal to x to A', although the customer value of A' is factually higher. The value of A' is higher for me than the value of A because A' does the job better (e.g., faster and more conveniently) for me than A. A' here has an objectively higher customer value than A although I—the customer—attribute a lower (or equal) value to it than to A. I attribute a lower (or equal) value because I do not know that A' does the job better (from my point of view) than A does. If I knew that, I would naturally come to a different subjective assessment—then I would ascribe a higher value to A' than to A (as I should). In this case, subjective value attribution and (objective) customer value would match.

The use of a product (or service) always has an "in order-to" logic. I buy a product (or service) in order to achieve something with it. So there is a means-purpose ratio here. The term "need" (/"need satisfaction") is not so well suited as a basic concept here, because there are many products that no one needs and that are bought anyway. Rolex is a company that exclusively develops, manufactures, and markets nice and expensive things that no one really needs. Today, everyone carries a smartphone that tells the time more accurately than a Rolex watch. Yet, when I wear a Rolex Daytona, I wear it for a reason. I am trying to get a job done, I am trying to achieve a goal by wearing (or collecting) a Rolex Daytona. But—and this is an interesting point—I do not have to be clear about what drives me to purchase a Rolex Daytona. Is it the aesthetic satisfaction I experience when I look at my left wrist?—do I want to impress the people around me?—express that I am wealthy?—gain more recognition in my golf club?—am I trying to make a smart investment? Or is it a combination of these (or some of these) goals? I do not have to explicitly know the goal (or goals) I want to achieve by wearing a Rolex Daytona, the way I know my zip code, date of birth, or phone number. These goals do not have to be consciously represented in my mind. They may be implicit mental goals, so that I am unable to name them when asked, even though they motivate my actions. I may imitate a person who impresses me and wears such a watch, without really being clear about why I am doing so. So it does not follow from the fact that I do not really know why I wear a Rolex Daytona (and not a Timex Waterbury) that there is not a job here that the expensive watch does for me. (That is just an example. I do not wear a Rolex Daytona or a Timex Waterbury.) I can also, of course, be deluded about myself and believe that I am wearing the Daytona to achieve a satisfying aesthetic perception, and in fact I am just trying to cover up my lack of self-esteem. In this case, the real job I want to get done is then consequently not the one I am stating, but the one I am not aware of. So the customer value resides in the actual job the product (or service) does for me—whether or not I am aware of what exactly that job looks like.

Assume that of two products, one does the job it is supposed to do clearly better. (Price, workmanship, purchase process, etc. are the same.) Will I then (if I am realistic about the situation) choose the product that does the job better in each case? That seems to follow from Christensen's JTBD theory. In fact, however, I will not always choose this product. Here's an example: I need a new espresso machine. Two products with different systems are on the shortlist: A Lavazzo Espresso Point capsule machine and a classical Gaggia espresso machine with a two-cup portafilter handle. With the Gaggia I can vary the amount of espresso, but not with the capsule machine. But with the capsule machine, the espresso is prepared faster, there is no dirt unlike the classic portafilter system, and the espresso quality is good, nice crema, intense aroma. Fast, clean, good. This is exactly what I want. So the decision should be easy. The Lavazza capsule machine does the job it should do in my kitchen, clearly better than the Gaggia. So do I purchase the Lavazza Espresso Point machine? That depends. The espresso that needs to be used here is in black plastic capsules. Two capsules each are shrink-wrapped in plastic cling film. So I produce a lot more waste if I choose to purchase the capsule machine. What does my purchase decision depend on here? Well, maybe I am a very environmentally conscious person, maybe not ... What is the case here? It is easy to figure out if you use "goal language." The job I want to get done is my core goal. But environmental protection is also more or less important to me. There is therefore a conflict of goals here. Not only is the core goal relevant to me, but I also want to produce as little waste as possible. If I decide in favor of the machine that, from my point of view, optimally achieves the core objective, then I will not achieve the waste avoidance objective. So I have to choose a trade-off here: The Gaggia, which is suboptimal with regard to the job to be done, but at the same time allows me to achieve the waste prevention goal, or the Lavazza, which is optimal with regard to the job, but causes me to miss the waste prevention goal. If waste reduction is very important to me, I will opt for the classic espresso machine, if not, then not.

7 Innovation: Necessarily a Trial and Error Process?

Clayton Christensen says companies do not know enough about these customer jobs.[37] And that has implications for companies' innovation processes. Innovation, he says, is commonly perceived as a trial and error process, because 80% of products that are launched fail. If a company funds 10 innovation projects, it knows that on average only two of them will lead to new products that will succeed on the

[37]For this paragraph cf. #EIE17: GENERAL SESSION - Competing Again [sic!] Luck with Professor Clayton Christensen – YouTube; https://www.youtube.com/watch?v=V603pf9s5WA&t=746s.

market—but of course it does not know which ones those are (otherwise it would only fund those). So innovations—like investments of venture capitalists—are a kind of gamble. You have to bet on ten innovation projects to end up winning two bets. If companies knew more about these jobs that customers want get done with their products, however, the chances of product launches being successful could be increased considerably, according to Christensen. Companies could then replace the trial and error process with a methodically controlled, systematic innovation process. This is because companies would then have a kind of innovation guideline as a result of this job-related customer knowledge. So the idea is this: If I know what the job looks like, and if I know that the current product is doing that job poorly, then I know in what direction I need to change it. And from Malcom McDonald's segmentation study, you can see that Christensen is correct in this view. Knowing the job scientific farmers want to get done gives a strong innovation clue: a new fertilizer that buyers can mix themselves and adjust to their particular soil conditions. That would not be trial and error innovation. The likelihood that scientific farmers would buy this new fertilizer product would be exceptionally high because it is very well suited to achieve their intended goal—to provide optimum nutrients to any soil.

Customer-type research therefore not only provides insights that are relevant for content marketing and for sales. It can change innovation processes as well and increase the probability of successful product launches. Such studies can also contribute to the alignment of marketing and sales, because they provide a common basis—customer knowledge—from which input can be derived for both areas. The entire customer journey, which consists of numerous (direct and indirect) touchpoints between the customer and the company and extends from the pre-purchase to the purchase and post-purchase phase, can be optimized with the help of experiential customer knowledge. Pain points can be identified and eliminated and pleasure points added. The buzzwords that are chosen for this—Customer Centricity Initiative, Customer Experience Management, Customer-Led Growth, etc.—are not important. I repeat myself: It is not the designation that matters, but what is designated.

8 Disruption Theory and the Voice of the Customer

In his book "The Innovator's Dilemma" (1996), Clayton Christensen developed the theory that made him famous—disruption theory. Steve Jobs, for example, was deeply influenced by this book.[38] That is also true for Amazon founder Jeff Bezos. Christensen's book is part of "Jeff's Reading List" which consists (or once consisted) of 12 books.[39] "The Innovator's Dilemma" has even had an impact on

[38]Cf. Walter Isaacson, "Steve Jobs", Abacus, paperback edition 2015 (first published 2011), p. 376.

[39]Cf. Brad Stone, "The Everything Store. Jeff Bezos And the Age of Amazon", Back Bay Books, 2013, Appendix, p. 347 ff.

Amazon's strategy.[40] In the book, Christensen says that the principle "*always listen and respond to the needs of your best customers!*"[41] is normally a principle of good management practice. However, there are certain situations—disruptive change—where following this principle is a bad idea. Since it has been argued here that it is beneficial for companies to listen to customers and align themselves with their expectations, desires, and goals, we now need to look at these disruptive situations where this approach—according to Christensen—is not only not beneficial, but even detrimental:

> The popular slogan ,stay close to your customers' appears not always to be robust advice.[42]

Christensen distinguishes between sustaining and disruptive innovations. Sustaining innovations improve the accepted performance metrics of products (or services) in established markets, in short, they make good products (or services) better.[43] Disruptive innovations often lead to new attributes, but these are irrelevant (or not important) for mainstream markets. In terms of the product (or service) attributes valued in these markets, these disruptive products (or services) perform worse than the established products (or services).

Sony's introduction of the transistor radio in the 1950s is an example of a disruptive innovation. The established products were large and expensive tube radios. The key established performance attribute was sound quality. A sustaining innovation would have improved sound (or increased the number of receivable stations). Yet the transistor radio had significantly poorer sound than tube radios. However, it had attributes that tube radio did not. It was very small and light, so you could take it anywhere, and it was cheap. These attributes were interesting for young people—people who were not buyers of tube radios. These were too expensive for them. From the point of view of the mainstream market, the transistor radio was a crummy product. But a bad-sounding radio was clearly better than no radio at all.

In "The Innovator's Solution" Christensen and Raynor call this a *new market disruption*—transistor radio has, in a sense, turned previous non-consumers into consumers. Christensen calls it: competing against non-consumption. Thus a new market emerged.

The two McDonald brothers introduced a so-called hybrid disruption with their fast food concept—they gained both non-consumers—people who had not previously eaten out—and patrons of low-end restaurants (low-end disruption).[44]

---

[40] Ibid., p. 243.

[41] Clayton M. Christensen, "The Innovator's Dilemma. When New Technologies Cause Great Firms to Fail", Harvard Business Review Press, 2016 (1996), Preface, p. 9 f.

[42] Ibid., p. 48.

[43] Sustaining innovations can be incremental or radical innovations (breakthrough innovations).

[44] According to Christensen and Raynor, there are exactly three types of disruption: new market disruption, low-end disruption, and hybrid disruption (a combination of the first two types). (Cf. Clayton M. Christensen, Michael E. Raynor, "The Innovator's Solution", op. cit., p. 45 ff.

The personal computer, most often referred to as the home computer or microcomputer in the mid-1970s, is also a disruptive technology—a new market disruption. Buyers of the Altair 8800, IMSAI 8080, Cromemco Z 1, Sol Terminal Computer, Apple II, etc. were electronic hobbyists, technology geeks—e.g., electrical engineering students—who had never bought a computer before. Before the PC, there were only mainframes and minimal or small computers (minicomputers). The minicomputers were the size of refrigerators. Mainframe computers cost up to $1,000,000 and minicomputers introduced in the late 1950s sold for well under $100,000. Digital Equipment Corporation's (DEC) PDP-8 transistor computer, introduced in the mid-1960s and selling very successfully, cost "only" $18,000—far too much dough for an average person. Minicomputers such as the PDP-8 were a category of computer below mainframes that was affordable to smaller businesses, government offices, and research and university institutes.[45] The Altair, introduced by MITS in 1975, cost just $397 as a kit.[46] And the Apple I (1976) sold for $666.66. In April 1977, the price dropped to $475. And the Apple II (1977) sold for $1298 at launch.[47] So the young personal computer companies like MITS, IMSAI, or Apple did not compete with the established minicomputer companies like Digital Equipment Corporation (DEC), Control Data Corporation (CDC), Wang Laboratories, or Packard Bell. MITS, IMSAI, Apple, Sol Terminal Computer, Processor Technology, etc.—the home computer makers—competed with each other for buyers who wanted to get their own computer for the first time and use it at home—competition against nonconsumption.[48]

Large established companies that develop disruptive technologies as prototypes often do not bring them to market. It is mostly entrants that market the disruptive

---

See also: Clayton M. Christensen, Scott D. Anthony, Erik A. Roth, "Seeing What's Next. Using the Theories of Innovation to Predict Industry Change", Harvard Business School Press, 2004, p. 6 ff).

[45]Cf. Der Tag als der Mini kam: 50 Jahre PDP-8 | heise online; https://www.heise.de/newsticker/meldung/Der-Tag-als-der-Mini-kam-50-Jahre-PDP-8-2582305.html and Rise and Fall of Minicomputers – ETHW; https://ethw.org/Rise_and_Fall_of_Minicomputers.

[46]Cf. Paul Freiberger, Michael Swaine, "Fire in the Valley", op. cit., p. 35.

[47]Cf. Christoph Dernbach, Apple I and Apple II › Mac History (mac-history.net), May 25, 2008; https://www.mac-history.net/computer-history/2008-05-25/apple-i-and-apple-ii and Suzanne Deffree, Apple II goes on sale, June 5, 1977 - EDN, June 5, 2019; https://www.edn.com/apple-ii-goes-on-sale-june-5-1977/.

[48]Christensen and Raynor correctly refer to the personal computer as a new-market disruption in "The Innovator's Solution", op. cit., of 2003 (p. 39): "The personal computer and Sony's first battery-powered transistor pocket radio were new-market disruptions ..." In "The Innovator's Manifesto" of 2011, however, Raynor then calls the personal computer a low-end disruption: "In the PC example above we see a 'low end' disruption, so called because the initial market segment targeted by the eventual disruptor settles for seemingly worse performance in exchange for materially lower cost."(Michael E. Raynor, "The Innovator's Manifesto. Deliberate Disruption for Transformational Growth", Crown Business 2011, p. 71.) This would mean that the early personal computer buyers would have come from the group of the least demanding minicomputer customers. Then Apple would have competed with minicomputer makers. But this has not been the case. Raynor here firstly expressis verbis contradicts his earlier assessment made together with Christensen and secondly is mistaken with this judgment.

products (or services). Steve Wozniak, co-founder of Apple, never wanted to start a company. He worked for Hewlett-Packard (HP) and wanted to stay there. HP "was producing everything from mainframes to pocket calculators."[49] Wozniak ("Woz") offered his computer designs to HP several times. After the fifth rejection, he decided after some hesitation to leave the company.[50] "Fire in the Valley" states:

> In their rejection, the HP engineers acknowledged that Wozniak's computer worked and could be built cheaply, but they told him it was not a product for HP. Wozniak eventually gave up on HP and built his computers in a start-up garage enterprise named Apple.[51]

Disruptive innovations introduced by entrants like Apple then get better and better via sustaining innovations: Apple I, Apple II, Apple IIGS, Apple III, Apple Lisa, Apple Macintosh, Power Macintosh ... Disruptors finally prevail in mainstream markets with their products—in this case only Apple—and marginalize the established large companies. The incumbents—in this case minicomputer manufacturers—are acquired, pushed into niches, or driven into bankruptcy (creative destruction, Schumpeter[52]):

> While the demise of classic minicomputers was clear by 1985, companies continued to offering them until the early 1990s, when the firms went bankrupt or were acquired by more astute competitors. Wang declared bankruptcy in 1992. Compaq bought DEC in 1998, and HP acquired Compaq in 2002. EMC turned Data General into a data storage business in 1999.[53]

The strength of large established companies is sustaining innovations. The minicomputer makers improved their machines. They developed more powerful and less expensive minicomputers. In contrast, entrant firms lead the way in disruptive innovations. Early home computer makers were all either startups (MITS, Processor Technology, Apple) or companies that had not previously made computers (Commodore, Atari, Tandy/RadioShack). Atari, for example, was a video game company that developed arcade video games that competed primarily with pinball machines in arcades.[54] The largest mainframe computer manufacturer

[49] Paul Freiberger, Michael Swaine, "Fire in the Valley", op. cit., p. 18.

[50] Cf. Apple-Mitgründer Steve Wozniak - HP lehnte seine Computer-Entwürfe fünf Mal ab (gamestar.de); https://www.gamestar.de/artikel/apple-mitgruender-steve-wozniak-hp-lehnte-seine-computer-entwuerfe-fuenf-mal-ab,3331612.html.

[51] Paul Freiberger, Michael Swaine, "Fire in the Valley", op. cit., p. 18.

[52] Cf. Joseph A. Schumpeter, "Capitalism, Socialism & Democracy" (1942), Routledge 2005, p. 84. According to Raynor and Christensen, disruptive innovation is likely the cause behind creative destruction, which Austrian economist Joseph Schumpeter identified as the primary driver of economic progress. Cf. Michael E. Raynor, "The Innovator's Manifesto", op. cit., p. 199 f. and Clayton M. Christensen, "The Innovator's Dilemma", op. cit., preface, p. 10.

[53] Rise and Fall of Minicomputers, op. cit.

[54] When Steve Jobs and Steve Wozniak started to develop the Apple II, they helped Atari to design the arcade video game "Breakout," which was released in 1976. Cf. Steven L. Kent, "The Ultimate

IBM introduced its home computer—called IBM Personal Computer—not until 1981.[55] That sustaining innovations is the preferred terrain of incumbents and disruptive innovations the terrain of entrants is well illustrated by the excavation industry. The transition from steam-powered excavators to gasoline-powered excavators had a sustaining logic, because gasoline-powered excavators were powerful enough from the start to move earth faster, more reliably, and at lower cost than most steam shovels. 23 of the top 25 steam shovel manufacturers successfully managed the transition to gasoline-powered excavators.[56] The later transition from cable-actuated excavators to hydraulic backhoes was quite different:

> Only four of the thirty or so established manufacturers of cable-actuated equipment in business in the 1950s (Insley, Koehring, Little Giant, and Link Belt) had successfully transformed themselves into sustainable hydraulic excavator manufacturers by the 1970s.[57]

Incumbents who develop disruptive prototypes early on and present them to their best customers usually receive negative reactions: no interest in this product—too poor a performance. From the perspective of the best (and often most demanding) customers, a disruptive product (or service) is an inferior product. They demand better performance—a better sounding radio—not a worse sounding one—a better minicomputer with more computing speed and more storage capacity—not a less powerful microcomputer. If incumbents listen to their best customers, they stop the disruptive innovation project and thus "sleep through" the new technology. It is the entrants who then introduce the disruptive technology. They find new buyers—a new market is created (new market disruption)—or (/and) they pull buyers from the lowest market tier of an established market (low-end disruption/hybrid disruption). Disruptors that successively improve their products (or services)—via sustaining

History of Video Games. From Pong to Pokémon and Beyond – The Story Behind the Craze That Touched Our Lives and Changed the World," Three Rivers Press, 2001, p. 71 f.

[55] In "Hypergrowth," however, Osborne and Dvorak write "IBM had already tried to enter the personal computer market ahead of everyone else with their highly unsuccessful model 5100." ("Hypergrowth", op. cit., p. 70.) IBM had in fact already introduced the IBM 5100 in 1975. The portable 5100 was unquestionably a microcomputer in terms of its dimensions. It was smaller than the IBM PC 5150 of 1981, but it was not really a home computer, because it cost between $8975 and $19,975 and was thus much too expensive for end users. (Cf. IBM Archives: IBM 5100 Portable Computer; https://www.ibm.com/ibm/history/exhibits/pc/pc_2.html.) Therefore, even though it is occasionally referred to as a personal computer, it is not considered a true home computer like the Altair, the Apple I and II, or the Commodore PET 2001.

[56] Clayton Christensen, "The Innovator's Dilemma", op. cit., p. 63.

[57] Ibid., p. 64. However, Christensen makes a mistake here. He erroneously includes the two German companies – Demag and Orenstein & Koppel (O & K)—among the hydraulic entrants (cf. ibid.). In fact, Demag and O & K are old companies that manufactured cable-actuated excavators before the transition to hydraulic technology. (Cf. History | Demag200; https://www.demag200.com/de/our-history and Orenstein & Koppel - Wikipedia; https://de.wikipedia.org/wiki/Orenstein_%26_Koppel.) So the success rate of incumbents is not quite as bad as Christensen claims. It is 50% higher than he assumes. Not four, but six incumbents have successfully mastered the hydraulic transition.

innovations—eventually conquer the higher tiers of established markets and displace the old technology that incumbents still rely on.

Because incumbents stay close to their best customers, they are marginalized or destroyed. So not listening to these customers, ignoring their negative reaction, and launching the disruptive product (or service) at an early stage would clearly be the better choice in this situation. After all, incumbents pay a very high price for listening to their best customers—they shrink, if they are lucky, and become niche players, or they disappear—i.e., they are bought out or have to file for bankruptcy.

So is it only beneficial in certain circumstances—in non-disruptive situations—to build up customer knowledge and act on it, and detrimental in others? No, not at all. It is better for companies in both disruptive and non-disruptive problem situations to align themselves with the expectations, wishes, and goals of actual or potential customers. But companies need to ask the right people—those who are actually potential buyers of these products. Seagate Technology, for example, has been a 5.25-in. disk drive maker in the 1980s, selling its hard drives into the desktop computer and workstation markets. The company developed 3.5-in. prototypes early on. When these smaller disks, which had less storage capacity than the 5.25 disk drives, were introduced to the market by Rodime, the buyers were the portable computer makers. Christensen writes about Seagate in "The Innovator's Dilemma":

> . . . engineers at Seagate Technology, the leading 5.25-inch drive maker, were, in 1985, the second in the industry to develop working prototypes of 3.5-inch models. [. . .] Seagate personnel showed working 3.5-inch prototype drives to customers for evaluation.[58]

To whom did Seagate submit these 3.5-in. prototypes for review? To its best customers—IBM's PC division, for example. Desktop computer manufacturers wanted disk drives with more storage capacity, faster read/write heads and a better price/performance ratio for their next PC generations. The fact that these new disk drives were smaller did not interest them. There was enough room in their computer cases to fit 5.25-in. disk drives. So this attribute was irrelevant to them. Why would they respond positively to prototypes with less memory and higher cost per megabyte? Surely they were not idiots. Were they? A positive evaluation simply does not make sense here. Christensen writes:

> Seagate's marketers tested the 3.5-inch prototypes with customers in the desktop computing market it already served—manufacturers like IBM, and value-added resellers of full-sized desktop computer systems. *Not surprisingly*, they indicated little interest in the smaller drive. They were looking for capacities of 40 and 60 megabytes for their next-generation machines, while the 3.5-inch architecture could provide only 20 MB—and at higher costs.[59]

Seagate listened to its customers and shelved the prototypes. The company did not bring 3.5-in. drives to market until 1988, when they were good enough for

[58]Clayton Christensen, "The Innovator's Dilemma", op. cit., p. 20/43.

[59]Ibid. (Italics added.)

desktop computer makers. They sold the 3.5-in. drives to their old customers, who now wanted them. But Seagate was unable to gain a foothold in the portable computer market that the 3.5-in. entrants had initially targeted. It was too late to gain market share there:

> Interestingly, according to industry observers, as of 1991 almost none of Seagate's 3.5-inch products had been sold to manufacturers of portable/laptop/notebook computers. In other words, Seagate's primary customers were still desktop computer manufacturers, and many of its 3.5-inch drives were shipped with frames for mounting them in computers designed for 5.25-inch drives.[60]

What blunder did Seagate's marketers make here? Well, that is actually obvious. They simply showed their 3.5-in. prototypes to the wrong people. If you are going to design a smaller 20 MB hard drive, you should not ask people who need at least 40 MB. You do not have to be an Einstein to anticipate that people who have no use for a small 20 MB disk drive will give you thumbs down if you ask them what they think about it. Seagate's marketers should not have asked their best existing customers, of course, but potential buyers of 3.5-in. disk drives—people who did not need more than 20 MB and for whom 5.25 or 8-in. drives were too big and too expensive. These potential customers would have been the portable computer makers. Seagate's marketers were looking in the wrong market.

When a company wants to develop and market a product (or service) that is attractive to market tier C (but not to market tier A or B), it should not submit prototypes to A or B customers for review—even if they are the company's best existing customers. If Seagate had presented their 3.5-in. prototypes to portable computer makers, they would certainly have been judged differently. The thumbs would have gone up.

I, therefore, come to the following conclusion: Staying close to *potential target customers* is not bad advice for incumbents in disruptive problem situations, but staying close to their *best existing customers* is—customers from a different market who are not potential buyers of the disruptive product (or service) at stake.

9 Conclusion

Clayton Christensen is a prominent business writer. "The New Yorker" once called him "the most influential business writer on earth."[61] But he is also a brilliant storyteller. He says that his research shows that listening and responding to the best customers is apparently not always good advice. Christensen's suggesting something here that sounds exciting, that makes you sit up and take notice. He makes the reader think that in disruptive situations, customer knowledge (in the sense meant here) tends to be misleading for companies. But this suggested reading

---

[60] Ibid., p. 21.

[61] See the cover of "The Innovator's Dilemma" (2016), op. cit.

is simply not true—and he knows this perfectly well. And yet Christensen, the storyteller, apparently cannot help himself. He suggests this reading because it leads to a more exciting story (I assume). The truth[62] is somewhat less surprising: *It is detrimental for companies to stay close to their customers if and only if they make judgments about something that is only attractive to a different set of customers.* And asking the wrong people is indeed bad management practice—in disruptive as well as non-disruptive situations.

It is a bit like what the screenwriter of "Apollo 13" did when he wrote the phrase "Houston we have problem!" The words actually spoken by Jim Swager, the Apollo 13 astronaut, were, "Okay, Houston, we*'ve had* a problem here."[63] Great storytelling but not completely accurate. Reality is often not quite as exciting as a good story.

References

#EIE17: GENERAL SESSION - Competing Again [sic!] Luck with Professor Clayton Christensen – YouTube. Accessed January 15, 2022, from https://www.youtube.com/watch?v=V603pf9s5WA&t=746s

"Project Purple": How the Motorola ROKR E1 became the first iPhone – ComputerBase. Accessed January 15, 2022, from https://www.computerbase.de/2021-10/apple-iphone-project-purple-motorola-rokr-e1/

Apollo 13 (film) – Wikipedia. Accessed January 15, 2022, from https://en.wikipedia.org/wiki/Apollo_13_(film)

[62]Note for constructivists among readers: Parenthetical note (for readers who know nothing about constructivists): Constructivists/relativists are people who write expressions like fact, truth, or discovery always in quotation marks because they believe that philosophers of science have shown that there are no facts and no true statements. Christensen, by the way, is not one of these people. Now to the main note: First, it was mediocre philosophers (and sociologists) of science who claimed this. They have believed to have shown it, but have not done so. Second, that there are facts and true as well as false statements can be demonstrated quite easily by simple cases. If I open a bottle of Heineken and say "I am opening a bottle of Heineken," I am making a true statement. If I open a bottle of Heineken and say "I'm opening a bottle of Budweiser," I am making a false statement. (And if I say "I decapitate an alien that looks like a bottle of Heineken," I am an idiot or a philosopher of science.) My opening the Heineken bottle is the fact or state of affairs—that which is the case. The utterance expressing that fact is the true statement. The utterance "I'm having a Heineken now" is true if and only if I am having a Heineken now. It is as simple as that. Truth is correspondence between fact and statement. Good ole correspondence theory of truth is not obsolete at all. For truth without correspondence makes no sense. Correspondence cannot be proved (in the logical-mathematical sense of proof), because the probability that an empirical statement is true is less than 1 (maybe the Heineken is an alien after all—it is unlikely, not impossible). But from that it does not follow that we cannot establish this correspondence (by evidence). If I hold a bottle in my hand that looks and feels like a bottle of Heineken and take a sip from it and the liquid tastes like Heineken, then in practice that is sufficient evidence for me that my utterance "I'm having a Heineken right now" is a true statement. I have then proven to myself beyond a reasonable doubt that I am telling the truth.

[63]Cf. Apollo 13 (film) - Wikipedia; https://en.wikipedia.org/wiki/Apollo_13_(film); (Italics added).

Apple-Mitgründer Steve Wozniak - HP lehnte seine Computer-Entwürfe fünf Mal ab (gamestar.de). Accessed January 15, 2022, from https://www.gamestar.de/artikel/apple-mitgruender-steve-wozniak-hp-lehnte-seine-computer-entwuerfe-fuenf-mal-ab,3331612.html

Bower, J. L., & Christensen, C. M. (1995). Disruptive technologies: Catching the wave. In J. S. Brown (Ed.), *Seeing differently. Insights on innovation*. Harvard Business Review Book, 1997.

Burkholz, R. (2008). Problemlösende Argumentketten. Ein Modell der Forschung. *Velbrück Wissenschaft*.

Cahn, L. *Here's what the McDonald's menu looked like the year you were born*. Updated: July 30, 2021. Accessed January 15, 2022, from https://www.rd.com/list/mcdonalds-menu-year-born/ [A Look Back at the McDonald's Menu Through the Years | Reader's Digest (rd.com)].

Chisholm, R. (1981). First person, Essay on reference and intentionality (studies in philosophy). *Branch Line*.

Christensen, C. M. (1996). *The innovator's dilemma. When new technologies cause great firms to fail*. Harvard Business Review Press, 2016.

Christensen, C. M., Anthony, S. D., & Roth, E. A. (2004). *Seeing what's next. Using the theories of innovation to predict industry change*. Harvard Business School Press.

Christensen, C. M., Hall, T., Dillon, K., & Duncan, D. S. (2016). *Competing against luck. The story of innovation and customer choice*. Harper Business.

Christensen, C. M., & Raynor, M. E. (2003). *The innovator's solution. Creating and sustaining successful growth*. Harvard Business Review Press.

Cooper, A. (2004). *The inmates are running the asylum. Why high-tech products drive us crazy and how to restore sanity*. Pearson Education US.

Deffree, S. *Apple II goes on sale, June 5, 1977 - EDN, June 5, 2019*. Accessed January 15, 2022, from https://www.edn.com/apple-ii-goes-on-sale-june-5-1977/

Der Tag als der Mini kam: 50 Jahre PDP-8 | heise online. Accessed January 15, 2022, from https://www.heise.de/newsticker/meldung/Der-Tag-als-der-Mini-kam-50-Jahre-PDP-8-2582305.html

Dernbach, C. (2008, May 25). *Apple I and Apple II › Mac History (mac-history.net)*. Accessed January 15, 2022, from https://www.mac-history.net/computer-history/2008-05-25/apple-i-and-apple-ii

Downes, L., & Nunes, P. (2014). *Big bang disruption. Business survival in the age of constant innovation*. Portfolio Penguin.

Dummett, M. (2014). *Origins of analytical philosophy*. Bloomsburg Academic.

Firsts: The Mouse - Doug Engelbart Institute. Accessed January 15, 2022, from https://dougengelbart.org/content/view/162

Frege, G. (1986a). Der Gedanke. In G. Patzig (Ed.), *Logische Untersuchungen* (3rd ed.). Vandenhoeck u. Ruprecht.

Frege, G. (1986b). Funktion und Begriff. In G. Patzig (Ed.), *Funktion, Begriff und Bedeutung* (6th ed., p. 19f). Vandenhoeck u. Ruprecht.

Freiberger, P., & Swaine, M. (1984). *Fire in the valley. The making of the personal computer*. Osborne/McGraw-Hill.

Hackett, S. (2017, December 14). *The Lisa*. Accessed January 15, 2022, from https://www.macstories.net/mac/the-lisa/ [The Lisa – MacStories].

History | Demag200. Accessed January 15, 2022, from https://www.demag200.com/de/our-history

IBM Archives: IBM 5100 Portable Computer. Accessed January 15, 2022, from https://www.ibm.com/ibm/history/exhibits/pc/pc_2.html

Isaacson, W. *Steve Jobs*. Abacus, paperback edition 2015 (first published 2011).

Kent, S. L. (2001). *The ultimate history of video games. From Pong to Pokémon and beyond – The story behind the craze that touched our lives and changed the world*. Three Rivers Press.

Learn How Apple's First Smartphone Came to Be (thoughtco.com). Accessed January 15, 2022, from https://www.thoughtco.com/who-invented-the-iphone-1992004

Levitt, T. (1960, July–August). *Marketing myopia*. Harvard Business Review.

McDonald, M. (2017). *On marketing planning* (2nd ed.). KoganPage.

No one wants a drill. What they want is the hole. Accessed January 15, 2022, from https://quoteinvestigator.com/2019/03/23/drill/#note-22083-9. [No One Wants a Drill. What They Want Is the Hole – Quote Investigator].

Orenstein & Koppel – Wikipedia. Accessed January 15, 2022, from https://de.wikipedia.org/wiki/Orenstein_%26_Koppel

Osborne, A., & Dvorak, J. (1984). *Hypergrowth. The rise and fall of Osborne Computer Corporation*. Idthekkethan Publishing Corporation.

Rackham, N., & De Vincentis, J. (1999). *Rethinking the sales force. Redesigning selling to create and capture customer value*. McGraw-Hill Education.

Raynor, M. E. (2011). *The innovator's manifesto. Deliberate disruption for transformational growth*. Crown Business.

Raynor, M. E., & Ahmed, M. (2013). *The three rules. How exceptional companies think*. Portfolio/Penguin.

Revella, A. (2015). *Buyer personas. How to gain insight into your customer's expectations, align your marketing strategies, and win more business*. Wiley.

Revella, A. (2018). *Personas: Everything you've heard is wrong*. Accessed January 15, 2022, from https://vimeo.com/270746719 [Personas: Everything You've Heard Is Wrong on Vimeo].

Rise and Fall of Minicomputers – ETHW. Accessed January 15, 2022, from https://ethw.org/Rise_and_Fall_of_Minicomputers

Schumpeter, J. A. (1942). *Capitalism, socialism & democracy*. Routledge 2005.

Searle, J. R. (1998). *Mind, language and society. Philosophy in the real world* (p. 141). Basic Books.

Snyder, T., & Kearns, K. (2007). *Escaping the price-driven sale. How world class sellers create extraordinary profit*. McGraw-Hill Education.

Steve Jobs introduces iPhone in 2007 – YouTube. Accessed January 15, 2022, from https://www.youtube.com/watch?v=MnJzXM7a6o

Stone, B. (2013). *The everything store. Jeff Bezos and the age of Amazon*. Back Bay Books.

Webster, F. E., Jr., & Wind, Y. (1972). *Organizational buying behavior*. Prentice Hall.

Xerox Star 8010 Information System – The Interface Experience: Bard Graduate Center (interface-experience.org). Accessed January 15, 2022, from https://interface-experience.org/objects/xerox-star-8010-information-system/

Zambito, T. (2013, May 27). *What is a buyer persona? Why the original definition still matters to B2B*. Accessed January 15, 2022, from https://tonyzambito.com//buyer-persona-original-definition-matters/; [What is a Buyer Persona? Why the Original Definition Still Matters to B2B - Tony Zambito].

Zambito, T. *Buyer insights research and market research that create opportunities*. Accessed January 15, 2022, from https://tonyzambito.com/engage/buyer-research-and-buyer-insights-that-create-opportunities/

Zambito, T. *Improving sales effectiveness with buyer personas. #SalesChats Episode 10*. Accessed January 15, 2022, from https://salespop.net/sales-professionals/buyer-personas-for-effective-sales/ [#SalesChats: Buyer Personas, with Tony Zambito by Tony Zambito - SalesPOP!].

Roland Burkholz holds a doctorate in philosophy and a post-doctoral qualification in sociology and has worked, among other things, as a research assistant, independent management consultant, university professor on a substitute basis, and marketing consultant. Since 2021 (until September 30, 2022), he has been a professor of marketing at the Department of Business at the Hochschule für Medien, Kommunikation und Wirtschaft (HMKW) (University of Media, Communication and Business) at the Frankfurt/M. location.

Valid Customer Data: The Foundation for Omni-channel Marketing

Simone Braun and Andreas Heißler

1 Digital Transformation Sets Customer Data into Focus

The digital transformation continues unabated and is bringing about a profound change in the economy, society, and politics. Information and communication technologies are comprehensively penetrating and connecting all areas of the economy and our daily lives (BMWi, 2017). This, together with developments such as artificial intelligence, cloud computing, or the Internet of Things, provides new innovative value creation opportunities for companies. To that end, data forms the foundation. Data has become an essential asset for new and competitive services, customer access, business models, and innovations (BVDW, 2018; Azkan et al., 2019).

A study by the European Commission revealed a market of 400 billion euros for the European data economy in 2019 for the EU27 plus the United Kingdom—a growth of 7.6% compared with the previous year. According to estimates, the European data economy (EU27 excluding the U.K.) is expected to reach a size of between 432 billion euros and 827 billion euros by 2025 (European Union, 2020). However, companies in Germany have only just started to exploit the potential of data. There are major weaknesses in the areas of data management and data governance, including data quality (DEMAND, 2019).

Communicating via social media platforms, managing finances from a smartphone, and shopping online at any time and anywhere have become a matter of course for many people. Users expect customized services in return for their

S. Braun (✉)
Offenburg University of Applied Sciences, Offenburg, Germany
e-mail: simone.braun@hs-offenburg.de

A. Heißler
Uniserv GmbH, Pforzheim, Germany
e-mail: andreas.heissler@uniserv.com

U. Hannig, U. Seebacher (eds.), *Marketing and Sales Automation*, Management for Professionals, https://doi.org/10.1007/978-3-031-20040-3_10

personal data. Kreutzer & Land (2013, p.47) characterize today's expectations on the customer side with the catchwords "I, everything, immediately and everywhere," with the smartphone becoming the personal communication center.

The buying behavior of consumers has changed dramatically. Today, prospects search, evaluate, and decide in a different way. Numerous studies show that recommendations from family and private contacts, e.g., via social media, and increasingly also by influencers, influence consumers' purchasing decisions (Bognar et al., 2019; Gafni & Golan, 2016; SPLENDID RESEARCH, 2018; Greven Medien & GfK, 2019).

More than half of online shoppers use customer reviews as decision support before making a purchase (Bitkom, 2020). This change does not only affect the Business-to-Consumers (B2C) sector but also Business-to-Business (B2B) procurement; the decision-makers transfer their private consumption and communication behavior to their professional contexts (van Bommel et al., 2014). Research, opinion-forming, and supplier selection increasingly take place online. More than half of the B2B purchasing decision process is already completed before contact is made with a supplier under consideration for the first time (Maycock et al., 2012; Google, 2016).

Thanks to modern Big Data methods, it is now easier than ever to collect data. This is especially true for customer data. Today, every contact a person has with a company is meticulously and precisely recorded. Marketers can read from the data, for example, how their customers are responding to the currently running campaign.

Digital marketing professionals have high expectations in artificial intelligence (AI), machine learning, and predictive analytics. According to the Digital Dialog Insights study, nine out of ten professionals surveyed see AI as a promising technology, particularly for personalization (Eichsteller & Seitz, 2019). The first approaches are already in use, e.g., to analyze customer data and recognize patterns from which customer segments are formed, suitable content is generated, and automatically displayed (Gentsch, 2017; Kröger & Marx, 2020). AI-based processes increasingly gain popularity, e.g., in e-commerce for dynamic pricing, customer dialog via chatbots, or personalized product recommendations (Bernhard & Mühling, 2020). Thus, B2C marketing decision-makers see data and analytics as a top priority (Myler, 2017).

But correct predictions of the next best action based on an immeasurable amount of data require clarity about what data is needed and whether it is of sufficient quality. AI-based approaches can only bring the best benefits if the data they use for learning is of high quality (Stern et al., 2021; Stevens, 2019; Weber et al., 2021). Any algorithm that is trained on incorrect data will come to wrong conclusions (Kessler & Gomez, 2020). For example, if customer data was collected with a wrong salutation, an online shop would, in simplified terms, recognize an increased interest in women's handbags for men—with corresponding consequences for the display of automated recommendations. If the date of birth is incorrectly recorded, a 35-year-old customer, for example, would be sorted into the 60+ age group and addressed as a sprightly senior citizen. If the date of birth is missing altogether, the customer might not be addressed at all (Wolters, 2020). Although there are certain data pre-processing techniques for AI-based methods to deal with missing values (i.e., imputation methods), these can only be used if missing values are unbiased, and a sufficiently large amount of data is available (Berthold et al., 2020). However, if there is a systematic error, e.g., the birth dates of a certain customer group are missing, this can lead to distorted results of the learning algorithms.

Besides ensuring a high quality of customer and prospect data, all such available data needs to be consolidated and made available to the AI system. However, the quality and completeness of data is the major challenge in marketing—a fact that marketers are well aware of (Eichsteller & Seitz, 2019; Lünendonk, 2019; Myler, 2017; Data IQ, 2017). This is also confirmed by a study commissioned by Uniserv in spring 2020[1] among decision-makers on the status of customer data management in corporations (Uniserv, 2020). Almost 15% of the participants stated that a lack of data quality leads to difficulties in projects involving artificial intelligence. Accordingly, 82% of respondents indicated that consistently high data quality is important. Seventy percent see a 360° customer view as important. In a study commissioned by Uniserv from 2019,[2] 51% of respondents also stated that there is a close connection between data quality and the success of AI-related projects (Uniserv, 2019).

For this reason, after initial euphoria, disillusionment spreads because desired results are not achieved. To get a 360° customer view in marketing automation and to develop a personalized cross-channel marketing strategy, reliable master, transaction, and behavioral data is of utmost importance. Data quality is not only essential for the relevance of marketing campaigns, but also for customer satisfaction. The following chapter gives an overview and understanding of different types of customer data.

2 Customer Data

Customer data can be divided into fixed data—master data or core data—and variable data—transaction data. The latter being one of the most important data assets, especially for analysis.

Definition of Master Data According to ISO 8000, master data is defined as entities "which are independent and fundamental to an organization; which must be referenced in transactions in order to perform them" (ISO, 2016).

Master data describes a company's core operational objects, also known as business objects, such as customers, business partners, suppliers, products, or

[1] Cf. Customer Data Management 2020 Practice Study, Uniserv GmbH/YouGov, 204 executives from German companies, survey May 22 to June 02, 2020, anonymous online survey.

[2] Cf. Trend Study Customer Data Management 2019, Uniserv GmbH/Grohmann Business Consulting, 154 participants from German companies, survey December 2019 to April 2019, anonymous online survey.

personnel (Piro & Gebauer, 2021). Master data is fundamental for ongoing business operations and is (semi-)static, i.e., it usually changes rarely. Personal master data includes, for example:

- The full name
- Title
- Date and place of birth
- Gender
- Residential, shipping, billing addresses
- Contact information, such as phone numbers, mobile numbers, and e-mail addresses
- Personal identification numbers, such as social security, passport, driver's license, tax
- Login/account data, such as bank details, loyalty card, Twitter handle, LinkedIn address, or company-specific IDs

Master data can be supplemented by other sociodemographic attributes that give a more comprehensive picture of the customers. These attributes vary widely between companies and include, for example, information about:

- Family such as marital status or number of children
- Professional history and related attributes such as income, industry, qualification, or position
- Lifestyle such as living situation, type of vehicle or pets
- Hobbies such as memberships in clubs, gyms, or subscriptions
- Special categories of personal data[3] such as
  - Ethnic origin
  - Political opinions
  - Religious or ideological beliefs
  - Union affiliation
  - Genetic data
  - Biometric data for the unique identification of a natural person
  - Health data
  - Data on sex life or sexual orientation

Definition Transaction data Transaction data is transaction-oriented and provides information about activities and individual transactions of the core business objects of a company (Otto & Österle, 2016).

[3]These data are particularly data worthy of protection. Their processing is prohibited (Article 9 (1) of the General Data Protection Regulation). Exceptions are, for example, the explicit consent of the data subject (Art. 9 (2) (a)) or medical diagnostics (Art. 9 (2) (h)).

Transaction data is created repeatedly, changes frequently in operational processes, and contains references to master data. Examples include invoices, orders, deliveries, returns, etc., with information on the number, type, time, and price of purchased or returned items, order and payment data, and others.

In addition to master data and transaction data, behavioral or user interaction data play an important role for marketing, retail and e-commerce and should be distinguished as a further group at this point.

Definition of behavioral data Behavioral data is any data about the behavior of an individual person that is collected or derived, especially, for marketing purposes.

This can be information on communication and purchasing behavior, brand preferences, or product usage. This category also includes information about:

- Online activities and interactions with online content such as website visits, click streams, retention time, product views or social media engagement; collected, for example, by cookies, session IDs, etc.,
- E-mail communications, such as openings, click-throughs, or replies to messages, or
- Customer service interactions, such as details of inquiries, communication time, details recorded by service personnel, and
- End devices used, IP addresses, and geolocations.

Behavioral data enables companies to understand how individual customers interact with a company, whether through specific actions or reactions. For example, the recency, frequency, monetary value (RFM) analysis (Bult & Wansbeek, 1995) is used to score a customer's value. Applied on transaction data, this can disclose information about how recently and how often purchases are made and how much is spent, and, derived from this, the preferences of an individual.

From a structural point of view, customer data can be divided into three categories: structured, unstructured, or semi-structured. "Structured data is data for which structuring information—metadata—is available" (Piro & Gebauer, 2021, p. 146). These are, for example, the format and permitted values of a date of birth data attribute. On the other hand, data from text, audio, video, and sensors exist in a non-formalized structure and is, therefore, referred to as unstructured. Semi-structured data is a hybrid of structured and unstructured data. That is, certain parts may have structure, but overall, there is no specific and unique structure. For example, an e-mail contains structured information about who sent it and who received it. However, the content of the e-mail, as a written message, is largely unstructured. Other examples include voice and text input when interacting with a chatbot, which is also collected in an unstructured way.

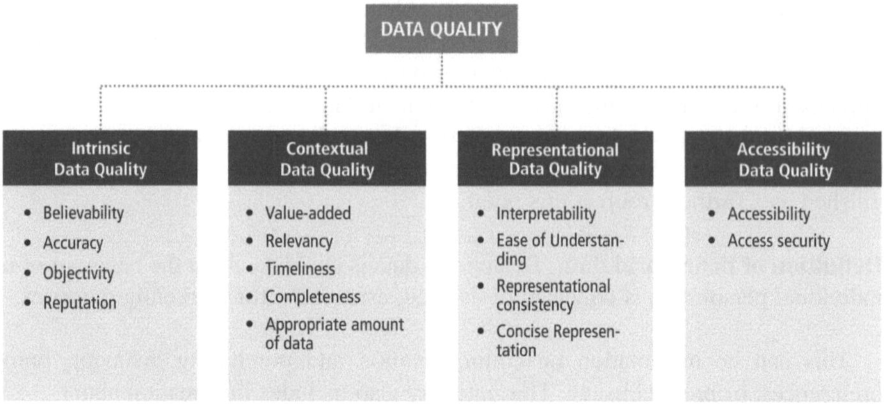

Fig. 1 Data quality dimensions according to Wang et al. (Source: Wang & Strong, 1996)

3 Data Quality Criteria

In order to optimize the value of corporate data, measures to improve data quality are of central importance in data management and data governance. However, despite numerous descriptions in the literature, there is no commonly accepted definition for the term "data quality".[4] Olson explains: "data has quality if it satisfies the requirements of its intended use. It lacks quality to the extent that it does not satisfy the requirement. [...] To satisfy the intended use, the data must be accurate, timely, relevant, complete, understood, and trusted." (Olson, 2003). Data quality is thus a metric that provides information about how well existing data can be applied in specific applications or business processes. That is, how well users of the data can apply the data for the respective applications' purpose ("fitness for use") (Wang & Strong, 1996). This fitness for use can change due to the varying needs of the users. Data quality thus depends on the time of observation and the available usage context (Weber & Klingenberg, 2020).

From a more technical perspective, data is of high quality if it is "error-free" and "meets specifications" (Fürber, 2016). Data quality is not a single characteristic, but multidimensional and context-dependent, i.e. "a set of data quality attributes that represent a single aspect or construct of data quality" (Wang & Strong, 1996, p. 6). Literature and practice provide a variety of different data quality dimensions (see, e.g., DAMA International, 2009; IQ International, 2017), with many approaches going back to Wang et al.'s dimensions published as early as 1992 (Wang et al., 1992). These were later condensed to 15 dimensions (Wang & Strong, 1996), which fall into four categories: intrinsic, contextual, representational, and accessibility (see Fig. 1).

[4]See, e.g., Ehrlinger et al. (2019), or Zulkiffli et al. (2019) for a discussion of terms.

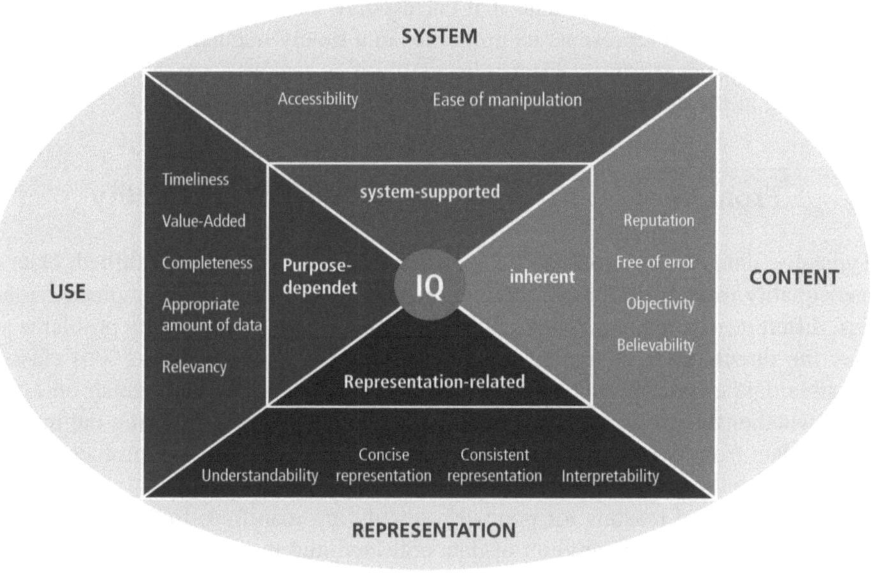

Fig. 2 15 dimensions of information quality according to DGIQ (Source: Rohweder et al., 2008)

Intrinsic data quality includes dimensions that deal with the quality of the data itself, such as accuracy or believability. Contextual data quality includes quality characteristics only observable when data is used. For example, relevancy can only be assessed in the context of the task at hand. The category of representational data quality includes dimensions related to the format and meaning of the data, such as representational consistency or ease of understanding. The category of accessibility considers dimensions related to the accessibility to data and access security.

Based on Wang et al. (1992) and a survey of IT users, the German Society for Information and Data Quality (DGIQ) developed a user-related definition (see Fig. 2), which categorizes data quality properties according to the (technical) system, the representation of the data, data use and content (Rohweder et al., 2008).

Since some of the definitions are fuzzy and, therefore, difficult to measure, dealing with overlapping criteria can be a costly problem. Consequently, practitioners often limit the assessment of data quality to a few selected dimensions—mostly focusing on the first four of the following dimensions:

- *Correctness/error-free:* Data is correct if it factually matches the attributes of the real-world reference object.
- *Completeness:* Data is complete if none of the necessary properties of the real-world object is missing.
- *Consistency:* Data is consistent if the attribute values of a data record are logically consistent and do not have logical inconsistencies with other data records of the same real-world object across different systems and sources.

- *Timeliness:* Data is up-to-date if it corresponds to the current state of the real-world object and represents its properties in a timely manner.
- *Availability/accessibility:* Data is available if it can be accessed by data users directly at the desired time.

4 From Content Accuracy to Mission-Critical Quality

Typically, data quality problems occur when requirements are not fulfilled. Data of poor quality implies duplicates, invalid or missing values. It is incomplete, erroneous, differently formatted, contradictory, and much more. Data quality problems are thus the direct result of unmet data requirements. Rahm and Do (2000) classify possible data errors by data source (see Fig. 3). The authors distinguish on a first level whether the problems occur within a single data source or during the integration of data from two or more sources. On a second level, whether problems affect the schema level or instance level.

The causes and reasons for poor data quality are manifold. In the age of social media and Big Data, the amount of data collected and the number of channels that can be used for collecting are constantly increasing. At the same time, data is often short-lived and changes quickly. Also, manual input often leads to incorrect or duplicate entries. For instance, when in a call center the name of the caller on the phone is misunderstood and thus re-entered in the system or not linked to existing customer information. In e-commerce, on average 19% of the customers do not remember their login data and therefore create a new account (Baymard Institute,

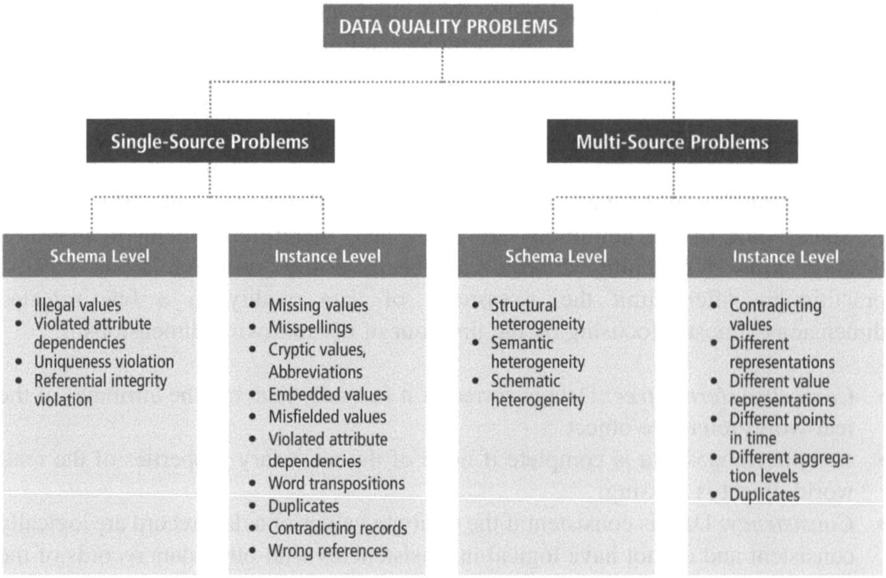

Fig. 3 Classification of data errors (Source: Rahm & Do, 2000)

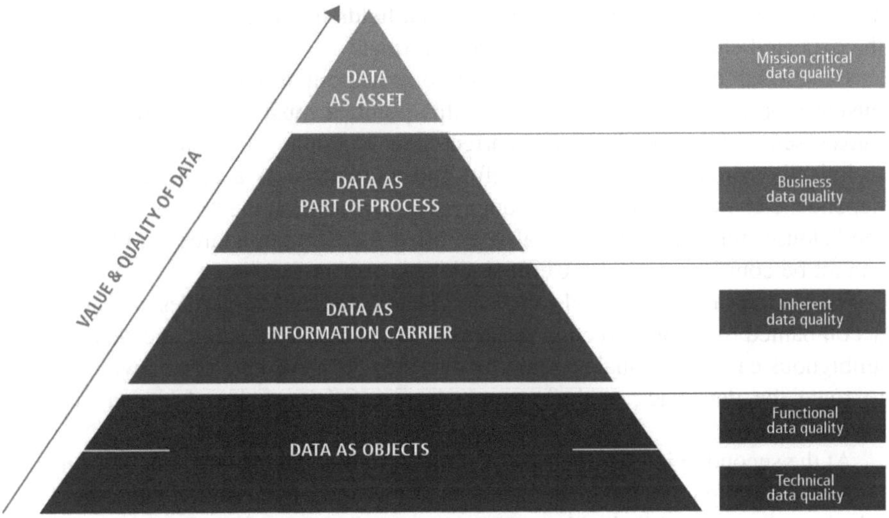

Fig. 4 Data quality and value pyramid (Source: Uniserv 2016a)

2017). When entering an address, users often select the country "Albania" because it appears at the top of the drop-down menu and can therefore be selected most quickly.

Within a company, a lack of communication between departments, too little awareness of data quality, difficulties in transferring data from other systems, a lack of technical support, or clear processes and guidelines for handling data can lead to poor data quality (Kraus, 2016). Rennhak (2006, p. 147) groups the different causes into the categories:

(a) Data entry—including incorrect, irrelevant, redundant, or even incomplete information
(b) Data transmission—technical errors or faulty data processing procedures during the transmission
(c) Data integration—flawed unification and consolidation processes
(d) Data storage—obsolete data attributes

Any of the above causes can hinder the success of a personalized cross-channel marketing strategy. When talking about data quality in relation to customer data, concepts such as address validation and duplicate cleansing, or matching come up quickly. But data quality is much more than just checking and, if necessary, correcting addresses or matching similar data records.

As the data quality and value pyramid illustrates, the quality of data can be ensured on four levels (see Fig. 4) and following up on all four will make data the ultimate asset for any company.

The first level is about technical and professional quality. Regarding technical quality, the data is viewed as a purely technical object without considering content.

Typical questions are, for example: Are data fields filled? Are the fields filled with the expected characters and in the correct format?

Functional quality is about content, but without looking at its relevance to business processes or applications. At this point, it must be ensured that the data makes sense, is admissible, and correct. For example, "February 31" would be technically correct but not meaningful and admissible as a date. A validation of dependencies must also be carried out at this stage, e.g., if the "Street" field is filled, the "House number" field must also be filled for German addresses. Otherwise, it cannot be considered a valid German address.

Validations at the first level can be automated, e.g., based on rules, and are ideally accompanied by error correction measures. These can be an automatic cleanup or, in ambiguous cases, a manual revision by data stewards. Another option would also be to route the data back to the person who created it so that they can make the correction.

At the second level, the focus is on validating that data is inherent. This includes address validation and duplicate cleansing. Only after it is ensured that a field for a telephone number is filled with correct characters in the specified format, a validation of the correctness of the telephone number is meaningful and necessary. Questions at this level can be: Is the address correct? Is the specified e-mail address accurate? Are there duplicates and how can they be merged?

Only inherent data can be a reliable basis for business processes. For example, article numbers are not just a piece of information in an order but must also be assigned to the right product. Only then, the order processing or shipping preparation can start.

To that end, rule-based validations of the content against specified references may be useful, which demand in-depth knowledge of business processes and business logic. Close collaboration with or direct involvement of the departments that have the required business know-how is indispensable for the successful development of such rules.

The eventual validation process for substantial correctness can largely be automated. Special validation processes, such as address validation or checking for duplicates, can be carried out in a similar way. For example, data about prospects transmitted from an internet portal can automatically be validated against existing data and, if necessary, marked as potential duplicates. Wrong data records that are neither automatically nor manually cleansed must be ejected so that they do not lead to errors, additional work, or inappropriate decisions in subsequent processes.

Once it is ensured that the data meets the basic quality requirements, the third level can address the question of their business utility. This step depends on the individual requirements of a company. Examples include finding out which products are in high demand in certain regions or which orders could not be fulfilled due to a lack of availability and what sales losses were associated with this. Are insights into cross-selling and up-selling potentials of interest? Legal requirements, such as age controls and embargoes, can also be monitored in this way. If the existing data cannot answer a company's questions, this may be due to incorrect or missing data.

In this case, the data on the prior levels must be revised in accordance with the requirements.

Finally, the fourth level contains data that supports mission-critical decisions. These are, for example, investments made based on predictive analytics. For this purpose, the data must meet the highest quality standards in order to minimize the risk of wrong decisions. If data meets these requirements, one can speak of data as an asset that creates added value for the company. Further steps on the way to an "all-encompassing data truth" in the context of customer data are, first, the "Golden Record" and, second, the so-called Golden Profile (Uniserv 2016b).

The Golden Record consolidates the existing information on a person, such as the postal address, e-mail addresses, telephone numbers, social login, and bank details, from various sources into a master data record. The Golden Profile enriches this record with transaction and interaction data. The Golden Profile is, therefore, composed of the following data:

- Customer behavior (e.g., orders, payment history, dwell time)
- Data describing the person (e.g., attributes, self-disclosures, demographics)
- Customer characteristics (e.g., opinions, preferences, needs, wants)
- Customer interactions (e.g., offers, results, context, clickstreams, notes)

With the Golden Profile, a complete, accurate, and up-to-date 360° view of customers is possible, enabling companies to make offers adapted to individual needs, as they are expected by customers in the digital age.

The Golden Profile can be viewed and further developed as the customer's digital twin (Braun et al., 2022). For example, detailed transaction data can be combined with interaction data from social media and usage or consumption data from Internet-of-Things-enabled products and devices to create a 360° view of customers that is expanded by many additional attributes (Hechler et al., 2020). This creates new opportunities to model customers more accurately in order to adapt products and services and improve the customer experience.

5 Data Quality Assessment

Ensuring a high quality of data so that it becomes a valuable asset is not a one-time process. As data changes over time, so does its quality. Making it a necessity that data quality is re-evaluated again and again. Deutsche Post Direkt GmbH (2021), for example, found in its "Address Study 2021" study that around 14 million relocations, 990,000 deaths, as well as 370,000 marriages and 150,000 divorces resulted in a large number of address and name changes every year. These changes, as well as changes in street names or changes in company names due to mergers and acquisitions, have to be maintained.

A company must know which data is collected, stored, and used by which systems for which purposes. In other words, data quality must be secured throughout the entire data life cycle. This requires specific organizational structures. This is

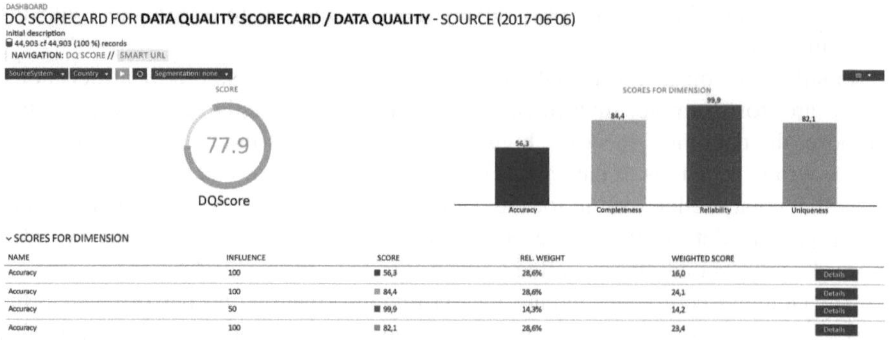

Fig. 5 Data Quality Scorecard of Uniserv GmbH

where data governance comes into play. It defines responsibilities, processes, standards, and metrics that ensure the efficient use of data as an economic asset and thus support the achievement of the company's strategic goals (Weber, 2012; DEMAND, 2019).

Data governance is a shared responsibility of corporate management, strategy, and specialist departments, such as customer service, sales, marketing, and IT. During its implementation, it is necessary to consolidate the knowledge of business processes and application systems distributed over the various corporate divisions. This goes hand in hand with a centralized definition and maintenance of business rules and a continuous monitoring of these rules during operations. In addition, companies need to keep a strategic and an operational perspective on data quality.

To ensure that the data precisely meets the required qualitative specifications, individual and application-specific business rules are defined that describe characteristics of data within the specific corporate contexts. These rules can then be used to validate entire data sets or individual data records. The rules thus operationalize the requirements that data users have on the data (Klingenberg & Weber, 2017).

Rules can address either one or more attributes of a data record. However, they can also refer to several data records across attributes and thus encompass the previously mentioned different levels of data quality. Rules are typically recorded for questions such as: "Are there empty data fields?" "Do the individual attributes, such as street, house number, postal code, and city, result in an accurate and existing address?" or: "Does each customer exist only once in the system?" If you want to check whether the existing customer data is sufficient for an e-mail marketing campaign, you need rules that evaluate whether the e-mail address field is maintained regularly.

For evaluating compliance with these rules, corresponding metrics are defined. These must be measured and monitored regularly. This is possible, for example, with a data quality (DQ) scorecard tool, as offered by various providers such as Uniserv GmbH (see Fig. 5). With a DQ scorecard, the entire data set can be validated against individual business rules. The validation results can be weighted and analyzed according to individual rules and are aggregated on different levels for a better overview and understanding. For example, custom metrics can be generated with the Uniserv DQ Scorecard by aggregation across a group of fields such as name and address elements to determine if these records are unique. The result is the Data Quality Score, which assesses the overall quality of all customer records across all defined rules.

During validation a distinction is made between rules that are "fulfilled," "not fulfilled," and "not applicable." For example, a syntax validation of an e-mail address would be "not applicable" if a previous rule shows that the field is not filled. Having such a "not applicable" status prevents multiple negative validations of a specific data attribute.

In addition, rules can be combined into rule groups and aggregated into hierarchy levels for these, for which a single data quality score can be calculated. For example, all rules related to address data are assigned to an "Address" group and all rules related to personal customer data are assigned to the "Personal data" group.

Drill-down functionality at group and field (i.e., attribute) level allows to see exactly which rules or entities have led to a lower data quality score—in other words, it shows where problems and weak points are hidden. Based on this knowledge, companies can define targeted measures to optimize data quality. By comparing different data quality scores, it is possible to evaluate which measures have led to an improvement in data quality. A comparison is also possible across different data sources, applications, and business areas.

6 Ensure Data Quality with the Help of the DQ Scorecard: A Practical Example

The DQ Scorecard allows data stewards to evaluate data quality in an easy and straightforward way, as presented in the following example.

A company sells household products worldwide. Direct access to customers is of particular importance. The products are sold via a large network of independent consultants. In addition, selected products are offered online and in stores. However, regardless of the sales channel, the product consultant remains the customer's first point of contact.

The subsidiaries in the individual countries operate largely independently. As a result, a complex system and process landscape that provides customer data has evolved over the years. Each country subsidiary utilizes its own databases and applications adapted to country-specific needs. In such a heterogeneous environment, professional customer data management is crucial to success.

For example, marketing campaigns must be optimally tailored to the needs of the customer base. A 360° customer view is recommended for effective customer loyalty measures. In order to create a golden customer profile, clarity about possible data quality deficiencies must be achieved. In our scenario, a heterogeneous system landscape might additionally complicate a cross-national overview of customer master data quality.

The DQ Scorecard from Uniserv is a solution that determines the quality of the customer master data for marketing measures across a complex system and process landscape. The first step is to create a uniform global view of the data from the various countries. This involves defining a uniform data structure with predefined fields so that the data landscape can be transformed into one consistent data format. This is followed by the definition of specific business rules that are used to validate the data records. This rule-based validation process forms the main component of the solution. The result is the so-called Data Quality Score. The Data Quality Score makes symptoms of bad data visible and measurable. Part of the definition is also how intermediate results are combined into the overall score, and with what weighting. Finally, the resulting set of rules is applied to the "global view" of all customer master data of all countries. The outcome of the rule check can be tracked on a browser-based dashboard. This gives decision-makers at the company the opportunity to efficiently compare and analyze the individual data quality scores.

In this way, the marketing department gains an overview of the current, overarching status quo of customer data quality across all subsidiaries and countries. Targeted measures to improve quality can be initiated, thus creating the prerequisite for the formation of Golden Profiles. With the help of the DQ Scorecard, employees in each country-specific organization can identify optimization potential, monitor the effectiveness of data quality measures, and initiate further improvement measures. Awareness about data and its quality can thus be significantly increased and, in turn, the data quality score permanently optimized. Marketing campaigns can be planned more effectively, as it is clearly visible whether the customer master data meets the respective requirements of the marketing campaign or not.

7 Summary

Together with digital transformation also customer data is moving into the focus of companies. As a result, data is becoming the number one competitive factor. Establishing good data practices requires not only long-term decisions by upper management but also daily decisions at the middle and lower levels of a company. The four-level pyramid shows how important adequate data quality is to utilize data as a valuable asset. If the data quality is inappropriate, corporate management decisions will be based on the results of incorrect data analysis and the digital transformation will be doomed to failure.

Akshay Tandon, Vice President and Head of Strategy and Analytics at LendingTree Inc., an American online financial services provider, also confirms the central importance of high-quality customer data in his statement (Burns, 2017): "It's like when you see a skyscraper: You're impressed by the height, but nobody is impressed by the foundation. But make no mistake, it's important. You have to have good data management to take advantage of AI."

Consequently, successful planning of future marketing and sales campaigns with the help of machine learning and predictive analytics is only possible if a 360° view of customers can be obtained. The "Golden Profile" integrates previously distributed customer data into such a 360° customer view and turns data into a valuable asset for any company.

Since the quality of the data can change over time, it should be measured continuously. A data quality scorecard clearly shows the status of data quality and where potential for optimization is hidden. Finally, a data quality score reveals the actual value of data for companies.

References

Azkan, C., et al. (2019). *Readiness Data Economy. Bereitschaft der deutschen Unternehmen für die Teilhabe an der Datenwirtschaft*. IW-Gutachten.

Baymard Institute. (2017). *Checkout optimization and reducing abandonments: 6 Ways to retain shoppers from 'add to cart' to order completion*. https://pages.amazonpayments.com/rs/846-RQB-314/images/Baymard%20Report%20-%20US.pdf

Bernhard, M., & Mühling, T. (2020). *Verantwortungsvolle KI im E-Commerce: Eine kurze Einführung in Verfahren der Künstlichen Intelligenz in der Webshop-Personalisierung*. Springer-Gabler.

Berthold, M. R., Borgelt, C., Höppner, F., Klawonn, F., & Rosaria, S. (2020). Data preparation. In *Guide to intelligent data science. Texts in computer science* (pp. 127–156). Springer.

Bognar, Z., Puljic, N., & Kadezabek, D. (2019). *Impact of influencer marketing on consumer behaviour*. Proceedings of the 42nd International Scientific Conference on Economic and Social Development, London, June 12–13, 2019, pp. 301–309. Varazdin Development and Entrepreneurship Agency (VADEA).

Bitkom. (2020, Juli). *E-Commerce und stationärer Handel: So digital shoppen die Deutschen. Ein Bitkom-Studienbericht*.

BMWi. (2017). *Weißbuch Digitale Plattformen*. Accessed March 20, 2017, from https://www.bmwi.de/Redaktion/DE/Publikationen/Digitale-Welt/weissbuch-digitale-plattformen.html

Braun, S., Follwarczny, D., & Heißler, A. (2022). Neue Kanäle – neue Daten: Die veränderte Rolle von Kundendaten im Handel. In T. Breyer-Mayländer, C. Zerres, A. Müller, & K. Rahnenführer (Eds.), *Die Corona-Transformation – Krisenmanagement und Zukunftsperspektiven in Wirtschaft, Kultur und Bildung* (pp. 133–159). Springer-Gabler.

Bult, J. R., & Wansbeek, T. J. (1995). Optimal selection for direct mail. *Marketing Science, 14*(4), 378–394.

BVDW – Bundesverband Digitale Wirtschaft. (2018). *Data economy*. Datenwertschöpfung und Qualität von Daten.

Burns, E. (2017). *Search Business Analytics: Analytics VP: AI projects must be built on a good data foundation*. http://searchbusinessanalytics.techtarget.com/feature/Analytics-VP-AI-projects-mustbe-built-on-a-good-data-foundation

DAMA International. (2009). *The DAMA Guide to the Data Management Body of Knowledge (DAMADMBOKGuide)*. Technics Publications.

Data IQ. (2017). *Royal Mail: 6 % Solution = How better customer data drives Marketing performance and business growth*. https://www.royalmail.com/sites/default/files/RMDS-Research-Report-2017-Six-per-cent-solution.pdf

DEMAND. (2019). *Data Economy. Status quo der deutschen Wirtschaft & Handlungsfelder in der Data Economy*. https://www.demand-projekt.de/

Deutsche Post Direkt. (2021). *Adress-Studie 2021. Untersuchung zur Qualität von Kundenadressen in Deutschland*. https://www.deutschepost.de/content/dam/dpag/images/D_d/DDP/Downloads/studien/dp-adress-studie-2021.pdf

Eichsteller, H., & Seitz, J. (2019). *Studie Digital Dialog Insights 2019*. Bundesanzeiger Verlag.

Ehrlinger, L., Rusz, E., & Wöß, W. (2019). *A survey of data quality measurement and monitoring tools*. CoRR abs/1907.08138, https://arxiv.org/abs/1907.08138

European Union. (2020). *The European data market monitoring tool: Key facts & figures, first policy conclusions, data landscape and quantified stories*. D2.9 Final Study Report. Publications Office of the European Union.

Fürber, C. (2016). *Data quality management with semantic technologies*. Springer.

Gafni, R., & Golan, O. T. (2016). The influence of negative consumer reviews in social networks. *Online Journal of Applied Knowledge Management, 4*(2), 44–58.

Gentsch, P. (2017). *Künstliche Intelligenz für Sales, Marketing und Service. Mit AI und Bots zu einem Algorithmic Business – Konzepte, Technologien und Best Practices*. Springer Fachmedien.

Google. (2016). *The B2B search landscape: Targeting the stages of your buyer journey to drive revenue*. Big Footprint Google Event, Oktober 2016. https://www.bigfootprintdigital.com/wpcontent/uploads/2016/10/Big-Footprint-Google-Event-FINAL-DECK.pdf

Greven Medien & GfK. (2019). *GfK-Online-Umfrage*. https://www.greven.de/bewertungen-gfk

Hechler, E., Oberhofer, M., & Schaeck, T. (2020). Applying AI to master data management. In *Deploying AI in the enterprise*. Apress. https://doi.org/10.1007/978-1-4842-6206-1_9

ISO International Organization for Standardization. (2016). *ISO 8000-100:2016 Data quality – Part 100: Master data: Exchange of characteristic data: Overview*. Standard. https://www.iso.org/standard/62392.html

IQ International. (2017). *Fundamentals of IQ*. International Association for Information and Data Quality. https://www.iqint.org/knowledge/fundamentals/

Kessler, R., & Gómez, J. M. (2020). Implikationen von Machine Learning auf das Datenmanagement in Unternehmen. *HMD Praxis der Wirtschaftsinformatik, 57*, 89–105.

Klingenberg, C., & Weber, K. (2017). Kundendatenqualität im Zeitalter der digitalen Transformation. In *IT-Governance. Fachzeitschrift des ISACA Germany Chapter e.V.* (Vol. 26, pp. 7–13).

Kraus, C. (2016). *Warum ein Online-Shop gute Datenqualität braucht*. COMPUTERWOCHE. Accessed January 02, 2016, from https://www.computerwoche.de/a/warum-ein-online-shop-gute-datenqualitaet-braucht,3217296

Kreutzer, R., & Land, K.-H. (2013). *Digitaler Darwinismus*. Springer.

Kröger, J., & Marx, S. (2020). *Marketing im Wandel. In Agile Marketing* (pp. 63–81). Springer Gabler.

Lünendonk, J. (2019). *Lünendonk-Studie 2019 – Künstliche Intelligenz*. Lünendonk & Hossenfelder GmbH in Zusammenarbeit mit GINKO Consulting Management.

Maycock, M., Spenner, P., Hamshar, R., & West, S. (2012). *Marketing leadership council: The digital evolution in B2B marketing*. http://www.thebluecollarmarketer.com/wp-content/uploads/2015/10/the-digital-evolution-in-b2b-marketing_research-studies.pdf

Myler, L. (2017). *Forbes: Better data quality equals higher marketing ROI*. Accessed July 12, 2017, from https://www.forbes.com/sites/larrymyler/2017/07/12/better-data-quality-equals-higher-marketingroi/#48e520b7b68d

Olson, J. (2003). *Data quality: The accuracy dimension*. Morgan Kaufmann; Elsevier Science.

Otto, B., & Österle, H. (2016). *Corporate Data Quality. Voraussetzung erfolgreicher Geschäftsmodelle*. Springer-Gabler.

Piro, A., & Gebauer, M. (2021). Definition von Datenarten zur konsistenten Kommunikation im Unternehmen. In K. Hildebrand, M. Gebauer, & M. Mielke (Eds.), *Daten- und Informationsqualität*. Springer Vieweg. https://doi.org/10.1007/978-3-658-30991-6_8

Rahm, E., & Do, H.-H. (2000). Data cleaning: Problems and current approaches. *IEEE Data Engineering Bulletin, 23*(4), 3–13.

Rennhak, C. (2006). *Herausforderung Kundenbindung*. Gabler Edition Wissenschaft. Springer-Verlag.

Rohweder, J., Kasten, G., Malzahn, D., Piro, A., & Schmid, J. (2008). Informationsqualität – Definitionen, Dimensionen und Begriffe. In K. Hildebrand, M. Gebauer, H. Hinrichs, & M. Mielke (Eds.), *Daten- und Informationsqualität*. Vieweg+Teubner Verlag.

SPLENDID RESEARCH. (2018). *Influencer: Einfluss auf die Kaufwahrscheinlichkeit*. Hamburg, Juli 2019. https://www.splendid-research.com/studie-influencer.html

Stern, P., Büllesfeld, E., & Bierkandt, J. (2021, March). *KI KI im Kundendatenmanagement – Einblicke in Anwendungsmöglichkeiten*. http://publica.fraunhofer.de/dokumente/N-630689.html

Stevens, J. (2019). Datenqualität bei algorithmischen Entscheidungen. In K. David, K. Geihs, M. Lange, & G. Stumme (Eds.), *INFORMATIK 2019: 50 Jahre Gesellschaft für Informatik* (pp. 367–380). Informatik für Gesellschaft.

Uniserv GmbH. (2016a). *Data Quality ist mehr als Adressvalidierung*. White Paper.

Uniserv GmbH. (2016b). *Digitale Transformation needs Kundendatenmanagement*. White Paper.

Uniserv GmbH. (2019). *Trendstudie Customer Data Management 2019*. Accessed June 06, 2019, from https://www.uniserv.com/unternehmen/blog/detail/article/ergebnisse-der-trendstudie-kundendatenmanagement-2019/

Uniserv GmbH. (2020). *Praxisstudie Customer Data Management 2020*. Accessed July 29, 2020, from https://www.uniserv.com/unternehmen/blog/detail/article/management-von-geschaeftspartnerdaten-nicht-oberste-prioritaet-bei-unternehmen/

van Bommel, E., Edelman, D., & Ungerman, K. (2014). *Digitizing the consumer decision journey*. McKinsey. http://www.mckinsey.com/business-functions/marketingandsales/our-insights/digitizing-theconsumer-decision-journey

Wang, R. Y., & Strong, D. M. (1996). Beyond accuracy: What data quality means to data consumers. *Journal of Management Information Systems, 12*(4), 5–33.

Wang, R., Reddy, M., & Kon, H. (1992). *Toward quality data: An attribute-based approach*. Massachusetts Institute of Technology (MIT). http://web.mit.edu/smadnick/www/wp2/1993-04-SWP%233515.pdf

Weber, K. (2012). Data Governance – Organisation des Stammdatenmanagements. *IT-Governance, 6*(13), 3–8.

Weber, K., & Klingenberg, C. (2020). *Data Governance*. Carl Hanser Verlag GmbH & Co. KG.

Weber, K., Otto, B., & Lis, D. (2021). Data governance. In K. Hildebrand, M. Gebauer, & M. Mielke (Eds.), *Daten- und Informationsqualität* (pp. 271–291). Springer-Gabler.

Wolters, H. M. (2020). Qualität von Kundendaten – Ansätze zur Analyse und Verbesserung als Basis für effiziente Marketingentscheidungen. In S. Boßow-Thies, C. Hofmann-Stölting, & H. Jochims (Eds.), *Data-driven marketing* (pp. 29–41). Springer-Gabler.

Zulkiffli, P. N. I. N., Akhir, E. A. P., Aziz, N., & Cox, K. (2019). The development of data quality metrics using thematic analysis. *International Journal of Innovative Technology and Exploring Engineering (IJITEE), 8*, 304–310.

Simone Braun is Professor of E-Commerce at Offenburg University of Applied Sciences. She teaches and researches in the field of omni-channel commerce, customer data management, and AI in retail and e-commerce. She has many years of experience in the field of innovation development with a special focus on customer data.

Andreas Heißler has worked for Uniserv GmbH, Pforzheim, for more than 20 years. His tasks in communications include press and public relations, content, lead management, and data protection. He writes about the importance of data as a valuable asset for companies in various industries, in the context of digital transformation and artificial intelligence.

Account-Based Marketing: Much More Than a New Automation Trend

Torsten Herrmann

1 Misconceptions About Account-Based Marketing

Account-based marketing is currently one of the most discussed online marketing trends. In the USA in particular, the approach has been considered "red hot" for about 5 years, i.e., a trendy topic to which experts are paying a great deal of attention online. But in Germany, too, more and more companies are taking an interest in this highly individualized marketing approach, which has given new impetus to the old dream of "1:1 marketing" (Peppers & Rodgers, 1993).

Although account-based marketing as a term has been heard for more than 10 years and the concept per se is not completely revolutionary—in sales, for example, the focus on individual customers in the context of key account sales has been known since the late 1970s (Kemna, 1979) and key account marketing is also in circulation as a term (Sidow, 2014)—opinions about this approach still differ in some respects. This can be seen in the fact that there is still no clear, universally applicable definition for ABM (Callahan, 2016). And it is also evident in the different spellings, which use different combinations of upper and lower case letters and hyphens (Baketaric, 2017).

Originally, the idea behind ABM was to treat each customer completely individually. This is shown, for example, by the early definition of the market analysis company ITSMA (Information Technology Services Marketing Association), which was the first to use the term account-based marketing in 2004 (ITSMA, 2018): "treating individual accounts as markets in their own right" (Burgess, 2017). In other words, *treating* individual accounts (customers) as markets in their own right.

Another definition comes from ABM software provider Engagio: "Account Based Marketing is a strategic approach that coordinates personalized marketing

T. Herrmann (✉)
chain relations, Frankfurt, Germany
e-mail: therrmann@chainrelations.de

U. Hannig, U. Seebacher (eds.), *Marketing and Sales Automation*, Management for Professionals, https://doi.org/10.1007/978-3-031-20040-3_11

and sales efforts to open doors and deepen engagement at specific accounts." Translated: *Account-based marketing is a strategic approach that coordinates personalized marketing and sales efforts to open doors and deepen engagement with defined accounts* (Engagio, 2018b, p. 9).

This second definition best illustrates the current direction of the approach. It clarifies which elements are characteristic of account-based marketing. According to this, ABM:

- *Strategic*, as it does not describe a single measure, but always includes a reorientation of the provider in marketing and sales.
- *Personalized*, because content and messages are targeted to the customer company (i.e., individual accounts) and its decision-makers.
- *Comprehensive*, as it involves both marketing and sales, both of which work closely together on winning the customer or order.
- *Goal-oriented* with regard to new customers, but also to the expansion of existing customers.

Basically, ABM is about the synchronization of marketing and sales in the sense of a marketing-and-sales alignment, about new access to defined accounts, and about a stronger dialog with all parties involved in a decision within a target company. A metaphor used by Engagio illustrates the approach: inbound marketing is like fishing with a trawl net, account-based marketing like fishing with a harpoon (Pakanati, 2018).

The fishing metaphor makes it clear: In contrast to inbound marketing, which exhibits characteristics of mass marketing with correspondingly large scatter losses, account-based marketing proceeds in a much more targeted manner. Software tools support this focused approach based on IP address ranges. These software systems recognize the visitor to a website as an employee of a target customer. This information is the trigger for subsequent actions.

In addition to these conceptual ambiguities, there are still a number of misconceptions circulating about account-based marketing. The most prominent of these have been summarized by Bev Burgess and Dave Munn in their book "A Practitioner's Guide to Account-Based Marketing" (2017) (Fig. 1):

One misconception that Burgess and Munn do not mention in their presentation concerns the role of software solutions and automated processes in account-based marketing (Goren, 2018). For example, consulting practice shows that companies think of ABM as a kind of "automated 1:1 marketing." They have had positive experiences with automation in inbound marketing and therefore assume that they can use ABM to set up a comparable, largely automated, individual marketing program.

To put it exaggeratedly, software systems specialized in ABM do the lion's share of the work for some potential users that has to be done within the scope of their programs. In their ABM programs, companies focus directly on implementation (even in the selection of service providers) without first properly handling strategy development. The result is half-baked ABM programs with which companies do not

Missverständnis	Realität
ABM ist ein eigenständiges Marketing-Programm, das von anderen Programmen abzugrenzen ist.	ABM ist eine kundengetriebene Marketing-Methode, die jede Marketing- und Vertriebs-Strategie einsetzt, die dazu geeignet ist, dem Kunden das zu geben, was er sich wünscht und braucht.
ABM ist lediglich eine andere Form der Account-Planung und hat für Vertriebs-Teams daher doppelte Arbeit zur Folge.	ABM ist kein Ersatz für bestehende Strategien, sondern baut auf einer guten Account-Planung auf, um machbare Marketing- und Vertriebs-Strategien zu kreieren.
ABM kann auch ohne Customer Intelligence erfolgreich durchgeführt werden.	Customer Intelligence ist das, was ABM zu einem account-basierten Ansatz macht. Ohne Customer Intelligence wäre es nur eine andere Form von "spray and pray"-Marketing.
ABM ist für jeden großen Ziel-Account passend.	ABM ist ein Investment und dementsprechend nur für Accounts geeignet, die einen angemessenen ROI liefern können.
ABM ist eine reine Marketing-Angelegenheit.	ABM muss Hand in Hand mit dem Vertrieb durchgeführt werden - stellen Sie es sich als entscheidenden Wegbereiter für Ihren Vertrieb vor.
ABM ersetzt Ihren gegenwärtigen Vertriebsansatz und den bisher genutzten Account-Planning-Prozess.	ABM ergänzt Ihr derzeitiges Vertriebsmodell, macht Account-Planung zur Realität, als gemeinsames, zu bearbeitendes Dokument.

Fig. 1 Misconceptions about account-based marketing (after Burgess/Munn)

achieve their goals as desired. This is because, as in key account management, it is not only a matter of optimally serving the target customers but always also of the strategic further development of the business relationship (Sidow, 2014, p. 12).

For this reason, this article focuses on the question of how much can actually be automated in account-based marketing with the help of software support—and how complex this approach really is in practice. The focus is on the most important fields of application in ABM and the opportunities that arise there through the use of software such as marketing automation systems.

2 Automation Within the Scope of the Main ABM Application Areas

However, the number of processes that can be automated in account-based marketing does not depend solely on the choice of software. More important is the question of the scope of the ABM program and how many accounts are to be addressed and processed. Various segmentation levels are conceivable here. In "The three types of account-based marketing" (2017), Bev Burgess, for example, advocates a threefold division (Fig. 2):

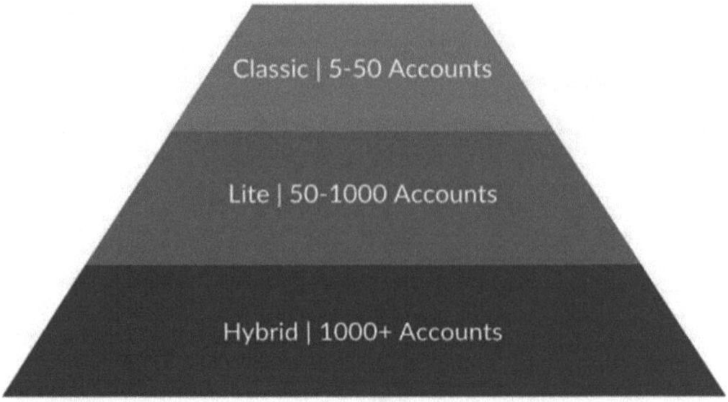

Fig. 2 Three types of account-based marketing

- Classic: 5–50 accounts
- Lite: 50–1000 accounts
- Hybrid: 1000 accounts and more

Another, equally appropriate, five-level structuring is provided by Simon Hall (Hall, 2017, p. 237):

- Strategic ABM—corresponds to the Classic level
- Segment-based ABM—defined segments, e.g., medium-sized companies segmented according to specific criteria
- Vertical account ABM—industry-oriented segmentation
- Campaign-based ABM—campaign-based processing of defined, researched accounts
- Product/solution ABM—based on previous purchasing behavior

The Classic stage corresponds to the original definition of ITSMA and largely to 1:1 marketing, actually a 25-year-old concept developed by Don Peppers and Martha Rodgers in "The One to One Future" back in 1993. With the appropriate software, it is actually feasible today in business-to-business relationships due to automation. But it goes without saying that such highly individualized marketing is only profitable for the most important customers. It is important to remember that setting up an individual marketing program with inbound and outbound measures, automated processes, and account-related content offers requires far more resources than marketing programs known to date.

Therefore, the choice of the appropriate ABM level is always at the beginning of any strategy development. This choice is directly related to the possible degree of automation as well as the effort required for each account (Burgess, 2017).

In the Classic variant, users develop a marketing plan for each individual customer. They must first fully understand this customer and ideally create individual buyer personas for each of them (Miller, 2016) or gather all available information in the sense of customer intelligence. Based on this, users then consider how they can address this individual customer individually, where they can meet him, what language he speaks, what arguments he responds to, etc.

In the Classic variant, the possibilities for automation are most limited. After all, this variant only targets a very limited number of top accounts, for which highly individualized content, landing pages, and dynamic websites have to be produced, among other things. In addition, there are e-mail campaigns and retargeting processes tailored to individual accounts.

For many, it may be unimaginable to invest so much effort in a single customer. But if this customer is so strategically important, if it brings in so much revenue and promises a good contribution margin, then the effort can be worthwhile.

This focus on a few target customers is excessive for many ABM users. For this reason, some companies prefer to use the ABM Lite and ABM Hybrid levels (also known as Programmatic, Burgess, 2017). Because here it is no longer about individual top accounts, but much more about target customer segments. For example, all banks in Germany or the largest industrial companies with production sites in Germany. In the hybrid stage, even coarser segmentations are conceivable: For example, all companies in Germany in five selected industries.

In the Lite and Hybrid levels, users no longer focus their marketing on individual target customers, but on similar companies that have certain things in common. For example, their industry affiliation or company size. The number of account segments at each level varies greatly: while in ABM Classic often 20–50 individual accounts are handled individually, at the Lite level these are up to 1000 accounts and at the Hybrid level sometimes 5–10 target segments with several thousand accounts, which are handled with more generalized ABM measures. Therefore, the effort for the users per account generally decreases with each level—because this effort increases strongly the fewer target accounts, but more individually, are to be served. The same applies to the opportunities that arise from the use of software in the area of automation.

Here is an exemplary selection:

- Automation of marketing processes
- Retargeting
- Website dynamization

Let us take a look at these three areas and consider the importance of automation with the help of software in each case.

2.1 Automation of Marketing Processes

In contrast to inbound marketing, ABM does not focus on individual persons who have previously registered, but on target accounts, i.e., all employees of a company.

Among other things, this opens up new possibilities in the field of marketing automation.

Let us assume that an employee of a target customer comes to the website of a consultancy that does account-based marketing and looks at some subpages on the services of this provider. Their ABM software now checks the visitor and scans their database to see if a contact from this company is already known. For example, it finds a project manager whose contact details are known from a past collaboration.

Let us further assume that the consultancy has developed a mechanism as follows: If an employee of an existing customer X comes to the website and looks at five predefined subpages, then the previous contact (in this scenario the project manager) receives a prepared e-mail.

Since all that is known at this point is that the visitor has used an IP address from the account pool, it is unclear whether this is the project manager. Nevertheless, as part of an automated process, the system sends her (and possibly all other known people in the company) an e-mail alerting her to offers that match what she—or possibly one of her colleagues—has just viewed on the website.

What the project manager from the example most likely does not know: she did not receive the e-mail with the offer notice without a reason. Instead, the message is part of an automated process. It was set in motion because the predefined mechanism is set up for the fact that this offer (or the challenge it is suitable for solving) is currently being discussed in the account company with a certain probability. However, for the consultancy as ABM user, it is unknown in which part of the company these discussions are taking place.

This approach circumvents a challenge of inbound marketing: More and more companies are engaging in inbound marketing and their own content is competing with more and more content on provider and media sites. Mark Schaefer therefore warned of a "content shock" as early as 2014 in his article "Content Shock: Why content marketing is not a sustainable strategy" (Schaefer, 2018). This must be having an impact on conversion rates for some providers.

2.2 Retargeting

Another important area of application in account-based marketing is retargeting. Traditionally, it works according to a simple principle that everyone knows all too well as a B2C customer: Internet users look at a product in an online store and are thus set a cookie. They then go to the website of their preferred news portal and see an ad there for the product they were just looking at. This often happens several days or even weeks after the person has become interested in a particular topic or product.

In B2B marketing, companies also rely on this approach. But with an ABM solution, they can go one step further. With appropriate software solutions, retargeting can be controlled throughout the company (Vajre, 2016). This means that if the system recognizes from the IP address that an employee of a company known to him has visited a product page, he is not the only one to see the corresponding ads. The same applies to his colleagues—although they can hardly know that the advertising is not being displayed to them without reason.

The big advantage of this approach is obvious. As in the case of marketing process automation, ABM in retargeting can be used to target an entire decision-making body with the help of similar ads. Both the managing director, who will later sign the contract, and the buyer (and all other people involved in the purchase decision) already get an impression of the name and the qualities of the product and the supplier.

In the IT industry, there is an old sales saying: "So far, no one has been fired for buying from IBM or SAP." Account-based marketing in retargeting works precisely against this effect. Because ABM can also do that: work on decision-making bodies and influence their buying decisions.

2.3 Web Page Dynamization

The greatest potential that companies can exploit with the help of automation in account-based marketing concerns the website of user companies. The following example uses the simplified structure of a website: In the navigation bar on the homepage, visitors will find the categories "Products," "Services," and "Customers," each of which is divided into individual sub-items (Fig. 3).

Suppose an employee of a truck manufacturer comes to the site of a quality management software provider. What she sees there is rather unspecific for most pages structured in this way. What she reads are relatively short, general statements about the company, its philosophy, and its products, services, focus, and experience. This may be sufficient for a first, rough impression—but if the visitor wants to find

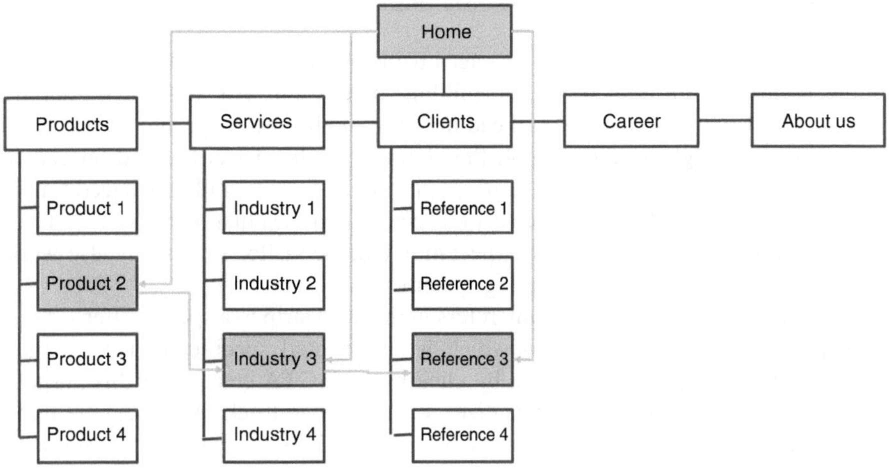

Fig. 3 Exemplary representation of a web page structure

out whether this provider has expertise in the truck sector, she has to click through the subpages and look for text passages that fit her industry.

Even if the software provider has a reference from this industry, it is by no means certain that her visitor will find this reference easily and therefore gain a good impression of the company. Then there is a high probability that she will continue looking for another provider. Someone who more skillfully conveys having experience with the challenges of her industry and, in the best case, has already worked with other companies from the same industry.

This is where account-based marketing opens up great potential. With the help of appropriate software, different versions of a home page can be configured, each of which is geared to a specific segment of target accounts or even a single company. If the ABM software recognizes which of these segments a visitor belongs to on the basis of his or her IP address, the appropriate version of the start page appears on his or her monitor. This dynamization thus always foregrounds the content that is most relevant to an identified contact.

In the aforementioned scenario, the software provider has defined truck manufacturers among its target accounts as part of its ABM program. Therefore, he has created a dynamic web page that aims to highlight industry expertise in vehicle manufacturing in text and images. In this way, the provider shortens the path of his visitor to the information that is of most interest to her. This is, for example, a product description focusing on the requirements of a vehicle manufacturer or a case study describing the cooperation with another truck manufacturer. So the visitor can easily skip the intermediate level about products, services, and customers. As a result, she gets a clear picture of the provider much faster and consequently also starts to build up a relationship of trust with him more quickly.

Suppose the software provider's home page includes a modern striped look, as simplified in Fig. 4. Normally, there would be general texts about each of these web page areas, perhaps an industry-independent image with people, or in the references, a selection of logos, usually from the very largest customers. As in the example text on the left side of Fig. 4:

When users dynamize their web pages using ABM software, they are basically doing nothing more than replacing building blocks 1:1. An image with another image, a text with another text, a heading with another heading, and so on. In the example on the right side of Fig. 4, the claim in the header is focused on general industry requirements. Of course, a more appropriate image would be placed for this in practice. The text design of the second section assumes that truck manufacturers usually work with SAP—with the expectation that the visitor's company also works with this enterprise resource planning system.

To do this, the software company refers in the third strip to a special offer—e.g., a whitepaper, a video, or e-book—which it has created specifically for the truck industry and which can be reached by clicking on a CTA created for this purpose. In this way, it suggests that it specializes so strongly in truck manufacturers that it already advertises relevant offers on the home page. This also ensures that its visitor gains confidence—especially since the reference list also shows the logos of renowned truck manufacturers especially for her.

Fig. 4 Example of web text dynamization

3 The Degree of Automation in ABM Depends on the Strategic Orientation

These three examples give an idea of what the use of dedicated software in account-based marketing means. In all likelihood, these opportunities will continue to grow in the coming years. This is because the market for ABM solutions is currently still very dynamic and complex, especially as it is still in a development process (Burgess & Munn, 2017, p. 44). Many specialized providers are only 2 or 3 years old. In addition, the marketing automation mechanisms mentioned, which are necessary for the approach, mostly make use of common solutions.

ABM solutions (just like CRM solutions) are integrated into an infrastructure with existing software systems (the so-called marketing tech stack). For example, if they connect their ABM tool to a marketing automation system, the latter's e-mail marketing functionalities can be used and e-mails can be sent to employees of a target customer on an account-wide basis. These systems then consequently provide the account view and, building on it, the optimization potential alluded to here—two things that are otherwise difficult to gain.

Conclusion

The success of inbound marketing has created a misconception: The view that online marketing will be largely automated in the future. In conversations about account-based marketing, this view is particularly common in practice. But as this article has shown, automated processes do play an important role in ABM. But this does not change the fact that this is an extremely resource-intensive approach that requires intensive planning.

There are, of course, tangible reasons why ABM is currently becoming more and more popular: Users are focusing themselves and their resources on their top accounts. They combine inbound and outbound marketing measures and thus target entire decision-making bodies. And they not only take care of closing new accounts but above all drive up-selling and cross-selling processes with their existing customers at the same time. As a result, ABM measures generate a higher ROI in most cases than more traditional marketing initiatives (Engagio, 2018a).

Nevertheless, users should always ask themselves whether the associated effort is really worthwhile. Unfortunately, even the best software cannot automatically create individual strategies, buyer personas, customer intelligence, and highly specific content. And if companies do not yet have any experience with account-based marketing, they ideally also need a partner who supports them at the operational, but above all at the strategic level right from the start.

Anyone who wants to address as many potential customers as possible as part of their marketing strategy, while accepting wastage because the ABM approach seems too resource-intensive, is probably better placed with methods such as inbound marketing. If, on the other hand, you want to build up specific marketing for small customer segments and address the questions of these customers as precisely as possible, ABM is a highly exciting, holistic marketing approach.

References

Baketaric, B. (2017). Account-based marketing with marketing automation systems. In U. Hannig (Ed.), *Marketing and sales automation – basics – tools – implementation. Everything you need to know*. Springer Gabler.

Burgess, B. (2017). *Three types of account-based marketing*. Accessed December 10, 2018, from https://www.itsma.com/pdfs/research/ITSMA_ThreeTypesofABM_TB059.pdf

Burgess, B., & Munn, D. (2017). *A practitioner's guide to account-based marketing: Accelerating growth in strategic accounts*.

Callahan, S. (2016). *What is account-based marketing? 10 Definitions from the EXPERTS*, 08.12.2016. Accessed August 16, 2017, from https://business.linkedin.com/marketing-solutions/blog/linkedin-b2b-marketing/2016/what-is-account-based-marketing-10-definitions-from-the-experts

Engagio. (2018a). *The clear & complete guide to account based marketing*. Accessed December 10, 2018, from https://www.engagio.com/clear-and-complete-guide-to-account-based-marketing

Engagio. (2018b). *ABM Outlook Survey 2018. An overview of the state of account-based marketing*. Accessed December 10, 2018, from https://resources.engagio.com/account-based-marketing/abm-outlook-survey-2018

Goren, M. (2018). *Myths and misconceptions about account-based marketing*. Accessed December 10, 2018, from https://www.pointtopoint.com/blog/myths-and-misconceptions-about-account-based-marketing

Hall, S. (2017). *Innovative B2B marketing*. KoganPage.

ITSMA. (2018). Accessed January 03, 2019, from https://www.itsma.com/account-based-marketing-hot-topic/

Kemna, H. (1979). *Key account management – sales success of the future through customer orientation*. Mi-Wirtschaftsbuch.

Miller, J. (2016). *How to generate relevant messages and content for account-based marketing*. Accessed December 10, 2018, from http://www.curata.com/blog/relevant-content-account-based-marketing/

Pakanati, E. (2018). *How to introduce account-based marketing into your B2B inbound efforts*. Accessed December 10, 2018, from https://www.thesmarketers.com/introduce-account-based-marketing-b2b-inbound-efforts/

Peppers, D., & Rodgers, M. (1993). *The one to one future. Building relationships one customer at a time*. Doubleday.

Schaefer, M. (2018). *Content shock: Why content marketing is not a sustainable strategy*. Accessed December 10, 2018, from https://businessesgrow.com/2014/01/06/content-shock/

Sidow, H. (2014). *Key account marketing & key account selling*. Springer Gabler.

Vajre, S. (2016). *Account-based marketing for dummies*. Wiley.

Torsten Herrmann is a Digital Marketing Consultant and Managing Director of the online marketing consultancy chain relations GmbH in Frankfurt am Main. For more than 25 years, he has been supporting B2B companies of all sizes in developing and optimizing their marketing and sales strategies. chain relations is a digital marketing agency with a consulting focus, specialized in online lead generation and demand generation in B2B industries. The company's competencies include inbound marketing, account-based marketing, content marketing, and marketing automation. The company's competencies include inbound marketing, account-based marketing, content marketing, and marketing Automation. Strategies and implementation rely on a thorough understanding of customer journeys based on customer interviews and surveys. Clients are primarily from B2B industries such as high-tech, professional services, traditional industries, and software-as-a-service.

Account-Based Marketing with CRM and Marketing Automation

Klaus Heinzelbecker

1 Account-Based Marketing Against the Background of the Digitalization of Marketing and Sales in the B2B Sector

In Germany, digitization in companies is closely associated with the term Industry 4.0. Accordingly, the focus is primarily on application areas in production and logistics (Dirks & Rohleder, 2016, p. 6). According to a Bitkom survey, four out of five German companies now have a digitization strategy (Berg, 2018), but only around half have a digitization strategy for marketing and sales (Hannig et al., 2019b, p. 16).

Although the use of CRM systems is now established almost everywhere in the field of marketing and sales (Hannig et al., 2017, p. 35; 2018; 2019b, p. 17; 2021, p. 48), but the development status of these systems is often still at the level of 10 years ago and can be described as CRM 3.0 or even only as CRM 2.0 (Heinzelbecker, 2017, p. 322ff.). The focus here is on optimizing relationships with existing customers. Improving efficiency and effectiveness in acquiring new customers and the use of IT in lead management have only recently been recognized as priorities and realized as part of CRM 4.0.

With the concept of inbound marketing and with the help of marketing automation, tried-and-tested tools are available today that ensure end-to-end optimization of the complete marketing and sales process, from lead generation as a marketing task, through various selection processes, to the conclusion of the sale by the sales department (Heinzelbecker, 2017, p. 326ff.). The optimized sales funnel combines the possibilities of marketing automation with the strengths of modern CRM systems (Fig. 1).

K. Heinzelbecker (✉)
Institute for Sales and Marketing Automation (IFSMA), Ludwigshafen, Germany
e-mail: heinzelbecker@ifsma.de

U. Hannig, U. Seebacher (eds.), *Marketing and Sales Automation*, Management for Professionals, https://doi.org/10.1007/978-3-031-20040-3_12

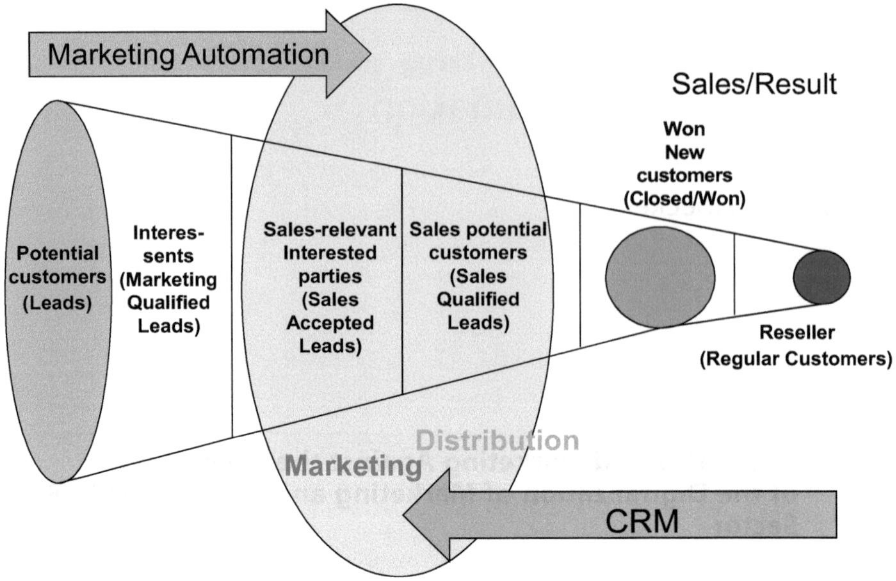

Fig. 1 Optimized sales funnel with marketing automation and CRM (Source: Heinzelbecker, 2017, p. 326)

However, marketing automation software providers soon had to recognize that they face special challenges in the B2B sector. The standard marketing automation solutions available are primarily suitable for those industrial companies that address a large number of customers and potential buyers with largely standardized products. The smaller the circle of customers and relevant prospects and the more explanation-requiring the products and services offered, the less marketing and sales automation appears to make sense.

However, with the linking of marketing automation and the concept of account-based marketing, which thus combines inbound marketing and outbound marketing, there is also the possibility of exploiting the potential for improving efficiency and effectiveness in marketing and sales with the help of modern IT solutions in the case of processing fewer customers and prospects. The providers of digital platforms for marketing and sales in particular, such as Adobe, Oracle, and Salesforce, have recognized these opportunities and have also closed the gap in their offerings with the help of cooperation with specialized consulting companies and software providers.

2 Account Management Versus Account-Based Marketing

Account management is the term used to describe the activity of a sales employee who maintains relationships with customers. In the case of important customers, this is usually referred to as key account management (Sidow, 2014). If the strategic side

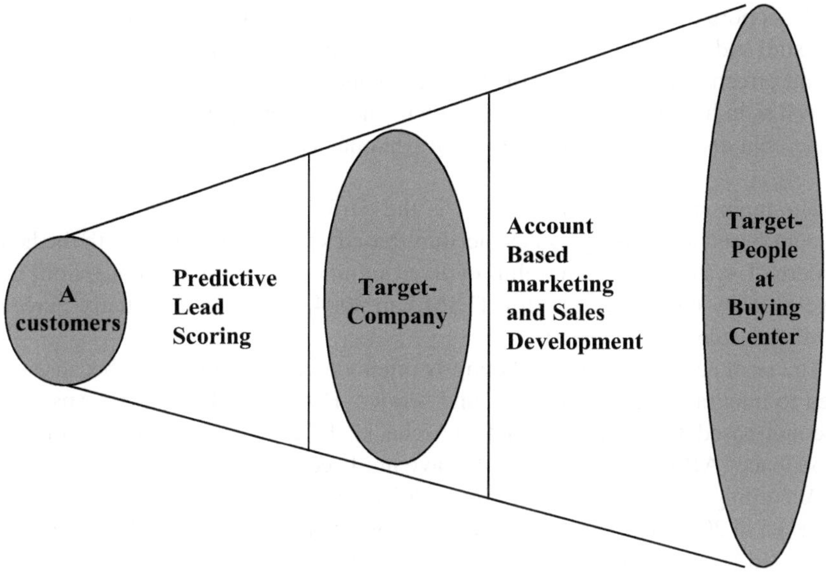

Fig. 2 Account-based marketing funnel (Own illustration)

is to be emphasized, the term Account Development Management is sometimes used in practice (Redlinger & Tonzi, 2016). The focus here is on strategic customer development on the basis of a longer-term account plan with targets, measures, and milestones, which are ideally defined together with the customer.

Typically, key account management focuses on handling so-called A-customers with high sales and earnings potential. Account-based marketing, on the other hand, is also about developing new customers with high potential and ultimately about the question of how marketing can support sales from customer acquisition to customer retention. The sales funnel optimized with marketing automation cannot be the appropriate approach here, because with ABM a targeted focus on the buying center of attractive customers is desired rather than a broad approach with individual contacts at potential customers. The striking formulation for this is: "Flip the Funnel" (Jaffe, 2010) or figuratively speaking with a German comparison "fish not with the net, but with the spear." The starting point can be the A customers from the existing customer base, whose characteristics are used to infer other potential customers (predictive lead scoring). This is followed by personalized customer processing with account-based marketing and sales development, including account-based advertising (see Fig. 2).

In summary, account-based marketing can be characterized as follows:

- ABM is a strategy for industrial business (B2B) that addresses the respective persons in the procurement circle (buying center) of specifically selected target customers and, in contrast to traditional key account management, also considers potential target customers (Heinzelbecker, 2020).

- IT-supported ABM uses the possibilities of modern CRM systems (basic prerequisite) and marketing automation as well as other marketing software for efficient and effective identification of the target persons among the target customers as well as individualized addressing with the help of personalized web pages, emails etc., but also with the targeted use of personal sales.

The main success factor of ABM is the perfect interaction of marketing (incl. account-based advertising), sales (account-based sales), and service with the help of modern IT systems. ABM has thus evolved significantly from the concept originally developed by the consulting firm ITSMA in 2004, in which IT initially played no significant role (Vajre, 2015).

The term account-based marketing is often viewed very critically because of the need to integrate marketing, sales, and service. However, alternative terms such as Account-based Engagement (ABE) (Archacki, R. et al., 2020) or Account-based Experience (ABX) (Miller, J., 2021) have not become widely accepted.

According to a study by Terminus (2021), around 50% of the U.S. companies surveyed in 2021 said they were already using an ABM strategy and another around 30% cited corresponding plans. According to the 2019 IFSMA study in Germany, only about 20% of respondents mentioned already implemented ABM strategies and another about 20% reported corresponding deployment plans (Heinzelbecker, 2019, p. 49). However, this situation has improved significantly in 2021. In the 2021 IFSMA survey, about 35% already mentioned the use of ABM and another about 20% said they planned to use it within the next 2 years. Thus, the status is comparable to the use of MAS but there is still a long way to go before CRM becomes widespread (Hannig et al., 2021).

3 The Process of Account-Based Marketing

The effort required for implementation depends on how many target customers are targeted by the ABM strategy. It has become common practice to distinguish between three types of ABM strategies: 1 to 1 ABM (with usually no more than 50 target customers), 1 to several ABM (with 50 to 100 target customers), 1 to many ABM (with more than 100 target customers). Especially in personalized targeting, these three types differ significantly, so they are often used in parallel with different gradations (Leavitt, R., 2021, p. 12).

According to Fig. 2, the account-based marketing process goes through the following stages:

1. Selection of the target customer area
2. Prioritization of target companies
3. Identify and prioritize targets in the buying center
4. Processing of the target persons
5. Success measurement and optimization

3.1 Selection of the Target Customer Area

It makes sense to start with the company's own customer base and look at its own existing A customers and possibly also its existing B customers. A pure ABC analysis based on sales or earnings is only useful to a limited extent. More meaningful is rather the purchase potential of the customers, which is to be estimated with the help of the selling coworkers and on the basis of specific demand indicators. In parallel, however, potential target companies can also be identified and taken as a starting point on the basis of general potential indicators, such as industry, production program, or company size (see Fig. 3).

An initial prioritization can be made with the help of a customer portfolio, which not only takes into account the assessment of current customer potential, but also considers future potential (see Fig. 4).

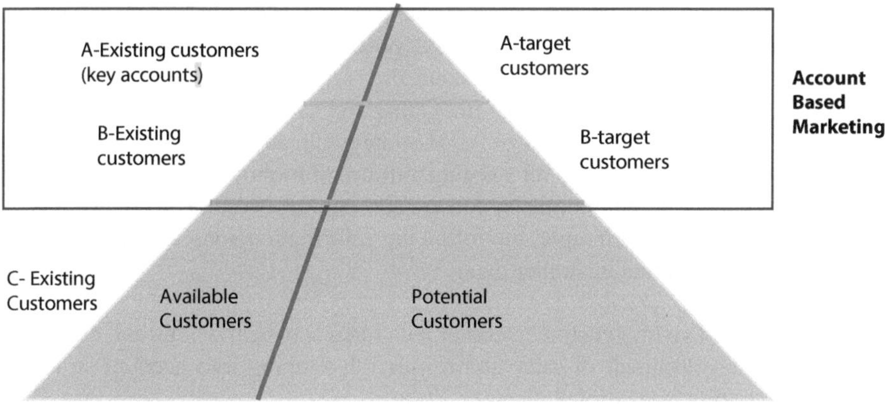

Fig. 3 The ABM target customer pyramid (Own representation)

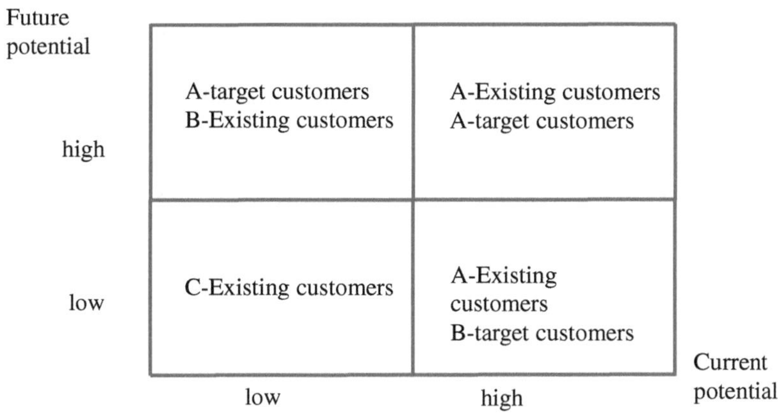

Fig. 4 The target customer portfolio (Own representation)

Accounting variables such as sales, contribution margin, and return on sales, but also payment behavior, order sizes, etc., serve as criteria for assessing the current potential of A-target customers. The assessment of the current potential of A-target customers is based on indicators such as product range, company size, company structure, market share, and financial situation. In addition, accessibility is to be assessed with the aid of indicators such as the competitive situation, contacts in the past, etc., as well as the current potential of the A-target customers, must be assessed. The future potential of existing A customers requires an assessment of:

- Customer growth (industry growth, strategy, innovation, etc.)
- Cross-selling potential
- Up-sell potential
- Purchasing share increase potential (competitive situation, contacts, etc.)

The future potential of A-target customers requires an assessment of future business growth (competitive situation in the industry, technological development, etc.) as well as accessibility (competitors' position with the customer, existing contacts, counter-business opportunities, etc.).

For IT providers from the areas of marketing and sales automation, the question of how to support companies with an ABM strategy already arises at this point. The first step here is the fusion of all existing information about the company's own customers. This is where the limits of data quality and data volume become apparent in many companies. In principle, the following information sources can be considered for merging internal customer data:

- Linking of all existing customer master data (also across divisions and countries)
- Historical development of sales and results (also taking into account structural breaks due to organizational changes, etc.)
- Customer relations in the past (offers, complaints, reminders, etc.)
- Data on payment behavior, ordering behavior, etc.
- Information about countertrade opportunities from the supplier file
- Use of all CRM data (sales force contacts, responses to promotions, trade show contacts, etc.)
- Recording of contacts at management level, etc. (formal, informal)

However, when it comes to potential customers and estimating future potential, the need for information enrichment with external data becomes clear. For company information, the following information sources come into question:

- External company databases (e.g., from Dun&Bradstreet, Kompass, Hoppenstedt/Bisnode, BvD/Moodys)
- Internet research (e.g., with Genios, Creditreform, etc.)
- Analyst reports
- Market Research Studies

- Company information from the Chambers of Industry and Commerce
- Address trading

In the USA, in addition to providers of classic company data (firmographics) on finances, production programs, etc., there are now also providers of technology data (technographics), such as Datanyze, on the systems, processes, etc. used by companies. (Batavia Research, 2015), there are now also providers of technology data (technographics), such as Datanyze, on the systems, processes, etc. used by companies (Zinsmeister, 2016) and on social media, such as LinkedIn (Hicks, 2017).

3.2 Predictive Lead Scoring to Prioritize Target Companies

The simplest way to prioritize the target companies is to create a scoring matrix based on the above criteria, which are weighted together with the sales department. In doing so, it is helpful to agree on a common idea of an Ideal Customer Profile (ICP) (Sears, T., 2019).

To support the prioritization of attractive target customers, machine-learning algorithms can be used today as part of predictive analytics. In this process, attractive A-target customers can be inferred from existing A-customers. The algorithm complements the traditional approach, in which the purchasing-relevant characteristics of the A-customers are determined by a team from marketing and sales on the basis of the following questions:

1. What are the general characteristics (industry, production program, locations, company size, technologies used, etc.) of the existing A customers?
2. Which special characteristics (willingness to innovate, internationalization, quality orientation, etc.) distinguish the already existing A-customers?
3. Which products/services are purchased together?
4. What are the special features (purchasing volume, seasonal effects, centralized/decentralized purchasing, use of countertrade, etc.) of purchasing behavior?
5. How is the buying center positioned (positions in the organization, special role of end users, influence of gatekeepers, etc.)?
6. What are the specific customer requirements (great importance of service, special requirements for logistics, etc.)?
7. What factors have led to sales success in the past (Won Sales Analysis)?

The more information on these questions is available in advance, the more accurate are the algorithms used, which are applied in an iterative process (see Fig. 5).

According to Forrester (Gualterie et al., 2017) and Gartner (Linden et al., 2017), the software vendors that excel in predictive analytics are: SAS Analytics Suite, IBM SPSS, RapidMiner, Angoss Knowledge Studio, Oracle Advanced Analytics, SAP Predictive Analysis, and FICO Analytic Modeller. However, there are also strong open-source vendors, such as Knime and Python. However, according to Forrester,

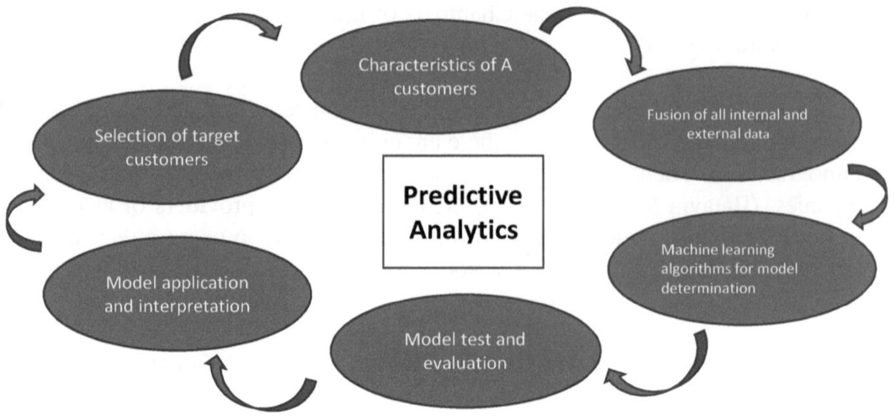

Fig. 5 The process of predictive lead scoring (Own illustration)

the specialists in predictive marketing analytics are vendors 6sense and Lattice Engines (Snow & Ramos, 2017).

The providers of comprehensive systems for marketing and sales (Marketing and Sales Cloud, Marketing and Sales Portals, etc.) now have their own tools with which they support the area of marketing analytics and predictive lead scoring. Salesforce says it offers Einstein Analytics, a tool for advanced analytics based on artificial intelligence (Salesforce, 2016). Adobe has the Adobe Analytics software package. (Adobe, 2017). Oracle partners with Leadspace on predictive analytics (Davenport, 2016). Marketo (now with Adobe) uses Infer software for predictive lead scoring, which is also compatible with Salesforce (Infer, 2016).

3.3 Identification of the Target Persons in the Buying Center

Purchasing decisions in the B2B sector have some special features:

- Especially in the case of larger investments and/or new suppliers and/or new products/services, several people are involved in the purchasing decision process; in particular, responsible persons from purchasing, production, research, and development as well as the management.
- According to CEB research, an average of 6.8 people are involved in an industrial purchasing decision, especially in larger companies (CEB, 2016).
- According to the different functions, the responsible persons fill different roles with different requirements. In addition, different personality traits must be taken into account. In this context, the concept of so-called buyer personas is significant. This refers to the description of relevant characteristics of different types of target persons, which are suitable for addressing them with tailored content in marketing and sales. As the IFSMA survey on digitization in sales showed, this

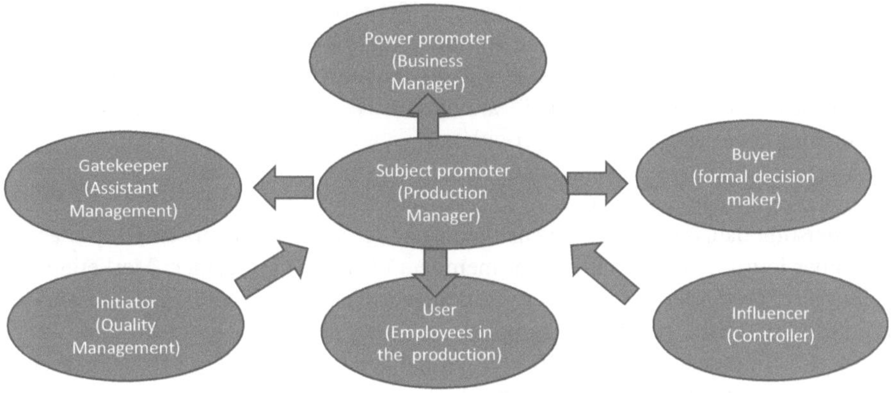

Fig. 6 Roles of target persons in the buying center (example) Own representation

concept has so far only been adopted by around a quarter of the companies surveyed in Germany (Hannig et al., 2019a).
- As the number of people involved increases, so does the time required and the complexity of the decision-making process. Today, the increasing need for information is satisfied primarily through the use of the Internet. In addition to information from providers, information from blogs, comments in social media, etc. is also used.

Of particular importance for ABM are the different roles of the people represented in the buying center. In addition to the buyer, who is often only the formal decision-maker, and the actual user, in many cases specialist promoters, power promoters, gatekeepers, influencers and the original initiator play an essential role in the purchasing decision (see Fig. 6).

The different roles result in different information requirements and different possibilities of influencing. For ABM, the question is not only which information and arguments are needed by which target person for their own information needs. The real challenge is rather to provide the right target persons with arguments in order to convince the ultimately relevant decision-makers.

Accordingly, the marketing and sales process takes place not only between the supplier company and the demand-side company, but also within the demand-side company. Identifying the advocates for one's own offering and understanding their needs and requirements is thus the first step. The next step is to understand what resistance and hurdles exist in the demand-side company and among the critical decision-makers and how these can be overcome with the help of the advocate or advocates in the sense of buyer enablement (Hess, 2016).

While knowledge about the buying center and the relevant target persons is usually at least partially available for existing A customers due to past contacts, no personal data is initially available for target customers. This data can initially be obtained via social media, such as Xing, LinkedIn, and Facebook, or via general

Internet searches. LinkedIn provides specific tools for personal targeting with Sponsored Content and Sponsored InMails (LinkedIn, 2017.) In the USA, where data protection regulations are more relaxed, the relevant target persons in the target companies can also be "targeted" anonymously via the networking of modern advertising tools with third data providers.

The use of content management in conjunction with a marketing automation system provides more information. Reactions to content offers are specifically linked with existing data on A-standing customers and A-target customers and thus map the customer journey for the individual members of the buying center. Marketing and sales can thereby deliver increasingly targeted personalized messages and address the specifics of the respective company or target person. A good example is the connection of Demandbase's B2B Marketing Cloud with Oracle's Eloqua marketing automation software (Akeroyd, 2016).

3.4 Personalized Customer Approach with Account-Based Marketing and Sales Development

The starting point for the personalized customer approach to target customers is an individual customer strategy (Heinzelbecker, 2021):

1. Define customer specific goals (short, medium, long term), overall and by product/region, e.g.:
   (a) Revenue performance
   (b) Market share or degree of potential utilization
   (c) Earnings performance
2. Definition of the initial situation:
   (a) Customer type (by target customer portfolio)
   (b) Target achievement level
   (c) Degree of penetration (knowledge of the buying center, etc.)
   (d) Degree of processing (success of previous marketing and sales measures)
   (e) ABM SWOT Analysis
3. Action Plan:
   (a) Marketing and sales activities (by person responsible)
   (b) Budget
   (c) Milestones
4. Measuring success according to ABM-specific criteria (Engagio, 2018):
   (a) Customer relationship-related key figures
   (b) Results achieved along the customer journey
   (c) ROI-related key figures

The following specific marketing and sales activities are typical for ABM:

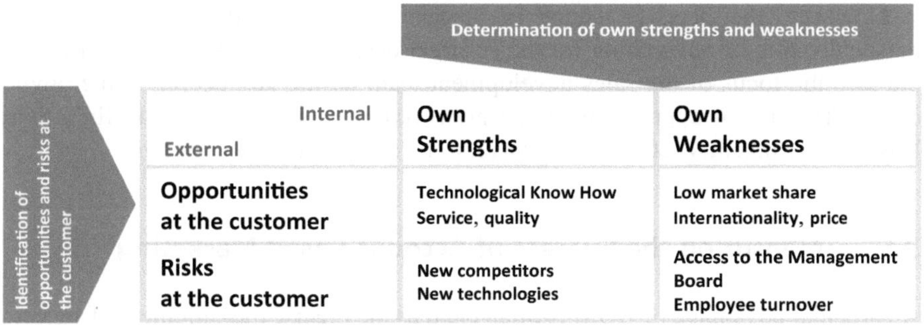

Fig. 7 The ABM SWOT analysis (example) Own illustration

- From the long-term strategic perspective of customer development, ABM goes as far as joint product development or even strategic alliances and other forms of cooperation.
- From a medium-term perspective, for example, the following measures are characteristic:
  - Customized presentations
  - Customer workshops
  - Customer Conferences
  - Customer fairs
  - Customer events (awards, cultural events, etc.)
- Under short-term operational aspects, it is about tailored activities such as:
  - Design of the webpage according to the target customer areas: Differentiation by industries, product range focus, technologies, etc.
  - Design of the webpage according to the target customers and target groups
  - Provision of content differentiated by target customer areas, target customers and target person groups (factsheets, whitepapers)
  - Capture prospect data by target customer area, target personas, and function in the buying center
  - Linking the new data with existing target customer data
  - Deploy Account Sales Development team to supplement target customer data
  - Processing of A-target customers with customized individual marketing concepts based on an ABM SWOT analysis (see Fig. 7)

Customized content marketing plays a major role. According to a benchmarking survey (Demand Gen, 2016), ABM companies used the following content variants:

- Content tailored to specific industries (75%)
- Role-specific content (51%)
- Personalized content per customer (49%)
- Standardized content with some customization (30%)
- Generic Content for All (8%)

However, the decisive factor in account-based marketing is not only the personalization of advertising for the A-target customers and A-existing customers but also the focus of the sales development team on the key people in the buying center. The use of appropriate social networking tools, such as LinkedIn's Sales Navigator (LinkedIN, 2013), has proven to be an essential tool for this.

3.5 Measuring the Success of Account-Based Marketing

A particular advantage of ABM is often cited as the precise measurement of success. (Miller, 2015; Demandbase, 2016). The measurement of success in the operational area includes, for example, the following traditional metrics:

- Account-based sales: number of initial contact calls, number of follow-up calls, number of successful contacts (connect rate), number of relevant leads (pass rate), number of accepted leads (pipeline rate)
- Account-based advertising: web contacts, email click-through and open rates, content views, completed contact forms, etc.

The only advantage of these metrics is the individual assignment to the defined target customers. However, as a study in the USA shows (Anderson, 2017), companies also measure the following key performance indicators with ABM:

- Success of individual campaigns 46%
- Customer conversion rates 46%
- Customer Activities 42%
- Influenced customers 37%
- Marketing Qualified Leads 34%
- Sales growth with customers 29%
- Acquisition costs 28%
- Customer acquisition rate 20%
- Customer Lifetime Value 19%

According to this study, ABM is much closer to achieving its goal of measuring marketing ROI than is otherwise the case.

4 Success Factors of Account-Based Marketing

The success of account-based marketing is highlighted in various studies, which, however, cannot be accurately verified methodologically and often have low case numbers:

- ABM delivers the highest ROI compared to any other B2B marketing strategy or tactic (Schwarz, 2014).

- When asked in 2016 how effective ABM is, about 25% of respondents answered "very effective" and about 70% answered "effective" (Con, 2016).

Surveys of this kind are probably the reason why ABM is already relatively widespread in the U.S., and in some cases, a certain hype has even established itself in this area there (Hilbert & Travis, 2017). At Google trend, it has now almost reached the level of awareness of key account management. In the German-speaking world, this concept has not yet been mentioned much. In Forrester's TechRadar from 2016, this topic is predicted to be highly successful, especially in the B2B sector (Casey et al., 2016). A benchmarking report from 2016 sees ABM already implemented in the USA in 2016 at 47% of the B2B companies surveyed and planned at 32% (Demand Gen, 2016). According to a more recent study, the percentage of B2B companies in the U.S. with ABM even rose to over 80% in 2017 (FlipMyFunnel, 2018).

There is widespread agreement on what conditions must be met for ABM to be successful (Engagio, 2016; Sweezey, 2015; Lattice, 2015; Burgess, 2017; Vajre, 2016):

1. Long-term marketing strategy
2. Close cooperation between marketing, sales, and service:
   (a) Common database
   (b) Common criteria for goal setting and performance evaluation (ROI)
   (c) Integrated Planning
   (d) Joint actions at the customer (e.g., at customer events)
   (e) Regular exchange of experiences and reviews
   (f) Some companies use written collaboration agreements analogous to service-level agreements (Roberge, 2015, pp. 151–161)
3. High demands on data management
   (a) The focus is not so much on the large number of corporate customers, but rather on detailed company profiles (organization, strategy, locations, production program, financial data, etc.), mapping of the buying center (people with functions and decision-making competencies) and personal profiles (decision-relevant personality traits, information behavior, etc.)
   (b) Verification of data quality, not only for external data (Uniserv, 2017)
   (c) Integration of data from marketing, sales, and service
   (d) Permanent updating of the data
4. Systematic recording of target customers (potential and accessibility) and target persons
5. Customized marketing programs (events, presentations, workshops, etc.)
6. Great importance of email marketing for targeting with the help of systematic content management (statista, 2020).
7. Communicating the right content to the right audience at the right time is "the holy grail" of account-based marketing. This makes content generation a critical bottleneck in many cases.

8. Depending on the number of selected target companies and target persons, both effectiveness and efficiency can be increased with the help of marketing automation.
9. Focused and networked use of IT tools, especially marketing automation and CRM, and increasingly the use of AI software (predictive analytics)

In many cases, the introduction of ABM involves a fundamental change in strategy and requires change management for the entire company and in particular for the cooperation between marketing, sales, and service. Particular importance is attached to the establishment of a common database to which all employees with customer contact have access and with which the customer status can be tracked from the target customer through the entire so-called customer journey to the existing customer and reseller.

Customer data platforms (CDP) are offered as a solution approach which, on the one hand, function like a kind of data lake in which all data is stored in the original format; regardless of whether the data originates from external sources or, for example, from the CRM system. On the other hand, this data can then also be cleaned, processed, and structured using appropriate tools (Glickman, 2018). Special software that supports these tasks is called demand orchestration software (Integrate, 2017).

Martech lists 22 providers of customer data platforms in its Marketer's Guide (Martech, 2018b). Gartner even speaks of hype in this area and arrives at 26 providers (Gartner, 2018). CDPs are sometimes confused with DMPs (Data Management Platform), which are used, for example, to manage campaign-related target customer data for online advertising (Bidel & Merlivat, 2017). However, the Customer Data Platform can provide input for the Data Management Platform.

5 ABM Systems Provider

ABM systems are offered by specialized consulting and software houses as well as by providers of marketing automation systems and as part of marketing and sales cloud platforms. In addition, there are marketing and advertising agencies that focus on ABM. Examples of ABM agencies are:

- Momentum (www.momentumabm.com)
- Radiate (https://radiateb2b.com)
- Spear Marketing Group (www.spearmarketing.com)
- Strategic Internet Consulting (www.strategic-ic.co.uk)
- The Rupicon Agency (www.therubiconagency.com)
- Iron Paper (www.ironpaper.com)
- Vendemore (www.vendemore.com)

Forrester distinguishes between (Forrester, 2016):

- ABM platform providers, such as Engagio, Integrate, MRP, Terminus, Triblio, Demandbase, ZenIQ
- Providers of specialized ABM solutions, e.g., Kwanzoo, LinkedIn, Madison Logic, Vendemore, Azalead, LeadGenius
- Data providers, such as Avention, Bombora, Datanyze, DiscoverOrg, InsideView, LeanData, Oracle Data Cloud, ReachForce, Salesforce Data.com, ZoomInfo
- Sales support, e.g. from Brainshark, CallidusCloud, Clear Side, LinkedIn Sales Navigator, Mediafly, Savo, Seismic, Showpad
- Content support, e.g. from Contently, Kapost, Oracle Content Marketing
- Marketing automation platforms, such as Act-On or Oracle
- Web personalization, e.g., from Marketo, Salesforce, Demandbase, Get Smart Content, Optimizely, Triblio
- independent consultants, such as Bizible, BrightFunnel, Full Circle Insights, Hlive9
- Customer research, from, e.g., InMoment, MartizCx, Medalia, Qualtrics

The landscape of these providers is in a permanent state of flux due to acquisitions and cooperations. In 2018, for example, ZenIQ and 6sense merged and Radius merged with Leadspace (separated again since 2018). Forrester was not yet able to take this into account in its New Wave classification of ABM platforms. It classified Demandbase and MRP as Leaders, Engagio, Jabmo, Lattice Engines, and TechTarget as Strong Performers, ZenIQ, Triblio, and Terminus as Contenders, and Madison Logic, 6sense, RollWorks, Radius, and True Influence as Challengers (Forrester, 2018). This picture has already changed significantly in 2020. The leader position of Demandbase and MRP has been confirmed, but new additions are 6sense and improved Terminus and Jambo (Azalead) (Casey, 2020).

Due to the strategic nature of ABM and the extensive consulting often required, specialized consulting and software houses are often involved in collaborations. Well-known ABM platform providers are Azalead (Jabmo), Demandbase, Engagio, Lattice Engines, MRP, TechTarget, Terminus, and 6sense with the following offerings according to company publications (see also Anthony, 2018).

Azalead changed its name to Jabmo in 2018. The platform primarily offers an account monitoring system that captures customer contacts of all types (on websites, via emails, etc.). Core elements include a real-time database based on IP addresses and cookie tracking, linking emails to IP addresses, and analytics software with machine learning. Areas of use include account-based advertising, personalization of websites, supporting account managers with email alerts about customer activity (account alerts) and via mobile ABM apps, and with customer-related metrics. Azalead software is compatible with CRM systems from Salesforce and Microsoft, for example, as well as with marketing automation systems from Salesforce, Oracle, Act-On, Hub-Spot and Marketo.

Demandbase sees itself as a leader in ABM with its artificial intelligence-based platform. This assessment is confirmed by Forrester's New Wave analysis.

(Forrester 3/2018) and also by the latest analysis from Gartner (Pun & Ferguson, 2022). Demandbase's Marketing Cloud supports:

- Marketing in identifying customers (using company data, behavioral data, contextual data), in personalizing websites, and in lead management
- Sales in the processing of target customers and target persons in the Buying Center
- Advertising in targeting promising target customers and target persons with personalized messages
- And provides meaningful analyses for the efficient and effective interaction of marketing and sales

With the acquisitions of InsideView and DemandMatrixin 2021, Demandbase is also expanding its position as a data provider.

Demandbase offers a comprehensive consulting service ranging from strategy consulting and implementation support to training with certification seminars in the USA and UK.

Demandbase partners with Adobe, SAP, Oracle, Hubspot, Marketo, and Salesforce, among others.

With the acquisition of Engagio in 2020, Demandbase was able to integrate the following modules:

- ABM Platform maps the organization of target customers and links them to data from Salesforce CRM and leads from the Marketing Automation system. In addition, data from emails, web monitoring, and other sources are used.
- ABM Analytics creates customized reports on target customer coverage, leads, and goal achievement. Lead generation is supported with the help of predictive analytics.
- PlayMaker is used to address target customers and target persons individually.

Lattice Engines (part of Dun & Bradstreet since 2019) has good marketing analytics tools for B2B marketing with the Lattice Predictive Insight Platform (LPI) (Snow, 2019) and is also suitable as a customer data platform for account-based marketing. In 2017, the platform was recognized as the best Sales and Marketing Intelligence Solution for ABM (siia Award 2017).

MRP Prelytics is ranked among the "Leaders" in ABM by Forrester in 2018 and 2020 (Forrester 3/2018; Casey, J., 2020). The core of the MRP platform is the Prelytics software for so-called Predicitve Marketing. Other solutions are offered for account-based advertising, email marketing (in cooperation with Oracle Marketing Cloud), insight-driven direct mail, lead conversion from marketing to sales, and pipeline management.

TechTarget is a leading provider of marketing data for B2B companies (Forrester, 3/2018) with a particular focus on IT buyers. By analyzing user behavior across its network of 140 technology websites, it can identify buyer intent, feed it into its ABM program, and prioritize it (Priority Engine). In 2021, TechTarget was ranked as a Market Leader by Research in Action (2021).

Terminus (ranked as a Leader by Gartner 2022) is an overarching ABM platform that offers its own solutions as well as integrates other partners. In terms of the tools provided, the platform follows the

Process of Account-based Marketing:

- Identify: Tools for identifying target customers in the traditional way or with the help of predictive analytics. Partners mentioned here are: DiscoverOrg, dun&bradstreet, bombora, 6sense, infer, Avention, ZenIQ, Mintigo, Datanyze, Social123, Kickfire, ReachForce, Everstring, InsideView, Lattice, leadspace, and Oceanus.
- Expand: Tools for broadening the customer base by enriching contact data, identifying email addresses, etc. In addition to its own software, the partners mentioned here are: DiscoverOrg, dun&bradstreet, bombora, Avention, ZenIQ, Datanyze, Social123, ReachForce, InsideView, leadspace, Oceanus, integrate, leandata, CaliberMind, and even Engagio.
- Engage: tools to deliver the right content to the target audience. In addition to Engagio's own software and that of Engagio, tools from the following partners are also mentioned: PFL, Sigstr, überflip, Triblio, evergage, Vidyard, KiteDesk, act-on, LookBookHQ, Captora, SalesLoft, SnappApp, and CaliberMind.
- Advocate: tools for persuading customers along the customer journey. Partners mentioned here are: Churnzero, Ambassador, Gainsight, and influitive.
- Measure: Performance measurement at the target customers. Partners here are: bizible, BrightFunnel, Engagio, LeanData, InsightSquared, KickFire, and Full Circle Insights.

In January 2018, Terminus also announced a partnership with LinkedIn (Shields, 2018) Terminus' comprehensive consulting offering also includes an education and training program marketed under the name ABM-University. In implementing ABM, Terminus leverages the company's existing software, specifically marketing automation, email systems, and CRM, as well as software to support events and webinars, content management, digital advertising, personalization, and direct mail (Terminus, 2018).

6sense (ranked as a Leader by Gartner 2022) has its focus on predictive analytics, which was strengthened by the acquisition of ZenIQ in April 2018. The central element of the offering is a Customer Data Platform (CDP).

As in other areas of marketing technology providers, the trend toward company acquisitions will continue in the ABM sector. For example, in spring 2018, ABM specialist ZenIQ (classified as a "contender" by Forrester) was acquired by 6sense (classified as a "challenger" by Forrester). In September 2018, Marketo was acquired by Adobe. In May 2019, SugarCRM acquired vendor Salesfusion. In July 2019, Dun &Bradstreet acquired platform provider Lattice Engines. And in June 2020, Demandbase acquired ABM specialist Engagio.

Most providers of marketing automation systems and/or CRM systems also offer solutions for ABM and also make these available as part of their cloud concepts. The focus here is on the options for data management, including synchronization with the CRM system, as well as the options for sending personalized emails, creating landing pages, and linking with social media channels. However, to regard ABM as a fundamental component of marketing automation only applies to a limited number of providers (Baketaric, 2017, p. 373).

Salesforce even talks about its ABM Cloud and relies on its AI system Einstein, which uses the Salesforce CRM system as the starting point for predictive lead management. It is based on the concept of Terminus and accordingly works with around 35 different partners (including LinkedIn) for the individual stages of the ABM process (Gorman, 2016). Salesforce also acquired the customer data platform Datorama at the beginning of 2018.

Marketo considers itself an industry leader in ABM. In early 2017, it formed the Alliance for ABM Success with DigitalPi, Elixiter, LeadMD, Fathom, and Perkuto (Marketo, 2017). Marketo was then acquired by Adobe in 2018.

Adobe has historically relied primarily on its data management platform within Audience Manager from Marketing Cloud for ABM, partnering with Demandbase and, for each stage of ABM, Dun & Bradstreet, ALC, Bombora, Cross Pixel, Eyeota, and TransUnion (Joshi, 2016). A new focus was formed with the acquisition of Marketo in 2018.

Oracle puts the Oracle Data Cloud at the center of ABM, emphasizing access to the data of more than 1 million U.S. companies and over 90 million users. For the process of ABM, Oracle offers the functionality of its marketing automation system Eloqua and cooperates with Demandbase and other service providers that can be used via Oracle AppCloud (Johnson, 2016).

For Microsoft, ABM is a possible complement to Microsoft Dynamics CRM. This connection is emphasized above all by Azalead (Jabmo) (Azalead, 2016). In addition, Microsoft also offers the ABM sales platform Folloze via its Azure Cloud as part of its scenarios (Microsoft, 2017).

HubSpot recommends the use of its Marketing Professional tool and integration with its CRM system for ABM. The importance HubSpot attaches to ABM can be seen in its involvement with Terminus (Coffey, 2017).

Act-on speaks of account-based marketing automation and cooperates with the companies Attend, Listenloop, PFL, oktopost, and siftrock for the individual stages of the ABM process in addition to Terminus (Musto, 2016).

Salesfusion (SugarCRM since 2019) considers the difference between targeting known customers and targeting potential customers in its ABM offering as part of its marketing automation software (Salesfusion, 2016).

Other marketing automation vendors with ABM capabilities include eTrigue, iContact Pro, and Infusionsoft (Martech, 2018a, p. 8).

6 Account-Based Marketing Is More Than Hype

As the many publications on ABM show, ABM in the USA is now out of the hype stage and for many companies in the B2B sector it is already an indispensable part of their marketing concept. Accordingly, all the major providers of software for marketing and sales are also involved in this area. In addition to the providers of marketing and sales cloud platforms, these are primarily the providers in the area of marketing automation and CRM. Most of these providers have recognized that three aspects in particular are crucial for the ABM concept:

- Analyzing existing customer data to derive patterns for finding similar customers and generating leads from them (predictive lead scoring)
- External sourcing of potential customer data to identify attractive target customers
- System support for individualized targeting

Since the implementation of the ABM concept often requires both a change in marketing strategy and entails organizational consequences regarding cooperation between marketing and sales, user support for system implementation is usually not sufficient. This has also led to system providers cooperating with the large ABM specialists and also working with many small specialists. This is probably also the reason why the ABM concept is still hardly represented in Germany. There are sales consultants on the subject of account management and account advertising is also well known, but consulting platforms such as Demandbase and Terminus are lacking in Germany.

A particular bottleneck lies in data procurement and German or European data protection law (Heukrodt-Bauer, 2017). This is particularly true since the EU General Data Protection Regulation (DSGVO) came into force, which places high demands on documentation and access in the case of personal data. However, the previously high German requirements for the use of data from potential customers are also being relaxed. According to this, publicly accessible data may be used for advertising purposes in the future even without the consent of the person (Marwan, 2017). This means that LinkedIn in particular, but also Xing, are increasingly being used for account-based marketing in Germany (Bredl, 2018).

In the USA, personal data from the decision-making bodies of the target companies, obtained via cookies or obtained via IP addresses, can be used without any problems. In addition, the intensive use of business-oriented social media, such as LinkedIn, is widespread. The specialists for data acquisition and data enrichment already mentioned several times taking advantage of this there.

Despite the above-mentioned limitations and the considerable effort required for implementation, account-based marketing is also a relevant approach for B2B companies in German-speaking countries. The author can confirm from his own positive experience that it is possible to draw conclusions about potential target customers from the patterns of existing A customers, thus identifying new business potential and tapping into it through personalized addressing.

The following approach has proven successful (Heinzelbecker, 2019):

1. Optimization of the processing of existing customers between marketing and sales:
   (a) Definition of target customers and target persons according to their role in the buying center
   (b) Review/update existing customer data in the CRM system or other systems (see also DSGVO)
   (c) Deployment of personalized sales programs
   (d) Use of individualized advertising measures
2. Optimization of the processing of potential target customers in coordination between marketing and sales:
   (a) Selection of potential target customers
   (b) Development of buyer personas
   (c) Obtaining the relevant customer data (company data, technology data, etc.)
   (d) Use of individualized customer data via social media (e.g., LinkedIn Sales Navigator)
   (e) Use of individualized advertising measures
3. Review of existing IT systems for marketing and sales:
   (a) Current status of the CRM system
   (b) Examine conversion to cloud solutions
   (c) Examine use of marketing automation
   (d) Consider use of a special ABM system

However, the starting point should first be the adoption of an ABM strategy, ideally based on a customer-centric vision and mission for the entire company.

References

Adobe. (2017). Accessed September 11, 2017, from http://www.adobe.com/de/data-analytics-cloud/analytics.html

Akeroyd, K. (2016). *Demandbase launches ABM solution for Oracle Eloqua Marketing Automation*. Accessed September 11, 2017, from https://blogs.oracle.com/marketingcloud/demandbase-launches-abm-solution-for-oracle-eloqua-marketing-automation

Anderson, B. (2017). *Marketing measurement and attribution*. DemandGen Survey Report.

Anthony, W. (2018). *Reviewing 9 of the best account based marketing softwares for 2018*. https://www.integrate.com/blog/reviewing-the-9-best-account-based-marketing-softwares-for-2018

Archacki, R., Andersen, P., Rhodes, S., & Mustaghni, B. (2020). *Moving beyond ABM to account-based engagement*. Accessed January 2, 2022, from Moving Beyond ABM to Account-Based Engagement | BCG

Azalead. (2016). *Azalead announces account based marketing for microsoft dynamics CRM*. Accessed September 11, 2017, from https://azalead.com/press-release/abm-for-microsoft-dynamics-crm/

Baketaric, B. (2017). Account-based marketing with marketing automation systems. In U. Hannig (Ed.), *Marketing and sales automation* (pp. 365–376). Springer.

Batavia Research. (2015). *Digital firmographics*. Accessed September 11, 2017, from http://bataviaresearch.com/wp-content/uploads/2015/04/BR-Digital-Firmographics-White-Paper-150218.pdf

Berg, A. (2018). *Digitizing the economy*. Accessed March 14, 2019, from https://www.bitkom.org/sites/default/files/file/import/Bitkom-Charts-Digitalisierung-der-Wirtschaft-06-06-2018-final.pdf

Bidel, S., & Merlivat, S. (2017). *The Forrester wave: Data management platforms*. Q2, 2017.

Bredl, M. (2018). *How to apply Account Based Marketing despite DSGVO*. https://www.takeoffpr.com/blog/fragen-zu-account-based-marketing

Burgess, B. (2017). *A practitioner's guide to account based marketing*. Kogan.

Casey, S., Ramos, L., & Wizdo, L. (2016). TechRadar. B2B marketing technologies. Q3, 2016.

Casey, S. (2020). *The Forrester new wave*. ABM Platforms Q2, 2020. Forrester Reprints.

CEB. (2016). *The revolution in B2B buying*.

Coffey, B. (2017). *Why HubSpot is investing in account based marketing firm ter*minus. Accessed September 11, 2017, from https://medium.com/@HubSpot/why-hubspot-is-investing-in-account-based-marketing-firm-terminus-16b1ba52aab6

Con, J. (2016). *State of Pipeline Marketing 2016*. Bizible.

Davenport, S. (2016). *Oracle launches "Largest B2B audience data marketplace"*. Accessed September 11, 2017, from http://thrivesearch.com/oracle-launches-largest-b2b-audience-data-marketplace/

Demandbase. (2016). *Expert ABM. The B2B marketer's guide to account based measurement*.

Demand Gen. (2016). *ABM Benchmark Survey Report 2016*.

Dirks, T., & Rohleder, B. (2016). *Digitalization of the economy*. Bitcom.

Engagio. (2016). *The Engagio Playbook*.

Engagio. (2018). *The clear and complete guide to ABM analytics*. Accessed March 19, 2018, from http://info.engagio.com/rs/356-AXE-401/images/the-clear-and-complete-guide-to-abm-analytics-20180201.pdf

FlipMyFunnel. (2018). *State of Account Based Marketing Survey 2017*. Accessed March 19, 2018, from https://flipmyfunnel.com/flipmyfunnel-account-based-marketing-survey/

Forrester. (2016). *Forrester vendor landscape account based marketing*. Q4, 2016.

Forrester. (2018). *The Forrester New Wave*. ABM Platforms. Q2, 2018. https://www.forrester.com/report/The+Forrester+New+Wave+ABM+Platforms+Q2+2018/-/E-RES134323

Forrester Q3. (2018). *The Forrester wave B2B marketing data providers*. https://reg.techtarget.com/rs/095-PCN 759/images/The_Forrester_Wave_B2B_Marketing_Data_Providers_2018.pdf?aliId=32937016

Gartner. (2018). *Market guide for customer data platforms for marketing*. https://www.gartner.com/doc/reprints?id=1-5WLZP4Z&ct=181206&st=sb

Glickman, R. (2018). *Enterprise customer data platform for dummies*. Hoboken 2018.

Gorman, P. (2016). *35 vendors join ABM Cloud for Salesforce partnership*. Accessed September 11, 2017, from http://www.fiercecmo.com/tech/35-vendors-join-abm-cloud-for-salesforce-partnership

Gualterie, M., et al. (2017). *The Forrester wave: Predictive analytics and machine learning solutions*. Q1, 2017. Cambridge.

Hannig, U., Heinzelbecker, K., & Aull, M. (2019a). *Sales in the digital age*. Ludwigshafen. IFSMA Whitepaper 2019.

Hannig, U., Heinzelbecker, K., & Foell, T. (2017). Marketing and sales automation in Germany. In U. Hannig (Ed.), *Marketing and sales automation* (pp. 19–37). Springer.

Hannig, U., Heinzelbecker, K., & Foell, T. (2018). *B2B marketing automation in the digital jungle 2018*. IFSMA Whitepaper 2018.

Hannig, U., Heinzelbecker, K., & Foell, T. (2019b). *Digital safety first. Marketing automation in DACH 2019*. White paper. Institute for Sales and Marketing Automation, Ludwigshafen.

Hannig, U., Heinzelbecker, K., & Foell, T. (2021). *Mission digital transformation*. IFSMA Whitepaper 2021.

Heinzelbecker, K. (2017). The integration of customer relationship management and marketing automation. In U. Hannig (Ed.), *Marketing and sales automation* (pp. 321–331).

Heinzelbecker, K. (2019). How to optimize your key account management. *SalesExcellence, 12*, 48–51.

Heinzelbecker, K. (2020). *Account-based marketing. The turbo for your key account management*. https://www.ifsma.de/2019/11/26/account-based-marketing-der-turbo-fuer-ihr-key-account-management/

Heinzelbecker, K. (2021). Digital personalization in the B2C and B2B sectors. In S. Lacher, P. Tachkov, & R. Völker (Eds.), *Digitalization in marketing*.

Hess, G. (2016). *The buying enablement guide*. Consensus.

Hicks, K. (2017). *Utilizing LinkedIn for account-based marketing*. Accessed September 11, 2017, from https://www.kunocreative.com/blog/linkedin-for-account-based-marketing

Hilbert, M., & Travis, T. (2017). *Hype cycle for CRM sales*. Gartner.

Heukrodt-Bauer, S. (2017). Legally compliant email marketing automation. In U. Hannig (Ed.), *Marketing and sales automation* (pp. 59–70). Springer.

Infer. (2016). *Marketo integration*. Accessed September 11, 2017, from https://www.infer.com/integrations/marketo/

Integrate. (2017). *A guide to demand orchestration software*. https://discover.integrate.com/hubfs/Content/Indices_Guides_Workbooks/Demand%20Orchestration

Jaffe, J. (2010). *Flip the funnel*. Wiley.

Johnson, D. (2016). *Oracle marketing cloud launches new account based marketing capabilities*. https://blogs.oracle.com/marketingcloud/oracle-marketing-cloud-launches-new-account-based-marketing-capabilities

Joshi, M. (2016). *Partnering Adobe drive successful B2B marketing* Accessed September 11, 2017, from https://blogs.adobe.com/digitalmarketing/advertising/partnering-adobe-drive-successful-b2b-marketing/

Lattice. (2015). *Predictive playbook: Account based marketing*.

Leavitt, R., & Schwartz, J. (2021). *Embedding ABM: ABM benchmarking study*. Accessed February 1, 2022, from https://www.itsma.com/research/embedding-abm-next-steps-for-market-leadership/

LinkedIn. (2013). *Social selling with LinkedIn sales navigator*. file:///D:/Update%20Final%20Update%202015/FinalUpdate2015/IFSMA/Account%20Based%20Marketing/LinkedIN/sn-step-by-step-guide-01282014.pdf

LinkedIn. (2017). *The sophisticated Marketers' Guide to LinkedIn* (2nd ed.). https://business.linkedin.com/content/dam/me/business/en-us/marketing-solutions/cx/2017/pdfs/Sophisticated-Marketers-Guide-to-LinkedIn.pdf

Linden, A., et al. (2017). *Magic quadrant for data science platforms*. Gartner.

Marketo. (2017). *Marketo and key partners establish the alliance for ABM success*. Accessed September 11, 2017, from https://www.marketo.com/newsroom/press-releases/2017-04-24-Marketo-and-Key-Partners-Establish-the-Alliance-for-ABM-Success/

Martech. (2018a). *B2B marketing automation platforms* (6th ed.).

Martech. (2018b). *Enterprise customer data platforms* (1st ed.).

Marwan, P. (2017). *Impact of the EU GDPR on B2B sales and marketing*. Accessed September 11, 2017, from http://www.silicon.de/41650029/auswirkungen-der-eu-dsgvo-auf-vertrieb-und-marketing-im-b2b-bereich/?inf_by=59b94452681db8205c8b45e4

Microsoft. (2017). Accessed September 11, 2017, from https://appsource.microsoft.com/en-us/product/office/WA104380681?tab=Overview

Miller, J. (2015). *The Big 5 Metrics for Account Based Marketing*. Engagio E-Book.

Miller, J. (2021). *The clear & complete guide to account-based experience (ABX)*. Accessed January 2, 2022, from The Clear & Complete Guide to Account-Based Experience (ABX) | Account-Based Marketing - Demandbase

Musto, P. (2016). *Act-on launches actual account-based marketing automation solution*. Accessed September 11, 2017, from https://www.act-on.com/press/press-releases/act-launches-account-based-marketing-automation-solution/

Pun, R., & Ferguson, C. (2022). *Magic quadrant for account-based marketing platforms*. Accessed February 10, 2022, from https://www.gartner.com/doc/reprints?id=1-28LGHNGR&ct=220105&st=sb

Research in Action. (2021). *Vendor selection matrix account-based marketing*. Reprint April 2021.

Redlinger, B., & Tonzi, M. (2016). *Account-based sales development playbook for revenue-driven teams*. Amazon eBook.

Roberge, M. (2015). *The sales acceleration formula*. Wiley.

Salesforce. (2016). *Salesforce Einstein – artificial intelligence for everyone*. Accessed September 11, 2017, from https://www.salesforce.com/de/blog/2016/09/salesforce-einstein%2D%2D-kuenstliche-intelligenz-fuer-jedermann.html

Salesfusion. (2016). *Salesfusion enhances account-based marketing offering*. Accessed September 11, 2017, from https://www.salesfusion.com/press/salesfusion-enhances-account-based-marketing-offering/

Schwarz, J. (2014). *Account based marketing and ROI: Building the case for investment*. ITSMA Online Survey.

Sears, T. (2019). *The framework for ideal customer profile development*. Accessed January 2, 2022, from https://www.gartner.com/en/articles/the-framework-for-ideal-customer-profile-development

Shields, T. (2018). *Announcing the terminus integration with LinkedIn*. Accessed March 19, 2018, from http://terminus.com/linkedin-terminus-account-based-marketing-integration/?utm_medium=email&utm_source=pardot-terminus-times&utm_campaign=linkedin-terminus

Sidow, H. (2014). *Key account marketing & key account selling*. Gabler.

Snow, A., & Ramos, L. (2017). *The Forrester wave: Predictive marketing analytics for B2B marketers*. Q2, 2017. Forrester.

Snow, A. (2019). The Forrester wave: B2B customer analytics. Q1, 2019.

Statista. (2020). *The content marketing study 2020*.

Sweezey, M. (2015). *Account based marketing: The key to B2B success*. DemandBase.

Terminus. (2018). *Blueprint to account based marketing campaigns*. Accessed March 19, 2018, from http://lp.terminus.com/blueprint-account-based-marketing-campaigns/

Terminus. (2021). *The state of ABM in Europe*. Accessed January 2, 2022, from https://terminus.com/blog/state-of-abm-europe-2021/

Uniserv. (2017). *2017 Customer Data Management Trend Study*.

Vajre, S. (2015). *The untold and fascinating history of account based marketing*. Accessed September 11, 2017, from https://www.martechadvisor.com/interviews/sales-enablement-3/the-untold-and-fascinating-history-of-account-based-marketing/

Vajre, S. (2016). *Account-based marketing for dummies*. Wiley.

Zinsmeister, S. (2016). *CMO's: Technographics is the new demographics*. https://venturebeat.com/2016/03/05/cmos-technographics-is-the-new-demographics/

Klaus Heinzelbecker Co-Founder and Member of the Board of the Institute for Sales and Marketing Automation (IFSMA).

With his book "Marketing Information Systems," published in 1985, he is considered to be a pioneer in the area of IT support in sales and marketing in Germany.

After studying business administration at the University of Mannheim, he received a Ph.D. at the technical university of Aachen (RWTH).

During the course of his management career, he worked as a marketing consultant in the electrical industry (ABB), as manager of marketing research, and as director of strategic planning in the chemical industry (BASF). He has many years of experience in international consulting in Europe, Asia, and the Americas and he has dealt with the challenges of many different industries, particularly in automotive, construction, packaging, nutrition, and healthcare.

After retirement, he worked as a strategy consultant and in the area of futuring for the German think tank Z-Punkt. His current focus is on new markets, new business models, online marketing, and digital transformation.

He is chairman of the Supervisory Board of the Future Management Group.

As a lecturer at the University of Business and Society Ludwigshafen, he teaches Strategic Management and HR Management.

Marketing Automation and Customer Loyalty

Janosch Baum

1 Possibilities of MAS

Leading CMOs of major international companies have understood for years that the planning and execution of marketing strategies are linked to customer data, the correct evaluation of which is crucial to success and thus linked to the prerequisite of obtaining this data as efficiently and validly as possible, with marketing technologies playing a supporting role.[1] As many different companies there are, as large is the selection of digital offerings. It is therefore not possible to provide an overview of all tools to this extent in their entirety, but there are websites that provide an insight into the various solutions offered by individual companies. Figure 1 visualizes the dimensions of the range of possibilities that can be found in various companies.

Although this listing does not claim to cover the full range of MAS, the topic-based categories give a clearer perspective.[2]

1. Lead tracking and nurturing: achieved through appropriate CRM systems that enable customer scoring, behavioral monitoring, and segmented customer targeting (e.g., Salesforce).
2. Social media marketing: here you can automate messages, likes and retweets, content postings, and influencer research (e.g., IFTTT).
3. Inbound marketing: there are supporting automation systems both in research (e.g., Google Alerts) and in the benchmark (e.g., Whatruns), up to the creation of

[1] Cf. Pattekwith et al. (2014): p. 13.

[2] Cf. Petersen (2018): o. p.

J. Baum (✉)
JB Design, Mainz, Germany
e-mail: contact@jb-design.net

U. Hannig, U. Seebacher (eds.), *Marketing and Sales Automation*, Management for Professionals, https://doi.org/10.1007/978-3-031-20040-3_13

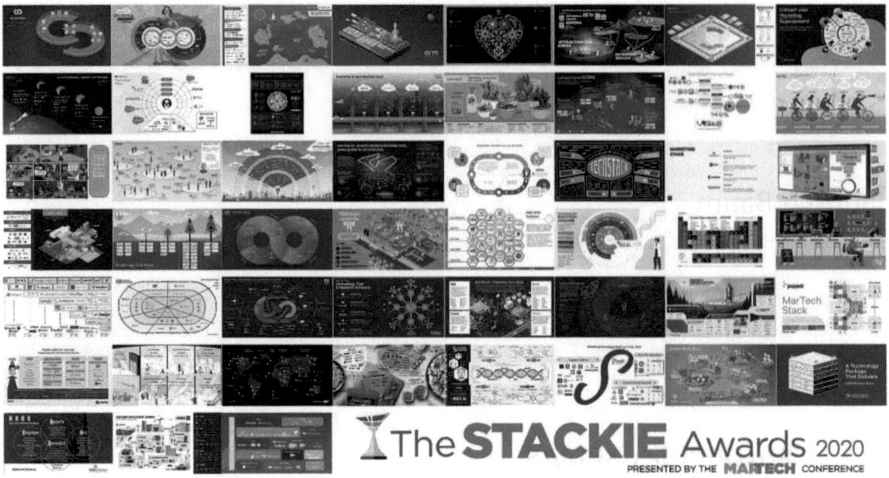

Fig. 1 Competition for MarTech stack visualizations (Brinker, 2020a: o. p.)

content (e.g., AX Semantics). MA processes also capture website optimizations, such as through SEO optimization tools or through A/B testing.

4. Programmatic out-of-home: In digital out-of-home advertising, data-driven target group clusters can also be addressed in one-to-many communication. Through geo-localization, individual customers can also be tracked.[3]
5. Data scaling and evaluation: the various CRM, ERP, or Google applications enable data collection that supports monitoring and strategic adjustments.

Thus, the operational services of MA are not only diverse but also cross-departmental. Sales and marketing, as well as other areas in an organization, are merging through overarching, digital data collection and data optimization, such as in new customer acquisition.[4] With regard to data, this is why marketers today speak of both Big Data and Big Ops, which means the conducive interconnection of Big Data.[5] The individual processes in MA intensify such promotions and have promising effects.

First of all, it is indispensable to define customer loyalty and its measurement values. Customer loyalty differs in terms of customer satisfaction, as customer satisfaction is measured only by the expectation criteria of the product or service. Customer loyalty, on the other hand, is also measured in terms of repurchase intention and recommendation. Loyal customers have a more emotional connection to the brand, buy products even if other offers are better value for money, and recommend them to others.

[3]Cf. Karc (2021): o. S.
[4]Cf. Pleßke (2021): p. 8.
[5]Cf. Malz (2021): o. S.

Customer loyalty can be determined using the survey method of Net Promoter Score, where customers are divided into different categories by survey results, i.e., promoters, passives, and detractors.[6]

With regard to the providers and developers of MAS, it is both beneficial to compare the repertoire of functions with one's own needs and important to recognize which providers provide the right integrations and which positions they hold in a global comparison. In addition, trends should be illuminated in order to know which global developments are influencing the market and how companies can benefit from them.

Providers of MAS have multiplied almost exponentially in the last decade. While in 2011 there were about 150 martech providers, by 2020 the number had reached around 8000. Developing new tools has never been so easy, thanks to the network of software providers who offer prefabricated solutions that can be integrated at all development levels.[7] Integration is the trend word here. According to a survey by Demand Spring, MA platforms were chosen most because of integration capabilities with other tools; only second in importance were the actual features. This is causing small tool providers in particular to aggregate more and more into the eco-systems of the big players.[8] These in turn acquired SaaS companies in the same industry in a big way: since 2018, Adobe, Salesforce, Facebook, and other organizations bought competing companies worth more than $16.3 billion, while beyond that, some acquisitions were not disclosed in terms of price.[9] These big players are now evolving their CRM systems into CDPs and consolidating tools even more. The big players are thus putting pressure on smaller vendors by buying them out or extending their own modules to increase their market share.

Capitalization in MAS is forecast to grow steadily in 2022. Important key points of the new trends remain in the creative-technical area of personalized content, AI, chatbots or automated social media, Internet of Things, digital out-of-home and voice.[10] Furthermore, according to Brinker, trends on the rise include no-code applications and apps, where software can be developed without having to code. He then describes the big app explosion, which represents an explosive growth in apps and services. According to IDC, there will be about 500 million of them on the market by 2023. Finally, in the data-related area, big ops, i.e., the proper integration of big data, are the big challenges that companies will have to overcome in the coming years, as well as connectivity of tools, and CDPs.[11]

---

[6] Cf. Boadum (2021): n.d.

[7] Cf. Brinker (2020b): o. p.

[8] Cf. Brinker (2021): o. p.

[9] Cf. Parker (2022): o. p.

[10] Cf. Shukla (2022): o. p.

[11] Cf. Davis (2020): o. p.

2 Customer Experience Management and MA

Modern CX management focuses primarily on customer centricity, so MAS is a standard part of a customer journey in order to be able to play out personalized content. Methods such as A/B testing of web pages, automatically generated, personalized content, and dialogs with chatbots are some examples that illustrate this.[12] In this field, there are two approaches to be distinguished, inbound and outbound marketing, which in the first case stands for the method of drawing consumers' attention to the company's website through relevant content and search engine optimization, letting them come to the website on their own and thereby promoting products. Outbound, in turn, is attributed to directly approaching customers through advertising.[13] While inbound marketing is the most inconspicuous way of advertising for the customer, outbound marketing involves penetrating customers "above and below the line," i.e., directly and indirectly with advertising. MAS promotes the possibility of addressing segmented target groups. Affiliate marketing, retargeting, social media advertising, SEM, and online advertising banners are further classified as outbound.[14] These advertising measures play a more significant role in the course of loyalty, as they are more susceptible to reactance.

In the course of the scientific and economic research, as well as in all the expert interviews, customer centricity was repeatedly identified as the anchor point of CX. Accordingly, the touchpoints of the customer journeys are to be aligned with it and thus MA processes are also to be subordinated to this strategy.

Thus, from a strategic perspective, MA is a sub-area of automation, in which sales and service must also be integrated, firstly, to record customer data in a standardized manner, which is a challenge for many companies, secondly, to better interlink the departments, and thirdly, to be able to personalize better as a result. The IT department plays the role of administration here. The interviews add to this the rethinking of campaign-based marketing concepts in addition to a time- and trigger-based approach, which is more in the sense of customer centralization and personalization and is optimized by MA processes. Audience management takes over the controlling authority for this. Thus, the implementation is done in the mentioned steps through customer centricity, data collection, segmentation, and personalization.

Accenture, the global service provider for business and strategy consulting, publishes an annual survey to identify the most important key indicators of successful customer engagement. In 2018, it was all about personalization, with one point in the survey specifically asking about automation processes and what customers think

[12] Cf. AX Semantics o. J.: o. S.

[13] Cf. Kuhlmann-rhinow (2021): o. S.

[14] Cf. Totka (2013): n.d.

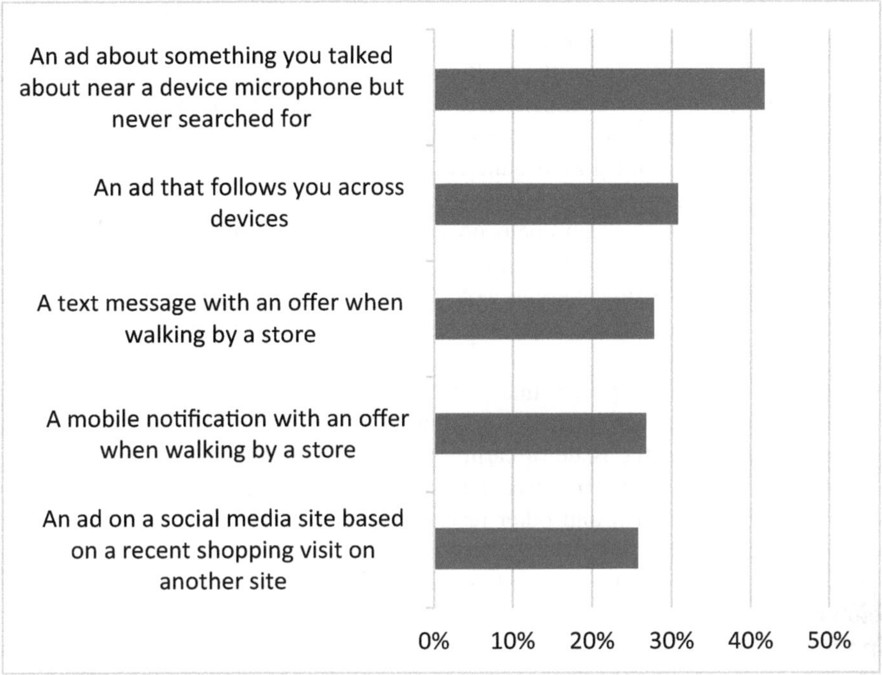

Fig. 2 Top five creepiest advertising techniques (Cf. Accenture, 2019: p. 6)

about them. With the introduction "Cool or Creepy," the automation processes with the most acceptance and the greatest reactance were contrasted.[15]

In the following year, 2019, the topic was covered on an even larger scale: The report was titled "See People not Patterns—Leading brands are using data to humanize their customer relationships and learning where to draw the line between invasive and inventive."[16] In it, it was confirmed that most algorithms did not reflect the purchase suggestions that customers intended. But a majority of consumers were willing to give up personal data if they could get better-tailored CX in return. Openness about the use of the data was another criterion in the course of this.[17] Figure 2 illustrates what consumers find strangest in connection with MA, showing the top five creepiest advertising techniques cited by European consumers.

Germany's respondents had the lowest rate of feeling that companies have become too personal compared to other European countries (20%), while 60%

[15]Cf. Accenture (2018): p. 5.

[16]Accenture (2019): p. 1.

[17]Cf. Accenture (2019): p. 5.

would stop trading if this feeling arose. In contrast, 95% find it important that interests and preferences are understood by a brand.[18]

In 2020, the focus was on the shift from "user experience" to a more holistic approach of the "business of experience." In the context of the paper, it is important to note in this study that consumers compare experiences with brands across industries.[19] The pandemic has also increased media usage time and changed buying behavior—expectations of digital standards must therefore be met.[20]

The study from 2021 again opens up a different sphere of influence. Customers no longer care only about price and quality; the values of a company are increasingly coming to the fore.[21] Conversely to MA, an even higher sensitivity with the use of user data is therefore to be expected, as consumers increasingly expect moral attitudes from companies.

The latest 2022 study proves that with the pandemic and its impact, a "Me over We" mentality is becoming more apparent.[22] In these times, brands should pay particular attention to the issue of caring, respond adequately to the new attitudes, and create a balance between individual needs and community responsibilities.[23]

The study by Qi Chen and other researchers from China further illustrates the paradox of personalization. The factors of gaining from personalized offers are opposed to giving up ownership of one's own data. They recommend that MA solutions should not only be geared to positive responses, but also to negative ones. Specifically, better-tailored personalizations, the concession of privacy protection and openness with data handling are aspects to be taken seriously, while attempts to conceal encroaching data use are to be avoided.[24]

In comparison with the interviews, it can be stated that the customer approach must be applied industry-specifically and, above all, played out accordingly at different frequencies. Constant impressions are just as important as the understanding of when direct automation should take place and when such processes may at best run in the background. Valued personalization can happen above all when customers have willingly decided to interact with the company, whereby the perspective of inbound marketing comes into play here again. In this context, customers must not be pushed but guided when approaching and handing them over to various touchpoints. Transparency in data use is not only mandatory by law, but also necessary in the spirit of customer centricity, because some measures can seem sinister and inhuman.

This is where the research results come in. Studies have shown quantitatively that customers want personalized addresses in the majority, but that there are differences

[18] Cf. Accenture (2019): p. 18.

[19] Cf. Accenture (2020): p. 8.

[20] Vgö. Accenture (2020): p. 2.

[21] Cf. Accenture (2021): p. 2.

[22] Cf. Accenture (2022): p. 2.

[23] Cf. Accenture (2022): pp. 12–14.

[24] Cf. Chen et al. (2019): p. 60.

in the perception of such measures. For example, geo-tracking and retargeting in particular have been classified as very unpleasant, which can be incorporated in the area of outbound marketing. Openness with data handling and securing privacy have been proven to have positive connotations, while obfuscation attempts and encroaching data use are to be avoided. In the context of the brand image, the connection to customer loyalty comes to light here, because as was stated in the definition of customer loyalty, this is not only rationally justifiable, but emotional in nature, especially with end customers. Against this background, the aforementioned transparency and the feeling of security with regard to MA processes are even more concise.

3 Legal Aspects of the MA

At first glance, MA and data protection are incompatible. For example, MA processes mostly aim to exploit personal data, while the GDPR counteracts this, aims to protect consumer data, and establishes regulations.[25]

MA relevant processes can be divided into two topics from a legal point of view: On the one hand, the declaration of consent for the storage of personal data and, on the other hand, the regulations for the permission of direct interaction and advertising measures with the customer, for example via email distribution lists. Both areas have widely differentiated applications and are therefore precisely regulated. Some of the most important functions and their limiting regulations must be explained in more detail here, since the possibilities are enormous on the one hand, but the regulations represent incisive and yet comprehensible barriers. In the following, these possibilities, which have become the focus of the GDPR, will first be shown in order to then describe their legal framework.

Since customers were first interested parties and are rarely interacted with directly, the subject area of personal data should precede. These are divided into three different categories: Personal master data, which in the case of B2C companies is usually stored by the direct input of the user himself. Transaction data is geared to processing and provides information on invoices, orders, deliveries, returns, etc. Linked to this is behavioral data, which includes information on purchasing behavior, preferences for brands, website visits, social media usage, etc.

Thus, there are four different sources for such data. In order to be able to use zero, first, second, and third data, different cookies are used, which are briefly described in detail. Normal cookies are text files that are stored in the browser and are either only exchanged between the user and the domain, or can also be used with third-party servers for advertising material. The super cookies are even more extensive, they can also retrieve data across browsers and forward user behavior to a detailed extent. Social widgets integrated into one's website can exchange user data between social

[25]Cf. Thorit (2019): o. p.

media platforms and the domain. App-based master and behavioral data is also stored by creating and tracking advertising IDs for customers. In addition, there are options such as cross-domain tracking, cross-device tracking, and mouse tracking on the company's own website.[26] Tools for establishing such data collection are led by Google Analytics, followed by Adobe Analytics. There are many other applications on the market that offer either partial or complete solutions, but a comparison is too extensive in this framework.

For consumer protection, the provisions of the GDPR have stipulated that personal data require direct consent from the user. Even cookies that do not collect personal data must be accepted voluntarily by the consumer, unless they are technically necessary for the website operator.[27] In addition, all data collected in the EU is required to be stored only on servers in the EU, so companies must screen tools for this restriction. The legal obligations further require companies to prepare a service contract with the MA service provider, which includes the access conditions, the handling of personal data, and the security measures. It must be stated which company will handle the data processing and also at which location it will then take place. The customer himself must be informed that cookies are set and, for example, click behavior is stored. They should always have the option of objecting to the storage and processing of their own data or having it deleted.[28] This should be cleverly described by companies in order, on the one hand, to decimate the number of customers who decide against cookies or, in the worst case, leave the website. On the other hand, the texts must meet legal requirements.

The scope of importance of automated interactions includes email distribution lists, remarketing, personalized content on the website, such as favorited products, but also phone calls, social media channels, and other touchpoints.

Automated email distribution lists offer a wide range of contact options, depending on the tool scope, which can be highly personalized through detailed customer profiles. In the basic function, A/B tests, cyclical mailings, monitoring of email delivery, etc. can take place. In extensions, for example, personalized product offers are sent, or recipient groups are addressed according to behavioral segmentation. The resulting improved click-through rates allow marketers to nurture higher-quality leads and collect and analyze behavioral data.[29] For such personalized e-mails, opt-in procedures are legally required and clear consent by the customer is mandatory. In the same way, customers must have the option of opting out of these advertising measures, but there is no time limit on the initial consent.[30]

Remarketing is mainly used to serve ads on various channels, which allow companies to use third-party cookies to draw the attention of potential customers to products across websites and browsers, which follow specific product allocations

---

[26] Cf. IT-WINGS (2020): o. p.

[27] Cf. Schirmbacher (2017): p. 295.

[28] Cf. Thorit (2019): o. p.

[29] Cf. Schoepf (2016): o. S.

[30] Cf. Schirmbacher (2017): p. 450f.

depending on the customer profile. According to the GDPR, such practices must also be permitted by the user via opt-in.[31]

Personalized content must be approved according to the same rules and can be expanded or restricted depending on permission. If users opt in completely, tailored products that have previously been searched for by users on other platforms can be displayed on the customer journey when they visit the company's own website. However, even with complete rejection of advertising permission, websites can at least import the products according to the pattern of the predecessors in the current search history.[32]

For telephone calls, there is the option of recording conversations, conducting automated customer surveys, and setting up call tracking. In the latter case, calls are analyzed automatically in order to record actual conversions if, for example, there is no online store and the sale has to be made over the phone. In any case, the customer's unambiguous consent to the recording of his or her call must be obtained. In some cases, such as when a contract is concluded verbally, this may also be required of the company.[33]

Interactions on social media networks can be greatly simplified by automation tools. They include, for example, linking pre-scheduled posts and blog content, tracking mentions and conversations, activity tracking, and all of this across platforms. But those who want to engage in such activities must legally obtain permission in two ways. On the way from the social network to the website, customers must consent about the storage of their data, as well as on the reverse way, when inviting to social media platforms on their own website. In addition, surreptitious advertising must be displayed as advertising material.[34]

In conclusion, the GDPR has imposed barriers on the marketing efforts of companies to protect users' data, but these are not insurmountable and self-determination of consent also gives users confidence and security.

This regulation was to come into force at the same time as the GDPR in May 2018, but negotiations continued until now. In February 2021, there was then a final draft, which will probably come into force in 2022/2023.[35] This regulation will bring the following six changes:

1. Encryption of user data must now also be ensured by the provider.
2. Spatial tracking by programs that are not actively used is prohibited.
3. Data providers may be required to disclose by government law enforcement requests.
4. Data processing will no longer be possible without consent.

[31] Cf. Datenschutz.org (2021): o. S.

[32] Cf. Hagemeyer (2018): o. p.

[33] Cf. Müller (2020): o. S.

[34] Cf. Schirmbacher (2017): p. 128.

[35] Cf. Winkler and Weick (2021): o. S.

5. Tracking protection measures are to be expanded.
6. Software and devices should be data protection-friendly by default.[36]

These provisions will impose deep restrictions on many companies, which is probably why the negotiations lasted so long. The economic reactions remain to be seen.

In summary, with regard to the GDPR, the consensus across research and interviews is to recognize and value the regulations on data protection. They reflect the interests of consumers and must be complied with at all costs. The ePrivacy Regulation as well as planned restrictions by Google will tighten these regulations again in the near future. Therefore, the focus on zero- and first-party data will be central in the future and will force companies to make better use of collected data, which may lead to existing inaccuracies in data analysis becoming more precise. With regard to customer centricity, the legal requirements mean above all that customer interests must be taken into account, and this is again related to customer loyalty.

4 Conclusion and Outlook

The results will now be summarized in the conclusion. It can be stated that the engine of the MA processes is customer centricity. For this reason, other departments must interlock in the same way in the automation network of a CDP and bundle data in it. This should be followed by a shift in thinking from campaigns to personalized triggers, which requires the segmentation of customers based on data from the CDP. In the end, the personalized customer journey will be a success if the rules of CX are observed. In doing so, each company must weigh up which tools are best suited to the customer journey. Large tool providers have the most mature systems and the most connections to other software. Predicted trends toward voice, AI, Internet of Things, digital out-of-home, and no-code developments, as well as data-related trends such as big ops, CDPs, and connectivity of tools are likely to be covered most comprehensively by these big players.

Furthermore, the final question to be answered is: What is the relationship between end customers' touch points with marketing automation processes and customer loyalty?

As was clearly evident, the easy-to-understand conclusion that well-applied MA processes promote customer loyalty, but poor ones can also harm it, has been substantiated by the experts' statements. It was possible to clarify more profound operational elements that enable a successful, personalized customer approach. On the other hand, emotional connections between the experience values of employees and customer loyalty were demonstrated. Such come about conducively when, in the process of gaining personalized content versus losing private data, a basis of trust has

[36] Cf. Datenschutz.org (2022): o. S.

been established that is based on transparency and security. This is further reinforced by the fact that studies have demonstrated the increasing need of customers for brands and products with corporate social responsibility. The boiling point of broken trust with regard to the use of personal data here lies in the individually intense willingness of customers to receive personalized content. A comparison of more acceptable and more off-putting addresses can be made with inbound and outbound marketing measures in the context of MA processes, whereby outbound tends to entail negative reputations. If customers remain uninformed about the use of their data, this is not conducive to promoting customer loyalty. This circumstance comes to a head again, especially with regard to the current legal situation. Anyone who is only forced by a company he/she trusts to provide information on data use and to sacrifice consent runs the risk of losing the loyalty of customers or not gaining it in the first place.

The second assumption, that without a clear added value of MA processes, reactances can arise and thus damage customer loyalty, can also be confirmed by the results.

With regard to the entire paper, it was particularly noticeable that research work as well as the expert interviews yielded the same results and complemented each other.

It can also be stated that in the context of MA, B2C companies only have significant differences in the approach to customer experience compared to B2B companies. As already known from theory, B2C companies have the special position in connection with MA processes of serving individuals who, in contrast to business customers, are usually left to their own devices in their decision-making process for product purchase and thus the brand image plays a much more important role. Thus, they generally need to be persuaded differently than in the B2B model. The otherwise generally illustrated findings are equally relevant for both industries. The focus is primarily on current impact mechanisms, which must always be expanded or reevaluated in the context of new circumstances. At the same time, the totality of the information content of these various dimensions reveals a new perspective on the strategic and operational options for action in the context of MA processes. This perspective is now to be rounded off by the outlook.

A practical implementation of good personalization can be illustrated using the example of Zalando's "Zalon." This platform deliberately offers customers personalized products as part of a style consultation based on previously collected zero-party data. In this sense, the win-win situation is very clear and beneficial. A step more progressive would be a conceivable introduction to personalization and data use in which the customer is presented in detail with the benefits of individual cookies, not in a data protection text on the smallest text size, but with an entertainment character and with the hopeful prospect that even cookies judged by the majority to be off-putting will be regarded as normal in the future, either through advancing digitization or simply through habituation effects. The final sentence, however, is left to an interview quote from Brinker, who gets to the heart of the relationship between MA and customer interests: "(Companies say) customers are number one and all these platitudes. Well, this is where you actually put your money where your mouth is: your customer is telling you how they want you to engage with them and how they don't want you to engage with them. And so if the customers are really number one, do things the way they want. It's not rocket science."

References

Accenture. (2018). *2018 personalization pulse check*. Accessed December 19, 2021, from https://www.accenture.com/_acnmedia/PDF-83/Accenture-Making-Personal.pdf#zoom=50

Accenture. (2019). *Interactive consumer pulse survey*. Accessed December 23, 2021, from https://www.accenture.com/_acnmedia/PDF-113/Accenture-Interactive-2019-Consumer-Pulse-Survey.pdf

Accenture. (2020). *Evolution of customer experience report*. Accessed December 23, 2021, from https://www.accenture.com/_acnmedia/Thought-Leadership-Assets/PDF-4/Accenture-Interactive-Business-of-Experience-Full-Report.pdf

Accenture. (2021). *Life-reimagined-full report*. Accessed December 23, 2021, from https://www.accenture.com/_acnmedia/PDF-161/Accenture-Life-Reimagined-Full-Report.pdf

Accenture. (2022). *Fjord Trends 2022*. Accessed May 7, 2022, from https://www.accenture.com/_acnmedia/PDF-169/Accenture-Fjord-Trends-2022-Full-Report.pdf#zoom=40

AX Semantics. (n.d.). *What is customer experience optimization?* AX Semantics. Accessed December 19, 2021, from https://en.ax-semantics.com/what-is-customer-experience-optimization/

Boadum, L. (2021). *Customer loyalty vs. retention: What's the difference?* Accessed January 28, 2022, from https://blog.hubspot.de/service/kundenloyalitaet

Brinker, S. (2020a). *51 martech stacks shared in the 2020 Stackie Awards, beautifully illustrated examples of modern marketing toolsets*. Accessed December 15, 2021, from https://chiefmartec.com/2020/10/51-martech-stacks-shared-2020-stackie-awards/

Brinker, S. (2020b). *Martech 2030 Trend #3: The Great App Explosion*. Accessed January 24, 2022, from https://chiefmartec.com/2020/12/martech-2030-trend-3-great-app-explosion/

Brinker, S. (2021). *2021: The year Martech shrank – just kidding (a year in review)*. Accessed January 24, 2022, from https://chiefmartec.com/2021/12/2021-the-year-martech-shrank-just-kidding-a-year-in-review/

Chen, Q., Feng, Y., Liu, L., & Tian, X. (2019). *International Journal of Information Management, 44*, 53–64. https://doi.org/10.1016/j.ijinfomgt.2018.09.001

Datenschutz.org. (2021). *Third party cookies and the GDPR I data protection 2022*. Accessed January 15, 2022, from https://www.datenschutz.org/third-party-cookies/

Datenschutz.org. (2022). *ePrivacy regulation: The supplement to the EU data protection regulation*. Accessed January 17, 2022, from https://www.datenschutz.org/eprivacy-verordnung/

Davis, K. (2020). Davis. *MarTech*.

Hagemeyer, C. (2018). *DSGVO und Personalisierung - Geht das?* Accessed January 15, 2022, from https://www.econda.de/2018/dsgvo-eprivacy-datenschutz/dsgvo-und-personalisierung-geht-das/

IT-WINGS. (2020). *Tracking tools: Info, functions & providers* I IT-WINGS Blog. Accessed December 28, 2021, from https://it-wings.de/blog/tracking-tools/

Karc, D. (2021). *Programmatic-out-of-home in a nutshell*. Accessed January 15, 2022, from https://www.adzine.de/2021/01/programmatic-out-of-home-in-a-nutshell/

Kuhlmann-rhinow, I. (2021). *Der Unterschied zwischen Outbound- und Inbound-Marketing*. Accessed January 25, 2022, from https://blog.hubspot.de/marketing/outbound-vs-inbound-marketing

Malz, C. (2021). *BSI LIVE I Big Ops: Interaction of automation, communication and data*. Accessed December 19, 2021, from https://www.bsi-software.com/de-de/live/post/von-big-data-zu-big-ops-prozessabstimmung-leicht-gemacht

Müller, J. L. (2020). *DSGVO: When and under what conditions is the recording of telephone conversations with customers permissible under data protection law?* Accessed January 16, 2022, from https://www.it-recht-kanzlei.de/aufzeichnung-von-telefongespraechen-nach-dsgvo-zulaessig.html

Parker, P. (2022). *What are marketing automation platforms, what do they do, and how is the vendor landscape changing?* Accessed January 24, 2022, from https://martech.org/martech-landscape-what-is-marketing-automation-software/#Who%E2%80%99s-who-in-B2B-Marketing-Automation

Pattekwith, S., Cooperstein, D. M., & Hayes, A. (2014). *The evolved CMO in 2014.* Accessed December 14, 2021, from https://de.slideshare.net/sebastianvogt/the-evolvedcmoin2014

Petersen, M. (2018). *Marketing automation: 5 processes you should automate.* Accessed December 25, 2021, from https://t3n.de/news/marketing-automation-5-prozesse-683962/?preview=true&pp=da2ce58775923015577fd1a22810235b

Pleßke, F. (2021). *Marketing automation.* SC-Networks.

Schirmbacher, M. (2017). *Online marketing and social media law: The comprehensive practical handbook for all legal issues in marketing* (2nd ed.). mitp, Ciando.

Schoepf, A. (2016). *Difference email marketing software to marketing automation.* Accessed December 21, 2021, from https://www.marketingautomation.tech/unterschied-email-marketing-automation/

Shukla, S. (2022). *9 Marketing automation trends of 2022.* Accessed January 24, 2022, from https://webengage.com/blog/top-marketing-automation-trends/

Thorit. (2019). *Marketing Automation & Datenschutz - das gilt es zu beachten.* Accessed December 27, 2021, from https://www.thorit.de/marketing-automation-datenschutz/

Totka, M. (2013). *Inbound marketing vs. "interruption marketing".* Accessed January 25, 2022, from https://www.business2community.com/marketing/inbound-marketing-vs-interruption-marketing-0655783

Winkler, L., & Weick, C. (2021). *Telecommunications – E-privacy regulation.* Accessed January 17, 2022, from https://www.bfdi.bund.de/DE/Fachthemen/Inhalte/Telefon-Internet/Positionen/ePrivacy_Verordnung.html

Janosch Baum is currently employed as a product marketing manager at the KATIMEX Cielker GmbH. His range of services includes design and IT implementations as well as analytical and strategic marketing skills within more than 11 years of work experience, most of it international. He completed his master's thesis while studying in the Design and Media Management Master program at RheinMain University of Applied Sciences in spring 2022, in which he researched the topic of marketing automation in B2C companies.

[illegible]

Marketing Automation for Tobacco Companies

Tobias Voigt

1 Welcome to the MarTech Arena

Since their inception, marketing departments have tried to sell their expenses as an investment in future sales. In principle, this is correct. But it's very hard to prove in euros and cents. Metric marketing stops where rationally conceived purchase triggers are supposed to lead to an emotionally driven purchase decision. The situation is completely different when it comes to marketing costs. If you vary them, the effects are immediately noticeable—or not. And that's exactly where resourceful company management comes in today.

The answer lies in digital transformation, which also affects marketing. MarTech is the name of the alchemy that is to ensure cost savings and efficiency increases of up to 30% in the future with digitally transformed marketing processes. VW recently announced this benchmark publicly. In this respect, the figure is not plucked out of the air, but quite possible, as a look at the results of more than 60 completed MarTech projects by markenautomat consultants shows (see Fig. 1). 100 marketing decision makers who have successfully implemented a MarTech automation tool were surveyed.

► Martech is the combination of marketing and technology and specifically refers to tools, platforms, solutions, and systems that use digital technologies to achieve marketing goals.

Specifically, it's about tools and software systems that make the life of the modern marketer easier. From agile collaboration in different teams, which well-known tools like Slack, Jira & Co. map quite well, to release routines, which can be handled quite smoothly with Workfront, Wrike, Hatchbuck & Co., to the production and programmatic distribution of advertising materials with SOCOTO, JobFlow,

T. Voigt (✉)
Markenmut AG, Frankfurt, Germany
e-mail: t.voigt@markenmut.de

U. Hannig, U. Seebacher (eds.), *Marketing and Sales Automation*, Management for Professionals, https://doi.org/10.1007/978-3-031-20040-3_14

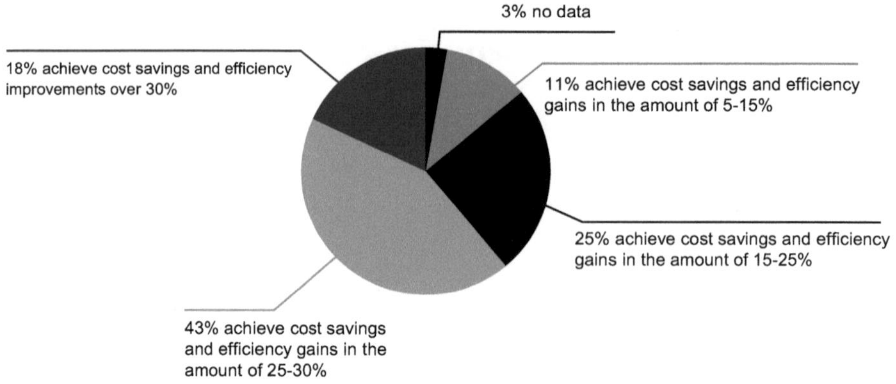

Fig. 1 Achieved results of completed MarTech projects (Source: Markenmut, 2022)

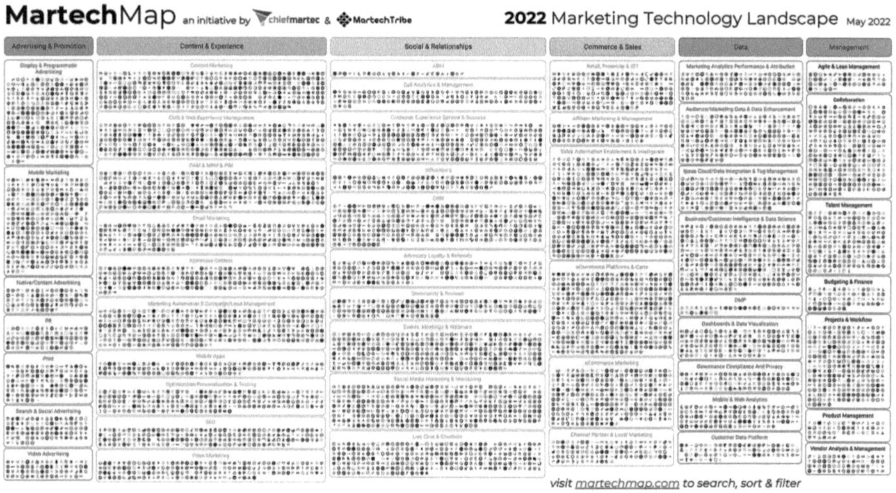

Fig. 2 Marketing technology landscape (Source: Chiefmartec, 2022)

Chilli-Publish & Co. And these are just three of the many disciplines offered for automation in the current MarTech Arena. Automated market research, AI-powered CRM systems, customer journey algorithms, and customer experience solutions, and of course all-in-one marketing clouds are on the wish lists of digital native CMOs these days. The problem with this is that there are simply many. For most people, clearly too many, because even the standard industry overview of the Chief Marketing Technologist blog "Martech Today" (see Fig. 2) with the significant name MarTech5000 lists meanwhile 9932 providers and also quite often forgets the one or other national solution provider.

2 The Right Toolstack Counts

The classification of tools is almost infinite: collaboration, release routines, conversion booster, programmatic distribution, all-in-one marketing systems, and so on. Once the call for MarTech has been raised in the company, processes must be audited and structures adapted before the selection of relevant and suitable tools, systems, and platforms can begin. As shown above, the current offering is huge and is supplemented by other smaller specialized providers, most of which have very mature and specific solutions for individual marketing operations in their quiver or, even more granularly, offer completely individually developed solutions.

At this stage at the latest, experts are needed who can make a suitable recommendation based on a requirements matrix. Requirements such as budget, work culture, networking of marketing and IT, existing processes, and resources as well as data flows quickly become a complex profile, which only specialized consultants with up-to-date MarTech know-how can combine into an individual best-of-breed toolstack recommendation.

In addition, there is the usually desired agile approach, in which not everything is fixed at the beginning, but rather keeps options open far beyond the horizon. In other words, systems that can be adapted sustainably and flexibly to the further and growing requirements of the respective marketing department. Once the right toolstack has been found, it's really "welcome to the MarTech arena," because even the providers are rapidly developing their systems on a daily basis. Staying up-to-date is a challenge in itself. But it is certainly the most important challenge for a successful marketing manager in the future.

3 Digital Transformation of Tobacco Operations

In the production and distribution of tobacco products, the "economy of scale" is firmly anchored in the entrepreneurial DNA. After all, there is no faster-growing crop, and the costs of the processing operation increase only slightly as the volume grows. So the step to automating recurring processes in marketing is not really that far either. The only disadvantage—but a decisive one—is the now extremely strict regulation of tobacco marketing and the associated considerable lack of customer-specific data.

In order to enjoy a cigarette or a cigarillo, the consumer, who is often willing to provide information in other industries, does not like to disclose his personal data. The value and benefit is often too low and, moreover, there are even customer segments that conceal their tobacco consumption under social pressure. So all that's left is to collect behavioral patterns and Big Data analytics to decipher customer flows, insights, and buying patterns. And before the creative agency picks up the ball and sings a plea for good old target group empathy, modern MarTech systems prefer to rely on statistics, psychometrics, or even AI-supported and graph-based data analytics. With skillfully placed pixels and cookies, tobacco consumers can at least be encircled today and even given a measurable momentum in the brand flywheel via user-generated content. Greetings from the Zero Moment of Truth.

Digital makes marketing more complex, but also more differentiated in its possibilities. Especially in daily consumption, where products are bought for immediate consumption, an impulse in real time is often the decisive stimulus. This is also the case when a digital brand presence is simply prohibited by law. Nevertheless, consumer dialogs to and about brands do take place. Anyone who has recognized this and not only automatically tracks the activities from user dialog and user-generated content to reaching for the shelf, but also reads and interprets the data set and uses it as a basis for decision-making for customer-centric packaging design as well as POS support, has arrived at digitally transformed tobacco marketing. At least for today.

The biggest changes in the digital transformation of tobacco marketing can be traced back to the Advertising Ban, which the WHO has massively promoted worldwide. Hardly any country in the world no longer restricts tobacco advertising. Most of them are even quite rigid, including plain packaging and a complete ban on any brand presence. What remains are customer dialogs and user-generated content. This, in turn, is difficult to control, and to make it even more difficult, it usually takes place on the social web. This means that tobacco-relevant target groups often only leave behind really meaningful psychometrics with the large walled garden providers. Anyone who thinks that the walled gardens want to see their very own MarTech stacks being used is in for a nasty surprise. Facebook, Google, Amazon and Co. also have their Tobacco restrictions on the surface, of course. In reality, however, there are often fans who communicate more or less on their own about tobacco products in social media.

Open MarTech systems and their interfaces to relevant customer data can therefore at least help to gain valuable insights into customers and their consumption behavior. Many tobacco marketers have already started to enrich their social listening with relevant psychometrics from third-party providers (Big Data) in order to generate insights about high-potential affinity spaces. Admittedly, not an easy task, but the right insights have been proven to help send more effective messages to the right recipients at the right time. Even in highly regulated markets. That's where the detail makes all the difference.

This is one reason, by the way, why modern tobacco marketing can be measured by business growth or slowed business decline and no longer by the very own marketing KPIs such as awareness and reach of their brands. In a perfectly digitalized world, one would be able to directly link all marketing activities across the entire customer journey up to the contribution to results of the respective customer touchpoint. In reality, this is not possible due to regulations, but the MarTech landscape and in particular AI-supported predictive graph-based analytics are constantly evolving here as well. For example, it has emerged that two metrics in particular are crucial for business success in tobacco marketing:

- What downstream influence on sales or earnings contribution do packaging optimizations, brand stages, and POS activities have?
- Do any of the actions help the tobacco trade?

As soon as you have a target image of your marketing processes in terms of data and desired results, there are currently a large number of digital helpers for identifying, conquering, and retaining a consumer who is willing to buy. And even customer lifetime values can now be predicted quite accurately on an individual basis using data.

Marketing automation is ultimately the cherry on the cake in the digital transformation of tobacco marketing. This is because digitally optimized tobacco marketing reaches the most profitable customers via the most cost-effective (and permitted) channels. Monitoring, analytics, programmatically purchased ad inventories, automatically adapted ads, and ultimately, on-target playouts lead to a definitive competitive advantage that will permanently transform the tobacco industry. Where brands like Marlboro, Camel & Co used to set the tone, smart price challengers with their data-driven marketing departments are now outpacing the former top dogs. The key is not only to understand the respective customer through experience and empathy, but also to scale such knowledge. This is the only way to continue to market products profitably, even in the face of constant price competition.

The good news is that as long as customer behavior continues to change and evolve, there is reason enough to be optimistic about an albeit immensely limited future for the tobacco marketing guild. After all, with the possibilities of digital transformation and the skillful use of individual MarTech advantages, the marketing of tobacco manufacturers can still contribute to a rewarding business model.

4 Best-of-Breed Marketing Automation Toolstacks

The global Tobacco industry is aggregating a variety of highly complex business models and is undergoing massive change with the introduction of e-cigarettes. The perceived disruption from new product offerings such as electronic vaporizers brings some breathing space—but does not solve the fundamental problems of a business model around health-hazardous stimulants.

That's why the marketing of a classic tobacco product is fraught with pitfalls in the regulated market as well as in the retail environment, and the same regulations will sooner or later apply to e-cigarettes and vaporizers. Therefore, it is almost impossible to give a clear recommendation for an optimal MarTech combination of systems, tools, platforms, and solutions. But there are recurring processes in tobacco marketing that we can illuminate quite well from the perspective of marketing automation.

Let's go straight to one of the most regulated markets in the world:

Cigarettes in the EU

Regulated production processes and plenty of insight market research provide tons of work before a product is even ready for the market. When it comes to "going to market," we are supposedly "back to the roots," having returned to a complete focus on specialist retailers, food stores, and outlets. But today, there is also a user-generated feedback loop around the ZMOT that cannot be ignored.

In addition, of course, as suitable as possible for different markets, different marketing structures and fundamentally different compliance, governance and risk requirements: From languages and approvals to regional productions and local requirements in—albeit very limited—advertising. There are indeed small but subtle differences between POS displays that may only be two-dimensional in one market and even three-dimensional in the next. And finally, please never forget the respective national law and its interpretation. For example, "A brand claim that is not allowed to be promotional" is a rule that can be interpreted broadly. Following this never-ending complexity, a best-of-breed marketing automation toolstack for tobacco manufacturers and distributors is bound to be one that offers something of each. An all-around package would actually be the order of the day here. The problem is that no marketing machine, no matter how perfect, will be able to do this. A complex quickly becomes a complex to the power of ten. That's why it's important to gradually extract the efficiencies from the individual marketing process modules.

►*Agile Insights:* The core of every tobacco product in the EU is the purchase intent and the question of its volume. This can only be answered by sophisticated market research, which is actually difficult to map in the current MarTech landscape. The only exception and therefore also here for once a concrete provider recommendation: QUANTILOPE. QUANTILOPE has developed an agile insights ecosystem and tool stack that can actually map the multi-layered market research in tobacco marketing in a partially automated way. All this in combination with a powerful social listening/monitoring tool that keeps its ear to the ground and can filter out user-generated content from the web just as well as derive relevant psychographics from it. In other words, the basic armamentarium of all tobacco marketing.

In tobacco markets with varying governance, compliance, and risk structures, it is worth taking a look at collaboration tools with mature approval processes to keep the complex legal requirements under control and to prevent integrated risk documentation from becoming an administrative nightmare. Once the product is ready for the market, a dynamic product information management system is recommended, which provides the most important communication credentials such as logos, packaging (pack shots), and brand stages for various stakeholders. Ideally in combination with a localization tool for automatic translation into all relevant languages.

A central platform for the CI-compliant production and distribution of the most important POS advertising materials, both analog and digital (displays, etc.), can make the underlying logistical and recurring processes significantly more efficient. At best, this should be multi-client capable for branch-based retailer structures and, if required, in combination with an advertising subsidy system that actively involves retailers in the production and distribution of POS advertising materials.

Important for ZMOT and the associated momentum in the feedback brand flywheel: a monitoring and social listening tool that analyzes brand loyalty in all user-generated content. Nothing is more important than brand reputation, which is influenced in a controlled way at best.

►*Conclusions:* An ecosystem of 2–4 tools, solutions, and systems connected by individual interfaces covers the basic marketing workflow for a present tobacco brand. More countries, more tasks and more possibilities are then offered by further extensions that an open platform can accommodate via interfaces.

The Cigarillo Manufacturers

The cigarillo manufacturers are actually not inferior to the cigarettes in anything—only that no one really throws an eye on these pleasure products. In this respect, some regulations are still relaxed here and the competition among each other is not so acrimonious as to threaten a legal sword of Damocles at every step.

Particularly in communication, which today takes place especially via communities on the social web, cigarillos and cigars are accorded less the status of a "gateway drug" for young people here, and more a role as a means of enjoyment for adults. Metrics are all the more the choice of the hour—even when it comes to such important topics as testimonials and influencers. Of course, this requires a variety of flexible and high-performance interfaces, which a marketing automation system must provide for a cigarillo brand. Starting with the Insight Mafo and ending with the Customer Experience.

Agile and automated market research lays the foundation of an efficient tool stack. As described earlier, the provider Quantilope is the first and unrivaled choice of the hour. This requires a collaboration tool that coordinates and sustainably documents the complex and numerous coordination processes of the stakeholders involved. At best, there is integrated risk documentation so that product development is always on the safe side.

Once the product has been developed, a dynamic product information management system is recommended, which provides the most important communication credentials such as logos, packaging (pack shots), and brand stages for a wide range of applications.

Customer journeys in the cigarillo and cigar segment often start in the inspiration phase in special interests, communities on the social web, or even special points on smoking desire (cigar lounges). So it is all the more difficult when the corresponding basic data is well protected at the walled gardens and can only be tapped with difficulty. And all the more important is a mature community and email management, which can identify and bind brand interested parties. The whole thing is then enriched with a central platform for the CI-compliant production of the most important advertising materials, both analog (advertising incentives, POS, etc.) and digital (displays, etc.). Ideally in combination with an advertising subsidy system, which actively involves retailers in the production and distribution of advertising materials.

Monetizing a complete customer lifetime value is also a decisive success factor for cigarillo and cigar manufacturers. After all, it is much easier and more cost-effective to persuade an existing customer to buy again than to acquire a new customer. In this respect, a customer experience extension with interfaces to bots and messenger services as well as an e-mail-based CRM system is a MarTech investment well spent when it comes to establishing a brand community.

►*Conclusions:* Of course, the basis of a cigarillo and cigar marketing automation system is initially the brand content. Due to the rapid development in influencer marketing, a very small-scale ecosystem is required, especially for social communications, in order to secure competitive advantages through marketing automation. Not an easy task for a suitable selection of possible tool stacks.

The International Perspective

Despite the numerous restrictions and regulations, there are still some interesting markets for potential advertising activities in the tobacco segment from an international perspective. Most industrialized countries are clearly regulated, but some developing countries still allow a range of activities.

In Asia, Indonesia is a market with fractal and small-scale trade structures, but overall it is high-volume and only partially regulated. Furthermore, there are still a considerable number of countries on the African continent in which the implementation of WHO-required regulations is slow, while there is considerable potential among the relevant target groups of adults. In addition, purchasing power is also rising sharply here, so that countries on the equatorial belt in particular deserve a closer look.

In terms of marketing, of course, the communication channels and trade structures are completely different here, so that even a MarTech toolstack must be viewed in a completely differentiated way. Ultimately, this does not make things easier, but rather more complex.

PIM and MAM incl. automatic translation into the numerous languages are mandatory for a tobacco brand. However, automated Mafo takes place on the street in the countries mentioned—so it is negligible. Done is better than perfect is the better option in such countries.

The highest automation potential is in the production of advertising materials. At best, a large combination system can completely cover the production of a wide variety of formats and advertising materials. From the display at the POS to the retailer-individualized sales booth system.

In addition, Africa has its own peculiarities when it comes to the most common communication channels: billboards and, above all, mobile notification. Cell phones are the communication lifeline of the African continent and the networks are developed in an exemplary manner. In addition, there are simple but highly efficient channels, such as the good old SMS, which is used a lot in Africa. Push notification tools are the basis for far-reaching advertising communication—combined with the most unusual promotions, incentives, and competitions.

Customer journeys with the help of notification messenger services and chatbots, which are based on a comprehensive customer experience system for high brand relevance or ZMOT provide momentum for the corresponding brand flywheel, which should not be underestimated.

►*Conclusions:* Particularly in individual international markets, it is worth taking a look at local conditions. In other words, the focus on customer mobile experience in combination with automated advertising production has a high potential for efficiency and success.

5 The Royal Road to the Right Toolstack

A common rule: It's easier written than done. Because marketing automation is not an easy task for marketing departments. It always involves uncharted territory. And if the setup is not configured correctly right from the start, marketing automation can quickly turn into a pipe burst. In addition, there are new processes that require new structures and, as with every transformation process, it is important to bring employees along with you instead of leaving them behind. In the end, it is the people who determine the success or failure of a transformation to marketing automation.

The most important first step is the marketing audit. After all, everyone involved needs to know how the existing processes actually work and what they were originally intended to achieve or what they actually do. And anyone who now thinks that an organization should know what it is doing is seriously mistaken. Only those who illuminate the furthest corners can really see what the status is and what can become of it. And in addition, a successful transformation toward marketing automation is always opposed by existing processes and structures that were never designed for automation. Auditing processes therefore also means questioning "we've always done it this way."

It is important to analyze exactly where and how automation can actually help to make processes faster and more efficient. At the same time, fears must be eliminated in a parallel change process. Silos have to be torn down and collaboration instead of competition has to be promoted. Even and especially with participating service providers, platforms, and system vendors. Once the change process has been planned and the processes audited, the next step is to select relevant and appropriate tools, systems, and platforms.

The current range of marketing systems includes around 10,000 providers and offers many other smaller specialist providers, from all-in-one systems such as Salesforce, Adobe & Co, which usually have very sophisticated and special solutions for individual marketing operations in their quiver. At this point at the latest, experts are needed who can make a suitable BEST-OF-BREED recommendation based on a requirements matrix.

Once you have defined your desired toolstack, it's time for purchasing and implementation. Here, it is not only experience in the MarTech market that helps with regard to possible conditions and compensation models. A look beyond the horizon of marketing budget allocation is also an important basis for a full cost calculation of a (partially) automated marketing process chain that can be expanded in a sustainable and future-proof manner (see Fig. 3).

Furthermore, the existing IT infrastructure must also be tested for its networking capability. What is the use of the next silo in marketing, when the actual goal should

Fig. 3 Pre-requisites for success (Source: Markenmut, 2022)

be to tear down silos? ERP systems, middleware, data sources, and existing supply chains need to be kept in view just as much as existing workplaces and data warehouses. A dash of healthy realism is always part of the equation. What good is a high-end marketing system if the marketing staff involved are working on outdated workstations whose operating systems are not capable of controlling MarTech tools in their full breadth? The same applies to human resources. Are there enough employees willing and able to actively use and support such an automation structure? Or does too large a best-of-breed system simply overwhelm them at the beginning? Ultimately, the truth lies between the perceived challenge and the perceived ability to accept it. A team in perma-powerstress mode doesn't help anyone in the long run. Just as little as underchallenges, by the way. That's why it's important to find the right mix and include it in strategic planning with the right toolstack.

At best, all of this must flow into an optimal, individual toolstack. A specification sheet with clear requirements for the system providers makes a lot of things easier. From the required interfaces to the test environment and training, this is the best way to find and put together the right partners.

The goal of automation is thus not only to improve the input/output ratio, but also to increase the effectiveness of the measures implemented, e.g., through personalized communication geared to individual needs. Automation is always useful when repetitive tasks are carried out more cost-effectively by a machine, freeing up time for more value-adding activities for the employees previously tasked with performing them.

When looking for processes to automate, it is important to keep the entire company in mind. Even a process that is triggered only once a year in a subsidiary company or is required in a branch office may well lend itself to automation if it is used at hundreds of locations worldwide. A campaign developed for one product can be used for several other products. Advertising can be created in one language and placed in several in different countries. Thus, the reusability of processes or process components represents a significant savings potential.

It is advisable to create a list of all recurring activities in marketing and sales sorted by their frequency, e.g. weekly, monthly, quarterly, or annually. The next step is to determine which processes or process steps can be automated. For these, the savings effects and the effort of automation must then be estimated. The corresponding comparison shows where automation is most worthwhile and thus with which processes to start.

6 Push the Button and Go!

The car is in the yard, but no one can drive it. To prevent this from happening, training and support should be clarified in advance. Many large systems also refer customers to specialized service providers. The marketing engineers by markenmut AG like to call it “Chauffeur services.”

Who takes care of the initial filling of the systems? The templating of running campaigns? The setup of dashboards and setting of the desired KPIs to be measured? Where can the system help even better and which interfaces to other tools are needed or are useful and helpful?

In advance, this should be deliberate and planned. As always, it is recommended to get professional help and support. At least for the introduction phase, until all employees are familiar and confident with the implemented toolstack. Because here, too, the last hurdle is always the marketing employee as the central interface between creative idea and automated realization. Best practice is achieved when in-house marketing uses an individual best-of-breed system and both develop dynamically. With continuous training and further education of those involved, because a good marketing automation system grows with the requirements. Marketing automation ultimately lives from the daily use and interaction of the marketing department with the systems and tools provided. A Trello board without entries is just as conducive as a team with individual offices without doors. Well-selected and implemented marketing automation systems have a similar usage intensity as a mail program (Outlook) in the company.

Therefore, “push the button and go” is a nice wishful thinking, but often has little to do with reality. It is important to keep the intensity of use as high as possible immediately after going live. Marketing automation process chains must become part of a company’s DNA. This is the only way to create sustainable cost savings potential and, even better, new freedom to do the right things instead of doing the same things right over and over again.

References

Chiefmartec. (2022). *Marketing technology landscape*. https://chiefmartec.com/wp-content/uploads/2022/05/martech-map-may-2022.pdf

Markenmut. (2022). *The markenmut whitepapers, cases and blogs*. https://www.markenmut.de/toolbox

Tobias Voigt is a member of the board and shareholder of markenmut AG, an established marketing boutique and the leading provider-neutral marketing engineering consultancy in Germany. He is responsible for the agency's creative product as well as the marketing engineering team for automation and growth marketing, which Tobias Voigt is setting up and expanding at the Cologne and Frankfurt locations. Although Tobias Voigt was born in 1970—and is therefore no longer a classic online hipster—he was Digital Native right from the start. He shows his footprint in over 25 social networks and his digital expertise is trusted by numerous best-in-class companies from FinTech, Tourism, FMCG, Tobacco, and Industry.

What Will Massively Influence the Automation of Marketing and Sales in the Future

Olaf Mörk

1 Automation of Marketing and Sales in Drastic Change

"Nothing is more constant than change," the quote from Heraclitus of Ephesus (535–475 BC), is more relevant in the course of digitalization and marketing than ever, even after more than 2500 years. The world is increasingly exposed to disruptive processes and this is suddenly the new normal. AI as part of digitization will once again enormously accelerate and redesign all processes.

In this environment, the smart way is to discover and automate content innovations and create relevant leads for sales. Contextual data is the perfect complement to outbound content marketing. Analytical models are rapidly evolving and creating NBA (Next Best Action) for users. Customer churn is avoided and perfect after sales support can be created. The Internet of Things (IOT) is rapidly evolving into an "Internet of THINK" (IOTk) and creating a revolutionary Customer Centricity. The goal of this new customer orientation is to offer a solution before the wish or problem even arises.

Example "Internet of THINK" (IOTk):
Shortly before a person feels hungry, the doorbell rings and the pizza is delivered. In terms of B2B, the machine notices, for example, that the oil change is due or that a tool replacement is due at the end of the operating time. Thanks to automation, the system can independently reorder the item on time or offer alternatives. During the sometimes considerably complex processes, marketing and sales gain insight into these events. In this way, further services and optimizations can be suggested to the customer, if at all necessary. Such applications already exist in offshore wind farms, for example, where a case of damage is associated with considerable repair costs.

O. Mörk (✉)
Mörketing Agency, Neumarkt, Germany
e-mail: olaf@mörk.com; o.moerk@gmx.de

U. Hannig, U. Seebacher (eds.), *Marketing and Sales Automation*, Management for Professionals, https://doi.org/10.1007/978-3-031-20040-3_15

1.1 Avatars Drive Marketing and Sales Automation

Processes for the future can and must be built or implemented today. Marketing and sales automation is increasingly moving from a passive to a proactive system. Skepticism among target groups about the technologies used will decrease more and more, thanks to emotionalization within digitization. "Everything that can be digitized will be digitized"[1] and "everything that can be emotionalized will be emotional".[2]

Chatbots have been around for more than 25 years, giving way to avatars more and more over time. A chatbot, or bot for short, is a text-based dialog system that allows chatting with a technical system in a simple way. It has one area each for text input and output. This allows communication with the system in natural language. The trend is that chatbots are increasingly being used in conjunction with an avatar, i.e., an artificial person or a graphical proxy of a real person. With the proliferation of virtual meetings due to the situational circumstance "corona pandemic," avatars are becoming more popular. Likewise, it is common in the gamer scene to replace one's own "self" with an avatar and endow it with all sorts of characteristics. The game Fortnite may serve as just one example. In May 2020, 350 million registered players were announced, of which 35% are female.[3] These gamers are now probably billions and the target groups of tomorrow. Often, they are already professionally active and can also be found in marketing and sales. As early as 2014, the global market leader Wanzl, for whose marketing the author was responsible for 5 years, was able to cause great amazement among the target groups with its innovative sales and marketing solutions. Augmented reality (AR) and virtual reality (VR) were already linked to automation at that time. At the time, these solutions could only be created with the help of insider knowledge from the gamer industry. Generation X is the term used to describe the vintages born between 1965 and 1980. Exactly these cohorts have long since arrived on the customer side and expect innovative solutions, use avatars, and are very technically savvy.

Chatbots that are more closely related to a full-text search engine than to artificial or even natural intelligence are no longer sufficient here. Thanks to steadily increasing computer power, chatbot systems can access ever more extensive databases ever more quickly. As a result, ever more intelligent dialogs are offered to the user. These systems are also known as virtual personal assistants.[4] By 2030, avatars will replace

[1] Gensheimer, Barbara. "Everything That Can Be Digitized Will Be Digitized." https://www. bme. com/everything-that-can-be-digitized-will-be-digitized-1427/. Published, 2016: Accessed 03/16/ 2022.

[2] Mörk, Olaf. Outlook and the situational content marketing strategy in 2030. In: Situational content marketing strategy. Springer Gabler, Wiesbaden, 2021. pp. 189–208.

[3] https://de.wikipedia.org/wiki/Fortnite. Accessed: 15.03.2022.

[4] Streicher, Hans Werner. "Appropriate Technologies for the Public Sector" Digital Transformation in Public Administration. Springer Gabler, Berlin, Heidelberg, 2020. 53–93.

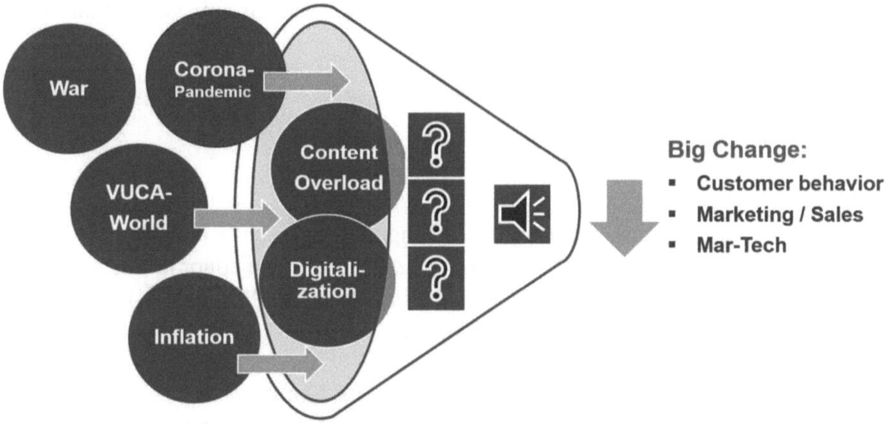

Fig. 1 Situational circumstances as favorable factors for a drastic change in customer habits and thus the use of Mar-Tech (Source: Mörk, 2022)

chatbots. A valuable assistant for sales and marketing experts will emerge. Customers will also increasingly use avatars for dialog with marketing and sales.

1.2 Changing Customer Habits Massively Thinning the Mar-Tech-Jungle

Currently, the question is which automation tools can be used from today's martech jungle with its more than 8000[5] different marketing channels and technologies. What are the chances of making the right choice here? One thing is certain, a wrong decision will be expensive and may even cost the company its existence. The answer comes from the future, what will be relevant for marketing and sales with regard to the target group(s) in the future.

"The world is in complete flux. Contingency factors such as digitization, new laws, and the corona pandemic are drastically changing the B2B marketing landscape. The event landscape alone has changed more in the last 12 months than it has in the past decade. Marketing budgets are being cut, sometimes drastically. Consequently, marketing must become more economical. Extensive changes are necessary for this.

Content that was once successful suddenly fails. Today, 60% of content is already irrelevant. The target group is now online longer than offline. Content overload and a VUCA world are also overwhelming the target audience."[6]

[5] https://chiefmartec.com/2020/04/marketing-technology-landscape-2020-martech-5000/. Accessed: 16.03.2022.

[6] Mörk, O. (2022). Situational content marketing is the new B2B guarantee of success. Glossary of bvik. https://bvik.org/b2b-glossar/situatives-content-marketing/. Accessed: 04/18/2022.

Figure 1 shows examples of some important situational circumstances that lead to major change in these three main areas:

1. *Customer behavior*
2. *Marketing and sales*
3. *Mar-Tech*

Customer habits and expectations changed significantly due to situational circumstances as shown in Fig. 1. *Marketing and sales* must adapt to this as quickly as possible. Otherwise, efforts will miss the target group. As a result, the measures within the *mar-tech strategy* must be adapted.

Example: Covid shutdown transforms distribution like never before:
Since March 2020, nothing has been the same in sales due to the Covid shutdown. 89% of companies were affected by the covid shutdown in 2020. Specifically, this was a time when no on-site visits could be made to customers.[7] *Numerous changes were implemented and undergone. Customer visits were suddenly no longer possible. Previously, an online conference with a customer was a rarity, but now it became the norm. Trade shows and events transformed into hybrid formats that will probably be retained forever.*

It is astonishing that despite this extreme situation, the sales targets were just achieved on average. This was only possible due to a drastic increase in online visits from previously 32.2% to 86.3% (e.g. with MS Teams, Zoom, Skype, ...). This corresponds to an increase of 171%.

New, innovative, hybrid processes were needed as quickly as possible. Although some things were digitized due to the enormous pressure, very little was automated in the process. This gap must be closed as quickly as possible. The wheel of time cannot be turned back here. It has been proven over the course of decades: a new marketing channel stays and does not suddenly disappear again. The art now is to define the benefit formula for marketing and sales within automation and to implement it in a targeted manner. Many projects of this kind still fail because people are not behind them and important strategic factors are simply overlooked.

1.3 Automation of Marketing and Sales in 5 Years more Radical than in the Last 25 Years

Human knowledge is becoming obsolete at an ever-faster rate: Every few years, human knowledge doubles (Mörk, O., 2021), leading to a content overload as shown in Fig. 1. Previous knowledge is constantly being revised. For example, the earth is not a disk. However, this was believed for hundreds of years. Galileo Galilei's claim

[7] Schmitz/Huckemann (2021), Hybrid Selling: More sales productivity through synchronized on-site and online visits, study Ruhr-Universität Bochum, n = 777 B2B companies.

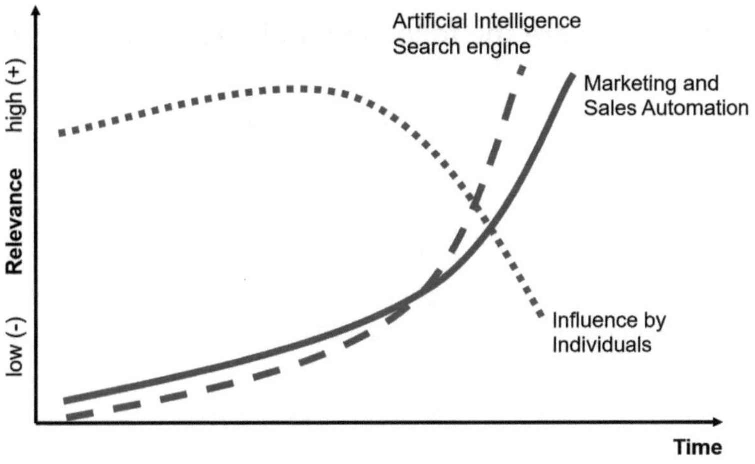

Fig. 2 The influence of the individual decreases over time in marketing and sales automation. The intelligence of search engines is increasing sharply (Source: Mörk, 2022)

that the earth revolves around the sun was declared false and unproven at the time. Every year, we lose about 10% of our knowledge—it simply becomes outdated and thus worthless. If you don't keep learning, you end up putting your job at risk. Whether it's IT, tax law, or marketing—more is changing than ever for their employees. Digitization, predictive touchpoints, marketing, and sales automation are the keys to success here. It is imperative that all of this be considered holistically under the aspects of the situational circumstances.

Marketing and sales automation increases drastically over time, as shown in Fig. 2. This is necessary because only top content has a chance with the search engines. Because "relevance is the new content king." At the same time, the influence of the individual on the automation processes decreases considerably. These processes are increasingly optimizing themselves by using AI. Those who do not take these circumstances into account will quickly lose market share!

2 Situational Content + Automation = Relevance for Marketing and Sales

According to Fig. 3, automation is given high importance at 53%. Influencers are at the top of the companies list of priorities with 60%, but they are relatively difficult to automate. In the future, "virtual influencers" or, more simply, chatbots will gain ground in this area, as they are already being used on a massive scale on Twitter. Elon Musk tried to buy Twitter for $44 billion in April 2022.[8]

[8] https://www.tagesschau.de/wirtschaft/musk-twitter-103.html. Accessed: 02.05.2022.

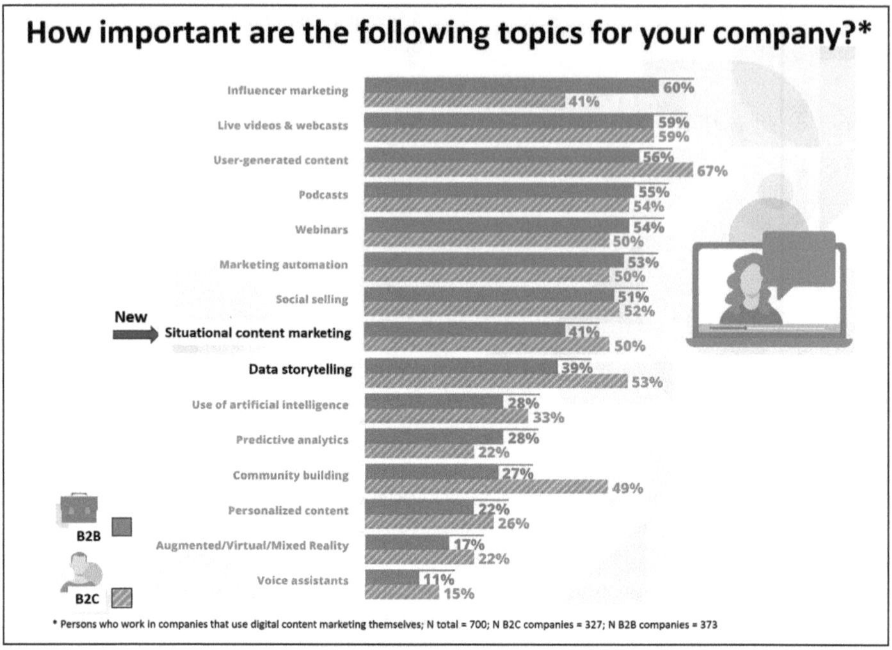

Fig. 3 Situational Content Marketing (SCM) rises high in importance as a new B2B marketing topic for corporate issues (Source: Statista, 2022)

More and more relevant marketing and sales topics from Fig. 3 rely on automation over time.

A great lever for automation lies in the new area of Situational Content Marketing (SCM). This enables companies to offer their target groups a tangible benefit. "This creates greater trust among the target group and ultimately higher sales (Mörk, 2021)." Already 41% of B2B companies and 50% for B2C attribute high importance to situational content marketing for their business purposes. Even AI is rated as less significant at B2B with only 18%.[9] It is remarkable that the new term "Situational Content Marketing" was asked for the first time in the study and is already classified as so significant.

2.1 Why Situational Content Marketing (SCM) is Becoming Increasingly Important for Companies

Already F. E. Fiedler (1967) points out in his leadership theory that situational influences are essential for success in achieving goals.[10] "Situational Content

[9]Statista (2022). The Content Marketing Trend Study 2022, 30.04.2022.

[10]https://wirtschaftslexikon.gabler.de/definition/kontingenztheorie-der-fuehrung-37489. Accessed: April 24, 2022.

Marketing (SCM), which is based on behavioral psychology belongs to the category of soft selling. Even content which worked well for many years is less and less effective with the target group. Product marketing, including its USP, suddenly no longer works as usual. The painstakingly created content seems like a rusting nail that is increasingly losing value, even ultimately becoming useless. "Content marketing in particular, will change more in the next 5 years than in the last 20 years before."[11]

This type of content demonstrates that psychosocial benefits are more often has greater relevance for customers than factual-functional benefits (Esch, 2016).[12]

The use of situational content increasingly makes use of industry-relevant information from the three core areas:

1. *Law: legal-political environment*
2. *Education: trend toward further training*
3. *Social: social environment*

2.2 The Positioning Creates Orientation

The company can position itself as a knowledge pioneer, innovation leader, or supporter with concrete benefits for the target group. In extreme cases, the company protects its target group from legal consequences. This approach creates a high level of trust among the target group. Ultimately, this results in higher sales of the company's products/services. This knowledge of situational content is literally the oil in the gears of automation. This in turn forms the engine in the company and ensures high efficiency of the processes.

Note *First, the benefit for the company must be determined. What is the goal of the measures? The three core objectives are predominantly:*[13]

1. *Strengthening the brand/image*
2. *Customer loyalty*
3. *New customer acquisition*

Once the benefit has been defined, the technology/software can be selected as shown in Fig. 4. This benefits the company as a whole. It also serves as an important strategic approach for marketing and sales.

[11] https://open.spotify.com/episode/1xsM4yAAzRGj9P98TH83fE. Accessed: 09.04.2022.

[12] Esch, F.R. (2016). Brand management strategy and technology. Munich: Franz Vahlen Verlag.

[13] Mörk in Seebacher (2021). B2B Marketing—A Guidebook for the Classroom to the Boardroom, Contingency-Centric Content Approach: Mastering Content Overload with Smart Content Marketing. Wiesbaden: Springer Fachmedien.

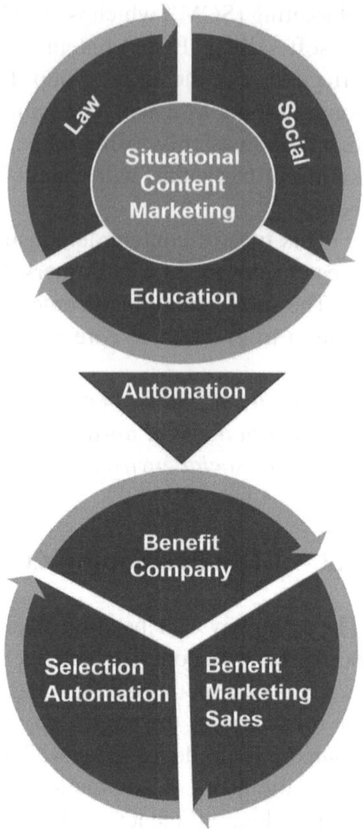

Fig. 4 The Situational Content Marketing Impact Model can also be used for automation. Easy to use, fast, and safe in practice (Source: Mörk, 2022)

Unfortunately, practice shows time and again that the exact opposite is the case. A powerful automation system often exists in the company. This tempts people to use the existing system, but it does not always optimally match the required benefit. Manual adjustments are made, which repeatedly lead to integration problems. This is noticed too late the project ends up in a dead end and is then discontinued. Automation systems make everyday marketing and sales work much easier, but only if the strategy fits. The good news is that automation systems are becoming more proactive and, thanks to the advent of AI, correspondingly more intelligent. However, these systems do not "think" completely on their own; that will take some time. The strategy for marketing and sales automation remains the responsibility of humans.

Example: Theoretical automation benefits cannibalize capacities
For a larger company, full automation of trade show reports for marketing and sales is to be implemented. This can provide multiple benefits, but in this case the devil was in the details. The system worked perfectly in demonstration mode, but not in practice:

1. The software was procured by the IT department and presented to marketing and sales afterward. The system did not consider important requirements of the contact persons. Manual adjustments were made, which not only became expensive, but also caused repeated problems with the constant updates of the software.
2. There was no clean introduction for the system users. There were acceptance problems and operating errors. A great deal of time, money, and trouble was wasted as a result.
3. The business cards of the trade show visitors were scanned and automatically transferred to the contact forms. This should create an enormous time advantage. Unfortunately, the software was only 99% reliable. Thus, 1% incorrect data was imported into the systems. In the end, all data had to be manually checked and reworked. Due to the situational circumstance of corona, there were almost no offline trade fairs for 2 years. The project was not discontinued but developed again and again. Capacities were burned on all sides without ever experiencing much benefit from automation. In the project, the software was selected first, only to define the benefits with the contacts afterward. The reverse order would have led to success and high profitability here.

3 Circumstances That Will Massively Influence the Automation of Marketing and Sales in the Future

As the chapter progresses, it becomes clear: disruption in marketing and sales suddenly seems to become the new normal. As a result of these situational circumstances, all automation processes throughout the company are being rapidly shaken up again and again. They need to be readjusted. Only with the help of AI and automation can this happen quickly. The hard rule here is that if you don't move with the times, you move with the times, and that goes for the brand and the company.

"In this environment, it is important to discover automation innovations in a smart way to create relevant leads for the sales department. Sales will lose its fear of contact with the technologies and will soon no longer want to miss this progress. AI-driven content is a new sidekick, not a rival. It enables real-time customer centricity combined with relevant and situational content. It makes customer hearts beat faster today and tomorrow."[14] For more than a decade, marketing and sales have been undergoing major changes. This has been drastically accelerated by covid, among other things, from 2020 onward, and since 2022 new war conflicts have additionally exacerbated this circumstance, as shown in Fig. 1.

[14] Mörk, O. (2021). What is situational content marketing (SCM)?. In: Situative Content Marketing Strategie. Springer Gabler, Wiesbaden. https://bit.ly/3uWvZo1

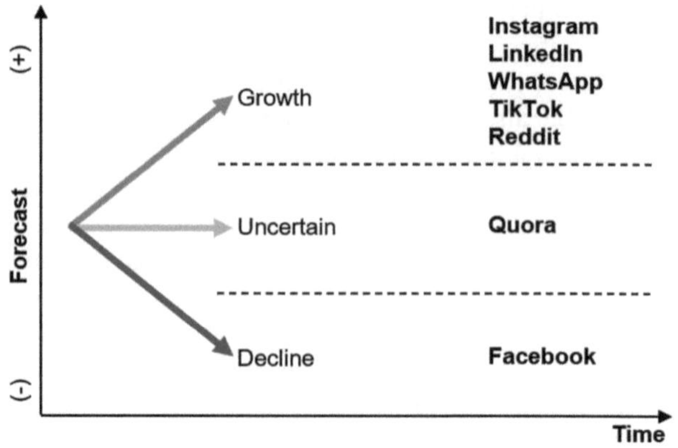

Fig. 5 Forecast Social media in B2B—the new channels in the jungle (Moseler, C., and Mörk, O. (2021). Social media in B2B: The new kids on the block. In *B2B marketing* (pp. 437–461). Springer, Cham)

3.1 Opportunities for Marketing and Sales in the Upheaval of Automation

Where many dangers lurk, there are almost always good opportunities. The disruption that seems to be hitting everywhere is even necessary. Digitalization would hardly have unfolded so quickly without this external pressure. Billions in subsidies were suddenly possible to avoid being drowned in the tsunami of digitization. The task now is to surf this wave of digitization and thus discover and implement new goals.

3.2 Three Important Core Areas within Automation Ensure Success

Social Media Always has an Open Ear

The target group can be reached anywhere, 7 days a week, around the clock. It is important to know which social media are booming, see Fig. 5, and which social media are gaining in importance from B2C for B2B. B2C is almost always ahead of B2B marketing here. Automation ensures convenient playout of content within these channels at the appropriate touchpoint. Automation also ensures rapid processing of leads and must be aligned with this. Predictive touchpoint management is becoming important. In other words, predicting at which touchpoint the opportunity for a lead, for example, is highest. Fig. 6 from the practical example, where SCM (Situational Content Marketing) was used effectively, shows how much qualified leads can be increased by over 1000% compared to before.

In this practical example, it was gratifying that the situational content marketing campaign worked so well. The automated playout of the campaign generated plenty of leads, cost less than ever before and was implemented in a flash. But there was a catch. No one had expected so many leads to flood marketing and sales in one fell swoop just before Christmas. Although a great deal was automated, not in the following areas:

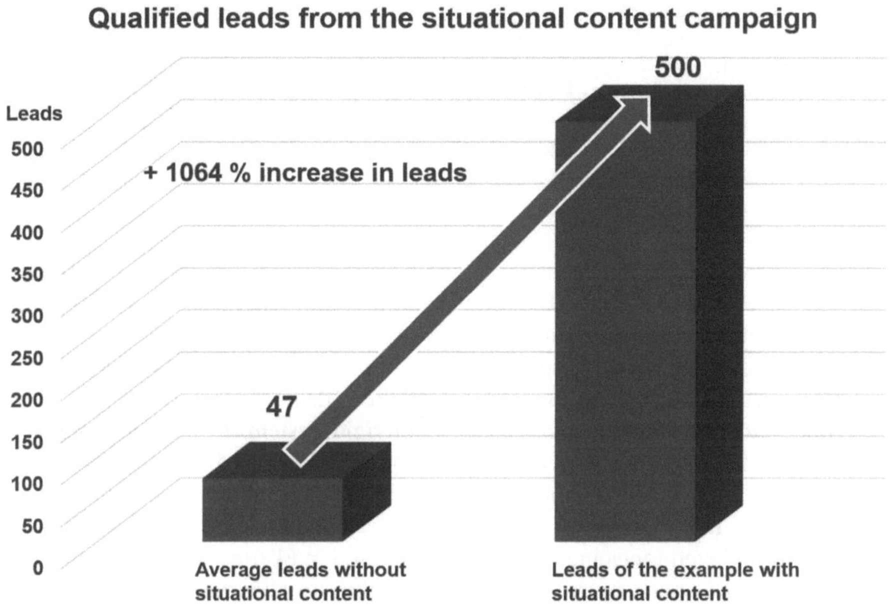

Fig. 6 Drastically increase leads through automation and situational content marketing (Mörk O, 2021)

1. Scheduling appointments with sales for product introductions.
2. Replying to numerous emails that are not intercepted automatically by, for example, a chatbot.
3. Not enough staff to provide desired customer training.
4. Sending out a wide variety of promotional materials and adding prospects to the CRM.

Within a few days, marketing and sales saw a tenfold increase in leads. Otherwise, this process took several weeks. Previously, the leads could be processed well in the normal course of everyday business. With a great effort and smart marketing actions, the sudden demand could still be satisfied. This practical example shows that it can be dangerous if sub-areas are not automated and thus jeopardize the entire project.

Emotionality is the New King of Automation

"What are your business hours? How can I order a product? And what deadlines apply in the event of a cancellation? More than one in four companies in Germany (27%) now answer such queries from customers and business partners via chatbot. Another 13% are planning to use these "little programs."[15] However, these chatbots

[15]https://www.bitkom.org/Presse/Presseinformation/Jedes-vierte-Unternehmen-in-Deutschland-nutzt-Chatbots. Accessed: 04/15/2022.

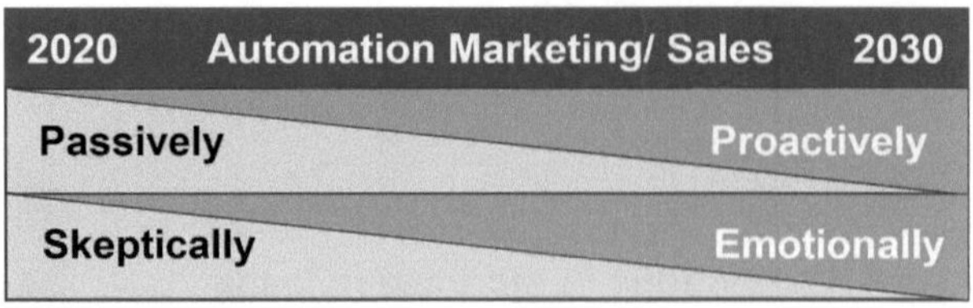

Fig. 7 Automation is shaping more and more proactive processes over time. Emotionalization within automation is steadily increasing in the process (Source: Mörk, 2022)

severely lack emotionality. As mentioned at the beginning of this chapter, avatars are much better at portraying this. Emotionalization within automation is an important building block for its success and is shown in Fig. 7. This builds trust and reduces fear toward fully automated processes. If this does not succeed, the systems are not accepted enough and success can thus be jeopardized.

While automation may have been a rather rigid system in the beginning, it is increasingly transforming into a proactive system. Increased use of AI and the simultaneous increase in computing power are creating entirely new automation opportunities. "Incorporating AI into marketing campaigns opens up the option of augmenting, or even replacing, traditional outbound marketing with the application of inbound and event-triggered marketing, opening up new, fast, customer-centric ways to optimize customer engagement."[16] The solutions created are packaged with plenty of emotion. Data is processed into lively infographics that can be grasped more quickly. Problems can be identified by the system before they even arise.

Talk to me and I know what to do

Another important component for emotionalization within automation is the form in which a query is presented to the system. Search queries via speech and voice assistance systems such as Siri, Alexa, or others are becoming increasingly popular. The Statista Trend Compass of 2020 reveals that voice assistance will increase by 320% in the USA by 2023 (Statista, 2020). Over 35 million of these units have been sold to date. Smart speakers understand much more than just voice, however. Based on the voice, the smart speaker can analyze with a high degree of accuracy not only the gender of the user, but also his or her age and emotional state. Later, gesture control will also be possible in addition to voice control.

Situational Content and AI Create Relevance for Automation

If only because of the new trends within social media and the increase in the emotionalization of content, automation will change greatly. However, the aforementioned areas are of little use if there is a lack of relevance for the target group. This is the third important building block for successfully leveraging technology. This topic will be considered in Sect. 2.

---

[16]https://www.openpr.de/news/1080506/Die-drei-Kernelemente-der-KI-Revolution-im-Kundendialog.html. Accessed: 04/14/2022.

Personalization in the context of content and automation
The target groups sense of entitlement is constantly increasing. Personalization across all channels is hardly conceivable without automation. Otherwise, at some point the processes can no longer be controlled, let alone continuously optimized. Self-learning systems are a great help here. Needs are derived in good time from the behavior patterns of users, automated, emotionalized, and played out. This even goes so far that the system recognizes the user's wishes before he does and provides the corresponding content. Depending on the reaction to this offer, the corresponding content is immediately adapted in turn. If the target person has a favorite color, for example, this is automatically incorporated into the communication if possible. After artificial intelligence, Artificial Creativity (AC) is increasingly being used. This has already advanced enormously and is often no longer distinguishable from human works. Through these automated measures in combination with situational content, customer wishes are recognized even more precisely and early, played out at the predictive touchpoint and satisfied. This leads to an unprecedented customer experience. Those who close their minds to these opportunities will lose market share. These processes must already be worked toward today.

3.3 Key Digitization Trends with High potential for Strong Changes in Marketing and Sales Automation

There are countless trends within digitization, some have already been described and it always depends on the individual case. Hardly anyone will be able to avoid the following four topics. It therefore makes sense to deal with them in good time.

Big Data - Gaining Valuable Knowledge from Unstructured Data and Identifying Predictive Touchpoints

Simply put, Big Data refers to larger and more complex data sets, especially from new data sources. These data sets are so large that classic data processing software can't manage them. But with these massive volumes of data, you can tackle business problems that you couldn't solve before.[17]

For example, the buying behavior of customers can be analyzed in this way. It is possible to offer the customer individual purchase recommendations that increase the probability of purchase. Amazon was one of the first providers of such systems. Customers and sales are increasingly expecting such systems. Big Data also recognizes social trends, can meaningfully evaluate newspaper articles and social media, and represents an important enrichment for marketing.

In the area of predictive big data, for example, device manufacturers can analyze how their products are actually used. This allows product improvements to be made and increases customer satisfaction. It is also quite easy to predict when a product in use needs to be serviced, which in turn is very helpful for sales and customers.

[17] https://www.oracle.com/de/big-data/what-is-big-data/. Accessed: 10.04.2022.

The recognition of predictive touchpoints is becoming increasingly important for marketing. Thanks to Big Data, unstructured data can be used to predict with a high degree of probability where the target group will be found next. This saves considerable costs. Figure 6 shows that leads can be increased dramatically in this way. Cognitive computing, subsection "Cognitive Computing: Artificial Intelligence Creates New Freedoms", is also a relevant component for achieving the highest possible hit probability.

Blockchain Technology: Much More than just Cryptocurrencies

Above all, it is about a secure and fast transaction between computers. Data manipulation is significantly more difficult here. This technology is best known from the field of cryptocurrencies such as Bitcoin or Ethereum. The requirements for data security will continue to increase enormously, so it is good to keep this technology in mind as a possible solution.

Cloud Computing: Location Independence for Maximum Efficiency

"Cloud computing includes technologies and business models for making IT resources available dynamically and billing for their use according to flexible payment models. Instead of operating IT resources, for example servers or applications, in company-owned data centers, these are available on demand and flexibly in the form of a service-based business model via the Internet or an intranet. This type of provision leads to an industrialization of IT resources, similar to what was the case with the provision of electricity."[18]

Cloud computing enables efficient collaboration between marketing, sales and customers. Files can be worked on easily and simultaneously. This ensures high flexibility in projects and also promotes agility in the company.

Cognitive Computing: Artificial Intelligence Creates New Freedoms[19]

In cognitive computing, the computer takes over routine human tasks and performs them. Areas of application include autonomous driving, automated stock trading, service hotlines, and the detection of credit card fraud. The service sector in particular offers unique opportunities for automation. The basis for cognitive computing is AI, speech recognition, machine learning, and vision. This creates completely new opportunities such as:

- Expert knowledge becomes available by machine, thus conserving scarce human resources. This opens up completely new possibilities for service hotlines.
- Analysis and processing of written and spoken texts. This is now increasingly used in the legal field. Tricky clauses are recognized and alternatives are suggested.

---

[18] https://wirtschaftslexikon.gabler.de/definition/cloud-computing-53360. Accessed: 04/10/2022.

[19] Hofmann, M. (2020). *Process optimization as a holistic approach.* Springer Gabler.

- Almost unlimited processing of video and image material by the computer in a short time. For example, knowledge databases can be built up and expanded. A great benefit for marketing, sales, and the customers.

The digitization trends described above have already become established in some industries but are often still considered “uncharted territory.” Over the course of the next few years, this will change significantly and merge more and more within automation.

4 Conclusion and Outlook on the Automation of Marketing and Sales in 2030

The possibilities and speed of digitalization and automation of marketing and sales are constantly increasing. As a result, everyone is facing the greatest challenge of the twenty-first century. Now it is important to look into the future. Processes that will become more important in the future must be strategically considered today. Otherwise, you end up running behind in the Mar-Tech world, which can be very draining.

Subchapter 3.2 explained the three most important core areas that have a significant impact on marketing and sales automation:

1. Social media
2. Emotionalization
3. Situational Content Marketing (SCM)

The goal is to create an intelligent and lasting connection between content marketing and marketing automation for the target groups. “However, it would definitely be too short-sighted to focus exclusively on the integration of the IT systems involved. This is of course a necessary, but not a sufficient condition for the lasting success of content marketing and marketing automation for the stakeholders marketing and sales. Ideally, however, the procedural and organizational connection of content marketing and marketing automation, together with the interaction of the website with e-mail marketing software and the CRM system, means the definition of a “lead pump”—provided that one also permanently generates the necessary relevant content alongside it.”[20] The quality of the content offered is and remains elementarily important.

Automation creates content relevance for content and design

Even the best system is of no use if the results end up falling through the cracks of the target group as a result of poor quality, or badly-prepared content. The question of what automation in marketing and sales must achieve in the future is a valid one.

[20]Hannig, T. (2021). Content Marketing Automation—What Lasts, Becomes Really Good. In: Hannig, U. (eds) Marketing und Sales Automation. Springer Gabler, Wiesbaden.

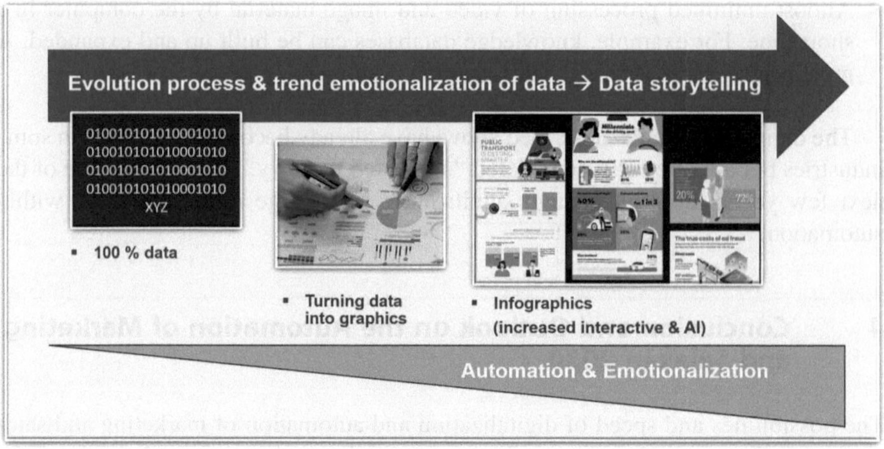

Fig. 8 New tasks in marketing and sales automation. Pure data becomes interactive infographics with infotainment character (Source: Mörk, 2022)

"Perfect automation is of little use if the presented content cannot be grasped quickly enough by the target group. Content must both convince and enchant its intended audience. Accordingly, it is important that the content is visually well prepared. Infotainment through infographics and videos, for example, is becoming increasingly popular. In general, content is being created, presented and evaluated more and more automatically," says Jan-Frederik-Ahrens.[21]

This trend is reinforced by using of AI. Future-oriented automation includes three important building blocks:

1. Recognizing and avoiding customer churn. After all, two out of five Germans have already boycotted a brand at some point because of some kind of misconduct.[22] Proactively proposing recommendations for action and creating a perfect customer dialog are the goal in order to retain regular customers.
2. Skillfully prepare content for the target groups as shown in Fig. 8 and play it out on the right channel. Figures become graphics. These continue to develop into infographics with increasingly interactive content and recommendations for action. Augmented Reality (AR) and Virtual Reality (VR) are already making increasing use of these elements.
3. Creation of a maximum Customer Experience (CX). This in turn leads to a higher purchase probability and ultimately secures the existence of the company.

---

[21] Interview with J.-F. Ahrens (2022), Statista Content and Design, 04/25/2022.

[22] https://www.horizont.net/marketing/nachrichten/yougov-studie-deutsche-verbraucher-sind-besonders-strenge-marken-boykotteure-186424?crefresh=1. Accessed: 01/05/2022.

The automation of marketing and sales goes far beyond pure business process optimization. Today, it is still too often understood as such. Now and in the future, it can ensure stable company growth. It is hardly surprising that 39% of startups are already using AI for their business processes and automation (Mörk, O., 2021).

References

Ahrens, J.-F. (2022). *Interview, statista content and design.*

Esch, F. R. (2016). *Brand management strategy and technology.* Franz Vahlen Verlag.

Fiedler, F. E. (1967). *A theory of effective leadership effectiveness.* McGraw Hill.

Hannig, U. (2021). *Content marketing automation – What lasts, becomes really good. Marketing and sales automation.* Springer Gabler.

Hofmann, M. (2020). *Process optimization as a holistic approach.* Springer Gabler.

Mörk, O. (2021). What is situational content marketing (SCM)? In *Situational content marketing strategy.* Springer Gabler.

Mörk in Seebacher. (2021). *B2B marketing: A guidebook for the classroom to the boardroom. Contingency-centric content approach: Mastering content overload with smart content marketing.* Springer Fachmedien.

Mörk, O. (2022). Das ist SCMS. Situativer Content schafft Vertrauen und sichert Erfolg. Mörketing. https://www.moerketing.com/was-ist-scms. Accessed: 02/05/2022.

Moseler, C., & Mörk, O. in Seebacher. (2021). *B2B marketing – A guidebook for the classroom to the boardroom, social media in B2B: The new kids on the block.* Springer.

Source study: Schmitz/Huckemann. (2021). Hybrid Selling: More sales productivity through synchronized on-site and online visits, Ruhr University Bochum, n = 777 B2B companies.

Statista. (2020). *Trend Compass 2020. The AI Market is expected to grow* (p. 107).

Statista. (2022, April 30). *The Content Marketing Trend Study 2022.*

Olaf Mörk studied economics and has been working as a marketing director, consultant, and lecturer in international B2B marketing for well-known companies for over 25 years.

For him, the focus of the digital transformation is the brand and the company, which must emerge stronger. The brand serves him as a stable anchor that provides support and orientation in the stormy digital sea.

As early as 1995, he specialized in digitization for industry, trade, manufacturers, IT, and services. Over 25 years ago, for example, he helped launch the Sparkasse as the second German direct bank and developed the first ever online configurators and chatbots. Later, he digitized and automated entire business areas. Numerous awards ensured a high level of international attention. The goal is to create innovative and new affordable solutions for tomorrow's success.

As author of numerous marketing publications and keynote speaker at leading marketing congresses such as CMCX, DMEXCO, Lead Management Summit, marconomy and editor of the free B2B marketing newsletter "#B2Better," he regularly reports on new sales and marketing strategies and digital marketing. His current book "Situational Content Marketing Strategy" (https://bit.ly/3uWvZo1) is at the top of the content marketing charts at Springer Professional.

Most recently, he initiated the "MÖRKETING" brand. Marketing strategies and impulses for the company and its brand are the focus here.

Part III

Customer Journey Management

From Email Marketing to Lead Management

Martin Philipp

1 Status Quo of the Use of Email Marketing

Sending emails has become an indispensable part of everyday life. Ray Tomlinson sent the first electronic letter in 1971—since then he is considered the inventor of email in today's sense. The triumph of email is unstoppable, because this way it is possible to send not only text messages, but also digital documents within a few seconds around the globe (Deutschlandfunk, 2016).

Emails are not only used in private, but also in business environments, for example in marketing. Email marketing is a part of direct marketing, which belongs to online marketing and refers to marketing work with digital messages. Companies use emails to draw customers' attention to new products, services, or offers and thus intensify customer loyalty. In email marketing, a distinction is made between one-to-one and one-to-many communication. The latter is often used as part of automation processes, as companies today can no longer afford to individualize and send out every email by hand (Deges, 2017).

Companies use email marketing, for example, in the form of a newsletter to inform their interested parties about news or current offers on a regular basis—for example, daily, weekly, or monthly. In addition, irregular mailings, so-called standalone mailings (see Fig. 1), are also used to announce an exciting promotion or news on a one-off basis. The structure and design of a newsletter or mailing should be professional and clearly structured.

> A good mailing or newsletter will contain specific calls to action, a call-to-action (CTA), to encourage the reader to click on linked buttons that will redirect them to the appropriate landing page of the company.

M. Philipp (✉)
SC Networks, Starnberg, Germany
e-mail: sales@sc-networks.com

U. Hannig, U. Seebacher (eds.), *Marketing and Sales Automation*, Management for Professionals, https://doi.org/10.1007/978-3-031-20040-3_16

Fig. 1 Example of a standalone mailing (Source: Evalanche | SC-Networks GmbH)

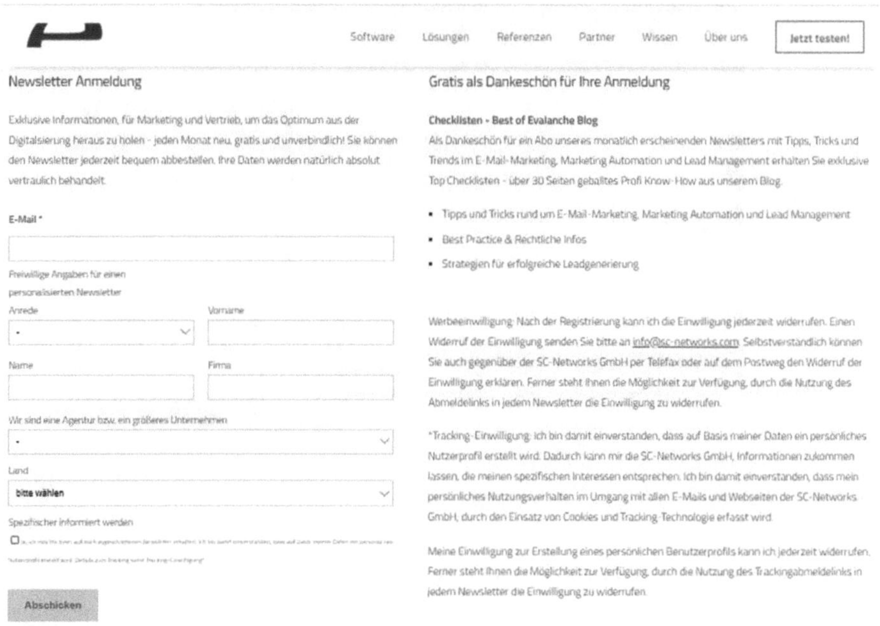

Fig. 2 Online form for granting consent (Source: Evalanche I SC-Networks GmbH)

In contrast to postal advertising media, the electronic equivalent may not be sent without the express permission of the recipient. An email may therefore only be sent to those recipients who have given their express permission for this or are among the company's existing customers and who are therefore likely to be interested in the content. The principle of permission marketing applies here (SC-Networks, 2018).

According to the General Data Protection Regulation (GDPR), the processing of personal data is generally prohibited, unless an element of permission applies (Art. 6 GDPR). The consent of a data subject is such an element of permission. Taking into account the EU-wide age limit of at least 16 years—in Germany according to the BGB still 18 years—the consent in an appropriate form is subject to proof (Art. 7, 24 DSGVO). In the case of minors, the consent or approval of the legal representatives must be guaranteed (Art. 8 GDPR). For the purpose of verifiability, it is practically necessary to have a consent given online confirmed by the data subject. This can be implemented by sending a confirmation link by email: By clicking on the link, the recipient confirms their email address and explicitly gives their contact permission for the second time—thus fulfilling the so-called double opt-in. This form of contacting as part of the permission process is legal. To ensure complete traceability, it is necessary to log every step of the double opt-in process in the system.

When designing the declaration of consent in an online form (see Fig. 2), care must be taken to ensure that it is provided with a corresponding reference to the right to object (Art. 21 GDPR)—this must also be provided in the form of an unsubscribe link in each individual email. Furthermore, the consent must be linked to a checkbox

Fig. 3 Display of a newsletter on mobile devices (Source: Evalanche I SC-Networks GmbH)

that has not been clicked on in advance in the immediate vicinity of the input window of the email address. The declaration of consent together with a reference to the right of withdrawal must be repeated in the general data protection information of the website.

Classic email marketing faces numerous challenges, in addition to the strict legal requirements. Nowadays, mobile use, social media, video marketing, segmentation, and various events or occasions also play a central role in the area of newsletter subscription. After all, smartphones and tablet PCs are common end devices today. It is therefore obligatory that digital messages can also be conveniently accessed on mobile devices (see Fig. 3).

In connection with mobile use, social media activities are also becoming increasingly popular. The communicative person wants to make his opinion known and keep his social environment up to date about his actions by liking or retweeting. Therefore, nowadays it is no longer sufficient to send out one's offers exclusively to the distribution list; instead, dialogue is required.

The content of electronic mail has also adapted. For example, topics or products that require explanation can be communicated very well through videos. Image and sound support the content and tell more than written words. Precisely because of the wide range of possibilities, there can be great fluctuations in interest among subscribers. One should therefore consider whether segmenting recipients for different newsletter content can increase the relevance and efficiency of email marketing.

Today, emails must be retrievable on different devices regardless of location and convince through optimal presentation. In addition, the content may also be supported by multimedia.

2 How Does a Prospect Voluntarily Give Out Their Contact Information?

Technological progress is unstoppable. Increasing digitalization in particular is leading not only to innovation, disruption, and dynamism, but also to shorter product and market life cycles and, above all, to a new power of the customer (SC-Networks, 2017). Because cold-calling by phoning company directories or flooding with print or broadcast advertising—i.e., classic outbound marketing activities—were yesterday. Today, it is the customer alone who decides when and how he wants to be approached by a company.

The potential customer starts his buying process independently by searching the Internet for relevant information. He reads product reviews and compares prices. This moment, when a prospective customer enters a specific search term online to find a product or service, is also known as the "zero moment of truth." At this point, no company knows about this purchase intention and consequently has no ability to influence the prospect. Or so it might seem.

But this is exactly where inbound marketing comes in, a marketing strategy based on the idea of being found, which is also highly relevant in the online sector. With a sophisticated content marketing strategy, a dialogue with the potential customer can be started online at an early stage. A provider can then accompany and support them throughout their entire purchase decision process, their customer journey.

The strategy is simple. Companies only need to be present on the Internet at the "zero moment of truth" with attractive content and relevant information. They have to attract the attention of potential customers so that they get in touch with the company of their own accord. After all, this is the result that a company initially works toward: The prospective customer must willingly give his or her permission to be contacted by the company via email on his or her own initiative.

Through qualitatively convincing and relevant content, a company can gain the trust of the prospective customer so that he is willing to disclose his name and email address in exchange for useful information (see Fig. 4).

The customer decides the timing, but the company can steer him in the right direction by means of high-quality and, above all, useful content. Good content consists of helpful and advertising-free content. It serves to attract the attention of potential customers without pushing them to buy a specific product. Therefore, the most suitable content is informative and relevant content that provides the reader with an actual benefit in their decision-making process. The content should be as high quality as possible, i.e. technically correct as well as error-free and understandable. Added value is the key word, because good content must not only be easy to find, but also offer the prospect an advantage.

A common concept in marketing is targeting. In this context, the content is adapted more in a blanket manner than individually to a customer type that is described rather vaguely. However, even in the business-to-business context, where multiple buying centers may need to be addressed, it is ultimately individual people that the provider needs to convince: CEOs, buyers, project managers, etc. Accordingly, it is necessary to win over the diverse decision-makers of a company.

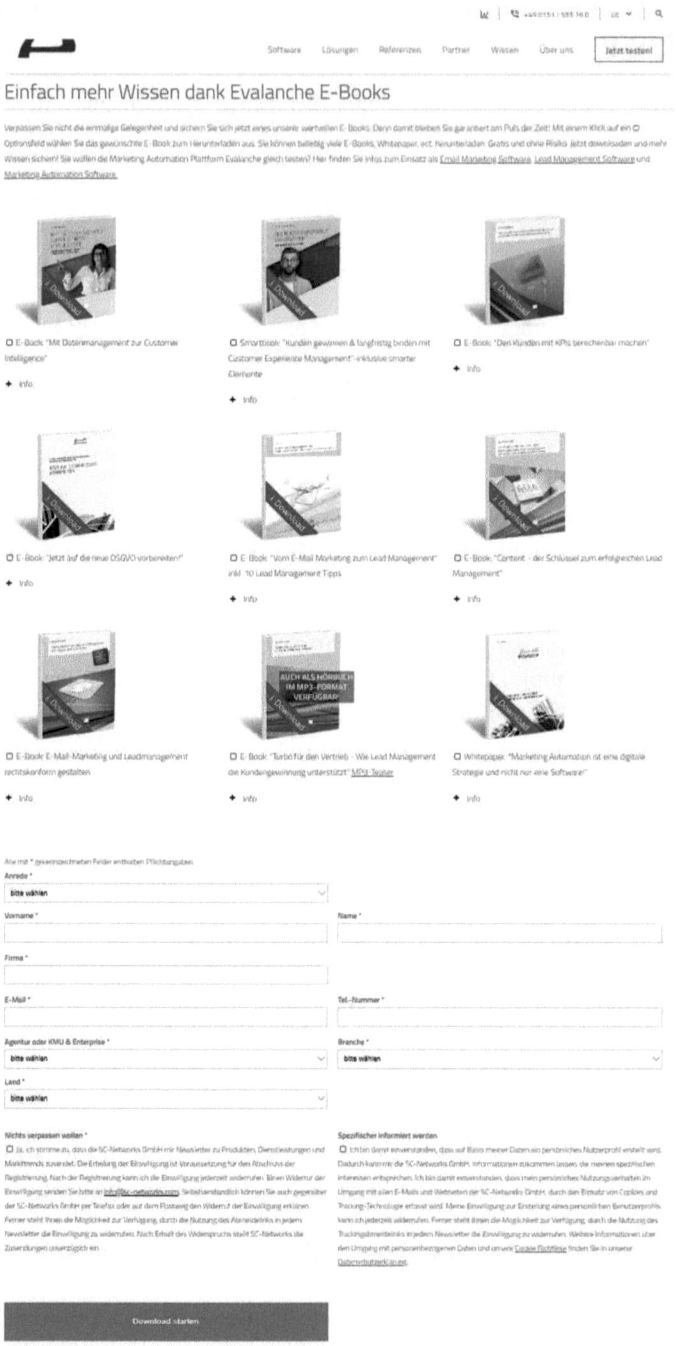

Fig. 4 Landing page with typical query form (Source: Evalanche | SC-Networks GmbH)

The buyer-persona concept offers a solution-oriented approach. Because a pure target group definition is no longer sufficient in the age of digitalization and individualization. It is better for marketing and sales employees to create their desired customer together: a buyer persona. Because sales attaches importance to different things than marketing, and their cooperation is indispensable for successful lead management. It requires creating profiles as detailed as possible of typical representatives of the decision-makers in the addressed companies.

A buyer persona is defined as a typical customer, a fictitious or real person with individual characteristics that exemplifies a certain type of customer. The characteristics should therefore apply to the majority of the desired customers. Otherwise you need several buyer personas. In addition to information on position, age, gender, educational background, professional career, and area of responsibility in the company, a persona profile also compiles personal interests, information behavior, and professional pain points of the desired customer. Even a fictitious portrait should be part of the persona profile for better illustration.

Based on the persona profile, it is possible to derive what moves the desired customer, what topics he is interested in, and what content is most likely to appeal to him. It can also be defined where and how this buyer persona can best find the company. Exactly these points of contact, the so-called touch points, must be carefully designed in order to offer the persona-relevant content there. Depending on the preferences and information needs of the buyer persona, a number of different content formats can be suitable.

There are some content formats that are more suitable for the initial contact at the beginning of the customer journey of a potential customer (ToFu = Top of the Funnel). Other content formats are better suited for the advanced status (MoFu = Middle of the Funnel) in the form of build-up content or even shortly before the conclusion of the contract (BoFu = Bottom of the Funnel) (see Fig. 5).

With the huge range of content formats, the choice is not easy. However, companies don't have to offer all formats right away. It is more important to focus on a few at first and to adapt these to the buyer persona in as high-quality a way as possible. Regardless of which content formats you choose, they must be media-appropriate. Text is not always necessary (SC-Networks, 2016).

Over time, a company can continue to add to its pool of information. In order to attract the attention of potential customers with the content, it is important to design the first touch points to the desired customer, such as the company website, the newsletter, and the social media presences, in a particularly appealing way. Otherwise, the prospect will not even get the idea to want to consume the content offered. If, however, in the "zero moment of truth" the prospect perceives the company's website as useful and feels addressed by it, he is also willing to download further content that promises him added value in exchange for personal data such as name and email address: he becomes a lead.

	ToFu*	MoFu*	BoFu*
Anwenderberichte, Case Studies & Success Stories	■□□	■■■	■■□
Audio-Content: Podcasts, Hörbücher & Co.	■■□	■■■	■■□
Bilder, Foto-Collagen & Slideshows	■■■	■■□	■■□
Checklisten, Listings & Tipps	■■■	■■■	■■■
Corporate Blog	■■■	■□□	■□□
E-Books	■■■	■■■	■■□
Erklärfilme & Video-Tutorials	■■■	■■□	■■□
Fachberichte	■■■	■■□	■■□
HowTos & Anleitungen	■□□	■■■	■■□
Infografiken & interaktive Visualisierungen	■■■	■■□	■□□
Interviews, Statements, Kommentare & Rezensionen	■■■	■■□	■□□
Newsletter & Mailings	■■□	■■■	■■□
Pressemeldungen	■■■	■□□	■□□
Product Sheets & Datenblätter	■■■	■□□	■■□
Produktproben, Probe-Abonnements & Demo-Versionen	■□□	■□□	■■■
Soziale Netzwerke	■■■	■□□	■□□
Spiele, Quiz & Tests	■■■	■■□	■■□
Studien, Umfragen & Forschungsergebnisse	■■■	■■□	■□□
Tools & Vorlagen	■□□	■■■	■■□
User Generated Content	■■■	■■□	■■■
Veranstaltungen & Begleitmaterialien	■■■	■■■	■■■
Webinare, Web-TV & Experten-Chats	■□□	■■□	■■□
Webseitentexte onsite/offsite	■■■	■□□	■□□
Whitepaper	■■■	■■■	■■□

** ToFu = Top of the Funnel, MoFu = Middle of the Funnel, BoFu = Bottom of the Funnel.*

Legende

optimal geeignet	■■■
gut geeignet	■■□
bedingt geeignet	■□□

Fig. 5 Content match matrix (Source: Evalanche I SC-Networks GmbH)

The aim is to provide content that is free of advertising, useful and of high quality, and only in exchange for personal data.

But you must not disappoint the interested party. Because if this first content does not convince him, he will possibly unsubscribe from the email distribution list right away. If, on the other hand, the first touch points were appealing and sparked further interest, the potential customer will be willing to form a bond with the company.

3 Lead Management as a Bridge from the Anonymous Prospect to the Lead

What counts for companies is the sale of goods or services. To do this, they need to win customers. However, buying behavior has changed, driven by digitalization. These changes also affect the acquisition of new customers.

Inbound marketing is the solution here. Today's buyers search for information on the Internet, often without a specific purchase intention. They start their customer journey highly individually and autonomously. If, during their research, they come across interesting content that offers them added value, they independently enter into a non-binding relationship with the company, for example by downloading a white paper or subscribing to the newsletter mailing list. No matter what they do, they leave their contact details.

Lead management in connection with content marketing is the approach behind it. The process of lead management can best be illustrated with a funnel, the lead management tunnel (see Fig. 6).

To generate revenue, a company needs paying customers at the end of the sales funnel. However, not every prospect who lands on the company's website in the

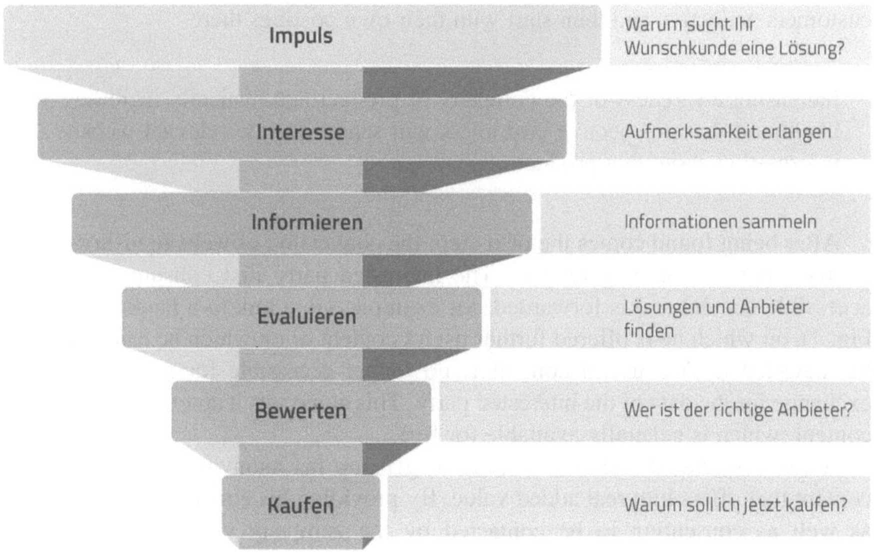

Fig. 6 The lead management funnel (Source: Evalanche | SC-Networks GmbH)

course of their customer journey is a lead that will eventually convert to a customer. On the contrary, the majority of prospects will fail to close the deal. Be it that the lead decides not to buy after all or buys from the competition. Both are crucial facts, the causes of which need to be explored.

Before the start of operational lead management, the marketing and sales staff must have already jointly defined the company's desired customers according to the buyer-persona concept and completed the associated content planning and creation. Only then does the first operational step follow: lead generation. As many prospects as possible should be convinced that it is worth giving up their anonymity in exchange for useful content. However, it is not the absolute number of leads that is decisive, but their relevance. After all, it's important for a company to get those prospects to its website and convert them into leads that could actually be considered for a purchase. This is where the buyer persona comes into play.

Companies need to ensure at this first stage of the sales funnel that their website or products are found on the Internet. Most of the time, the potential customer enters a keyword in a search engine. In order to be found here, the persona and search engine optimized website of the company counts first and foremost. In addition, a corporate blog can also improve the ranking in search engines. On top of that, such a blog offers a company the opportunity to establish itself as an expert in certain specialist topics or industries. Despite the focus on the Internet, offline touch points such as trade fairs or print trade magazines also help to attract the attention of potential customers.

With the help of social media, popularity can be driven further. Through convincing and high-quality content, a product or company can also become popular in the social media area—for example, on Facebook, Twitter, Xing, or LinkedIn. However, companies should first check in which social networks their desired customers are active and then start with their own postings there.

Increasing awareness of the company or product automatically increases the likelihood that prospective customers will search for the relevant website or information about that product.

After being found comes the next step: the conversion of website visitors, social media followers, or blog readers. The interested party first consumes the freely accessible content and is forwarded, for example, via a link to a landing page (see Fig. 7), on which he is offered further useful content or on which he can sign up for the newsletter. This useful content is no longer accessible for free, but only in exchange for the data of the interested party. This alone sets it apart from advertising content, which is generally available for free.

A truly interested visitor is willing to give up his anonymity for high-quality content that offers him real added value. By providing his email address and name, as well as consenting to be contacted by the company via double opt-in, the interested party is no longer an unknown. He becomes a lead that the company is allowed to address via email.

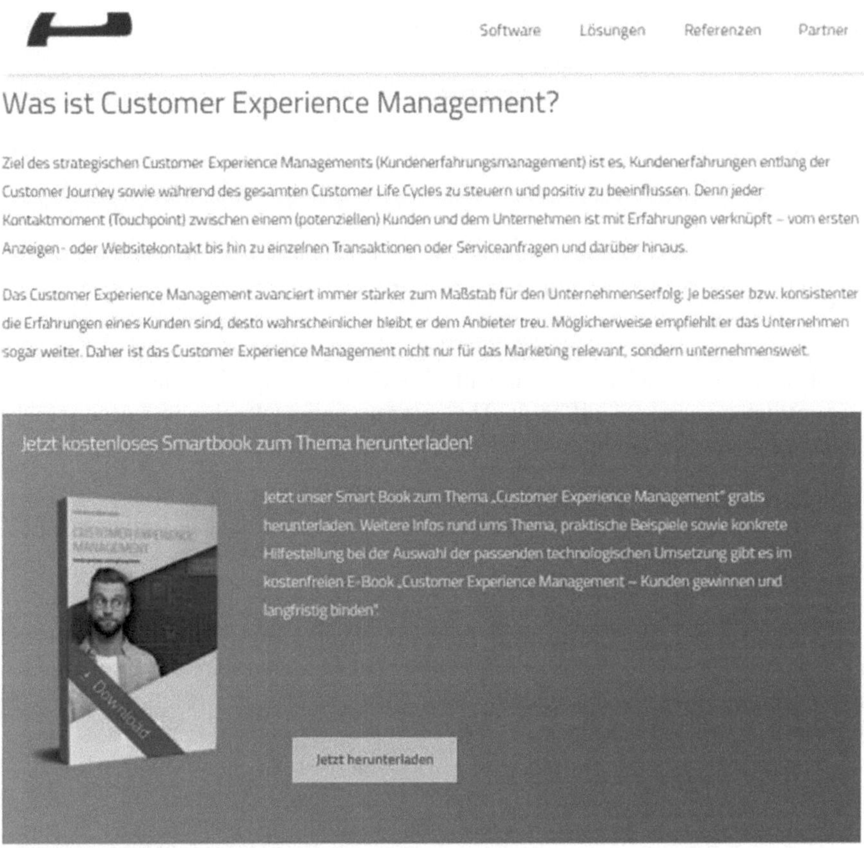

Fig. 7 Example of a blog post that links to another content module (Source: Evalanche I SC-Networks GmbH)

Lead management is basically based on a barter transaction: relevant content for personal data. The principle of data economy (Art. 5, 25 DSGVO) must be taken into account.

4 From Lead to Paying Customer Through Lead Nurturing

The first prospects have left their contact information and have become leads that the company can work with. Nevertheless, it would be ineffective to immediately forward this information to a sales representative, even if he or she ultimately has to take care of closing the deal.

It is already a great success to have generated a lead. But if this lead is contacted too early by the sales department, this can quickly lead to frustration on both sides. The lead may not even be ready to buy. He may have received useful content, but this does not equate to an immediate purchase intention. So far, he has only shown interest in a certain topic.

Lead Nurturing, the second major step in the lead management process, is used to develop the leads generated online until they are finally ready to be contacted by a sales representative. However, with sophisticated, automated nurturing, the company succeeds in developing its just-generated leads until they are ready for sales. In this context, one also speaks of lead qualification.

This process is individual for each lead, because the respective initial stage does not necessarily have to be the same. One lead has requested a whitepaper, the next an e-book, and the third a guide. Even if all these leads correspond to the buyer persona, their customer journey is different. The company must take this into account when planning its nurture campaign.

Immature leads are of little use to sales, but lead nurturing can further qualify leads to sales maturity.

A nurture campaign is basically nothing more than a sequence planning of further emails (and content offers) to a lead. A nurture campaign therefore comprises several emails whose content and timing are coordinated in advance (Philipp, 2017). The beginning is always the same.

The new contact is welcomed with a Welcome Nurture. In addition to a greeting that is as personal as possible, this first email usually contains a selection of information or links to various content and—in the case of a specific content request—of course the link to the download. Software solutions for marketing automation allow such emails to be sent out automatically. Marketing automation solutions support modern email marketing and—provided that each individual Nurture stage has been created—facilitate the work of marketing enormously.

The further emails of the campaign are each based on the actions of the lead and always refer to them before offering the prospect further useful content. Through these, the profile of the lead is refined more and more. This is because the lead leaves behind traceable indications through his activities, such as clicking on a link or downloading further content modules.

For lead qualification, the download of further content is linked to the query of new customer-specific data. Here, the principles of transparency, purpose limitation, data economy, and limited storage must also be observed (Art. 5, 25 GDPR). Therefore, the purpose of the data query must be precisely defined at each individual Nurture stage. The collected information can be bundled and used for further personalization of the customer. The lead is continuously further qualified and matures. At the same time, the company can also refine the definition of its buyer persona.

Lead Nurturing promotes getting to know each other. The lead receives relevant content and provides the company with information through his actions and his personal data, which serves the company to refine not only the individual lead profile, but also the basic persona profile.

5 Assessment of the Degree of Maturity by Means of Lead Scoring

The lead not only leaves more and more personal data in the course of his customer journey, but also receives certain scores for his behavior, i.e. for each action—the sum of which represents the maturity level. This process of lead scoring (see Fig. 8) takes place according to the defined criteria.

The evaluation process is two-stage. On the one hand, the company receives explicit data, including information such as position, department, role in the decision-making process, interests of the person, but also information about the company, such as company size, annual turnover, industry, location, and so on. According to this data, an explicit scoring (profile scoring) can take place.

On the other hand, you also implicitly give lead scoring points for their behavior (activity scoring). For example, this could be 14 points for visiting the website, 14 points for downloading a whitepaper, 20 points for downloading an e-book, 14 points for signing up, or −5 points for unsubscribing from the newsletter. So you quantify the activity index for each lead.

If the lead is finally passed on from marketing to the sales department as ready for sales, the results of implicit and explicit scoring are of enormous importance for the sales employee. This is because they can use them to accurately assess the lead in order to make them a tailor-made offer.

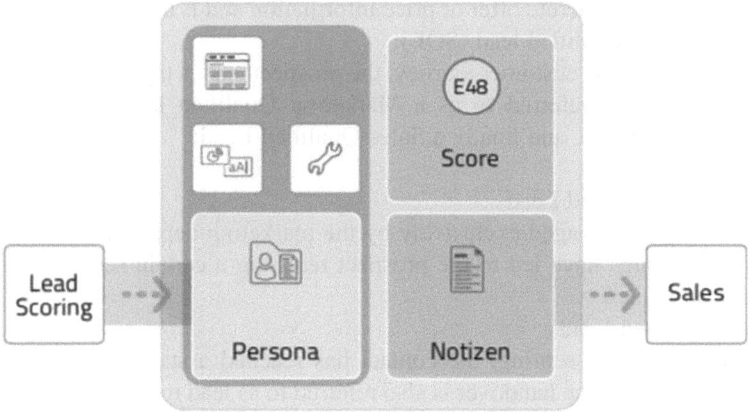

Fig. 8 Scoring matrix (Source: Evalanche I SC-Networks GmbH)

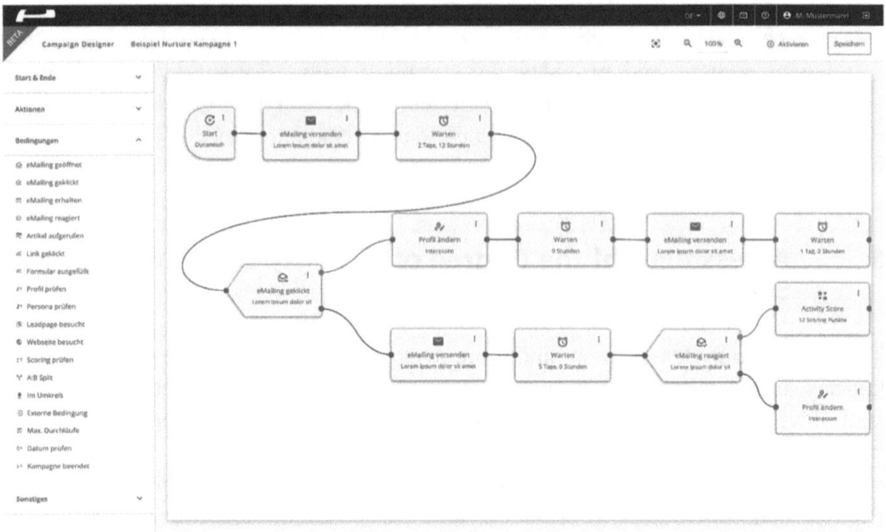

Fig. 9 Example of a nurture campaign (Source: Evalanche I SC-Networks GmbH)

Each lead follows its individual path along the nurture campaign (Fig. 9). The company's goal is always to first develop the lead to sales maturity and then, at best, to bring it to the conclusion of the contract, the closing.

First of all, every single lead is important for the company. If a lead does not respond to the company's emails for a longer period of time, the company can send him a so-called wake-up nurture. This email refers to the last registered activities as well as the lead's behavior during the initial contact phase. It is intended to reactivate the lead.

If a lead shows strong interest in concrete prices and offers at an early stage, it can also be directly qualified for sales with a Booster Nurture. With this booster email, the lead receives a concrete offer or price information and is thus directly transferred to sales as a sales-qualified lead (SQL).

In the course of the customer journey, the prospect passes through different stages and is successively referred to as a Marketing Qualified Lead (MQL), a Sales Accepted Lead (SAL), and finally a Sales-Qualified Lead:

1. Marketing Qualified Lead
   The contact is managed exclusively by the marketing department. Various marketing measures have led to the prospect reaching a certain scoring value. The lead has matured.
2. Sales Accepted Lead
   According to lead scoring, the contact has reached a state that qualifies it for handoff to sales. The handover is also referred to as lead routing. The lead is now further qualified by the sales department, which also estimates the success rate.
3. Sales-Qualified Lead:

The contact has reached sales maturity. It is now ready for a concrete offer by a sales representative.

But even in the sales department, the Nurture campaign is not over yet. Leads that have already been handed over to sales can continue to be provided with relevant information through sales nurtures in the course of the contact phase or through warm-up nurtures. This includes information such as product and price updates. It is imperative to coordinate the content and dispatch times with the sales department.

The following applies to all Nurture emails: The content should be short, concise, personalized, and focus on one topic. A clear call-to-action must be integrated. The principle of data economy applies to the data query (Art. 5, 25 GDPR).

6 Cross-Selling and Up-Selling Lead to Increased Sales with Existing Customers

It is also important to convince existing customers again and again—otherwise the competition might do this. In order to encourage existing customers to make repeat purchases, you should also provide them with emails beyond the closing. This already starts with the after-sales nurture, which on the one hand serves as an order confirmation, but on the other hand can also offer the customer supplementary products.

Cross-selling is the effort to convince an existing customer of complementary products or services. Equally relevant is the so-called up-selling, which, for example, offers the customer a higher-quality product or a more extensive service than before.

Business with existing customers pays off, because the effort is usually many times less than with new customer acquisition. Existing customers can be kept up to date not only with the newsletter, but also through standalone mailings or event nurtures. Special wake-up nurtures are also suitable for reactivating existing customers.

In addition, the so-called trigger emails can be sent, for example on the occasion of birthdays, name anniversaries, or anniversaries, which contain a special preferential offer and thereby encourage the customer to purchase again. As a result of the purchase, the company has specific information up its sleeve that it can follow up on. For example, the existing customer can be offered a maintenance contract or spare parts.

7 Event Nurture Campaign Combines Outbound and Inbound Marketing

With an event nurture campaign, outbound and inbound activities can be combined. An event, for example a trade fair or an "open day," is aimed at both new and existing customers.

Leads or customers of the company receive the invitation to the event via a standalone mailing. With a QR code, the event visitors are finally directed to a landing page where the Nurture campaign starts. Or the new contact reveals their contact details during a personal conversation and is added to the campaign after a successful double opt-in.

But also non-acquired customers can still be interesting for the company. These can also be kept up to date with wake-up nurtures or standalone mailings as well as the newsletter, provided they do not unsubscribe (opt-out). There may even be an opportunity to specifically follow up with these lost customers to find out why. This information is of great importance for the optimization of marketing measures. Because, if the reasons are known, there may be another opportunity and the provider has a new starting point to inspire these lost customers for the products or services of their own company after all.

After each contract is signed, it is important to reveal the cards and draw conclusions from the respective customer journey. A range of key performance indicators (KPIs) make it possible to measure and assess the company's marketing and sales measures. Only when the pure numbers are known can the entire process be profitably optimized.

The most important KPIs include the conversion rate, the opportunity amount, the sales cycle, the customer acquisition costs, and of course the return on investment (ROI). In addition, there are many other key figures that also play a role in the context of email marketing and allow conclusions to be drawn not only about the content quality but also about the timing of a campaign.

In particular, companies should at least check how many recipients have read the newsletter (open rate) or clicked on linked elements (click rate) (see Fig. 10).

Based on graphical statistics, the user receives updated information about common KPIs around the newsletter, such as open and click-through rates, as well as hard and soft bounce. This tells the company whether the content was appealing and the timing was right. Furthermore, the complaint rate, delivery rate, spam mark rate, or unsubscribe rate as well as the bounce rate—hard and soft bounce—provide important insights and open up optimization potential in email marketing.

Link tracking also has an importance that should not be underestimated. By analyzing the click behavior of the recipients, the company receives information about whether, for example, the newsletter is optimally structured and whether its length and content appeal to the readers.

A clickmap makes the evaluation of this data even more vivid because it displays the results graphically. The company also does not remain hidden whether a recipient has retrieved the email via a mobile device. Thanks to geotargeting, the location of the retrieval is also no longer a secret. It is important to note that any user-related

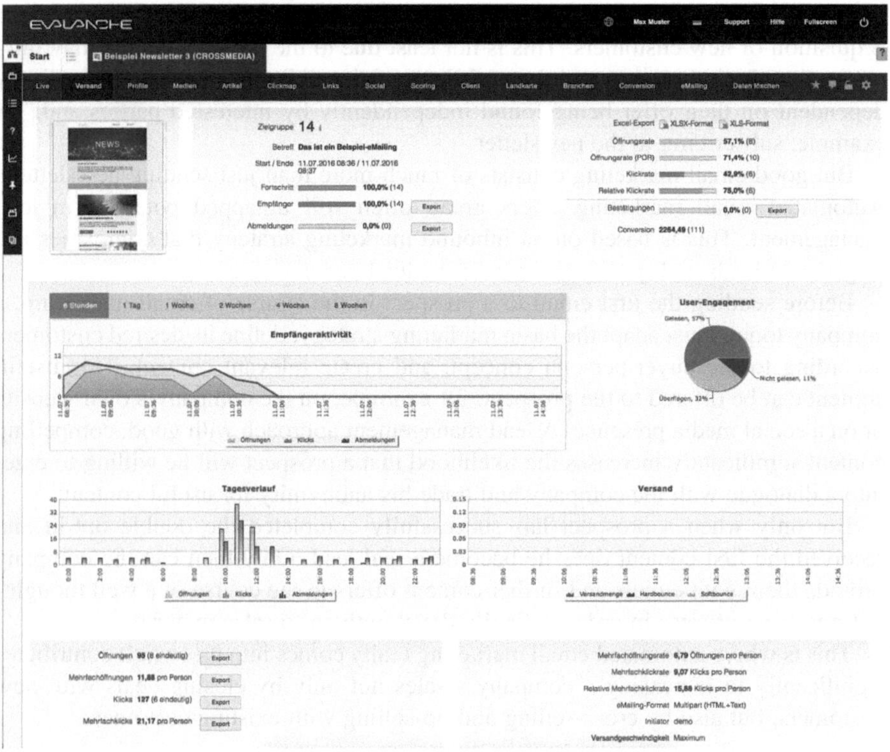

Fig. 10 Statistics on newsletter distribution (Source: Evalanche I SC-Networks GmbH)

tracking also requires the consent (opt-in) of the person concerned and that there must also be a possibility of revocation (opt-out) at any time.

KPIs make the customer, their individual buyer journey and the entire internal company process transparent. In this way, KPIs offer the company plenty of opportunities for campaign optimization, so that deals and sales increase.

8 Conclusion

The change in buying behavior and digitalization make it necessary for companies to still generate sufficient contacts and leads through a contemporary approach. Accordingly, emails have become an indispensable part of our everyday lives and in many cases shape our actions.

Email marketing is now also firmly anchored in the marketing mix of many companies. However, many companies still fail to recognize the true potential of this form of communication. They limit themselves to sending individual emails or newsletters. Email marketing then usually plays only a subordinate role in the acquisition of new customers. This is not least due to the fact that emails may only be sent with the express consent of the recipient. Companies are accordingly dependent on their offer being found independently by interested parties and, for example, subscribing to the newsletter.

But good email marketing consists of much more than just sending newsletters. Automated email marketing offers great, often still untapped potential in lead management. This is based on an inbound marketing strategy that companies use to generate leads and qualify them until the lead becomes a customer.

Before sending the first email to a prospect in the course of email marketing, a company today must adapt the basic marketing strategy, define its desired customers according to the buyer-persona concept, and create relevant content. This useful content can be offered to the prospect, for example, on the company's own website or on a social media presence. A lead management approach with good, compelling content significantly increases the likelihood that a prospect will be willing to enter into a dialogue with the company and trade his anonymity for useful content.

But only when a prospect has successfully completed the double opt-in and received the first content does he become a real lead. Only then can the company provide them with emails and further content offers in the course of a well thought-out nurturing process in order to finally develop them to sales maturity.

This is where automated email marketing really comes into its own. It contributes significantly to increasing a company's sales not only by closing deals with new customers, but also by cross-selling and up-selling with existing customers.

References

Deges, F. (2017). *Email marketing*. https://wirtschaftslexikon.gabler.de/definition/e-mail-marketing-119012

Deutschlandfunk. (2016). *The inventor of e-mail and his elephant ear*. https://www.deutschlandfunk.de/zum-tod-von-ray-tomlinson-der-erfinder-der-e-mail-und-sein.691.de.html?dram:article_id=347713

Philipp, M. (2017). Marketing automation ensures efficient lead nurturing. In U. Hannig (Ed.), *Marketing and sales automation* (pp. 223–243). Springer.

SC Networks. (2016). *Content – The key to successful lead management*. https://www.sc-networks.de/download/?dl_id=372239

SC Networks. (2017). *Turbo for sales – How lead management supports customer acquisition*. https://www.sc-networks.de/download/?dl_id=400384

SC Networks. (2018). *Email marketing and lead management legal compliance*. https://www.sc-networks.de/download/?dl_id=347291

Martin Philipp is co-managing director of SC-Networks GmbH, producer of the "Made in Germany" marketing automation platform Evalanche, and responsible for new customer acquisition and customer enthusiasm. He has over 20 years of experience in online marketing and digital sales of sophisticated products and solutions that require explanation.

Keep in Touch: Evaluating Touchpoint Performance Along the B2B Customer Journey

Fabienne Halb and Uwe Seebacher

1 Change in B2B Buying Behavior

Regardless of the differences between the individual industries, the business environment today is more dynamic and complex than ever before. New technologies and concepts, such as Marketing Resource Management (MRM) (Seebacher & Güpner, 2021), Internet of Things (IoT), smart devices and sensors, artificial intelligence, machine learning, cloud computing, 3D printing, predictive maintenance, and remote service are shaping business processes in many industries. As a result, companies are facing increasing market uncertainty (Mora Cortez & Johnston, 2017, p. 99; Schüller, 2015, pp. 14–20). All these technologies lead to the enablement of data-driven management (Seebacher, 2021a) and based on this, Predictive Intelligence (Seebacher, 2021b). Applying this approach is the door opener into the upcoming cookie-free world in the sense that in All-2-All (A2A) communication arenas the predictive touchpoint optimization is done via data from brain scans, AI, and interactive tracking and recognition of buying behaviors on all touchpoints and on all kinds of outlet.

Customer satisfaction alone is no longer enough today. In order to remain in customers' memories, companies have to inspire and surprise them. Nowadays, companies compete on the basis of customer experience (Salesforce Research, 2017, p. 5). B2B marketing has changed dramatically in response to this (Hall, 2017, p. 7).

Industry-leading companies are increasingly putting customer centricity and experience at the heart of their strategies to respond to intensifying global

F. Halb
Technology industry, Graz, Austria

U. Seebacher (✉)
University of Applied Sciences Vienna, Vienna, Austria
e-mail: us@uweseebacher.org; uwe.seebacher@edu.fh-wien.ac.at

U. Hannig, U. Seebacher (eds.), *Marketing and Sales Automation*, Management for Professionals, https://doi.org/10.1007/978-3-031-20040-3_17

competition and ultimately be selected as supplier in the B2B decision-making process. In addition, the battle is on to intelligently combine digital and non-digital transformation. After all, this is the only way to ensure a seamless customer experience across all channels (Maechler et al., 2017). In this context, the last few years have been characterized by the rise of content marketing, the increasing use of digital technologies, data generation and management in marketing, and the changing buying behavior of customers when using channels during their information and purchase process (Hall, 2017, p. 107).

Purchasing behavior in the B2B sector (Seebacher, 2021c) is increasingly converging with that of B2C customers. The battle for customers has long since ceased to be fought on the basis of long-established purchase decision criteria such as price, delivery time, technical standards, safety standards, location and origin of the company, familiarity with the company, service agreements, or other contractual terms. Thus, in addition to rational technical and economic criteria, subjective soft factors such as the brand and image of a company, the length of the business relationship, cultural affinities, the level of education of the purchaser, previous experience with certain companies, and also the personal interests and motivation of the decision-makers are becoming increasingly important in terms of their influence on the final purchase decision (Malaval, 2001, p. 39f.).

The amount and speed of information and the variety of choices are increasing rapidly. As a result, B2B customers are overwhelmed by the ever-increasing wealth of information and choices they are confronted with and have difficulty making the right purchase decisions. To win them over, companies need to develop strategies and tools that facilitate purchasing and help customers at every stage of the buying process (Toman et al., 2017, p. 120).

B2B customers are also demanding a better customer experience, according to a survey of 1000 B2B decision-makers conducted by McKinsey. The results show that the lack of speed in interaction with their suppliers is the biggest pain point for customers (Maechler et al., 2017).

The buying patterns of B2B customers are more complex, yet many companies do not realize that B2B customers are only marginally different from their B2C counterparts. Although corporate purchases are usually based on more in-depth research and discussions in a buying center as well as a higher budget, they are still made by people who go home every day and then "transform" into "normal" consumers. This means that their expectations of B2B customer experience are heavily influenced by their B2C activities (Shaw, 2018; Maechler et al., 2016). For this reason, creating a strong customer experience has become a leading management objective. This development is also reflected in new professional roles, such as Chief Customer Experience Officer, Vice President Customer Experience, or Customer Experience Manager (Lemon & Verhoef, 2016, p. 69).

In order to create such unique customer experiences, companies need to understand the customer journey. This refers to the phases that customers go through in their relationship with a company or brand along the purchase decision process (Morgan, 2018). On their path to the final purchase, they interact with companies via several contact points, so-called touchpoints (Lemon & Verhoef, 2016, p. 82).

2 The Measurement of Customer Experience

Touchpoints are the moments of truth: whether customers buy and become loyal is decided at the touchpoints of a company (Schüller, 2015, pp. 13–15). Although most B2B companies recognize the importance of creating exceptional customer experience to stay ahead of the competition, only a few actively implement this (Morgan, 2018). According to the Digital Brand Leadership Study, only 34% of the companies surveyed capture customer journeys holistically and 24% do not consider the customer journey at all (Esch et al., 2016, p. 16).

To make it easier for customers to buy, marketers must not only understand the course of the customer journey, but also tackle the biggest challenges customers face at each touchpoint on their path to purchase. For this reason, the goal at the beginning of any customer experience initiative should be to identify and assess the touchpoints that are relevant to customers. Based on this, the distribution of marketing resources per touchpoint can be optimized and their effectiveness improved in order to ultimately sustainably increase the number of new customers and maintain relationships with long-standing customers and keep them profitable. Schüller structures the customer touchpoint management process into four steps (see Fig. 1) (Schüller, 2016, pp. 154–157).

Before a marketing strategy can be aligned with experience and corresponding communication measures can be adapted, a survey of the current touchpoint situation from the customer's point of view must be carried out.

The development of a B2B touchpoint evaluation tool enables an interactive and multidimensional assessment of individual touchpoints not only from an internal perspective, but also from the customer's perspective, thus helping to derive customer-oriented recommendations for action for the future management of the identified touchpoints. For the evaluation of touchpoints, an examination of at least four dimensions from the customer's perspective is necessary:

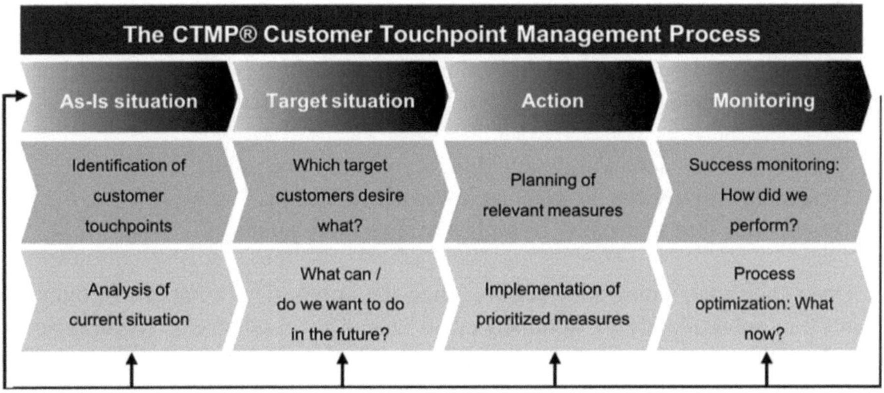

Fig. 1 The four steps of the CTMP® Customer Touchpoint Management process (Source: Schüller, 2016, p. 157)

- Touchpoint Awareness (Reach),
- Touchpoint Importance (Relevance),
- Touchpoint Quality and
- Touchpoint Impact (Influence of a touchpoint on decision-making).

The basis for the evaluation is to conduct a primary survey to find out how customers perceive touchpoints previously defined in an internal analysis. Initially, 50–100 people are sufficient for such a survey (Schüller, 2016, p. 184). The opinions of the customers can be recorded using various methods and instruments, for example questionnaires, focus groups, or personal in-depth interviews. Based on the four evaluation dimensions, individual touchpoints can be specifically queried, and their performance evaluated from the customer's perspective.

The awareness dimension is intended to identify which touchpoints are perceived by customers and which are not known. This provides insight into the touchpoint reach, i.e. whether the touchpoint reaches a large proportion of potential and existing customers or is only perceived by a small niche segment (Ott, 2017, pp. 73–76).

Touchpoint relevance shows the importance of the respective touchpoints for customers, allowing the company to identify critical moments of truth, so-called super touchpoints, across a person's entire customer journey. The third dimension, touchpoint quality, measures the performance of touchpoints in terms of customers' best and worst experiences at each touchpoint (Schüller, 2016, p. 184).

Combined with the importance of the touchpoints, the fourth dimension, the influence on the final decision-making process, allows conclusions to be drawn as to which touchpoints the focus should be placed on in order to ultimately be preferred to competitor providers. These four dimensions can then be used to identify the so-called love points and pain points in the individual phases of the buying process and thus derive appropriate marketing measures to improve the customer experience along the entire customer journey (Schüller, 2016, p. 184). Table 1 shows an excerpt of questions on the respective dimensions of the touchpoint evaluation of a B2B company.

Once the customer perspective has been examined for each touchpoint, each contact point can be awarded one, two, or three points depending on its performance. The distribution of points can be derived from the percentages achieved in the survey results. For example, categories can be structured as follows:

- Touchpoints that score less than 34% receive only one point.
- Touchpoints that score 34–66% are awarded two points.
- Touchpoints that score 67% or higher receive three points.

Once each touchpoint has been assigned the appropriate number of points, all points can subsequently be summed up to a final touchpoint effectiveness score. Based on this total score, all touchpoints can be arranged in a matrix or along a customer journey illustration.

As a final step in the evaluation process, the result can be compared with the company's internal view to identify deviations. In terms of internal cross-checking,

Table 1 Touchpoint evaluation dimensions (Source: Own presentation)

Touchpoint evaluation dimension	Questions
Touchpoint awareness	Which sources of information would you use when searching for *<product or service>*?
	How did you find out about Company XY?
	Which contact points of company XY are you aware of? *(multiple selection of touchpoints)*
Touchpoint importance	Which five contact points are the *most important* to you in each stage of your purchase decision process *regarding <product or service>?* *(multiple answers structured according to pre-purchase, purchase and post-purchase phase)*
	Which five contact points are generally the *least important* to you in your purchase decision process regarding *<product or service>*? *(multiple selection of touchpoints)*
Touchpoint quality	With which five contact points of company XY have you had the *best* experience so far? *(multiple selection of touchpoints)*
	What made your experience with these contact points so special?
	Which *positive* moments do you remember when you were in contact with company XY?
	With which five contact points of company XY have you had the *worst* experience so far? *(multiple selection of touchpoints)*
	What has made your experience with these contact points unsatisfactory?
	Which negative moments do you remember when getting in touch with the company XY?
Touchpoint impact on purchase decision	Which five contact points ultimately convince you to buy from company XY? *(multiple selection of touchpoints)*
	Why are *<name selected contact points>* particularly important to you?
	What is important to you regarding these contact points?
	What are your expectations of these contact points that are particularly important to you?

no general key performance indicator (KPI) structure can be provided to measure each dimension, as customer journeys are too diverse. Therefore, the identification of appropriate KPIs depends on the type of touchpoint customers face at each stage and the data a company has access to.

However, the evaluation tool (see Fig. 2) suggests a number of metrics that can be used to measure specific aspects of a touchpoint with data available at each stage. Depending on the touchpoint, each company must decide for itself which KPIs are appropriate for measuring each dimension. It is recommended to use a mix of future as well as past-oriented metrics.

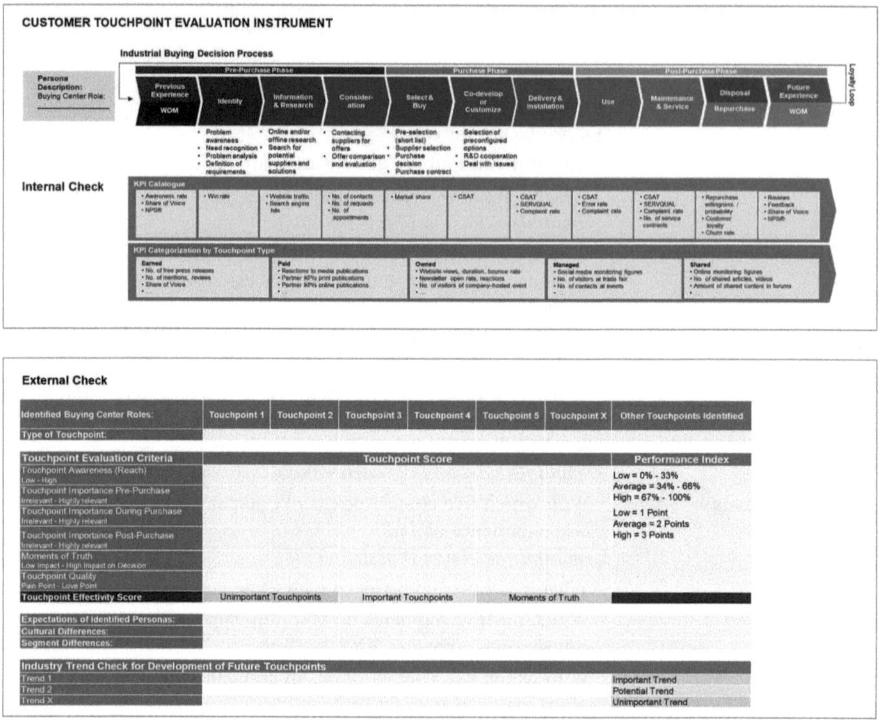

Fig. 2 B2B touchpoint evaluation tool (Source: Own presentation)

Classic metrics, such as customer satisfaction, customer loyalty, SERVQUAL, or the Net Promoter Score®, can be combined to cross-check corresponding results from touchpoint surveys. In order to obtain a 360° view of the selected touchpoints, all information, including internal data from the company as well as external data from the customer, must be integrated into a touchpoint or customer experience dashboard in the longer term. Combined with the customer relationship management and marketing automation system as well as other outside insight tools, a sustainable marketing management cockpit can be developed.

The main goal of tracing the experience at each customer touchpoint is to develop an understanding of how to optimize the experience for customers throughout their entire decision-making process. This starts with needs assessment, then moves through information search and processing to final selection and purchase transaction, followed by the post-purchase phase where the product or service is used until a new solution is required, and where opinions about the product or service are also shared. At each stage of this decision-making process, customers come into contact with the company through touchpoints, for which it is necessary to evaluate what information and what experience customers want at each point and what turns out to be an obstacle for customers (Schmitt, 2003, p. 68).

Touchpoint identification and evaluation are part of the analysis phase of the customer touchpoint management process. Only when the performance of each individual touchpoint has been evaluated from the customer's point of view the next process step can be tackled. Once the as-is situation has been outlined, companies can derive goals and—according to prioritization—develop appropriate measures to optimize and improve their current touchpoint landscape in order to achieve the defined target situation.

All results can be summarized and presented in the aforementioned 360° customer experience dashboard providing information on relevant buyer personas, the visualized customer journey, and the results of the touchpoints at a glance. By combining all available data and metrics, an overall customer experience index can ultimately be defined, which serves as a new KPI allowing to continuously review the company's performance in terms of customer experience.

In the case of the touchpoint analysis of the selected international B2B group, it turned out that contact with the sales force is traditionally still the most important touchpoint in terms of its influence on decisions at all stages of the B2B buying process under study. For this reason, the development of the sales and service team is a critical success factor in creating unique customer experiences throughout the buying process.

The other important touchpoints are mainly online touchpoints. Therefore, the focus is on investing in the optimization of the online presence. It should be noted that a broad mix and thus a choice of a variety of alternatives to get in touch with a potential supplier is of high importance for customers. This means that despite an increased online focus, essential offline touchpoints must not be forgotten.

In terms of marketing budget allocation, resources need to be invested in channels that are actually relevant to customers. These are those channels where they spend time, prepare to buy and make the transactions, and where recommendations are reinforced. The focus is on super touchpoints that increase customer enthusiasm for the product or service, the reputation of the company, customer loyalty as well as the willingness to recommend the product and the provider (Schüller, 2016, p. 156).

As part of a sustainable, strategically oriented marketing automation approach, the customer experience management tool presented here makes a significant contribution to optimizing the marketing return on investment as well as lead and demand generation with regard to order acquisition and sales optimization.

References

Esch, F.-R., Brendel, D., Klaus, A., Adler, N., & Thunig, C. (2016). *Digital brand leadership. Brand leadership in a digitally transformed world.* Accessed December 16, 2018, from https://www.esch-brand.com/wp-content/uploads/2018/04/2016-ESCH.-l-Digital-Brand-Leadership-Studie.pdf

Hall, S. (2017). *Innovative B2B marketing. New models, processes and theory.* Kogan Page.

Lemon, K. N., & Verhoef, P. C. (2016). Understanding customer experience throughout the customer journey. *Journal of Marketing, 6*, 69–96. Accessed June 09, 2018, from https://

www.ama.org/publications/JournalOfMarketing/Pages/understanding-customer-experience-customer-journey.aspx

Maechler, N., Poenaru, A., Rüdt Collenberg, T., & Schulze P. (2017, April). *Finding the right digital balance in B2B customer experience*. Accessed August 11, 2018, from https://www.mckinsey.com/business-functions/marketing-and-sales/our-insights/finding-the-right-digital-balance-in-b2b-customer-experience

Maechler, N., Sahni, S., & Van Oostrum, M. (2016, March). *Improving the business-to-business customer experience*. Accessed July 03, 2018, from https://www.mckinsey.com/business-functions/marketing-and-sales/our-insights/improving-the-business-to-business-customer-experience

Malaval, P. (2001). *Strategy and management of industrial brands. Business to business products and services*. Springer Science + Business Media.

Mora Cortez, R., & Johnston, W. J. (2017). The future of B2B marketing theory. A historical and prospective analysis. *Industrial Marketing Management, 66*, 90–102. Accessed August 31, 2018, from https://www.sciencedirect.com/science/article/abs/pii/S0019850117300263

Morgan, B. (2018, March 24). *Build a compelling B2B customer journey*. Accessed July 03, 2018, from https://www.forbes.com/sites/blakemorgan/2018/03/24/build-a-compelling-b2b-customer-journey/#51fe716d6a13

Ott, C. S. (2017). Selling successfully in a digitalized world. Paradigm shift in touchpoint management. In B. Keller & C. S. Ott (Eds.), *Touchpoint management. Acting successfully along the customer journey* (pp. 65–86). Haufe-Lexware.

Salesforce Research. (2017, June 15). *Fourth annual state of marketing. Insights and trends from 3,500 global marketing leaders*. Accessed November 09, 2018, from https://www.salesforce.com/form/pdf/2017-state-of-marketing.jsp?nc=7010M000000u6f2&d=7010M000000u6ex

Schmitt, B. H. (2003). *Customer Experience Management. A Revolutionary Approach to Connecting with Your Customers*. Hoboken: Wiley.

Schüller, A. M. (2015). *Touchpoints. In touch with today's customer. Management strategies for our new business world* (6th ed.). Gabal.

Schüller, A. M. (2016). *Touchpoint. Victory. Communication in times of digital transformation*. Gabal.

Seebacher, U., & Güpner, A. (2021). *Marketing resource management – How marketers storm to the top of the company* (7th ed.). AQPS.

Seebacher, U. (2021a). *Data-driven Management: A primer for modern corporate decision making*. AQPS.

Seebacher, U. (2021b). *Predictive intelligence for data-driven managers: Process model, assessment-tool, IT-blueprint, competence model and case studies*. Springer.

Seebacher, U. (2021c). *B2B marketing guidebook*. Springer.

Shaw, A. (2018, March 15). *B2B businesses need a customer experience overhaul*. Accessed July 03, 2018, from https://www.forbes.com/sites/forbescommunicationscouncil/2018/03/15/b2b-businesses-need-a-customer-experience-overhaul/#39326f8b2993

Toman, N., Adamson, B., & Gomez, C. (2017). The new sales imperative. B2B purchasing has become too complicated. You need to make it easy for your customers to buy. *Harvard Business Review, 3–4*, 119–125. Accessed September 24, 2018, from https://hbr.org/2017/03/the-new-sales-imperative

Fabienne Halb is heading global customer relationship management for the marketing and communications department of an international technology group. In the course of her master's thesis on B2B customer experience, she specialized on touchpoint management with a focus on touchpoint analyses and developed a touchpoint evaluation tool specifically for industrial B2B companies in this context.

Uwe Seebacher is a methods and structural scientist. He holds a doctorate in economics and business administration and is Professor for Predictive Intelligence at the University of Applied Sciences Munich, Professor for Marketing and Communications at the University of Applied Sciences for Marketing and Communication at Vienna and Professor for Data Science, Predictive Intelligence, Sales and Distribution Management at the Institute of Management Technology Ghaziabad and Dubai. He has more than 30 years of experience as a business angel and investor, consultant, leader but also entrepreneur in the media, manufacturing, and service industries. He is a popular keynote speaker and panelist.

He has authored more than 50 books in many leading publishing houses, such as "Reengineering Corporate Communications" (Springer Cham), "Assets-as-Service" (Springer Gabler 2021), "Data-driven Management" (Springer Gabler 2021), "Predictive Intelligence for Managers" (Springer 2021), "B2B Marketing Guidebook" (Springer 2021), "Marketing Resource Management" (AQPS 2021), "Leadership Development" (Linde 2006) or "Template-based Management (Springer 2020) or "European Human Resource Management" (HBM 2009).

For his innovative concepts and initiatives, e.g., with Allianz, the European Union, the Austrian Federal Economic Chamber, Bayer Leverkusen, and BASF, he received various awards, such as the Diskobolos Innovation Award of the European Chamber of Commerce and the 2016 Export Award of the Austrian Federal Economic Chamber. For more information, visit www.uweseebacher.org.

Interaction of Lead Management and CRM Along the Customer Journey

Alexander Woelke

1 Alignment of Marketing and Sales

With a lot of effort and creativity, marketing develops relevant content and addresses suitable channels and target groups to generate leads. Unfortunately, depending on the business model and average deal size, an operational flurry then starts in many companies, because the interest of the leads could be hot. Therefore, without the time for sufficient prioritization, qualification, and documentation, too many leads are often handed off to sales at a mediocre quality level. In the best case, they return these leads; in the worst case, the leads go completely unprocessed because Sales does not have adequate opportunities to follow up with the contacts in a meaningful priority.

Either Sales judges the result as "too few leads with good quality" or Marketing reads it as "ignorance of Sales to further qualify the contact requests." It's usually a frustrating result for everyone involved. Lots of inbound just doesn't equal lots of results.

To solve the dilemma between marketing and sales, the systems and processes must be coordinated and interlinked. To do this, the goals must be defined, the strategies and activities for achieving them derived from them, and responsibilities defined. In this context, it is very important to develop a common understanding of when a lead is actually "sales ready."

In order to integrate lead management and CRM conceptually and procedurally, one ideally starts with the conception of the big picture. Because without understanding in detail the internal and external requirements for the strategy and aligning the content conception and the processes to it, the implementation will fail in

A. Woelke (✉)
Cloudbridge Consulting GmbH, Munich, Germany
e-mail: a.woelke@cloudbridge.eu

U. Hannig, U. Seebacher (eds.), *Marketing and Sales Automation*, Management for Professionals, https://doi.org/10.1007/978-3-031-20040-3_18

practice. In the analysis for the preparation of the strategy, the following areas should be considered in particular:

- Corporate goals, departmental goals, and personal goals of individual stakeholders;
- Strengths, weaknesses, opportunities, and threats of the existing lead process in inbound marketing and nurturing;
- Strengths, weaknesses, opportunities, and threats of the existing CRM setup.

Before getting into the details of the customer journey strategy, it's important to consider the following:

- Alignment of corporate goals, goals of individual teams, and goals of individual players in the company (e.g., marketing, sales, operations, IT);
- Definition of the customer journey from initial contact to the management of existing customers through after-sales services;
- Determine the strategic and operational responsibilities of each manager.

It is advantageous to document the results of the analysis as well as the strategy in writing and thus get all internal stakeholders on board.

2 Customer Journey Management

The optimal interaction of marketing and sales in an end-to-end view concerns the following five efficiency fields (see Fig. 1):

- Marketing and Lead Generation;
- Lead Scoring and Nurturing;
- Sales and CRM;

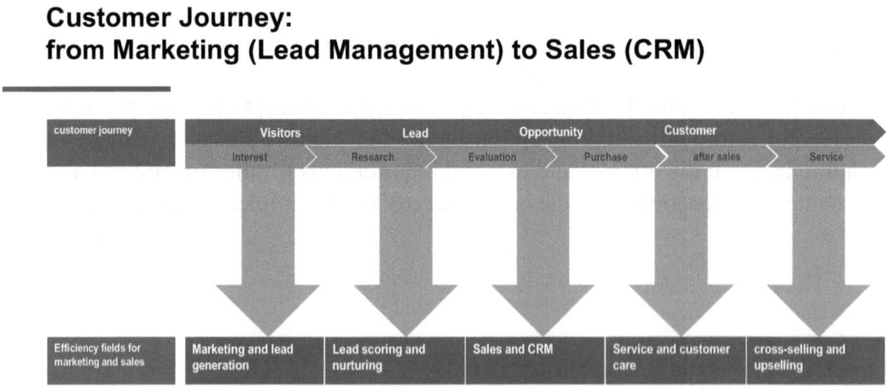

Fig. 1 The five central efficiency fields for marketing and sales (Source: Cloudbridge Consulting)

- Service and customer care;
- Cross-selling and up-selling.

2.1 Marketing and Lead Generation

Sales departments work according to the system of a sales funnel. This divides the sales process into individual stages. In each stage, the number of leads decreases, while their quality increases. From an initial high number of contacts with loose interest, the funnel narrows with each stage. Qualified contacts become leads with buying interest and finally buyers and regular customers.

Marketing can benefit from this methodology. For this purpose, the marketing organization must be oriented to the structure of sales. Then a marketing funnel is to be developed (see Fig. 2). Unlike the sales funnel, the goal is not to close the deal, but to handover sales-ready leads to the sales department.

Now it's time to develop marketing stages and measures that lead stakeholders with different levels of maturity through the customer journey. Because not every subscriber is a lead that can be developed into a buyer. Lead management must therefore be subjected to an end-to-end consideration—from the unknown member of the target group to the potential customer to the buyer, regular customer, and lost customer.

At the top level of the funnel in online and web marketing, suitable touch points and instruments must be defined in order to lead the leads from stage to stage. Furthermore, operational goals, key figures, and success criteria must be defined in order to be able to check and optimize the effectiveness of measures and campaigns.

Fig. 2 The marketing funnel as the basis for a sustainable sales pipeline (Source: Cloudbridge Consulting)

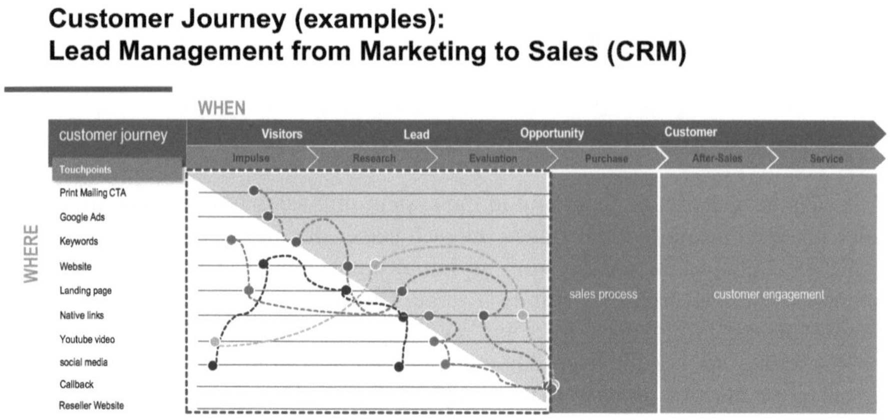

Fig. 3 Lead management in marketing (Source: Cloudbridge Consulting)

Examples of a touch point from the first funnel stage are blogs and newsletters about products and solutions. These must be search engine optimized in order to be found by information seekers in the impulse phase.

Appealing content attracts returning readers who are willing to exchange more detailed information, such as white papers, guides, and webinars, for personal data. In this way, unknown visitors become leads (see Fig. 3).

Ideally, a call-to-action (CTA) should be built into all marketing steps to automatically and relevantly nurture leads based on the recipient's key interest.

2.2 Lead Scoring and Lead Nurturing

The classification of leads according to their maturity level in the respective stage of the marketing funnel enables efficient cooperation between marketing and sales and gives both sides the highest possible transparency about the existing pipeline. For this purpose, it is necessary to discuss the benchmarks and evaluation points together with the sales and marketing management. Lead scores are the only way to decide when a lead is "sales ready" and can be handed over to the key account manager, for example. The scoring model should be dynamically adaptable to the respective requirements of sales, inventory pipeline, and company situation.

The so-called Behavior Score is used to evaluate which product or offer of the company the person behind the lead is interested in and with what intensity, which can be derived, for example, from the surfing, downloading, or webinar behavior. These activities can be easily measured at the respective touch points. In addition to this behavior score, it should be possible to evaluate whether the prospect also corresponds to the target group and is therefore seriously interesting for the sales department.

For a better assessment of these facts, corresponding key data should already be requested in the marketing funnel, such as personal data, position and area of responsibility, decision-making category, company size as well as budgets and requirements. While these factors can be collected at individual touch points, other essential information arises within the customer journey. They concern, for example, surfing and search behavior, the will to download or participate, as well as the switch to the offline world, for example, during a visit to a trade fair.

Goal-oriented scores are to be assigned for each attribute, for example a high number of points for direct purchase decision-makers and participants in product presentations. Negative scores should also not be neglected, for example for leads who unsubscribe from newsletters or reject contact requests.

The scored leads are automatically transferred to further measures and stages with the help of corresponding systems. The leads are processed in the marketing funnel until they are "sales ready" according to the previously defined definition. In this context, it must also be determined how to proceed with leads that have already been transferred to sales but have not yet been successfully processed in the sales funnel.

2.3 Sales and CRM

At the latest at the point where a lead is transferred from the marketing funnel to the sales funnel, it becomes clear how important coordination between both areas is, both technically and in terms of content. Elementary and measurable factors for the lead transfer are:

- Timeliness and quality of the data, e.g. current key figures on the company and the contact details of the decision-maker;
- Data to be transferred to CRM: Sales colleagues need at least basic information on specific needs and possible budgets;
- Self-explanatory Behavior Score.

But less hard factors are also valuable:

- Interactions with the contact on the way to the lead handover, e.g. time and type of contact at the first touch point, date of the last interaction;
- Striking behaviors of the lead;
- Information recently sought by the lead: Sometimes this can reveal important connection points, such as attending a webinar on a particular topic or using a free trial of a product.

However, lead management is not a one-way street from marketing to sales. In the course of processing the sales funnel, further insights about leads arise that play a decisive role for the marketing team. For example, negotiations can result in approaches for further processing in a new topic area. Sales employees also personally meet customers whose names are stored in the CRM system, but who are completely unknown in the marketing system. Information therefore flows in both directions via an account and via a contact, i.e. from the marketing automation or lead management system into the CRM and vice versa.

A Service Level Agreement (SLA) must be concluded between Marketing and Sales for the processing of leads. This could include the following parameters, for example:

- the Behavior Score or Qualification Quality, where leads are passed from Marketing to Sales;
- the type of transfer between the systems, e.g. automated, push-pull;
- The period of time in which leads are processed by Sales in a particular processing stage and the result of this processing (for example, lead accepted by Sales, sales opportunity created, lead rejected, lead passed on to partner) is stored in the system;
- The way leads are returned to marketing when they cannot be further processed by sales;
- the necessary information, e.g. opportunity too small, target group does not fit, no suitable solution to offer, to submit a lead.

2.4 Service and Customer Support

Very valuable for an effective lead and customer management that is thought through to the end are after sales and customer service. The most important milestone in lead management is certainly the closing. But after that, the process continues. Only if the customer is professionally taken care of in the long term after the contract has been signed will there be lasting customer loyalty. Depending on the complexity of the solution, after sales and customer service are key factors influencing customer loyalty, churn rate, cross-selling, and up-selling.

A positive experience during the implementation and onboarding of new products and solutions often lays the foundation for a long-term customer relationship. For example, after registering the hardware, one receives extensive newsletters from Apple with tips and tricks for use. Support requests are directed to a perfectly maintained information portal that makes it possible to answer most questions yourself. If there are still questions, the customer can get in touch with a support team via different channels, which usually provides quick and uncomplicated answers.

Negative experiences due to poor execution and poor accessibility of customer service, on the other hand, are often the beginning of the end of a successful customer relationship. It starts with not finding the contact options for support either in the service contract or on a website. The response times of the service team, the waiting times for a phone call, a technically poorly implemented online chat, or an email request with response times of several days lead to frustration among customers.

In any case, the employees are essential for the quality of the service. It is recommended to direct the requests to different teams with different skills and experience according to their level of complexity. 80–90% of all questions to service teams, help desks, and technical support are standard questions that can be solved easily. For the more complicated queries, specialists or workflows should be available for escalations. In the CRM system, selection fields should be included for the respective customer categories—complex solution in use, medium complex, standard—which are filled in by the sales department and are available to the service department to assess the cases.

The after-sales and service teams must always be equipped with the most important information from the CRM along the customer journey. Only those who know what is important can act accordingly. Here, too, a flow of information in all directions must be ensured. After all, the information about service cases, annoyance, or satisfaction is a valuable input for marketing.

Today, after sales and customer service must not only reliably handle difficulties and complaints, but also keep an open ear for other topics and developing needs. Therefore, it is elementary that service management is integrated systemically, organizationally, and process-driven into the customer journey just like marketing and sales. Today, there are already service management systems that are seamlessly integrated with marketing automation, lead management, and CRM. If the systems used today do not yet achieve this, the requirements must be met through interfaces or at least through regular data exchange.

2.5 Cross-Selling and Up-Selling

In order to exploit the full customer potential through cross-selling and up-selling, all relevant data must be stored in the systems used. For example, it is rarely the case that someone who buys screws also needs a drill or a drill. After all, anyone who ventures into DIY does not buy the screws first and foremost. The necessary technical equipment is usually available, but perhaps dowels or putty is missing to iron out mistakes. The screws can also be used, for example, to fix an awning for the patio. If the DIY store and garden center operator now knows that his customer is currently re-equipping his terrace, he can certainly offer him suitable products, such as a barbecue or garden furniture, automatically.

To take advantage of such opportunities, you need to know your customers across all business units. Those who combine lead management and CRM have this knowledge. The end-to-end view not only provides information about products actually purchased, but also about deals not closed, interest not followed up and the development of the customer. This is because new opportunities for selling adjacent services sometimes arise years later. Therefore, it is important to sustainably evaluate the collected information about the customer journey and the customer relationship.

► The three most important findings are:

- A customer journey is not a one-way street from marketing to sales to service management. A customer is unique along his life cycle. All points of contact with the customer must be documented. This information must be consistently mapped in systems and made accessible, evaluable, and usable for all stakeholders.

- The interaction of marketing, sales, and service management along the customer journey can be solved to a large extent through common goals, consistent data management and intelligent systems, SLAs and workflows. However, it must not be forgotten that people are responsible for this overall work. The clean coordination of common goals and individual goals as well as the definition and delimitation of responsibilities is elementary for success as a team.
- Regardless of whether a company has ten large industrial customers or more than a million consumers among its clientele, these customers are unique and the engine of a company. Accordingly, they must be treated well from the first point of contact throughout the entire customer journey. Focusing on the customer should always be one of the most important corporate goals.

Alexander Woelke is CEO of the Munich-based marketing consultancy Cloudbridge Consulting. He is an expert in B2B marketing, sales, and digital business for companies that want to consistently align themselves with sustainable revenue growth. Together with his team, Woelke develops the "big picture," creates specialist concepts for customer journey, CRM, marketing automation, lead management, and helps select the relevant technologies.

Boosting Marketing and Sales Automation's Effectiveness: Strategies to Increase Lead Quality

Hannes Huttelmaier and Julia Heigl

1 Introduction

Advances in digitalization and a changing buying behavior among B2B decision-makers have since long affected companies' marketing and sales approaches (Andersen et al., 2017; Marketing Leadership Council, 2012). Covid-19 has been a catalyst to this development, leading to significant changes, as businesses were forced to review and adapt their marketing and sales strategies to inbound-based approaches (Corsaro et al., 2021). This development often goes hand in hand with the introduction of marketing automation, which is becoming an increasingly important building block in marketing (Huttelmaier et al., 2022). According to a study by McKinsey & Company, 51% of US B2B companies have invested in resources and capabilities to drive personalized marketing. In addition, 45% of respondents said they have recently reevaluated the role of marketing in their organization (Harrison et al., 2021). Likewise, our discussions with decision-makers show that they would like to see a more prominent role for marketing in their organizations in general and in generating sales in particular. Against this background, corresponding investments are made in people, systems, and structures. However, these investments to date often do not yet lead to the desired outcomes (Harrison et al., 2021). Marketing teams may be great in shaping brand images, attracting the attention of potential customers, or even generating leads by, e.g., successful advertising campaigns, social media activities, search engine optimization, or events. Traditional marketing-related performance indicators such as view or engagement

H. Huttelmaier (✉)
Technical University of Applied Sciences Würzburg-Schweinfurt, Schweinfurt, Germany
e-mail: hannes.huttelmaier@fhws.de

J. Heigl
Eastern Bavarian Technical University Amberg-Weiden, Weiden, Germany
e-mail: j.heigl@oth-aw.de

U. Hannig, U. Seebacher (eds.), *Marketing and Sales Automation*, Management for Professionals, https://doi.org/10.1007/978-3-031-20040-3_19

rates, whitepaper downloads, or website visits may show excellent scores. Still, in many cases, these activities do not transform into sales. This, however, is what many decision-makers in B2B expect their marketing teams to deliver.

Often the problem stems from non-existent or at least inadequate lead management. Significant and increasing resources are spent on marketing to generate leads (Gregoriadis, 2021; Olenski, 2012). Often, however, these leads are not systematically developed, followed up, qualified, and handed over to a sales specialist at the right moment. Beyond this background, it is not surprising that these leads generated with great effort are often ignored or never contacted by sales (Sabnis et al., 2013). Marketing efforts in lead generation are worthless and, thus, a waste of time and money, if leads are not properly managed (Ohiomah et al., 2019). Without effective lead management, marketing-generated leads can even hurt downstream sales outcomes because of wasted effort on poorly qualified leads or delays in following up with them (Smith et al., 2006).

Thus, setting up an effective lead management system or optimizing it is of major importance (Ohiomah et al., 2016). Prior research has shown that an effective use of lead management systems has a significant and positive effect on sales performance (Ohiomah et al., 2019). Therefore, many companies have introduced lead management processes and invested in Marketing & Sales Automation (MSA) to increase the effectiveness and efficiency of their lead management (Huttelmaier et al., 2022). However, in many cases, they still end up with either too many low-quality or not enough leads passed on to sales. In the first case, this results in sales being spammed, leaving them having to follow up on too many leads that they are not able to turn into customers and, thus, wasting their time (Stevens, 2011). The reasons for this are manifold and include issues such as leads being passed on to sales without any qualification, qualification based on wrong criteria, or wrong timing of the handover. Especially timing is critical and often leads are routed to sales too early or too late. As hot leads—prospects that are ready to buy—will "cool down" fast, the timeframe for passing leads on from marketing to sales is limited while the conversion ratio increases significantly with the right timing (Stevens, 2011; Ohiomah et al., 2016; Carroll, 2006). In fact, immediacy is found to be the most important factor in lead follow-up on sales performance (Ohiomah et al., 2019). Not passing on enough leads to sales, on the other hand, will lead to a low return on investment and doubts about the effectiveness of marketing's activities.

Therefore, implementing strategies to improve the quality of leads passed from marketing to sales is of crucial importance for any company following a lead management approach with MSA. In the following, we will outline some simple but very effective best practices to systematically increase lead quality.

2 Important Elements of Lead Management and Areas to Increase Lead Quality

Lead management refers to all strategies, processes, and actions of a firm to systematically turn unknown potential into actual customers (Seebacher, 2021; bvik, 2022). The objective is to find the optimal balance between quantity and quality of leads passed on from marketing to sales to maximize sales conversions. Typically, lead management is divided into the sub-processes lead generation, lead nurturing, lead scoring, and lead routing (see Fig. 1).

Lead generation involves all measures to identify prospective customers (Stevens, 2011). Typically, these potential customers start their information journey on their own, for example by entering a keyword in a search engine. Companies pursuing an inbound marketing strategy try to be present at this so-called zero moment of truth with attractive and relevant content by providing content that matches the search query, and SEO or SEA activities. Of course, lead generation is not restricted to this exemplary channel and inbound approaches. Trade shows, social media activities, "cold" calls via phone or physical visits, public relations, webinars, podcasts, and many more are further examples of channels and activities used to generate leads. In all cases, the objective is to attract potential customers' attention so that they are willing to exchange some sort of contact data (e.g., email address, name, etc.) for useful information. At this point, the unknown person turns into an identified prospect or lead (Philipp, 2021).

Some identified prospects qualify right away. In most cases, however, forwarding such a lead directly to a salesperson is not successful, as the lead has only shown a certain interest in a topic but is usually not yet ready to buy (Stevens, 2011). At this point lead nurturing comes into play. It is defined as the process of moving leads along the customer journey until they are ready to buy by having consistent and meaningful dialogue with valuable information at the right time via the right touchpoints with them (Carroll, 2006).

Lead nurturing is typically accompanied by lead scoring, which is about ranking a lead's maturity level regarding interest and sales-readiness. The goal is to identify each lead's position in the customer journey to decide if they are ready to be passed on to a salesperson or—in case they are not ready yet—which nurturing activities would be best suited to move them forward. There is no one right scoring system.

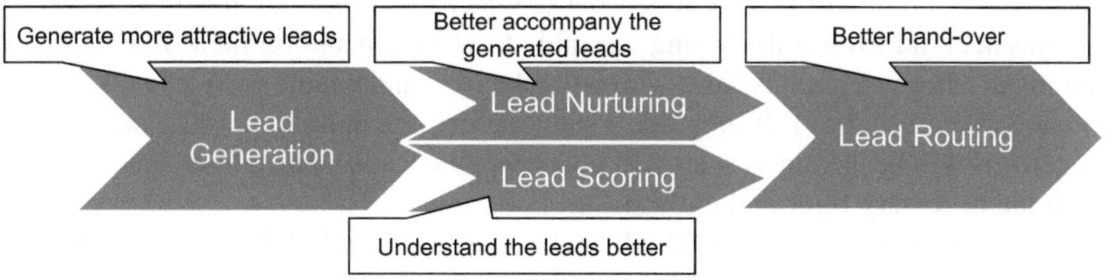

Fig. 1 Overview of lead management elements and areas to improve lead quality (Source: Own representation)

Companies can, e.g., use a numerical system, terms like cold lead, warm lead, and hot lead, or a grading system using letters. Regardless of the chosen method, lead scoring typically incorporates a combination of different factors (Marketo, 2019).

Finally, especially when they have been qualified as "sales-ready," leads have to be routed to the right channels or persons of contact to follow up on them. This is called lead routing (Stevens, 2011).

Beyond this background we can identify four areas to improve lead quality: (1) generate more attractive leads, (2) better accompany the generated leads, (3) better understand them, and (4) better pass them on to sales (see Fig. 1).

In this chapter, we will focus on "(3) Better understand them", as from our experience this is the main aspect companies are struggling with and the area where companies can improve lead quality significantly with relatively low effort.

3 Increasing Lead Quality by Meaningful Lead Scoring

3.1 Strategic Actions

Clear Definition of the Ideal Customer and Lead Stages

What is a high-quality lead? Put simply and from a high-level perspective, this is a lead that sales accepts and which converts into a customer. Or, from a customer-oriented perspective: A high-quality lead is a contact who is happy to talk to a salesperson.

However, a major problem in many companies struggling with their lead management is that there is no common understanding in the company of what they consider a high-quality lead. Very often, different functions or organizational units (such as marketing and sales, but also, e.g., subsidiaries), and even different people within these units understand something completely different under a lead. It is, however, impossible to increase lead quality without a detailed understanding of what characterizes a high-quality lead. Therefore, lead quality starts with a clear and consistent definition of the ideal customer and the different lead stages; with a special focus on leads that are ready to be passed on to sales. It is of utmost importance that these definitions are jointly worked out and agreed upon by marketing and sales together. Marketing is generally not able to do this alone. It is salespeople who know customers, their journey, and the nature of the sales process best. Nobody else will be able to tell better which customers are most likely to turn into a sale. And even if marketing was able to work this out on their own, it would not make any sense, as it is sales who will take over and handle each lead taking it to closure (Stevens, 2011). If they don't stand behind the definition 100%, all marketing efforts will be in vain as sales will not accept the leads handed over and follow up with the necessary rigor and enthusiasm.

Therefore, companies are well-advised to start at the end of the process by having marketing and sales define jointly what the "perfect" customer would look like and then—step by step—working their way up the sales channel (see Fig. 2). Thereby, it makes sense to first define which stages the company wants to build its lead

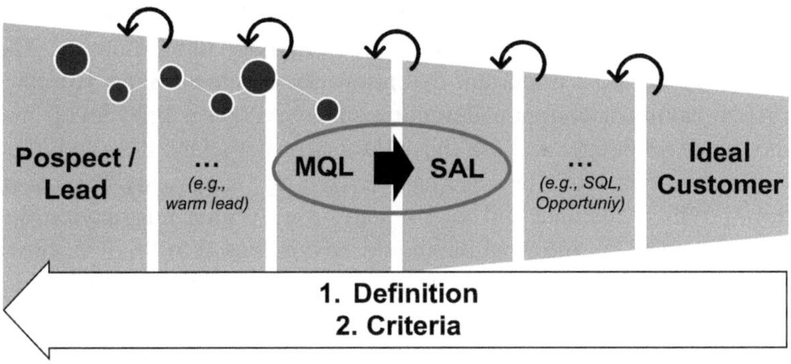

Fig. 2 Sales funnel with exemplary lead stages (Source: Own representation)

management on, to, in a second step, get specific by describing the criteria which indicate the stage of a lead.

The name for leads being passed on from marketing to sales—like for all other stages in the sales funnel—differs from company to company. Most commonly, however, they are called "Marketing Qualified Leads (MQLs)", which includes companies or contacts that marketing has qualified as ready for the sales team. An MQL that was accepted by sales is commonly known as "Sales Accepted Lead (SAL)", often followed by a stage called "Sales Qualified Lead (SQL)"—a company or contact that was accepted and qualified as a potential customer by sales (e.g., by using the BANT criteria, which is budget, authority, need, time). When discussions with this company or contact are about a specific project, they might move to an additional stage called "Opportunity" until they buy and from this time on will be considered as "Customer."

The first step should be a definition of the "ideal" or target customer. Because, only by having a common understanding of which types of customer profiles the lead management process should attract, marketing is able to target, generate, and further develop the right leads until sales-readiness (Schuster, 2022). The definition of the ideal customer is typically worked out in one or several workshops with sales managers or experienced sales reps. They could, e.g., be asked to describe one or two real customers that were a perfect fit for them or what characterizes the most attractive from the worst customers. Of course, the specific information required depends on the respective business, but it might, for example, include the industry of the customer, available budget, the role of the contact person (decision-maker, buyer, user, ...?), the timeframe to purchase, and so on. To keep the descriptions realistic, it might help to ask them to focus on the five critically, most important characteristics and not take everything they come up with as gospel (Stevens, 2011; ActiveCampaign, 2022; Carroll, 2006). Also, and this is true for all further definitions, marketing teams must not accept vague definitions and criteria, but zoom in deeply, perhaps also interview some customers themselves to get a detailed understanding of their characteristics. Once they have a clear understanding of the ideal customer, they should move the sales funnel upwards and—of course only, if the sales team uses these stages, or, if it makes sense with regard to the business they are in—define stages such as Sales Qualified Leads or Opportunities. Then they should move to the most important definition: the so-called Sales Accepted Lead (SAL). After having a common definition of a SAL on a high level, marketing should go one level deeper and ask the sales team what a lead they would accept is characterized by: When is a lead is characterized as "sales-ready"? What do these leads know? Which channels did they already use? Which information have they already consumed? This information should be condensed to the 3–5 most critical criteria that sales will from now on use to judge whether they will accept a lead or send it back to marketing. These criteria should also be the basis for the definition and description of a marketing qualified lead.

Of course, to build up an effective lead management, marketing must not stop at this point but gain an in-depth understanding of the jointly defined target group's customer journey, including jobs-to-be-done, pains, questions, and preferred channels at each of the identified touchpoints. Based on this analysis, it is often valuable to add further lead stages before leads are finally considered as marketing qualified leads. The stages might be labeled "prospect", "lead", or "cold lead", followed by stages such as "warm lead" and "hot lead" or similar—the number and naming of the stages differ from company to company. What is important is not the name, but that these stages are clearly defined and characterized by unambiguous criteria so that everyone in the organization has a clear understanding of their meaning. For each stage, marketing must assess what characterizes a lead in this specific stage as well as what potential customers need at this stage and what they need to move on to the next stage. Based on these insights marketing can set up effective lead generation and nurture strategies as well as specific actions.

Combining Demographic with Behavioral Scoring

Obviously, there exist many potentially useful criteria for each stage, and in consequence for a high-quality lead. They, however, can be classified in two dimensions, which form the basis for an effective lead scoring system: demographic information and behavioral information (see Fig. 3). Companies are well-advised to include criteria of both dimensions when setting up a lead scoring.

Demographic scoring is typically used to assess the fit of the lead with the company's target group. The higher the score, the closer the lead's profile matches the ideal customer the company is looking for and, consequently, the more relevant the lead is for the company (Wenger, 2021). Information typically considered for demographical scoring is industry, job title, location, company size, or similar. In most cases, it is information that the lead provides directly to the company, which is why scoring based on demographic information is often also referred to as explicit scoring (Adobe, 2020a).

Behavioral scoring, on the other hand, is typically based on information that a company observes or infers about the lead (therefore it is also referred to as implicit scoring) and includes information such as which pages a lead visited, whether they downloaded a whitepaper, requested demo access, etc. Such behavioral scoring, thus, tracks a lead's online behavior to assess its level of interest in buying the

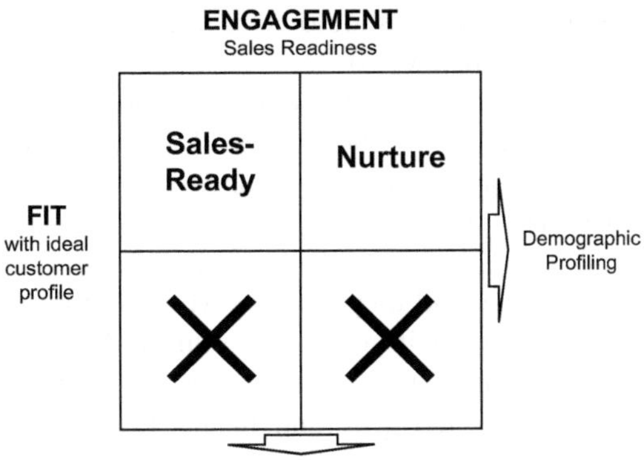

Fig. 3 Exemplary lead scoring matrix with profile and behavioral information (Source: Own representation based on Adobe, 2020a; edynamics, 2011)

company's offerings—its readiness to buy. A well-designed behavioral scoring will therefore help companies to determine whether someone is an early-stage prospect who is just looking for general information or entertainment or an active lead who is considering a purchase (Adobe, 2020b).

After the criteria have been set, it is time to decide on a scoring scale and—based on the defined scale—to assign a value to each criterion (in other words: to weight the criteria). Thereby, the absolute values are not important. A company can decide to score on a scale of 1–100, 10–1000, or differently. What is important is the ratio between the values assigned to the criteria: Behavioral activities indicating high purchase interest or demographic characteristics which are very important to the company should receive relatively higher values than criteria with lower impact. Also, companies should keep their scoring as simple as possible (ActiveCampaign, 2022; Robinson, 2021).

By combining behavioral and demographic scores it is possible to either come up with a total score or—if behavioral and demographic information are kept separate—with a matrix with the desired granularity, e.g., a 2×2 matrix as indicated in Fig. 3. This will help companies to determine the right actions for each lead, most importantly to decide which leads should be passed on to sales. In our matrix, we distinguish four groups based on

- the level of engagement (low/high), i.e., how much a lead wants to talk to the company, and
- the level of fit with the ideal profile, i.e., how much the company wants to talk to the lead.

Leads assigned to the upper left quadrant are leads that are a good match with our ideal profile and ready to talk to a sales rep, thus, they should be passed on to sales. Leads in the upper right quadrant are also a good fit, however, their behavior indicates that they are not sales-ready yet, thus, marketing should continue to further develop them with targeted nurturing campaigns. Finally, leads who fall into the two bottom categories should be segmented out, as they do not match the defined target profile (edynamic, 2011).

To classify leads in the different quadrants of the matrix and the lead stages, we need to define threshold values for each quadrant and stage. To come up with the right threshold values, companies may ask themselves what ideal or typical customers did, until they reached a certain stage (e.g., when they are sales-ready)—i.e., which information did they assess, which channels did they use, which pages did they visit, to whom did they talk to, etc. Summing up the values of each action will result in the threshold value. A special focus should be on when an MQL will be passed on to sales or—in the matrix—when a lead will be classified in the upper left quadrant. In this respect, it is important to note that companies should make sure that the maximum achievable demographic score will not exceed 50% of the threshold value. Otherwise, it would be possible that a lead is classified as sales-ready just based on a great fit, which does not make sense (Adobe, 2020a; edynamic, 2011).

Alternatives to Explicit Progressive Lead Profiling

Many companies base their scoring on demographic information of the lead which they collect via forms (explicit lead profiling). However, scoring on such explicitly entered information in forms is problematic due to low validity (Adobe, 2020a). Especially in the early stages of the customer journey users often enter fake information, because, at this point, they do not want to receive further information from the respective company or simply do not want to provide the requested information. This problem can be reduced by asking only for the most basic data at the beginning of the journey and requesting more detailed, more personal, and harder-to-assess information later in the journey—step by step. Form fields should be displayed dynamically, depending on data that already exist. In this way, leads are only asked for information that does not yet exist (explicit progressive lead profiling). Still, chances are high that the collected data is biased. Which alternative approaches do companies have to collect high-quality and useful data?

The key to answering this question is to ask yourself when leads have an interest in providing correct information. This is the case when this information is an important input for a result they want to get. This could, for example, be:

- Calculators: This could be, e.g., ROI, consumption, or benchmarking calculators. For example, Laserhub (a platform that combines inquiry, ordering, and delivery of metal parts in one lean, digital process) offers a price calculator on its website. After registering, companies can simply upload their CAD files and receive a quote in a few seconds (Laserhub, 2022a, 2022b).
- Configurators: Companies could offer a self-service configurator on their website or via apps where potential customers can configure a product/service to get an approximate price. Liebherr, for example, offers a "crane finder." After registering and providing basic company information, potential customers can access this free-of-charge web application to find the right crane by entering information such as height, load, radius, etc. (Liebherr, 2022).

- Free trials: Especially in the software industry many providers offer free trials. To start such a free trial phase, potential customers typically must open a demo account and provide some basic information such as email, telephone number, industry, etc. to set up the demo appropriately.
- Free services such as free SEO or website audits, audits to assess improvement potentials in a factory or similar do not only offer basic information about a lead but also detailed insights into his business which might help to later draft a customized offer taking specific requirements into account.
- Shortcuts: What is the best sign that a lead is ready to talk to a salesperson? When the lead explicitly asks for it. Therefore, many companies integrate shortcuts to sales such as "request offer", "talk to a sales rep", "book a demo", or similar on, e.g., their website. Leads requesting such next steps of course are willing to provide accurate information such as email address, industry, or telephone number.

Instead of relying on explicit information, companies could also use implicit information to collect profile data. One possibility is Content Profiling. Here, content is evaluated according to the characteristics of leads who interact with this content. I. e., which characteristics or motives they have, where in the buying process they are, etc. This can then be compared with the ideal customer profile to assess how relevant these leads are.

3.2 Tactical Actions

Sort Out "Spam Leads"

To achieve a decent lead quality, a very basic, but in reality often not trivial, measure is sorting out "spam leads", i.e., contacts which do not match the defined target group at all. Examples are students, competitors, investors, own employees, job candidates, etc. They might perform the same activities as potential customers but will never turn out to be the same. Therefore, it is important to identify and filter them out. Otherwise, these low-quality leads would spam the sales pipeline.

Typically, leads with certain job titles, company sizes, private email addresses, email addresses with certain domains (of competitors, .edu, etc.), or similar receive negative values. We, however, recommend being careful with resetting scores to zero or decreasing scores based on certain characteristics. Otherwise, chances are high to filter out leads that would actually be of high quality. For example, just because someone does register a private email address does not mean that she is not a potentially interesting lead. In China, for example, it is quite usual to enter private email addresses. Also sorting out leads just because of the job title might not be a good idea. It is not unusual that important decision-makers do not give their real job title at the beginning of their information journey. Therefore, we recommend to better start with an open mesh to tighten it step by step.

Distinguish Between "High-Value" and "Low-Value" Behavior for Behavior Scoring

To improve the quality of the scoring model in place and to, in consequence, improve lead quality, companies are well-advised to distinguish between "high-value" (indicating high interest and purchase intention) and "low-value" (indicating only general interest early in the customer journey) behavior for behavior scoring. Examples of low-value behavior are, e.g., interaction with early-stage content, registration for a low intent webinar (very general webinar focusing on a problem/ need or general information, but no product-focused content), or newsletter registrations. Interaction with mid-/late-stage content, regular visits to pricing or product pages, or attendance of a "high intent" (product-focused and/or highly technical) webinar are typical examples of high-value behavior. While low-value behavior should only receive a low number of points ($<10\%$ of maximum score), high-value behavior should be scored high (20–100% of maximum score) (Robinson, 2021).

Distinguish Between Active and Passive Leads (Recency)

A high-quality lead is a hot lead—someone who is showing a certain, desired behavior at the current time. Therefore, it makes sense to distinguish between active and passive buying behavior. Active buying behavior—an indicator of high interest and, at least to a certain extent, sales-readiness—involves high engagement activity with leads recently performing many high-value actions in a relatively short timeframe. Passive buying behavior, on the other hand, involves lower engagement activity over a longer timeframe. Active leads should receive a higher score than passive leads or be marked as more active. There are various means to achieve this. One possibility would be to divide the score of the last 2 months by the total score. The higher the ratio, the more active the lead (Adobe, 2020a).

Include a "Decay Scoring Model" Instead of a "Reset Scoring Model"

Following the same rationale, companies want to see current, real-time signals to interact with their leads based on these signals. This is why actions taken some months ago are not worth as much as those taken today. Therefore, if leads are inactive for a certain amount of time and, thus their score is not going up, it should be going down. This can be achieved by either resetting their scores to zero or by decreasing their scores step by step. We highly recommend not using a reset but a decay scoring model. Resetting scores to zero after some time of inactivity or after a failed contact approach from sales does not reflect the actual buying behavior of a potential customer. Take this example: A potential customer browses a company's website. After some time, she hits the threshold and is contacted by a salesperson. However, she was not ready to buy, only browsing to gather information. Three weeks later, however, she is again browsing the website, this time, though, not looking at as much content as before, since she already knows a lot. Let's assume she is now ready to buy. In case of a reset after the failed MQL alert, we would not recognize it. We would miss the subtle signals of when it is time to reach out to her

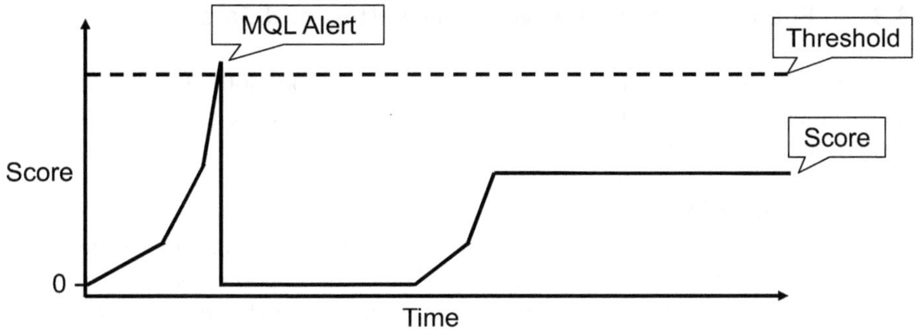

Fig. 4 Reset scoring model (Source: Own representation based on Robinson, 2021)

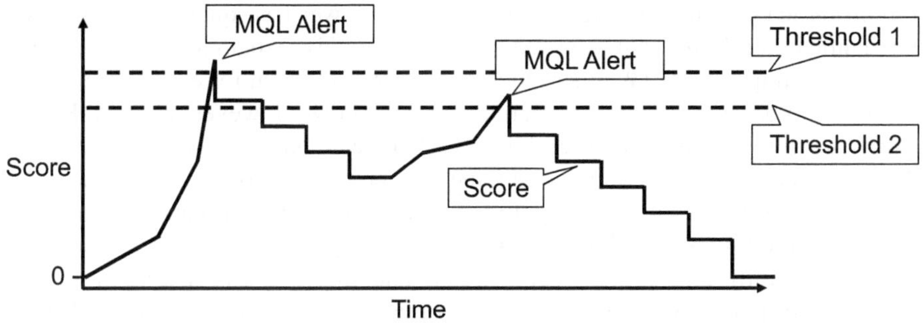

Fig. 5 Decay scoring model (Source: Own representation based on Robinson, 2021)

again (see Fig. 4)—the respective lead would not have a chance to reach the MQL threshold again. This is different in the case of a gradual reduction of the scoring value: Here our lead has a good chance to qualify as MQL again—especially, if we decrease the threshold for leads with a failed MQL alert, as indicated in Fig. 5 (Robinson, 2021).

Define Upper and Lower Limits for Scores

To set up an effective lead scoring, it is important to define upper and lower limits for scores. Otherwise, leads who interact intensively with a company may accumulate an extremely high score from which they will never come down, despite any point deductions for inactivity or the like. The same is true for negative scores: Without a lower limit, leads might end up with very negative scores from which they will never be able to recover. Therefore, limiting total scores to certain top and bottom values is recommended to realize a decent lead quality (Robinson, 2021).

3.3 Feedback Loops Between Marketing and Sales

How does marketing know whether they are doing a good job regarding their lead management activities? They need to implement a systematic process to measure, control, and improve lead quality.

Measurement of Lead Quality

The measurement of lead quality is quite simple, and it is important to not overcomplicate lead management controlling. The most important key performance indicator (KPI) to measure lead quality is the ratio of marketing qualified leads (MQL) to sales accepted leads (SAL)—the "MQL to SAL conversion ratio". The closer to 1 or 100% the ratio, the higher the quality of leads passed on from marketing to sales—or in other words: the better the fit to what sales considers as promising leads. The closer to zero the ratio, the lower lead quality, and the more unqualified, non-fitting, not sales-ready, or—put simply—spam leads are passed on from marketing to sales (Wenger, 2021). Of course, the goal for every organization should be to bring this indicator to a ratio close to 100%. However, as for all KPIs, it is first and foremost not about reaching a certain value but continuously improving. Therefore, consistent, ongoing measurement and review are of great importance. At this point, it becomes obvious why it is of such importance that marketing and sales have a common understanding of what defines a high-quality lead, that they have defined it jointly and continuously discuss and improve this definition and the respective criteria: Sales has the power to reject any lead sent to them. Without mutual trust, feedback loops, and a common goal, this ratio will not be meaningful, and its score will be at a low level without any improvement potential.

To permanently improve its lead management, an organization should, however, go beyond the "MQL to SAL conversion ratio" and analyze further indicators. As ratios tell nothing about the number of leads, also the absolute quantity of leads passed on from marketing to sales should be tracked and continuously increased or at least be kept constant—with the ratio remaining constant or increasing. A declining number of MQL—if not intentionally reduced—is a sign of ineffective lead generation and nurturing activities: e.g., campaigns or content do not reach the envisaged target group, do not fit their needs, are not timed correctly, or are delivered through the wrong channels.

Sales typically tracks the "opportunity win rate"—how many opportunities transform into actual customers. For marketing, it might be interesting to understand how many and which MQLs turn into actual customers ("MQL win rate") to learn from these insights and further refine their lead generation and nurturing activities. In this context, it is also recommended to track lead quality indicators on a campaign-, channel-, and content-level. Such analyses allow identifying, e.g.,

- which campaigns were most successful in generating and developing high-quality leads,
- which channels and which content in which stages have been well received by fast- or well-converting leads (Adobe, 2020a).

Building on this, marketing could allocate more time and budget to developing similar campaigns and improving their channel and content strategy. This, in consequence, will increase the likelihood of a growing number of high-quality MQLs which actually transform into customers.

The Importance of Feedback Loops

Since ultimately only sales can assess the quality of leads and transform leads into actual customers organizations should install feedback loops and monitor how well marketing and sales work together. Because, to ensure that lead management efforts translate into actual revenue and profit, it is important that MQLs are timely qualified, followed up, and served by sales. Moreover, marketing needs timely and high-quality feedback about each MQL accepted and rejected. Only then do they have the necessary data basis to continuously optimize their lead management efforts. It makes sense to distinguish between instant feedback on every single lead passed on from marketing to sales and more strategic feedback rounds.

Instant Feedback

If sales were to decide on which leads they provide feedback to marketing, this would typically result in them only providing feedback on leads they judge to be an excellent fit and—probably in a much larger quantity—on leads they judge to be non-fits. Therefore, to avoid an incomplete picture, organizations must make sure that marketing receives feedback on every single lead being passed on to the sales team. Moreover, they must ensure timely feedback. Only then sales is able to provide high-quality feedback and marketing able to react (Robinson, 2021).

Thus, it is of importance that sales and marketing agree upon a time limit, within which sales must follow up on every MQL and provide feedback to the marketing team. This commitment is often formalized in a service level agreement between the teams involved. The difference between the agreed time limit and the actual time needed to follow up or provide feedback on MQLs might then serve as an indicator of compliance with the agreements. To ensure that this commitment is also practiced in daily operations, it helps to raise the visibility of leads that were not followed up on time or with pending feedback. More importantly, however, organizations should put great effort into making both follow-up and feedback as easy as possible (Adobe, 2020a; Robinson, 2021; Hubspot, 2018).

The first step to making feedback provision as simple as possible is to only ask for the most important information. Indispensable information is whether the transmitted lead was "good" (i.e., accepted and followed up by sales) or "bad." We, however, suggest a more detailed feedback query after sales has followed up upon and qualified the lead, which—if implemented correctly—does not require additional effort from sales, but provides marketing with much more detailed, relevant information (see Fig. 6). Marketing needs to understand (a) whether the lead they forwarded to sales was a fit regarding the profile sales is looking for, and (b) whether the lead was ready to buy. This leads to a 4×4 matrix with the sectors

		Target Group Fit?	
		Yes	No
Sales-Ready?	Yes	Good	Bad Fit
	No	Bad Timing	Junk

Fig. 6 Feedback on MQL quality (Source: Own visualization based on Robinson, 2021; edynamic, 2011)

- good lead: lead matched the target profile and was ready to buy
- bad timing: lead matched the ideal profile, however, was not ready to buy
- bad fit: lead was interested in the company's offering, however, did not match the target profile (e.g., prospect too small to benefit from offered solutions, prospect too big to be served, industry that the company does not serve, . . .)
- junk: lead was far from matching the target profile and did not show interest in the company's offering (e.g., spam, a competitor, a student, a job candidate) (Robinson, 2021).

While marketing should strive for a high share of "good leads" and should carefully assess which characteristics contacts belonging to this group share, analyzing the other three sectors will lead to insights that can no less be used to optimize the lead scoring approach. In case of a high share of "bad fits", marketing should either come up with ideas on how to prevent "bad fits" from being attracted by their offerings and campaigns and make sure that this type of lead is sorted out and not passed on to sales. They, however, could also assess whether it would make sense to extend their offering to a potentially attractive new target group.

Leads reported as "bad timing" should receive special attention. Being a match with the target group, they were passed on to sales even though not ready to buy yet. Such leads should be directly sent back to further nurturing until they are actually ready to buy. Moreover, analyzing leads that fall into this group provides important information about the implicit scoring model: It is likely that the current scoring is based on the wrong criteria or wrong weights are assigned to the right criteria. Also, a high share of leads in the "bad timing" sector might indicate a slightly too aggressive scoring model with the threshold for lead routing being set too low.

In order to make it easy for sales to provide the requested feedback, organizations could set up an automated campaign sending a request for feedback to sales directly with the lead notification, some time after the notification, at the moment when sales has accepted or rejected the lead, or similar. This message should be sent via the channel or system that the sales team uses for their daily work, which could be the CRM system, email, or any chat/messenger service. The request for feedback itself should also be kept as clean as possible. The example in Fig. 7, e.g., only contains

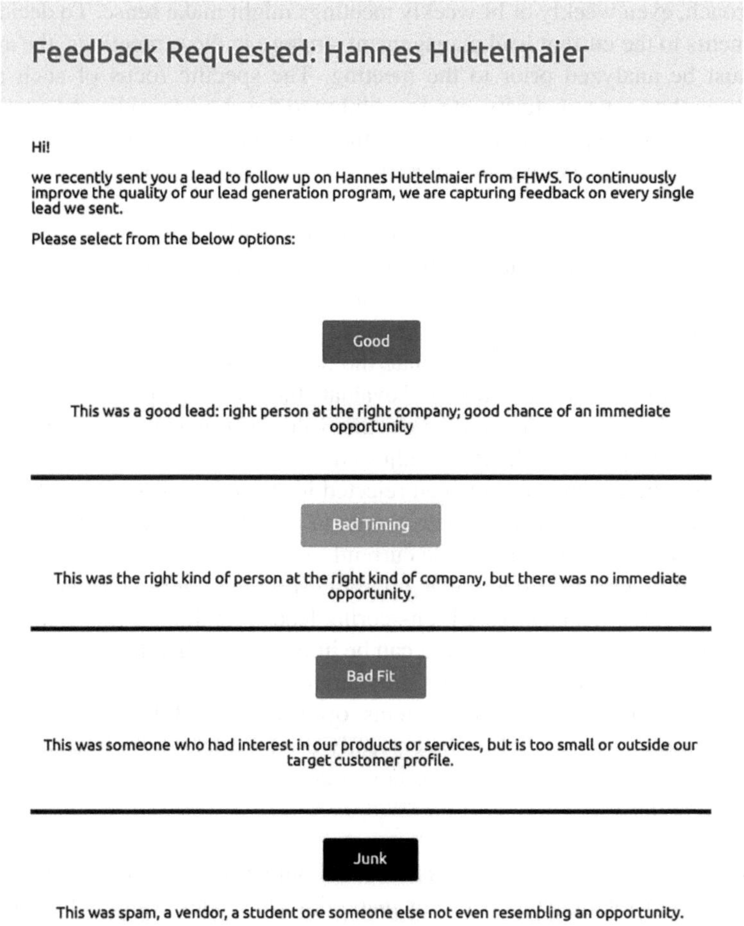

Fig. 7 Example of feedback request (Source: Own representation based on Robinson, 2021)

the name of the lead and four buttons with explanations—allowing the respective salesperson to transmit his feedback with one click directly to the system. We suggest sending requests for feedback to the respective salesperson until feedback has been provided.

Strategic Analysis and Feedback Rounds

Instant, campaign-based feedback allows marketing to react in a timely manner. However, it also provides the necessary data to trigger and support discussions in regular workshops between marketing and sales about lead quality as well as adjustments to the current lead scoring and routing strategy.

Such workshops should be scheduled at least quarterly (Adobe, 2020a). If an organization just recently implemented lead management or fundamentally adjusted its approach, even weekly or bi-weekly meetings might make sense. To decide about adjustments to the current lead management strategy in these meetings, the available data must be analyzed prior to the meeting. The specific focus of such analysis depends on the scope, maturity, etc. In addition to the above-mentioned analysis, the following assessments—among many other possibilities—might create valuable insights (Marketo, 2019; Adobe, 2020a):

- Analyzing the share of leads that fall into a specific scoring segment (e.g., that have scores between 0 and 15, 16 and 30, etc.) to see where the majority of leads fall, and to detect leads with low, negative, or very high scores indicating problems regarding the scoring approach.
- It might also make sense to evaluate the demographic scores of the latest leads that transformed into customers and evaluate their demographic scores against the set threshold to see if they fall below this value. If this is the case, this indicates that the scoring model should be adjusted.
- Assessing the differences between rejected leads and leads that transformed into opportunities might help to detect criteria which are better suited to predict conversion probability than those currently used.
- Comparing scores of lost and won opportunities might help to better predict sales success. Moreover, analyzing high-scoring leads that did not turn into customers could be valuable to see if scoring can be improved so that these leads do not end up appearing as a top priority for sales anymore.
- Many marketing automation systems offer the possibility to run additional scoring models in parallel to the currently used model. Organizations could use them to discover models and criteria that better predict lead conversion than the default model.

Besides these formalized approaches, we should not underestimate the impact of a good, trusted relationship between marketing and sales teams which results in informal conversations about lead quality and valuable ideas on how to improve.

4 Conclusion

In many companies marketing goes to great lengths to generate leads and has even invested in MSA to further develop these generated leads. Still, in many cases, these leads are never followed up by sales, who complain about either receiving too many low-quality or not enough leads. Implementing strategies to improve the quality of leads passed from marketing to sales is key to solving this issue. In this chapter, we therefore outlined some simple but effective ways to systematically increase lead quality with relatively low effort.

We showed that companies can increase lead quality on a strategic level by clearly defining the ideal customer profile and lead stages as well as by setting up a meaningful lead scoring with criteria based on both demographic and behavioral information. As the quality of information gathered with explicit progressive lead profiling is often low, we recommend using more creative alternatives.

On a more tactical level companies can increase their lead quality by systematically sorting out spam leads, by distinguishing between high-value and low-value behavior, as well as by distinguishing between active and passive leads. Also, using a decay scoring model as well as defining upper and lower limits for scores will help to better understand the leads.

In general, we believe that the best results can be achieved with an agile approach: Companies should start with simple models and carefully assess the effect of single strategies to increase lead quality to continuously, step by step, refining their strategies and tactics. For this, feedback loops are crucial. Only by continuously monitoring, analyzing, and discussing lead quality with all relevant parties involved, marketing can systematically and sustainably improve the quality of leads being passed on to sales. This again is one key aspect in improving both marketing's and sales' effectiveness and efficiency.

References

ActiveCampaign. (2022). *7 Steps to creating the optimal lead scoring system*. Accessed May 20, 2022, from https://www.activecampaign.com/learn/guides/7-steps-to-creating-the-optimal-lead-scoring-system

Adobe. (2020a). *The definitive guide to lead scoring*.

Adobe. (2020b). *The definitive guide to lead nurturing*.

Andersen, P., Archacki, R., Bellefonds, N., & Ratajczak, D. (2017). *How digital leaders are transforming B2B marketing*. BCG Insights. Accessed May 20, 2022, from https://www.bcg.com/publications/2017/marketing-sales-how-digital-leaders-transforming-b2b.aspx

bvik. (2022). *Was bedeutet Leadmanagement?* Accessed May 20, 2022, from https://bvik.org/b2b-glossar/lead-management/

Carroll, B. J. (2006). *Lead generation for the complex sale – Boost the quality and quantity of leads to increase your ROI*. McGraw-Hill.

Corsaro, D., Maggioni, I., & Olivieri, M. (2021). Sales and marketing automation in the post-Covid-19 scenario: Value drivers in B2B relationships. *Italian Journal of Marketing, 4*, 371–392. https://doi.org/10.1007/s43039-021-00024-x

edynamic. (2011). *Lead scoring best practices*. Accessed May 20, 2022, from https://www.slideshare.net/edynamic1999/lead-scoring-best-practices-9081991

Gregoriadis. (2021). *The state of B2B lead generation 2021*.

Harrison, L., Plotkin, C. L., Stanley, J., & Reis, S. (2021). *B2B sales: Omnichannel everywhere, every time*. Accessed April 20, 2022, from https://www.mckinsey.com/business-functions/marketing-and-sales/ourinsights/b2b-sales-omnichannel-everywhere-every-time

Hubspot. (2018). *Holding your teams accountable with a service-level agreement*.

Huttelmaier, H., Hesselbach, N., & Heigl, J. (2022). *Stand von Marketing Automation 2022: Einsatz und Nutzung in deutschen Unternehmen*. https://doi.org/10.57714/H41W-2H59

Laserhub. (2022a). https://laserhub.com/plattform/preise/

Laserhub. (2022b). https://laserhub.com/ueber-uns/

Liebherr. (2022). https://www.liebherr.com/en/int/products/mobile-and-crawler-cranes/service/crane-finder.html

Marketing Leadership Council. (2012). *The digital evolution in B2B marketing*. Accessed May 20, 2022, from https://www.thinkwithgoogle.com/_qs/documents/677/the-digital-evolution-in-b2b-marketing_research-studies.pdf

Marketo. (2019). *Lead scoring cheat sheet.*

Ohiomah, A. A., Benyoucef, M., & Andreev, P. (2016). Driving inside sales performance with lead management systems: A conceptual model. *Journal of Information Systems Applied Research, 9*(1), 4.

Ohiomah, A., Andreev, P., Benyoucef, M., & Hood, D. (2019). The role of lead management systems in inside sales performance. *Journal of Business Research, 102*, 163–177. https://doi.org/10.1016/j.jbusres.2019.05.018

Olenski, S. (2012). *When it comes to inbound marketing time is definitely of the essence*. Accessed May 20, 2022, from https://www.forbes.com/sites/marketshare/2012/05/22/when-it-comes-to-inbound-marketing-time-is-definitely-of-the-essence/

Philipp, M. (2021). Vom E-Mail-Marketing zum Lead Management. In U. Hannig (Ed.), *Marketing und Sales Automation*. Springer Gabler. https://doi.org/10.1007/978-3-658-21688-7_14

Robinson, S. (2021). *Lead scoring (points) best practices in Mautic*. Accessed May 20, 2022, from https://www.youtube.com/watch?v=Ze_y8sTc0P0

Sabnis, G., Chatterjee, S. C., Grewal, R., & Lilien, G. L. (2013). The sales lead black hole: On sales reps' follow-up of marketing leads. *Journal of Marketing, 77*(1), 52–67. https://doi.org/10.1509/jm.10.0047

Schuster, N. (2022). *Digitalisierung in Marketing und Vertrieb: Richtige Strategien entwickeln und Potentiale der Digitalisierung für mehr Umsatz nutzen*. Haufe Lexware. https://doi.org/10.34157/9783648158661

Seebacher, U. G. (2021). The B2B marketing ecosystem: Finding your way through the world of colorful B2B terms! In U. G. Seebacher (Ed.), *B2B marketing. Management for professionals*. Springer. https://doi.org/10.1007/978-3-030-54292-4_2

Smith, T. M., Gopalakrishna, S., & Chatterjee, R. (2006). A three-stage model of integrated marketing communications at the marketing-sales interface. *Journal of Marketing Research, 43*(4), 564–579. https://doi.org/10.1509/jmkr.43.4.564

Stevens, R. P. (2011). *Maximizing lead generation: The complete guide for B2B marketers*. Pearson Education.

Wenger, S. (2021). Successful lead management: Nothing's gonna stop us now. In U. G. Seebacher (Ed.), *B2B marketing. Management for professionals*. Springer. https://doi.org/10.1007/978-3-030-54292-4_10

Hannes Huttelmaier is a Professor of Business Administration and Technical Sales at Technical University of Applied Sciences Würzburg-Schweinfurt. His main research interest lies in the field of digital B2B marketing & sales with a focus on aspects at the intersection of humans and machines in B2B markets. Besides his research and teaching activities, he is a co-founder of Aggredi Consulting and a strategic advisor to decision-makers in B2B companies. Before joining academics, he held various positions in industrial companies.

Julia Heigl is a Professor of B2B-Marketing and Intercultural Management at the Eastern Bavarian Technical University Amberg-Weiden. Her professional background includes various positions in industrial and commercial companies in product management, marketing, sales, and corporate development. Besides her research and teaching activities, she is a co-founder of Aggredi Consulting which advises companies on digital business models, product & service management, marketing & sales.

Lead Management Automation Unites Marketing and Sales

Uwe Hannig

1 The Compulsion to Automate Lead Management

Lead management has the task of guiding a prospect through the buying process with the aim of turning him into a customer.

In general, automation is the state achieved by transferring repetitive activities from humans to machines or IT systems. When looking for processes to be automated, one must keep the entire company in mind. Even a process that is triggered only once a year in a subsidiary or is required in a branch office may well lend itself to automation if it is used at hundreds of locations worldwide. The definition of lead management automation is analogous to the definition of marketing automation (Hannig, 2016, p. 27).

Lead Management Automation is the IT-supported execution of recurring activities within the lead management process with the aim of efficiently converting prospects into customers.

Automation always makes sense when repetitive tasks can be performed more cost-effectively by a machine than by the employees, who thereby gain time for more value-adding activities. Since the inclination to work in sales is becoming less and less prevalent in Germany, the workload of the remaining sales staff is increasing in many companies. By relieving them of routine tasks in the context of lead

U. Hannig (✉)
Institute for Sales and Marketing Automation (IFSMA), Viernheim, Germany
e-mail: hannig@ifsma.de

U. Hannig, U. Seebacher (eds.), *Marketing and Sales Automation*, Management for Professionals, https://doi.org/10.1007/978-3-031-20040-3_20

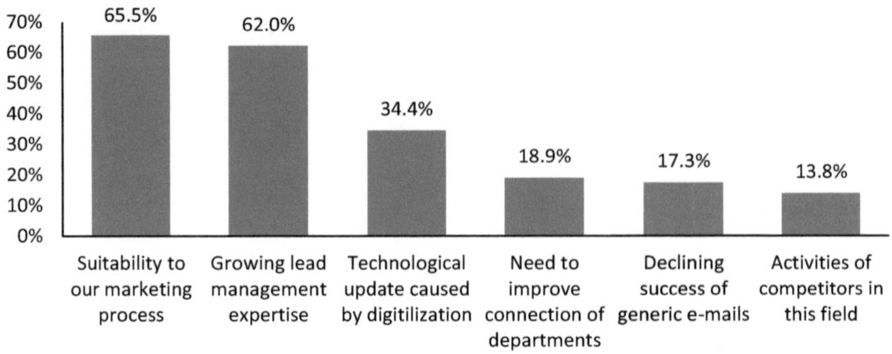

Fig. 1 Reasons for implementing a marketing automation system (Source: Hannig et al., 2021, p. 34)

management automation, they can concentrate on the prospects and customers who are ready to close the deal and thus work much more effectively.

In the USA, marketing automation was initially often equated with lead management (Born, 2013, p. 26). The reason for this was that all conventional marketing automation tools support lead management in its core task of turning potential buyers into customers. Although this understanding of the term is incorrect, the use of the most widely used tools in lead management at the moment is still the most important. Thus, the two most important drivers for the companies surveyed by the Institute for Sales and Marketing Automation 2021 to enter marketing automation are the suitability for the current marketing process and the increasing expertise in the area of lead management (see Fig. 1).

For most companies, automating lead management is therefore a good way to get started with marketing automation in general. It is now high time for this in Europe, and especially in Germany, if companies do not want to fall behind the global competition. According to Gartner's Digital Marketing Hype Cycle, we were already in the mainstream adoption phase in 2015 with regard to the IT-supported implementation of lead management activities (see Fig. 2). In the meantime, the plateau of productivity has been reached for the longest time.

The need to automate lead management arises primarily from the changed search and purchasing behavior of the majority of consumers. It is not only the generation of digital natives born after the year 2000 who mostly gather information about interesting offerings on the web. Google alone processes more than 3.5 billion search queries a day (Live Encounter, 2022). Of course, this also includes a large number of searches from purchasing staff.

And it often does not stop at the information search. As early as 2016, the Corporate Executive Board estimated that 57% of the sales process in the B2B sector is already completed before a sales representative gets involved (Corporate Executive Board, 2016). The success of sales platforms, such as Amazon, proves that more and more buyers are completing a large part of their relationships with suppliers without interpersonal communication or interaction.

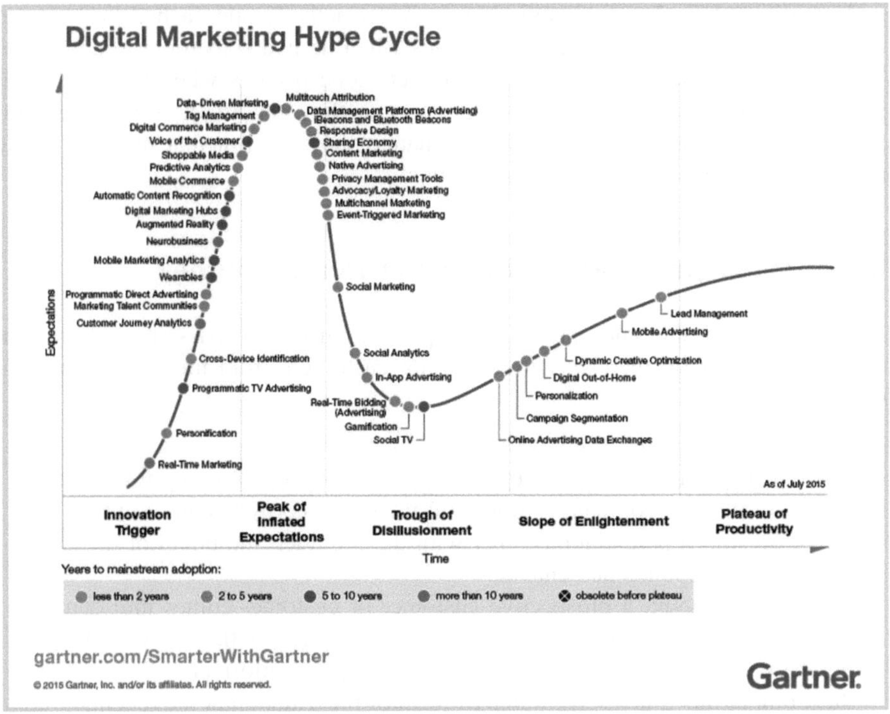

Fig. 2 Lead management automation reached the plateau of productivity (Source: Gartner, 2015)

And they are quite happy to do so. After all, purchasing staff often regard any form of unsolicited contact by suppliers as undesirable disturbances. Contact with supplier employees is avoided as long as possible these days. When a question arises, people prefer to look for an answer in forums rather than contact the sales department directly. In more and more companies, this raises the question of whether a sales force is still needed at all, or what it still has to do. In the past, at least in the B2B sector, this was literally everything related to selling.

The change from push or outbound marketing to pull or inbound marketing, which has been forced by changes in demand behavior, the General Data Protection Regulation in Europe, and the use of spam filters and ad blockers, requires a completely different type of market communication.

Inbound marketing describes strategies and tactics that help prospects find a company that offers a solution to their problem. The goal of inbound marketing is to ensure that the potential customer approaches the company on their own initiative.

In traditional market cultivation, the provider actively approached the selected target groups with his advertising messages when he had something to announce. Today, the customer or prospective customer alone decides when their customer journey or buyer's journey begins. As soon as they set off, it is important for providers to be there and offer the information they want at that moment in the right form via the currently preferred channel.

2 Qualifying Leads Along the Customer Journey

In the course of the sales process, prospective customers pass through several successive stages on their way to becoming customers from the supplier's point of view.

The customer or buyer's journey describes a prospect's journey toward purchase. From the company's point of view, it represents the sum of all interactions of a potential customer with the provider, the brand or the offer across all touchpoints and channels.

At a touchpoint, a prospective customer or customer comes into contact with the company, the brand, or the product or service. On the way to making a purchase, the potential customer expects exactly the information he wants at this point at this time in his preferred form of presentation at the touchpoints.

The sales funnel model is often used to visualize the qualification process of a potential customer along the buyer's journey from contact to buyer because of its clarity. The number of stages differs from author to author. However, the principle is the same everywhere.

The sales funnel, also called sales or revenue funnel, is used to visualize the qualification process of the potential customer from contact to buyer.

According to Leung, 57% of B2B companies see the conversion of qualified leads into customers as the top priority when using the sales funnel concept (Leung, 2014). Figure 3 shows how the prospects with low purchase probability and low sales potential are filtered out step by step. This allows the sales department to concentrate on processing the most attractive leads.

Users on the path to the customer go through several stages that build on each other. If a prospective customer is concerned with a topic for which we have an offer and comes into contact with our website during a Google search, for example, he or she is in the "Engaged" stage. If there is then another indication, e.g., the call-up of a specific page, that it could be worthwhile to specifically process the contact, he becomes a lead. If the contact shows a basic interest in our offer, the lead becomes a prospect, i.e., a potential new customer.

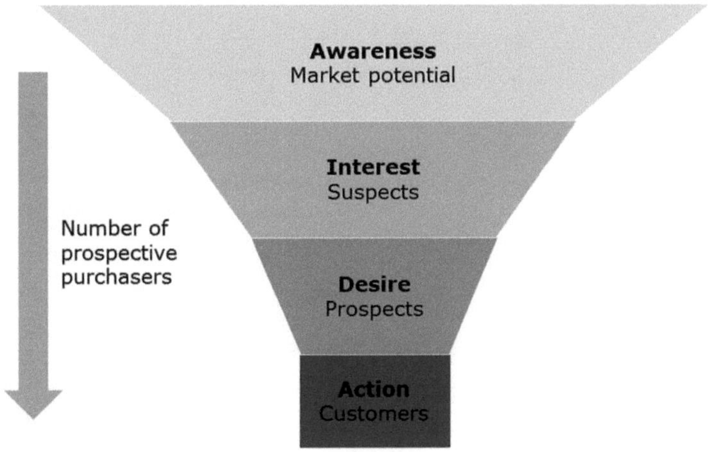

Fig. 3 Sales funnel (Source: onlinemarketing.de, 2022)

The goal is now to develop the prospect into a marketing qualified lead (MQL). This can be achieved, for example, if the prospect discloses his e-mail address and data that indicate an interest in buying in exchange for access to a white paper. Because that is the DEAL with the LEAD: there is a reward for giving up data. During their next online visit, the marketing automation system can then direct them to a landing page with up-to-date content tailored to them on the basis of the information they now know.

The Marketing Qualified Lead is automatically "nurtured" with additional information and offers that are of interest to him.

Lead nurturing is the process of providing potential customers with information that is useful to them in their search or buying phase.

An example from SC-Networks is used below to illustrate what a lead nurturing process looks like in practice with the support of a marketing automation system. The example from the first edition of this book (Philipp, 2017, pp. 232–241) is reproduced below in abbreviated form for reasons of space.

In the first step (Step 1), a white paper is offered for download to interested parties who, for example, have searched for initial information on a topic in a blog and discovered the corresponding link there (see Fig. 4). The link takes the interested party to a landing page (Step 1.0.0) and requests the white paper by filling out the data form (F) and agreeing to the terms of use.

Sending the data triggers a trigger e-mail (Step 1.2.0.0: TM) with the link to the PDF. By clicking on the link, he confirms his e-mail address in the sense of a double opt-in and can download the white paper. If there is no download or no activity, the prospect will receive another trigger e-mail within a period of 90 days. In case of further inactivity, this contact will expire from the data pool.

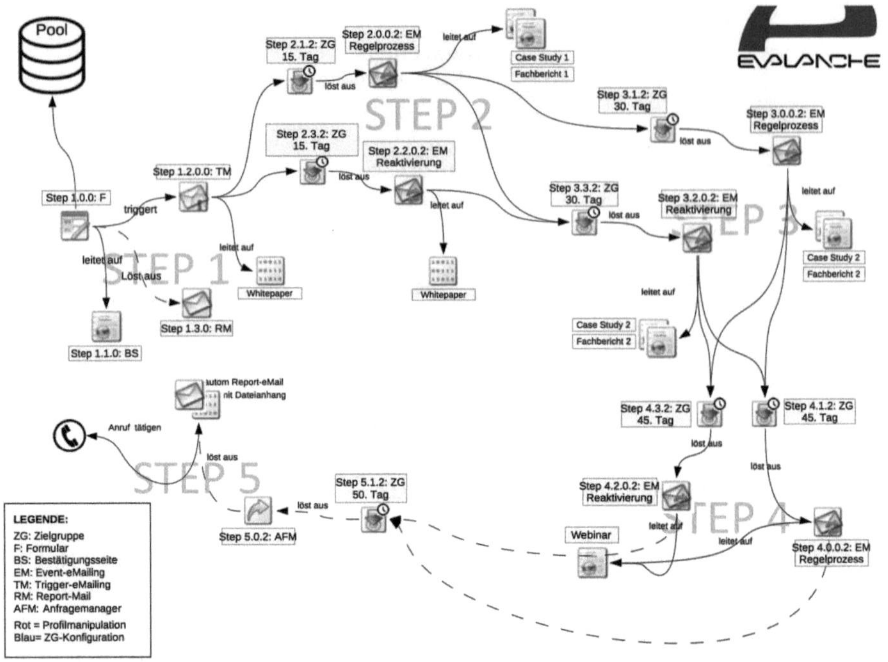

Fig. 4 Plan of procedures of a nurturing campaign (Source: Philipp, 2017, p. 233)

Since the prospect has consented to being contacted for advertising purposes, he can now be sent the monthly newsletter, for example. The case studies contained in the newsletter can be used to provide purchasing arguments (Step 2). An alert is set for the 15th day after the white paper request and the data pool is split into two target groups (ZG) (Step 2.3.2 and Step 2.1.2). The prospects who requested the white paper but did not click the link in the trigger e-mail (TM) receive another e-mail (EM) reminding them once again to download the white paper. This is for reactivation (Step 2.2.0.2). Those who have already downloaded the white paper receive an e-mail (EM) in a regular process (Step 2.0.0.2), which offers them a technical report and a case study as further content.

In the third step (Step 3), further content about the product and its functions is delivered. The downloaded content provides guidance on how to deploy the solution. The leads who have downloaded the white paper, the first technical report and the first case study receive an e-mail (EM) with a link to a second technical report and a second case study on the 30th day after the first white paper request (Step 3.1.2), in the regular process (Step 3.0.0.2). Those leads who either did not download the white paper until the reactivation step (Step 2.2.0.2) or did not download Case Study 1 and Technical Report 1 will instead receive a reactivation e-mail (Step 3.2.0.2: EM) on the 30th day after the first white paper request, but this e-mail will also link to the second technical report and the second Case Study.

In Step 4, a webinar is offered to the potential customer. The link to this is sent on the 45th day after the white paper request (Step 4.1.2) by e-mail (Step 4.0.0.2: EM) to the prospects who have downloaded the second technical report and the second case study. Those leads who downloaded only the white paper or the white paper plus technical report 2 plus case study 2 (Step 4.3.2) will receive a reactivation e-mail (Step 4.2.0.2: EM) referencing the webinar.

On the 50th day after the white paper request, in the fifth step (Step 5), an e-mail is automatically sent to the one sales employee (AFM = request manager) with all relevant information about the previous activities and the data of the lead. How the lead is to be addressed based on its data and activities was determined in advance between Marketing and Sales. Sales also receives information on when the lead should be contacted by phone. Thus prepared, it is now easy for the sales representative to make a concrete offer with good prospects of success.

Three out of four leads prefer different, coordinated content on their customer journey (Leung, 2014). It is therefore essential for success to provide prospects and customers with consistently positive experiences.

The customer experience (abbreviated to CX) encompasses all experiences that a prospective customer or buyer has with a company. This applies to the period before the purchase as well as afterwards.

Managing the customer experience is the task of customer experience management, which can be supported by marketing automation systems.

The goal of customer experience (CX) or customer experience management is to provide current and potential customers with a consistent customer experience at all interfaces or contact points and to create positive experiences with the company and its offerings.

The activities or behavior of leads on their customer journey can be registered and scored by a marketing automation system. The system takes into account the lead's extensional characteristics, such as contact data or role in the purchasing committee, as well as their activities during the customer journey, such as visiting a website or downloading specific content.

The maturity of a lead thus comprises the components of grading and scoring. Grading is the classification of the prospect into a category on the basis of the data available about him, e.g., decision-maker for our product area.

Lead scoring involves scoring or rating the activities of the lead, i.e., their information behavior and responses, during the Buyer's Journey.

Fig. 5 Scoring of activities (Source: Kanpp, 2017)

Activity	Points
Form/Landing Page Submission	+ 5
Submitted "Contact Me" Form	+25
Received an Email	0
Email Open	+1
Email Clickthrough	+3
Registered for Webinar	+3
Attended Webinar	+10
Downloaded a Document	+5
Visited a Landing Page	+2
Unsubscribed from Newsletter	-2
Watched a Demo	+8
Contact is a CXO	+5
Visited Trade Show Booth	+3
Visited Pricing Page	+10

The more the lead engages, e.g., visits the price list or a webinar, and the more data he reveals about himself, the more points he receives (see Fig. 5).

Determining the point values for the individual activities is a process in which the insights gained over time lead to optimization. The determination of the initial values, for example, for the execution of a download, is to be carried out jointly by marketing and sales.

Once the lead has reached the right level of maturity, the Marketing Qualified Lead is forwarded by Marketing to Sales. Sales must first consider it worthwhile for further processing and accept it. Reasons for Sales to reject a lead are in practice (Famico, 2012):

- Unavailability: Despite several attempts, it is not possible to contact the lead personally
- Incorrect data, e.g., incorrect name or telephone number
- No suitable offer: The customer requirements cannot be met

To be classified as a Sales Qualified Lead, the BANT criteria must also be met (Hegewald, 2013):

- Budget: The funds for the purchase of our offer must be available.
- Authority: The lead must have decision-making authority.
- Need: There is a need or a concrete intention to purchase.

- Time: There is no intention to buy in the foreseeable future. The lead will be involved in a nurturing program until then.

Sales now has the task of persuading the Sales Qualified Lead or Opportunity to close the sale.

3 Cooperation Through Automation

Successful lead management requires close and trusting cooperation between marketing and sales. But in German companies in particular, the relationship between the two departments is anything but harmonious. Marketing is often certain that the campaigns it has developed cannot develop their potential because Sales is not properly involved. And sales has the feeling that the marketeers are only keeping them from their core task of closing deals.

Instead of working closely together, they compartmentalize and create data silos that are not made accessible to the respective other department. For around half of all companies that took part in a study by the Institute for Sales and Marketing Automation, improving collaboration between marketing and sales was an important goal with regard to the introduction of a marketing automation system (Hannig et al., 2021, p. 39). Around 90% of the companies with above-average success recorded more effective collaboration between the two departments after the MAS introduction.

Although it is the sales force that benefits from the use of MAS, the implementation of a marketing automation system by the marketing department without the involvement of the sales force does not improve the situation. The pioneers of marketing automation had to learn painfully that the early integration of the sales force is critical for the success of the implementation of a marketing automation system.

Marketing automation projects require joint efforts and a lot of communication across departmental boundaries. In the process, one often finds that people live in different conceptual worlds. Another complicating factor is that there is no clear definition of the term "lead" and its characteristics in the literature, which is why it is first necessary to define common meanings of terms at the company level (Brüggen, 2013). Here, one must not shy away from time-consuming discussions. One point here will usually be that the quality of the leads generated by marketing often did not meet the expectations of sales in the past. The reason for this often turns out to be that leads were passed on to Sales regardless of their quality, because the number of leads generated was used as an indicator of marketing's performance. Accordingly, the incentive system must also be critically examined and revised if necessary as part of the implementation process. Against this backdrop, too, it is worth the effort to exchange views intensively and to review the past in order to work together with realistic expectations in the future.

In addition to a shared understanding of the lead, there must be agreement on the target customers to be acquired. Marketing and sales must consider together which demanders they would prefer to come into contact with and with what content.

Content marketing has the task of providing content that is of interest to a current or potential customer in an entertaining and benefit-oriented manner at the right time via the right channel.

In order to develop the content to attract the searching ideal customers in an entertaining way, it is necessary to have as concrete an idea as possible of the target customers. After all, prospective customers will only respond if the content provided precisely satisfies their needs. The buyer persona concept (Burkholz, 2017; Kusinitz, 2014; Revella, 2015; Köhler, 2016) virtually brings the ideal or target customers to life.

Buyer personas are fictitious representatives of real buyer types, so-called archetypes. They go far beyond classic customer profiles in that they contain typical expectations, wishes, and characteristics of real target customers. The number of buyer personas depends on several factors, such as the industry or the product or service.

With the image of a buyer persona in mind, it is easier to imagine what a desired customer will do at which fork in his customer journey and with which content he can best be reached at which touchpoint (Köhler, 2016). In order to compile an information offer that activates a buyer persona, it is necessary to know their sociodemographic characteristics, their interests and preferences, their information and media usage behavior, as well as the course of their search and purchase decision process.

In contrast to the approach often found in companies for determining target groups, which is to have sales describe the most attractive customer types, buyer personas should be determined systematically. Exploratory interviews are a good way to do this, focusing on obtaining information relevant to purchasing decisions. Current and potential customers who were involved in the decision-making process not long ago, e.g., as members of a buying center, are interviewed.

With the opening question, respondents are asked to mentally move back to the starting point of the decision-making journey. Move back to the beginning of the decision-making journey. At this point, it is important to find out what initiated the search for a problem solution.

The follow-up questions result from the answers received. The respondents are asked to go through the decision-making process again and describe it in detail. Of course, it is interesting to find out at which touchpoint they would have liked to receive what information or support and where their expectations were met and how. Revella recommends collecting the following five buying insights (Revella, 2015):

- The investment trigger, i.e., the trigger responsible for starting the Buyer Journey
- The success factors in the form of the most important results hoped for from the purchase
- The obstacles, i.e., the aspects that spoke against a purchase
- The influencers and the influences on decision-making during the buyer journey
- The decision criteria, i.e., the offer features that are decisive for the buyer's purchase

The interviews are recorded. During the evaluation, a search is made for overlaps and patterns, e.g., unfulfilled expectations that led to annoyance (Burkholz, 2017, p. 55). The individual buyer personas are created over time from the commonalities found.

In this process, dealing with the hypotheses of the other parties involved from marketing and sales about why a buyer persona acts or reacts to an input in the way it does leads to a deeper understanding of the search and decision-making process of the target customers on both sides as part of the discussions to be held, but also for the way of thinking and work of the colleagues from the respective other department. However, despite the advantages of the buyer persona concept, not all companies are currently using it. In the study by the Institute for Sales and Marketing Automation, only around one in two companies dealt with the topic (Hannig et al., 2021, p. 29).

Furthermore, the success metrics and key performance indicators as well as the point values for scoring the individual activities on the customer journey must be defined in the interaction between marketing and sales. A particularly hotly debated issue in this context will be when a lead is passed on from marketing to sales with which accompanying data. As with setting point values for individual activities, this is a process in which insights gained over time lead to optimization. Here, too, the initial value must be determined jointly by marketing and sales experts.

Lead routing is the transfer of a Marketing Qualified Lead to Sales.

Once the formal prerequisites for the marketing automation project have been created, it proves advantageous to start with a manageable pilot project in an area in which both departments have a strong interest and any systematic approach to the processes will lead to an improvement over the previous, conventional approach. In the case of B2B companies, for example, lead management in the context of trade show participation is a good example of this, since the probability of achieving quick wins, at least in the form of efficiency improvements, is high here.

The introduction and operation of a MAS and thus the automation of processes in marketing and sales is a process that itself must be constantly optimized. Accordingly, the costs for the marketing automation tool make up only a fraction of the total costs of automation. Within the framework of an elaborate change management, the fears of a change in the daily work routine or even the loss of the job must be dealt with intensively. Thus, shying away from the adaptation of processes in marketing and sales are two of the four biggest obstacles to the implementation of a marketing

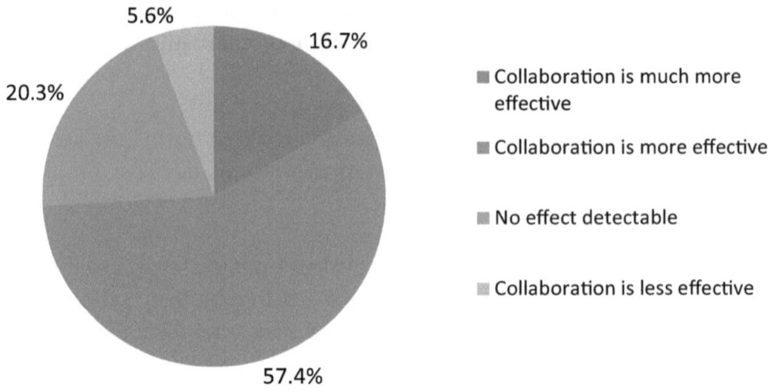

Fig. 6 Change in the collaboration of marketing and sales department (Source: Hannig et al., 2021, p. 39)

automation system. Once these are overcome, the use of MAS leads to more effective collaboration between marketing and sales in almost three quarters of companies (see Fig. 6).

In this respect, the outperformers benefit most from the introduction of marketing automation. Around 90% of the outperformers note that sales and marketing work together more effectively after MAS implementation.

References

Born, A. (2013). Marketing automation – applications with aha experience. *absatzwirtschaft, 3*(2003), 24–29.

Brüggen, P. v. d. (2013, September 13). *Always the same song with the leads!* http://philippsmarketing.com/2013/09/immer-das-gleiche-lied-mit-den-leads/

Burkholz, R. (2017). Development of a buyer persona. In U. Hannig (Ed.), *Marketing and sales automation – Fundamentals, tools, implementation* (pp. 49–58). Springer Gabler.

Corporate Executive Board. (2016, November 21). *Leading B2B sales organizations challenge, align & prescribe to get deals done.* http://www.multivu.com/players/English/7427254-ceb-challenge-align-prescribe-b2b-sales-strategy/

Famico, J. (2012, December 17). *Sales accepted leads – Disqualification reasons.* https://www.siriusdecisions.com/Blog/2012/Dec/Sales-Accepted-Leads-Disqualification-Reasons

Gartner. (2015, October 14). *Five key trends in Gartner's 2015 digital marketing hype cycle.* http://www.gartner.com/smarterwithgartner/five-key-trends-in-gartners-2015-digital-marketing-hype-cycle/

Hannig, U. (2016). More than basic mental attitude. *acquisa, 11–12*(2016), 26–27.

Hannig, U., Heinzelbecker, K., & Foell, T. (2021). *Mission digital transformation. Automation in Marketing and Sales 2021.* White Paper, Institute for Sales and Marketing Automation, Viernheim.

Hegewald, T. (2013, September 8). *BANT – Qualifying B2B leads professionally.* http://www.callcenter-wissen.de/2013/09/bant-b2b-leads-professionell-qualifizieren/

Knapp, S. (2017, April 19). *How to use lead scoring to ensure success from your content efforts.* Accessed March 03, 2020, from https://marketing.sfgate.com/blog/how-to-use-lead-scoring-to-ensure-success-from-your-content-efforts

Köhler, K. (2016, November 4). *What is the difference between target groups and buyer personas.* http://blog.hubspot.de/marketing/was-ist-der-unterschied-zwischen-zielgruppen-und-buyer-personas

Kusinitz, S. (2014, March 8). *The definition of a buyer persona [in under 100 words].* https://blog.hubspot.com/marketing/buyer-persona-definition-under-100-sr#sm.0001mzpxiw3ppe1qyj721b52tdl8p

Leung, S. (2014, May 20). *Sales funnel management – Simplify by cutting steps, not corners.* https://www.salesforce.com/blog/2014/05/sales-funnel-management.html

Live Counter. (2022). *Google search queries.* http://www.internetlivestats.com/google-search-statistics/

Onlinemarketing.de. (2022). *Encyclopedia.* Funnel. https://onlinemarketing.de/lexikon/definition-funnel

Philipp, M. (2017). Marketing automation ensures efficient lead nurturing. In U. Hannig (Ed.), *Marketing and sales automation – Fundamentals, tools, implementation* (pp. 223–243). Springer Gabler.

Revella, A. (2015). *Buyer personas – How to gain insight into your customer's expectations, align your marketing strategies, and win more business.* Wiley.

Uwe Hannig is scientific director of the Institute for Sales and Marketing Automation (IFSMA) in Ludwigshafen. The professor for Information and Performance Management has many years of experience in marketing and sales in theory and practice.

The Institute for Marketing and Sales Automation has set itself the goal of paving the way for sales and marketing automation in the DACH region. It monitors the market, promotes the exchange of experience and knowledge transfer at specialist events, and takes care of the training of urgently needed specialists. The common focus of the institute's activities is to improve efficiency and effectiveness in marketing and sales with the help of scientific and practice-relevant methods, instruments, and systems.

Integration of Sales Partners into Lead Management

Philipp Baron von der Brüggen

"Marketing is the New Sales" was the title of an article in Forbes. More than ever, people expect marketing to make a clearly measurable contribution to the company's success. However, when companies market their products indirectly, i.e., through sales partners, the manufacturer's marketing campaigns repeatedly come to nothing. The transfer of inquiries to the partner's sales department rarely works smoothly and the data feedback to the manufacturer almost never!

The manufacturer usually suffers the damage to its image if, for example, a test drive is requested on the website of the car manufacturer but no dealer contacts the interested party. Or the dealer who does get in touch cannot even offer the car for a test drive. So how does the manufacturer best respond when it receives no information from the customer service department? There is no alternative: the distibution partner must be integrated into the lead management process in the best possible way (see Fig. 1).

If a lead has been developed by marketing into a real prospective buyer, an opportunity, according to criteria to be defined in advance, this is often referred to as a Marketing Qualified Lead (MQL). This is usually passed on to sales immediately. When Sales accepts the lead and begins to process it, it becomes a Sales Accepted Lead (SAL).

1 Opportunity Management in the Channel

The lead management process is simpler in most companies with direct sales, as marketing and sales often work together on a technical platform, the customer relationship management system (CRM system). The processing of leads is

P. B. von der Brüggen (✉)
Nurture Flow, Weyarn, Germany
e-mail: brueggen@nurture-flow.com

U. Hannig, U. Seebacher (eds.), *Marketing and Sales Automation*, Management for Professionals, https://doi.org/10.1007/978-3-031-20040-3_21

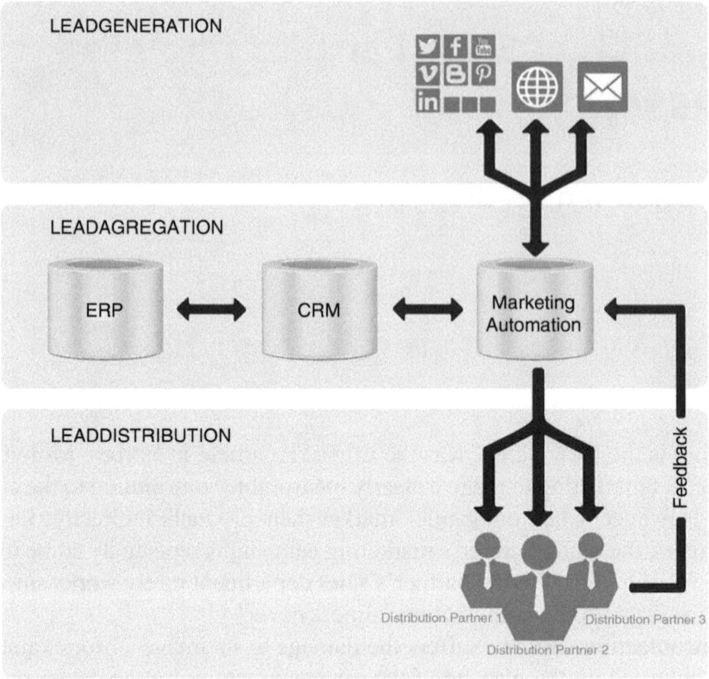

Fig. 1 From lead generation to lead distribution (Source: leadtributor)

considerably more complicated in the case of indirect sales via partners. They are not part of the company's own organization. And manufacturers and sales partners hardly ever work on a common database. This is the reason why there are rarely well thought-out, coherent, and efficient processes for customer care between manufacturers and sales partners. But these are precisely the processes that are eminently important for shaping the customer journey in a positive way.

In this context, lead management is understood as a holistic process. In this context, many experts speak of a 360-degree view of the customer. The customer's behavior is recorded, collected, and evaluated in order to optimize communication on this basis. Algorithms analyze where the customer is in the buying process and what next steps need to be taken. The central challenge here is to provide the prospect or customer with the right information at the right time via the right channel.

Signals that indicate that the customer should be processed by sales lead to a transfer to the sales department. If the inquiry is passed on to a sales partner, the transparency gained up to that point usually comes to an end. This would be extremely important at this point in time. Because only if the provider knows what the negotiations with the partner have produced can he react, for example, in the form of follow-up programs, so-called Nurture Flows.

Many products, such as mobile communications contracts or security software, are sold by subscription. The services are made available to customers over a fixed contract term. This applies to software just as it does to the leasing of cars or machines. If, in these cases, marketing receives information from the sales partner that the customer has unfortunately bought from a competitor, this is certainly annoying, but it also offers another opportunity. Because all the work was not in vain. We know the buying center, we know when we have to approach the customer again (contract term), and we also know how to crack it (competitive information).

The marketing department then has the opportunity to develop follow-up programs with the aim of turning the lost prospect back into a customer at the latest when the contract with the competitor ends. Of course, this is much easier if all the information from the previous sales process is available. All the information from the channel is also needed to build up and expand any newly acquired customers.

2 Challenges in Lead Management with Sales Partners

Experts know that lead management often works bumpily in interaction with the company's own sales department. A recent study by the software provider Lean Data, for example, shows a bleak description of the state of customer development (LeanData, 2017). 500 B2B sales and marketing experts gave a status report on the lead processes in their companies. In the process, more than 57% of respondents were convinced that their processes cannot generate good customer experiences. In addition, one in four customer inquiries make extra rounds because they end up in the wrong department or with the wrong sales person. 66% of respondents said that sales does not follow up at all on prospects generated at great expense by marketing. 38% currently have no way of distributing IT-supported inquiries to suitable sales staff.

These are figures that essentially result from working with in-house sales. How much more difficult is lead management with sales employees who are not part of your own organization? The challenges here are quite mundane. Most discussions with sales partners already arise when defining the term lead, as there is no industry standard.

In practice, the word leads are used very differently. From an address without information to a serious prospect with a budget and a short-term purchase intention, everything is included. In this context, one also likes to speak of contacts, prospects, customer inquiries, suspects, or opportunities.

The list of descriptions could be extended at will. If you do not ask very precise questions here, you produce misunderstandings. And not only in the cooperation between sales and marketing. Especially between manufacturer and sales partner, these inaccuracies are the cause of false expectations and disappointments.

The solution to the dilemma is a clear definition of terms. Ultimately, it does not matter what the address data to be developed is called. The main thing is to ensure that everyone involved means the same thing.

► In the Anglo-Saxon world, the following terms have become established, which make a somewhat clearer and finer distinction:

- *Suspect*
  The literal translation of suspect is "suspected offender" or "suspicious person." However, what is actually meant by this is the relevant target group. Target persons whom we "suspect" to be interesting for us. These are neither customers nor have they had any contact with us so far. But our product "should" be interesting for these people according to the target group definition.
- *Lead*
  The word lead is generally translated as "tip," "lead," or "clue." In marketing, a lead is a person where there are indications that the contact is worth following up. This could be a click on a website or a download of a white paper.
- *Prospect*
  Translated, prospect means "expectation," "perspective," or "possible candidate." In lead management, one speaks of a prospect when an interest in the product or service has been expressed. This includes, for example, the retrieval of product documentation, a trade fair contact or participation in a product demo. The prospect has a basic interest in the product. However, information is missing as to whether the person has decision-making authority, whether there is a budget, and whether a purchase is being considered.
- *Opportunity*
  If you consult the dictionary, you will see that opportunity is translated as "chance" or "opportunity." A prospect becomes an opportunity when the prospect has expressed a need, a project is imminent, and budget has been allocated.

Ultimately, it does not matter how you name the statuses, as long as you make it very clear what who can or must expect. It is therefore important to define each level precisely and to enforce it within the company.

In terms of an optimal customer journey, it is crucial that the partner deals with the request promptly and competently. If this does not happen, escalations and processes must ensure that the end customer nevertheless receives perfect support almost imperceptibly. Sales partners who have no desire, time, e.g., due to vacation, or the necessary know-how must not receive any leads. Last but not least, it must be ensured that the information obtained during the external process steps flows back into the company's own systems in such a way that it can be used for the next steps.

3 Motivation of the Distributors to Participate in the Lead Management of the Manufacturer

The distributor is happy about every lead that comes from the manufacturer, you would think. And that is generally the case. But only as long as there are no conditions attached to the handover of the prospects. After all, sales partners are fundamentally skeptical of their manufacturers. After all, they are interesting to the manufacturer primarily because they have access to the customers.

The value of the partner increases for the manufacturer the more contacts and access the partner has to the market. Any form of transparency in this partner/customer relationship could possibly make a partner superfluous. This is especially true where manufacturers operate the indirect and direct sales channels side by side. There is a latent fear that a customer contact that has been painstakingly built up will be lost to the manufacturer's direct sales force if customer information is disclosed.

But it is not only competition from possible direct sales that is feared. Technical developments can also be natural enemies of distributors. Adobe used to distribute its products via partners, but now it does so via the cloud (Creative Cloud). The same is true for Microsoft's Office 365.

Customers have always had to register with Adobe. Customer data was collected and maintained through the Adobe registration process. In the age of the cloud, it was only a comparatively small step to bypass the sales partners. The complete sales channel for some products was replaced by web-based services and a strengthening of the company's own marketing. Today, Adobe is "almost" a direct sales company.

Such examples make it difficult for distributors to build trust with manufacturers and to disclose their customer contacts to them to a large extent. If they give up contact with the customer, the partners fear, they will be easier to replace. As long as the manufacturer does not know who is working on which cases, the sales partner believes he is safe.

Especially in large, complex systems, partner leads often disappear into anonymity. This is especially true for sales partners who also sell the manufacturers' competitor products. It is not uncommon for leads from one manufacturer to be sold products from another. An opportunity management system makes it much easier to monitor partner activities more closely during lead processing.

Every manufacturer uses partner portals in which tools are offered for a wide variety of applications: From "event out of the box" to "marketing material generator" to lead management. The variety of tools makes it difficult for partners to keep track of everything. In addition, partners often have their own systems, e.g., CRM systems, which also need to be maintained.

Distributors' reservations about using manufacturers' tools are only set aside by them if the benefits for the distributor are so great that they are happy to be part of the manufacturer's lead process. First and foremost, this is the prospect of more business. For this to happen, the manufacturer must produce leads of high quality. The better the leads are, the more likely the channel partners are to follow through with motivation.

The prospect of getting leads according to objectively suitable criteria, such as regional proximity or project size, is also tempting. For this, it must be ensured that only the right partner receives the inquiry tailored to him.

There are requests for complex or simple projects for small or large companies. If you give the wrong projects to the wrong partners, the sales success is low. Small projects, for example, are treated stepmotherly by large partners, while large projects overtax small partners. The key to success therefore lies to a not inconsiderable extent in the perfect matching of inquiries.

Above all, successful opportunity management in the channel must be child's play. Partners only use the manufacturer's tools and portals if it is really simple, fast and, at best, fun. The distribution partners find it particularly interesting when the manufacturers channel the respective prospects according to rules, i.e., offer lead routing. If a partner is already in initial talks with a company, he can be informed in the future about all activities, inquiries, and opportunities regarding this customer.

Powerful opportunity management systems remember which partner is already working on which company and route all information, such as downloads, website visits, participation in events, and inquiries, about that lead through to the processing partner. It is this capability that convinces many partners to work with a vendor's opportunity management tool.

Lead routing protects partners' negotiations with end customers because the manufacturer can better channel all inquiries and information gained. This creates less competition among a manufacturer's sales partners and more trust.

With the transparency gained from an opportunity management system, manufacturers have the opportunity to reward partners who work actively and successfully. These can be incentives, advertising cost subsidies or more or better leads.

The more information (e.g., industry, number of employees, sales development, extract from the commercial register, names of the members of the buying center, the last press mentions, etc.) the data set contains, the more valuable it appears to the partner sales department. If, on the other hand, data is only sparsely available, the data set appears less interesting. This picture emerges quite independently of the actual value of the opportunity. For this reason, it makes sense to provide the lead with all the information that could be relevant for the partner. Technically, this is easy to solve today. There are service providers who enrich leads with information such as turnover, number of employees and industry via completely automatic processes.

Sales partners use manufacturer tools when they can provide concrete support in initiating or closing business. But this is precisely where sales partners are often made far too difficult.

As a rule, argumentation aids, studies, competitive comparisons or objection treatments are available to sales partners in the partner portals. There, they can find everything they need to sell the respective products: from video training and marketing brochures to technical specifications. Here, too, the pull method applies according to the motto: "Come and find what you need yourself."

But the vast majority of partner portals are confusing or overloaded. Partners often spend hours searching for relevant information. To solve this problem, an entire industry for sales enablement tools has already emerged. Although it is easier and faster for the sales partner to find what he is looking for after entering various parameters, the partner is again the one who has to become active.

The solution to the dilemma is to link opportunity management and sales enablement. If the manufacturer uses a solution to provide the leads, then he naturally knows the industry, company size, etc., of the lead. Based on this information, offers have to be made to the sales partner.

If manufacturers take the trouble to define profiles that show which content supports the partner in which phase of the sales process, the process can be changed from pull to push. Partners do not have to spend a lot of time and effort researching what information they can use for their initial meetings or appointments. Instead, they actively receive offers based on the lead profile. The sales partner is accompanied and supported by the opportunity system in the sales process.

4 Control of the Processing of Leads from the Sales Partners

The first step in the targeted control of the processing of the acquired leads provides for the setting of the distribution of the leads. Partners do not receive opportunities, but have to pick them up on a web platform or on their Android or IOS client in a push/pull process. Reversing the usual process ensures that only the partner who has the time and inclination to handle inquiries takes the lead.

If you simply distribute the opportunities by e-mail, you run the risk that the leads will not be noticed or will be processed too late. If, on the other hand, you use the picklisting process, you can build in escalations for leads that have not been picked up. Only when leads are picked up is it ensured that the partner actively wants to work on the lead. To do this, they must be able to see in the web portal what kind of lead it is in detail.

Good opportunity management requires timely feedback on the status of lead processing. This can easily be enforced by the system stopping the retrieval of new leads if predefined work steps have not been carried out or feedback has not been given. The platform thus exchanges feedback for leads and rewards partners who handle opportunities responsibly.

On the other hand, the manufacturer can do everything possible to ensure that the partner can work on his lead in peace. Further inquiries or interactions from this lead can be routed directly to the partner. Partner sales successes can be rewarded via motivation systems. Close-meshed reporting ensures that nothing is left undone and that difficulties or bottlenecks are identified and eliminated as quickly as possible.

Servicing customers under maintenance or leasing contracts also yield opportunities for successful lead management with sales partners. If a manufacturer receives a notice of termination or a renewal of the contracts is pending, it can make these requirements available as quickly as possible to the partner who concluded the deal. The partner can then try to dissuade the customer from terminating the contract or sell him a successor product.

But this only works if there are processes and escalations and both parties work on the same database. The system must know which customer is served by which partner and which deal must be concluded with which partner. Also, all escalations in terms of deadlines, e.g., contract renewal, must be controlled centrally. The advantage for the partner is that he can concentrate on sales and implementation.

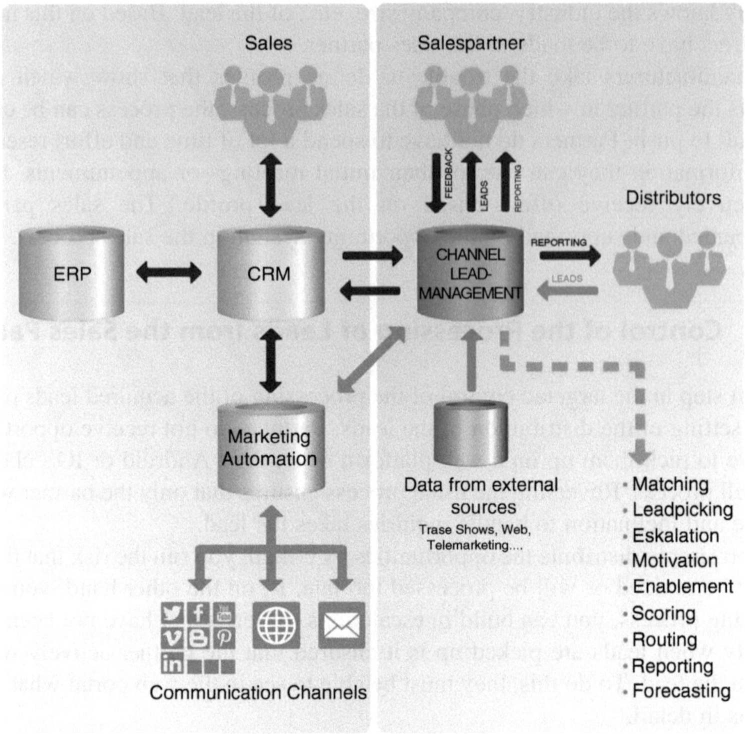

Fig. 2 Channel lead management (Source: leadtributor)

Set-up and expansion are driven by automated processes that the manufacturer maintains and operates (Fig. 2).

Often you can find initiatives in affiliate programs, such as deal registration programs. This is the possibility to register an opportunity with the manufacturer. The manufacturer does not provide address information to the partner, but the process is the other way around.

The partner can reserve the target company for itself through the deal registration program. In this case, the manufacturer ensures that no competitor pressures the prices at the end customer. As a rule, partners are motivated to deal registration by additional margin points. The manufacturer thus collects valuable data and, above all, can continuously analyze and evaluate its current pipeline in the sales partner channel.

The partner not only has the advantage of lead protection, but all information on past and current interactions, downloads, inquiries, event participations, etc., of the target customer can be forwarded to the partner in charge. This actively supports the partner in the sales process and makes all activities between the end customer, the manufacturer and the sales organizations transparent for everyone. In this way, the sales partner is constantly aware of all the reactions of the customer he is looking after. For this purpose, it is necessary to provide a technical platform that makes it

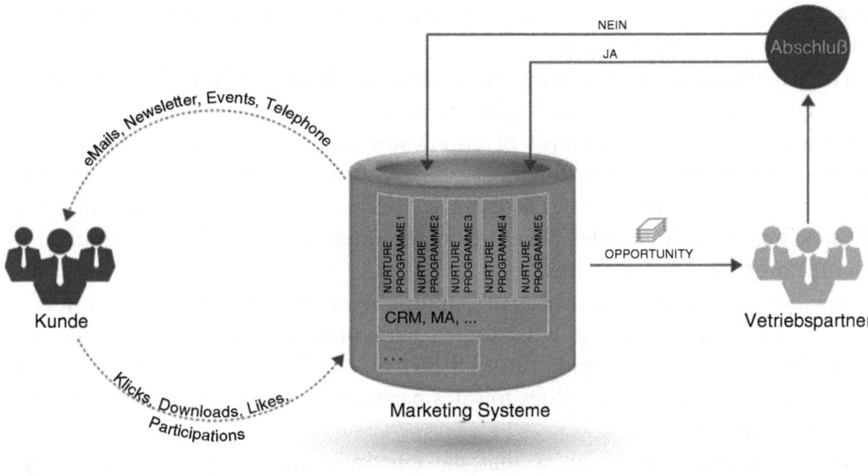

Fig. 3 Informing channel partners about their opportunities (Source: leadtributor)

possible to provide a partner with all the information from the marketing automation. In principle, sales partners and manufacturers trade lead protection for transparency to create forecasts and pipelines.

Here, too, there are a number of legal obstacles to be considered. The end customer must know transparently where his data is located and who does what with it. In addition, they must also agree to this procedure.

Sales partners often do not have a large organization. They rarely have significant marketing budgets. Accordingly, it makes sense to use the manufacturer's processes, methods, and tools for your own lead generation. If sales representatives are used or if there are clearly definable sales territories, there are many opportunities to support the partner in his territory. Customer development via marketing automation in conjunction with a channel lead management tool creates an environment in which the manufacturer can systematically generate leads for the partner.

Especially in such a structure, it is imperative that the sales partner provides quick and easy feedback on the outcome of his efforts with the opportunity. Depending on their feedback, opportunities run into various follow-up programs or nurture flows. Such programs enable manufacturers to systematically produce leads for their channel partners. The advantages for the partner are that he receives high-quality leads and does not have to build a large technical infrastructure for lead management (Fig. 3).

When using such support programs for sales partners, it is conceivable that the partner hands over his data to the manufacturer, who then develops the partner's customers in a structured lead process. However, this usually only works in sales representative structures.

Again, there are some legal pitfalls to consider. For example, the end customer must not only be informed about the management of data by the manufacturer, he must even explicitly agree to it. The clear and unambiguous separation of data must also be technically guaranteed.

The sales partner then benefits from the manufacturer's know-how, the elaborately developed communication processes and receives MQLs. In return, the manufacturer remains in control of end-customer communications. This is very attractive for many manufacturers, especially from the point of view of brand communication and messaging, as the sales partners very rarely adhere to CI and CD specifications. Both sides benefit from the integration of sales partners into the manufacturer's lead management.

Another very important aspect of opportunity management is data protection. Information collected about a customer may only be passed on to specialist distributors under certain conditions; whether by telephone, fax, or e-mail. In order to be able to pass on opportunities to sales partners, a number of prerequisites must therefore be met.

The most important thing is that the customer knows that his data will be forwarded before it is passed on. The customer must expressly agree to this forwarding. It is not enough to write in the data protection provisions: "We will pass on your data to our sales partners." The partners in question must be named. Including long lists of partners in the data privacy policy is not a solution. This has already been prohibited by the courts in individual cases. Experts assume that 3–5 explicitly named partners would be reasonable. This means that the lead management process must include a step in which the customer expressly approves the transfer of his data to the partners in question (see Fig. 4).

The legislator sets clear limits for the disclosure of data to third parties (in our case sales partners). Two extremely important things are required for the forwarding of inquiries to sales partners:

1. The leads come from the distributing manufacturer
   Note: When purchasing leads from third-party sources that the manufacturer distributes to resellers, different rules apply.
2. The lead has given consent to receive advertising by e-mail or telephone.
   This is a mandatory prerequisite, since contact, at least by e-mail (and also by telephone to end consumers), is generally only permissible if there is a declaration of consent. It must be clear to whom "exactly" consent is given and, above all, for what. The legislator does not provide for unspecific "free rides." Accordingly, permission to make promotional contact always relates to a company and to one or more specific products/services/topics. In most cases, it will therefore only be possible to contact the interested party if such consent has been given.

If these basic conditions are met, the following options can be considered for passing on the leads to sales partners with legal protection.

- Leads may only be contacted by e-mail or phone for the purpose of closing their own business.

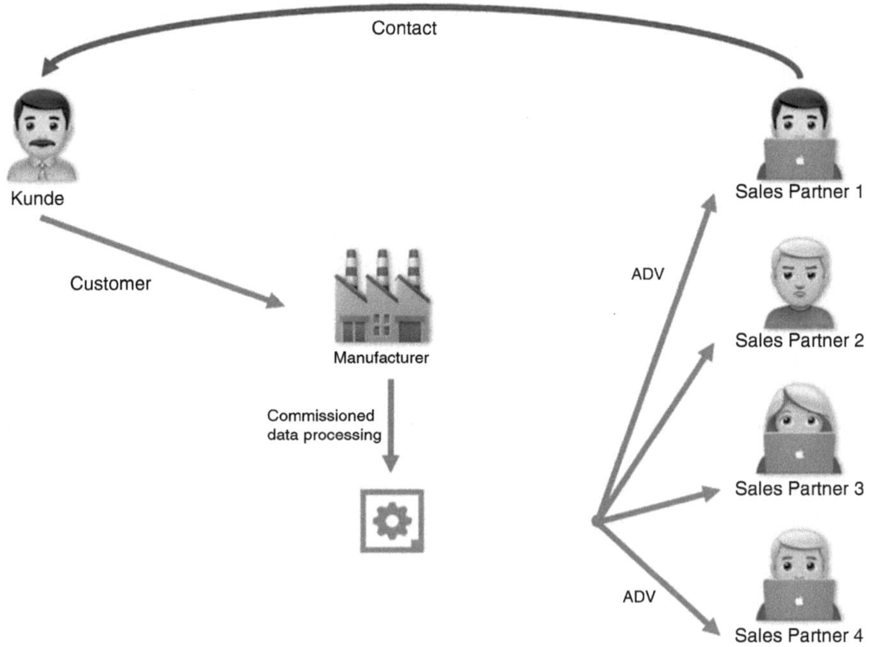

Fig. 4 Ensuring data privacy (Source: leadtributor)

- In any case, consent must be obtained before the lead is passed on to a sales partner!

5 Obtain Sufficient Consent Before Sharing Leads with Channel Partners

If you want to choose the legally safest way to share lead data with your sales partners, make sure you have explicit permission from the customer to contact them. Please remember that this consent only ever relates to the connection between you and the clearly defined customer. Furthermore, this consent also only relates to a specific product, service, or topic.

There are several ways to design the process:

- Customer chooses the partner who will take care of them
  It would be perfect if you could ask for permission to give the data to a sales partner for further processing as early as the query stage in a form. This process can be designed in a legally compliant manner as follows: The customer selects a partner on the manufacturer's website and confirms in the contact form that the manufacturer may forward the data to the sales partner in the course of processing

his interest in product XYZ. Via direct assignment in the leadtributor, only the selected sales partner is then offered the inquiry.

- The distributor who responds the fastest gets the lead's data
  If you want to offer a lead to several partners, you use the possibilities of matching and picklisting in leadtributor. Based on profile data (static or dynamic profile data), leadtributor automatically searches for the perfectly matching partners for the request and offers them to several. Accordingly, the supervising sales partner is not yet determined when the customer gives his consent.

Such disclosure to distribution partners is somewhat more difficult because consent must be obtained not for a clearly defined distribution partner, but for as many distribution partners as possible. It should be noted that general consents that do not precisely define the scope of the consent are inadmissible. It must therefore always be precisely defined to which companies and products the consent relates. However, case law does not define any explicit restrictions in terms of the number of distributors to whom the request may be offered. For this reason, lawyers consider lists of potential sales partners that the lead may receive to be permissible in principle. With one condition: It must be possible and, above all, reasonable for the person giving consent to review the list of all sales partners in question. If the customer discovers a sales partner on the list to whom he does not want to give his data under any circumstances, he does not confirm the consent or cancel it.

The term "reasonableness" is important here. Unfortunately, the legislator does not define what is reasonable and what is not! However, it is clear that the blanket statement "... we will pass on your request to one of our sales partners ..." is inadmissible. The sales partners in question must be provided in a list. Lists of 500 or even 1000 sales partners, for example, would probably be unreasonable. The customer would have to check these lists if he wants to ensure that his data does not fall into the hands of unwelcome sales partners. The following or similar consent text would therefore be conceivable: "I consent to receiving information about product XYZ from a sales partner [link to the list of eligible sales partners].

A simple reference to a blanket list of all sales partners somewhere in the privacy policy is by no means sufficient. It is conceivable to link to a list as part of the respective consent (see proposed consent text). However, there are already the first examples on record of how not to do it. A link to a partner list that gave the impression in the consent text itself that one could easily select one's desired partners was considered inadmissible. In this case, however, it was necessary to declare a kind of opt-out from an unusually long list of sales partners by clicking away previous check marks. In the opinion of the court, however, the decisive factor was interestingly not so much the length of the sales partner list as the fact that the consent text conveyed an inaccurate impression with regard to the easy and simple possibility of opting out.

6 Sales Partner Contacts Leads as Part of Commissioned Data Processing

Contacting by the sales partners is also possible without a separate consent. The only condition: Contact may only be made within the framework of commissioned data processing (ADV) for the manufacturers. Such processing could be handled by the leadtributor through appropriate contracts in the context of subcontracting relationships. Figure 5 illustrates this construction.

This enables the sales partner to contact interested parties on behalf of the manufacturer. The German Federal Court of Justice (BGH) has also confirmed that such contacting on behalf of the manufacturer (e.g., by a call center) is permissible. In practice, this is hardly relevant, but there is still a small flaw. Strictly speaking, contacting is only permitted for the manufacturer's products and only for sales by the manufacturer. Unless express consents, as shown above, have also been granted for the sales partner.

If there are corresponding ADV agreements between manufacturers and sales partners, the call or contact on behalf of the manufacturer is permitted. However, the permission does not automatically apply to selling the manufacturer's products to the customer in their own name and for their own account. Within the framework of an ADV, the sales partner can therefore establish contact and initiate the transaction. Only the manufacturer itself is "allowed" to sell.

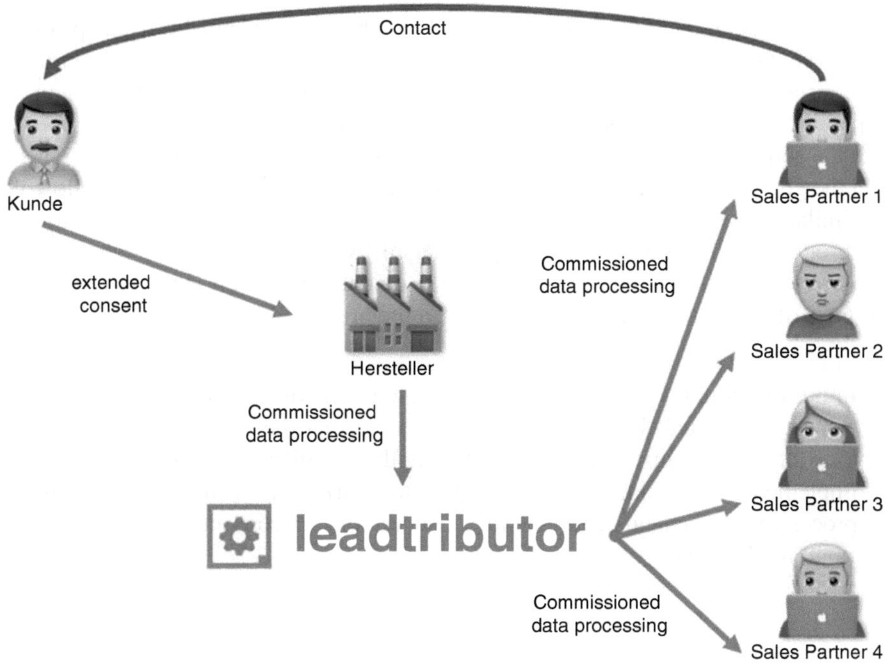

Fig. 5 Handling of subcontracting relationships (Source: leadtributor)

It is also doubtful so far whether the request for extended consent alone (which would allow not only the manufacturer but also the distributor to sell the product to the prospective customer) by the distributor would be permissible in the context of this call. Of course, this is more of a legal issue. In practice, the following two scenarios arise:

- No interest
  The sales partner calls the customer on behalf of the manufacturer or contacts him by e-mail. In the course of this contact (conversation or e-mail communication), the customer declares that he is no longer interested after all. In this case, it would be quite absurd for the sales partner to ask for consent to sell the manufacturer's products on his own behalf in the future.
- Interest
  The distributor calls or contacts the customer by mail on behalf of the manufacturer. The customer confirms his interest to buy the product. If the sale is handled by the manufacturer, there is no problem. However, in the narrower sense, it is not permitted for the sales partner to ask the customer for permission to remain in contact with him in order to sell him the product in his own name. This case is legally shaky, but hardly relevant in practice. This is because customers who are in intensive contact with the sales partner are unlikely to invoke the law if the sales partner sells the manufacturer's product in his own name. In most cases, the customer even expects this!

Strictly speaking, however, this would not be covered by the usual process. However, this problem could also be solved by means of an extended declaration of consent. The consent would have to be extended to include permission to expressly address the sales partner in advertising (in the future). It is also important that the consent is limited to only one sales partner (even if not yet named) to ensure that the group of companies advertising is sufficiently clearly defined. The following or similar consent text would be conceivable: "I consent to receive information on the product xyz from one of the sales partners of ABC GmbH on their behalf. I also consent to this sales partner requesting me to contact me myself in the future for the purpose of providing further information on the aforementioned products."

In our opinion, the safest way is to obtain explicit consent in advance. In this respect, a residual risk only exists in the event that the reseller lists are very long and confusing. To the extent that this is difficult or impossible to implement, it would also be possible to work with commissioned data processing agreements and extended declarations of consent, leaving a very small residual risk.

Reference

LeanData. (2017). *The state of lead management. A survey of B2B sales and marketing professionals*. Accessed September 01, 2020, from http://learn.leandatainc.com/h/i/344545596-the-state-of-lead-management

Philipp Baron von der Brüggen started his career in a small Munich advertising agency after graduating in communications. He quickly moved to an English software provider. In 1994 he left the company after 4.5 years to start his own marketing agency. The goal: marketing services and consulting for complex technical products in B2B segment. His agency "technology marketing people gmbh" served customers like Weidmüller, Samsung, VMware, Citrix, Oracle, Kaspersky, Unify, Infineon, SAP, or Adobe. In 2016, he sold his agency. Since 2016, he supports start-ups with advice and assistance! He is CMO of Natuvion GmbH, Walldorf, an international IT consulting company since fall 2020.

Philipp von der Brüggen is an expert in B2B marketing communication, structured lead generation using modern online tools, lead management and the establishment, operation and optimization of indirect sales systems.

Funnel Performance Management

Jan Beco and Egemen Zeren

1 Increasing Challenges for Marketing and Sales

The good old marketing and sales playbook is now outdated and has taken its place on the shelf of the old economy. Customer journeys have changed radically, and classic cold calling has long since ceased to achieve the desired and required leads and prospects. In addition, GDPR and DSGVO have not made outbound activities any easier. The inevitable result is sales cycles are lengthening and the contributions to achieving marketing and sales goals are becoming increasingly difficult to realize.

One reason for all these symptoms are the significant changes in customer journeys. Where guidance was necessary in the past, we are now faced with a self-confident, highly informed customer who knows exactly what to buy, where and at what price. According to findings by SiriusDecision (SiriusDecisions, 2020, see literature), more than 80% of the buying process is already complete when a potential customer makes initial contact with the sales department.

Therefore, the opportunity to personally advise and influence a prospect early in the sales process is eliminated. Accordingly, approaches such as the Zero Moment of Truth (ZMOT) coined by Google (Google, 2011), in which needs are initially awakened, are becoming increasingly important. To achieve this, it is necessary to adapt all marketing activities to the changed behavior of consumers at an early stage and to align the entire sales and marketing value chain appropriately.

Just a few years ago, a buying journey looked utterly different. In a world of information scarcity, lead generation meant marketing using various campaigns to identify potential buyers at an early stage of their buying journey and directing them

J. Beco (✉)
Jan Beco Advisory, Sigmaringen, Germany
e-mail: email@janbeco.ch

E. Zeren
Nagarro, Freiburg, Germany

U. Hannig, U. Seebacher (eds.), *Marketing and Sales Automation*, Management for Professionals, https://doi.org/10.1007/978-3-031-20040-3_22

to sales, unqualified. On the other hand, Sellers had significant influence over the buying process and could steer demanders very early in the buying cycle and get them to the desired conclusion.

Its an entirely different story these days: buyers have a wide range of decision-making tools at their disposal. From Google to authentic recommendations and reviews in social media to comparison portals. Through content, produced and distributed by vendor-independent organizations, prospects can learn a lot about a product or service before they even contact a salesperson. They are already well aware of which vendors exist and which are relevant to them. They know the advantages and disadvantages of the individual products and services and already have a very clear opinion of providers and offers via numerous reviews, forums, and blogs; straight through to insights into the values of the company and its reputation as an employer. Accordingly, with all these points taken into consideration, companies should carefully build and expand their digital presence on all conceivable channels and always in a well-thought-out manner.

Against this backdrop, it is not very helpful that sales and marketing are continuously flooded with new lead and demand generation approaches. New service providers and specialists are constantly trying to make their mark in the still young lead and demand generation market. In addition to various innovative methods and processes, they often present very individual glossaries that are difficult to bring down to a common denominator. All that new lingo aside, do not get confused, the traditional sales funnel is still working just fine.

It is much more important to accept change as a constant. You can be better prepared for the future by continuously adapting to changing external influences. This also applies to all lead and demand generation processes. Existing internal processes and the entire sales and marketing organization must be continuously scrutinized. The motto here is: Evolve or die.

2 The Funnel Is (Still) Alive!

Today, executives demand countable contributions to results from marketing and sales:

- What percentage of revenue should we invest in marketing?
- What portion of the pipeline should marketing drive?
- What lead conversion rates can we expect from marketing?
- How much time should sales invest in revenue-generating activities and how much in administrative activities?
- What do the processes look like at successful companies with the highest growth and revenue numbers? In order to be able to answer these questions in the best possible way, a plan is needed for dealing with prospects, leads, and existing customers. And despite many new approaches and methods, it is still a good idea to map the processes in a funnel (see Fig. 1).

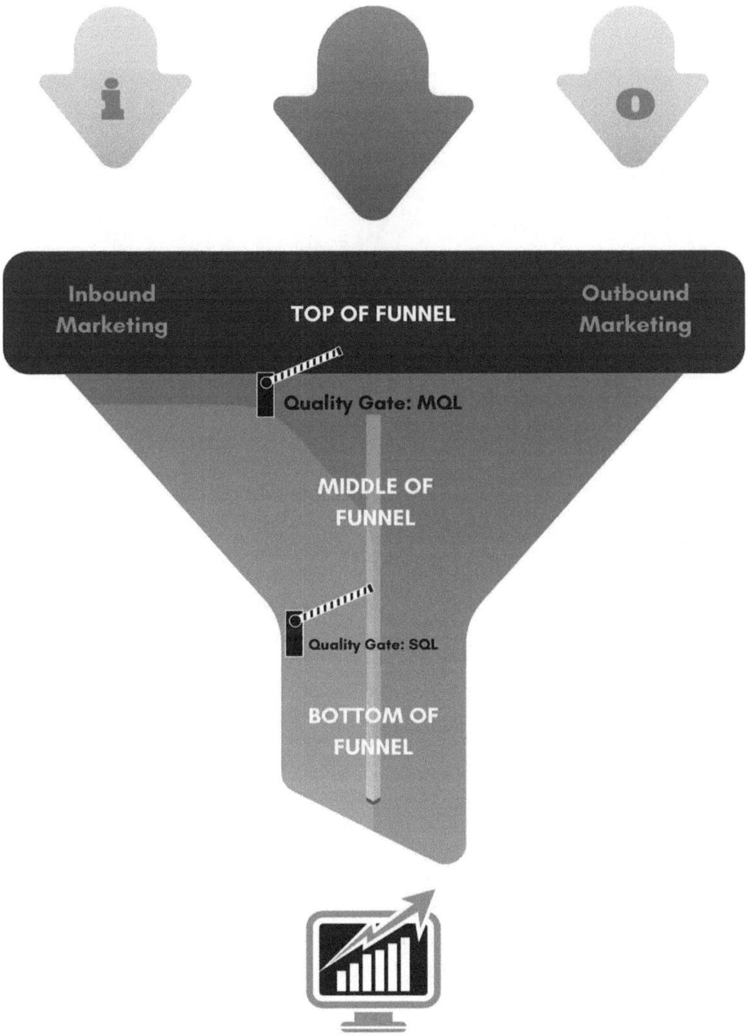

Fig. 1 The sales and marketing funnel (Source: Own illustration)

The ground rules have not changed significantly over the last few years. At the top of the funnel, there must be high-quality, disruptive, and always engaging content that potential customers either find (inbound marketing) or which gets actively distributed to them (outbound marketing). A structured approach is required: "to be able to cut through the noise" (Gillett, 2016). By this, it is meant that one's marketing activities attract the attention of the target customers. This is where the content marketing strategy comes into play. It must be possible to stay in contact with the leads generated this way along their very individual customer journeys to act as a constant source of advice. Potential customers must be provided

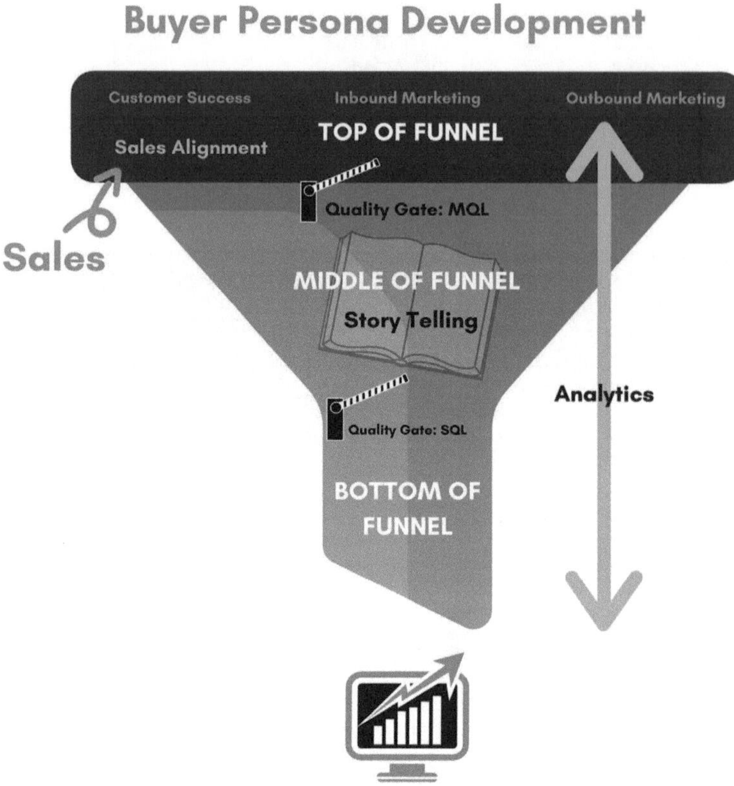

Fig. 2 Continuous optimization of the funnel based on various initiatives (Source: Own illustration)

with personalized content at the right time and in the suitable form across all channels and quality gates (Marketing Qualified Leads—MQLs—and Sales Qualified Leads—SQLs).

Only a consistent "play" on a prospect ensures that he or she is "top of mind" for the upcoming purchase. At best, the prospect already feels that they have made the right decision. Strategically, this means dealing with the development of buyer personas, thinking about messaging and differentiation at the top of the funnel, trying out storytelling in the middle of the funnel, actively practising funnel analytics, and continuously bringing sales and marketing together (see Fig. 2).

However, it would be too short-sighted to now simply entrust individuals within the company with these tasks. The entire sales and marketing organization must be reorganized to meet these challenges, and this requires management commitment right from the start. Whoever permanently expands, optimizes, repeats and continuously scales such a complex marketing process will be able to do profitable business in the long term.

Companies that increasingly strive for and implement a focused and structured process sell more because, among other things, sales can concentrate on the actual business. Companies maximize sales by ensuring that only the best-qualified leads are being passed from marketing to the sales department. In such an ideal situation, sales can spend more time developing highly qualified leads and focus on closing deals. An account manager can be far more successful because it allows them to focus on their main strength, selling.

But when marketing floods sales with low-quality leads, salespeople get frustrated and decide to generate leads on their own to meet their annual goals. This often means they waste time researching databases, creating their own marketing materials that do not always meet internal guidelines, and in the worst-case duplicating work already done by the marketing department. In short, when expensive salespeople spend their time developing marketing campaigns, it thwarts the business imperative to strengthen strengths and weaken weaknesses. One way out of such a predicament is to implement a lead scoring model that manages the marketing team to ensure that leads are correctly qualified, developed, and handed over to sales at the right time.

Lead scoring models require continuous updates. Ideally, they are based on predictive ranking. The aim is to determine which contact attributes are exhibited by the potential customers who are most likely to buy. Since the sales department knows its customers the best, it can contribute important information, such as how and when they want to be contacted and what information they are looking for.

However, in many companies, the motto is still: more leads automatically mean more sales. However, in the real world, this is usually not the case. Often, companies do not have the problem of generating leads. Still, they do not attach enough importance to continuously optimizing the follow-up process to improve conversion rates to opportunities constantly. To do this, all key figures at every point of the buying journey must be identified and continuously monitored.

The following list shows key figures for successful funnel performance management:

- Sum of all leads from all sources per month
- Sum of all leads from all sources this month compared to last month
- Sum of all leads from all sources this month compared to the same month 1 year ago
- Sum of all leads from all sources this month compared to the set goal for this month
- Sum of all visitors to own website per month
- Sum of all visitors to own website this month compared to last month
- Sum of all visitors to own website this month compared to the same month 1 year ago
- Sum of all visitors of own website of this month compared to the set target for this month
- Sum of generated leads of own website per month
- Sum of generated leads of own website of this month compared to last month

- Sum of generated leads of own website of this month compared to the same month 1 year ago
- Total leads generated from own website this month compared to the set target for this month
- Percentage of all leads that become Sales Qualified Leads (SQLs)
- Percentage of all Sales Qualified Leads (SQLs) that convert to opportunities
- Percentage of all opportunities to which a quote is sent
- Percentage of all quotes that are accepted
- Percentage of all inbound leads
- Percentage of all inbound leads this quarter compared to last quarter
- Percentage of all outbound leads
- Percentage of all outbound leads this quarter compared to last quarter
- Percentage of all leads per source (organic/paid search, social, email, referrals, word-of-mouth, events, outbound marketing, etc.)
- Percentage of all opportunities per source (organic/paid search, social, email, referrals, word-of-mouth, events, outbound marketing, etc.)
- Percentage of all new customers per source (organic/paid search, social, email, referrals, word-of-mouth, events, outbound marketing, etc.)
- Percentage of revenue per source (organic/paid search, social, email, referrals, word-of-mouth, events, outbound marketing, etc.)
- Cost per lead this month
- Cost per lead this quarter vs. last quarter
- Cost per lead this month compared to the same month last year
- Cost per new customer this month
- Cost per new customer this quarter compared to last quarter
- Cost per new customer acquired this month versus the same month last year
- Overarching Funnel Conversion Rate
- Conversion rate on the landing page with the most visitors per month
- Total of all blog subscribers
- Blog subscriber growth rate

The list of commonly used key figures and performance indicators is long. In order to achieve above-average performance, the following key figures should also be taken into account:

- Percentage of outbound (email) activities with reply (connect rate)
- Comparison of the connect rate this month with that of last month
- Proportion of cases where a positive Reply resulted in a dialog (Engagement Rate)
- Engagement rate this month compared to last month
- Open rate for lead nurture email campaigns
- Click-through rate for lead nurture email campaigns
- Engagement rate for lead nurture email campaigns
- Average customer lifetime value (CLV) of a new customer
- Current average CLV compared to that of the previous year

- Average revenue per new customer
- Current average revenue per new customer compared to that of the previous year
- Development of customer retention rate
- Current sales cycle in days
- Current sales cycle in days compared to last month
- Current sales cycle in days compared to last quarter
- Current sales cycle in days compared to the same month last year
- Total pipeline value in the current month compared to last month

This data is available in most marketing automation tools and CRM systems, and they can be extracted more or less easily and reported daily, weekly, monthly and quarterly. It is crucial to find out and individually define which data is performance relevant and when it should be evaluated. In addition, not only the business department should know the sales and marketing metrics, but also every CEO, CMO, and VP Sales and COO. Only then will there be opportunities to realize optimization potential in a timely manner.

In addition, to get a fully integrated approach, you need to know how the sales team is using the company's internal CRM system. Only when you have a focused view of everything from tracking sales quotas and routing leads to revenue forecasting processes can leads be better managed, filtered through the funnel, and tracked. The associated key figures provide even more insights (see Fig. 3).

For the Aberdeen Group, the marketing contribution to the sales forecasted pipeline and the value of the marketing funnel are of particular importance. The sales forecast pipeline attributed to marketing is important because it is not directly related to the marketing funnel but rather to both funnels' outcome and the collaboration between sales and marketing (Aberdeen Group, 2012). This data is a reminder that marketing in lead management involves more than managing interactions with potential customers and prospects. Marketers must equally fulfill other internal expectations.

3 Become Successful Through Marketing Automation

A funnel managed jointly by Sales and Marketing provides the basis for introducing a funnel performance management process. The approach further develops the Revenue Performance Management (RPM) created by Oracle in the 1990s as a subarea of marketing process automation (Oracle, 2019). The idea was to better measure marketing success and to optimize marketing activities throughout the sales cycle.

With RPM, marketing had a set of basic information and tools to evaluate marketing activities continuously. Funnel performance management is now about using RPM and a holistic approach to guide prospects through the funnel as optimally as possible.

It is essential to realize that Funnel Performance Management is a strategy and not a technology. That being said, marketing automation tools are required for

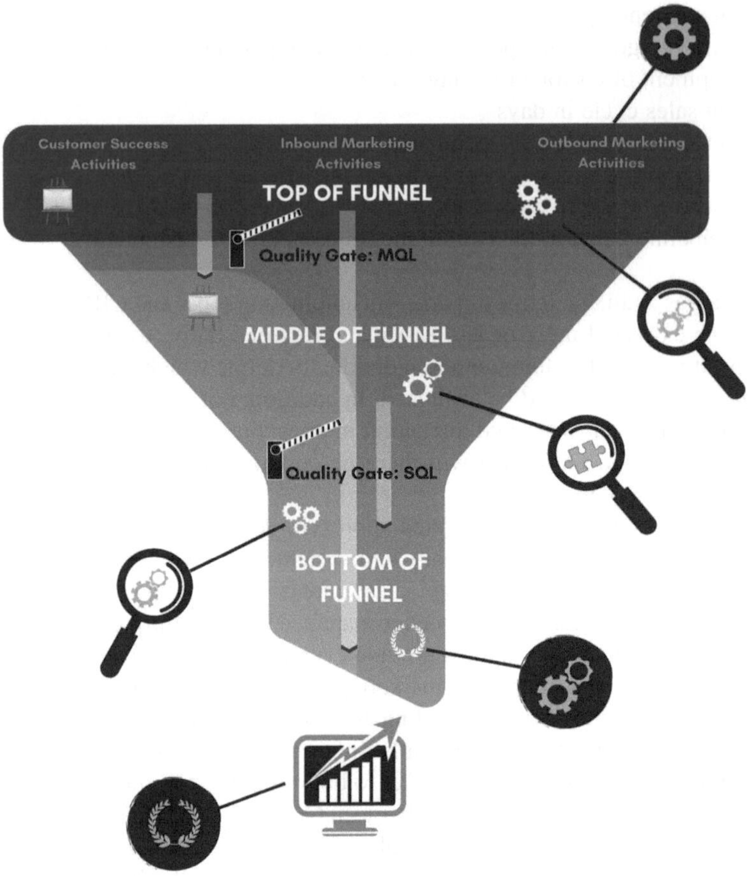

Fig. 3 Analysis of individual funnel activities (Source: Own illustration)

implementation so that funnel performance management can be used consistently throughout the company. Accordingly, sales and marketing automation tools are essential for leveraging the identified potential.

Just as important as investing in marketing automation systems is developing business practices that are scalable and widely accepted. It is no longer enough to manage website visitors, downloads, leads, webinar registrants or opportunities in isolation. Today, the entire buying cycle, from ZMOT to order entry, must be planned, managed and optimized continuously. This also requires sales, marketing, and service to work closely together. Effective sales and marketing alignment is reflected in a common funnel that constantly identifies improvement actions based on current data.

By looking at the entire funnel, irregularities in the pipeline can be identified and optimized promptly. With the right metrics, analytics, and customer interaction information, companies gain the ability to forecast long-term growth and identify revenue opportunities. A well-deployed funnel performance management system makes it possible to monitor prospects' behavior throughout the entire buying process. From lead quality as a function of content, identifying core target groups with high purchasing power, and predicting which offer customers will take up.

Last but not least, production capacities can be adjusted to the expected demand, and the required resources can be optimized. This gives marketing and management a relatively accurate picture of future sales trends and enables them to respond to them at an early stage. If, for example, a decline in sales is foreseeable for the next two quarters, quick-win campaigns can be launched and the focus in sales and marketing can be directed to the associated investments.

Suppose marketing also takes care of pipeline activities, such as lead nurturing and lead scoring, thereby generating good-quality leads. In this case, sales can focus on hot leads and opportunities and close more deals. Experience shows that companies generate customers from only a small proportion of top-of-funnel leads. Conversion rates can be significantly improved through an optimized strategic revenue generation thinking approach, re-orchestration, and continuous optimization of the funnel.

Ultimately, everything relies on having a deep understanding of how efficiently the funnel is set up; continuously identifying and analyzing the lowest conversion rates. Based on the results, further improvements must be analyzed and developed. If there are problems primarily in the lower part of the funnel and opportunities are not closed, this may be due, for example, to the fact that formal contracts and offers tend to create more uncertainty or raise even more questions than sealing the purchase pragmatically.

Only by taking a hard look at the orchestration of all lead and demand generation disciplines can you assess how far you are from the goals you have set and how fundamentally sales and marketing need to be reorganized. Better forecasting makes it easier to identify new business opportunities and implement the necessary actions.

Building a revenue generation program that consistently exceeds KPI targets requires experience. Reliable best practices are very individual and do not (yet) exist.

The following prerequisites should be met for the successful introduction of Funnel Performance Management:

- A well-designed funnel, jointly managed by sales and marketing
- Defined activities, touchpoints and/or interactions within the funnel
- Ongoing lead scoring adapted to the company, and
- Deliberately selected KPIs and metrics along the entire funnel that are continuously measured

A proven approach to optimizing the funnel is to reverse the customer journey and derive the funnel activities from the set sales targets in a back-planning approach. For example, suppose revenue needs to be increased by 30%. In that case, it is possible to determine how the individual activities and processes in the funnel should look based on the known key figures and conversion rates. We know that if X specific activities are carried out in the top of the funnel, Y leads will be

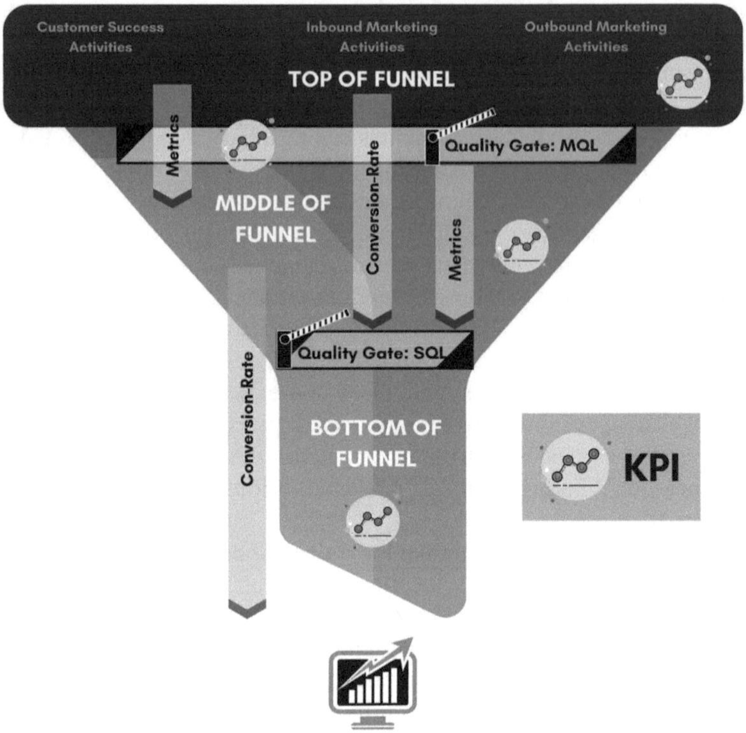

Fig. 4 Determination of KPIs (Source: Own illustration)

converted into opportunities and Z deals can be expected within a specific time frame (Fig. 4).

Based on a new target Z, we can now reverse engineer how many and of which activites need to be planned in the top of funnel in order to even be able to achieve the set target (see Fig. 5).

The theoretical explanations are illustrated below using an example: A company measures around 15,000 visitors per month on its website. Experience shows that these result in around 204 MQLs and approximately 12 SQLs per month after successfully processing the leads. These 12 SQLs results in about four new customers with whom an average of 100,000 euros are generated (see Fig. 6).

Management is increasing the revenue goals now by 30% to 130,000 euros. Based on the available key figures and conversion rates, it is now easy to calculate that at least 19,500 website visitors are required to achieve these sales targets (see Fig. 7).

It is essential to recognize that Funnel Performance Management is a process, an approach and a discipline. Even companies that do not have mature end-to-end marketing processes defined, implemented and instrumented today could and should approach Funnel Performance Management successively and roll it out internally.

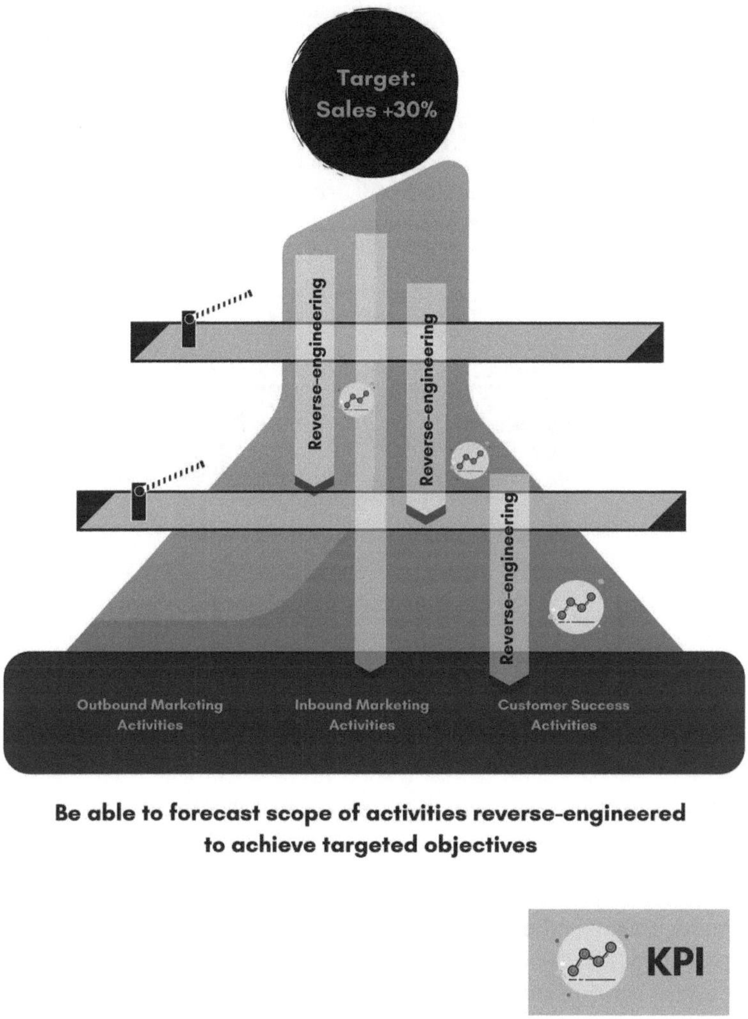

Fig. 5 Forecast of top-of-funnel activities for target achievement (Source: Own illustration)

A good starting point is an audit of existing marketing processes. Building on this, even small steps towards a funnel performance management strategy can bring initial success. The key performance indicators in the entire sales process should be defined jointly by sales and marketing. Otherwise, the qualification gates MQL and SQL in particular are always a cause for discussion. As soon as a lead is handed over to sales, marketing can have little or no influence on further processing.

Cleanly set up and unanimously defined processes and metrics provide the basis for continuously expanding a funnel performance management strategy and transparently managing both the resulting investments and their ROI. In addition, FPM provides extremely valuable information on the health of the entire company and

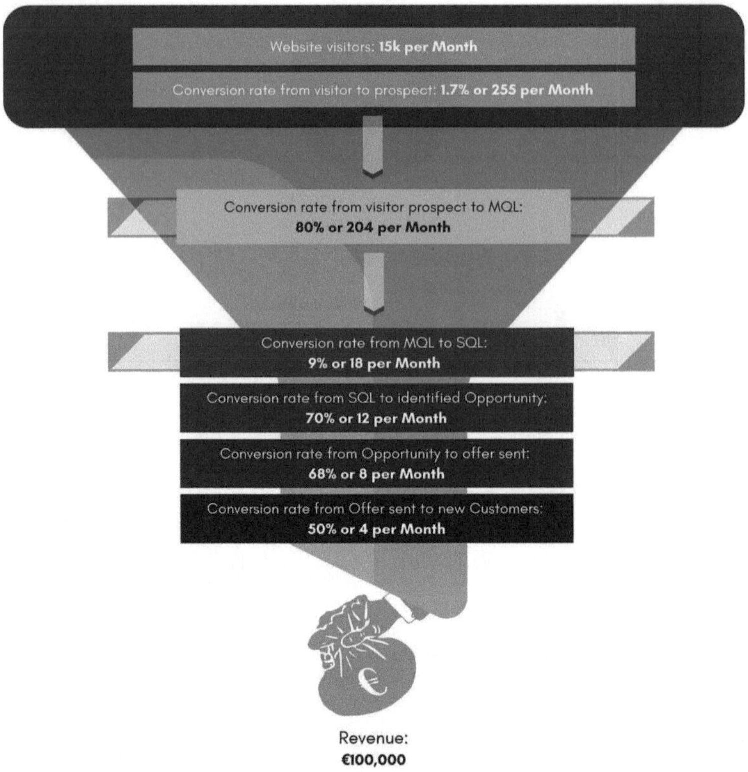

Fig. 6 Initial situation in the practical example (Source: Own illustration)

offers the opportunity to make data-based decisions on future marketing investments and programs. Behavioral economics is effectively being cheated.

However, more data is needed to identify which metrics have the most significant impact on sales performance, such as email and campaign metrics. Despite AI and Big Data, it is up to marketing management how to interpret the results of the analysis and which measures to take. Continuous testing is mandatory because every company is unique. In this respect, best-practice approaches are of limited help.

Especially for Funnel Performance Management, the saying of the French philosopher Charles Pépin applies: "Try again. Fail again. Fail better" (Pépin, 2017, p. 203). The key is to achieve constant improvements based on insights from marketing and sales, and this requires ensuring that everyone in the company knows how their work contributes to success.

Start with Funnel Performance Management in the short term, but take your time setting it up and expanding it. Because the degree of complexity requires a well-thought-out plan before investing money in tools and employees. Because the mantra of successful funnel performance management is: manage thoughtfully!

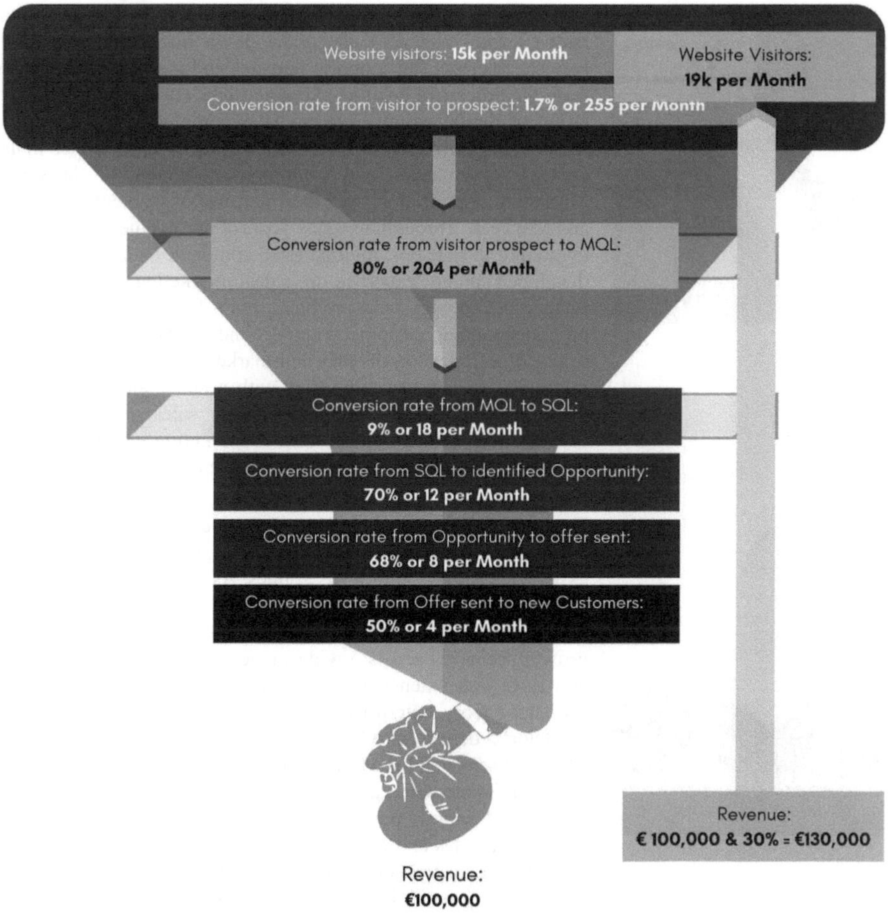

Fig. 7 Necessary website visitor input to reach the goal (Source: Own illustration)

References

Aberdeen Group. (2012). *Was Unternehmen im deutschsprachigen Raum über Revenue Performance Management wissen sollten.* http://docplayer.org/7940340-Was-unternehmen-im-deutschsprachigen-raum-ueber-revenue-performance-management-wissen-sollten.html

Gillett, A. (2016). *Cut through the noise.* Accessed July 15, 2016, from https://www.quora.com/What-is-the-exact-meaning-of-this-phrase-cut-through-the-noise

Google. (2011). *Zero moment of truth.* https://www.thinkwithgoogle.com/marketing-resources/micro-moments/zero-moment-truth/

Oracle. (2019). *Revenue performance management.* https://www.oracle.com/marketingcloud/resources/revenue-performance-management.html

Pépin, C. (2017). *Die Schönheit des Scheiterns. Kleine Philosophie der Niederlage. Aus dem Französischen von Caroline Gutberlet.*

SiriusDecisions. (2020). *Align the revenue engine.* https://go.forrester.com/research/siriusdecisions/

Jan Beco is an "In-between Generation X and Millennial Digital Native" with over 25 years of hands-on marketing, sales, and service expertise. Jan supports start-ups and mid-sized companies from the process of creative planning to the successful implementation of digitalization projects. After completing his Executive MBA at the University of Rochester, Jan further specialized in the strategic optimization and continuous alignment of Sales and Marketing organizations and the smart use of Content Marketing and MarTech. Through his many years of involvement in sales and marketing in start-ups, multinational companies, and agencies, he developed broad expertise in sales, marketing, management, finance, technology, and products. Jan's focus has always been on understanding customer journeys and needs as well as future-oriented optimization of sales and marketing organizations. Jan's mission is to provide companies with a better understanding of disruptive influences, optimally align sales and marketing organizations through smart sales & marketing engineering, and thus help the company achieve more revenue and success.

Egemen Zeren brings in over two decades of domestic and international business development, marketing, and management experience across multiple disciplines. As a well-recognized "analytical creative" within all levels of his former and current teams and organizations; Egemen thrives in digital transformation and growth scenarios across a wide range of industries in both B2B and B2C with extensive experience in retail, CPG, professional services, energy, enterprise software and IT. While completing his bachelor's degree in Computer Science at the University of Massachusetts and his Master's program in Information Technology and E-commerce at Istanbul Technical University, Egemen Zeren held various positions in business development, demand generation, sales and marketing roles until he found his ultimate niche in Digital Marketing, in the early 2010s. Backed up with his agency background, Egemen brings in holistic expertise in creating digital presence from strategy and conceptualization to funnel building, marketing automation implementation and optimization. Currently, he is responsible for the marketing automation infrastructure, inbound marketing engine and the launch of the pilot Account Based Marketing program at Nagarro for the DACH region.

How Customer-Led Growth Solve Typical Lead Management Problems of B2B Companies

Thorsten Herrmann

1 Introduction

In B2B companies, lead management and new customer acquisition are becoming increasingly complex. Potential customers who want to improve their online marketing are coming under pressure: falling conversion rates, disappointing access figures to the blog and website, and fluctuating quality of the leads generated. These experiences may be subjective—to my knowledge, there are no reliable figures on this. However, the fact that the goals associated with strategies such as inbound marketing are more difficult to achieve today than they were 5 or 10 years ago is only logical in view of the increasing spread of digital lead management approaches.[1]

The reasons for this development are manifold. In competitive industries in particular, the content shock predicted by marketing consultant Mark Schäfer in 2014 is already becoming apparent.[2] For some topics, there are now a large number of high-quality, freely accessible content offerings that are often very similar in terms of structure and argumentation. Filtering the right information from this mass is becoming more and more of a challenge for decision-makers, especially since there is often more than one solution on the market for their problems.[3]

At the same time, many people have had bad experiences with methods such as inbound marketing in recent years. Those who were immediately contacted by the provider's sales team after downloading a white paper or who were bombarded with e-mails and personalized ads on a topic almost daily may be more cautious when

[1] Cf. Kergl, Raphaela (Et.al): Marketing Automation Study 2021.

[2] Cf. Schäfer, Mark: Content Shock - why Content Marketing is not a sustainable strategy.

[3] Cf. Adamson, Brent: Sensemaking for Sales, p. 124.

T. Herrmann (✉)
Chain Relations, Frankfurt, Germany
e-mail: therrmann@chainrelations.de

U. Hannig, U. Seebacher (eds.), *Marketing and Sales Automation*, Management for Professionals, https://doi.org/10.1007/978-3-031-20040-3_23

dealing with offers that require registration. This may also be a reason for the poor results that some companies have recently achieved in online marketing.

2 Lack of Customer Knowledge Makes It Difficult to Acquire and Maintain New Customers

However, the main reason for the current problems in B2B marketing lies deeper. What characterizes modern lead management at its core is the claim to help customers make decisions with the help of information offers. This service character requires a deep understanding of the challenges and needs of potential customers—and this is precisely what B2B organizations lack. This is reflected in a disappointing customer experience from the customer's point of view:[4] In a study by the US consulting firm Bain & Company, for example, 80% of the providers surveyed said they provided excellent service. Conversely, however, only 8% of customers confirmed that they were satisfied with these service providers.[5]

A strong discrepancy between self-perception and reality is typical when it comes to the topic of customer knowledge or customer insights. Almost every company believes that it understands the requirements of its customers and aligns its offerings and processes accordingly. In practice, however, many companies find it difficult to act in a customer-centric manner. This is evident from advertising messages and content offers that focus more on the provider than on the situation of potential customers and in which the advantages of an offer that are attractive from their point of view are insufficiently described. But it is also symptomatic that customer satisfaction is often not measured systematically. Instead, managers focus on KPIs that do not allow any statement about the quality of the customer experience (e.g., the number of leads generated).[6]

The fact that companies find it difficult to align themselves with their customers is absurd in some respects. Many of them were only able to occupy their competitive niche because they recognized an important task at the time of their founding for which no adequate solution was available to their customers. Nonetheless, this strong focus on the situation of potential customers is being lost as most organizations grow. Increasingly, they define their business in terms of the products or services they offer, not the task they solve for their customers.[7]

[4]The use of the term "customer experience" is based on Brian Meredith's definition: According to this definition, the customer experience is the product of the interactions that a customer experiences with a provider over the course of the customer life cycle—from the first contact to the use of the product and associated services (cf. Brian Meredith: Customer Experience – A key marketing element, p. 50).

[5]Cf. Allen, James; Reichheld, Frederick F.; Hamilton, Barney; Markey, Rob Markey: Closing the delivery gap.

[6]Cf. Rice, Mae: Welcome to the Era of Customer-led Growth.

[7]Cf. Christensen, Clayton M.: Better than Chance: "Jobs to Be Done" – the Strategy for Successful Innovation, p. 227.

3 Why Do Large Gaps Open Up in the Area of Customer Knowledge?

Why do companies lose focus on their customers? The reasons are diverse. Basically, deep gaps in customer knowledge open up in many organizations over time. Even the customer-facing departments only partially understand how the decision-making process is structured on the demand side. Sales, for example, knows which phases the sales process involves from the first personal contact with decision-makers of the prospective customer. On the other hand, Sales does not know what hurdles these people overcame before the sales meeting, what their preferences were in the pre-selection of suppliers, or how they interacted with competitors. The situation is even worse where personal customer contact itself is weak (e.g., in software-as-a-service companies). Here, direct experience with the customers' decision-making processes is almost completely lacking.

In addition, customer insights are usually available at certain points, but are only rarely transported into the organization in a structured manner. However, this is an important prerequisite for making the insights usable. For example, many companies have salespeople who have gathered immense knowledge about the challenges and needs of customers. However, it is difficult to transfer this information to the stages of the buyer's journey of the various customer segments, especially since very few companies have processes for internal knowledge transfer and, above all, for structuring them. Instead, information silos are created that are inaccessible to areas such as marketing, service, and product development.[8]

To understand why companies are losing focus on their customers, it also helps to take a look at go-to-market approaches that can be summarized under the term "X-led growth." Here, the "X" stands for different growth drivers that make the largest contribution to total sales. A distinction is usually made between *sales-led growth* (growth through intensive sales activities), *product-led growth* (growth based on product features), *engineering-led growth* (growth through advertising-financed platforms) and *marketing-led growth.* The latter stands for companies in which lead management strategies such as inbound marketing make a significant contribution to the acquisition of new customers.

The distinction makes it clear which perspective companies take when dealing with new and existing customers. In principle, almost every organization can be assigned to one of the X-led approaches mentioned. These, in turn, all have two fundamental weaknesses that prevent companies from realizing their full revenue potential. On the one hand, each X-led approach focuses on one growth driver and neglects other areas or the interaction of several, be it marketing, sales, or service. On the other hand, strategies for new customer acquisition and revenue growth in these approaches emerge from an inside-out perspective. These are "inside-out" concepts, in which strategies for market development are the result of internal considerations.

[8]Cf. Herrmann, Torsten: Customer-led Growth – knowing what customers want.

Differentiation from the competition is difficult under these circumstances, especially since internal company views often differ only slightly within an industry.[9]

4 Customer-Led Growth Helps Companies Regain Customer Focus

Regardless of how and when the focus on the customer is lost: In the long run, this can endanger the competitive position of a company. This is especially true in competitive industries where products and services differ little in terms of quality and consequently the customer experience becomes the decisive differentiation factor.[10] After all, customer relationships are the best lever compared to product features (which can be copied very quickly) and price (which is under constant pressure).[11] The market research company Forrester Research speaks not without reason of the "Age of the Customer."[12] Due to product reviews, testimonials and the mass of freely available content, customers sometimes know at least as much about a product or service as the sellers do. At the same time, large B2C providers such as Amazon and Apple have set the bar for a good customer experience extraordinarily high in recent years. B2B providers must also orient themselves to this, whereby even small mistakes can lead to customers deciding in favor of the competition.[13]

In this context, a further, still relatively new approach is interesting, which focuses on a different growth driver: Customers. Customer-led growth (CLG) was developed primarily by the US marketing consultants Georgiana Laudi and Claire Suellentrop. It is a growth strategy in which companies use methodically acquired customer knowledge to consistently align all customer-related processes within the organization with the customer journey of potential customers and existing customers. The logic behind this is simple: if companies enable a precisely tailored customer experience, this leads to an optimal buying and user experience. This, in turn, should increase customer loyalty—and thus their willingness to switch to higher product versions, to do further business with the provider, and to recommend the provider to acquaintances and business contacts.[14]

Unlike all other X-led approaches, CLG does not follow an inside-out logic, but an outside-in logic. Companies systematically develop insights into the challenges and needs of customers, carry these insights into all customer-facing areas, and then tailor their processes and messages to potential customers in order to optimize their

[9]Cf. Hague, Nick; Hague, Paul: B2B Customer Experience: A practical guide to delivering exceptional CX, pp. 61–62.

[10]Cf. Webster, Bryce: The Power of Consultative Selling, p. 3ff.

[11]McDonald, Malcolm: On Marketing Planning, p. 37

[12]Cf. Gazala, Michael: Winning in the Age of the Customer.

[13]Cf. Bodine/Manning: Outside In – The Power of putting customers at the center of your business, p. 15ff.

[14]Cf. Mouzakitis, Aggelos: What is Customer-led Growth?

buying experience. The idea behind this is not revolutionary. The consultative selling approach, for example, is familiar from sales. For decades, this approach has been aimed at increasing the number of sales by providing customers with the most personalized service possible. Accordingly, sales employees score less with their sales skills than with their consulting and problem-solving skills.[15]

In addition to Consultative Selling, there are comparable approaches from other areas of the company. For example, the AARRR method, which is familiar from marketing, aims to optimize the customer experience at every touchpoint that can be influenced by marketing.[16] However, these strategies always focus only on sub-areas and not on the entire customer journey. This is the qualitative difference compared to customer-led growth, which aims to tailor each individual touchpoint to the customer's requirements. To achieve this, not only must all customer-facing areas be brought into line. At the same time, CLG can only be realized if companies develop a deep understanding of the challenges and needs of their customers and systematically transfer this insight knowledge into the organization.[17]

5 How Do Companies Develop the Customer Knowledge Needed for CLG?

At this point, we encounter the first major challenge in implementing CLG: generating insight knowledge about customers. Internal brainstorming is not suitable for this task, as it inevitably leads to assumptions that in practice are surprisingly often different from the reality of the customers. Collecting quantitative data—whether via market research, standardized questionnaires, purchasing from data providers, or recording online interactions—is also not sufficient for CLG. These essentially focus on "who" counts as a company's customers or "what" they think about a product or service. For Customer-led Growth, however, we need to understand "why" the customer's decision-makers made the choice for a product or service and remain loyal to it. This is best understood when we elicit the reasons for the decision in a personal conversation.[18]

Developing customer insights for customer-led growth works using the Jobs-to-be-Done (JTBD) methodology developed in the 1990s by Clayton M. Christensen at Harvard Business School. JTBD is a strategic approach to analyzing customer goals and requirements. Using quantitative customer surveys (e.g., online questionnaires) and qualitative interviews, providers seek to understand what needs and goals their customers want to fulfill when they purchase a product or commission a service.[19]

[15] Cf. Hanan, Mack: Consultative Selling, p. 25ff.

[16] Cf. Mivekannin, Maurice: AARRR – in 5 steps to becoming a growth hacker.

[17] Cf. Mouzakitis, Aggelos: What is Customer-led Growth?

[18] Cf. Bob Moesta/Chris Spiek: Jobs-to-be-Done – The Handbook, p. 34.

[19] Cf. Christensen, Clayton M.: Better than Chance: "Jobs to Be Done" – the Strategy for Successful Innovation, p. 35.

Elementary for the understanding of the method is the term "jobs." In the JTBD context, this is not a simple work task, but rather a dynamic process that is intended to lead to a specific end result under certain circumstances. This can take numerous forms, from fulfilling an extrinsic need (e.g., a job instruction) to satisfying an intrinsic need (e.g., satisfying hunger) to abstract (e.g., entertainment). Ultimately, then, a customer's job-to-be-done is an overarching goal that one or more people in the customer organization want to achieve. This goal is fundamentally solution-neutral, because the customer does not care how he or she achieves it. The provider's offer is merely one way among many to achieve the goal.[20]

It is important that a customer's job does not just involve functional aspects. For example, someone who buys a sports car does not just want to get from A to B, but associates emotional (freedom, pride, etc.) and social (external image, etc.) needs with the vehicle. These need to be filtered out during the interview process.[21] To do these jobs, more is needed than just good products or services. In the same way, providers must succeed in making the customer experience high-quality, personalized and simple from the very first contact. In this sense, every job-to-be-done is like a service, even if the company actually offers products.[22]

JTBD is associated with a change of perspective ("outside-in"), which is most comparable to the concept of buyer persona development developed by Adele Revella.[23] Here, too, the focus is not on who the customers are (income, family status, etc.), but on why they made a purchasing decision. At the same time, both methods involve a structured process in data collection and evaluation. In other words, they rely neither on the individual brilliance of individual employees nor on the factor of chance.

What distinguishes both methods is the focus of the investigation. Buyer personas focus on the purchase decision process. Companies use them to find out why customer archetypes have chosen a product or service. JTBD, on the other hand, scrutinizes the deeper motivations. The focus is on the question of what problems customers face and how providers can best help them here.[24] This orientation predestines JTBD for the implementation of a customer-led growth strategy, especially since the basic idea of both approaches is almost identical.[25]

At the same time, the Jobs-to-be-Done framework takes a more structured approach to analyzing the data collected. This applies to both the interviews and the questionnaires used to gather customer insights. The reason for this is the strong

[20] Cf. Christensen, Clayton M.: Better than Chance: "Jobs to Be Done" – the Strategy for Successful Innovation, p. 98.

[21] Cf. Ulwick, Anthony: What Customers Want, p. 25ff.

[22] Cf. Christensen, Clayton M.: Better than Chance: "Jobs to Be Done" – the Strategy for Successful Innovation, p. 152.

[23] Cf. Revella, Adele: Buyer Personas.

[24] Cf. Christensen, Clayton M.: Better than Chance: "Jobs to Be Done" – the Strategy for Successful Innovation, p. 107.

[25] Cf. Mouzakitis, Aggelos: What is Customer-led Growth?

focus on the jobs that customers want to achieve with the help of a product or service. This leads to a dynamic, process-related perspective that reveals correlations between influences on a decision-making process and opens up new insights with regard to the segmentation of target groups. For example, companies that are firmographically similar (e.g., size, industry) are often assigned to different segments in JTBD. Organizations that at first glance have nothing in common, on the other hand, are grouped together because they want to do the same job-to-be-done.

6 How Are Customer Insights Operationalized at CLG?

Companies use customer interviews and quantitative customer surveys to create the informational basis for customer-led growth. The second major challenge is to use the insights gained in a targeted manner to improve the customer experience in all customer-related areas. For this task, CLG creates so-called customer experience maps. This process attempts to sketch the customer journey of representative customer types for each job and define the transitions to the next stage in the form of meaningful key figures. Based on the sketch, companies can define compact guides for content, measures, and messages so that they fit the customer's needs exactly.[26]

Operationally, customer experience mapping is essentially about structuring customer insights in a meaningful way. The focus is on how customers feel at each individual touchpoint to a company's sales funnel and its offering, what they think and do, and what needs they exhibit at these touchpoints. The goal is to make each of these touchpoints feel like part of a cohesive, holistic process. From the customer's point of view, the customer journey is a journey that providers need to prepare in detail, from first contact to after-sales. In this way, they create the greatest possible added value for their customers.[27]

Characteristic of Customer-led Growth is that it rejects traditional thinking in sales funnels. The sales funnel, according to the thesis of CLG inventors Georgiana Laudi and Claire Suellentrop, primarily represents the economic goals that a provider wants to achieve, and accordingly usually ends with the successful conclusion of the sale. What added value is generated for customers in the individual stages is not the focus of this view. However, this is precisely what CLG wants to move to the center of entrepreneurial thinking. Accordingly, customer experience mapping is about structuring the customer journey in a meaningful way with a view to customer insights, which not only includes all touchpoints, but also orients its structure to the customer's goals.[28]

In order to be able to reconstruct the customer journey, companies must divide it into phases with a view to the insights gained, at the end of each of which added

[26] Cf. Hermann, Torsten: Customer-led Growth – knowing what customers want.

[27] Cf. Broadbent, Andrew: Customer Experience Mapping – What it is and how to do it

[28] Cf. Rice, Mae: Welcome to the Era of Customer-led Growth.

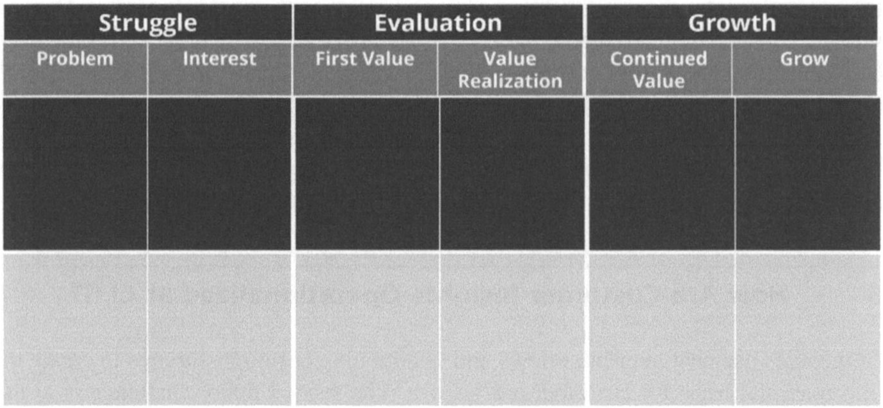

Fig. 1 Exemplary representation of a customer experience map. In the top two large columns, enter the key preferences and jobs of the customer type. You underline your findings in the column below with striking statements from the surveys

value is created for the customer (so-called Customer Success Milestones[29]). The JTBD perspective is helpful here, because a Customer Success Milestone is often a job that the customer has completed at a certain point in time.[30] Each defined phase is then assigned the touchpoints at which customers come into contact with the provider's brand and offering. This creates a structure that can be clearly visualized using a multi-column map (see Fig. 1). Companies then assign the most important findings and customer statements from the interviews and questionnaires to the appropriate phases and touchpoints in the individual fields.[31]

The great advantage of Customer Experience Mapping is that it allows a transparent view through the customer's glasses. All actions, thoughts, feelings, and preferences that customers experience during contact with a touchpoint at a specific point in the buyer's journey are systematically recorded and visualized in the form of a structured map. This makes it easier to analyze every action taken in contact with the customer from the customer's perspective and to optimize it on this basis. At the same time, the customer experience map makes it easier for companies to carry the findings from interviews and questionnaires into the company and to systematically implement customer-centric thinking in all departments, especially in marketing, sales, service, and product development. The customer experience map is intended to serve as a foundation for all strategic and operational decisions.[32]

In order to understand what outcomes customer companies want to achieve at what point in the Buyer's Journey, providers need to understand what metrics their

[29]Cf. Mouzakitis, Aggelos: What is Customer-led Growth?

[30]Cf. Rice, Mae: Welcome to the Era of Customer-led Growth.

[31]Cf. Broadbent, Andrew: Customer Experience Mapping – What it is and how to do it.

[32]Cf. Mouzakitis, Aggelos: What is Customer-led Growth?

customers use to measure when a job is considered done.[33] An essential part of customer experience mapping is therefore the development of metrics that match the defined customer success milestones. KPIs that supposedly underline the success of one's own measures (e.g., click and download numbers, registrations) are unsuitable for CLG because they do not allow any statement about the added value generated for customers. Instead, there is a need for metrics that illustrate how a customer perceived his customer experience at a specific point in his customer journey. These metrics do not represent the behavior in a phase, but describe the transition to the new phase (e.g., "test account created").[34]

In this context, companies can draw on various metrics that primarily rely on regular surveys. These include the Customer Satisfaction (CSAT) system, in which the individual dimensions of the customer experience (offering, processes, services, etc.) are reviewed as part of satisfaction surveys. The Customer Effort Score (EFS) can also be used for CLG. Here, customers are asked to rate the statement "The company made it easy for me to solve my problem" on a scale of 1–7. The Loyalty and Net Promoter Score (NPS) is more suitable for analyzing existing customers. Here, companies focus in surveys on the extent to which their customers would recommend them as a provider.[35]

7 Why Is Customer-Led Growth Worthwhile for B2B Companies?

Customer-led growth helps companies to consistently align all strategies, processes, and messages, as well as existing products and services, with the needs of their customers. From an operational perspective, this facilitates the day-to-day business of product development, services, marketing, and sales. For example, the customer experience map provides marketing with precise input on how measures and messages must be designed at each touchpoint in order to promote customer trust. Marketing teams receive precise information on which methods, arguments, and terms should be used to generate a positive emotional response from the customer. This not only impacts customer satisfaction and loyalty, but leads to better leads, greater sales opportunities, and more revenue.[36]

In addition, customer-led growth promotes a shared understanding of customers and customer segments—and thus the transformation to a customer-led organization.[37] Customer insights are systematically collected, structured, and visualized with the help of the customer experience map, and then made available to all areas of the company. This not only makes it easier to align measures with the customer

[33] Cf. Ulwick, Anthony: What Customers Want, p. 16ff.

[34] Cf. Rice, Mae: Welcome to the Era of Customer-led Growth.

[35] Cf. Villani, Isabella: Transform Customer Experience, p. 151ff.

[36] Cf. Mouzakitis, Aggelos: What is Customer-led Growth?

[37] Cf. Mouzakitis, Aggelos: What is Customer-led Growth?

journey across all departments. At the same time, it improves collaboration between the departments. At CLG, for example, marketing and sales are imperative to communicate more and better. By consistently focusing on the customer, CLG becomes a driver of marketing and sales alignment, which in turn has a positive effect on the customer experience.[38]

Another advantage of CLG is that it usually does not require a revolutionary reorganization of the company. What changes is primarily the focus. However, this change is what makes CLG so attractive to B2B companies, because it provides real differentiation from the competition.

Internal company ideas about customers and target groups often differ only rudimentarily within an industry, as most companies focus on their product or service. Customer-led growth, on the other hand, focuses on the company's real customers and surveys them in order to align products, services, service processes, and all marketing and sales activities with their needs. Organizations thus move away from a crude understanding of the target group, which offers no added value for real customers, and stand out from the crowd of providers with precisely tailored content offerings, services, and sales conversations.[39]

8 Customer-Led Growth Is a Culture Change

Whether it is developing a new product, improving an existing service, or evaluating a strategic partnership: A CLG organization is always focused on helping its (potential) customers achieve their goals and orients all its strategies and actions toward meeting those needs. CLG is therefore always a dynamic process. Companies committed to the approach must constantly evolve with their customers in mind, taking into account new insights and trends, and optimizing what already exists where necessary, in order to continue to offer customers a consistent, simple, and personalized customer experience.[40]

In customer-led growth, it is important that companies invest in their philosophy and culture. This involves a change process that is ideally carried top down into the organization. Instead of leaving marketing and/or sales alone with this task, executives should exemplify customer-centric thinking and support the operational forces in gaining customer insights and applying them as best they can.[41] It also makes sense for one or more people to be responsible for creating and implementing the CLG strategy and for collecting and updating customer insights.[42]

[38] Cf. Herrmann, Torsten: Customer-led Growth – knowing what customers want.

[39] Cf. Hermann, Torsten: Customer-led Growth – knowing what customers want.

[40] Cf. Villani, Isabella: Transform Customer Experience, p. 7.

[41] Cf. Hague, Nick; Hague, Paul: B2B Customer Experience: A practical guide to delivering exceptional CX, p. 103.

[42] Cf. Villani, Isabella: Transform Customer Experience, p. 147.

Customer-led growth is a cultural change that can apply to all areas and processes of an organization. At the same time, culture is the factor most likely to cause the transformation to a CLG company to fail. A good way to embed the CLG mindset (and systematically disseminate customer insights) is to use storytelling elements. Case stories or short stories that depict the customer's situation help to make the insights fixed in the customer experience map tangible and communicable to employees.[43]

Managers should not underestimate this point. Customer-led growth requires intensive cross-functional collaboration. For this to work, all areas involved in the CLG program need the same idea of customers and their jobs. At the same time, the customer-facing areas in particular need to be better linked. For example, suitable processes are needed for communication as well as workshops and cross-team events in which the CLG idea is strengthened and promoted. This is the prerequisite for a customer experience that offers minimal friction and maximum customer-added value from start to finish.[44]

References

Adamson, B. (2022). Sensemaking for sales. *Harvard Business Review, 01/02*, 122–129.

Allen, J., Reichheld, F. F., Hamilton, B., & Markey, R. M. (2005). *Closing the delivery gap*. https://www.bain.com/contentassets/41326e09188834cd1a0102fdd0810535d/bb_closing_delivery_gap.pdf

Bodine, K., & Manning, H. (2012). *Outside in – The Power of putting customers at the center of your business*.

Broadbent, A. (2016). *Customer experience mapping – What it is and how to do it*. https://www.startupgrind.com/blog/customer-experience-mapping-what-is-it-and-how-to-do-it/

Christensen, C. M. (2017). *Better than chance: "Jobs to be done" – The strategy for successful innovation*

Gazala, M. (2015). *Winning in the age of the customer*. https://www.forrester.com/report/Winning-In-The-Age-Of-The-Customer/RES119546

Hague, N., & Hague, P. (2018). *B2B Customer Experience: A practical guide to delivering exceptional CX*.

Hanan, Mack: Consultative selling. , 1999.

Hermann, T. (2022). *Customer-led growth – Knowing what customers want*. https://www.chainrelations.de/customer-led-growth-wissen-was-kunden-wollen/

Kergl, R., et al. (2021). *Marketing Automation Studie 2021*. https://www.sc-networks.de/blog/marketing-automation-studie/

McDonald, Malcolm: On marketing planning. , 2017

Meredith, B. (2016). *Customer experience – A key marketing element* (p. 50). NZ Business + Management.

Mivekannin, M. (2020). *AARRR – In 5 steps to becoming a growth hacker*. https://www.appvizer.de/magazin/marketing/online-marketing/aarrr

[43]Cf. Bodine, Kerry; Manning, Harley: Outside In – The Power of putting customers at the center of your business, p. 153.

[44]Cf. Hague, Nick; Hague, Paul: B2B Customer Experience: A practical guide to delivering exceptional CX, pp. 113ff.

Moesta, B., & Spiek, C. (with Fowlkes Jr., E.). (2014). *Jobs-to-be-done – The handbook.*
Mouzakitis, A. (2021). *What is customer-led growth?* https://www.growthsandwich.com/resources/what-is-customer-led-growth/
Revella, A. (2015). *Buyer personas.*
Rice, M. (2021). *Welcome to the era of customer-led growth.* https://builtin.com/marketing/customer-led-growth
Schäfer, M. (2014). *Content shock – Why content marketing is not a sustainable strategy.* https://businessesgrow.com/2014/01/06/content-shock/
Ulwick, A. (2005). *What customers want.*
Villani, I. (2019). *Transform customer experience.*
Webster, B. (1987). *The power of consultative selling.*

Torsten Herrmann is a Digital Marketing Consultant and Managing Director of the online marketing consultancy chain relations GmbH in Frankfurt am Main. For more than 25 years, he has been supporting B2B companies of all sizes in developing and optimizing their marketing and sales strategies. Chain relations is a digital marketing agency with a consulting focus, specialized in online lead generation and demand generation in B2B industries. The company's competencies include inbound marketing, account-based marketing, content marketing and marketing automation. The company's competencies include inbound marketing, account-based marketing, content marketing and marketing Automation. Strategies and implementation rely on a thorough understanding of customer journeys based on customer interviews and surveys. Clients are primarily from B2B industries such as high-tech, professional services, traditional industries, and software-as-a-service.

Part IV

Beyond Sales and Marketing Automation

Predictive Intelligence as a Success Factor in B2B Marketing

Thomas Geiger and Uwe Seebacher

Big Data and Artificial Intelligence (AI) have already dominated the professional world for several decades. What is new, however, is the fact that huge amounts of data can be stored more easily and, above all, more cheaply thanks to immense advances in the field of information technology. Thanks to cloud services, this storage capacity no longer even has to be physically provided within the company itself. In addition, the enormous computing power of modern computers makes it possible to collect, cleanse, and evaluate huge volumes of structured and unstructured data in a very short time (Lyytinen & Grover, 2017, p. 207208).

In an increasingly turbulent, digitized business environment, organizations are seeking to gain a strategic advantage through large-scale investments in information technology to respond more quickly and adequately to opportunities and changes in their market environment. With the emerging era of Big Data in particular, organizations are investing more and more resources in business intelligence, analytics, and communications technologies to anticipate changing customer needs, new technologies, and product innovations or activities of direct competitors (El Sawy & Fiss, 2017, p. 23).

1 From Business Intelligence to Predictive Intelligence

Business Intelligence (BI) basically deals with events in the past and their effects on the present. In doing so, BI attempts to quantitatively and qualitatively explain questions about what happened, but also the possible causes of events. The tools

T. Geiger
Graz, Austria

U. Seebacher (✉)
Institute of Management Technology (IMT), Ghaziabad/Dubai, India/UAE
e-mail: uwe@fynest.at; us@uweseebacher.org

U. Hannig, U. Seebacher (eds.), *Marketing and Sales Automation*, Management for Professionals, https://doi.org/10.1007/978-3-031-20040-3_24

	STATISTICS	DATA MINING
DATA	Manageable data volumes from a case number of 30	Big Data
TRANSFERABILITY	Conclusions are drawn based on a sample of the population	- Basic population often does not exist - Sample is not defined - Data sets change constantly
EVALUATION	Also feasible with paper and pencil	Restricted to computers only
TIME SPAN DATA COLLECTION - RESULTS	Evaluations often take many years, such as in the case of clinical studies	Results must be available promptly to the survey such as in the case of criminology
PREREQUISITES	Prerequisites must be checked very precisely for procedures used	- Data mining methods are no longer theoretically justifiable - Instead, data mining methods are used in parallel - based on this, the best of the different methods is selected in each case
TARGET	Testing hypotheses	Generating hypotheses

Fig. 1 Distinction between classical statistical methodology and data mining (Source: Grünwald, 2019)

used for this purpose include, for example, reporting using KPIs, automated monitoring, dashboards or OLAP (Online Analytical Processing).

Business analytics (BA) extends classic BI to include a view into the future. BA provides answers to questions about the causes, effects, interactions, or consequences of events. BA relies primarily on statistical analyses of company data. Predictive Intelligence (PI) (Seebacher, 2021a) can be considered the royal class of applied AI applying multi-segment as well as multi-level combinations of AI-systems and techniques enabling dynamic and most precise predictions for all possible dimensions. University-based start-up Predictores.ai demonstrates the power and enormous gain in knowledge in the context of Predictive Intelligence. It all starts where OLAP or reporting stop. Data models are used to make predictions about scenarios that may occur in the future. There is a close connection with data mining (Mauerer, 2017).

Classic data mining methods include regression analysis, classification (clustering), neural networks and association analysis to identify patterns in data sets. In addition, predictive intelligence also uses

- Statistical calculations
- Machine learning
- Methods of Operations-Research
- Elements of game theory and
- Simulation method

In addition to these mathematical and statistical approaches, linguistics and text mining for the analysis of non-structured data in blogs, tweets, etc., are increasingly finding their way into this field.

The relevance of data mining results from the fact that evaluations on paper are simply no longer possible due to the occurrence of Big Data. Big data describes both the

- Accumulation of millions of records (volume)
- The increasing elevation speed (velocity) as well as the
- The diversity of data structures, such as videos, images, text, etc. (Variety)

The goal of data mining is to generate and generalize previously unknown, useful information from the available data material. Figure 1 shows the demarcation to general statistics deliver (Grünwald, 2019).

In summary, business analytics describes the scientific process within which accruing data is transformed into insights in order to make better strategic business decisions. BA is applied to the data- or fact-based discussion of solutions, with the goal of making the best possible decision for the business situations at hand (Camm et al., 2019).

Although predictive analytics is the most commonly used term when it comes to using external as well as internal data for business management and strategy development, it is on an equal footing with descriptive analytics and prescriptive analytics. Descriptive analytics serves as the first step in gaining new insights into data. The goal is to understand relationships between products and customers or macroeconomic developments and sales figures. The insights are to be used to make better decisions for the future. Although these analyses reveal correlations, they say nothing about cause-and-effect relationships.

Building on the acquired knowledge, predictive analytics enables the estimation of the probability of an event occurring. Statistical models and algorithms are used to identify relationships in various data sets. Prescriptive analytics additionally provides explanations as to why a future event will occur and makes recommendations as to how to respond. Decisions are thus to be evaluated before they have even been made (Martin, 2015).

Business analytics can be divided into the following development stages or maturity levels:

1. Business Intelligence or Market Intelligence is the original form, where data is used non-interactively and only singularly dimensional. Only external market data and information are used. This means that information is drawn from one or more data sources on a situational and occasion-related basis and then qualitatively evaluated either by an expert or also by a team, discussed and evaluated in relation to a business decision to be made.
2. Descriptive Intelligence, to which form, or level Descriptive Analytics also belongs, integrates internal company information into the analysis. However, the process still does not take place interactively, which means that data is drawn once and cannot be dynamically updated, filtered, and evaluated multidimensionally.
3. Predictive Intelligence is the highest level of maturity – as also can be seen in the Intelligence Maturity Model (Seebacher 2021a, p. 122ff), where both internal and external data and information, interactively and multidimensionally drawn from many different data sources, are then linked, and processed by defined specific algorithms, thus enabling either semi- or fully integrated short-, medium-, and also long-term business planning, action, and optimization.

The crucial point is that these three rough maturity levels must be passed through in order to be able to design, structure and implement an accepted and functioning predictive intelligence tool. This is not an IT project, as is often mistakenly assumed, but rather data science and management projects. The IT basis is a subsidiary and merely supporting subject area in this context. Successful predictive intelligence initiatives are always started analogously by means of Excel pivot tables and only migrated step by step to a more performant database and also analytics technology as the complexity of the algorithms and also the amount of data increases.

Everyone is talking about data-driven decision-making and data-driven management (Seebacher 2021c). However, the value-creating use of information in everyday business is still in its infancy. The focus is primarily on internal figures, such as incoming orders, sales, and profitability, which are presented on a quarterly or monthly basis. The vast amounts of external information, some of which is freely available, are still neglected.

However, blind faith in internal financial data and key figures carries the risk of tunnel vision. Experience shows that key performance indices (KPIs), such as order intake or EBIT, are assessed on the basis of their development compared to the previous period. But how is performance validated? An increase in sales of 3% sounds positive in principle, but if this is put into context with the development of the relevant market or industry, only then does one get an overview of the actual performance of one's own company. Assuming that the largest competitors consistently achieve a plus of 5% in terms of their order intake, the result implies a clear underperformance. The company is performing worse than the market and its market share is shrinking, but this only becomes clear in the context of a relational analysis (Lyseggen, 2019, pp. 52–57).

2 What Data Is Useful at All?

In addition to the fundamental value of external data in terms of determining the position of companies, it plays an equally important role when it comes to formulating an appropriate competitive strategy. An essential part of strategy formulation is to relate a company to its environment. According to Porter, competition is composed of the five drivers of market entry, threat from substitute products, bargaining power of suppliers, and rivalry among existing competitors (Porter, 2013, p. 37–39).

In order to get a realistic overview of one's own position and to build the foundation for any form of business analytics, a broad spectrum of diverse data from various information entities, such as the competition or product types, must be acquired and related. An exemplary process for this is demonstrated in the business case that follows later. According to Lyseggen, the three defining cornerstones of modern business analytics are:

1. The use of external data
2. The availability of real-time information and
3. Direct comparison with the competition (benchmarking)

Only those who draw on data from the corporate environment, i.e., from outside, can clearly clarify the following questions:

- Are the internal assumptions supported by the findings that emerge from external data?
- Do managers know about current market developments?
- Do existing strategies make sense at all in view of prevailing developments?

The information needed to answer these questions is often freely available. Institutions such as the World Bank or the International Monetary Fund offer vast amounts of data on macroeconomic developments for download. Financial data from corporations can be accessed via their legally required publications, while specialized market research companies can be used for more disaggregated data for a fee.

Furthermore, news portals, competitors' websites, social media activities, spending on online advertising, and job offers must not be underestimated under any circumstances in terms of the information they provide about the competition or the market (Lyseggen, 2019, pp. 41, 85–90, 136–137). The art is to match collected information and discover patterns. However, to enable data mining, it is first and foremost necessary to store data successfully within the company's internal IT infrastructure.

Our predictive intelligence projects and experiences have shown that, especially when purchasing special databases but also complete and comprehensive market studies, unfortunately more and more often the well-known and renowned, very expensive providers deliver only very little reliable data and evaluations. However, this can only be recognized if one already has internal comparative or reference data on the basis of which external evaluations can be validated and verified. Caution is therefore advisable if you want to close your own data gaps by purchasing data for which you often have to pay five- to six-figure sums.

With regard to the numerous market reports offered on the market, it can be assumed that around 60–75% are useless and not reliable. The decisive success factor here is not to invest in external services for figures, data, studies, and reports, but rather in building up expertise within the company. In the long term, this leads to an increasingly complete data picture by means of data science, which enables increasingly precise extrapolations in terms of operational and strategic planning not only for the company, but also for its business units and country organizations.

3 From Transaction Processing to Decision Support Systems

Today's status of data and information as the most valuable asset, even before the actual personnel, naturally also requires an infrastructure that is as professional as possible. Only in this way can data be stored, retrieved, processed, and subsequently visualized without losing quality and significance. So-called transaction processing systems (TPS) generate data through interactions with customers (for example,

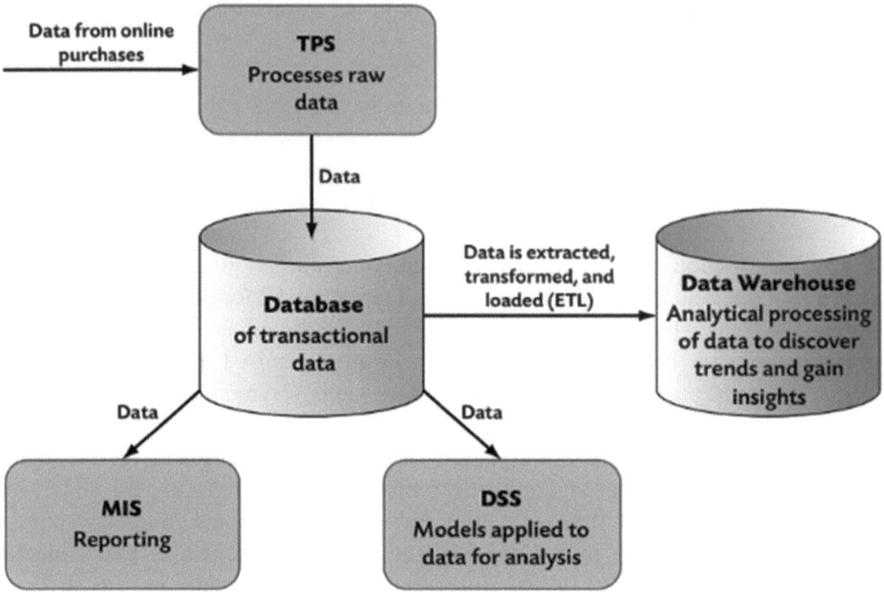

Fig. 2 Information systems and their interactions (Source: Turban & Volonino, 2011, p. 31)

online orders or data from potential customers who download a white paper from the company website) and store it in a database. In this form, the stored data is still very confusing and must first be transferred to a standard format before it is stored in the data warehouse for further processing.

This data is then loaded into the Management Information System (MIS) and used for classic reports for management. In addition to the MIS, there is also the option of loading data into decision support systems (DSS) using statistical models and procedures in order to obtain direct recommendations for action (Turban & Volonino, 2011, p. 31f.). Figure 2 schematically depicts the interaction of the various IT-supported information systems within a company.

Especially in the business-to-business (B2B) sector, the profits of companies correlate very strongly with external macroeconomic factors. These include fluctuating prices for raw materials required in the production process, energy, tendering activities or construction projects in target markets and the general economic situation in relevant markets (Lyseggen, 2019, p. 129130). Of course, the personal assessments of experienced employees from sales or business development are a valuable additional source for future planning. However, it would be risky to blindly rely on this information.

Too many renowned companies have shown over the past few years where insisting on past success formulas and intuition can lead to. Prime examples in this context include Nokia, Blackberry, Polaroid.

BA and PI technologies, such as enterprise-wide integrated databases, visualizations, outlier handling and data mining, expand the ability of companies to make the best use of data and the information generated from it. The danger of an unmanageable flood of data due to Big Data is reduced to a minimum, while decision-makers always have their finger on the pulse in terms of their knowledge of their own position in the market and the competition.

Data is automatically processed through the developments of recent years and specially tuned algorithms, allowing real-time monitoring or the sending of information or recommendations for action to relevant people within the organization. This increase in agility for business management is a valuable competitive advantage in modern business (El Sawy & Fiss, 2017, p. 9).

4 Predictive Intelligence for Corporate Planning: The Supreme Discipline of B2B Marketing

For a long time, the classic responsibilities of B2B marketing (Seebacher, 2021b) were limited to the production of product brochures, advertising materials and the organization and implementation of events such as trade shows or conferences. In many large, traditional B2B companies, this is still the case today. This is due to outdated ways of thinking, rigid, non-transparent structures and the resulting complex processes and workflows, but also marketers who are not yet aware of the new opportunities and possibilities offered by Marketing 4.0.

However, the starting position for marketing has changed drastically in the twenty-first century. Whereas the profitability of advertising campaigns was difficult to assess before the advent of digitization, today every single action can be analyzed down to the last detail. Page impressions, click rates, social media activities, etc., provide real-time information on whether a measure was worthwhile (Lyseggen, 2019, p. 149–151).

External market data can be obtained from market research institutions at any time and linked to internal data from ERP, CRM, CPQ, PLM, and other IT systems. Thus, in addition to purely quantitative factors, the field of qualitative, behavioral aspects, which is becoming increasingly important under the aspect of user experience (UX) or customer experience (CX), can be observed, evaluated, and interpreted numerically.

To illustrate an exemplary process for the effective and efficient use of data, a fictitious medium-sized company will be used. It is a globally active company in the field of mechanical and plant engineering. The approach used to date to define target markets and strategies is based on the order intake of the previous year and the individual assessments of the business development managers and sales managers. Based on the defined key industries, marketing activities are determined, such as trade shows or media selected (Kamps & Schetter, 2018, p. 11–15), and performance determined.

However, sales figures have been stagnating for some time and have recently even declined slightly. The sales management emphasizes that these developments are due to the tense situation in global economic policy and that the competition would also be affected. However, figures confirming this development are not available. The Board of Management therefore decides to set up a central business intelligence unit to keep a closer eye on the business environment.

The aim is to make relevant information on market developments available to responsible managers and employees throughout the company at all times in order to identify changes in the market at an early stage in the future and to be able to act proactively instead of just reacting. In addition, this central information hub is expected to reduce marketing costs by targeting individual activities more effectively.

Against this background, three different use cases are used to illustrate how predictive intelligence can make a sustainable contribution not only to securing a company, but rather to effective, natural corporate growth and thus success:

1. Short-term optimization of sales or net working capital
2. Medium-term market expansion (Lorette, n.d.)
3. Medium- to long-term operational and strategic corporate development

Marketing, with its interface character to external as well as internal stakeholders, represents a huge portfolio of data. Therefore, it is only logical to locate the analysis of this data in the same department, as long as this is possible with regard to the available capacities.

In the first step, it is necessary to map one's own company in detail with regard to all available information as well as relevant external data and their potential sources. One variant for doing this is the entity relationship model (Jung, 2019), in which the individual data objects (e.g., customers, sales managers, products) and their relationships to one another are represented graphically.

Each data object is assigned several attributes, in the sense of properties or column labels in a relational table, and a clearly defined primary key is defined (Ferstl & Sinz, 2006, p. 140ff.). We refer to a primary key as a value that defines a record, such as the customer number. The graphical representation is intended to provide an overview of a company's information landscape and to facilitate the transfer to a relational database without creating redundancies within the database.

Now that the basic overview has been created and the data model has been created, the real work of creating added value for the company with data through a professional approach must begin.

At the outset, it is essential to understand the key drivers of one's own business or within the industry and to map their impact. In this case, it is advisable to obtain input from leading forces within the organization, as they have a broad expertise as well as some experience in the industry. Another pragmatic method is the regression analysis of potential influencing factors with internal sales developments (Lyseggen, 2019, p. 132–137).

Once the external factors that significantly influence the company have been determined, they can be visualized in the form of dashboards using modern BI or OLAP software, such as Microsoft Power BI or Tableau. The aforementioned software solutions are cloud-based, which means that access can be granted quite simply via the e-mail addresses of the relevant persons. Alternatively, if the cloud is considered too insecure, a dedicated server within the company can be used to manage all data. There are hardly any limits to the way of visualization here, both in terms of the individual parameters and interactivity.

The roll-out process within the company is particularly important in this context. Regardless of the strategic importance of such a solution, it is important to proceed thoughtfully in terms of acceptance and understanding. Otherwise, the project is doomed to failure from the outset. It makes sense to inform the relevant internal customers at an early stage about the background and additional benefits of the planned PI solution. This can be done, for example, as part of a regular newsletter. This should be followed by targeted training sessions with end users.

The development of a so-called PI key user network, which provides a trained PI contact person at each individual site so that rudimentary user support can be provided quickly and easily on site, has also proved helpful. Valuable feedback can be obtained here, which promotes further development as well as access to the new system. The communication of the planned innovations in the PI area must be supported above all by the top management in order to ensure successful change management (From, 2003).

4.1 Use Case 1: Short-Term Optimization of Sales or Net Working Capital

The decisive factor in day-to-day business is to always be on target. This means that you must be able to react to deviations—especially negative ones—at any time and immediately and initiate or implement countermeasures. Until now, hectic actionism was the order of the day in most cases. Using predictive intelligence, one or more countermeasures can now be derived at any time and for any organizational unit—be it a site, an application or even just a single product—based on numbers in the following steps:

1. The rolling forecast generated on an ongoing basis from CRM can be used to identify sales deviations in both positive and negative areas at an early stage. On this basis, corresponding divergences from the budget can be precisely defined for organizational units. Let us assume an example in which significant downward sales deviations are indicated for two locations.
2. For these two locations, the CRM extracts the relevant products as well as their average sales times. If, for example, this analysis shows significant deviations during the Q2 review, there are still 6 months left in the same fiscal or budget year. Thus, in the sequence, those products must be identified whose lead times are between 4 and 6 months, then those with 2–4 months and correspondingly shorter.
3. Based on these defined products, the aggregated and extrapolated data is now evaluated in the Marketing Intelligence Cube with regard to market and sales potential, regions, industries and applications. This analysis provides a ranking of relevant markets or segments.

4. In the next step, these are matched in Event and Media Intelligence (EMI) with the strongest and fastest converting marketing and communication channels. This results in a list of events and media to be used as part of the Go-To-Segment (GTS) strategy for short-term revenue optimization. Taking into account the information and data from the CX and UX areas, the corresponding customer journeys or nurturing campaigns are defined together with the campaign managers and the responsible sales or product managers. For this purpose, the existing content database and the assets it contains for the respective product—such as LinkedIn post, one-pager, white paper, technical article, video snap, video trailer, video clips, among others—are used to set up the most effective optimization campaign possible.
5. If it is a product or application that can also be placed in the area of large customers or key accounts, the previously extracted information is matched with the account-based marketing (ABM) manager, which can itself import corresponding optimization campaigns based on the defined campaigns (see step 4) into the ABM and then play them out via the relevant, automatically generated and highest-performing touchpoints.

PI campaigns of this type deliver the first qualified leads after just 2–4 days and—depending on the product type and Lead-2-Sales (L2S) times—also concrete sales in the sense of Order Intake (OI) after a short time. The result of another campaign was a request from a board member to present the product within the company. With properly set up predictive intelligence, much can be achieved at a highly attractive cost-per-lead or cost-per-sales factor that is significantly below conventional benchmarks.

This use case can also be used for upcoming events. Such campaigns are also used for short- to medium-term optimization of net working capital (NWC) (Controlling Portal, 2019). Reference campaigns in the food industry have brought in the corresponding results within 4–6 weeks after the start of the campaign. For example, the focus campaigns developed using PI reduced six-figure inventories and thus significantly optimized the NWC of two sites within a short period of time.

In the specific case of a medium-sized mechanical engineering company, essential components for certain products are purchased from external suppliers. However, in order to be competitive in terms of the end product and its selling price, these components must be ordered and purchased in larger quantities. As a result, a larger number of machines are ultimately manufactured than customers currently order. These machines are thus "on stock" as a dead chapter and have a negative impact on net working capital. Against this background, the following steps are taken in PI (see also Fig. 3) to counteract this situation:

1. In the Market Intelligence Cube (MIC) area, the current market potential, the competitive situation, the local purchasing and investment power and other socio-economic and also geopolitical factors are extracted and aggregated for the relevant machine. In the specific case, three countries (Greece, Italy, and Spain) were defined as regions that appear most attractive in the short term.

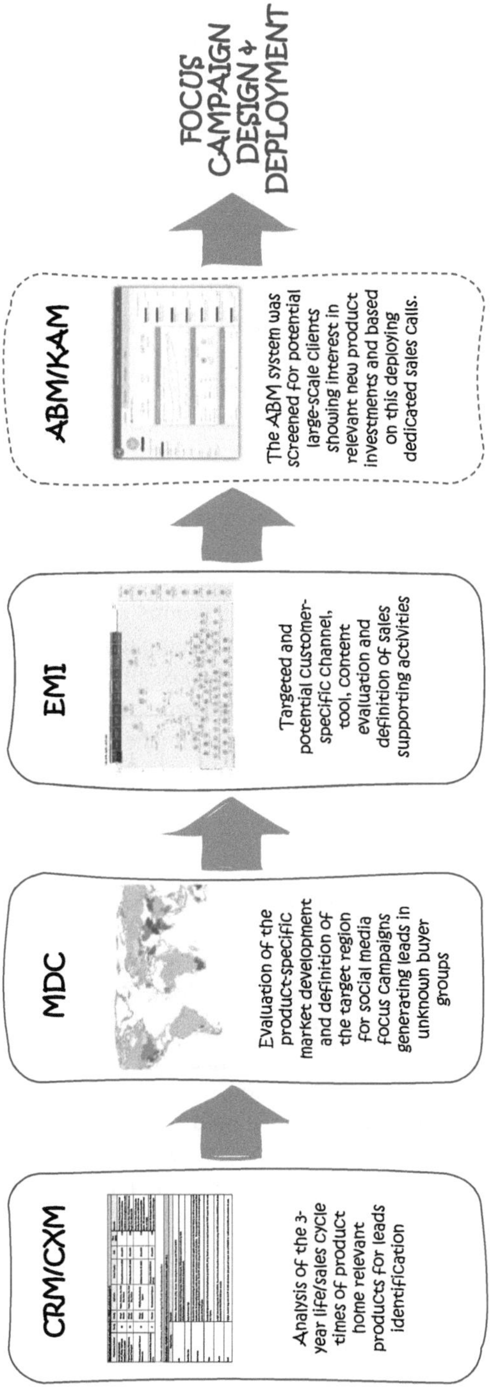

Fig. 3 PI-based short-term revenue optimization (Source: Own representation)

2. In parallel, the CAPEX and OPEX in the countries were determined on the basis of the value chains that always underlie the PI. This is because it would be insufficient to look at the absolute market volumes of an industry or a specific process in each case for such an optimization measure, since a pump, for example, represents only a small subsection of a production process in the food industry. If the total market were taken as the market potential in this case, this would lead to an incorrect picture. However, if one takes only that share of the investment that falls to a specific pump in a process, a realistic, valid market volume (the "relevant" market) can be shown. This evaluation makes the respective percentage of the identified total market clear, since production processes can be different in different countries, which in turn affects the relevant market volume for the product in each case. Based on this, the relevant market volume for the product in stock can be extracted in addition to the absolute market potentials in the three target countries.
3. Based on these relevant market volumes, the previously compiled country list is then verified once again. In this specific case, Italy and Greece were ultimately the most attractive target regions.
4. The EMI was used to identify the relevant media and events, although neither a media partner nor an event was defined as useful and relevant in the underlying case study due to the urgency. The channel judged to be most effective was LinkedIn. With the help of EMI, the relevant touchpoints and the corresponding content assets were defined for the target groups selected with the responsible sales staff and transferred into two concrete campaigns.
5. A comparison with the ABM brought two possible key accounts into play for which the "on stock" products could be relevant.
6. In the final step, the focus campaigns were launched and also played out via the ABM. After 6 weeks, the products were sold, and the goal of the PI measure was thus achieved.

4.2 Use Case 2: Medium-Term Market Development

Another use case for predictive intelligence is aimed at a no less essential operational business topic, namely PI-based business development or the opening up of new markets. The specific use case relates to an internationally active company in the field of machinery and plant engineering with around 30,000 employees and around 5 billion in sales per year. Under discussion was the market entry into the Middle East. Since the company had already generated business without a local presence, the management was faced with the question of whether its own location in Dubai would pay off against the background of the relevant market volumes extracted from the MIC and, if so, in what timeframe or with what ROI. The following steps were chosen:

1. The basic analysis aggregated those countries in the region that could be covered with a location in Dubai. Ten specific countries were defined from the MIC.

2. However, since the company can only serve parts of the value chains underlying the industries in the four core industries with its own products, the absolute current and future market potentials had to be disaggregated in order to be able to calculate the relevant market volumes.
3. This data was stored in the Automated Business Planner (ABP) and the business development managers were required to store realistic product sales figures for each individual product in each of the ten defined target countries on the basis of the current sales achieved there in the countries, but also on the basis of empirical values relating to market share developments from previous market entries. Based on this, the ABP generated a business plan that was backed up with gross margins from CRM as well as price sensitivities. On the part of Marketing, the defined costs for personnel, premises, and other items were also stored in order to be able to finalize the 10-year business plan with the three scenarios Worst Case, Neutral Case and Best Case.
4. Using EMI, relevant events and media partners and their costs were integrated into the business plan in terms of time.
5. From the ABM, relevant key customers were filtered who had viewed, opened, downloaded, or used content assets of the defined key products for market entry in the last 6 months. Using the PI, further sales potential was determined on the basis of the ABM data. In this specific case, the business plan was only marginally changed by this, as the extracted purchase probabilities of the key customers showed too low a value for the defined period.

Based on these PI activities, the market entry business plan (see Fig. 4) was presented to the management and immediately confirmed by them. Since then, the PI-based business plan has been the basis for the semi-annual reviews and enables immediate identification of deviations so that proactive countermeasures can be taken.

4.3 Use Case 3: Medium- to Long-Term Operational and Strategic Corporate Development

In the long term, predictive intelligence can also make a significant contribution to sustainable and successful corporate development since PI can be used to evaluate and view everything multidimensionally on the basis of figures and data in time series. Against this background, PI has become the core of operational as well as strategic corporate management within various business units of a multinational company based in Europe.

On the basis of a clearly defined annual process (see Fig. 5), the entire planning and monitoring activities are continuously recorded using PI. For example, coordinated templates are sent to the Business Development, Research and Development, and Product Management teams in the third quarter. These templates are used to request relevant information on developments and changes from the various

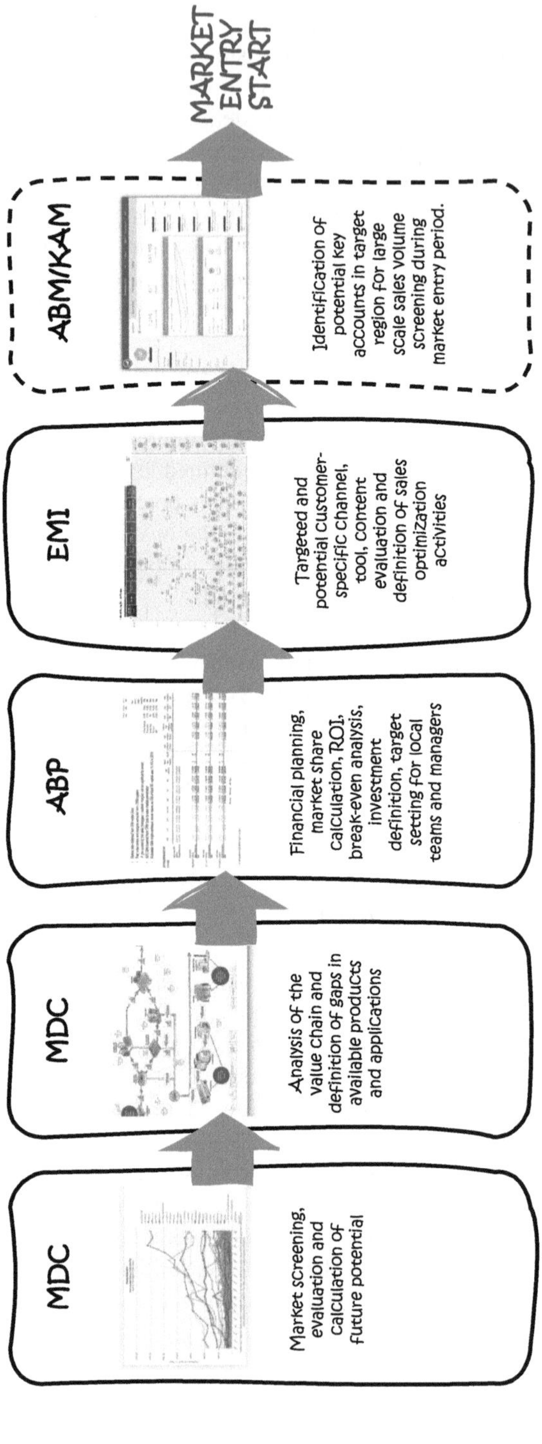

Fig. 4 PI-based medium-term market development (Source: Own representation)

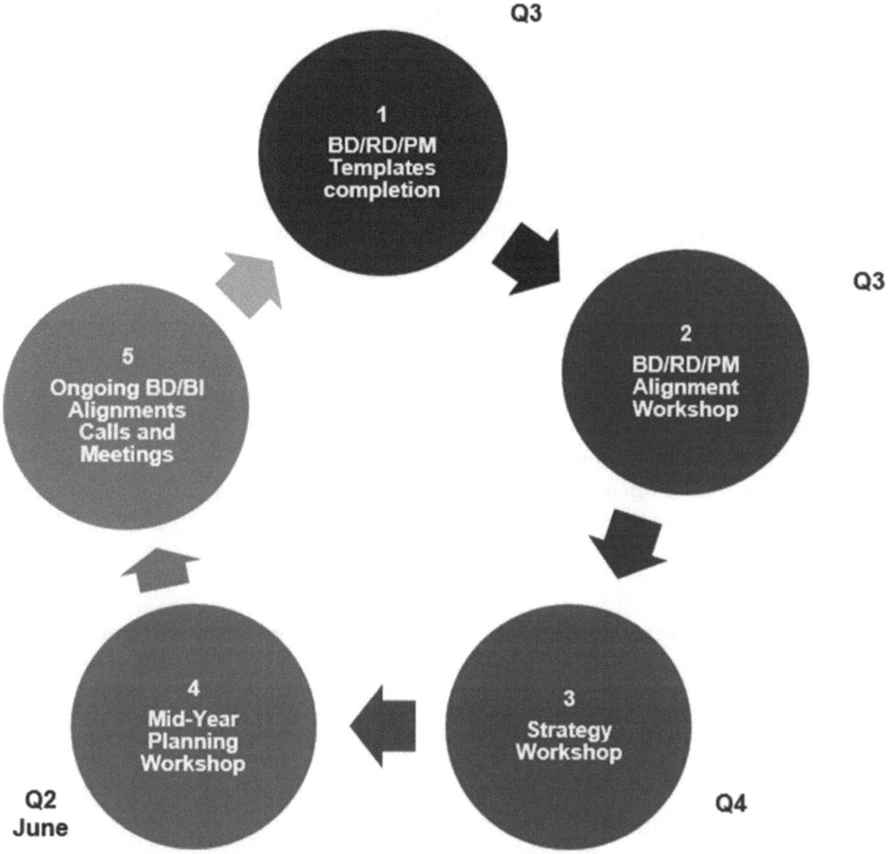

Fig. 5 PI-based management process for corporate control (Source: Own representation)

stakeholder groups in a standardized form. This data is evaluated and collated by the PI team. The result is analyzed and validated using PI.

The PI team prepares the analyses and chairs the coordination workshop with the relevant internal stakeholders that takes place in the third quarter in order to make joint strategic decisions on products, applications, and individual regions. For this workshop, too, both the agenda and the form of preparation and decision-making are defined as part of the PI process. This creates transparency and clarity and ensures high process efficiency.

The jointly made decisions regarding products, industries, applications, and regions are then incorporated by the PI team into a strategy document that includes a multidimensional, number-based strategy plan. The budget, which is calculated top-down and also bottom-up, takes into account margins, products, and realistic market share developments in terms of validity and reliability.

The half-yearly meeting is then held in May of each year. In this workshop, positive and negative divergences are identified for each strategic segment—similar to the previously described use case 1. Again, on the basis of previously defined templates, the PI team works out the divergence analysis in collaboration with Controlling and relates it to corresponding market developments. Based on this analysis, the PI team designs possible measures for each negative divergence before the workshop and adapts the strategic plan defined in Q3. The background to this is that, at their meeting at the end of June, the management would like to be presented with a detailed quantitative and qualitative measure for each negative deviation on the basis of the half-year figures. Experience has shown that in most cases, the optimization measures derived were confirmed by management and then implemented.

Predictive Intelligence can be a turbo for a sustainable and solid company development and management. With PI, nothing is left to chance and every single discussion in the company can be substantiated and based on numbers. However, PI must grow slowly in order to create sustainable added value for all stakeholders through acceptance and transparency.

Experience has shown that the thirst for facts and figures in companies is enormous and internal customers very quickly begin to actively work with the information provided.

In order to successfully establish predictive intelligence in companies, the following factors are crucial:

- Right from the start, the data model must be coordinated and discussed with Sales, especially with regard to the value chains and the relevant markets derived from them. Otherwise, the generated figures on markets will always be called into question.
- The processes and templates must initially be discussed with all the designated stakeholders in the companies, debated, possibly adapted, and then finally confirmed. This is crucial for the quality and validity of the content generated with them.
- From the very beginning, a PI capacity-building measure must be set up in order to be able to inform and train internal customers and users in a timely manner. If reports and analyses are still created manually by the PI team at the beginning because the PI does not yet run interactively and dynamically, this does not pose a problem, but is a good opportunity to enter into dialog directly with the internal customers and to obtain unfiltered feedback in this way.
- In terms of information technology implementation, one can ideally start with conventional tools, such as MS Excel, and only subsequently migrate to higher-quality database and analysis systems. In this way, PI grows consistently in terms of both content and technology. On the other hand, you can start without a separate budget, show initial successes in the form

(continued)

of analyses and reports after a short time, and let PI grow step by step based on acceptance and demand.
In the cases presented, a cloud-based solution was used in a first step in each case, which provides data on macroeconomic indicators and developments, trading activities and relevant market volumes. In addition, internal figures from the customer relationship management system (CRM) were included to contrast internal external developments.

Clearly defined functionalities will be activated for users, enabling them to generate relevant information on their own with the help of "slicers" and then save it locally in various formats for further use and reuse. In a next step, key figures of the direct competition will also be included in the system and the possibility of a programming interface to the externally drawn data will be discussed in order to enable a live connection and to react even faster to changes. In addition to this holistic view of the market, data on events such as trade fairs and congresses, as well as recorded media, will be collected and evaluated using the same tools in order to obtain the best price/performance ratio for future activities. This also achieves the goal of the desired cost savings and reduces the price per lead.

With PI, we can confidently leave behind the times of supposedly omniscient salespeople who are far superior to marketers. The marketing return on investment (MROI) in the sense of the marketing resource management (MRM) approach (Seebacher & Güpner, 2021) can be significantly optimized and continuously evaluated by means of EMI. Through the MIC, short-, medium-, and long-term corporate policy decisions can be prepared, and measures can be quantified objectively, reliably, and validly.

The topic is not new, but digitalization and the new technological possibilities—from crawlers to social bread crumping to artificial intelligence—have given it new perspectives that innovative and prudent companies will not allow to go unused. The early bird catches the worm and to be able to implement PI in your own company, you do not need an external agency, a consultant or an IT company.

References

Controlling Portal. (2019, January 05). Retrieved from Controllingportal: https://www.controllingportal.de/Fachinfo/Grundlagen/Kennzahlen/Net-Working-Capital.html

Camm, J. D., Cochran, J. J., Fry, M. J., Ohlmann, J. W., & Anderson, D. R. (2019). *Business analytics*.

El Sawy, O. A., & Fiss, P. C. (2017). The role of business intelligence and communication technologies in organizational agility. A configurational approach. *Journal of the Association for Information Systems, 9*, 648–686.

Ferstl, O., & Sinz, E. (2006). *Fundamentals of information systems*.

From, I. (2003). *Overcoming speechlessness*. Retrieved March 07, 2003, from https://www.computerwoche.de/a/die-sprachlosigkeit-ueberwinden
Grünwald, R. (2019). *Data mining methods. An understandable overview of the most important methods*. Retrieved January 21, 2019, from https://novustat.com/statistik-blog/data-mining-methoden-ueberblick.html
Jung, R. (2019, February 02). Retrieved from Encyclopedia of Information Systems Online Encyclopedia: http://www.enzyklopaedie-der-wirtschaftsinformatik.de/lexikon/daten-wissen/Datenmanagement/Daten-/Entity-Relationship-Model%2D%2D/index.html
Kamps, I., & Schetter, D. 2018. *Performance marketing*.
Lorette, K. (n.d.). *Business development strategies in accessing new markets*. https://smallbusiness.chron.com/business-development-strategies-accessing-new-markets-1410.html.
Lyseggen, J. (2019). *Outside insight. How to recognize your business of tomorrow in the data jungle*.
Lyytinen, K., & Grover, V. (2017). Management misinformation systems. A time to revisit? *Journal of the Association for Information Systems, 9*, 206–230.
Martin, W. (2015). *What you need to know about predictive analytics*. Retrieved May 27, 2015, from https://www.computerwoche.de/a/praktische-anwendung-von-predictive-analytics
Mauerer, J. (2017). *What's what in predictive analytics*. Retrieved December 11, 2017, from https://www.computerwoche.de/a/was-ist-was-bei-predictive-analytics
Porter, M. E. (2013). *Competitive strategy methods for analyzing industries and competitors*.
Seebacher, U. (2021a). *Predictive intelligence for data-driven management*. Springer.
Seebacher, U. (2021b). *B2B marketing: A guidebook for the classroom to the boardroom*. Springer.
Seebacher, U. (2021c). *Data-driven Management: A primer for modern corporate decision making*. APQS.
Seebacher, U., & Güpner, A. (2021). *Marketing Resource Management. How marketers storm to the top of companies!* APQS.
Turban, E., & Volonino, L. (2011). *Information technology for management. Improving strategic and operational performance*.

Thomas Geiger works as a Market Data Analyst in an international technology group. In addition to his activities in the B2B area, he was able to acquire valuable knowledge in the area of Management Information Systems as well as Data Mining within the scope of his Joint Degree Masters at the Chungbuk National University in Cheongju/South Korea.

Uwe Seebacher is a method and structural scientist. He holds a doctorate in economics and business administration and is a Professor for Predictive Intelligence at the University of Applied Sciences Munich, Professor for Marketing and Communications at the University of Applied Sciences for Marketing and Communication at Vienna and Professor for Data Science, Predictive Intelligence, Industrial (B2B) Marketing, Sales and Distribution Management at the Institute of Management Technology (IMT) in Ghaziabad and Dubai. He has more than 30 years of experience as a business angel and investor, consultant, leader but also entrepreneur in the media, manufacturing, and service industries. He is a popular key note speaker and panelist.

He has authored more than 50 books in many leading publishing houses, such as "Reengineering Corporate Communications" (Springer Cham), "Assets-as-Service" (Springer Gabler 2021), "Data-driven Management" (Springer Gabler 2021), "Predictive Intelligence for Managers" (Springer 2021), "B2B Marketing Guidebook" (Springer 2021), "Marketing Resource Management" (AQPS 2021), "Leadership Development" (Linde 2006) or "Template-based Management (Springer 2020) or "European Human Resource Management" (HBM 2009).

For his innovative concepts and initiatives, e.g., with Allianz, the European Union, the Austrian Federal Economic Chamber, Bayer Leverkusen, and BASF, he received various awards, such as the Diskobolos Innovation Award of the European Chamber of Commerce and the 2016 Export Award of the Austrian Federal Economic Chamber. For more information, visit www.uweseebacher.org.

Artificial Intelligence: The Revolution in Marketing

Claudia Bünte

1 AI Has Come to Stay

AI has arrived in the economy: Among the ten largest companies based on market capitalization in 2021, there are only three companies that do not live primarily from software, data, and consumer insights (pwc, 2021, S. 22). All the others—Apple, Amazon, Facebook, Alphabet, Microsoft, Tencent, and Alibaba—have a business model based on systematically collecting customer data and analyzing it using AI. That is why it is commonly said that data is "the oil of the 21st century."

AI is becoming an important economic factor at an unprecedented speed: The McKinsey Global Institute (MGI) calculates a global average increase in gross domestic product (GDP) of 1.2 percentage points per year by 2030 due to AI alone—an impressive impact of a single technology on GDP. At the time, the steam engine added 0.3 percentage points, industrial robots 0.4, and information and communication technologies 0.6 percentage points (McKinsey & Company, 2018; Bughin et al., 2018, S. 23.

Marketing managers also share the obvious importance of AI for the economy. 91% of the marketing managers surveyed in 2021 within the study "AI—the future of marketing" in D-A-CH say that AI is already important for marketing today—an increase of around 12 percentage points compared to 2019 (Fig. 1).

AI is also here to stay in marketing. Artificial intelligence enables companies to analyze customer data faster and better than a human can. A competitive advantage in marketing. Because those who better understand the wishes of their customers can align products and services more precisely to these very wishes, and are thus more likely to be chosen, used for the purchase. More customers become familiar with the brand, come back, and talk more about the product experience. This in turn generates

C. Bünte (✉)
SRH Berlin University of Applied Sciences, Berlin, Germany
e-mail: cb@kaiserscholle.com

U. Hannig, U. Seebacher (eds.), *Marketing and Sales Automation*, Management for Professionals, https://doi.org/10.1007/978-3-031-20040-3_25

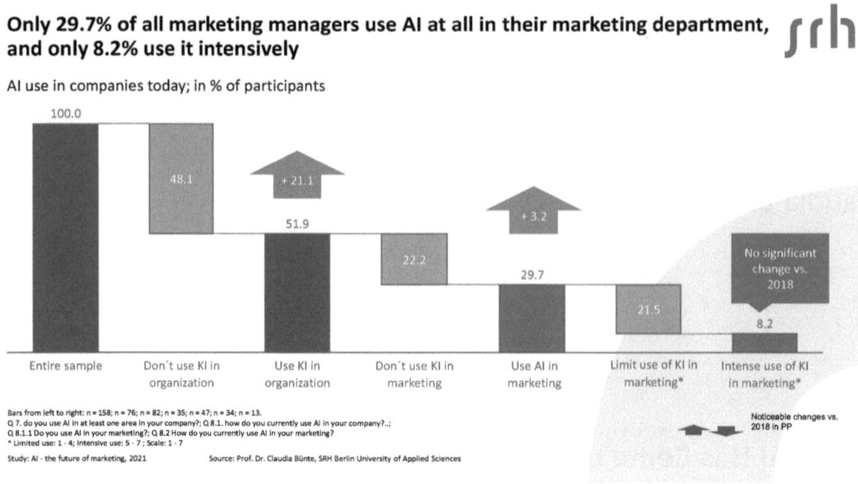

Fig. 1 Current use of AI in companies and marketing 2021

more data that an AI can analyze. A positive learning curve for the company that uses AI in marketing—and a competitive advantage.

But only 29.7% of all respondents in 2021 use AI at all in their marketing work, according to their own statements, and only 8.2% use it daily—compared to 2018, this is a stagnation (Fig. 1) (Bünte, Studie KI - Die Zukunft des Marketings, 2021, S. 11; 2019, S. 10; 2018, S. 12).

However, this hesitant use does not appear to be specific to marketing. Rather, this cautious approach to a new technology apparently also exists in other industries, as McKinsey found in three studies in 2019, 2020, and 2021, among others (McKinsey & Company, 2019, 2020, 2021). In the most recent study from 2021, 56% of the companies surveyed worldwide are using AI in at least one of the business areas, but this also means, conversely, that 44% are not yet doing so.

A study of European electrical wholesalers conducted by the author together with partners also shows a similar picture in 2020, namely that around 70% believe AI is important for their company, but only 39% use AI in at least one area and only 9% intensively (Bünte et al., 2020, S. 18 ff).

2 Five Reasons Prevent Marketing Managers from Using AI

Why is AI being used in marketing? The analyses of the current study "AI—the future of marketing" show that there are five reasons that prevent managers from using AI according to its actual potential: (a) the knowledge of AI is rather low according to their own assessment, (b) although attitudes toward AI are changing positively, there are still skeptics and neutrals, (c) the AI assessments of managers and employees in the same team differ significantly, (d) the focus on data is in part only slightly pronounced, and (e) experience with AI has so far been at a low level

(Bünte, Studie: Künstliche Intelligenz - die Zukunft des Marketings, 2021, S. 32 ff). Removing these obstacles seems comparatively straightforward, which this article will address. And a look beyond Europe's borders shows that the use of AI is revolutionizing marketing, commerce, and the economy as a whole. Therefore, "business as usual" in Europe does not seem to make sense in the long run.

3 Best Practice China

Traditionally, people in Europe like to look to the USA when it comes to economic progress. In fact, however, it is China that is developing into the leading economic nation, driven not least by artificial intelligence. There are three reasons for this (Stefanov et al., 2021, S. 58 ff):

First: Many inhabitants, many data
With 1.4 billion inhabitants, China has the largest population in the world. Almost 1 billion people here are "mobile only," meaning they are online and do so with their smartphones. This results in a very large amount of unstructured usage data that, if analyzed correctly, can provide new insights into everyday needs for retailers and manufacturers.

Second: A data protection law that allows linked data analysis
China has a data protection law that allows data to be analyzed in a linked way. Combined with AI, this creates deeper insights into customer preferences than in other countries. To be sure, China has just been tightening personal data protections since January 2021 and most recently in November 2021, following the GDPR. Nevertheless, the analysis possibilities for Chinese companies remain greater than those of other companies.

Third, a clear government focus on AI development.
The one-party government in China has developed its own 5-year plan for AI. The stated goal: China wants to be the world leader in AI by 2030. Part of this strategy are many, very detailed measures. And: China spends about as much money on basic AI research per citizen and year as Germany—but China is about 17 times larger than Germany (Colvin et al., 2020, S. 27; Bundesministerium für Wirtschaft, 2018, S. 5). Experts therefore attest that China is around 3–5 years ahead of Europe in digitization (Bünte, 2020, 17ff.).

Companies such as Alibaba, Tencent, WeChat and Co. are making intensive use of this deep digitalization of everyday life in China with the help of AI—also in optimizing communication and marketing measures for their hundreds of millions of customers (Bünte, Die chinesische KI-Revolution. Konsumverhalten, Marketing und Handel: Wie China mit Künstlicher Intelligenz die Wirtschaftwelt verändert, 2020, S. 81 ff). They offer their goods and services in integrated, so-called platform ecosystems. These platforms make it possible to retain and analyze customers from search to payment in a single ecosystem. Through linked data analysis using AI, these companies understand their customers better, plan advertising strategies more individually, design campaigns more creatively, address them individually, down to the so-called segment of one, and measure performance down to the individual.

This is how a so-called new marketing is developing, i.e. marketing in real time. Customer data is evaluated in real time by AI, immediately converted into campaigns with the help of AI, deployed on an individual basis, and the success of each individual communication measure immediately measured by an AI.

The result is inevitable: customers feel better understood, appreciate that shopping has become easier for them, and therefore buy more in this ecosystem, the system receives more data, and an analysis and optimization cycle starts. Those who operate in China without AI in their advertising lose out because their offers are not as perfectly aligned with the wishes of their customers or are not played out as punctually as the increasingly spoiled customers have come to expect. Chinese companies are just learning to understand their customers really well with the help of AI.

Once the Chinese market is saturated, the same companies will want to continue to grow, including in Europe. These companies will (have to) comply with European data protection, but their offerings will be so optimized on the basis of Chinese customer data that they will in all likelihood also be better suited to the needs of customers here than the offerings of European companies, which are only slightly AI-optimized. It is therefore worthwhile to gain experience with AI in Europe now in order to be prepared for competition from China. Alibaba is already showing ambitions to gain a foothold in Europe—and brings its own extensive, sophisticated AI ecosystem toolkit. If these assessments are correct, it doesn't seem like a real option to wait too long to try your own hand at AI in marketing and advertising. This is also reflected in the experience of the managers who already use AI in D-A-CH: 78.2% of the respondents who already use AI in marketing see AI in marketing as a decisive factor for the success of the company, 12.8% THE decisive factor. And those who use AI in their company say they are significantly more successful than those companies that do not use AI (Fig. 2) (Bünte, Studie: Künstliche Intelligenz - die Zukunft des Marketings, 2021, S. 9 f).

4 How to Use AI in Marketing with Success

The barriers to the effective use of AI in marketing described above are, on closer inspection, surmountable obstacles. The challenges require good management skills alone. No executive needs to learn to code, for example, or go back to university to become a Data Scientist. Here are a few practical tips on how to get started successfully with AI:

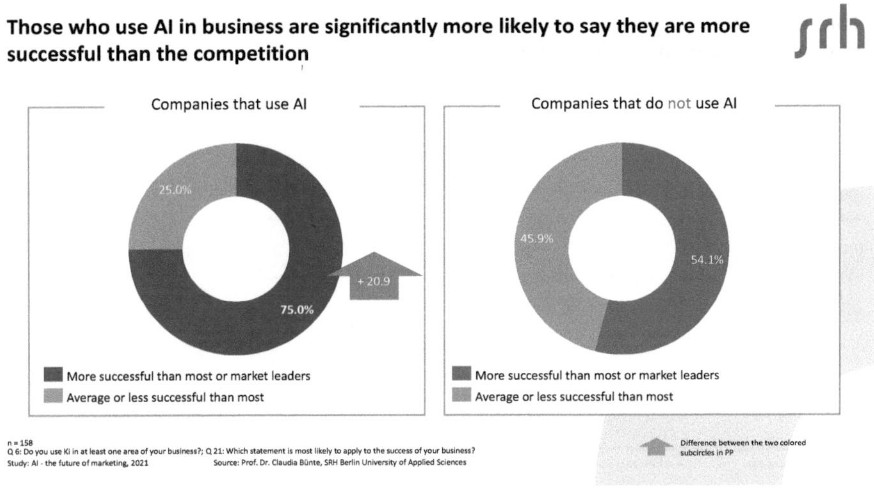

Fig. 2 Use of AI in the company and success according to respondents' assessment

(a) *knowledge of AI is rather low according to own assessment*

According to their own assessment, the respondents' knowledge of AI is only low—that of their own marketing department even lower: on a scale of 1 (low knowledge) to 7 (high knowledge), the average of all marketing experts is a meager 3.93 according to their own statements, and that of their marketing departments is an even lower 3.33 points (Bünte, Studie KI - Die Zukunft des Marketings, 2021, S. 34). Those who believe they are not well versed in an innovative topic are reluctant to invest money and human resources (Fig. 3).

For this self-attested knowledge gap, there are already very good solutions, some of which shall be mentioned as examples:

Good knowledge and learning platforms in English, also free of charge, e.g.

- https://kirevolution.com/—Free knowledge platform on AI in marketing, retail, advertising, with best practice examples, key notes available online and many tips and hints
- https://www.plattform-lernende-systeme.de/startseite.html—Free knowledge platform with explanatory videos, good, clear, and entertaining; funded by BMBF; topics include technology, mobility, society—not marketing-specific
- https://ki-campus.org/; https://www.udemy.com/; https://iversity.org/de—Three paid online learning resources

Anyone who wants to read up should take a look at these publications:

General insight into AI and digitization in business:

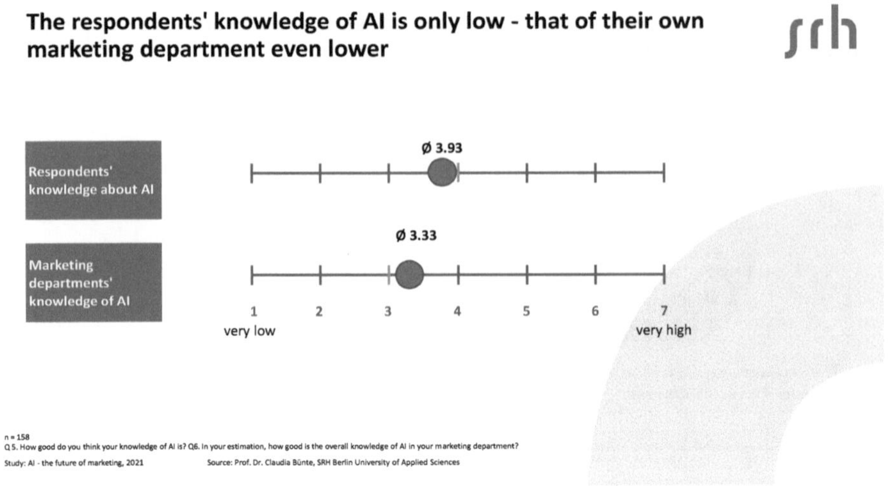

Fig. 3 Assessment of own knowledge about AI

- Kai Fu Lee, AI Superpowers. China, Silicon Valley, and the New World Order, Houghton Mifflin Harcourt, 2018
- Max Tegmark: Life 3.0: Being Human in the Age of Artificial Intelligence, Penguin, 2018

Artificial intelligence applied in practice:

- Rajkumar Venkatesan, Jim Lecinski: The AI Marketing Canvas: A Five-stage Road Map to Implementing Artificial Intelligence in Marketing, Stanford Business Books, 2021.

In-house workshops tailored to your own situation

Many digitization consultants offer tailored in-house training, including Future Candy with innovation workshops (https://www.futurecandy.com/), Kaiserscholle GmbH (https://kaiserscholle.de/de/kuenstliche-intelligenz/) with master classes on AI in marketing, Hundertmark with practical workshops on chatbots (https://www.hundertmark.ch/).

(b) *attitudes toward AI are changing positively, but skeptics remain*

A segmentation, calculated with the data of the study "AI—the future of marketing," shows three different types of AI managers (Fig. 4): The "AI optimists" have a positive attitude toward AI and account for 61.4%. The so-called AI neutrals with 28.5% look at AI with a little distance are not against or for it for now, but also not among the first to try AI. The so-called AI skeptics, on the other hand, are fundamentally opposed to AI. Among other things, they fear job losses and do not believe

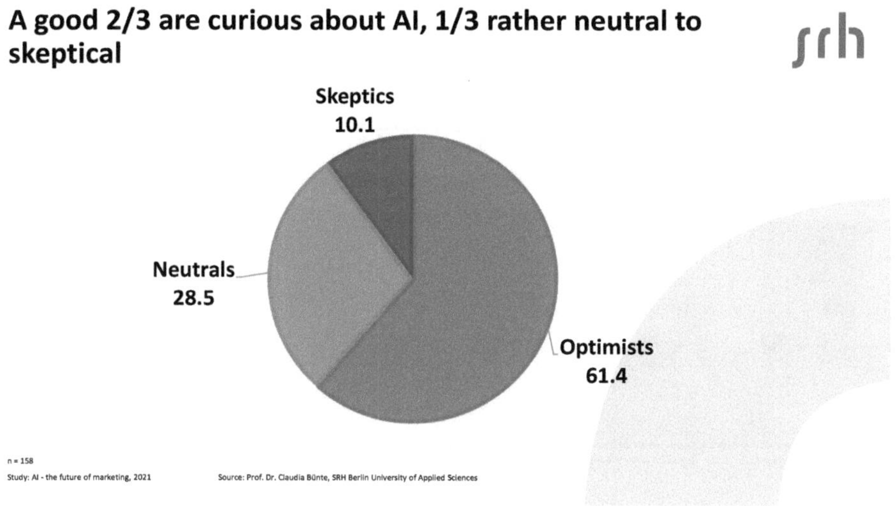

Fig. 4 Types of AI managers

that their company will be more successful as the result of AI usage. Their share amounts to around 10% of respondents in 2021 (Bünte, Studie KI - Die Zukunft des Marketings, 2021, S. 36 ff).

It can also fluctuate in marketing teams: The study team developed an AI type test based on segmentation and conducted it with various marketing departments. The number of skeptics varies between zero and 30%. The problem: If you have too many skeptics in your team, the successful use of AI as a tool will be difficult or impossible. In this case, it would be important to work out together with the team, and in large companies with the HR department, how the use can succeed before piloting AI.

Anyone who wants to know which segment he/she falls into can take the free, anonymous quick self-test here: https://kaiserscholle.de/de/ki-typomat/. Test for the entire team plus recommendations or individually, each in English, can also be conducted: Email requests to KI@kaiserscholle.com.

(c) *the AI assessments of managers and employees in the same team differ significantly*

The study suggests that executives tend to see more value in AI than their employees and that the challenges are not so much in downsizing, but in AI training of the team (Bünte, Studie KI - Die Zukunft des Marketings, 2021, S. 44 f). The problem with this is that if the team and the manager start from different premises when it comes to AI as a tool, expectations can thereby diverge. Bosses may expect everything to be implemented and work very quickly, employees may want more transparency about the goal, purpose, and KPIs for the deployment. The solution is simple: Teams should create transparency about the actual use of AI in the company,

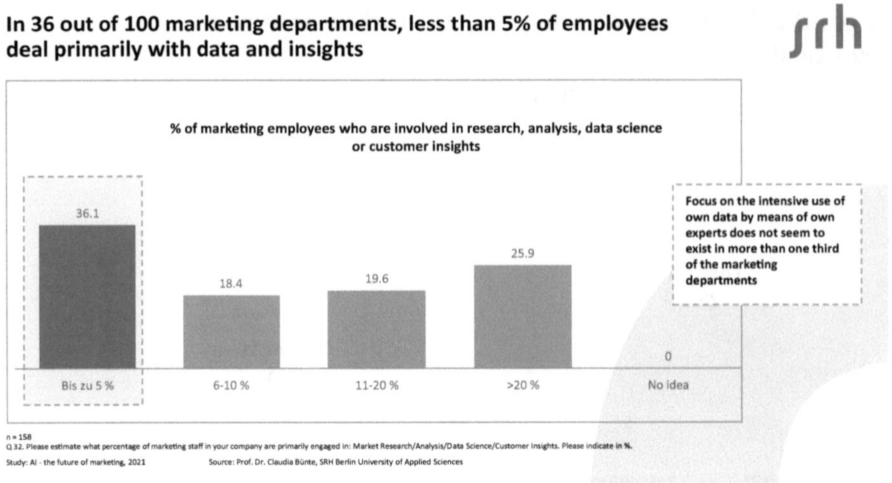

Fig. 5 Use of data in own marketing team

regularly put AI on the internal—Jour-Fixe agenda and actively discuss the status of AI projects.

(d) *the focus on data is in part only slightly pronounced*

In 36 out of 100 marketing departments, less than 5% of employees deal mainly with data and insights (Bünte, Studie KI - Die Zukunft des Marketings, 2021, S. 46). This rate seems significantly too low. If data is the new oil, 36% of companies are deploying too few resources to extract it (Fig. 5).

In this context, the use of data is the most important factor for being competitive in the future. The reasons for non-utilization may be manifold—one of the most frequently cited: People don't know where to start because the data is unstructured and building a data strategy seems too long and too difficult. Some also point out that data protection, especially in Europe with the GDPR, is so difficult to understand or so fraught with penalties that people would rather not analyze data than make any mistakes that could be costly.

Uwe Seebacher found with his 2020 study amongst B2B marketing that only about 50% of B2B marketers are responsible for the content of market and business data, and a third of all B2B marketing managers do not even know where and by whom in their companies this important information is collected, processed, and validated (Seebacher & Graz, 2021, S. 63).

To overcome these obstacles, a two-stage approach is recommended: Stage 1 would be the simple start by means of a pilot that defines 2–3 core questions in marketing without data strategy and data landscape and is worked through in a cross-functional team, if necessary, with external support from specialist companies (e.g., Analyx GmbH or XQ-Digital GmbH). With the learning experience of the pilot and

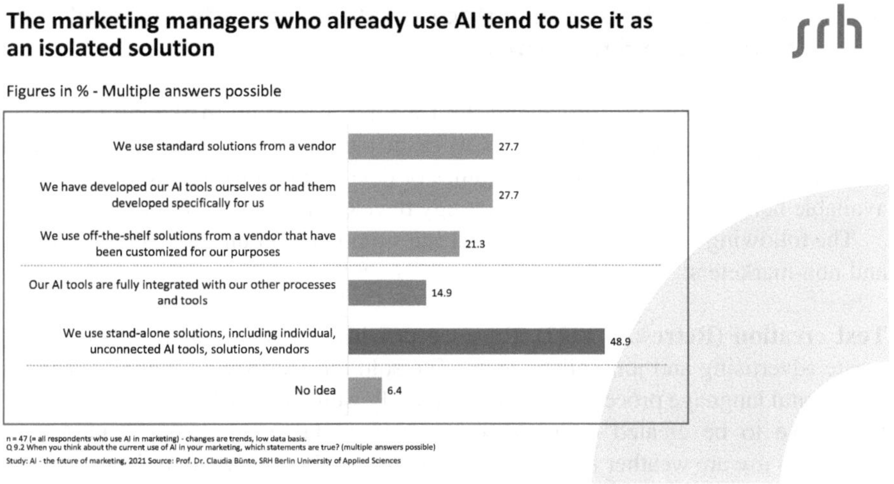

Fig. 6 Use of AI solutions in marketing

associated experience in one's own team, stage 2 can then begin: The establishment of a data strategy and a structured and comprehensive data landscape in one's own company. And in case one does not have the data at all, one can buy data. However, if choosing to buy data, make sure it is of high quality (check validity) and do not just buy whatever is available. Have a clear analytic goal in mind to avoid unnecessary data costs. (Seebacher & Graz, 2021, S. 63 ff.).

(e) *the experience with AI is so far on a low level*

This is the result of the four previous hurdles. Nearly 70% of respondents have no on-the-job experience with AI tools in marketing. And nearly half of the remaining roughly 30% of respondents, those who are already using AI in marketing, are using isolated solutions, with only about 15% of AI tools fully integrated. In other words, even among those who already use AI in marketing, AI is far from being an everyday occurrence, but rather ekes out an existence as a special solution (Fig. 6).

At the same time, very good software-as-a-service solutions (SaaS solutions) exist, especially in marketing. With these solutions, you or your employees must only be able to use and control the tool, but not necessarily program the software themselves.

5 Successfully Use AI Without Having to Code Yourself with These SaaS Tools

AI tools already exist in Europe and the USA for almost all marketing tasks. The tools for supporting communications work in particular are more mature than in other task areas because the large volumes of data required for AI are often already available here, unlike in product or strategy development, for example (Fig. 7).

The following examples show how AI can support communications professionals and non-marketers:

Text creation (Retresco, 2022) Retresco provides AI solutions to automatically create advertising and journalistic texts. The solution works with machine learning and natural language processing. It is particularly well-suited when relatively similar texts have to be created over and over again in large numbers. Examples for Retresco's use are weather reports, soccer results, or descriptive texts for apartments on online real estate platforms. The software replaces the tedious writing of very similar texts. Retresco also automatically creates product descriptions for clothing on the platform of a German online department store, for example. In doing so, the application reduced the time for text creation, the cycles of editing until text approval, and rework in the high double-digit percentage range. In addition to Retresco, other companies, such as Conversionmaker (2022), offer such text automation solutions.

Social Media Optimization (Keyhole, 2022) Keyhole analyzes reports and improves social media activities of companies. It uses machine and deep learning from Google subsidiary TensorFlow. The aim is, among other things, not only to

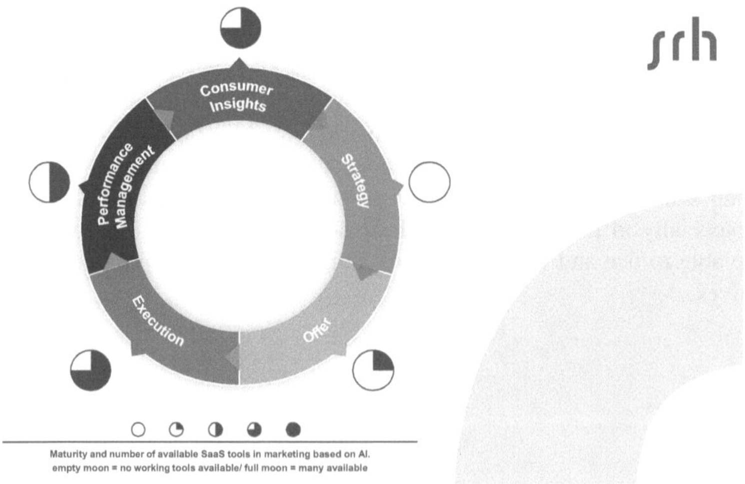

Fig. 7 Five core tasks in marketing and assessment of availability of working AI tools as SaaS (own figure)

observe and report on negative sentiment or even the so-called shitstorms on the Internet, but also to predict them and suggest the tone of the corresponding corporate communication.

Automated advertising impact measurement in pre-testing (Affectiva, 2022) Affectiva measures the advertising impact of a video clip by scanning the faces of the viewers. In the process, small changes in facial muscles (so-called micro-expressions) are detected and evaluated using AI. Affectiva provides a data-based overview of the reactions per scene, giving clues as to when something is boring, annoying, exciting, or funny. The application analyzes whether a spot is the right length, whether it should be shortened or optimized at certain points. Here, too, there are other providers with similar offerings, such as Real Eye.

Campaign control and performance management (Albert, 2022; Campello, 2019) Albert is a software tool for planning and executing online campaigns. Various social media and online applications can be integrated. It uses an algorithm that learns from the data collected from each advertiser and provides suggestions for optimized budget use. In this way, media is automatically bought and campaign content is autonomously targeted. Cosabella, a high-end lingerie brand from Italy, used Albert (Bünte, Studie KI - Die Zukunft des Marketings, 2021) to promote the brand internationally and generate sales via its own online store. Cosabella defined KPIs, budget, creative ad copy and ad visuals. Albert used AI to analyze the customer journey and find patterns in search and buying behavior. It then tested various campaigns via A/B testing, enabled channel and ROI analysis, and additionally improved budget efficiency through automated media buys. The result, according to Cosabella's CEO: 12% lower ad spend, 335% higher return on advertising spend after 3 months, 20 times higher sales through social media channels and 155% more revenue—albeit coming from a low base.

6 But AI Also Has Limits and Risks

Not all AI tools are already fully developed or sufficiently thought through. Artificial intelligence is often a so-called black box, where even trained data scientists are not always clear how the self-learning AI arrived at its results. Especially, but not only, in the area of "Deep Learning," where input and output are clear—but the so-called layers in between, which elaborate the results, are not.

Examples also show that AI algorithms can learn in an undesirable direction. For example, AI tools were recently found to discriminate against women and people with dark skin over time, when the human team did not actively counteract (Bünte et al., Künstliche Intelligenz und Ethik: Wen und warum diskriminiert KI eigentlich – und wie kann das verhindert werden?, 2021, S. 2 ff.).

AI in particular and digitalization in general are also under discussion because their use can result in the reduction of jobs. Depending on the source, between 1% worldwide (McKinsey Global Institute, 2018, S. 45) and 10 and 47% of all jobs in

Germany could be on the line—the exact figure cannot yet be calculated precisely at the present time (Pabst, 2019, S. 14 ff.). A large number of white papers, studies, and literature from the German government, government agencies, and the private sector revolve around the topics of "Work 4.0," "New Work," or "New Work." For example, the "White Paper on Work 4.0—How we will work." (Bundesministerium für Arbeit und Soziales Abteilung Grundsatzfragen des Sozialstaats, der Arbeitswelt und der sozialen Marktwirtschaft, 2017). Concerns about job retention are contrary to many beliefs not unjustified: Every technological innovation, from the steam engine to the Internet, has cost jobs or caused a reallocation of tasks, on the one hand, while creating new jobs, on the other.

There are, as shown, many working AI tools with proven impact in advertising, but also limitations and risks.

7 Weighing the Options and Tips for the Practical Use of AI with Impact

All in all, the question at hand is what should managers do? Wait and see or try out AI? AI is obviously here to stay. Those who use AI have competitive advantages—those who don't, disadvantages over time. Therefore, it would make sense to try AI now, test it, adapt it, and learn for yourself. Establish the following key points with your team before a deployment of an AI project:

- Define clear goals—what should AI as a tool help with?
- Get results from other AI tool customers of the tool provider and then choose the right one for your needs.
- Check within your team how high the willingness to use AI is. Those who are AI skeptics will not be happy to participate (see AI Typomat). If there are too many skeptics in the team, it is worthwhile to seek the support of the HR department or to coach the employees through external parties.
- As with any important project, manage milestones with priority. Make AI implementation a boss issue, too.
- Monitor the results of your AI tools for unwanted effects (keyword discrimination).
- Back the piloting with sufficient budget and time.
- Have the courage to make mistakes in order to learn from them.

8 Management Take-Away

AI is here to stay. Those who use AI in marketing understand customer wishes better and can tailor and offer their products and services to better meet these wishes. A look at China shows that this type of AI use has a major impact on the success of companies and the economy as a whole. This realization has also arrived in the USA and Europe, but too few marketing managers are yet leveraging these benefits. There are five obstacles in the way. To remove these obstacles, managers don't need to know coding or become AI experts. There are already many working SaaS tools that have proven impact. Rather, managers can rely on their usual management skills: Aim cleanly, select tools based on what their benefit is for achieving goals, take employees along on the journey, and give the topic a special focus in piloting, i.e., attention also to undesirable developments, budget, and time. Then the use of AI can succeed and make the marketing department ready for the future, which definitely will be built using AI.

References

Affectiva. (2022, March 6). *Affectiva media analytics*. Retrieved March 6, 2022, from https://go.affectiva.com/affdex-for-market-research

Albert. (2022, March 6). *Is your self-learning digital marketing ally*. Retrieved March 6, 2022, from https://albert.ai/

Bünte, C. (2018, April 30). *Studie KI - Die Zukunft des Marketings*. Retrieved January 15, 2021, from https://kaiserscholle.de/de/kuenstliche-intelligenz/

Bünte, C. (2019, April 30). *Studie KI - Die Zukunft des Marketings*. Retrieved January 15, 2021, from https://kaiserscholle.de/de/kuenstliche-intelligenz/

Bünte, C. (2020). *Die chinesische KI-Revolution. Konsumverhalten, Marketing und Handel: Wie China mit Künstlicher Intelligenz die Wirtschaftwelt verändert*. Springer Gabler.

Bünte, C. (2021, April). *Studie KI - Die Zukunft des Marketings*. Retrieved March 6, 2022, from https://kirevolution.com/

Bünte, C., Beutin, N., Kirchner, P., & Vogler, O. (2020, September 30). *Digital transformation in B2B – The role of AI and pricing automation*. Retrieved January 16, 2021, from https://kirevolution.com/

Bünte, C., Poths, L., & Schubert, T.-H. (2021, February 2). *Künstliche Intelligenz und Ethik: Wen und warum diskriminiert KI eigentlich – und wie kann das verhindert werden?* Retrieved February 26, 2021, from https://kirevolution.com/wp-content/uploads/2021/01/Whitepaper_Diskriminierung-final6

Bughin, J., Seong, J., Manyika, J., Chui, M, & Joshi, R. (2018, September 5). *Künstliche Intelligenz: Größeres Potential als die Dampfmaschine*. Retrieved August 20, 2020, from https://www.mckinsey.de/news/presse/2018-09-05-ki-studie-mgi-dampfmaschine

Bundesministerium für Arbeit und Soziales Abteilung Grundsatzfragen des Sozialstaats, der Arbeitswelt und der sozialen Marktwirtschaft. (2017, March). *Weißbuch Arbeiten 4.0 - wie wir arbeiten werden*. Retrieved October 15, 2018, from www.arbeitenviernull.de

Bundesministerium für Wirtschaft. (2018, November 13). *Strategie Künstliche Intelligenz*. Retrieved August 20, 2020, from https://www.bundesfinanzministerium.de/Content/DE/Downloads/Digitalisierung/2018-11-15-Strategie-zur-Kuenstlichen-Intelligenz.pdf?__blob=publicationFile&v=2

Campello, G. (2019, April 12). CEO Cosabella. (C. Bünte, Interviewer).

Colvin, T., Liu, I., Babou, T., & Wong, G. (2020, February). *A brief examination of Chinese Government Expenditures on Artificial Intelligence R&D*. Retrieved January 24, 2021, from https://www.ida.org/-/media/feature/publications/a/ab/a-brief-examination-of-chinese-government-expenditures-on-artificial-intelligence-r-and-d/d-12068.ashx

Conversionmaker. (2022, March 6). *Erfolgreiche Produktbeschreibungen: schnell, einfach, effizient!* Retrieved March 6, 2022, from https://conversionmaker.ai/

Keyhole. (2022, March 6). *Enterprise-Grade Social Listening & Analytics Simplified*. Retrieved March 6, 2022, from https://keyhole.co/social-listening/?from=homeHeroSplit

Lee, K. F. (2018). *AI superpowers. China, Silicon Valley, and the new world order*. Houghton Mifflin Harcourt.

McKinsey & Company. (2018, November 13). *AI adoption advances, but foundational barriers remain*. Retrieved February 26, 2021, from https://www.mckinsey.com/featured-insights/artificial-intelligence/ai-adoption-advances-but-foundational-barriers-remain

McKinsey & Company. (2019, November 22). *Global AI Survey: AI proves its worth, but few scale impact*. Retrieved May 14, 2021, from https://www.mckinsey.com/featured-insights/artificial-intelligence/global-ai-survey-ai-proves-its-worth-but-few-scale-impact

McKinsey & Company. (2020, November). *Global survey: The state of AI in 2020*. Retrieved May 14, 2021, from https://www.mckinsey.com/~/media/McKinsey/Business%20Functions/McKinsey%20Analytics/Our%20Insights/Global%20survey%20The%20state%20of%20AI%20in%202020/Global-survey-The-state-of-AI-in-2020.pdf

McKinsey & Company. (2021, December 2021). *The state of AI in 2021*. Retrieved from https://www.mckinsey.com/business-functions/mckinsey-analytics/our-insights/global-survey-the-state-of-ai-in-2021

McKinsey Global Institute. (2018, September). *Notes for the frontier: Modeling the impact of AI on the world's economy*. Retrieved February 26, 2021, from https://www.mckinsey.de/~/media/McKinsey/Locations/Europe%20 and%20Middle%20East/Deutschland/News/Presse/2018/2018-09-05%20-%20MGI%20 AI

Pabst, E. (2019, June 25). *Künstliche Intelligenz im Marketing - Ängste nehmen und Akzeptanz schaffen (Bachelorarbeit SRH Hochschule Berlin)*.

pwc. (2021). *Global top 100 companies by market capitalisation*. Retrieved January 3, 2022, from https://www.pwc.com/gx/en/audit-services/publications/assets/pwc-global-top-100-companies-2021.pdf

Retresco. (2022, March 6). *PIONEERING NATURAL LANGUAGE TECHNOLOGIES*. Retrieved March 6, 2022, from https://www.retresco.de/

Seebacher, U., & Graz, A. (2021). *Predictive intelligence for data-driven managers. Process model, assessment-tool, IT-blueprint, competence model and case studies*. Springer.

Stefanov, A., Bünte, C., & Schubert, T.-H. (2021). *Digitalisierung Made in China. Wie China mit KI und Co. Wirtschaft, Handel und Marketing transfomiert*. BoD.

Tegmark, M. (2018). *Life 3.0: Being human in the age of artificial intelligence*. Penguin.

Venkatesan, R., & Lecinski, J. (2021). *The AI marketing canvas: A five-stage road map to implementing artificial intelligence in marketing*. Stanford Business Books.

Claudia Bünte is a proven AI expert and management consultant. She has held international positions at leading global companies, including for McKinsey clients and as a manager at Volkswagen and Coca-Cola. She runs the marketing consultancy Kaiserscholle GmbH, as a professor she teaches marketing at international universities, and researches artificial intelligence. Her three most recent books deal with the role of AI in business and marketing.

Application of AI in Customer Experience Management

Merve Kacar

1 Artificial Intelligence as Critical Success Factor

Barely any other field of informatics causes as much confusion as the field and associated terms of AI. Most likely, this is the reason why there is currently no uniformly established definition in the literature. However, a core statement can be recognized in many definitions.[1] Basically, intelligence is "the ability [of humans] to think abstractly and rationally and to derive purposeful action from it."[2] Thus, there are many different approaches to definitions of AI, which have different emphases according to their technical and historical origin.[3] However, this book is oriented toward the practical definition. To start with the following definition by Rich, which is essentially intended to provide a basic understanding: "Artificial Intelligence is the study of how to make computers do things at which, at the moment, people are better."[4] This definition of AI illustrates that the limits of the possible are constantly being redefined. Autonomous driving can be mentioned as an example here.[5] In this sense, AI is best described as the field of computer science that deals with the acquisition of the above-mentioned cognitive abilities which are usually attributed to human intelligence.[6] So broadly speaking, AI is a simulation of human intelligence respectively human behavior by machines. This simulation includes "planning, reasoning, problem-solving, learning, knowledge representation, motion,

[1] Cf. Gentsch, 2019, p. 17.

[2] Bibliographisches Institut GmbH, 2021.

[3] Cf. Gentsch, 2019, p. 17.

[4] Rich et al., 2009, p. 2.

[5] Cf. Kreutzer & Sirrenberg, 2019, p. 3.

[6] Cf. Bünte, 2018, p. 5.

M. Kacar (✉)
Independent Solution Consultant, Leipzig, Germany

U. Hannig, U. Seebacher (eds.), *Marketing and Sales Automation*, Management for Professionals, https://doi.org/10.1007/978-3-031-20040-3_26

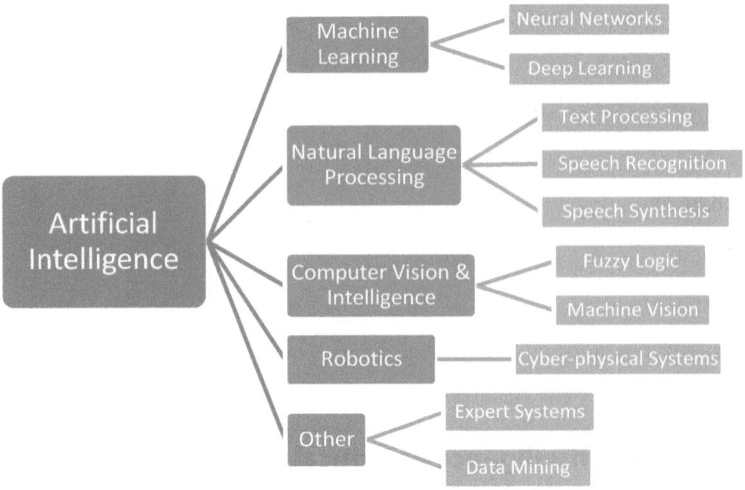

Fig. 1 Subfields of AI. Source: Own representation based on Mullion, Marc: What's AI Anyway? (Online, n.d.). Internet: https://www.aus.com/de/node/5726 (hit: 04/20/2021, 14:48 MEZ)

perception, manipulation, and to a certain extent social intelligence and creativity." The three main functions of AI are description, prediction, and prescription. The chart in Fig. 1 shows the main subfields of AI.

Thus, AI is based on three pillars: Understanding, feeling, and acting. In this context, "understanding" means the processing of input by the so-called natural language processing (NLP) programs that understand written and spoken language and the language itself. "Feeling" is understood as the acquisition of impressions from the environment, through computer vision, sensors, or microphones. Finally, AI is supposed to implement what it understands and perceives. Here, robotics provides the necessary hardware, so that action is made possible for the software, e.g., by using autonomous robots, humanoid robots, or service robots.[7] In the financial sector, NLP is an essential business tool. Fields of application include spam detection, virtual assistants and chatbots for customer service, as well as financial advisory, social media sentiment analysis, and analysis of big amounts of customer data.

Machine learning is basically the most advanced and comprehensive subfield of AI. At the bottom, the term "machine learning" encompasses methods that use learning processes to identify correlations in existing data sets to make predictions.[8] In machine learning and in the development of increasingly powerful algorithms, basically three different types of learning can be distinguished: Supervised, unsupervised, and reinforcement learning. Supervised learning proceeds within clearly

[7]Cf. Brutkasten Media GmbH, 2017.

[8]Cf. Murphy, 2012, p. 1–3.

defined boundaries.[9] It includes algorithms that are trained with a variety of "labeled" data to make decisions independently.[10]

The key difference between supervised and unsupervised learning is that unsupervised learning does not depend on labels in datasets and does not require any external input to classify data.[11] Hence, it is the task of algorithms to identify commonalities in datasets to then form clusters or compress data. It is therefore usually a matter of discovering hidden patterns in data that operators are unaware of.[12] Unsupervised learning algorithms can be applied, e.g., to customer and market segmentation. Furthermore, unsupervised learning algorithms can identify and cluster different behavior on social media which later can be used to offer customized product and services.[13]

Alongside supervised and unsupervised learning, reinforcement learning is the third major pillar of machine learning. The terminology "reinforcement learning" is derived from psychology and behaviorism and works similarly. Meaning, that an optimal strategy is to be developed for a given problem.[14] The system must try out solutions iteratively through a trial-and-error process to subsequently discard and/or further develop them. This iterative process is driven by "rewards" for good solution approaches and "punishments" for bad approaches. Thus, the algorithm optimizes its actions autonomously, by constantly correcting itself. It can also be applied in online marketing to control marketing tools and communication.[15]

Another important subfield of machine learning is deep learning: "Deep Learning is a type of machine learning that can extract progressively higher-level features" from a wide range of data sources.[16] This subfield of machine learning can witness many human characteristics and behavioral databases to perform supervised learning.[17] Examples include the detection of different human emotions and signs, image, speech and voice recognition, conversion of video and voice into text data, and the identification of right or wrong gestures.[18] In summary, it can be emphasized that the core of machine learning is to independently process big amounts of data, recognize patterns in it, and to take autonomous decisions and predictions based on this data.[19] Some of the most crucial implementations of machine learning in the finance sector are portfolio management, advisory services, loan underwriting, fraud

[9] Cf. Gentsch, 2019, p. 37.
[10] Cf. Buxmann & Schmidt, 2019, p. 9.
[11] Cf. Wennker, 2020, p. 15.
[12] Cf. Gentsch, 2019, p. 38.
[13] Cf. Kreutzer & Sirrenberg, 2019, p. 7.
[14] Cf. Wennker, 2020, p. 16.
[15] Cf. Wennker, 2020, p. 17.
[16] Oxford University Press, 2021.
[17] Cf. SoftwareTestingHelp, 2021.
[18] SoftwareTestingHelp, 2021.
[19] Cf. Kreutzer & Sirrenberg, 2019, p. 9–15.

detection and prevention, and algorithmic trading, which will be dealt with in more detail in the following chapters.[20]

A further important subfield of AI is computer vision, also known as natural image processing or machine vision. Computer vision describes the ability of computers or subsystems to identify objects, scenes, and activities in images.[21] Machine vision enhances customer experience in the finance sector for instance, through biometrics identification when opening a bank account and is being widely implemented for further security purposes.[22] Robotics is a further symbolic branch of AI: Robots are artificial agents that behave and move like humans. They are "built for the purpose of manipulating the objects by perceiving, picking, moving, and modifying the physical properties of objects or to free manpower from doing repetitive functions."[23] In this book, the focus will be on humanoid, collaborative service robots, which will be used in the financial sector primarily for consulting activities in the future.

The AI subfields "expert systems and data mining" will be briefly touched on, as they are not very relevant to the rest of the research. Rule-based expert systems are computer programs designed to assist human beings in complex issues.[24] Their knowledge originates from experts and it is used to derive conclusions based on input variables.[25] The term data mining refers to a sub-process of knowledge discovery in databases, i.e., the nontrivial extraction from previously unknown and potentially important information from databases.[26] Exact areas of application range from risk monitoring to market analysis.[27] It is noticeable that the subfields of AI are closely linked, as most of the applications rely on the models and methods of all the subfields mentioned above to perform the main tasks of AI, such as deduction, reasoning, problem-solving, perception, knowledge representation, and planning/ predicting.[28]

2 Distinction Between Human and Artificial Intelligence

An interesting phenomenon occurred during the development of AI. The first tasks of AI were difficult for humans but easy for AI systems to process, such as complex calculation processes. Working through a large amount of data using given mathematical formulas is one of the easiest tasks for AI systems. In contrast, it is usually

[20] Cf. Corporate Finance Institute Education Inc., n.d.

[21] Cf. Kreutzer & Sirrenberg, 2019, p. 36.

[22] Cf. SAS Institute Inc., 2021.

[23] Singh, 2018.

[24] Cf. Kreutzer & Sirrenberg, 2019, p. 40–46.

[25] Cf. Gentsch, 2019, p. 32.

[26] Cf. Brighterion Inc., 2017.

[27] Cf. Brighterion Inc., 2017.

[28] Cf. Kreutzer & Sirrenberg, 2019, p. 51.

much harder for computers to handle such tasks that are easy for humans, such as speech and object recognition. Human beings can very easily recognize physical objects, while AI systems must go through numerous trainings and still often fail to recognize the actual meaning of the objects.[29]

There are basically three main types of AI: Artificial general intelligence, artificial narrow intelligence, and artificial super intelligence. Artificial narrow intelligence (ANI) is machine intelligence that exceeds human intelligence in narrowly defined tasks. ANI is the most widely used AI technology in the industry. An existing example of such automatic system that performs beyond human reach is Watson. The supercomputer of the International Business Machines Corporation is an expert in mimicking the cognitive competences of humans.[30] Artificial general intelligence (AGI) is the capability of a machine to meet the full spectrum of human performance across any task to the same standard as humans. Unlike, general intelligence—narrow intelligence focuses on a specific group of tasks or abilities to outperform humans in that area. Hence narrow intelligence is also known as "Weak AI," whereas general intelligence is known as "Strong AI" or "Human Level AI." Once AGI is achieved, the next and final step that AI could theoretically reach is artificial superintelligence (ASI).[31] Here, machine intelligence would be able to surpass human intelligence in any task.[32] As previously stated, AI has evolved strongly toward machine learning in recent years, which corresponds to the most important enabling technology of the era. At present, only ANI technologies, that outperform humans in special areas, are well-matured.[33] AGI technologies are expected to be holistically possible by 2040, meaning that AI research is practically at the beginning of exploration and development.[34]

One main difference between human and artificial intelligence can be clearly stated: Above all, human intelligence is flexible. It can always adapt to new situations. AI systems are specialists, they can perform some tasks with higher efficiency and accuracy. But the facets of human intelligence are so diverse that many years of development work and high budgets are needed to get anywhere close to human intelligence, at least at the present stage.[35] In the future, a machine or a program may succeed in being flexible, creative, or innovative. But whether it succeeds or not, will be decided by human beings.[36] In the big picture, it is human intelligence that shapes the emergence and adoption of AI and the solutions associated with it.[37] Again, it is human intelligence that questions possible scenarios

[29] Cf. Kreutzer & Sirrenberg, 2019, p. 3–4.

[30] Cf. Allan, n.d.

[31] Cf. JuPantarhei GmbH, n.d.

[32] Cf. De Spiegeleire et al., 2017, p. 30.

[33] Cf. Buxmann & Schmidt, 2021, p. 7–12.

[34] Cf. Ahmet, 2018, p. 9.

[35] Cf. Kreutzer & Sirrenberg, 2019, p. 15.

[36] Cf. Lenzen, 2018.

[37] Cf. Buchkremer et al., 2020, p. 5–11.

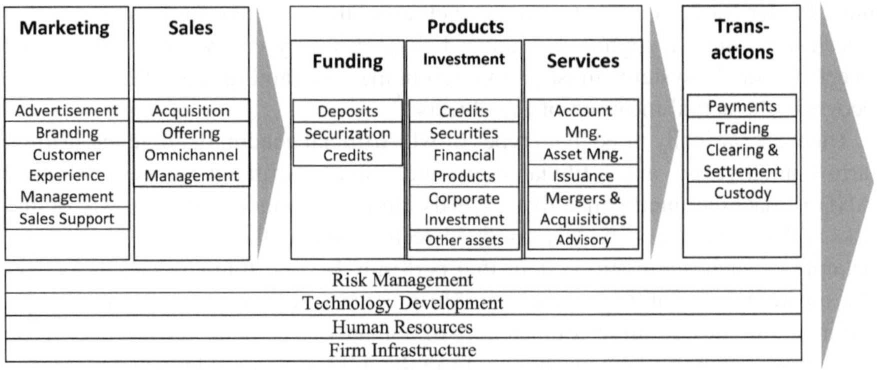

Fig. 2 Value chain of a bank. Source: Lammers, Markus: Strategic Sourcing in Banking – A Framework. (text file, October 2004). Internet: https://slidetodoc.com/strategic-sourcing-in-banking-a-framework-markus-lammers/ (hit: 07/05/2021, 20:48 MEZ)

through critical thinking,[38] as humanity is always seeking meaning in everything they do. Machines will most likely not be able to do that in the foreseeable future. Presently, they can only think as far as mortals program them.[39]

3 Application of AI Tools Along the Value Chain of a Bank

In this subsection, the functional areas of the AI tools listed above are analyzed in more detail in the individual stages of the value chain. The (typical) banking value chain in Fig. 2 will be used for this purpose.

What distinguishes this value chain from other industrial value chains (see Porter) is the fact that it begins with the customer side. Thus, the service is first offered/ advertised in the market, sold, and provided to customers, and ultimately the corresponding transactions are carried out. An additional difference is risk management as supporting activity.[40] This is one reason why the banking sector was chosen as the research object for this chapter.

AI modifies service value chains essentially in four dimensions: The (further) development or complete reinvention of business model structures, reinvention of the service concept, optimization of service systems (internal processes), and the reorganization of customer interfaces.[41] To start with the marketing and sales unit, i.e., those that are most involved in customer service. Here, opportunity and risk assessment and the operational use of AI are most pronounced.[42]

[38] Cf. Aurecon Group Pty. Ltd. n.d.

[39] Cf. Schenk & Tietze, 1993.

[40] Cf. Lammers, 2004.

[41] Cf. Bruhn & Hadwich, 2021, p. 16–25.

[42] Cf. Bünte, 2018, p. 7.

An important application of AI in marketing is lead prediction and lead profiling. Based on large data sets (predictive analysis), current core customers and potential new customers are being compared to identify so-called look-alike audiences. In this way, forecasts about purchase probabilities and customer values can be made. The company succeeds in optimizing marketing planning and channel management, as the information gained here can be entered into dynamic profiling.

This leads to the next major field of AI application, which is targeting.[43] Targeting is the goal-oriented addressing of a user with individually tailored, "promotional content, within the much-cited parameters, at the right time, with the right proposition."[44] Automated recommendations can make a significant contribution to increasing customer satisfaction and simultaneously increase sales and, above all, profits by improving the conversion rate. This is also partly enabled by AI-supported content creation, which automatically searches the internet and inserts the content that is most likely to appeal to the recipient to persuade them into a purchase at any touchpoint.

Some studies indicate that for many customers, irrelevant content in the sales approach is the main reason for a lack of interaction with manufacturers.[45] In addition, AI-based content marketing can draft articles from digitally available information. For example, short news from the financial world, such as reports on the development of stock market prices, can be written in real time and distributed in the appropriate channels (content distribution). Here, speed (real-time information) and cost-effectiveness are major advantages.

Another function AI performs in marketing and sales that has already been addressed is conversational commerce. These systems execute tasks from the basic provision of customer service to the placement of the purchase. Interestingly, all processes can be performed in real-time without leaving the messaging application if the following performance fields are seamlessly linked: Messenger services, marketing automation software, predictive analytic tools, customer relationship management systems, enterprise resource planning systems, e-commerce store systems, and data warehouses. AI also offers significant support in monitoring, especially in the monitoring of communication in social media. Social media monitoring or, more comprehensively, web monitoring can be used to identify problems with products and services as well as general changes in the customer perception of the company and its offerings at an early stage. The tonality of the statements is determined by means of sentiment analysis.

AI algorithms are also increasingly being implemented in pricing.[46] AI-based dynamic pricing provides customers not only with individualized content but also with individual prices. It is reported that in some cases AI has even increased

---

[43]Cf. Kreutzer & Sirrenberg, 2019, p. 156 f.

[44]Wennker, 2020, p. 40.

[45]Cf. Jugel, 2017.

[46]Cf. Kreutzer & Sirrenberg, 2019, p. 157–167.

revenue and margin by 3–12%.[47] All efforts supported by AI should have a customer-centric focus. After all, customers will only remain loyal to a brand if they can identify individual added value for themselves. In the operational area (products and transactions) AI can help with regulatory compliance, portfolio management, capital optimization, market impact analysis, and with supervision.[48] They are primarily used to increase efficiency when offering services such as account closure validations or asset management advisory. In the credit and insurance business, applications can be processed faster, more accurately, and more cost-effectively using AI systems—achieving a reduction of 88% in processing time.[49]

AI is a crucial factor in the risk management of financial institutions respectively banks, as this sector is particularly exposed to risks. It has been estimated, that in 2020 the total amount of credit card fraud worldwide exceeded $30 billion for the first time. In the area of fraud detection, AI has quickly gained a foothold. Supervised, unsupervised, and reinforcement learning can quickly spot parameters that make a transaction fraudulent across multiple channels.[50] It then sends alerts about potentially fraudulent activity to a virtually unlimited number of bank customers and employees simultaneously. Credit risk is a further challenge that banks must deal with. Here, AI applications support to better assess, e.g., customers' credit histories. Many companies that are specializing in this area state that they can reduce default rates by approximately 20% through AI-based models. When it comes to reducing risks in market trading, AI technologies like machine learning identify trading patterns across several markets to forecast more accurately. Besides that, AI-supported back testing (in risk management) can also detect cyberattacks in time. In this way, risks can be identified and avoided in advance. AI tools that minimize or avoid risks also overlap with AI use in banks' main services.[51]

AI accompanies an employee life cycle in all stages from recruiting to promotion. In recruiting, intelligent systems undertake tasks such as optimizing the application process for both parties (applicants and HR staff) by answering inquiries,[52] analyzing applications, and interpreting applicants for word choice and body language during interviews. During onboarding process, digital assistants and RPA are used to support employees and even train them in some cases. For qualifications and promotion purposes, employees' internal data is analyzed to identify (unused) skills or good job matches so that these can be forwarded to the employee or HR personnel. IBM claims that this system has so far saved the group $300 million in retention costs through early intervention. Also, feedback from staff happens in a completely automated way. Here, AI examines the various strengths and weaknesses

[47] Cf. Dilmegani, 2017.

[48] Cf. Financial Stability Board, 2017, p. 11–19.

[49] Cf. Kreutzer & Sirrenberg, 2019, p. 241–244.

[50] Cf. Wennker, 2020, p. 108 f.

[51] Cf. Chalopin & Trehan, 2020.

[52] Cf. Buxmann & Schmidt, 2021, p. 124 f.

of the company according to employees' opinions and works out suggestions for improvement.[53]

4 AI Solutions in Customer Experience Management

According to research by Gartner, it is expected that soon 70% of customer interactions in banking will take place with emerging technologies such as machine learning apps, chatbots, and mobile messaging.[54] Today, 65% of customers already search for financial services such as loans, credit cards, deposits and insurances digitally, and around 50% even buy them digitally. Another survey of Gartner reveals that 81% of financial institutions mostly compete on customer experience management (CXM), making customer experience a key differentiator.[55] Consequently, 51% of the banks surveyed stated that they are focusing on improving the customer experience as a second priority, besides holistic digital banking transformation at 75%.[56] AI provides CXM systems an accurate presentation of customer insights, easy engagement, at-scale personalization, proactive recommendations, and rapid innovation cycles.[57]

In the following, the current application of AI in banking worldwide is explained based on the touchpoints of the customer journey. In general, it can be concluded from research that AI is currently serving banks in a human-accompanied rather than a fully autonomous manner. What is also striking at this point is that in their quest for greater efficiency, banks seem to focus primarily on AI applications that can take over costly, labor-intensive, and repetitive activities. They are looking to improve operational risk management, e.g., through fraud detection or better know your customer (KYC) processes, and to reduce costs, e.g., through chatbots or robo advisors.[58] For banks to fully transform themselves, AI must be embedded in all areas—including front, middle, and back office.[59] The front office uses costumer facing offerings such as client-focused interaction and credit scoring.[60] The middle office is operations-focused. Here, AI helps to optimize business models and internal processes, including capital optimization, model risk management, and market impact analysis. In the back office, AI provides administrative and support services for trading and portfolio management as well as for regulatory compliance, mostly based on machine learning. "The complete integration of AI into business processes enables financial institutions to become more competitive and improve their ROI.

[53]Cf. Wennker, 2020, p. 57–61.

[54]Cf. Dudovicz, 2021.

[55]Cf. Dudovicz, 2021.

[56]Cf. Berry, 2020.

[57]Cf. Marous, 2020, p. 3– 2.

[58]Cf. Kaya, 2019, p. 5–7.

[59]Cf. BeyondMinds, 2021, p. 1.

[60]Cf. Financial Stability Board, 2017, p. 10–13.

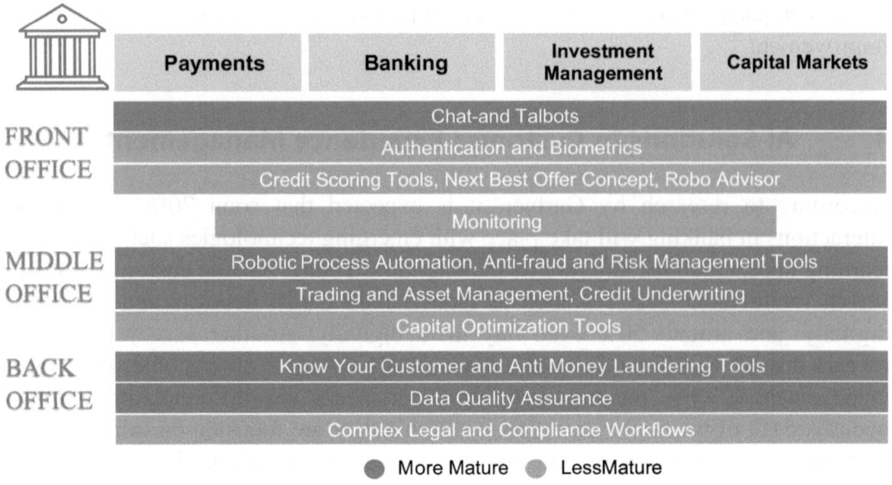

Fig. 3 Overview of AI applications in each area of the bank. Source: Own representation based on Marous, Jim: Building an AI-Powered Financial Institution. (WWW-Site, July 2019). Internet: https://thefinancialbrand.com/86455/ai-digital-banking-customer-experience-fraud-risk-trends-artificial-intelligence/ (hit: 07/20/2021, 13:16 MEZ)

According to Statista, business value derived from AI in the global banking industry is projected to reach $300 billion by 2030."[61] This represents a cost reduction of 22% corresponding to $1 trillion in total savings, according to a report by Autonomous Next.[62] The chart in Fig. 3 provides an overview of AI applications in each bank area.

Among these, the most widely used AI tools are robotic process automation (RPA) with 36% for structured operational tasks, conversational interfaces with 32% for customer interaction, and machine learning with 25% for fraud detection purposes.[63] In the following an example of a fully AI-based customer journey, including the individual touchpoints and the respective AI applications, can be found. Since AI applications largely overlap, no clean separation can be made between the touchpoints, but the function or advantage of the respective tool for the banking industry is emphasized and simultaneously assigned to the front, middle and back office systems (Fig. 4).

One thing that has changed significantly in the first step (awareness) in contrast to the traditional customer journey is that instead of individuals themselves recognizing that they need a new banking provider, analytics-based tailored advertisements are used to awaken the need in the potential client. AI is applied to monitor customer behavior to create the next frontier of personalization—the so-called hyper-personalization. "Compared to standard personalization, which uses data analytics

[61] BeyondMinds, 2021, p. 1.

[62] Cf. Marous, 2019.

[63] Cf. Biswas et al., 2020.

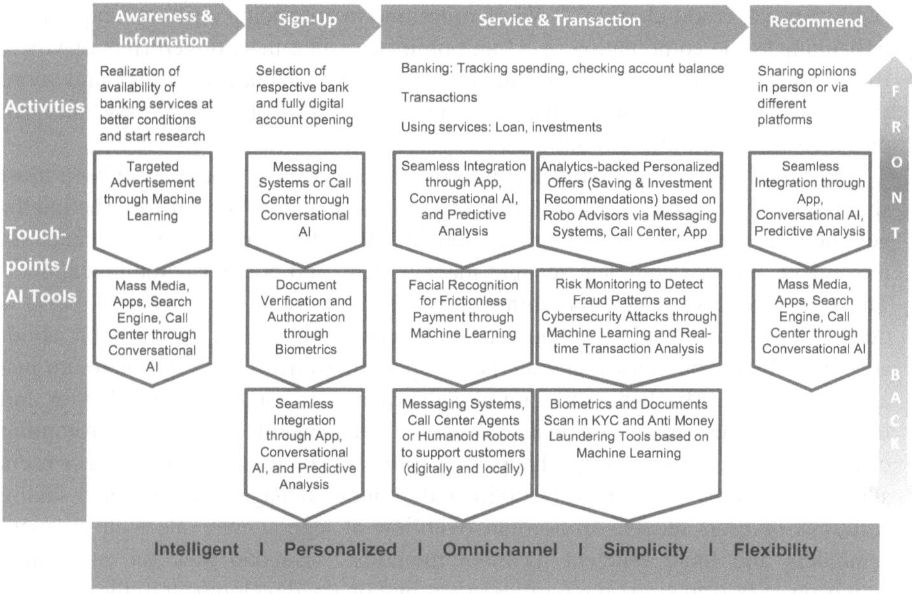

Fig. 4 AI-based customer journey in banking. Source: Own representation based on Biswas, Suparna et al: AI-bank of the future: Can banks meet the AI challenge? (WWW-Site, September 2020). Internet: https://www.mckinsey.com/industries/financial-services/our-insights/ai-bank-of-the-future-can-banks-meet-the-ai-challenge (hit: 07/22/2021, 11:49 MEZ)

to deliver targeted marketing and sales messaging to different customer segments, hyper personalization drills down to the individual customer."[64] This can be achieved by combining predictive analytics and machine learning. Therefore, real-time usage data, such as individual customers' search history, preferred content, geographical location, and further personal information is monitored to queue more targeted, one-to-one marketing campaigns and offers.

Research from the Boston Consulting Group indicates that well-done personalization can increase revenue by 10%.[65] Once the bank succeeds in attracting the attention of the accurate target group, they try to convince them using messaging services such as chatbots or smart agents on the site, via an app or on social media platforms based on NLP processes and predictive analytics. These processes basically run completely autonomously without intervention by employees. The next stage of the customer journey, namely the sign-up, has been completely modified. With AI-based customer service the process of opening a bank account can drop down to 15 min instead of 22 days, as the physical presence of the customer and his documents are not required anymore. AI-based customer service "can authenticate the validity of IDs, auto populate form fields, perform live face recognition, and

[64] Dudovicz, 2021.

[65] Cf. Dudovicz, 2021.

conduct quick credit checks."[66] A key milestone in enhancing customer experience in banking is the combination of AI and biometrics like face, fingerprints or voice. Biometric scanning systems can identify and verify documents faster and more securely by utilizing vast amounts of data.[67] Here, as well, virtual assistants can provide support during account setup.[68]

The actual usage of the bank account, i.e., the services of a bank have been most shaped by AI-powered chatbots and virtual assistants in the front office. The intelligent bots can be distinguished by functionality: Bots for information about account movement, bots for complete account management, and bots for communication.[69] The first category, which represents most of the current generation of bots, is designed to inform simply about account activity, including information about account balance, purchases, and alerts for upcoming bills. Currently, there are just a few bots in use by banks that are already capable to analyze user behavior and thereby become more personal providing independent advice or prompting customers to act.[70] This might happen as follows: For instance, bots detect users spending patterns and suggests optimized money management tips and saving solutions or users receive an account overview at regular intervals with payment reminders and more efficient payment methods.[71] Beyond that, the automated provision of information on securities prices and on the development of the portfolio are also available.[72] The Russian bank "Tochka" was the first bank ever to use a chatbot to enable its small and medium-sized customers to completely manage their accounts in 2017. Besides simple functions like querying account balance, it includes, finding ATMs in the respective area using geolocation, the ability to call the bank, and contact customer support.[73]

Meanwhile, various banks widely implement account managing bots to walk customers through more complex banking tasks such as making international transfers, canceling credit cards,[74] checking credit lines, applying for loans, and accepting orders in the trading area or redirect them to the appropriate banking officers that can help.[75] AI-based transactions usually make use of biometric scanning systems for frictionless payment. Here, for instance, clients can use a "smile-to-pay" function to initiate transactions or command the bot to execute the money transfer via banking app. While doing so, all transactions are being monitored and analyzed in real-time making the back office processes more secured.

[66] BeyondMinds, n.d.

[67] Cf. Trang, 2020.

[68] Cf. Schüssler, 2021.

[69] Cf. Smolinski et al., 2017, p. 239.

[70] Cf. Financial Stability Board, 2017, p. 14–16.

[71] Cf. Biswas et al., 2020.

[72] Cf. Schüssler, 2021.

[73] Cf. Smolinski et al., 2017, p. 231–233.

[74] Cf. Trang, 2020.

[75] Cf. Schüssler, 2021.

Bots, which are primarily used for communication, are mostly used in customer service. They enable consumers to directly interact with the bank for servicing requests and to solve problems.[76] The request proceeds as follows: To identify the intention behind the message and then trigger the action to be performed, bots access the knowledge base where the answers are already stored. By entering the customer number, e.g., if the interaction takes place via the bank's website, the virtual assistant can immediately assign the customer and provide suitable answers by analyzing its data in milliseconds. If the customer communicates in the app or by phone, the system recognizes the customer, as it is connected to the bank's database.[77]

The data obtained via conversational AI can also be used to improve sales and marketing activities. If the virtual assistant is aware of which customer it is dealing with, it can offer further contract options based on a conversation.[78] "While outdated infrastructure for client data storage has slowed the development of chatbots in financial institutions in many jurisdictions, Asian financial institutions and regulators have developed more sophisticated chatbots that are currently in active use."[79] However, it must be noted that customers only perceive a chatbot or talkbot as intelligent or positive if it also able to answer individual and complicated questions helpfully and correctly. Otherwise, there is a risk of an essentially negative customer experience.[80] But internally—in the middle office—there is also a broad spectrum of chatbot applications, ranging from IT and the HR service desk to finance and supply chain. Besides taking over various inquiries, from product research to the conclusion of a purchase, digital assistants also serve as assistants for agents. For complex requests, they can do the groundwork so that human agents can take care of the core tasks. This ensures that customer concerns are handled more efficiently and with minimal effort.[81] For example, chatbots support human clerks with complex customer concerns by analyzing customer data and pinpointing it in a sorted order or even by calculating probabilities about customer behavior, performing as a help desk like a search engine for employees.[82] In summary, it can be said that chatbots or virtual assistants can bring significant improvement to banks, starting with 24/7 accessibility and availability across all channels to enabling fast and hassle-free customer service.[83] In fact, according to estimates of Gartner chatbots will be responsible for cost savings of over $8 billion per year by 2022. Furthermore, it could allow banks to save 862 working hours by 2023, which equals half a million working years.[84]

[76] Cf. Biswas et al., 2020.
[77] Cf. Smolinski et al., 2017, p. 235 f.
[78] Cf. Schüssler, 2021.
[79] Financial Stability Board, 2017, p. 15.
[80] Cf. Buxmann & Schmidt, 2021, p. 55.
[81] Cf. Schüssler, 2021.
[82] Cf. Ulusoy, 2020.
[83] Cf. Trang, 2020.
[84] Cf. Maynard & Crabtree, 2020.

In addition, AI systems support customer service by, e.g., automatically answering e-mails or forwarding them to the relevant team sorted by importance. The same applies to customer requests by phone calls. However, if customers still want to visit the branch, there are also humanoid robots that serve customers holistically, although very few banks are currently providing this service. And in cases where there are no interfaces to third-party systems, requests can be executed by integrating RPA solutions.[85] As stated previously, RPA solutions are the most widely implemented AI systems in the middle and partly back office. There are basically two different types of RPA—AI-driven and normally automated RPA tools. Just a few of the AI-driven RPA can support in the front office with the functions described above, e.g., sending e-mails, or advising customer by phone in interactive voice response. But mostly RPA systems focus on assisting human employees by supporting existing systems. Here, RPA largely serves to process the previously insufficiently structured input by relying on machine learn-based techniques such as optical character recognition (OCR) and NLP. OCR can recognize texts and images; NLP can understand and evaluate them. In this way, e.g., scanned documents, salary statements, and identification documents can be processed by RPA applications.[86] In addition to process optimization of routine tasks, such as accounting for incoming and outgoing payments, RPA can also analyze transactions in the back office and forward unusual patterns "such as multiple transactions made in a short time or substantial increases in cash deposits or withdrawals."[87] Very mature RPA systems can even help decide on individual customer matters, such as calculating the interest rate in relation to customers' risk.[88]

As already explained, loans can be applied for via app or via virtual assistants without having to physically visit the bank branch with numerous documents. Getting a credit approval nowadays can happen in only 2 days instead of 10–15 days due to AI, which can significantly enhance customer satisfaction.[89] In retail banking and in the already largely automated lending business, further AI use cases arise from the voluminous transaction data available. AI software can facilitate data collection for creditworthiness checks for both the bank and the customer. For financing inquiries or before signing a lease, banks generally require a so-called confidential self-disclosure. In largely standardized questionnaires, the prospective customer must disclose data on his/her person, assets, current income and expenses, and other liabilities. Here, several banks have implemented a solution with an AI component, which automatically derives and structures the required information from all available transaction data. To do so, customers' incoming and outgoing payments are analyzed and assigned to the relevant categories through intelligent tagging, e.g., income, rent payments or existing financing installments. This

[85] Cf. BeyondMinds, 2021, p. 2.

[86] Cf. Buxmann & Schmidt, 2021, p. 56 f.

[87] Trang Linh, 2020.

[88] Cf. Ulusoy, 2020.

[89] Cf. BeyondMinds, n.d.

eliminates the need for individual process steps such as submitting proof of income. As a result, an automatically filled-in self-disclosure minimizes the effort for the prospective customer and accelerates the process up to the loan decision. The bank saves manual process steps in importing and checking the information that is already available and can optimize the risk assessment by taking all known data into account.[90]

However, a more new and efficient way of credit scoring is to analyze additional, unstructured, and semi-structured data sources, including social media activity, mobile phone use, and text message activity. Banks are increasingly acquiring these credit scoring tools as it captures a more nuanced view of creditworthiness and improves the rating accuracy of loans. However, the increased risk regarding the use of personal data must be handled with a high level of caution. The implementation of AI in credit scoring models brings several advantages. Since the credit assessing process is faster, more efficient, and less costly, more clients can access loans more easily. Whereas in the past a weak or incomplete credit story led to loan refusal, today people without a credit story have significantly more financing options. The current state of machine learning-led credit scoring models is that it has not yet been proven that intelligent models outperform traditional ones in assessing creditworthiness.[91] Nevertheless, the Smava borrower study shows that the conclusion of loans in bank branches is now declining and that this trend will continue. Thus, 7% of respondents have already taken out a loan online at least once, and as many as 25% can imagine doing so in the future. The reasons given for the increasing popularity of online offers are better conditions, constant availability, transparency of offers, and short processing.[92]

Apart from borrowing, another common business of banks is investment. The main AI tool applied for this purpose is robo advisors. Banks can deploy automated investment advice in two variants: Complete solutions, in which the investment is handled entirely by the advisor within the framework of the user's specifications and advisory software that merely calculates a proposal for the customer on how to invest his money. The customer then purchases the securities himself. In both cases, the investor must answer a few questions online about own financial situation after choosing a provider. On this basis, they receive a proposal for the appropriate composition of their securities account—i.e., regarding the securities, such as funds, that may be most suitable in their individual situation and for their investment goals.

Subsequently, the securities account is constantly monitored by the robo advisor. Transparency plays a major role here. The advantages of intelligent investment advisors are, on the one hand, that the effort required to compile and maintain a securities account is relatively low. Investors do not necessarily have to follow

[90]Cf. Buxmann & Schmidt, 2021, p. 55–57.

[91]Cf. Financial Stability Board, 2017, p. 12.

[92]Cf. Smolinski et al., 2017, p. 246 f.

developments on the international capital markets, as portfolio adjustments are either completely automatic or require only a few mouse clicks.

On the other hand, relatively small amounts can already be invested with many providers. Furthermore, many investors tend to act emotionally when investing, which is impossible with robo advisory. However, long-term investment success cannot be guaranteed due to the short time of deployment of robo advisors in the market.[93] In the meantime, operational risk management is carried out in the middle office so that customers can conduct secure online banking, including credit and asset management.

Credit card fraud has become one of the most prevalent forms of cybercrime in recent years and this trend is exacerbated by the strong growth in online and mobile payments.[94] Here, FinTechs, e.g., offer banks AI-supported solutions to prevent payment fraud. Payment instructions via credit cards or online banking are checked for plausibility in real time. Among other things, the payment recipient, amount, and location are compared with historical transaction data. If the AI system detects significant discrepancies or other risks, the payment can be blocked and a corresponding check order issued to a bank employee.[95]

In the back office, AI-based risk management tools such as KYC and anti-money laundering systems, focus more on providing support in meeting regulatory requirements and increasing efficiency and quality. For companies in the banking and finance sector, the term KYC refers to the regulatory requirement to obtain sufficient knowledge about new and existing customers. Compliance with this requirement is regularly monitored by national regulators (e.g., BaFin for Germany). Possible non-compliance can quickly lead to penalties and reputational risks for the bank in question.[96] This means that in order to comply with monetary sanctions and prevent money laundering and terrorism financing, banks must continuously verify that their customers' personal and corporate data is correct and up to date.[97] To do so, AI algorithms scan customer records and compare them with information on the internet to determine how reliable the records are.[98] In case of any contradictions or out-of-date data such as data that contradicts entries from publicly accessible media such as a company's website, an employee is assigned to perform an individual check. In a further development stage, the automated correction of incorrect data and the addition of data that is not yet available is conceivable to improve the data quality of a bank.

As already stated, banks are required by law to check all payment transactions for suspicious patterns and to report them to the respective authorities. According to BaFin, the annual volume of money laundering in Germany alone is estimated at

[93] Deutsche Postbank AG, 2021.

[94] Cf. Kaya, 2019, p. 6.

[95] Cf. Buxmann & Schmidt, 2021, p. 56–58.

[96] Cf. Smolinski et al., 2017, p. 281.

[97] Cf. Buxmann & Schmidt, 2021, p. 51, 57.

[98] Cf. Kaya, 2019, p. 6 f.

between 50 and 100 billion euros. Anti-money laundering tools are also based on a combination of the analysis of monitored data and historical customer data,[99] but considering the above-mentioned volume, a distinction can be made between two automated checking procedures for preventing money laundering. These procedures are based on detection rules defined by experts. In some cases, the procedures relate to individual transaction characteristics. At the same time, it is possible to systematically bypass the defined rules, e.g., by deliberately falling below the known thresholds.

Moreover, these models can only be adapted to new and more complex money laundering methods with a time lag. Against this background, various banks are testing machine learning approaches in the form of consistent feedback on current detection rules and based on this, the derivation of new, previously unknown detection patterns. Using AI, the number of baseless suspicions and the manual follow-up effort can thus be reduced in the target image and previously hidden money laundering cases can be uncovered.[100] Which in turn "not only improves security, but also increases customer trust, protects the brand's reputation, and reduces customer churn."[101]

The main objective of using AI in CXM is primarily to address customers individually at the right time via the right channels to offer personalized products or services, as already addressed. Due to the pandemic, consumers even expect a higher level of personalized treatment.[102] In this section, a few examples will be given to demonstrate how banks are using continuous monitoring and advanced analytics tools to proactively offer clients assistance with financial management or suggest opportunities to grow their wealth based on their (financial) situation.

This type of proactive engagement should take place on any offered service and their touchpoints.[103] The usage of predictive analysis systems can be categorized into client facing purposes in the front office, tailored communication and services in the middle office, and ultimately into bank-internal purposes in the back office with forecasts for the banking business itself, from which the customer ultimately still benefits.

A widespread concept of product recommendation for addressing individual customer needs is the so-called next best offer concept. Based on known characteristics such as age, occupation, place of residence, spending (propensity), consumer behavior, and (liquid) assets, customers are assigned to specific profiles, to which they receive a correspondingly suitable product offer. The advantage here is that with machine learning, previously unnoticed interdependencies can be identified and, as a result, both the quality of recommendations and the closing rate can be

[99] Cf. IVXS UK Limited, n.d.

[100] Cf. Bruxmann & Schmidt, 2021, p. 51–58.

[101] BeyondMinds, n.d.

[102] Cf. Biswas et al., 2020.

[103] Cf. Hüffner, 2020.

increased.[104] For example, if the search data indicates that a customer is frequently looking for houses or researching home loans and mortgage rates, the algorithms recognize that the customer wants to buy a house and is therefore a good candidate for a home loan. Based on this information, the software generates a home loan offer with a low interest rate for this customer and proposes it either directly to the customer or, in some cases, (first) to the bank employee.[105]

In another use case from Commerzbank AG, the software searches through thousands of articles a day from up to 8000 newspapers worldwide for risk-relevant information on the bank's own corporate customers, to be able to support a company in financial difficulties at early stage. For this purpose, NLP is used to identify words and word sequences that may represent company names to then compare these with the bank's own database entries. If the company is indeed a customer, the newspaper articles are forwarded to the responsible risk or credit manager. In this way, the latter always remains informed about potentially critical developments—even with a large customer portfolio. One use case of advanced analytics, which primarily serves internal bank purposes, is historical account data evaluated by machine learning to preview future balances to avoid potential shortfalls.[106] Especially in unforeseen situations like the current corona-induced pandemic, AI can be a crucial support in inventory management.[107]

For the final stage of the customer journey—the recommendation step—, social media monitoring is increasingly being deployed to influence or even avoid bad customer experiences or negative criticism at an early stage. Monitoring customer feedback on social media is carried out for reasons including opinion research, market research, trend analysis, press review, early warning system, and competitive analysis. Here, the monitoring tool continuously searches social platforms for certain keywords, such as the name of the bank, which is also known as social listening.[108]

A deep knowledge of customers and their opinions enabled by social listening results in improved engagement and assisted intelligent decision-making.[109] Hence, the introduction of AI in CXM is success critical, as it clearly modifies each customer touchpoint in a positive way. It can be concluded that AI in the front office enables faster, more flexible, and highly customized service, while in the middle office it tends to boost operational efficiency. In the back office, AI eventually guarantees compliance with the regulatory framework. However, one fact seems to be certain, in the competition for direct customer contact, the banks with the best customer experience will most likely prevail.[110]

---

[104] Cf. Bruxmann & Schmidt, 2021, p. 56.

[105] Cf. Hüffner, 2020.

[106] Cf. Bruxmann & Schmidt, 2021, p. 55–57.

[107] Cf. Trang, 2020.

[108] Cf. Smolinski et al., 2017, p. 288 f.

[109] Cf. Mentionlytics Inc. n.d.

[110] Cf. Bruxmann & Schmidt, 2021, p. 55.

5 Summary: AI Digitalizes the Business Model of Banks

The numerous AI applications at (German) banks show that AI is no longer a technological fad, but is increasingly being implemented to fully digitalize the business model of banks. Although most banks are in the test phase or at an early stage of transformation, they have high expectations of the possibilities offered by AI, as it is opening new application areas that until recently were considered either too complicated or too expensive to automate. Predominantly, conversational AI (NLP), predictive analysis tools, and credit scoring tools are enabling banks to provide personalized customer support, offer tailored services in real time, and guarantee greater security during the banking process.

The research results show that AI makes customers' lives considerably easier. According to the interviews conducted, customers appreciate the fact that they no longer must appear on site to open an account, e.g., or wait several weeks for their loan decision.

The banks also benefit from AI potential: In middle office systems, most current AI use cases are aimed at a higher level of automation to reduce the workload of employees and thus increase efficiency.[111] In the back office area, AI is becoming a necessity in order to comply with the regulations with which banks in particular have to contend. Here, a noticeable phenomenon has emerged: The research results show that banks are clearly limited in the implementation of AI technology due to strict regulations.

On the other hand, it is the regulatory regimes, especially regarding cyberattacks and transactions, that require the adoption of AI. This seems to pose a dilemma for banks. However, each bank implements AI technology differently to satisfy individual needs, as there is no standardized approach.

Although self-learning algorithms are already capable of performing certain activities better than humans, they are sometimes pushed to their limits, as the complexity of the human brain represents an insurmountable obstacle for AI systems. As a result, there remains a degree of mistrust in AI among the banks surveyed. They are firmly convinced that AI can currently only be deployed to assist humans and is mainly used to serve employees. Although this works successfully, AI can currently be described more as a tool for humans than as a substitute for them.[112]

References

Ahmet, C. (Ed.). (2018). *Artificial intelligence. How advanced machine learning will shape the future of our world* (1st ed.).

Allan, S. (n.d.). *The three tiers of AI. Automating tomorrow with AGI, ASI & ANI.* (online). Internet: https://www.aware.co.th/three-tiers-ai-automating-tomorrow-agi-asi-ani/ (hit: 04/07/2021, 20:11 MEZ).

[111] Cf. Buxmann & Schmidt, 2021, S. 49–57.

[112] Cf. Segesser, 2018, p. 16.

Aurecon Group Pty. Ltd. (Ed.) (n.d.). *Artificial intelligence vs human intelligence – a competition or collaboration?* (online). Internet: https://www.aurecongroup.com/expertise/digital-engineering-and-advisory/artificial-intelligence-vs-humans (hit: 04/18/2021, 19:30 MEZ).

Berry, C. (2020, November). *Journey mapping in banking* (online). Internet: https://www.smaply.com/blog/journey-mapping-banking (hit: 07/17/2021, 00:24 MEZ).

BeyondMinds. (Ed.) (2021). *AI potential. For customer-facing services in finance.* (text file). Internet: https://hs.beyondminds.ai/hubfs/BM_Financial_whitepaper_2021Q1.pdf?utm_medium=email&_hsmi=111366822&_hsenc=p2ANqtz-9idUPsQZmgfRVXwiIlXFw4-YhE7d1d5Y12FomOomCMQX6mhPT6A02jgALzb1xIK7BwHsJZE8fQAClkscp3m_NFp4ie64vproVlWBrtA9a11EX3_vo&utm_content=111366822&utm_source=hs_automation (hit: 07/19/2021, 22:17 MEZ).

BeyondMinds. (Ed.) (n.d.). *Financial AI to improve customer service: The future of the customer experience.* (online). Internet: https://beyondminds.ai/blog/financial-ai-to-improve-customer-service-the-future-of-the-customer-experience/ (hit: 07/15/2021, 15:33 MEZ).

Bibliographisches Institut GmbH. (Ed.) (2021, April). *Die Intelligenz.* (online). Internet: https://www.duden.de/rechtschreibung/Intelligenz (hit: 04/05/2021, 09:53 MEZ).

Biswas, S., et al. (2020, September). *AI-bank of the future: Can banks meet the AI challenge?* (online). Internet: https://www.mckinsey.com/industries/financial-services/our-insights/ai-bank-of-the-future-can-banks-meet-the-ai-challenge (hit: 07/20/2021, 13:34 MEZ).

Brighterion Inc. (Ed.) (2017, January). *A closer look at AI: Data mining.* (online). Internet: https://brighterion.com/data-mining/ (hit: 05/10/2021, 00:10 MEZ).

Bruhn, M., & Hadwich, K. (Eds.). (2021). *Künstliche Intelligenz im Dienstleistungsmanagement. Geschäftsmodelle – Serviceinnovationen – Implementierung* (1st ed.). Springer Gabler.

Brutkasten Media GmbH. (Ed.) (2017, August). *Verstehen, Fühlen, Handeln – Die Grundlagen künstlicher Intelligenz.* (online). Internet: https://brutkasten.com/venionaire-kuenstliche-intelligenz-teil2/ (hit: 04/20/2021, 23:14 MEZ).

Buchkremer, R., Heupel, T., & Koch, O. (2020). *Künstliche Intelligenz in Wirtschaft & Gesellschaft. Auswirkungen, Herausforderungen & Handlungsempfehlungen* (1st ed.). Springer Gabler.

Bünte, C. (2018). *Künstliche Intelligenz – die Zukunft des Marketing. Ein praktischer Leitfaden für Marketing-Manager* (1st ed.). Springer Gabler.

Buxmann, P., & Schmidt, H. (Eds.). (2019). *Künstliche Intelligenz. Mit Algorithmen zum wirtschaftlichen Erfolg* (1st ed.). Springer Gabler.

Buxmann, P., & Schmidt, H. (Eds.). (2021). *Künstliche Intelligenz. Mit Algorithmen zum wirtschaftlichen Erfolg* (2nd ed.). Springer Gabler.

Chalopin, J., & Trehan, R. (2020, June). *Applying AI to risk management in banking and finance. What's the latest?* (online). Internet: https://www.deltecbank.com/2020/06/15/applying-ai-to-risk-management-in-banking-and-finance-whats-the-latest/ (hit: 07/10/2021, 23:36 MEZ).

Corporate Finance Institute Education Inc. (Ed.) (n.d.). *Machine learning (in finance).* (online). Internet: https://corporatefinanceinstitute.com/resources/knowledge/other/machine-learning-in-finance/ (hit: 04/24/2021, 15:27 MEZ).

De Spiegeleire, S., Maas, M., & Sweijs, T. (2017). *Artificial Intelligence and the Future of Defense. Strategic Implications for Small- and Medium-sized Force Providers* (1st ed.). The Hague Centre for Strategic Studies.

Deloitte GmbH. (Ed.) (2020, June). *State of AI in the enterprise – 3rd edition. Ergebnisse der Befragung von 200 AI-Experten zu Künstlicher Intelligenz in deutschen Unternehmen 3rd ed.* (text file). Internet: https://www2.deloitte.com/content/dam/Deloitte/de/Documents/technology-media-telecommunications/DELO-6418_State%20of%20AI%202020_KS4.pdf (hit: 05/11/2021, 23:26 MEZ).

Deutsche Postbank AG. (2021). *Robo-Advisors – die neue Art der digitalen Vermögensverwaltung.* (online). Internet: https://www.postbank.de/themenwelten/geld-finanzen/artikel_robo-advisor-anlageberatung-vom-computer.html (hit: 07/24/2021, 15:04 MEZ).

Dilmegani, C. (2017, November). *Dynamic pricing: What it is, why it matters & top pricing tools*. (online). Internet: https://research.aimultiple.com/dynamic-pricing/ (hit: 07/09/2021, 19:23 MEZ).

Dudovicz, P. (2021). *10 Banking customer experience trends to watch in 2021*. (online). Internet: https://global.hitachi-solutions.com/blog/banking-customer-experience-trends (hit: 05/31/2021, 19:27 MEZ).

Financial Stability Board. (Ed.) (2017, November). *Artificial intelligence and machine learning in financial services. Market developments and financial stability implications*. (text file). Internet: https://www.fsb.org/wp-content/uploads/P011117.pdf (hit: 05/17/2021, 21:14 MEZ).

Gentsch, P. (2019). *Künstliche Intelligenz für Sales, Marketing und Service. Mit AI und Bots zu einem Algorithmic Business – Konzepte und Best Practices* (2nd ed.). Springer Gabler.

Hüffner, E. (2020, April). *Was ist Customer Experience und warum ist sie wichtig?* (online). Internet: https://www.zendesk.de/blog/why-companies-should-invest-in-the-customer-experience-2/ (hit: 07/29/2021, 22:35 MEZ).

IVXS UK Limited. (n.d.). *Knowledgebase AML Transaktions-Monitoring. Was ist AML Transaktions-Monitoring?* (online). Internet: https://complyadvantage.com/de/knowledgebase/was-ist-anti-geldwaeschepraevention-aml/anti-geldwaesche-aml-transaktions-monitoring/ (hit: 07/27/2021, 17:36 MEZ).

Jugel, V. (2017, December). So verändert KI das Marketing. (online). Internet: https://www.onetoone.de/artikel/db/oto_49307.html (hit: 07/08/2021, 22:08 MEZ).

JuPantarhei GmbH. (Ed.) (n.d.). *ANI, AGI and ASI – what do they mean?*. (online). Internet: https://jupantarhei.com/ani-agi-and-asi-what-do-they-mean/ (hit: 04/07/2021, 17:39 MEZ).

Kaya, O. (2019, July). *Künstliche Intelligenz im Bankensektor. Ein bisher kaum genutzter Hebel für Rentabilität*. (text file). Internet: https://www.dbresearch.de/PROD/RPS_DE-PROD/PROD0000000000496371/K%C3%BCnstliche_Intelligenz_im_Bankensektor%3A_Ein_bisher.PDF;REWEBJSE SIONID=9EB8C08010C7D67E3638A7F345C28B67?undefined&reaload=NAhZGWMsORrgxRqxQoju9ejqYh5zmdFw/P~ppDeyo~DXf~MPQ8SOPTK1ut5vtYa (hit: 05/31/2021, 19:48 MEZ).

Kreutzer, R. T., & Sirrenberg, M. (2019). *Künstliche Intelligenz verstehen. Grundlagen – Use-Cases – unternehmenseigene KI-Journey* (1st ed.). Springer Gabler.

Lammers, M. (2004, October). *Strategic sourcing in banking – A framework*. (text file). Internet: https://slidetodoc.com/strategic-sourcing-in-banking-a-framework-markus-lammers/ (hit: 07.07.2021, 23:17 MEZ).

Lenzen, M. (2018, May). *Kurzinterview: Worin sich menschliche und Künstliche Intelligenz unterscheiden*. (online). Internet: https://mindtheprogress.de/aktuelles/kurzinterview-worin-sich-kunstliche-und-menschliche-intelligenz-unterscheiden/ (hit: 04/18/2021, 19:26 MEZ).

Marous, J. (2019, July). *Building an AI-powered financial institution*. (online). Internet: https://thefinancialbrand.com/86455/ai-digital-banking-customer-experience-fraud-risktrends-artificial-intelligence/ (hit: 07/20/2021, 13:16 MEZ).

Marous, J. (2020). Banking transformed white paper. Transforming the digital customer journey. In *White Paper Special Edition December 2020*. DBR Media.

Maynard, N., & Crabtree, G. (2020, October). *AI & automation in banking: Adoption, vendor positioning & market forecasts 2020 – 2025*. (online). Internet.

Mentionlytics Inc. (n.d.) *Social media monitoring for financial institutions*. (online). Internet: https://www.mentionlytics.com/social-media-monitoring-for-financial-institutions/ (hit: 07/28/2021, 14:00 MEZ).

Mullion, M. (n.d.). *What's AI anyway?*. (online). Internet: https://www.aus.com/de/node/5726 (hit: 04/20/2021, 14:48 MEZ).

Murphy, K. P. (2012). *Machine learning: A probabilistic perspective* (1st ed.). The MIT Press.

Oxford University Press. (Ed.) (2021). *Definition of deep learning*. (online). Internet: https://www.lexico.com/en/definition/deep_learning (hit: 05/01/2021, 14:08 MEZ).

Rich, E., Knight, K., & Nair, S. B. (2009). *Artificial intelligence* (3rd ed.). Tata McGraw Hill Education.

SAS Institute Inc. (Ed.) (2021). *Artificial intelligence. What it is and why it matters.* (online). Internet: https://www.sas.com/en_us/insights/analytics/what-is-artificial-intelligence.html (hit: 04/20/2021, 21:12 MEZ).
Schenk, C., & Tietze, U. (1993). *Halbleiter-Schaltungstechnik* (10th ed.). Springer Gabler.
Schüssler, S. (2021, April). *Neue Wege im Kundenservice durch Conversational AI. Wie virtuelle Sprachassistenten die Kundeninteraktion verändern.* (online). Internet: https://www.der-bank-blog.de/neue-wege-kundenservice/technologie/37676373/ (hit: 06/02/2021, 17:20 MEZ).
Segesser, P. (2018, June). *Was ist eigentlich KI – Künstliche Intelligenz? Und wie wird sie unser Leben in Zukunft verändern?* (text file). Internet: https://friedrich.dzbank.de/fileadmin/user_upload/Friedrich-Ausgabe2-Ki.pdf (hit: 08/30/2021, 11:06 MEZ).
Singh, N. (2018, December). *Artificial intelligence and it's sub-fields.* (online). Internet: https://medium.com/@neha49712/artificial-intelligence-and-its-sub-fields-a5a63d8263e8 (hit: 05/09/2021, 00:29 MEZ).
Smolinski, R., Gerdes, M., Siejka, M., & Bodek, M. C. (Eds.). (2017). *Innovationen und Innovationsmanagement in der Finanzbranche* (1st ed.). Springer Gabler.
SoftwareTestingHelp. (Ed.) (2021, June). *What is artificial intelligence: Definition & sub-fields of AI.* (online). Internet: https://www.softwaretestinghelp.com/what-is-artificial-intelligence/ (hit: 07/02/2021, 17:46 MEZ).
Trang Linh, T. (2020, April). *Adopting RPA in response to COVID-19 pandemic.* (online). Internet: https://blog.fpt-software.com/adopting-rpa-in-response-to-covid-19-pandemic (hit: 07/23/2021, 13:05 MEZ).
Trang, T. (2020, November). *How artificial intelligence enhances customer experiences in bank*ing. (online). Internet: https://blog.fpt-software.com/how-artificial-intelligence-enhances-customer-experiences-in-banking (hit: 07/22/2021, 17:49 MEZ).
Ulusoy, M. D. (2020). *KI und RPA bei Banken: Mit Bots Kundenanfragen in Echtzeit beantworten.* (online). Internet: https://www.ki-note.de/einzelansicht/ki-und-rpa-bei-banken-mit-bots-kundenanfragen-in-echtzeit-beantworten (hit: 06/04/2021, 18:47 MEZ).
Wennker, P. (2020). *Künstliche Intelligenz in der Praxis. Anwendung in Unternehmen und Branchen: KI wettbewerbs- und zukunftsorientiert einsetzen* (1st ed.). Springer Gabler.

Merve Kacar is a solution developer at one of the Big Four consulting companies. She is responsible for consulting in the areas of digitalization and risk management.

As a solution developer, she supports companies in the implementation and operation of compliance, risk and performance management systems. In her academic as well as professional career, she has been dealing with the digital transformation of business processes over the past years.

The Future of Marketing and Sales Automation

How Smart Glasses, the Metaverse and Algorithmic Commerce Impact the Next Evolution of Marketing and Sales Automation

Markus Rach

1 Technological Evolution of Marketing and Sales Automation

Marketing and Sales Automation (MSA) marks one of the most notable and fundamental digital transformation processes within organizations. While much of it happens in the background, contrary to the more public omnichannel content evolution, or much notable e-commerce efforts, MSA revolutionized marketing and sales operations. However, it was not an abrupt revolution, such as the impact of the smartphone on customer communication, or the recent growth of short video as a dominant content format. It was a silent revolution, that began with the invention of customer relationship management (CRM). CRM is a philosophy, a methodology, a process, and a business tool. It is essential to understand the interplay of CRM and marketing in the context of the ongoing technological and cultural transformation of organizations. As the saying goes "a fool with a tool is still a fool," one must appreciate the intertwined nature of process thinking, organizational culture, and the deployment of technological advances in the history of MSA.

When talking about MSA, twenty-first-century technology comes to mind. Yet the journey started in the earliest days of human-to-human trade relationships. Over 20,000 years ago, traders in Papa New Guinea acknowledged, that to trade obsidian successfully, much knowledge was needed about the trading partner's needs and context. Book-keeping in accounting fulfilled a very similar role, essentially marking a codification of trading records; who owns what to whom.

Jumping forward, Rolodexes took over this role in the 1950s, see Fig. 1, long before CRM manifested itself as a well-researched and widely applied business philosophy.

M. Rach (✉)
Shenzhen Technology University, Shenzhen, China
e-mail: markus.rach@sztu.edu.cn

U. Hannig, U. Seebacher (eds.), *Marketing and Sales Automation*, Management for Professionals, https://doi.org/10.1007/978-3-031-20040-3_27

Fig. 1 Rolodex deck (Source: Princeton University, 2021)

The Rolodex mirrored the wealth of a salesman. The more cards, the more Rolodexes, the more outgoing, connected and relationship-driven a salesman seemed to be. Contact cards did not just contain names, companies, and phone numbers, but also personal details. Birthdays, the name of a contact's kids, business drivers, and much more. It marked the unspoken beginning of CRM as a tool and as a philosophy, long before scholars emphasized CRM as a business mantra. Up to this point, marketing and sales functioned in silos. The marketing function, despite the many definitions and the emergence of the 4Ps, remained fundamentally focused on promotion and marketing communication. Although not much has changed in that regard, if one believes current research, the emergence of information technology was about to impact this very silo-relationship. Driven by Moore's Law, computers started to emerge as a daily tool within the business landscape. Although unaffordable to SMEs at first, computers became a standard business tool in the 70s. They quickly replaced the typewriter and gave way to an increasing flood of applications, rendering office work more productive than ever. While the cost of computing kept crumbling, computer power increased. So did their impact on the now-dominating CRM philosophy in many organizations. Rolodexes were digitally transformed into databases. Database marketing, which got later replaced by CRM tools, provided huge productivity gains. However, the marketing—sales gap remained. The first baby steps in MSA did in fact occur in sales and not in marketing.

The 1990s saw an explosion of CRM solutions, alongside the growth of enterprise resource planning (ERP). A very competitive battle began, with big named players like Siebel, IBM, and others competing to become the dominant CRM solution. It was however a cloud service founded in 1999, who took the CRM market by storm. Salesforce.com. Its naming is almost ironic, considering the acronym SFA (Sales Force Automation) was used to bridge the gap between a pure database, contact management and what is today known as a full-fledged CRM system.

The 1990s did also mark the beginning of marketing automation. It became clear, that both marketing and sales must align to unleash the full potential of the CRM movement. Thus in 1992, Unica, later IBM Campaign, was one of the very first marketing automation attempts. It took however until the middle of 2000 for marketing automation to truly take off. It was not for the availability of computing power, but the emergence of the Internet to disrupt brand interactions with the marketplace. Although web2.0 was not born yet, E-Mail marketing started to emerge, quickly creating the first meaningful use cases demanding the integration and alignment of CRM and marketing automation. Through the emergence of social media and thus the web 2.0 era, marketing automation evolved and truly exploded in offering and application. Use cases widened from E-Mail marketing to full journey marketing, integrating mobile and becoming the marketers' go-to tool to manage much of their set and forget customer interaction. Market consolidation by the leading players, in the CRM and MA field, did the rest to morph CRM systems and marketing automation into true all-in-one marketing platforms.

Why is this short historical recap of the technological evolution of MSA relevant? Its relevancy can be found in the fact that, until around 2010, the adoption and use case of MSA were driven by technological advances on the application side and end-user adoption behavior of technologies. To the most part, MSA functioned as a support system to the organization. Allowing more efficient brand to market interactions. It mitigated the data-processing limitations of humans and assisted the interpretation of larger datasets to plan relevant automated marketing campaigns. Set-and-forget strategies emerged and dominated the MSA use case scenario. The introduction of AI to MSA started to open new playing fields from 2010 onward. Suddenly, MSA systems became more capable than the human mind. Predictive and prescriptive capabilities emerged. This meant that the data-processing ability of humans became second to that of MSA systems. However, the involvement of systems within decision-making processes remained another issue.

Although over 20 years ago, Bucklin et al. (1998) argued that the impact of technology in marketing was to progress from supporting decision-making to automated decision-making. This state is not yet achieved, despite the many advances. In most instances, it is still the human factor governing the ultimate decision-making process of the MSA setup, process definitions, and extend of usage. Support for this argument can be found in the research of Mero et al. (2020), who argue for a highly causal mode of reasoning during the MSA implementation phase, in contrast to a rather effectuation-based mode of reasoning during the selection, and a balanced mode of reasoning during the post-implementation, phase. Further support can be found by Rach (2021) discovering decoupled managerial decision-making processes from organizationally available marketing technology data. For this very reason, understanding the interplay of technology, the human factor, the activity to be achieved and the context of application remains vital to contextualize the current and future impact of technological developments on MSA systems. Likewise, it is vital for managers to understand how the breadth of

MSA systems might change to prepare their organization from both a human, technological, and application perspective for the MSA roadmap ahead.

2 Understanding Technology in the Context of Human Limitations

To further elaborate on the role MSA systems play within the current technological context, the Human Activity Assistive Technology Model (HAAT) has been applied (Fig. 2). The HAAT, based on Bailey's (1989) human performance model, allows to understand the previously mentioned interplay, within a defined business context. Although the model is mostly used to frame assistive technologies in a non-business context, it can help to understand the context and breadth of MSA system applications (Cook & Polgar, 2014).

The HAAT focuses on two important and interlinked perspectives: Human beings aiming to conduct an activity within a given environmental context. Thus, this model assumes an interface between technology and the environment. At the same time, it acknowledges limitations on the human side to achieve set activities. While its application to physical undertakings is obvious, it helps to categorize knowledge-driven tasks by recognizing cognitive limitations of the human factor. In the light of MSA systems, these include data collection, data handling, and data interpretation capabilities, alongside the use of data for decision-making processes. The context, defining the environment and thus the relevant environmental interface, constantly broadens. Whereas in the mid-1990s, activities centered around record keeping, the context was limited to human-to-human interactions, before adding E-Mail. Only 5–10 years later, the context of both application and the environment changed

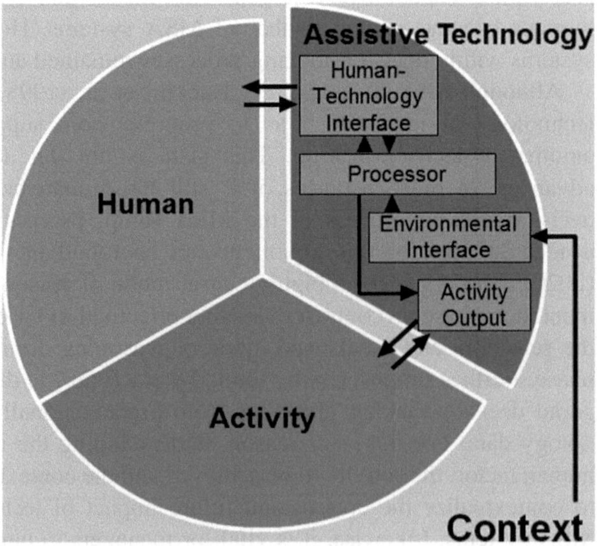

Fig. 2 HAAT model (Cook & Hussey, 1995)

dramatically through web2.0 and thus a new flood of mostly unstructured data points. Customer journeys became more complex, yet also more digital. The Social-CRM development emerged as a result. Omnichannel and multiple screens became the norm. The 360 view of the customer was not bound anymore to human-to-human only but embraced human to web interactions. Even in the beginning stages of the Social-CRM and thus Social-MA campaigns, the cognitive limitation of humans was exceeded by far. The reliance on technology for effective organizational decision-making within the marketing and sales function manifested itself.

Alternative models, such as the Human Technology Organization Model (HTO), attempt to equally classify the interaction of humans and technology (Karltun et al., 2021; Berglund et al., 2020; Baruch, 1997), yet miss the granularity of context. As technologies change, their context of usage and thus application changes. While MSA systems function today largely on the dimension of the Human-Computer-Interaction (HCI), the widening of use cases through new end-consumer and enterprise technologies, is pushing the need to also understand the dimensions of Human-Machine Interaction (HMI) and Human-Technology Interaction (HCI). The latter offers a novel contextual structure of application, e.g., through Web 3.0, Virtual and Augmented Reality, or comprehensive autonomous systems (Fig. 3).

Context Aware Assistive Systems (CAAS) take the notion of HAAT further, yet only in the perspective of technology (Korn et al., 2014). CAAS applications can be found in daily appliances, such as GPS systems in cars or in smartphones. It is only recently that the notion of HAAT and CAAS has been used to understand the human to technology interaction in a work- or business-related context. It is, therefore, that a model, extending the notion of HAAT, HTO and CAAS is suggested, integrating the HCI, HMI and HTI dimension, to conceptualize how innovative technologies will impact MSA systems.

3 Shortfalls and Optimization Opportunities of Current Marketing & Sales Automation Solutions

Before continuing, it is important to know where current MSA solutions fall short to integrate new technology. Figure 4 provides a system's perspective, applying the HAAT model nomination. As can be seen, the link between an organization, its MSA technology stack, and the market is provided through the contextual linkage of systems.

As evident in Fig. 4, at least three contextual links can be drawn. As per the HAAT model, the governing technology interaction perspective is the HTI, yet in current MSA applications, which are governed by the HTO model, HCI applies. This imposes a limitation by assuming the independence of the environment, the organization, and the organization's technology stack. While these three dimensions are independent by themselves, their interaction is not. A change in the context of the environment impacts the functional ability of the organization's technology stack and thus likewise the decision-making ability of the same organization's management. Thus, contextual changes must be noted and linked to step-changes in the

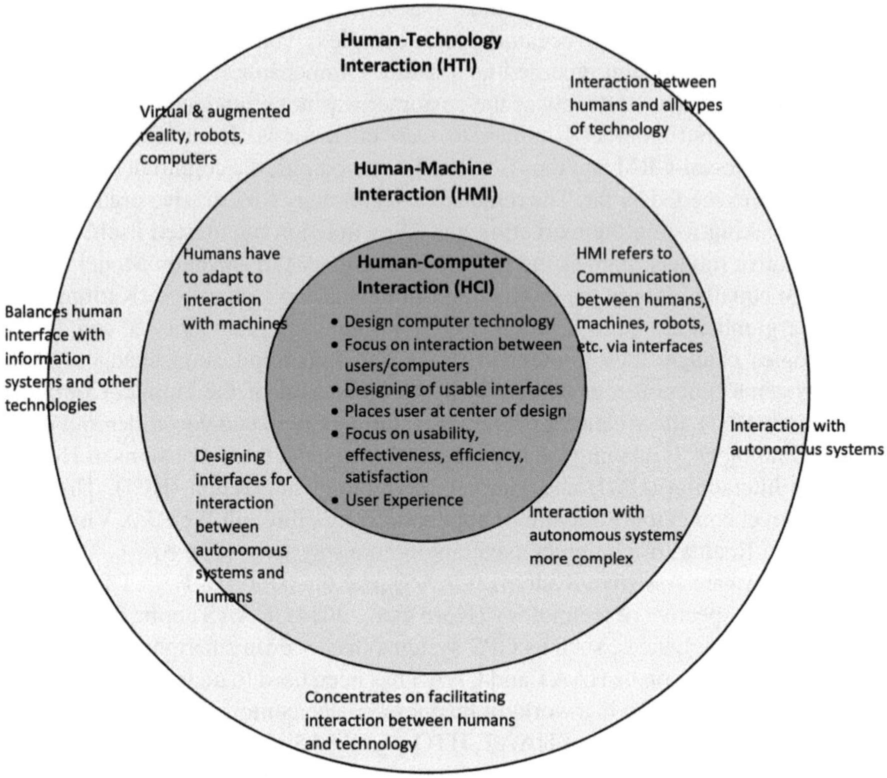

Fig. 3 Exemplary comparison of HCI, HMI and HTI (Coetzer et al., 2020)

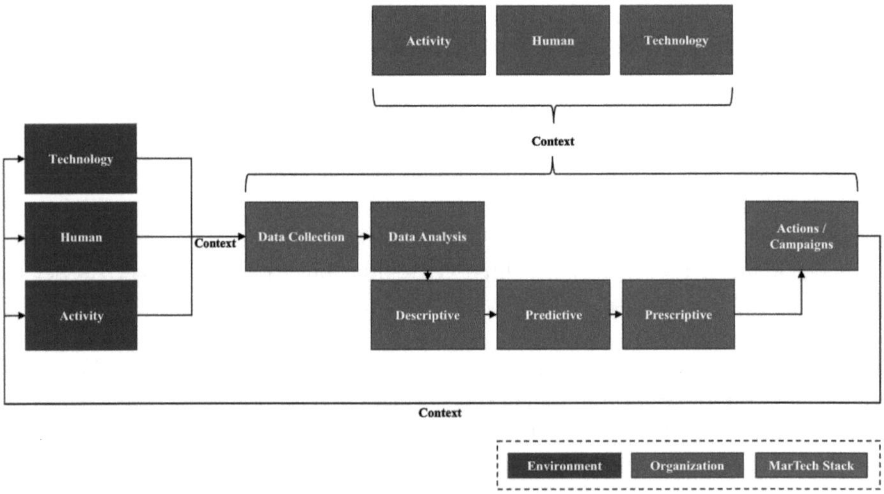

Fig. 4 MSA within the context of HAAT model dimensions

evolution of technologies, both on the environment and enterprise side. These step-changes include but are not limited to the evolution of the Internet from web1.0 to web2.0 and web3.0. It also encompasses developments in mobile computing, such as the increasing penetration of the smartphone as a de-facto cyber-technological extension of humans (Ricker, 2016). Thus, the change in available technology, its market penetration, and the adaption of human behavior to the use of technology create a constant force of change to the context of application. One could describe this flux of technological transformation as a constant rat race between organizations as a system and their environment. A good example is the use of mobile computing, both in the forms of smartphones, tablets and/or laptops. While years ago, it was often businesses that pioneered the adoption on scale, this has now much shifted toward the consumer (Undrell, 2020). A potential reason for this shift in adoption cycles can be found in the technology adoption behavior of enterprises vs. private consumers. While the latter is treating technology as a stable for entertainment and communication purposes, adoption is driven by needs, wants and thus many external forces, such as marketing and advertising efforts to stimulate purchases. Technology on the consumer side is often regarded as standalone solutions. Thus, purchasing decision-making processes are quick, externally biased, and often more on an emotional vs. a functional level.

Enterprises on the other hand experience many barriers in the adoption of emerging technologies (Chouki et al., 2022; Buttler & Sellbom, 2002). These barriers include organizational politics, such as the feud between marketing and IT with regard to the governance of the technology stack or technology investments. It was only in 2017 when marketing technology spending surpassed that of IT for the first time (Cameron, 2017), highlighting both the importance of technology to market facing organizational functions, yet also a growing organizational need for aligned technology investment planning and management. Scott Brinker's (2021) regularly published Marketing Technology Landscape Supergraphic, which was for the first time in over 10 years not updated in 2021, due to the sheer explosion of tools, is a further testament to spending willingness of organizations. Further barriers to organizational technology adoption include shrinking budgets, growing top management impatience to see investment results, the missing interplay of technological solutions within the organizational technology stack, missing market transparency of existing solutions, data management capabilities within organizations and of course indirect costs such as learning and implementation costs. Thus, despite the many SAAS components of MSA systems, at the very least, learning and adaptation costs occur, rendering organizations often hesitant to quickly adopt new solutions.

As a result, MSA systems are prone to have a delay in technological adaption based on organizational and human fallacies. This causes MSA systems to produce inefficiencies in resource allocation processes. The human factor impacting decision-making processes between the environment, the organization, the relevant and adopted technology stack, as well as actions and campaigns, extrapolates the above technologically caused inefficiency even further.

4 MSA Contextual Technology Model

The following model has been proposed (Fig. 5) to counterbalance the ineffective and inefficient MSA system state during technological step-change imbalances between an organization and its environment. The model entails digital and non-digital data. An example of a non-digital dataset includes a phone call of a sales-rep with a customer, or a walk-in for a retailer. Digital data sets include any relevant customer to brand interaction using technology. The structured or unstructured nature of data is second to its codified nature to allow technology-based processing without the further need for human interaction.

Figure 5 scaled on the level of autonomous decision-making through assistive technologies and the spectrum of assistive technologies deployed. The spectrum of assistive technologies has been extended from HTI to Automated Technology Interaction (ATI) to depict autonomous technologies.

The potential breadth of these technologies can be seen in Fig. 6. ATIs must be understood as autonomous systems, operating within defined boundaries. Examples include notions of algorithmic commerce, or a-commerce. A term coined by NYSU professor Scott Galloway (2020). The level of autonomous decision-making ranges from manual, thus fully human based, to automated and eventually autonomous technology based. The difference between automated and autonomous is important to understand the next conceptual evolution of MSA systems. Automated decision-making involved decision-making processes without human assistance, yet within prior set, human-defined processes (Heimbach et al., 2015). These are likely to include trigger points. An example of the latter could range from a pre-defined set-and-forget campaign in MA, to an automated chatbot. Autonomous decision-making on the other hand includes a performance-based decision-making process without human intervention under significant environmental uncertainties. It requires the ability of a system to compensate for these uncertainties (Stein & Gregoire, 2019; Furnham, 2019; Vilchis-Medina et al., 2021).

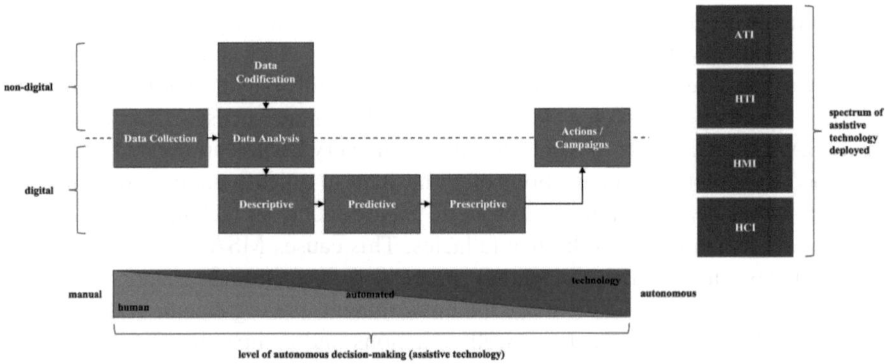

Fig. 5 MSA and spectrum of technology interaction

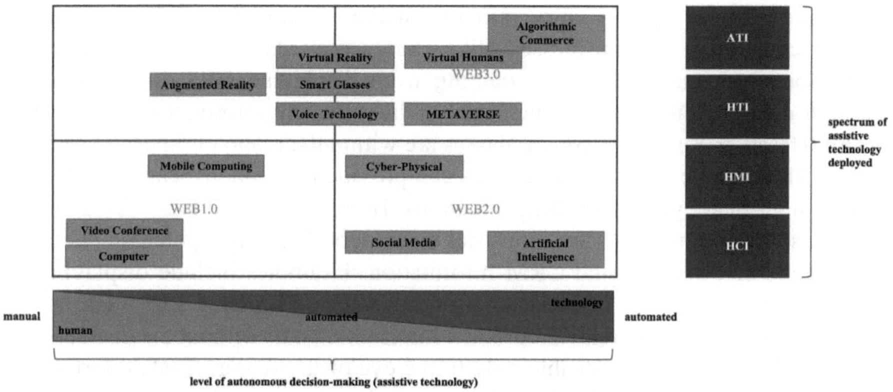

Fig. 6 Current and future technology mapping

The distinct placement of technologies is hard, as Moore's Law does not only apply to much advancement of technological developments, but also to the reciprocal impact technologies have on the creation and adoption of new technologies. The smartphone revolution serves as the simplest example. Mobile phones paved the way, while the increase in computing power and reduction in cost made the modern smartphone possible. Metcalfe's network effects enhanced adoption rates due to the increasing value of connected technologies and thus connected users (Briere, 2006). Metcalfe's law also explains the growth of applications, based on the adoption of the smartphone (Zhang et al., 2015). AI and many more technologies follow the same cycle and build upon technology adoption cycles, or market penetration rates of previous generations of technology. Thus, many technologies cannot be regarded as isolated technological instances, but causal states within the technological evolution.

5 Current and Future Technologies Impacting Marketing and Sales Automation

This section highlights some current and future technologies, which are likely impacting a further step-change scenarios for MSA systems, as shown in Fig. 6. It must be noted, that mentioned technologies can only be of exemplary nature due to rapid and unforeseeable technological innovation patterns. All technologies are being portrayed from the perspective of an MSA using party, thus the seller side.

Smart Glasses

Smart glasses combine the use of augmented reality (AR) and mixed reality (MR), mobile computing, AI, 5G, and of course any underlying web technology. Smart glasses can be classified as wearable technology, overlaying real-world sensory input, such as vision and sound with digital information (Rauschnabel et al., 2015). Ranging from the earliest days of Google Glass in 2013 to the latest speculation about Apple's entry into the market, smart glasses have fascinated private consumers and businesses alike (Sawyer et al., 2014). The application range for smart glasses is wide, ranging from displaying GPS data to navigate through cities or buildings, to messages or literally any information its user may desire (Hasan & Yu, 2017). Smart glasses are within the realm of the HCI spectrum.

For MSA applications, smart glasses can provide tremendous leaps in effectiveness in high-ticket personal selling situations. Both in B2B and B2C. Assuming its wearer is the sales manager for industrial machinery. Meeting a potential client, the smart glass can display vital CRM information. Examples include displaying the client's name, pronouns, or pronunciation assistance. Further, CRM track records can be displayed, next to relevant product information. All without the distraction of a tablet, phone, or laptop. Visible only to the eye of its wearer. If taken further and within the notion of the HAAT model as introduced previously, smart glasses can assist by providing an artificial interface to the wearer's environment. This allows to literally analyze anything from the client's tone of voice, use of semantics, facial expressions, and much more. Based on cloud-computing technology and AI services, this data can be used to predictively model alternate courses of actions to provide prescriptive input. Depending on the underlying dataset available, its wearer could be constantly displayed the closing probability based on the real-time processing of the meeting's unstructured data flow (Vincent, 2019). Additionally, hints, clues, or argument suggestions can be provided to the wearer. The sole objective of the application is to continually increase closing probabilities. The real-time codification and analysis of environmental data provides the necessary foundation. While this might still sound like science-fiction, television shopping, or its digital twin live-stream commerce (Wohn & Freeman, 2020), mark the earliest forms of real-time data usage in sales situations. The only difference is the skewed ratio of sellers to buyers and its non-personal nature. The integration of smart glasses into MSA systems provides therefore an interesting perspective from an assistive technology perspective (Yang & Kang, 2019). The use of smart glasses within service, manufacturing, or construction environments has already been proven beneficial to organizations (Niemöller et al., 2019; Dalenogare et al., 2019). Its application in pure sales and marketing situations is however still underdeveloped.

Nevertheless, the availability of technology and thus the true adoption behavior for MSA system providers remains unclear at this point. Further, privacy and data protection laws might render much of the described real-time assistive use unrealistic (Bertarini, 2014; Hofmann et al., 2017).

Virtual Reality, HMDs, and the Metaverse

Virtual Reality and the current understanding of the metaverse, although distinct in nature, go somewhat hand in hand with regard to their MSA impact. For simplicity purposes, this chapter defines virtual reality and the metaverse as a 3D generated computer environment for communication, entertainment, and commercial purposes. This definition seems to match most perceptions of the metaverse at the time of writing (Chen, 2022). It must be noted that the metaverse and its depiction is still in a fluid phase and likely to change in depth, perception, and direction in the years to come (Park & Kim, 2022).

To use virtual environments, the availability and acceptance of wearable technologies is essential. So-called head-mounted displays (HMD) are required to allow users to dive into a virtual environment. While HMDs' low market penetration is one of the biggest obstacles to boarding users to virtual worlds, virtual reality concepts also require organizations to understand the language narrative of virtual reality (Ivanova, 2018). The latter differs tremendously from other media formats.

Using virtual realities for sales activities is far from new (Bourlakis et al., 2009) but must yet prove its longevity beyond a hype. The first attempt of a metaverse-like world, Second Life, is largely accepted to have failed for various reasons, despite many companies actively investing in a virtual presence to reach consumers in novel ways (Kaplan & Haenlein, 2009). Sales staff were virtualized (Berthon et al., 2010), store locations in virtual worlds were researched (Krasonikolakis et al., 2014) and advertising flourished. Yet consumers did not adopt Second Life as companies expected. Over 10 years later, Facebook's 2021 keynote and its subsequent renaming into META has sparked novel interest in virtual reality applications and thus the metaverse (Kraus et al., 2022; Shen et al., 2021).

The metaverse, virtual worlds, and the application of HMDs can have a profound impact on MSA systems. First, it allows to extend brand spaces from the physical world to the digital world. Thus, inevitably connecting further sensory and semantic experiences. This includes the monitoring of customer to brand interactions and thus gaining new understandings of customer behavior at scale. This will include spatial movement, gaze-tracking, direct interaction, and much more. Particularly the expected evolution of HMDs to master eye and full body tracking is assumed to provide more granular insights into consumer behavior, otherwise invisible to the human eye. This manifests a true HTI application. To unlock the full potential of its contextual application, advances in automated decision-making processes are required to allow for seamless application use cases.

The usage of HMDs for virtual meetings, as promoted by Microsoft and Meta, through the Horizon Workroom initiative, must be seen in the context of f2f meeting substitution. While this will hold some advantages in terms of data collection and application, it is likely not going to advance MSA toward a higher level of automation (McVeigh-Schultz & Isbister, 2021).

Virtual Humans

In contrast to the metaverse and virtual reality, virtual humans present semi-autonomous, or autonomous virtual beings with the ability to present an organization in 2D and 3D digital worlds. Virtual humans, often also metahumans, have become more popular in recent years, mostly due to increases in computing power, making them a valuable alternative to real humans. Latest developments let literally everybody create their own virtual being, for example with EPIC's Metahuman Creator Engine (Gault, 2021). An increasingly popular example of virtual humans is to be found in virtual influencers (Moustakas et al., 2020). Studies have shown how virtual influencers, despite their non-human nature, have positive impacts on both brand awareness and purchase intent (Molin & Nordgren, 2019). Some of the most famous virtual influencers have already millions of social media followers and showcase a constant stream of brand-endorsed posts (Chitrakorn, 2021). China currently leads the application development in the virtual human and virtual influencer space, rendering virtual beings as close as one could imagine to real humans (Lorenzana, 2022). The very latest developments promoted AI-driven real-time semantic and animation capabilities. An impressive undertaking, which Samsung used to unveil its recent flagship smartphone. The brand partnered with a virtual being called ZERO, displaying live interaction with a metahuman, which went as far as to ask ZERO for a group selfie during the live-streamed event (Kulp, 2022). Offbeat Media, the technology company behind ZERO, confirmed upon request that all interaction shown was in non-scripted and in real time.

Based on powerful AI engines, virtual humans provide various brand extension opportunities within MSA environments. Their application range pushes the boundary from text-based chatbot interactions, to visual and virtual metahuman to human interactions. Thus, entering the Autonomous Technology Interaction (ATI) sphere. This allows to enhance the contextual situational analysis of customers, enhance the contextual understanding of interactions, and provide an equally contextual extension of the brand's autonomous interaction with the market. This could include live video interaction with customers to answer questions or enhance purchase intent. It could also include autonomous post-purchase service or loyalty programs to increase live time values. Most importantly, ignoring ethical and privacy restrictions for the argument, it allows reducing the human availability limitation to zero. A sales manager can have a real, as well as an infinite number of virtual, existences. Customer response delays, or interaction waiting times, can thus be rendered a problem of the past.

The above requires however the integration of deep-customer analysis, including semantics, in the CRM, further to the implementation of autonomous characters and the relevant underlying technology. To take this leap and gain experience in the MSA-ATI extension, a trial application is highly suggested. This allows companies to understand and investigate technologies, processes, and cultural change needs. Further, it lets companies, and their customers experiment with this technology, gain adoption behavior insights, before aiming to integrate virtual humans into mission-critical processes. A chatbot with a virtual human interface can be trial accessed via the following link: https://iamsophie.io

Algorithmic Commerce

A move into a fully autonomous decision-making process and autonomous technology application can be found in the term algorithmic commerce. This term, although still ambiguous in nature, assumes to not only automate data gathering, analysis, and potential post-analysis campaigns but almost the entire customer interaction process. This includes the gathering of information, the analysis, autonomous closing processes, with the extension of automated product deliveries. Such an effort extends the breadth of any MSA system far beyond the CRM and MA dimension. It requires a redefinition of the organizational technology stack, as an extension of the ERP,

CRM, and MA into a full 360 suite of applications. It also demands the digital transformation and automation of fulfillment processes. Thus, the notion of algorithmic commerce is only truly viable, if MSA systems are being extended into Organizational Automation (OA) systems. Amazon, one of the globe's leading e-commerce businesses is on the forefront of organizational automation and thus the extension beyond MSA systems (Delfanti & Frey, 2021). Another company that has also extended into organizational automation is the Chinese fashion retailer SHEIN. Through its large-scale automated test and re-order (LATR) model, SHEIN has essentially created the first full value chain automation (Matsakis et al., 2021). Particularly SHEIN's integrative approach, at making autonomous decision-making processes the heart of its automation efforts, shine light on a potential future for MSA systems in time-critical markets (Greeven, 2021).

Being on the very top dimension of autonomous decision-making and autonomous technology interaction (ATI), as shown in Fig. 6, OA systems represent the highest level of human-factor limitation mitigation in any system environment. As one expert, interviewed for this very chapter stated, OA systems with a full value-chain integrated autonomous decision-making capability, define the notion of intuitive AI.

6 Conclusion and Outlook

This chapter discussed how MSA systems underly a constant transformational force, fueled by ongoing technological innovation and adoption processes. It is therefore imperative for MSA governing managers to assess the state MSA application within the context of their organization's respective environment. To do so, it is vital to understand the interplay of components within the HAAT model, to acknowledge and plan for incongruencies between the current state of application and the contextual environment of a given MSA application. The biggest limitation of MSA systems lies within the human factor as a decision-making instance, both on the design, yet also the effective operation, of the MSA system. New technologies provide a means to mitigate mentioned technological, human and process limitations. Particularly technologies extending the collection, interpretation, and decision-making impact of contextually relevant datasets.

This elevates MSA systems from HTI to ATI. The interplay of both autonomous technology interaction with a given environment and the semi-autonomous to autonomous decision-making process based on the context of the environment holds much potential to achieve sustainable competitive advantages through principles of automated organizations. The latter however requires not just the alignment of marketing and sales, but all value-chain relevant organizational processes.

Though fully autonomous organization will likely remain limited to sectors of high environmental dynamics and non-relational customer interactions, other technologies, as discussed in this chapter, do allow to increase the collection of contextual information, and to extend automated market interaction. It remains however case-dependent for organizations to determine the likelihood of a technology's market adoption and thus value provision to their respective MSA system.

References

Bailey, R. W. (1989). *Human performance engineering: Using human factors/ergonomics to achieve computer system usability*. Prentice-Hall.

Baruch, Y. (1997). High technology organization-what it is, what it isn't. *International Journal of technology management, 13*(2), 179–195.

Berglund, M., Karltun, A., Eklund, J., & Karltun, J. (2020). HTO-a concept of humans, technology and organisation in interaction.

Bertarini, M. (2014, January). Smart glasses: Interaction, privacy and social implications. In *Ubiquitous Computing Seminar FS2014 Student report*.

Berthon, P., Pitt, L., Halvorson, W., Ewing, M., & Crittenden, V. L. (2010). Advocating avatars: The salesperson in second life. *Journal of Personal Selling & Sales Management, 30*(3), 195–208.

Bourlakis, M., Papagiannidis, S., & Li, F. (2009). Retail spatial evolution: Paving the way from traditional to metaverse retailing. *Electronic Commerce Research, 9*(1), 135–148.

Briere, D. (2006). First Moore's Law, then Metcalfe's Law, now McGuire's Law. *Network World Canada, 16*(5), 8.

Brinker, S. (2021). *2021: The Year Martech Shrank — Just Kidding (A Year in Review)*. Accessed April 04, 2022, from https://chiefmartec.com/2021/12/2021-the-year-martech-shrank-just-kidding-a-year-in-review/

Bucklin, R., Lehmann, D. R., & Little, J. D. C. (1998). From decision support to decision automation: A 2020 vision. *Marketing Letters, 9*(3), 235–246.

Butler, D. L., & Sellbom, M. (2002). Barriers to adopting technology. *Educause Quarterly, 2*(1), 22–28.

Cameron, N. (2017). *Gartner: How CMOs will spend more on technology than CIOs in 2017*. Accessed April 04, 2022, from https://www.cmo.com.au/article/612861/gartner-how-cmos-will-spend-more-technology-than-cios-2017/

Chen, B. (2022). *What's all the hype about the metaverse?*. Accessed March 05, 2022, from https://www.nytimes.com/2022/01/18/technology/personaltech/metaverse-gaming-definition.html

Chitrakorn, H. (2021). *What influencer marketing looks like in the metaverse*. Accessed March 05, 2022, from https://www.voguebusiness.com/technology/what-influencer-marketing-looks-like-in-the-metaverse

Chouki, M., Talea, M., Okar, C., & Chroqui, R. (2022). Barriers to information technology adoption within small and medium enterprises: A systematic literature review. *Emerging Issues And Trends In Innovation And Technology Management*, 369–412.

Coetzer, J., Kuriakose, R. B., & Vermaak, H. J. (2020, July). Collaborative decision-making for human-technology interaction-a case study using an automated water bottling plant. *Journal of Physics: Conference Series, 1577*(1), 012024.

Cook, A. M., & Hussey, S. M. (1995). *Assistive technologies: Principles and practice*. Mosby.

Cook, A. M., & Polgar, J. M. (2014). *Assistive technologies-e-book: Principles and practice*. Elsevier Health Sciences.

Dalenogare, L. S., Baseggio, M. M., Ayala, N. F., Le Dain, M. A., & Frank, A. G. (2019). The contribution of Smart Glasses for PSS. *Procedia CIRP, 83*, 318–323.

Delfanti, A., & Frey, B. (2021). Humanly extended automation or the future of work seen through Amazon patents. *Science, Technology, & Human Values, 46*(3), 655–682.

Furnham, P. (2019). Automation and autonomy of big data-driven algorithmic decision-making. *Contemporary Readings in Law and Social Justice, 11*(1), 51–56.

Galloway, S. (2020). *The rise of the rundle & algorithmic-commerce*. Accessed April 04, 2022, from https://www.youtube.com/watch?v=un3c1yMs1F8

Gault, M. (2021). *Epic Games will soon let you design and download photo-realistic humans on demand*. Accessed March 05, 2022, from https://www.vice.com/en/article/3anen3/the-metahuman-creator-wants-to-produce-digital-humans-easily

Greeven, M. (2021). *China's Shein has taken the womenswear world by storm. Now what?*. Accessed March 06, 2022, from https://asia.nikkei.com/Business/Business-Insight/China-s-Shein-has-taken-the-womenswear-world-by-storm.-Now-what

Hasan, M. S., & Yu, H. (2017). Innovative developments in HCI and future trends. *International Journal of Automation and Computing, 14*(1), 10–20.

Heimbach, I., Kostyra, D. S., & Hinz, O. (2015). Marketing automation. *Business & Information Systems Engineering, 57*(2), 129–133.

Hofmann, B., Haustein, D., & Landeweerd, L. (2017). Smart-glasses: Exposing and elucidating the ethical issues. *Science and Engineering Ethics, 23*(3), 701–721.

Ivanova, A. V. (2018). VR & AR technologies: Opportunities and application obstacles. *Strategic Decisions and Risk Management, 3*, 88–107.

Kaplan, A. M., & Haenlein, M. (2009). *Consumers, companies and virtual social worlds: A qualitative analysis of Second Life*. ACR North American Advances..

Karltun, J., Karltun, A., & Berglund, M. (2021, June). Activity–The core of human-technology-organization. In *Congress of the International Ergonomics Association* (pp. 704–711). Springer.

Korn, O., Funk, M., Abele, S., Hörz, T., & Schmidt, A. (2014). Context-aware assistive systems at the workplace: Analyzing the effects of projection and gamification. In *Proceedings of the 7th International Conference on Pervasive Technologies Related to Assistive Environments* (pp. 1–8). https://doi.org/10.1145/2674396.2674406.

Krasonikolakis, I., Vrechopoulos, A., & Pouloudi, A. (2014). Store selection criteria and sales prediction in virtual worlds. *Information & Management, 51*(6), 641–652.

Kraus, S., Kanbach, D. K., Krysta, P. M., Steinhoff, M. M., & Tomini, N. (2022). Facebook and the creation of the metaverse: Radical business model innovation or incremental transformation? *International Journal of Entrepreneurial Behavior & Research*.

Kulp, P. (2022). *Samsung's live shopping event was hosted by a virtual influencer*. Accessed March 04, 2022, from https://www.adweek.com/commerce/samsung-live-shopping-event-virtual-influencer/

Lorenzana, P. (2022). *China's top virtual influencers on social media*. Accessed March 04, 2022, from https://www.virtualhumans.org/article/the-top-virtual-influencers-trending-on-chinas-social-media-platforms

Matsakis, L., Tobin, M., & Chen, W. (2021). *How Shein beat Amazon at its own game – and reinvented fast fashion*. Accessed March 06, 2022, from https://www.theguardian.com/fashion/2021/dec/21/how-shein-beat-amazon-at-its-own-game-and-reinvented-fast-fashion

McVeigh-Schultz, J., & Isbister, K. (2021). A "beyond being there" for VR meetings: Envisioning the future of remote work. *Human–Computer Interaction*, 1–21.

Mero, J., Tarkiainen, A., & Tobon, J. (2020). Effectual and causal reasoning in the adoption of marketing automation. *Industrial Marketing Management, 86*, 212–222.

Molin, V., & Nordgren, S. (2019). *Robot or human? The marketing phenomenon of virtual influencers: A case study about virtual influencers' parasocial interaction on instagram.*

Moustakas, E., Lamba, N., Mahmoud, D., & Ranganathan, C. (2020, June). Blurring lines between fiction and reality: Perspectives of experts on marketing effectiveness of virtual influencers. In *2020 International Conference on Cyber Security and Protection of Digital Services (Cyber Security)* (pp. 1–6). IEEE.

Niemöller, C., Metzger, D., Berkemeier, L., Zobel, B., & Thomas, O. (2019). Mobile service support based on smart glasses. *Journal of Theoretical and Applied Information Technology, 20*(1), 4.

Park, S. M., & Kim, Y. G. (2022). *A Metaverse: Taxonomy, components, applications, and open challenges*. IEEE Access.

Princeton University. (2021). *My Rolodex, no password needed.* Accessed March 02, 2022, from https://graphicarts.princeton.edu/2021/08/04/my-rolodex-no-password-needed/

Rach, M. (2021). *The impact of marketing technologies on the marketing return on investment.* Maastricht School of Management.

Rauschnabel, P. A., Brem, A., & Ro, Y. (2015). *Augmented reality smart glasses: Definition, conceptual insights, and managerial importance.* Unpublished Working Paper, The University of Michigan-Dearborn, College of Business.

Ricker, T., (2016). *Elon Musk: We're already cyborgs.* Accessed March 04, 2022, from https://www.theverge.com/2016/6/2/11837854/neural-lace-cyborgs-elon-musk

Sawyer, B. D., Finomore, V. S., Calvo, A. A., & Hancock, P. A. (2014). Google Glass: A driver distraction cause or cure? *Human factors, 56*(7), 1307–1321.

Shen, B., Tan, W., Guo, J., Zhao, L., & Qin, P. (2021). How to promote user purchase in metaverse? A systematic literature review on consumer behavior research and virtual commerce application design. *Applied Sciences, 11*(23), 11087.

Stein, H. S., & Gregoire, J. M. (2019). Progress and prospects for accelerating materials science with automated and autonomous workflows. *Chemical Science, 10*(42), 9640–9649.

Undrell, J., (2020). *Are business users really that different to consumers?* Accessed April 04, 2022, from https://businessblog.o2.co.uk/2020/09/29/are-business-users-really-that-different-to-consumers/

Vilchis-Medina, J. L., Godary-Dejean, K., & Lesire, C. (2021). Autonomous decision-making with incomplete information and safety rules based on non-monotonic reasoning. *IEEE Robotics and Automation Letters, 6*(4), 8357–8362.

Vincent, J. (2019). Facial recognition smart glasses could make public surveillance discreet and ubiquitous. *The Verge, 10.*

Wohn, D. Y., & Freeman, G. (2020, June). Audience management practices of live streamers on Twitch. In *ACM International Conference on Interactive Media Experiences* (pp. 106–116).

Yang, K. C., & Kang, Y. (2019). Augmented, mixed, and virtual reality applications in cause-related marketing (CRM). *Cases on Immersive Virtual Reality Techniques*, 217–240.

Zhang, X. Z., Liu, J. J., & Xu, Z. W. (2015). Tencent and Facebook data validate Metcalfe's law. *Journal of Computer Science and Technology, 30*(2), 246–251.

Markus Rach is an Associate Professor of marketing at the Shenzhen Technology University in China. He further lectures at the Swiss Marketing Academy and is a guest professor at the kdG in Belgium. His research interests include disruptive marketing technologies and the notion of algorithmic commerce. From 2020 to 2022, Markus ran a 650k follower strong TikTok experiment, resulting in various book and paper publications.

Before transitioning into academia, Markus served as the head of marketing for various multinationals. He holds several active board seats and serves on the CMO council as an advisory board member. Markus is a thought-after speaker on disruptive marketing, TikTok, and the future of marketing and actively consults brands in Europe and China on marketing.

Marketing and Sales Automation as Enabler for Reengineering Corporate Communication

Uwe Seebacher

1 Why Do We Need Reengineering Corporate Communication?

In the last 50 years, the world of communication has changed completely. There has been a shift from mono-dimensional direct communication to multi-dimensional interactive interaction around the clock and around the world. This process of change was both shaped and driven by the digitalization and automation of processes. Operational processes were automated through the introduction of so-called ERP systems. In the further course, CRM systems found their way into the world of companies. This development also gave rise to the so-called CRM paradox, named after these systems.

This phenomenon results from the fact that information technology systems or products are acquired and purchased by decision-makers in organizations without taking into account that corresponding organizational prerequisites must be created for the meaningful use of such systems. Such prerequisites include appropriate procedural analyses and documentation as well as the corresponding adaptation of position descriptions and, in this context, also the adaptation of the respective organizational unit. These elements are necessary in order to be able to compare and subsequently match the organization's own processes currently being implemented with those of the processes stored in such CRM systems within the framework of the implementation of CRM systems, for example.

If such a comparison is not possible due to a lack of existing documentation, systems are implemented and rolled out top-down in organizations, and the

U. Seebacher (✉)
University of Applied Sciences Vienna, Vienna, Germany

University of Applied Sciences Munich, Munich, Germany

Institute of Management Technology (IMT), Ghaziabad/Dubai, India/UAE
e-mail: uwe.seebacher@edu.fh-wien.ac.at; uwe.seebacher@hm.edu; us@uweseebacher.org

U. Hannig, U. Seebacher (eds.), *Marketing and Sales Automation*, Management for Professionals, https://doi.org/10.1007/978-3-031-20040-3_28

organizations stumble into a process-related chaos and stagger between their own, lived processes and the processes imposed by the system. Based on the illustration or description of the CRM paradox, it quickly becomes clear that this paradox now appears to be relevant for almost most implementations of externally purchased IT solutions. Every company can point to at least one failed implementation of an IT solution, with the consequence that the results and savings defined at the beginning of the respective IT solution could never be realized.

In spite of all this, the development of software technology has led to an enormous development of the ecosystem of enterprise IT systems. This rapid development is reflected not only in the annual increase in the number of relevant products but also in the enormous diversity of content. All experts in the field of marketing know about the regularly published illustrations of the colorful and dazzling Marketing Technology Stack (MarTechStacks) and the incredible growth rates of available products and systems in the field of marketing automation shown therein. The same applies to the area of sales automation, but also to the accelerating growth rates of the solutions offered in the area of data management or predictive intelligence (Seebacher 2021b, p.196).

These developments were the result of a symbiosis of American entrepreneurship and a creatively innovative ecosystem in the lap of Silicon Valley. The goal was to make internal processes even leaner and more effective by mapping them in corresponding products. On the other hand, the aim was to be able to understand, read and serve the customer ever better with stringency and consistency. This requires the ability to manage and measure the entire customer journey. With this information, it became possible to collect more and more data on the customer, his wishes, and motivations, in order to use this information to predict the intended customer behavior more and more precisely and to be able to implement it unerringly through corresponding Call-2-Actions (C2A). After all, the old saying applies that you can only manage what you can also measure.

In this context, the areas of marketing and sales have developed brilliantly. Today, there are appropriate solutions and products for almost all areas in these fields of activity to automate processes and integrate information along the entire customer journey. The danger is that the two areas of marketing and sales are each developing their own ecosystems of IT solutions that are characterized by ever greater redundancy and overlap. In the context of the silo mentality that still prevails, this circumstance poses an enormous risk for companies, namely in terms of the development of redundant IT ecosystems that are not coordinated with one another and are even less integrated in terms of data and processes.

But what is really striking about the entire situation is the fact that a significant part of corporate activity has apparently been completely left out of the equation by these developers so far. This is because, based on a research study conducted in 2021 under the direction of the author, it became clear that the entire area of corporate communications has not yet been automated or digitized. In only a small percentage (10%) of the total of more than 300 companies studied worldwide, initial repetitive activities have already been automated. In a comparable percentage, the corporate communications departments use the term "customer" in the sense that the customers of corporate communications are the recipients of the information sent out. In the reverse conclusion, this means that the product of the enterprise communication represents the sent-out information.

If one continues this thought, then experienced marketing and sales experts very quickly come up with catchwords such as an *information journey* resulting from the customer journey or, following on from user excellence, *information excellence*. Against this background, many of the concepts and instruments already established in the area of marketing and sales can be very quickly and easily adapted and adopted directly for the entire institutional communication. So, too, is the all-important theme of account-based marketing (ABM), which in the context of corporate communications is the all-important framework construct for *segment-based communication* (SBC), as a strategically targeted, programmatic communication with selected key stakeholders, which in turn are divided into segments.

This means that against the backdrop of the enormous developments in the automation of marketing and sales, the area of corporate communications must now be taken into account and included as quickly and as effectively as possible. Why this is so can be clarified very quickly on the basis of a few points (Seebacher, 2022, p. 15ff):

- Establishment of a contemporary communication structures
- Realization of optimized processes
- Building on this, automating repetitive activities in the area of communication and interaction
- Enabling the use and application of always up-to-date concepts, tools, methods, and systems for interaction
- Increasing the efficiency and effectiveness of the entire interaction process
- Optimization of resource utilization through (partial) automation and digitization and the resulting redistribution of freed-up resources and employees to activities and tasks with higher added value.
- Risk minimization with regard to emerging communication crises and the resulting material and immaterial damage to the respective organization.

In addition to these qualitative arguments, many number-based results can also be cited for the enormous potentials of corporate communication reengineering (RCC) based on various practical examples:

- Cost savings of up to 50–60%.
- Minimization of the number of employees required for classic corporate communications by up to 30–40%, enabling redistribution to new, additional activities as part of the newly established corporate interaction.
- Optimization of processing times by up to 40–50% through automated, digitized processes, systems, interfaces, and the use of artificial intelligence.
- Optimization of brand activation by 5–10% annually through agile-predictive enterprise interaction.

- Demonstrable, increasing contribution to respective company results (image, profit, survey scores, etc.) from approx. 6 months after the start of reengineering activities in corporate communications

These two listings, therefore, underline that the question is not whether reengineering corporate communication is necessary, but that it must actually already be considered more than overdue when realizing what currently is not working (Seebacher, 2022, p. 16f):

- In terms of communication efficiency and effectiveness, stringently documented and continuously optimized process documentations are not available (87%).
- There is a lack of adapted position descriptions and generally new positions and designations in the context of the changed contingency situation of corporate communication (76%).
- Too little automation and digitization of activities in the area of corporate communications as a consequence of the aforementioned aspects (84%).
- Frequent lack of awareness of the new, diverse possibilities of automated and digitized communication and interaction (89%).
- Predominant silo thinking and the resulting lack of joint and coordinated action with the marketing and sales departments (73%).
- Lack of goals for corporate communications or their measurement, also and especially with regard to economic added value and the direct and indirect contribution to organizational success (88%).

2 What Are the Challenges?

Against this background, it is now more crucial that proven experts in the field of marketing and sales automation now initiate, promote, support, and accompany the integration of corporate communications in the activities of automation and digitization. This is the only way to prevent the gap between corporate communications and sales and marketing from widening in the future, not only technologically but also ideologically, but also to prevent the development of another redundant technology stack—a ComTechStack.

The challenges can be summarized into the following points:

- *Organizational:* Against the backdrop of the tedious and always ongoing discussions about which department in the triad of communications, marketing, and sales must be in charge, this structural discussion must be stringently avoided. Only a joint and coordinated approach at eye level will work in the long term and also be able to form the basis for realizing the enormous potential. With regard to any informal leadership, this can and must only be considered in the context of the respective aspect. As such aspects are on the one hand the content-conceptual and on the other hand the product-system-technical level, which comes into play. The first level focuses on who has the most experience and competence in dealing with concepts such as Customer Journey, Account-based Marketing, Performance Marketing, Sales Intelligence, Sales Qualified Leads (SQL), and other relevant concepts and models, among others. The second level focuses on competence in the area of selection, implementation, adaptation but also integration of possible products and solutions.

- *Content:* Another success factor is the required transfer of knowledge within the organization toward colleagues in the area of corporate communications. Only if the opportunities and potentials are sufficiently discussed through this transfer can awareness also arise of the importance of corporate communication reengineering for the corporate communication area itself but also for the entire organization. After all, efficient and effective integration of corporate communications can only work on the basis of an organizational learning process in which marketing and sales raise their colleagues from corporate communications to the same level in terms of competencies in as short a time as possible.
- *Technical:* Building on the previously outlined content challenge that needs to be solved, it is then crucial to create awareness that Reengineering Corporate Communication defacto does not require a separate TechStack. This is based on the fact that all the necessary concepts and models for automating and digitizing corporate communication can be adopted directly from marketing and sales. Conversely, this means that the systems that already exist in marketing and sales or are currently being introduced can also be used directly for corporate communications.
- *Management:* The fourth challenge is to position this topic appropriately, especially at the management level. From the background of risks, cost savings to the possibilities of predictive, orchestrated corporate interaction, this should be relatively easy to do, especially if the triad of communications, marketing, and sales act and communicate in concert on the issue. Of course, this is about sustainable change management because, on the one hand, corporate communication has to deal with the concept of the customer in a completely new way and, on the other hand, the nature of corporate communication is significantly changed as a result. It is no longer about informing investors or interest groups, but about forward-looking, dynamic 24/7 interaction in the environment of All-2-All interaction arenas. Corporate communications will become the powerhouse of interaction management with the various groups of information recipients and will require a state-of-the-art interaction technology stack (InTechStack) based on predictive interaction intelligence (PII) (Seebacher 2021b, p. 193).

If these four challenges are mastered, this will be the basis for successfully, efficiently, and effectively realizing the realignment of corporate communications in the context of marketing and sales automation. Once again, success is the result of many small steps. Because it is only through many small steps that the necessary intrinsic organizational learning process can be initiated and run through as the basis for this sustainable but essential change process.

3 From Corporate Communication to Corporate Interaction

In order for experienced experts in the field of marketing and sales automation to be able to accompany their colleagues from the field of corporate communications in the best possible way on the journey toward corporate interaction, it is first of all necessary to place familiar concepts from marketing and sales in the context of today's corporate communications. Therefore, in the first part of this section, the conceptual world from marketing and sales is transferred to that of corporate communications. On this basis, a four-stage maturity process is then outlined, which schematically represents this development process. In the third part of this section, the procedure for reengineering corporate communication is then described in very concrete terms in the form of 12 modules and critically appraised. A more detailed description of the process model with its own templates for do-it-yourself implementation in companies can be found in the author's publication on which this article is based, entitled "Reengineering Corporate Communication" (Seebacher, 2022).

3.1 The New Eco-systems for Corporate Communication

In the previous section of this article, various concepts from marketing and sales have already been dealt with selectively and it has been indicated how these must be modified in the context of corporate communications. Much of what is presented here and introduced into the discourse will seem more than logical to experienced experts from marketing and sales when they read through it. This is also all too understandable against the backdrop of developments in these areas in recent years, but it should not obscure the fact that many experts in the field of corporate communications are not yet familiar with these terms and concepts. Therefore, the aim of this section is to show marketing and sales professionals how concepts and terminology can be explained and transferred to the context of corporate communications in cooperation with colleagues from corporate communications.

In order not to go beyond the scope of this publication, only basic and essential terms and concepts will be discussed here. In any case, the authentic development of one's own conceptual world for one's own communication is crucial for a sustainably successful change process. Once a common basic understanding with a jointly agreed and defined objective has been established in the triad of communications, marketing, and sales, this ecosystem of terms and concepts will automatically and intrinsically continue to develop dynamically, always in the context of the further development of the organizational maturity level.

From the Buyer Journey to the Communication Journey

The basis is, as in the automation of marketing and sales, the concept of the customer's journey from not knowing the company to becoming a loyal companion. In contrast to the classic customer, the customer buys the information and the content in the sense of the product. A goal of enterprise communication must be that the

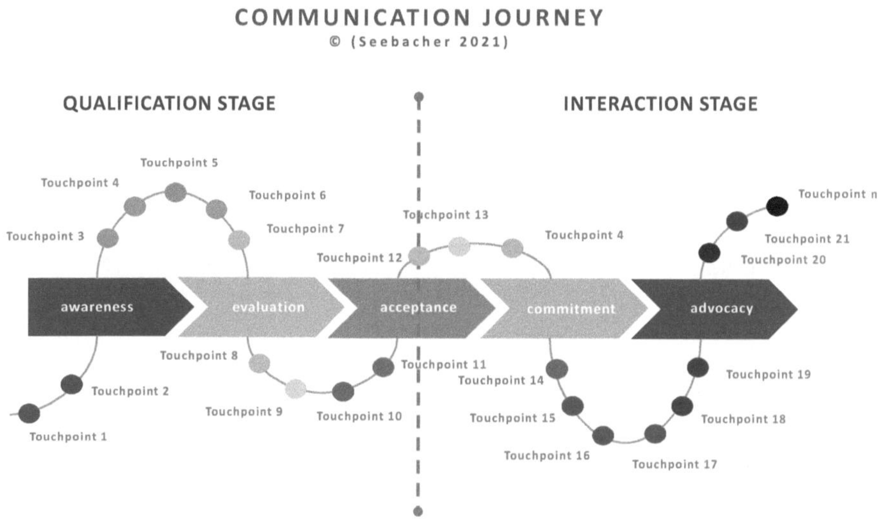

Fig. 1 Communication journey (Source: Seebacher, 2022, p. 120)

respective information receiver uses the contents in the sense of the enterprise, renders and further distributes. Regardless of this, of course, the content-related interpretation sovereignty of the respective information recipient remains untouched. However, as in the area of marketing and sales, the aim is to constantly increase the probability of the intended behavior of the respective customer, regardless of whether he is a product customer or an information customer (Fig. 1).

This communication journey and the entire concept of reengineering corporate communication can also be applied directly to the part of internal communication inherent in corporate communication. The internal communication journey shows how the individual touchpoints fit in along the various maturity levels of the journey (Fig. 2).

Of course, the experts involved are free to define further customer journeys based on the concept of the communication journey. For example, the following journeys could be formulated and defined:

- External Communication
  - Investors Journey (siehe auch Fig. 3)
  - Journalist Journey
  - Influencer Journey
- Internal Communication
  - Onboarding Journey
  - Employer Branding Journey
  - Blue collar Journey
  - Alumni Journey

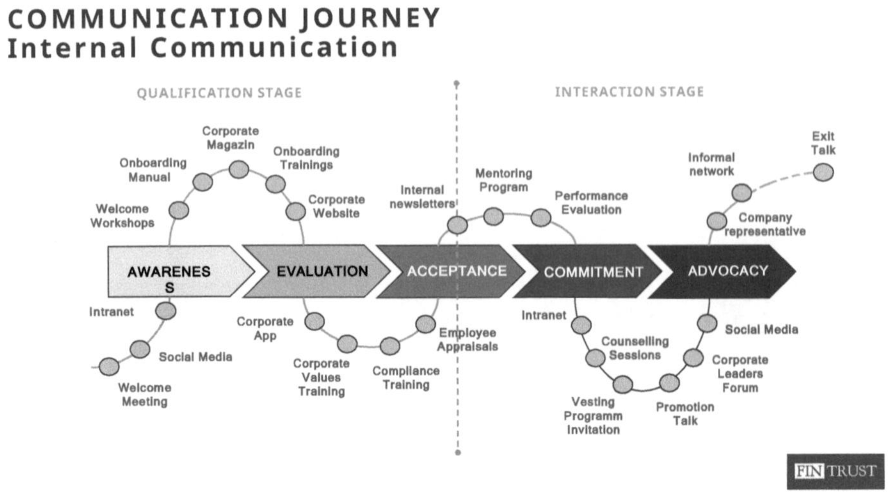

Fig. 2 Internal communication journey (Source: Seebacher, 2022, p. 122)

In principle, there are no limits to disaggregation, but the criterion for further segmentation should always be whether there are really significant deviations in terms of maturity levels but also contact points. Once the concept of the customer journey is established, the need for the appropriate classification around segmentation of the different types of information customers becomes logical and obvious. This in turn is the basis for the next step in the development process.

From the Communication Journey to Communication Personas

Another important aspect in the evolution from classic corporate communications to A2A corporate interaction is the adoption of the *persona* concept from marketing to corporate communications. Based on the research work, it has been shown that many organizations already have profiles on various information recipients. However, the level of detail and design of these profiles varied greatly between the companies studied. Moreover, in the absence of the communication journey concept, these profiles seem not to be stringently incorporated into corporate communications activities.

For the experts from marketing and sales, this means that the transition of the concept of personas from marketing and sales to the field of corporate communications can be completed very quickly. The main task will be to transfer the existing information to templates used in marketing or sales (Seebacher, 2021a). Within the framework of this transfer, corresponding information gaps with regard to the various personas of the various information recipients can then be eliminated together. Such information gaps mostly result in less professionally prepared and designed templates for customer segmentation in the area of corporate communications compared to those of marketing and sales.

It is important that colleagues in corporate communications feel that they are being met and that they do not feel overrun or overwhelmed by the joint transfer of information from the templates of corporate communications to those of marketing and sales. From the very beginning, it should be ensured that there is the greatest possible consistency between communications, marketing, and sales in terms of concepts, models, and templates. This makes it much easier to share products, interfaces, databases, and systems.

If there are no predefined templates or profiles on the part of corporate communications, it is necessary to carefully explain and introduce the persona concept in the context of the communication journey.

With Communication Personas to Communication Touchpoint Management

Once the various information recipients have been archetypically recorded and documented, the large area of contact points can be developed and processed on the basis of the communication journey. The diagram of the Internal Communication Journey (Fig. 2) already shows some customer-specific contact points. Once again, the aim is to pick up colleagues in corporate communications at the current level of knowledge as best as possible and to make the best possible use of everything that is already available in terms of relevant materials and knowledge and to incorporate it into the new world of terms and concepts. In any case, the experience already gained and documents created from marketing and sales should be presented and discussed in the area of customer touchpoints to ensure the appropriate transfer of knowledge between the departments.

The four-step process for managing contact points according to Schüller (2016, p. 157) has proven to be very helpful, as it makes the interrelationships and modes of action easy to understand and comprehend (Fig. 4).

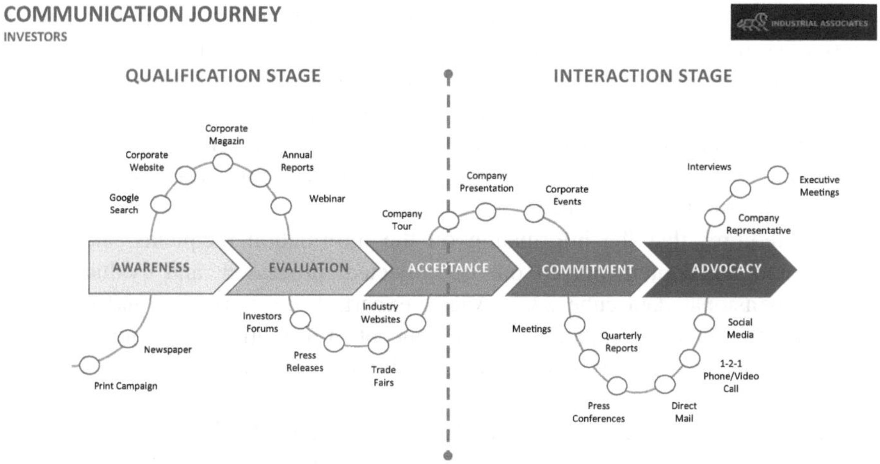

Fig. 3 Investors' journey (Source: Seebacher, 2022)

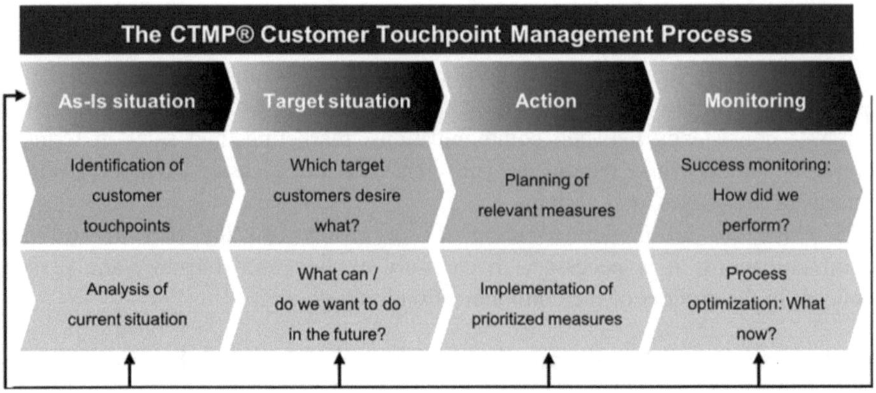

Fig. 4 The four steps of the CTMP ® (Source: Schüller, 2016, p. 157)

Touchpoint Management as the Basis for Communication Excellence

The next step is to address the issue of customer experience. Like every product customer, the information customer ideally wants to be approached in the best possible way. In terms of communication, this aspect of the customer experience has so far been insufficiently mapped or taken into account. Based on the current research results, this is probably due to the fact that the necessary concepts and instruments in this regard have been largely unknown in the context of corporate communications and therefore do not exist.

As part of the joint approach between communications, marketing, and sales, all these instruments and concepts are now also available to corporate communications, and measuring the perception of the customer in relation to the various customer contact points becomes stringently possible for the first time. According to the motto "perception is reality," the quality and grade of the contact points can be automated and optimized for the first time by measuring the communication experience in the sense of communication excellence (CE). Until now, the customer experience could not be measured, which meant that it could not be developed further. If corporate communications now know when, where, via which end device, and in which form the respective information recipient would ideally like to receive relevant information and news about the company, the perception of the information recipient can be subtly and positively influenced.

This requires that the information on the information recipients, the contact points, and the content played out be collected, processed, and evaluated in a multi-dimensional data cube 24/7. Again, experts from marketing and sales will recognize that this is comparable to the concept of a multi-dimensional data cube (MDC) (Seebacher, 2021b, p. 60f), which is familiar from marketing and sales.

From Communication Excellence to Interaction Intelligence

What has been best practice in the area of sales for years and has also been adopted in marketing for about 10 years, has apparently not yet arrived in the area of corporate

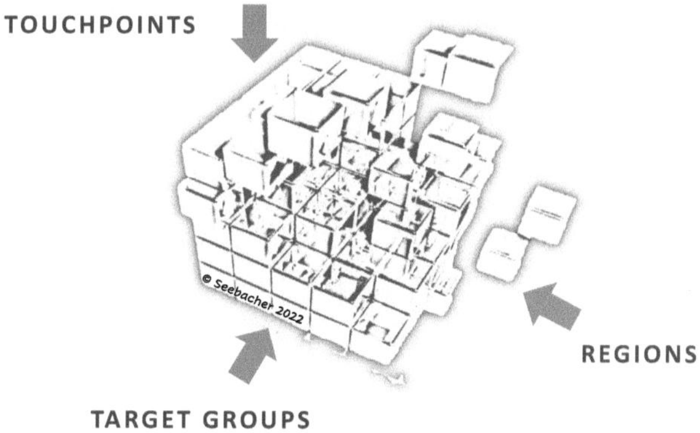

Fig. 5 Multi-dimensional-data-cube for interaction intelligence (Source: Seebacher, 2022)

communications. We are talking here about stringent and structured collection, documentation, processing, and analysis of all relevant communication data. These are necessary in order to be able to act and interact professionally in the context of data-driven management (Seebacher, 2021c) in the long term. This MDC (Fig. 5) is structured according to the three parameters of regions, target groups, and contact points and should also have access to the information of an event media intelligence (EMI) (Seebacher, 2021b, p. 256), which contains all relevant company-specific information on trade shows and events but also all off- and online magazines, media, and journals.

In combination with the Event-Media-Intelligence (EMI) information could be generated continuously but also and above all used at any time and situationally (Seebacher, 2022), for example, to:

- Long-term branding and corporate communications campaigns can be planned precisely not only in terms of content but also in terms of budget on the basis of EMI data.
- Plan and prepare corporate information efficiently and effectively in the medium term with a precise focus on the respective target groups in the different regions up to
- Automated playout of necessary crisis communication at short notice in the event of any kind of imminent danger.

The entire field of data management must also always be carried out in the context of the joint approach of communications, marketing, and sales with the aim of building up predictive intelligence in the long term, as described on the basis of the multi-stage maturity model according to Seebacher (2021b, p. 15) (Fig. 6).

Interaction Intelligence Needs Interaction Automation

Once the previously outlined basics have been established, only then does it make sense to start automating the processes and activities in the corporate communications environment as part of the activities for automating marketing

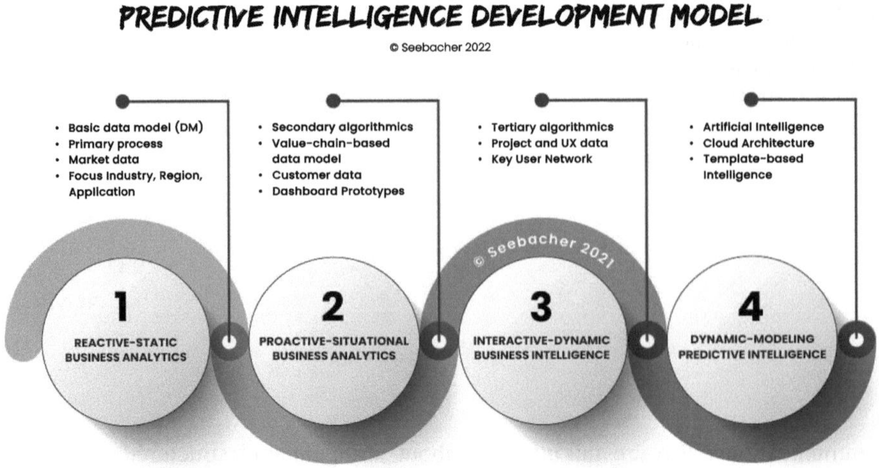

Fig. 6 Growth model for predictive intelligence (Source: Seebacher, 2021a)

and sales. The reason for this is that only then is the necessary, precisely defined frame of reference for IT-based automation and digitization in place. If this basis is missing, it is like shooting at moving targets and the risk of missing the target is very high in this scenario.

On the other hand, the more data is collected from an ever-increasing number of sources and incidents, at a certain point this can no longer be done manually in a valid and reliable way. The situation is similar in the environment of data-driven management with the use of artificial intelligence to cope with large volumes of data. In a figurative sense, the automation of interactions or their management thus represents so-called artificial intelligence in the context of data management. Interaction automation enables interactive, agile, but also predictive interaction management of all ongoing interactions around the clock and around the globe. This automation transforms corporate communication into an A2A corporate interaction, which:

- Identifies and defuses communicative crises at an early stage
- Delivers omni-channel-based screening, documentation, and analysis of interactions 24/7
- Supports marketing and sales activities interactively in a coordinated manner
- Turns internal, rigid communication into an interactive, agile, responsive interaction arena, and
- Transparently monitors brand activation, employer branding, and interaction performance

And it is precisely with regard to interaction automation that close collaboration with marketing and sales is essential, because this is the only way to avoid the need for corporate communications to develop its own ecosystem of required IT solutions and systems. If the activities described here are carried out rigorously, it automatically becomes clear to everyone involved that the three areas of communications, marketing, and sales need to make use of a common interaction technology stack (InTechStack) in order to have the best possible level of information on the one hand and to be able to learn from each other and thus deliver better on the other. By sharing systems, templates for content, processes, and campaigns can be directly adopted and reused, and data can be evaluated and extracted according to the relevant criteria or parameters in a situation-elastic manner. All this would not be possible with two or three separate TechStacks.

With Interaction Automation to Segment-Based Interaction

The next step is then to implement the strategic concept of segment-based interaction (SBI). This concept was developed on the basis of the Account-based Marketing (ABM) model (Bacon, 2021). It involves targeted and coordinated communication with particularly critical and important stakeholders. Based on the ABM concept, SBI is divided into three different levels (Fig. 7) (Seebacher, 2022):

- *Strategic SBI:* Inform key groups specifically, build relationships, deepen or win them over
- *Lite SBI:* Clusters of key information customers in areas, regions, and segments of particular importance to the organization
- *Programmatic SBI:* Focused campaigns on a group of information recipients who have a common content or regional context

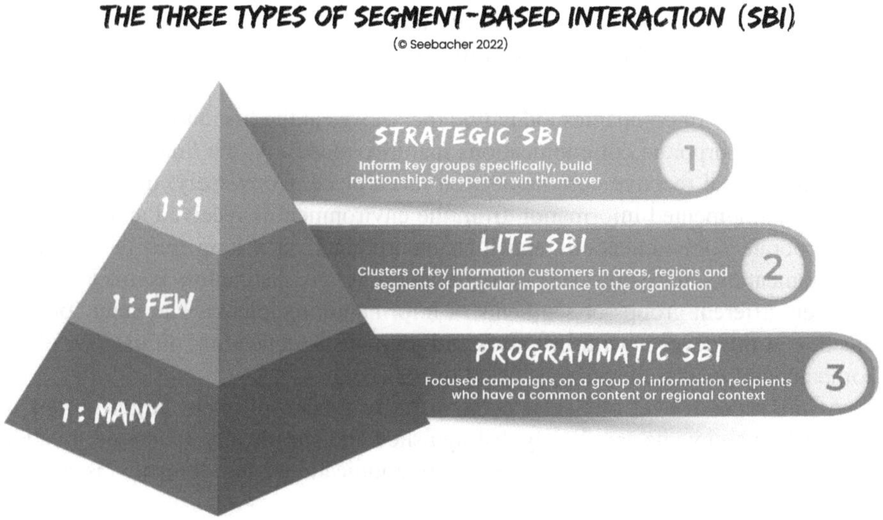

Fig. 7 Three types of segment-based interaction (Source: Seebacher, 2022)

Against this background and considering the fact that IP tracking plays an important role for ABM or SBI and the current developments in the area of increasingly strict data protection regulations, attention must be paid to the buzzword "cookie-free world." In this context, thought must be given to predictive contact point optimization based on findings from the field of neuro-interaction as well as brain scan research in order to become independent of external data providers as well as third-party cookies. Here, the European Competence Center for Neurointeraction is leading the corresponding basic research, which will be highly relevant for A2A Corporate Interaction in the near future.[1]

3.2 The Four-Stage Growth Process

In the previous section, the development from classic corporate communication to modern corporate interaction was illustrated using various terminologies. The transfer of terminology from marketing and sales to the context of corporate communications is intended to help marketing and sales professionals immerse themselves in the linguistic world of corporate communications and, against this background, to be able to enter into discourse with their colleagues from corporate communications departments.

Based on this, only in this part of the article, the structural change process is described and critically assessed on the basis of four schematic representations using four maturity levels. The following four levels of maturity are distinguished (Seebacher, 2022):

1. One-dimensional reactive maturity level
2. Multi-dimensional situational maturity level
3. Multi-dimensional interactive maturity level
4. Multi-dimensional interagile maturity level

The majority of companies today find themselves at the first and second maturity levels of the corporate communications maturity model. At the first maturity level, one-dimensional reactive communication takes place. Conversely, this means that only very fragmented information from the environment is received and processed by corporate communications and then incorporated in a loop into the outgoing communications measures (Fig. 8). In addition, no distinction is made per se between different groups or segments of information recipients. The main communication at this level is with investors and journalists, depending on the size of the company and its classification as listed or unlisted.

At the second level of Seebacher's maturity model, different target groups of information recipients are already distinguished and specifically addressed. In addition to intrinsically initiated corporate communications, the company is already

[1] www.cdpnc.org. Accessed: February 3, 2022.

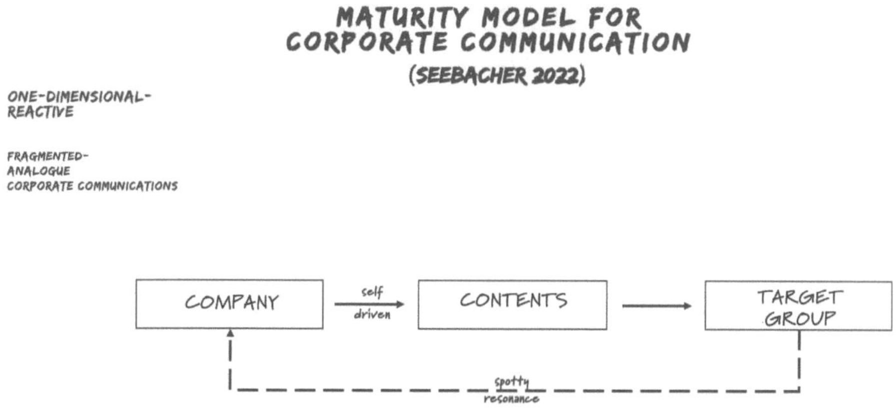

Fig. 8 One-dimensional reactive corporate communication (Source: Seebacher, 2022)

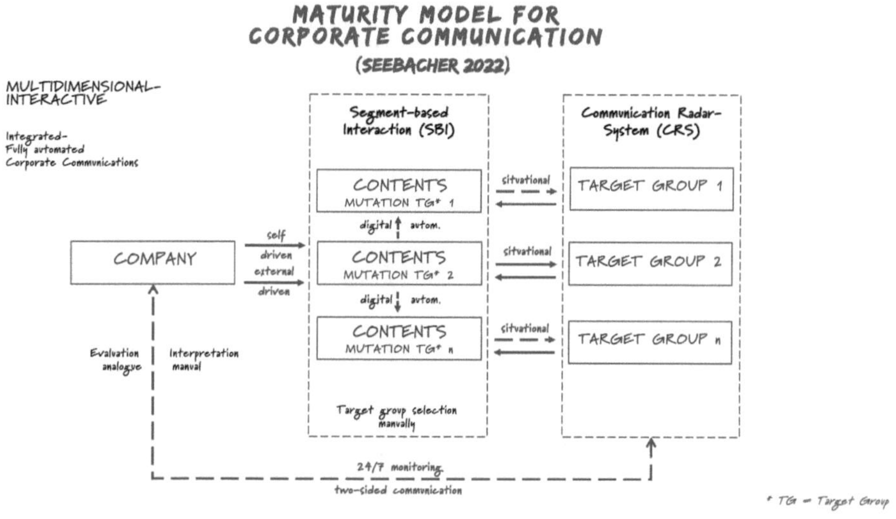

Fig. 9 Multi-dimensional-situative corporate communication (Source: Seebacher, 2022)

responding to external impulses and signals in terms of communications technology. However, everything is not yet fully automated, from adapting content to specific target groups to evaluating feedback in direct and indirect environments. In addition, there is no structured data collection and processing in the sense of the interaction intelligence already introduced into the discourse (Fig. 9).

With the development toward the third stage of the model, the shift toward fully integrated and automated corporate communications is taking place. This also enables the implementation of the concept of Segment-based Interaction (SBI) and the Communication Radar System (CRS) by using the previously described Interaction Intelligence. This technological ecosystem forms the basis for then multi-

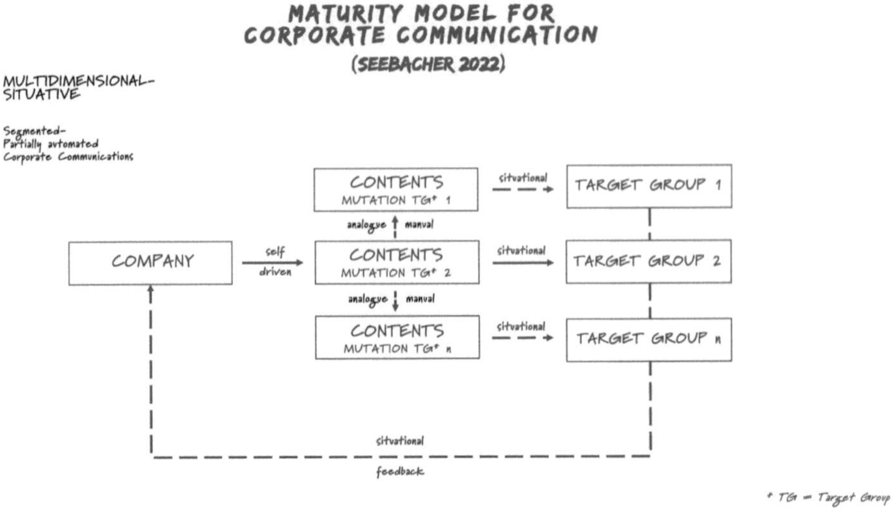

Fig. 10 Multi-dimensional interactive corporate communication (Source: Seebacher, 2022)

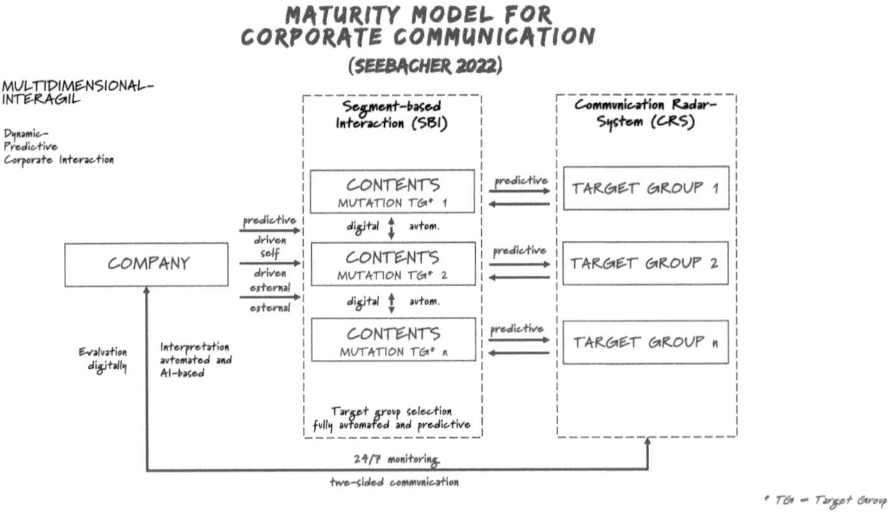

Fig. 11 Multi-dimensional interagile corporate communication (Source: Seebacher, 2022)

dimensional interactive enterprise communication with 24/7 monitoring and bi-directional exchange. This monitoring and evaluation of all converging data and information still takes place without the integration of artificial intelligence (Fig. 10).

With the development of the fourth stage of the maturity model, artificial intelligence will be integrated into the entire system in order to be able to process, evaluate and interpret the ever-increasing volumes of internal and external data in a timely, omni-dimensional manner (Fig. 11). In the long term, this will enable and realize predictive, interactive, and dynamic optimization of customer contact points.

These four schematic diagrams were used to outline and describe the changing mechanisms. The following is a brief description of the operational process model based on these four maturity levels. A more in-depth and detailed description can be found in Seebacher (2022) in the book of the same name on the subject of "Reengineering Corporate Communication," also published by Springer Group.

The Approach to Reengineering Corporate Communication

Based on the research work and our own practical studies, we developed our own process model for the new direction of corporate communications in the context of automation and digitization. This was based on the latest findings from the field of B2B marketing (Seebacher, 2021d) and a model was developed that not only makes parallel implementation together with marketing and sales possible but also makes sense. The reason for this is that both models have the three structural elements of process, organization, and data in common and thus fit together perfectly.

Operational modules were derived and defined for each of these three dimensions. This results in the following process structure (Fig. 12):

- Process Structure
  - Communication Process Library (CPL)
  - Communication Optimization
  - Communication Integration

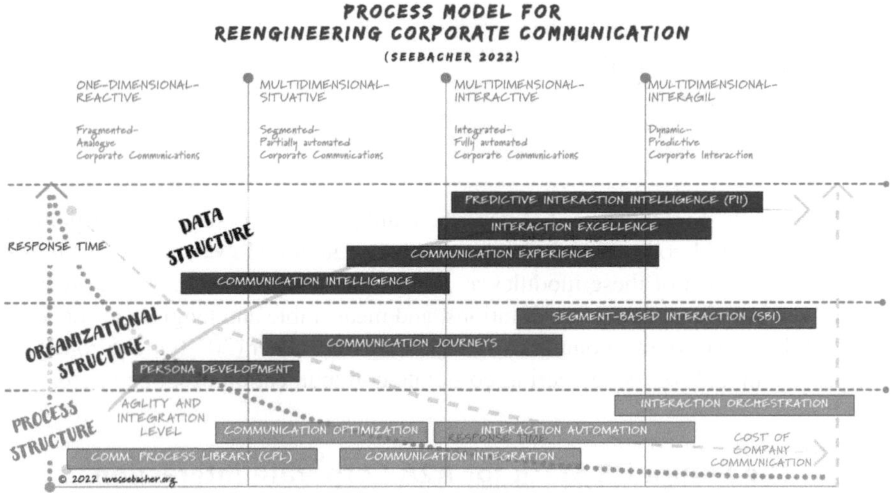

Fig. 12 Process model for RCC (Source: Seebacher, 2022)

Procedure model for
Reengineering of corporate communications (CC)

Jens Müller
(Call Uwe!)

PHASE 1 | MODULE 1 COMMUNICATION PROCESS LIBRARY (CPL)

NR.	DESCRIPTION ACTIVITY	START DATE	END DATE	DESCRIPTION STEPS	TASK OWNER (TO.)	RESULT
1.1.1	Screening of existing documents	1.4.21	14.4.21	• Screening of quality management documents (QM Handbook) QM Dept → Michael H. • Collection of own and existing process documents (Exec, Matteo, Clara, Jens)	Peter Noll	• Availability of relevant documents • Analysis report
1.1.2	Creation/addition/ update of the CPL	15.4.21	30.4.21	Agenda • Conduct 1st team workshop (15.4.21, Meeting Room 3.2.4, of Agenda) • Designation of all CC processes and final format of the CPL • Distribution of processes to team members • Joint development of an example process Sample process • Planning next steps with start/end dates • Creation/addition/update of all processes (online, cross check with Marketing) • Conduct 2nd team workshop for final coordination (28.4.21, invite Marketing) • Proofreading, final layout and final production	Peter Noll	• WS Documentation • List and decisions • Process owners • Finished processes • Project plan • CPL Draft 1 • CPL Draft 2 • CPL Vs 1
1.1.3	Communication of the CPL	3.5.21	28.5.21	• Definition of internal customers (Exec. Team, Mark., Sales, Bus. Unit Heads) • Operational communication of the CPL (pres. In MGT meeting, intranet, 1.2.1) • Recording feedback, evaluation and, if necessary, incorporation into CPL	Peter Noll	• List with names and way of addressing
1.1.4	Continuous updating of the CPL	17.5.21	28.5.21	• Create annual plan with calendar weeks, coordinate in team, and name of task owner (define process and integrate in CPL, per team on TO!) • Broadcast for the submission of updates (eMail, annual CC meeting) • Aggregation of inputs either virtually or in team-workshop • Incorporation and publication of the updated CPL	Peter Noll	• Deadline list and task owner • eMail • List with input • CPL Vs n

Fig. 13 Sample template of RCC process model (Source: Seebacher, 2022)

- Interaction Automation
- Interaction Orchestration

• Organizational Structure
  - Persona Development
  - Communication Journeys
  - Segment-based Interaction (SBI)
• Data Structure
  - Communication Intelligence
  - Communication Experience
  - Interaction Excellence
  - Predictive Interaction Intelligence (PII)

The individual modules are not described and presented in detail in this publication, as this would go beyond the scope of this document. However, a template was developed for each of these modules as part of the research work, which precisely defines the individual activities, durations, and measurable and tangible results to be realized (Fig. 13). All this content can be found in Seebacher (2022) in the context of the process model for reengineering corporate communication described here.

4 The Future HR Stack for A2A Corporate Interaction

There is no doubt that the field of corporate communications must defacto completely reinvent itself. This has been made drastically clear by the detailed analyses of the most current, scientific works and publications (Seebacher, 2022).

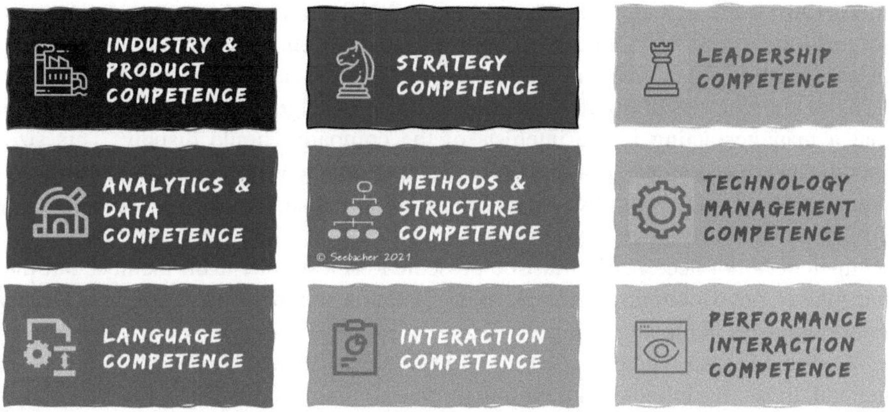

Fig. 14 Competence model for A2A corporate interaction (Source: Seebacher, 2022)

Corporate communicators who do not recognize the signs of the times will simply be overrun in the long term by the changes in the areas of marketing and sales and will see their raison d'être evaporate. With the changes already described in detail, the requirements for future employees in the field of corporate communications will also change completely. On the one hand, personal competencies (Güpner & Seebacher, 2022) will gain in importance, and on the other hand, completely new professional competencies will become relevant in the context of digital skills.

In this context, four meta competences can be defined for practitioners, which they have to perceive in order to be able to establish *Predictive Interaction Intelligence* in the companies:

- Speaking and living *Predictive Interaction* (Seebacher, 2021a)
- *Managing data* in interaction as a strategic resource
- Building *data-driven corporate interactions*
- Building competitive advantage through *Predictive Interaction*

Based on these four meta competences, the following nine core competences (Fig. 14) can be derived for A2A Corporate Interaction teams and their professionals:

- Industry and Product Competence (Turner, 2021)
- Strategy Competence (Gersch & Sundermeier, 2019)
- Leadership Competence (Güpner & Seebacher, 2022)
- Analytics and Data Competence (Seebacher, 2021b)
- Methods and Structure Competence (Seebacher, 2021a)
- Technology Management Competence (Peris-Ortiz & Lindahl, 2016)
- Language Competence (Cook & Wei, 2016)
- Interaction Competence (Spencer & Franklin, 2009)
- Performance Interaction Competence (Seebacher, 2021e, p. 47f)

Already from the beginning, a responsible RCC team must have the ambition to set itself up according to the size of its own organization. The approach often found in conservative structures of defining one's own significance and importance on the basis of the number of employees assigned to a manager contradicts the ideology that a manager acting in the interests of the company should display. This size-specific awareness should shape RCC activities from the very beginning. This means that also a team of two or three practitioners is more than sufficient to run RCC very efficiently and effectively. Conversely, this means that the above-mentioned competences not necessarily must be presented each by one team member but that one player has to combine two or more of the required skills. This is especially important right at the beginning.

And this is also where Marketing and Sales Automation comes into play as, in general, those disciplines and their practitioners are already further down the growth road and can therefore assist the Reengineering Corporate Communication with the required skills and experience. The early a human resource and competence masterplan is present and followed, the better the different team members can be trained and developed in a specific direction. This also positively impacts the RoI of RCC as in regard to Strategic Workforce Management (Weiss, 2016) *make* is always much better compared to *buy* best-trained people. Seebacher (2022) provides a fully developed competence matrix with defined behavioral anchors for initial but also ongoing employee appraisal and training and development. The competence model defines these anchors on the four major competency levels:

- E1: graduate, entry-level
- E2: Advanced knowledge and (sub-)project management level
- E3: In-depth and proven knowledge and expertise (team leadership)
- E4: Corporate Communication director/manager (head of department)

5 The Future Corporate Interaction Technology Stack

Good things first: The research work focusing on methods and structures in the context of RCC has not yet revealed any aspect that cannot be covered by products and solutions available from the field of marketing and sales automation and already in use. This circumstance offers enormous opportunities for providers of corresponding solutions, but can also entail risks in this respect. This is because resourceful providers will approach corporate communicators under the guise of a communication technology stack (ComTechStack) with dazzlingly colorful solutions and make them believe how important their own ComTechStack is.

A similar situation has also taken place in the area of sales and marketing, where we now find relatively large and ever-increasing, functional overlaps in the various offerings in the area of the MarTechStack and the SalesTechStack, as Seebacher (2021b, p. 185ff) also discusses and critically validates. A responsible approach from all sides demands being aware of the fact that a separate ComTechStack is not required, but that existing IT ecosystems in the area of marketing and sales

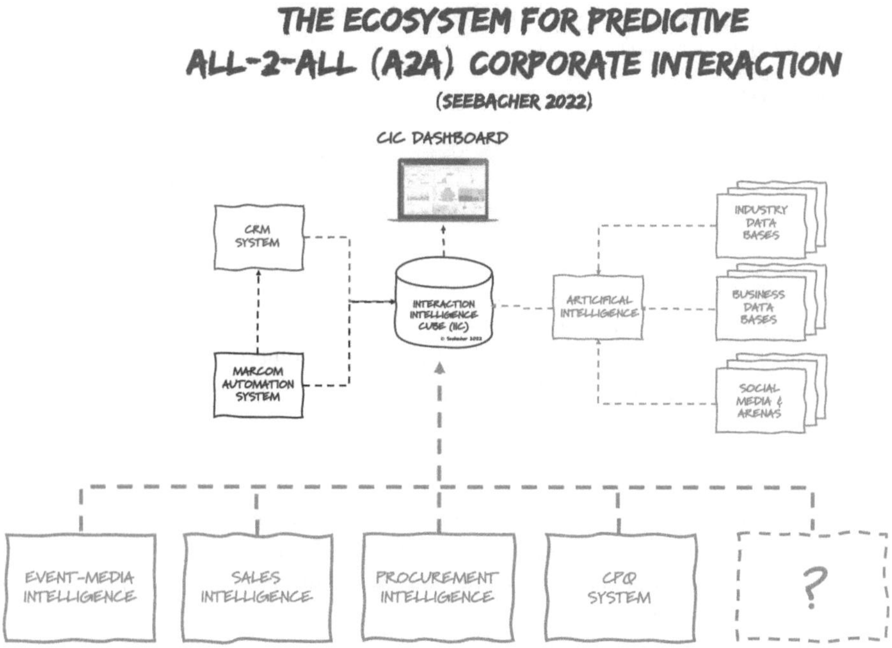

Fig. 15 Blueprint of the InTechStack for A2A corporate interaction (Source: Seebacher, 2022)

automation must now grow together and be integrated in the course of automating communication to form an interaction technology stack (InTechStack) (Fig. 15). This creates an information technology "MetaVerse" which, in addition to the OperationsTechStack (OpsTechStack) consisting of ERP systems and other systems required to ensure efficient and effective handling of the day-to-day operations of an organization, covers everything relating to necessary internal and external, direct and indirect interactions around this OpsTechStack in an integrated manner.

When developing such InTechStack within the company, this only makes sense if an aligned development process can be ensured by focusing on and actively considering the organizational learning process. The experience has shown that less is more. At the beginning of an RCC more should be invested in structures and their development as well as in basic competencies and alignment between the different stakeholders than in systems and products. The most important elements of an A2A InTechStack are the integration with the CRM system and the re-use of already available marketing or sales automation systems.

Such marketing and sales automation (eco-)systems cover all required functionalities in the narrowest sense that an A2A InTechStack needs to provide to its users in Corporate Interaction department. This is because for example marketing automation solutions per se can track information on client behavior at all different and defined customer contact points. In addition, also queries and research activities can easily be monitored and tracked in the context of the already-mentioned

Fig. 16 Three-step-approach for A2A corporate interaction InTechStack (Source: Seebacher, 2022)

Predictive Touchpoint Optimization. Also, the function of Segment-based Interaction (SBI) plays an important role, especially for multi-national companies (MNCs).

This now brought into discourse A2A InTechStack blueprint offers many different advantages (Seebacher, 2022):

- Cost minimization
- Incrementally achievable
- No serious information technology interventions in existing structures
- Applicable for all possible organization-specific IT strategies
- Greatest possible independence from external solutions
- Greatest possible, long-lasting adaptability with regard to the course of the project

Further detailed information on the process of the development of this A2A InTechStack can be found in the management book on "Reengineering Corporate Communication" (Seebacher, 2022) providing a three-step approach consisting of Structuring, Aligning, and Purchasing (Fig. 16).

Based on the development process described, it becomes clear that the path for corporate communicators to achieve interaction excellence is long and complex. The maturation process is accompanied by that of the MarTechStack and InTechStack development of a corporate communications department. Internationally recognized IT industry veteran Peter O'Neill[2] has used his experience—like the Marketing Maturity Model (Seebacher, 2021d)—to map an organization's IT development in relation to its MarTech stack. According to O'Neill, this results in a five-stage process in which the various systems and solutions are arranged in an S-shaped curve. Based on this model by O'Neill, an S-curve model was developed that operationally represents how to proceed step-by-step in relation to the instrumental level (Fig. 17). This model shall be considered by marketing and sales automation professionals when screening their eco-systems in the context of RCC.

[2] http://marchnata.eu/. Accessed 12/2/2021.

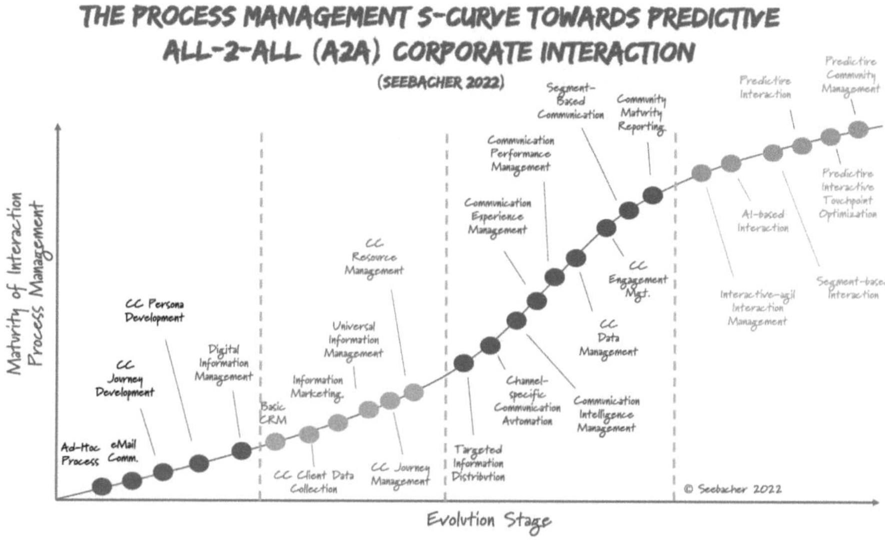

Fig. 17 S-curve model InTechStack (Source: Seebacher, 2022)

After marketing and sales automation, the next step is to automate corporate communications. Organizations must succeed in moving away from classic analog, multi-dimensional communication toward digital, omni-dimensionally agile corporate interaction. In this context, the responsible executives could decisively benefit from the developments and experiences of the past years in the field of marketing and sales. In order for Reengineering Corporate Communication to be successfully initiated and realized efficiently and effectively, the following factors are crucial from the perspective of Marketing and Sales Automation and its experts:

- From the outset, awareness must be established that the enormous potential and synergies can only be realized if the silo mentalities that still prevail among all those involved are thrown overboard.
- On the part of the experts from marketing and sales, a proactive approach to corporate communications is the first important step toward initiating the necessary joint activities. Particular care must be taken to first understand where corporate communications currently stand in relation to the basic structures described in the article, but also to any automation or digitization that may already have taken place.
- It is crucial that RCC is first and foremost a content-related or process-related project and not an IT issue. IT must follow the processes and

(continued)

structures. IT is the enabler, but the drivers are the departments of communications, marketing, and sales.

- In order for collaboration to occur at eye level, knowledge transfer is one of the most important aspects right from the start. It is therefore crucial for the marketing and sales experts, against the background of their own in-depth experience, to pick up the proverbial content from their colleagues from corporate communications and take them by the hand.
- The basic principles of *trust-building communication* authenticity, empathy, and logic (Frei & Morriss, 2020) are three pillars for a coordinated, orchestrated approach in the course of RCC.
- Clearly defined processes are the necessary basis so that existing solutions in the area of marketing and sales can be validly and reliably analyzed in terms of their applicability to corporate communications activities.
- Success lies in many small, coordinated steps. Minimizing risk means always trying things on a small scale, evaluating them, building on this to optimize the procedure, and only then scaling up.

The aim of this article was to create awareness of the enormous potential opening up in front of us with regard to the involvement of colleagues from corporate communications in the so important activities for the automation and digitization of marketing and sales. However, this article also makes an attempt to provide a valid process model in a very concentrated manner in order to provide marketing and sales experts with a tool to enable them, for their part, to start thinking about and possibly also initiating activities. This is because it requires the commitment of both sides, namely marketing and sales on the one hand and corporate communications on the other. For the further course of RCC it is insignificant who takes the first step. It is crucial that the first step is taken as soon as possible, because the risk of inaction will increase with each passing day in the context of A2A 24/7 interaction arenas with their uncontrollable mechanisms and dynamics.

It must be the goal of all stakeholders to act here in a concerted and orchestrated manner in terms of resource optimization, risk minimization, and sustainable yield maximization. The detailed description and many further argumentations, derivations, thoughts, models, and templates can be found in the author's specialist book on "Reengineering Corporate Communication" published by Springer Cham (2022), on which this article is based.

References

Bacon, A. (2021). In U. G. Seebacher (Ed.), *Strategic account-based marketing: How to tame this beast* (B2B marketing. Management for professionals ed.). Springer.

Cook, V., & Wei, L. (2016). *The Cambridge handbook of linguistic multi-competence (Cambridge Handbooks in Language and Linguistics)*. Cambridge University Press.

Frei, F., & Morriss, A. (2020). *Unleashed: The unapologetic leader's guide to empowering everyone around you*. Harvard Business Review.

Gersch, M., & Sundermeier, J. (2019). *Journal of Competences, Strategy & Management, 10*. Rainer Hampp.

Güpner, A., & Seebacher, U. (2022). *Cracking the code for successful career entry: With the 7 all decisive personal competencies, many tips, templates and checklists!* AQPS.

Peris-Ortiz, M., & Lindahl, J. M. (2016). *Sustainable learning in higher education: Developing competencies for the global marketplace (innovation, technology, and knowledge management)*. Springer.

Schüller AM (2016) Touch. Point. Win. Communication in Times of Digital Transformation. Offenbach. Gabal

Seebacher, U. (2021a). *Template-based management. A guide for an efficient and impactful professional practice*. Springer.

Seebacher, U. (2021b). *Predictive intelligence for data-driven managers: Process model, assessment-tool, IT-blueprint, competence model and case studies*. Springer.

Seebacher, U. (2021c). *Data-driven management: A primer for modern corporate decision making*. AQPS.

Seebacher, U. G. (2021d). The B2B marketing maturity model: What the route to the goal looks like! In U. G. Seebacher (Ed.), *B2B marketing. Management for professionals*. Springer.

Seebacher, U. G. (2021e). The B2B marketing ecosystem: Finding your way through the world of colorful B2B terms! In U. G. Seebacher (Ed.), *B2B marketing. Management for professionals*. Springer. https://doi.org/10.1007/978-3-030-54292-4_2

Seebacher, U. (2022). *Reengineering corporate communication: A marketer's view with process model, self-assessment and more than 20 templates*. Springer.

Spencer-Oatey, H., & Franklin, P. (2009). Intercultural interaction competence (ICIC). In *Intercultural interaction. Research and practice in applied linguistics*. Palgrave Macmillan. https://doi.org/10.1057/9780230244511_3

Turner, P. (2021). *The making of the modern manager: Mapping management competencies from the first to the fourth industrial revolution*. Palgrave Macmillan.

Weiss, C. (2016). Human resources strategy and change: Essentials of workforce planning and controlling. In M. Zeuch (Ed.), *Handbook of human resources management*. Springer. https://doi.org/10.1007/978-3-662-44152-7_111

Uwe Seebacher is a methods and structural scientist. He holds a doctorate in economics and business administration and is Professor for Predictive Intelligence at the University of Applied Sciences Munich, Professor for Marketing and Communications at the University of Applied Sciences for Marketing and Communication in Vienna and Professor for Data Science, Predictive Intelligence, Industrial (B2B) Marketing, Sales and Distribution Management at the Institute of Management Technology in Ghaziabad and Dubai. He has more than 30 years of experience as a business angel and investor, consultant, leader but also entrepreneur in the media, manufacturing, and service industries. He is a popular keynote speaker and panelist.

He has authored more than 50 books in many leading publishing houses, such as "Reengineering Corporate Communications" (Springer Cham), "Assets-as-Service" (Springer Gabler 2021), "Data-driven Management" (Springer Gabler 2021), "Predictive Intelligence for Managers" (Springer 2021), "B2B Marketing

Guidebook" (Springer 2021), "Marketing Resource Management" (AQPS 2021), "Leadership Development" (Linde 2006) or "Template-based Management (Springer 2020) or "European Human Resource Management" (HBM 2009).

For his innovative concepts and initiatives, e.g., with Allianz, the European Union, the Austrian Federal Economic Chamber, Bayer Leverkusen, and BASF, he received various awards, such as the Diskobolos Innovation Award of the European Chamber of Commerce and the 2016 Export Award of the Austrian Federal Economic Chamber. For more information, visit www.uweseebacher.org.

MIX
Papier aus verantwortungsvollen Quellen
Paper from responsible sources
FSC® C105338

If you have any concerns about our products,
you can contact us on
ProductSafety@springernature.com

In case Publisher is established outside the EU,
the EU authorized representative is:
Springer Nature Customer Service Center GmbH
Europaplatz 3, 69115 Heidelberg, Germany

Printed by Libri Plureos GmbH
in Hamburg, Germany